W9-BMO-582

Cisco Internetwork Troubleshooting

Laura Chappell
Dan Farkas

Cisco Press
201 West 103rd Street
Indianapolis, IN 46290 USA

Cisco Internetwork Troubleshooting

Laura Chappell
Dan Farkas

Copyright© 1999 Cisco Systems, Inc.

Cisco Press logo is a trademark of Cisco Systems, Inc.

Published by:
Cisco Press
201 West 103rd Street
Indianapolis, IN 46290 USA

Printed in the United States of America 6 7 8 9 0

6th Printing March 2001

Library of Congress Cataloging-in-Publication Number: 99-61691

ISBN: 1-57870-092-2

Warning and Disclaimer

This book is designed to provide information on Cisco internetwork troubleshooting. Every effort has been made to make this book as complete and as accurate as possible, but no warranty or fitness is implied.

The information is provided on an as-is basis. The author, Cisco Press, and Cisco Systems, Inc., shall have neither liability nor responsibility to any person or entity with respect to any loss or damages arising from the information contained in this book or from the use of the discs or programs that may accompany it.

The opinions expressed in this book belong to the author and are not necessarily those of Cisco Systems, Inc.

Trademark Acknowledgments

All terms mentioned in this book that are known to be trademarks or service marks have been appropriately capitalized. Cisco Press or Cisco Systems, Inc., cannot attest to the accuracy of this information. Use of a term in this book should not be regarded as affecting the validity of any trademark or service mark.

Feedback Information

At Cisco Press, our goal is to create in-depth technical books of the highest quality and value. Each book is crafted with care and precision, undergoing rigorous development that involves the unique expertise of members from the professional technical community.

Readers' feedback is a natural continuation of this process. If you have any comments regarding how we could improve the quality of this book, or otherwise alter it to better suit your needs, you can contact us through e-mail at ciscopress@mcp.com. Please be sure to include the book title and ISBN in your message.

We greatly appreciate your assistance.

Publisher	John Wait
Executive Editor	John Kane
Cisco Systems Program Manager	Jim LeValley
Managing Editor	Patrick Kanouse
Acquisitions Editor	Brett Bartow
Development Editor	Kitty Wilson Jarrett
Project Editor	Dayna Isley
Technical Editors	Henry Benjamin, CCIE
	Steve Kalman
	Doug MacBeth
	Steve Wisniewski
Team Coordinator	Amy Lewis
Book Designer	Regina Rexrode
Cover Designer	Karen Ruggles
Proofreaders	Debra Neel
	Megan Wade
Layout Technician	Wil Cruz
Indexer	Craig Small

About the Authors

Laura Chappell is the senior protocol analyst for the Network Analysis Institute, LLC. She is an established speaker, writer, and consultant who focuses on protocol-level communications to provide troubleshooting, design, and optimization information throughout the world. Laura has been providing Cisco SE/CSE training on IPX/SPX protocol implementation, troubleshooting, and analysis since 1992 and has written numerous books and articles on a variety of networking subjects. She is the editor of the Cisco Press books *Introduction to Cisco Router Configuration* and *Advanced Cisco Router Configuration.*

Dan Farkas is a Cisco Certified Internetwork Expert and a Certified Cisco Systems Instructor. He teaches a variety of router and switch configuration classes, including the CIT class. He performs both internal training for Cisco engineers, technicians, and programmers, as well as training for Cisco end users through several international training partners. Dan also works with Information Innovation to provide seminar presentations at Cisco University events. Dan is also a consultant to both small and large organizations for network design, implementation, and troubleshooting issues.

About the Technical Reviewers

Henry Benjamin is a senior network consultant for a large organization specializing in IP routing protocols and SNA. He is a Cisco Certified Internetwork Expert and has planned, designed, and implemented large networks including IGRP, EIGRP, and OSPF. Over the past two years, he has focused on large SNA networks, including the largest Cisco DLSw+ network in the world. Henry holds a bachelor of engineering degree from Sydney University.

Steve Kalman is the principal officer for Esquire Micro Consultants. Steve is a seasoned professional with more than 30 years' experience in data processing. His main strength is in the area of network design and implementation. Steve teaches several classes on Cisco routers; Windows; and infrastructure issues such as Fast Ethernet, WAN and Telecom, and wide-area networking.

Doug Macbeth is an IOS documentation manager at Cisco Systems, Inc. He has more than 15 years' experience in technical documentation and has worked for Cisco Systems since 1993. While at Cisco, Doug has been an editor and project leader for the Cisco IOS documentation set. Doug lives in San Jose, California, and holds a bachelor's degree in technical and business communications from San Jose State University.

Steve Wisniewski has a masters of science degree in telecommunications management from Stevens Institute of Technology and is currently working toward his Ph.D. in information management systems. He is a full-time instructor in telecommunications management for Devry Technical Institute. Steve is also a System Network Administrator Consultant.

Acknowledgments

Special thanks to Carol Lee for her help in content organization and input. Thanks also to Jill Poulsen of Network Analysis Institute for her assistance on the coordination of this project on behalf of Ms. Chappell. Thanks to Henry Benjamin, Steve Kalman, Steve Wisniewski, and Doug MacBeth for their time and effort on the technical review of this material.

This book is the product of many contributors within Cisco's Education Department, including, but not limited to, Cisco course developers, course editors, and instructors. We would like to acknowledge the efforts of training developers Bob Martinez, Priscilla Oppenheimer, and Elwin Smith, as well as Mark Powell, Marty Adkins, Matt Lyons, Merwyn Andrade, Robert Leonis, Tong Ma, Teh Cheng, Hai Doan, and Thierry Martens.

We are also grateful to the efforts of Cisco Press in developing this title and bringing it to press. Specifically, we would like to thank Brett Bartow, Amy Lewis, John Kane, Kitty Jarrett, Dayna Isley, and Patrick Kanouse.

Contents at a Glance

Table of Contents

Foreword

In April 1998, Cisco Systems, Inc., announced a new professional development initiative called the Cisco Career Certifications. These certifications address the growing worldwide demand for more (and better) trained computer networking experts. Building on Cisco's highly successful Cisco Certified Internetwork Expert (CCIE) program—the industry's most respected networking certification vehicle—Cisco Career Certifications enable you to be certified at various technical proficiency levels.

Cisco Internetwork Troubleshooting presents in book format all the topics covered in the challenging, instructor-led certification preparation course of the same name. The Cisco Internetwork Troubleshooting (CIT) exam is one of four required to become a Cisco Certified Network Professional (CCNP). Whether you are studying to become CCNP certified or you just need a better understanding of error detection and troubleshooting methodologies, you will benefit from the insights this book offers.

Cisco and Cisco Press present this material in text-based format to provide another learning vehicle for our customers and the broader user community in general. Although a publication cannot replace the instructor-led environment, we must acknowledge that not everyone responds in the same way to the same delivery mechanism. It is our intent that presenting this material via a Cisco Press publication will enhance the transfer of knowledge to our audience of networking professionals.

This is the third in a series of course supplements planned for Cisco Press, following *Introduction to Cisco Router Configuration* and *Advanced Cisco Router Configuration*. Cisco will present existing and future courses through these coursebooks to help achieve Cisco Worldwide Training's principal objectives: to educate Cisco's community of networking professionals and to enable that community to build and maintain reliable, scalable networks. The Cisco Career Certifications and classes that define these certifications are directed at meeting these objectives through a disciplined approach to progressive certification. The books Cisco creates in partnership with Cisco Press will meet the same standards for content quality demanded of our courses and certifications. It is our intent that you will find this and subsequent Cisco Press certification and training publications of value as you build your networking knowledge base.

Thomas M. Kelly
Director, Worldwide Training
Cisco Systems, Inc.
May 1999

Introduction

The networking world is becoming more complex every day as we attempt to add bandwidth and capability to our LANs and WANs overnight. The alarming rate of growth requires a solid understanding of how to quickly and efficiently spot communication and configuration problems. Cisco Systems, the premier designer and provider of internetworking devices, is committed to supporting network administrators, designers, and builders in the use of its products.

The content, organization, and goals of this book are based on Cisco's highly successful Cisco Internetwork Troubleshooting course. The book provides a comprehensive guide for troubleshooting LANs and WANs that use TCP/IP, IPX/SPX, and AppleTalk protocols. In addition, the book details switched and VLAN network troubleshooting.

Configuration examples demonstrate management and troubleshooting techniques for numerous LAN and WAN designs. If you are using this book as a study aid in preparing for one of Cisco's certification exams, you will find the end-of-chapter exercises useful. The exercises are designed to help you evaluate your understanding of the concepts contained in the chapter and your ability to apply the configuration techniques available for Cisco routers. Chapters also contain sidebars in the form of tips, notes, and cautions to help emphasize critical details.

The previously published titles in this series, *Introduction to Cisco Router Configuration* and *Advanced Cisco Router Configuration*, also offer basic through advanced technical details on internetworking devices.

Who Should Read This Book

This book provides basic through advanced information on networking technology, practices, and troubleshooting for TCP/IP, IPX/SPX, and AppleTalk LANs and WANs. If you are pursuing CCNP certification and anticipate taking the CIT exam, this book is a logical starting point.

Even if you are not using Cisco routers, this book can increase your understanding and efficiency in isolating and troubleshooting internetworking problems.

Part I: Troubleshooting Tools and Methodology

Part I lays the foundation for the book. It provides the guidelines for troubleshooting, including a problem-solving model that can be used regardless of what the network trouble may be. This section focuses heavily on the protocol characteristics (primarily the various Layer 2 protocols, TCP/IP, NetWare IPX/SPX, and AppleTalk). You'll learn about the basic packet structures and be able to identify frames based on their unique characteristics. This section also details Cisco's router functionality, including the route processor mechanism, the switch processor mechanism, and the various levels of cache that reside within router. You are also presented with an arsenal of tools you can use for solving your network's problems. Some of these are third-party devices, but many of them exist within the Cisco IOS itself. You'll learn about the appropriate tools for solving specific problems.

We recommend that you spend some time becoming familiar with the technology defined in Part I of this book. Parts II, III, and IV assume that you have completed Part I successfully.

Part II: Routing and Routed Protocol Troubleshooting

In Part II, you'll learn which tools can be used to troubleshoot the most common networking environments today, including TCP/IP, Novell, and AppleTalk networks. In each of the chapters in Part II, you'll find diagnostic commands and tools that can be used to troubleshoot each of these environments, as well as problem resolution and isolation suggestions for each of these environments.

Upon completion of Part II, you should have the knowledge to attack any network problem, regardless of the protocol type or location of devices in the internetwork.

Part III: Campus Switch and VLAN Troubleshooting

Part III focuses on switch and VLAN communications, with an emphasis on spotting common problems and helpful tools.

Chapter 10 provides the necessary foundations by detailing Catalyst 5000 functionality and general Catalyst switching technology. This chapter also provides definitions of the spanning-tree process, which is a must-read for anyone working in looped networks.

Chapter 11 focuses specifically on VLAN technology and troubleshooting. In this chapter, you learn how VLANs work and the format of frames that are tagged for interswitch communications.

Upon completion of this part, you should be comfortable with the troubleshooting methods and tools for switched networks that use VLAN technology.

Part IV: WAN Troubleshooting

Part IV focuses on Frame Relay and ISDN BRI WAN technologies specifically and the primary steps required to troubleshoot WAN activity. In each of the chapters in Part IV, you'll find diagnostic commands and tools that can be used to troubleshoot each of these environments, as well as problems, resolutions, and isolation suggestions for each of these environments.

Upon completion of Part IV of this book, you should have the knowledge to identify problems due to line faults, protocol incompatibilities, and configuration errors. You should also be familiar with the most useful troubleshooting tools and utilities.

Part V: Appendixes

The appendixes contain the answers to each of the chapter tests as well as details on how to work with Cisco Support. The appendixes also contain numerous references and recommended reading that will help you keep up with and further your studies of internetwork technology and troubleshooting. Finally, Appendix D contains a problem-solving checklist and worksheet that can help you organize and document your troubleshooting steps.

Troubleshooting Tools and Methodology

CHAPTER 1

Troubleshooting Methodology

Today, the complexity of internetworks is growing, and multiprotocol environments are presenting more problems. Internetwork troubleshooting has become an important issue to many organizations. There are crucial reasons a systematic approach is necessary to resolve internetworking problems. This chapter gives you a standard problem-solving model that will help you begin troubleshooting.

This chapter is the core around which this book is built. Effective and efficient growth of troubleshooting expertise can only result from a systematic and logical approach. Whenever you approach a network problem, you should use a problem-solving model— a logical step-by-step method of eliminating the causes.

It is also important to document the network and relevant devices and configurations before and after making changes. Understanding and documenting your network reduces the time required to troubleshoot problems that arise.

After reading this chapter, you will be able to

- Use a problem-solving model, which will be useful for systematically troubleshooting problems.
- Outline the steps you took to isolate potential causes of problems and the steps you took to determine possible solutions.

Using a Systematic Troubleshooting Method

The costs of an internetwork failure can be disastrous. Generally, the average cost of a production network disability—using lost productivity due to loss of host or client/server access as the basis of the calculation—can range from tens of thousands of dollars to several million dollars per hour. For a growing number of organizations, an extended production network outage can cause the end of the organization.

Restoring an internetwork that has failed or has become impaired puts incredible pressure on network engineers and network administrators. Given this pressure, use of special expertise and known shortcuts to rapidly restore network functionality is valuable. If you know how to solve a production network problem directly, do so. Use your expertise.

However, this expertise requires a technical depth and a detailed breadth of knowledge about the internetwork. Not often does this depth and breadth result from isolated, scattered, and unsystematic troubleshooting.

Unless you already know how to solve a problem, an unsystematic approach to troubleshooting can result in wasting time lost in the network's maze of symptoms, interdependencies, and contingencies. A systematic troubleshooting method, on the other hand, can help you understand the network's maze of details by going through a process that can help you identify facts, consider possibilities, act on likely causes, and observe the results of your testing.

The general idea of a troubleshooting model is to systematically reduce a large set of possible causes of trouble to a small set of causes or a single cause. Then you can fix the problem and restore network function. After the problem is resolved, a systematic troubleshooting method of documenting the case helps to capture, preserve, and communicate the experience gained while solving the problem.

The use of such a systematic troubleshooting model increases the expertise of the organization and reduces the time to solve similar, future problems. This evolution of improving expertise and collaboration can help mitigate the pressures of supporting crucial, complex internetworks.

The Complexity of Internetworks

As more advanced technologies and services are introduced into the fields of information processing and communications, the tasks of designing, managing, and maintaining the resulting internetworks are becoming increasingly complex.

Historically, network architectures were host-centric. Mainframe-based architectures have evolved to distributed processing systems with an emergence of the client/server paradigm. New applications such as CAD/CAM, video, audio, and multimedia, are gaining popularity and are feasible due to the increase in processor power on clients and servers. The result has been users that need high-speed links such as dedicated 10-Mbps Ethernet, 100-Mbps Ethernet, 100-Mbps FDDI, or greater to the desktop. To accommodate the transport of the increased load, carriers are implementing services such as ISDN, Frame Relay, and ATM. As shown in Figure 1-1, different networks require different designs and different levels of complexity.

Figure 1-1   *Data flow and throughput needs often define the design and complexity of a network.*

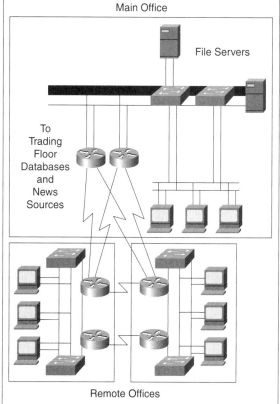

The variety of proprietary protocols adds complexity to the internetwork. A goal of the International Organization for Standardization (ISO) Open System Interconnection (OSI) reference model (see Figure 1-2) is to provide compatibility and operability between different vendors' systems, theoretically providing a common architecture and removing intercommunication problems. Although many vendors model their protocol structures on the seven-layer OSI model, attaining a seamless interrelationship between all vendors' products is far from a reality.

Figure 1-2   *Most network troubleshooting takes place at Layers 2 and 3 of the seven-layer OSI reference model.*

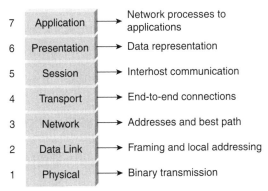

As a result of these factors, today's internetworks are complex. Internetworks have become a mixture of protocols, technologies, media, and topologies. With this added complexity comes the potential for difficult connectivity and performance problems. Difficult problems require a systematic problem-solving model.

In this chapter we'll examine how a problem-solving model can be the most effective way to reduce the time required to troubleshoot the network.

The Problem-Solving Model

The complexity and crucial uptime requirements of modern networks intensify the pressures to solve connectivity and performance problems. The best way to approach an internetworking problem is to develop a standard troubleshooting methodology. The problem-solving model presented in Figure 1-3 is one example of such a methodology. Using an ordered pattern of thought when troubleshooting helps you solve any problems you encounter. It also helps you and your organization improve overall expertise as your organization supports its internetwork.

Figure 1-3   *This reliable problem-solving model is only one of many, and is the one we work with in this book.*

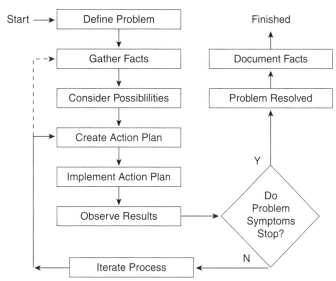

Figure 1-3 shows a sequence of steps. These steps can be grouped into a small number of troubleshooting phases:

- Make sure you have a clear, sufficient definition of the problem.
- Gather all the relevant facts and consider the likely possibilities.
- Create and implement an action plan for the most likely possibility, and then observe the results.
- If the symptoms do not stop, try another action plan (or gather additional facts).
- If the symptoms do stop, document how you resolved the problem.

NOTE   This problem-solving model is one of many such models you can use. If you are already using another model (based on an alternative model or learned through experience), you should continue to use it. If in your past experience you have not approached problems systematically and not considered using a problem-solving model, you should adopt a scheme such as the one outlined in this chapter.

The goal of this chapter is to establish a methodical mindset—an ordered pattern of thought to use when troubleshooting. The model described in this chapter takes a multistep approach to problem-solving. In the next sections, we will examine each of these steps in detail to see how it can be used in a troubleshooting example.

Step 1: Define the Problem

When analyzing an internetwork problem, make a clear problem statement by defining the problem in terms of a set of symptoms and associated causes. Form problem statements with reference to the baselines that you have established for your networks. To do this, identify the general symptoms and then ascertain what possible kinds of problems (causes) could result in these symptoms. For example, consider the sample network troubleshooting scenario shown in Figure 1-4.

Figure 1-4   *Hosts 1 and 2 cannot get a response from Host A or B.*

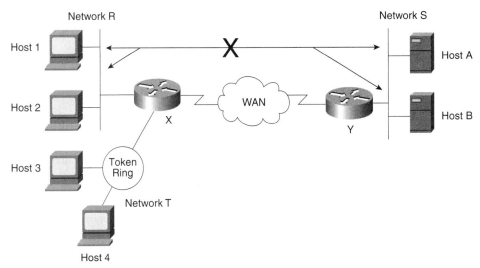

This network uses the TCP/IP protocol suite, and a problem is occurring. The symptom of the problem is that users at Host 1 and Host 2 cannot get any response from Host A or Host B. How do you solve the problem?

At this point in the methodology, you define the problem by identifying associated general symptoms and identifying possible causes. Try to form opinions of possible causes and document them. Many answers might arise, but concentrate on those that could be considered major contributors to the problem.

At this point, the aim is to consider possible causes. Subsequent steps in the methodology allow you to ask questions (that is, gather facts) such as whether Host 3 and Host 4 are getting any response from Host A and Host B, whether Host 1 can communicate with Host 2, whether the WAN link is operational, and so on.

A systematic approach to troubleshooting consists of a sequence of steps. The first grouping of these steps is to make sure you have a clear, sufficient definition of the problem, and then to gather all the relevant facts. In this group of steps, you should use (and at the same time, be skeptical of) the initial diagnosis made by the end users. What the end user reports is important; however, the full definition of the problem may have a broader basis. If possible, proceed from your own knowledge about your internetwork and try to see the problem for yourself.

As part of the systematic approach to troubleshooting, many support teams have developed a set of primary questions and processes to use when getting problem report information from end users. Among the primary questions are "How often has this problem happened?" and "When did it start?" and "Can you readily reproduce the problem condition, and if so, how?"

The problem statements that you form must be with reference to the baselines that you have established for your networks. You should know what your network indicators look like when the network is performing as you expect it to. Also, you must have knowledge of the network aspects that have changed since the last evidence of baseline performance.

To define the problem, identify the general symptoms and then ascertain what possible kinds of problems (causes) could result in these symptoms.

The following might be possible causes of the communications problems at Host 1 and Host 2:

- Faulty interface cards installed in Host 1 and Host 2.
- Host 1 and Host 2 require a default gateway, and this has not been configured.
- Misconfigured subnet masks exist on Host 1 and Host 2 or in Router X.
- Network R has a faulty device attached to it that causes excessive collisions on the Ethernet cable.
- Either Router X or Router Y has a misconfigured access list, causing traffic from the affected hosts to be blocked.
- There is a problem with the WAN link.
- The routers are not configured with valid mapping statements for the protocol.
- Host A and Host B are not configured to recognize Host 1 and Host 2.

There might be several other possibilities, but first you should concentrate on those that could be considered major contributors to the symptom.

Step 2: Gather the Facts

The second step in troubleshooting is to gather the facts you need to help isolate possible causes.

Ask questions of affected users, network administrators, managers, and any other key people involved with the network. Try to ascertain whether anyone is aware of anything that has been changed. (How many times has this question been asked and the answer "Nothing!" been given?) Thoroughly document all information received.

Depending on the nature of the reported symptoms, collect facts from sources such as network management systems, protocol analyzer traces, output from router diagnostic commands such as **debug** privileged EXEC commands and **show** EXEC commands, or software release notes. It might be necessary to collect this information at discrete times or over extended time periods, such as an overnight data capture.

It is always a good idea to document and keep on record copies of the configurations of hosts, routers, servers, and any other configurable network devices to be able to compare configurations and determine whether anything has changed.

Returning to our sample problem, you need to gather facts in an attempt to focus on the possible causes. In analyzing the problem, let's assume that the following facts have been gathered:

- Host 3 and Host 4 can communicate with Host A and Host B.
- Host 1 and Host 2 can communicate with Host 3 and Host 4.
- Host 1 can communicate with Host 2.
- Host A and Host B are correctly configured to recognize and communicate with Host 1 and Host 2.

Step 3: Consider the Possibilities

Using the data you gathered and your knowledge of the Cisco Systems products and other devices in your internetwork environment, you can set the boundaries that help you begin to isolate the problem cause(s). By setting the boundaries, you focus on only those portions of the product, media, or host that are relevant to the specific problem or failure mode.

One of the most important outcomes of a systematic troubleshooting approach is to narrow the possibilities—remove irrelevant network details from the set of items that you need to check. You can eliminate entire classes of problems associated with system software and hardware. You can eliminate several possible causes based on the facts gathered for the sample problem. Consider the possible causes identified earlier (see Figure 1-5).

Figure 1-5   *You can rule out possible problems one at a time.*

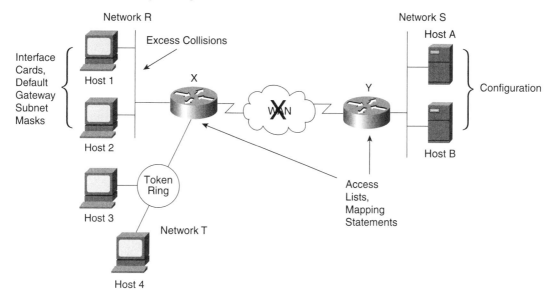

- Faulty interface cards installed in Host 1 and Host 2.

  You can eliminate this possible cause because Host 1 can communicate with Host 2.

- Host 1 and Host 2 require a default gateway, and this has not been configured.

  You can eliminate this possible cause because Host 1 and Host 2 can communicate with Host 3 and Host 4.

- Misconfigured subnet masks exist on Host 1 and Host 2 or in Router X.

  You can eliminate this possible cause because Host 1 and Host 2 can communicate with Host 3 and Host 4.

- Network R has a faulty device attached to it that causes excessive collisions on the Ethernet cable.

  You can eliminate this possible cause because Host 1 and Host 2 can communicate with Host 3 and Host 4. Also, Host 1 can communicate with Host 2.

- Either Router X or Router Y has a misconfigured access list, causing traffic from the affected hosts to be blocked.

  This is still a possible cause. You cannot eliminate it based on any of the facts gathered.

- There is a problem with the WAN link.

  You can eliminate this possible cause because Host 3 and Host 4 can communicate with Host A and Host B.

- The routers have not been configured with valid mapping statements for the protocol.

  You can eliminate this possible cause because Host 3 and Host 4 can communicate with Host A and Host B.

- Host A and Host B are not configured to recognize Host 1 and Host 2.

  You can eliminate this possible cause because Host A and Host B are correctly configured to recognize and communicate with Host 1 and Host 2. We checked this when gathering facts.

The scope of the problem has been narrowed down to the following: An access list configured in either Router X or Router Y might be blocking traffic to or from Host 1 and Host 2.

Step 4: Create an Action Plan

You can devise an action plan based on the set of possibilities that were just created. From these possibilities, you can implement a "divide and conquer" policy. Consider the most likely possibility, and determine a plan in which only one variable is manipulated. This approach allows you to reproduce a given solution to a specific problem. If more than one variable is altered simultaneously and the problem is solved, how can you identify which variable caused the problem?

- Use a partitioning effect. Split your troubleshooting domain into discrete areas that are logically isolated from each other. This approach allows you to determine which side of the partition (if not both sides) keeps the problem after the partitioning.

- Determine where in the network the problem exists. Use a series of tests to pinpoint where network failure occurs. Begin from a source device and try a sequence of tests to determine whether proper functioning occurs from the source to successively more distant, intermediate network devices. This approach allows you to gradually trace a path from a source along the way to the ultimate destination and possibly isolate the part of the path that contains the problem.

- Collaborate with others and share rules-of-thumb action plan approaches. The more of these logical problem-solving approaches you learn, the more tools you have. Tools help you test a given problem situation. As you gain experience, you improve your ideas on how to relate the given possibilities and your troubleshooting tools to a specific and systematic action plan.

From our analysis of the sample problem, the most possible cause has been determined to be an incorrect access list configured in one of the routers that may be blocking traffic to or from Host 1 and Host 2.

An action plan for this cause is to look at each router's current configuration and determine whether any access lists that are present are correct. (You should always be aware of the implicit deny that exists at the end of *every* access list.) Figure 1-6 shows the access list configuration on Router X.

Figure 1-6   *Router X is configured with an access list that could be part of the problem.*

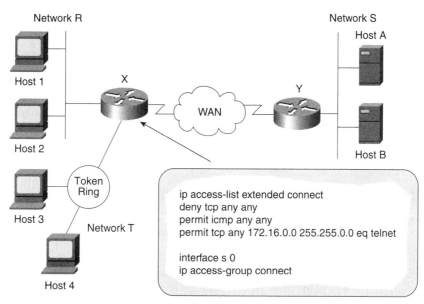

After analyzing the configurations, either try to fix a misconfigured list or temporarily disable the access list (by removing the **access-group** command that applies to an interface).

NOTE   Remember that disabling the access list removes the security that the list was meant to provide.

Step 5: Implement the Action Plan

It is important to be very specific in creating and executing the action plan; the plan must identify a set of steps to be executed, and each step must be carefully implemented. Keep track of exactly what you are testing. Try not to change too many variables at the same time.

As you implement your action plan, also try to

- Make sure that what you implement does not make the problems worse or add new problems.

- Limit as much as possible the invasive impact of your implemented action plan on other network users.

- Minimize the extent or duration of potential security lapses during your action plan implementation.

It is important to have a backout plan (for example, a saved configuration file) to return the network to a known previous state. For this sample problem, connect to one of the router's command consoles—the console of Router X, for example—to view its configuration. (Connect either by using Telnet, by attaching a terminal to the console port, or by connecting to the router's auxiliary port.)

If the access list configuration is deemed to be incorrect, reconfigure the access list or temporarily disable it by changing the last line to **no ip access-group connect**.

To ensure that not more than one variable is manipulated at a time, the results of the changes made must be observed before any changes are made to the configuration of Router Y or any other device.

Step 6: Observe the Results of the Action Plan

After manipulating a variable to find a solution to a problem, be sure to gather results based on this action plan. Generally, you should use the same method of gathering facts that you used in step 2 of the methodology.

After you have analyzed the results, you must determine whether the problem has been resolved. If it has, then this is the exit point of the iterative loop in the problem-solving model. If the problem has not been resolved, then you must use these results to fine-tune the action plan until a proper solution is reached.

For the sample problem, having manipulated one variable—namely, reconfiguring the access list or temporarily disabling it—observe the results. Can Host 1 and Host 2 now access Host A or Host B? If they can, then the problem has been resolved, and the process is terminated. (If the action plan were to temporarily disable the access list, and as a result the problem were resolved, the administrator would have to reconfigure the access list.) If, however, Host 1 and Host 2 are still unable to access Host A or Host B, then you must move on to the next step.

Step 7: Repeat the Problem-Solving Process

In order to reach a point where you can exit this problem/solution loop, you must strive to make continuous progress toward a smaller set of possibilities until you are left with only one.

So after narrowing your possibilities list (as a result of implementing the previous action plan and observing the results), repeat the process, starting with a new action plan based on a new (possibly shorter or longer) list of possibilities. Continue the process until a solution is found. Problem resolution can involve many iterations of modifications to host configurations, router configurations, or media.

Remember that it is very important to undo any "fixes" you made that did not work. Remember that you want to change only one variable at a time. Also, if too many changes are made at one time in the network, it could result in a degradation of network performance and policy. This is why it is always important to have a backout plan to undo your changes and restore the network to its previous state.

For the sample problem, having considered Router X first and finding that reconfiguring or disabling the access list did not solve the problem, you must repeat the process loop.

You must now implement the next step of the action plan. Check to see if your work results in a legal access list that accomplishes the intended traffic filtering. Make additional changes as required.

A further iteration of the process to consider is the configuration of Router Y (see Figure 1-7). Perhaps the access list on Router X is working but the problem is an inbound access list at the other end of the internetwork. The loop must be repeated, making necessary configuration changes to Router Y and again observing the results.

The iterations must continue until the problem is solved. Systematically eliminate each of the possible causes until you isolate and confirm the cause or causes so you can fix the problem.

Figure 1-7   *Now that Router X has been eliminated as the problem, you can **telnet** to Router Y. Notice that on Router X you can restore the original configuration by reapplying the access list to the interface.*

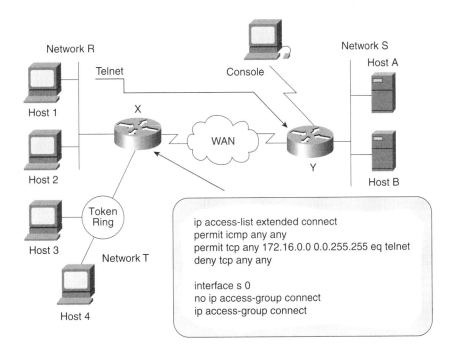

Step 8: Resolve the Problem

If you have located the true source of the problem, then you can finish up and document the problem. If, however, you exhaust all common causes and actions for your environment as you attempt to resolve a network problem, then your last recourse is to contact your router technical support representative. You should have available necessary information about your problem that will help the support representative determine the possible cause of your problem.

One of the aims of this book is to help you develop your own processes for gathering data, resolving problems, and preventing problems from recurring with a minimum of downtime and external intervention. Even though the recursive progression through this model may seem time-consuming, as your troubleshooting skills mature, this process will become more automatic, and you will not need to follow a flow diagram step-by-step.

As soon as the problem symptoms stop, chances are that you have resolved the problem. At all times you need to document your work, which involves the following:

- Maintaining a record of which steps you have already taken (for example, whether you involve others, such as other engineers or administrators in your organization or Cisco Technical Assistance Center).

- Providing a backout trail if it turns out that you must reverse the actions you took (for example, if you solved the problem at hand but inadvertently caused some other problem).

- Establishing a historical record for future reference (for example, to help you remember and help others to learn about what occurred). This record can provide a shortcut to solving a similar future problem.

Appendix D, "Problem-Solving Checklist and Worksheet," provides an outline of a checklist and worksheet that you can use to document progress through a problem resolution cycle.

NOTE   If you intend to take the test to become a Cisco Certified Internetwork Expert (CCIE), one of the components of the CCIE lab test is to check that you document all your work while being tested.

Preparing Yourself to Troubleshoot

As you troubleshoot, isolate problem causes, and restore your network to its normal functioning, you apply your expertise about your own network. In order to troubleshoot effectively, you should know your network well and be able to communicate efficiently and effectively with all key people involved in network administration and those people affected by the problem. Consider the network shown in Figure 1-8 and ask yourself the following questions:

Figure 1-8   *Today's networks are complex. Are you up to the challenge?*

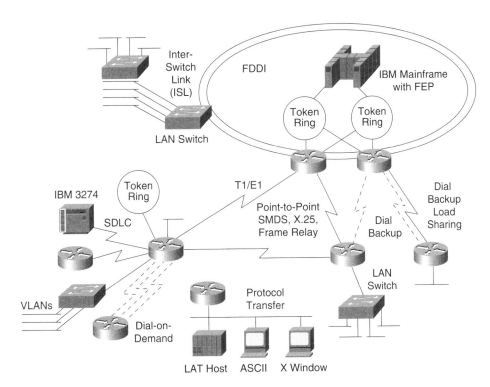

- Do you have an accurate physical and logical map of your internetwork? Does your organization or department have an up-to-date internetwork map that outlines the physical location of all the devices on the network and how they are connected, as well as a logical map of network addresses, network numbers, subnetworks, and so on?

- Do you have a list of all network protocols implemented in your network? For each of the protocols implemented, do you have a list of the network numbers, subnetworks, zones, areas, and so on that are associated with them?

- Do you know which protocols are being routed? For each of these protocols do you have a correct, up-to-date router configuration?

- Do you know which protocols are being bridged? Are there any filters configured in any of these bridges, and do you have a copy of these configurations?

- Do you know all the points of contact to external networks, including any connections to the Internet? For each external network connection, do you know which routing protocol is being used?

- Do you have an established baseline for your network? Has your organization documented normal network behavior and performance so that you can compare current problems with a baseline? What constitutes the normal baseline functioning that you expect when your network is running well? What events, new equipment, software, or reconfiguration have been added since the last baseline?

- What specific application characteristics and traffic demands are involved (and which are not involved) in the problem? What past troubleshooting cases (if any) might apply to or assist with the current situation?

A systematic troubleshooting method helps overcome the time that is often wasted trying to work through the maze of complex, interrelated network details. Because networks are strategic tools in your organization, it is a practical reality to look for shortcuts. These shortcuts usually come from prior expertise, which in turn probably resulted from systematic troubleshooting.

If you already have a systematic troubleshooting method that works well for you, continue using it to troubleshoot your networks. However, if you have not adopted a systematic troubleshooting method, consider using the one presented in this chapter.

To grow and communicate what is learned during network problem solving, use a process for documenting your troubleshooting details. Both now and in the future, this documentation step can help you, help others in your team, and help the engineers in Cisco's Technical Assistance Center (TAC).

Summary

In this chapter you have learned how to follow a standard problem-solving model. You have also learned how important it is to document your findings and actions. Now you should refer to Appendix D.

Chapter 2, "Protocol Characteristics Overview," focuses on how protocols such as TCP/IP, AppleTalk, and NetWare's IPX/SPX operate on the network. The protocol-level foundation knowledge should help you identify and eliminate the most common communications problems.

Chapter 1 Test
Troubleshooting Methodology

Estimated Time: 15 minutes

Complete all the exercises to test your knowledge of the materials contained in this chapter. Answers are listed in Appendix A, "Chapter Test Answer Key."

Use the information contained in this chapter to answer the following questions.

Question 1.1

What are some of the factors that can be considered when you calculate downtime costs?

_____

_____

_____

Question 1.2

What are the eight steps of the sample problem-solving model defined in this chapter?

1. _____

2. _____

3. _____

4. _____

5. _____

6. _____

7. _____

8. _____

Question 1.3

Where can you collect the facts when you approach a network problem?

_____

_____

_____

Question 1.4

If upon implementing an action plan, the network problems aren't resolved, what must you do before proceeding to the next action plan?

_____

_____

_____

Question 1.5

When addressing an access list problem, what additional concern must be taken into account as part of your action plan?

_____

_____

_____

CHAPTER 2

Protocol Characteristics Overview

This chapter compares connection-oriented and connectionless protocols and identifies commonly used protocols as being one or the other. It also focuses on the operation of Ethernet/IEEE 802.3, Token Ring/IEEE 802.5, Fiber Data Distributed Interface (FDDI), and serial protocols such as High-Level Data Link Control (HDLC), as well as routed protocols and routing protocol families such as Transmission Control Protocol/Internet Protocol (TCP/IP), Novell Internetwork Packet Exchange (IPX), and AppleTalk.

This chapter is divided into two main sections:

- Basic protocol characteristics
- Detailed protocol characteristics

The first section provides an introduction to protocols as a foundation or core set of communication elements. The second section provides in-depth details on the data link, network, and upper-layer protocols.

To become a successful troubleshooter, it is important that you understand how protocols behave under normal circumstances. This will help you recognize abnormal behavior when it occurs. Understanding the complexities of protocols will help you understand what is likely to break or not perform optimally.

Most protocols have common characteristics. For example, they are either connection oriented or connectionless and reliable or unreliable. Understanding in theory how these functions work helps you understand all connection-oriented protocols. Even though you may not currently work with some of the protocols in this chapter, in the future that might change. New protocols might be added to your internetwork or you might move to another job that requires you to understand new protocols. Consider, for example, the number of IPX NetWare networks that are now pure TCP/IP.

Basic Protocol Characteristics

As previously mentioned, protocols can be distinguished as either connection oriented or connectionless and reliable or unreliable.

A reliable protocol is a protocol that has error correction, flow control, and retransmission functionality built into it. Unreliable protocols depend on higher-layer protocols to provide reliability. An example of sending data reliably is sending a letter via certified mail with a return receipt. Unreliable data delivery would simply be dropping the letter in the mail box and having best-effort delivery.

Most connection-oriented protocols are reliable, and most connectionless protocols are unreliable, but there are exceptions. For example, Frame Relay is a connection-oriented protocol. It requires virtual circuit connectivity before data can be sent, but there are no reliability mechanisms built into Frame Relay. Likewise, Open Shortest Path First (OSPF) is connectionless. When OSPF sends out routing updates, it sends multicast packets (which are by definition connectionless), yet it still expects to see acknowledgments from its neighbors.

All the connection-oriented protocols discussed in this section are reliable protocols.

An entity can transmit data to another entity in an unplanned fashion and without prior coordination. This is known as *connectionless data transfer*, in which each packet stands alone. The receiving software entity that is part of the Open System Interconnection (OSI) reference model protocol stack sees that the packets received are complete, but a higher-layer application must put them in the proper order, manage timeout counters, and request the retransmission of missing packets.

Connection-Oriented Services

A connection-oriented data transfer is conceptually similar to a telephone call in which the caller initiates the call, knows when the connection is made because a person is heard at the other end of the line, and hangs up and terminates the call when the information exchange is complete.

A connection-oriented protocol has some method for connection establishment, flow control, error control, and session termination. TCP and Asynchronous Transfer Mode (ATM) are examples of connection-oriented protocols.

A connection-oriented protocol ensures that packets are in order and manages timeout counters. That connection-oriented protocol also requests retransmission of missing packets.

With connection-oriented data transfer, a logical association, or connection, is established between protocol entities. As shown in Figure 2-1, this type of data transfer has a clearly distinguishable lifetime, consisting of three distinct phases:

- Connection establishment
- Data transfer
- Connection termination

Figure 2-1   *The connection establishment phase (which occurs first in connection-oriented services) is often referred to as a* handshake.

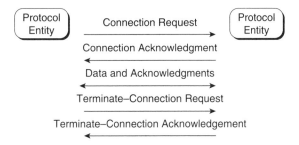

Depending on the protocol, a specific protocol entity might always establish and terminate the connection. However, in some protocols, either side can initiate these functions.

Connection-oriented data transfer is preferable to connectionless data transfer when stations require a lengthy exchange of data or certain details of their protocol must be worked out dynamically. TCP is an example of a connection-oriented protocol, and Asynchronous Transfer Mode (ATM) is another.

When troubleshooting connection-oriented protocols, check whether there are multiple retransmissions of segments of data. If there are, determine why the higher-layer protocol is requesting them. Verify that sequence numbers, acknowledgments, window sizes, and other parameters associated with this type of protocol are appropriate and are being incremented or managed correctly.

NOTE   Refer to the section "Detailed Protocol Characteristics" later in this chapter for more specific examples of connection-oriented communications.

Connectionless Services

With connectionless services, there is no connection setup between the two communicating protocol entities (see Figure 2-2). Each data unit is transmitted independently of previous and subsequent data units. A connectionless data transfer is conceptually similar to a set of postcards, each postcard handled separately. So, too, each packet stands alone. An entity can transmit data to another entity in an unplanned fashion and without prior coordination.

Figure 2-2   *Connectionless communications, shown here, are much simpler than the three-part connection-oriented communications. Notice that there is no connection made before data transfer begins.*

The receiving software entity that is part of the OSI reference model protocol stack sees that the packets received are complete, but a higher-layer application must put them in the proper order and request the retransmission of missing packets. A connectionless data transfer is efficient, is simple to implement, and has relatively low demands for network traffic.

When troubleshooting connectionless data transfer, look for problems where data is not acknowledged, where errors in the data are not reported to the sender, where data may arrive out of order (because it is not sequenced), and where there is no flow control.

When connectionless protocols are used at lower layers, upper layers are usually connection oriented to ensure reliable transfer of data. For example, in the TCP/IP protocol suite, IP is a connectionless Layer 3 protocol, but TCP is a connection-oriented protocol up at Layer 4.

Sample Connection Sequences

After you have identified and corrected any physical-layer or data link-layer troubleshooting targets, you can proceed to consider higher-level troubleshooting targets.

Failures at these lower layers propagate to the higher layers. For example, a bad Ethernet data link affects the connected router Ethernet interface, which in turn affects the TCP/IP routing tables, which in turn affects the connection made by an application.

Sometimes there can be multiple potential causes for a network problem, especially where there are multiple technologies, protocols, and data-link hops that the application will use.

NOTE   For the protocol suites covered next, the sending host on a network cannot get higher-layer data to a destination side until a network connection is made.

If users are having trouble making connections on the network, check the specific network and upper-layer protocol troubleshooting targets.

At the network layer are two types of protocols. Rout*ed* protocols send user data between hosts. Rout*ing* protocols communicate information between routers about the network paths to use. The connection sequences that protocol suites use involve both of these types of protocols as well as higher-layer protocols within the protocol suites. This chapter describes the following concepts:

- TCP/IP using Address Resolution Protocol (ARP) and synchronization (SYN) packets
- Novell NetWare Core Protocol (NCP) using Routing Information Protocol (RIP), Service Advertising Protocol (SAP), and Get Nearest Server (GNS) requests
- AppleTalk using several of the protocols in its protocol suite, including Routing Table Maintenance Protocol (RTMP), Zone Information Protocol (ZIP), Name Binding Protocol (NBP), and AppleTalk Transaction Protocol (ATP).

Let's take a look at the different connection sequences that occur with TCP/IP, NetWare, and AppleTalk. Each protocol set has a unique connection establishment routine.

The TCP Connection Sequence

TCP is an example of a connection-oriented protocol. The TCP connection establishment sequence is often called a *three-way handshake*, as shown in Figure 2-3.

Figure 2-3   *The three-way handshake must be completed successfully before data can be exchanged.*

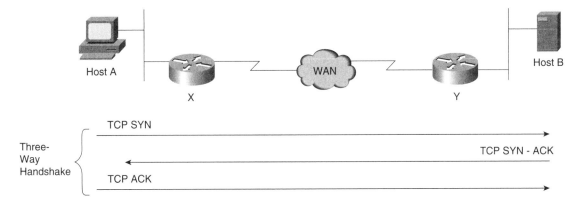

A three-way handshake consists of three stages:

- The host that wants to initiate the session sends a TCP synchronization (SYN) packet.
- The receiving host acknowledges the SYN and in the same packet sends its own SYN.
- The original host acknowledges the receipt of the SYN from the other host.

Figure 2-3 also shows Host A sending an ARP request and receiving a reply. The ARP frames are not part of a TCP session establishment, but are necessary for Host A to reach Host B.

Until Host A receives an ARP reply, it only knows the IP address of Host B. A MAC address must be determined in order to transmit data. Our example assumes that Host A's software sends ARP frames even when the destination is not local and the router responds to ARP frames for hosts on the other side. (The router runs proxy ARP, which is the default for Cisco Systems routers.)

A different, but correct, interpretation of the ARP frames shown in Figure 2-3 is that Host A is configured with Router X as its default router and must send an ARP to learn the MAC address of Router X.

ARP establishes correspondences between network addresses (an IP address, for example) and LAN hardware addresses (Ethernet addresses). A record of each correspondence is kept in a cache for a predetermined amount of time and then discarded.

When you are troubleshooting, use the **show ip arp** command to check for any anomalies (such as duplicate routes) and to see whether the host(s) in question is appearing in the ARP table.

NOTE   See the section "Detailed Protocol Characteristics" later in this chapter for more information on the TCP/IP protocol suite.

The NetWare Connection Sequence

NetWare has two types of connection sequences: Sequenced Packet Exchange (SPX) and NCP connections. NetWare uses SPX to provide transport-layer, connection-oriented services. In a manner similar to TCP, an SPX client requests synchronization with a peer SPX device. An acknowledgment reply completes SPX's two-way handshake process. SPX ensures the guaranteed delivery of data in order, just as TCP does.

Novell's NCP is also a connection-oriented protocol used by file servers and clients. Before a client can log in to an NCP file server and start requesting or sending data, the client first broadcasts a SAP GNS request, as shown in Figure 2-4.

Figure 2-4   *NetWare clients must perform service discovery before connecting to a server.*

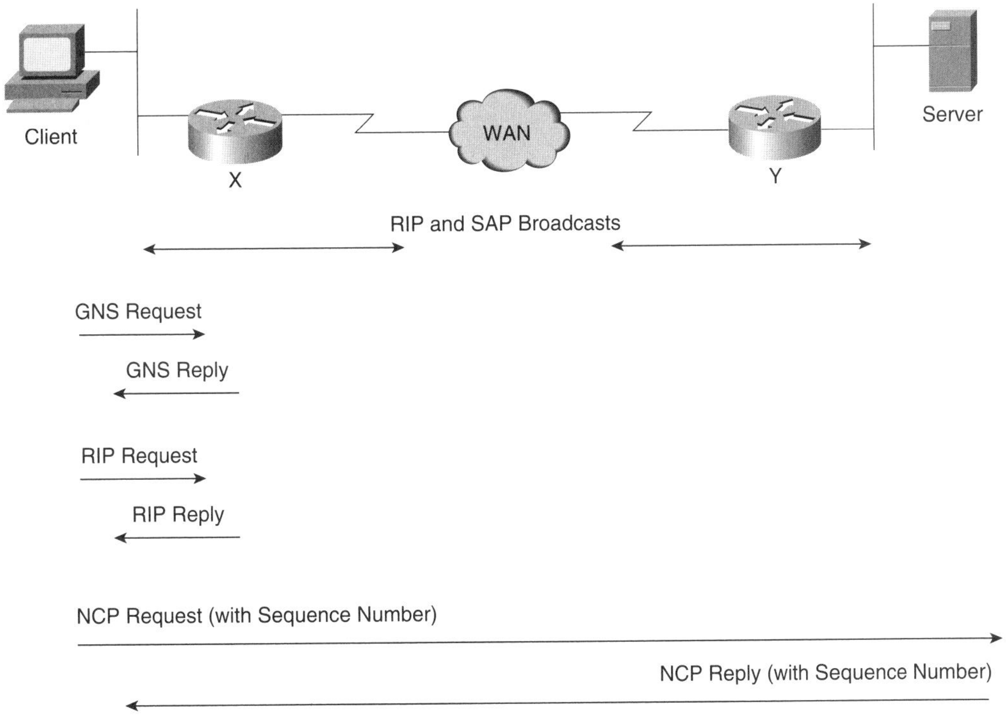

A router or server can respond to the request. Routers learn about services by listening to SAP broadcasts from servers and other routers. After a client learns about a server, it sends a RIP request to find a route to the server. Finally, the client can send NCP requests to log in and send and retrieve data.

NCP requests and replies contain a sequence number field to ensure that packets arrive in order and that no packets are missing.

NetWare versions 3.x and 4.x use IPX for Layer 3 connectivity, addressing, and routing. Interconnecting NetWare clients on LANs running IPX face a variety of problems that can impair connecting to a server over a routed Internet. These can include mismatched network numbers and encapsulation types. It is important to proceed with a systematic troubleshooting method to obtain facts to help you isolate the problem or problems. Among the several Cisco Internetwork Operating System (IOS) tools to help you isolate problems is the **show ipx interface** command. This command can be used to verify network and encapsulation configurations as well as the status of the router interfaces. The **show ipx traffic** command can be used for verifying the sending and receiving of packets from the protocols described previously in this chapter.

The interfaces should indicate that the interface is up and that the protocol is up.

NOTE See the section "Detailed Protocol Characteristics" later in this chapter for more information on the Novell NetWare protocol suite.

The AppleTalk Connection Sequence

ATP is a transport-layer, connection-oriented protocol that is used by both AppleTalk Filing Protocol (AFP) and Printer Access Protocol (PAP). It provides reliable transport of data when a client attaches to an AppleShare file server or printer.

Before a client can attach to a file server (or printer), it must locate the server through a process called *service discovery*. A Macintosh computer sends a GetZoneList request to the local router to fill the Chooser window with zone names. When the user clicks on a zone name and type of service, the Macintosh sends an NBP broadcast request, as shown in Figure 2-5.

Figure 2-5 *AppleTalk uses a combination of protocols to locate and connect to a service.*

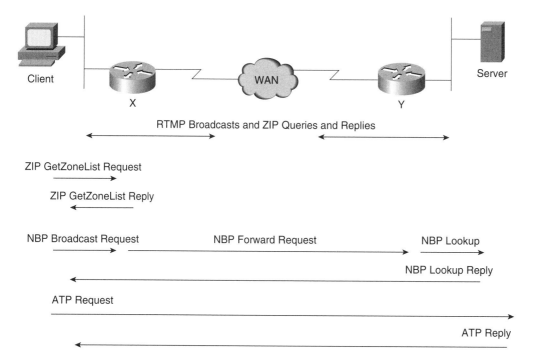

The router looks in its zone information table to determine which networks are in the requested zone. The router forwards the request to a router for each network in the zone. The receiving router then sends an NBP lookup request onto its local network. All servers of the requested service type respond to the original requesting Macintosh. (The address of the original requesting Macintosh is carried inside the NBP frames.)

When the client Macintosh knows how to reach a file server, it sets up a connection using ATP and AFP. It may also send an Echo frame in order to determine how much time it takes to reach the server. This information can be used for setting ATP timeout values.

A variety of problems can block access to servers and services on an AppleTalk network. For example, the Cisco IOS software command **show appletalk traffic** provides a good high-level overview of the AppleTalk activity on the router.

Another source of troubleshooting information is to look for an AppleTalk configuration mismatch. A mismatch occurs when the following rule of AppleTalk is violated: "All routers on a given cable must agree on the configuration of that cable (meaning that all must have matching network numbers, cable ranges, zone names, or zone lists)." The router declares a port configuration mismatch in the output of the **show appletalk interface** command.

NOTE	See the following section "Detailed Protocol Characteristics" for more information on the AppleTalk protocol suite.

Detailed Protocol Characteristics

Although this section starts in quite general terms, it quickly delves into the complexities of the protocol sets and operation of 802.3, 802.5, FDDI, Point-to-Point Protocol (PPP), Synchronous Data Link Control (SDLC), Frame Relay, ISDN, TCP/IP, NetWare IPX/SPX, and AppleTalk networks.

Let's start this discussion with the infamous OSI reference model. When discussing communication between or among computer systems, it is helpful to adopt a common set of standards or conventions. The International Organization for Standardization (ISO) developed the OSI reference model as a framework for defining standards for linking heterogeneous computers.

The OSI reference model includes a vertical set of layers. Each layer performs the functions required to communicate with the associated layer of another system. Each layer relies on the next lower layer to provide a set of services and at the same time provides services to the next higher layer. ISO finalized a reference model that has seven layers, and then defined each layer and the services to be performed there. Figure 2-6 shows the seven layers of the OSI model.

Figure 2-6   *The OSI model has seven layers.*

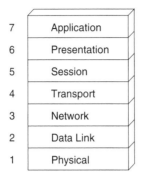

7	Application
6	Presentation
5	Session
4	Transport
3	Network
2	Data Link
1	Physical

The OSI layers and their functions are as follows:

- Layer 7, the application layer, specifies the user interface and the application program interface and is concerned with the meaning of data, job management, and data exchange.

- Layer 6, the presentation layer, accepts data from the application layer and negotiates data syntax, representation, compression, and encryption with peer systems.

- Layer 5, the session layer, adds control mechanisms such as checkpoints, terminations, and restarts to establish, maintain, and synchronize communication between applications.

- Layer 4, the transport layer, provides end-to-end accountability and ensures reliable data delivery using acknowledgments, sequence numbers, and flow control mechanisms.

- Layer 3, the network layer, specifies network routing (using symbolic addressing) and communication between network segments.

- Layer 2, the data link layer, is responsible for data transfer over a communication channel by consolidating data into frames, detecting and recovering from transmission errors, and defining physical device addresses.

- Layer 1, the physical layer, deals with the mechanical, electrical, functional, and procedural interface between user equipment and the network communications system— in other words, "getting bits onto the wire."

The intent of the OSI model is that protocols be developed to perform the functions of each layer to enable communication between corresponding (peer) entities at the same layer in two different systems.

Regardless of the nature of the applications or entities attempting to exchange data, there is usually a requirement that data be exchanged reliably; that is, all the data should arrive at the destination process in the same order in which it was sent.

Connection-Oriented Versus Connectionless Protocols

In order for applications or entities in different systems to communicate with each other, some form of protocol must define a set of rules (that is, the syntax and semantics) governing the exchange of data between the two.

A fundamental aspect of any communications architecture is that one or more protocols operate at each layer of the architecture, and that two peer protocols at the same layer but in different systems cooperate to achieve the communication function.

A set of functions forms the basis of most protocols. These functions might be present in protocols at the different conceptual layers. Although we are looking at the concept of protocols within the seven-layer OSI model, some vendors' protocols are proprietary. However, these protocols can be viewed as fitting within one or more of the OSI model's layers.

Protocol functions can be grouped into the following categories:

- Data segmentation and reassembly
- Data encapsulation
- Connection control
- Ordered delivery of data
- Flow control
- Error control
- Multiplexing

This section focuses on aspects of a protocol's connection characteristics that cover connection control, ordered delivery, flow control, and error control. Earlier in this chapter we talked about two types of protocols—connection oriented and connectionless. The connection-oriented protocols are likened to a telephone call, where we make certain there is a user at the other end before sending data, whereas connectionless services are more like a postcard in the mail, with no guarantee of delivery.

Connectionless Data Transfer

An entity can transmit data to another entity in an unplanned fashion and without prior coordination. This is known as *connectionless data transfer*, in which each packet stands alone. The receiving software entity that is part of the OSI protocol stack sees that the packets received are complete, but a higher-layer application must put them in the proper order and request the retransmission of missing packets. Although this mode can be useful, it is less common than connection-oriented transfer.

With connectionless data transfer, no logical connection is established and each PDU is transmitted independently of any previous or subsequent data unit. Figure 2-7 illustrates this concept.

Figure 2-7 *Connectionless data transfer has low overhead compared to connection-oriented services.*

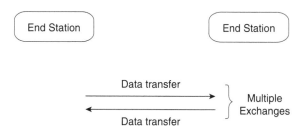

The stations make an *a priori* agreement with each other, but not with the lower-layer services, about transmission of protocol data units (PDUs).

Because no connection is established, each data unit is transmitted with a single service access, and this access must contain all the information necessary for the unit to be delivered to its destination (destination address, services required, and so on). As a result of this single-service access, no negotiation of parameters occurs. Also, because the PDUs are transported by the service provider, which knows no relationship between current, previous, or subsequent data units, they do not include ordered delivery, flow control, or error control.

The following are examples of connectionless protocols:

- IEEE 802.2 (often referred to as Logical Link Control [LLC]) offers three types of service, two of which are connectionless: Type 1 provides unacknowledged connectionless service, and Type 3 provides acknowledged connectionless service.

- OSI offers both a connectionless and connection-oriented network-layer service. The connectionless service is described in ISO 8473 (usually referred to as Connectionless Network Protocol [CLNP]).

- Internet Protocol (IP) is the network-layer connectionless protocol in the TCP/IP suite. User Datagram Protocol (UDP) is the connectionless transport-layer protocol in the TCP/IP suite.

- AppleTalk's primary network-layer protocol is Datagram Delivery Protocol (DDP). DDP provides connectionless service between network sockets.

- Novell's IPX is a connectionless network-layer datagram protocol for NetWare networks functioning on IPX/SPX. NetWare 5 can run directly over TCP/IP and replaces IPX functionality with UDP in that case.

- DECnet uses CLNP and Connectionless Network Service (CLNS) for connectionless service.

- Fast Sequenced Transport (FST) is a connectionless, sequenced transport protocol that runs on top of IP. FST uses the IP header to implement sequencing without violating the IP specification. FST transports remote source-route bridging (RSRB) packets to peers without TCP or UDP header or processor overhead.

Connection-Oriented Data Transfer

As mentioned earlier in this chapter, connection-oriented data transfer is preferable if stations require a lengthy exchange of data or certain details of their protocol must be worked out dynamically.

With connection-oriented data transfer, a logical association, or *connection*, is established between the entities. This type of data transfer has a clearly distinguishable lifetime, consisting of three distinct phases:

- Connection establishment
- Data transfer
- Connection termination

Connection establishment begins when one of the stations issues a connection request to the other. The two end stations might be the only devices involved, or a central authority might be involved as well.

As shown in Figure 2-8, during the connection establishment phase, the two end stations must make an agreement with each other and with the underlying protocol layer to exchange data. While the connection is in place, the parties agree on the acceptance of every error-free data unit that is transferred. There might be negotiation of parameters and options that will affect the subsequent data transfer (such as the maximum data or window size). The negotiation might result in the rejection of the connection, if one of the parties is unable to provide the connection configuration that has been requested.

Figure 2-8   *Connection-oriented data transfer has three phases.*

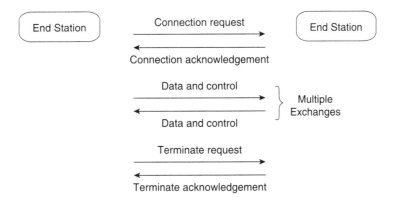

After the logical connection has been established, the data transfer phase is entered, when data and any relevant control information such as flow control or error control are exchanged between the end stations. A connection identifier can be used to identify that data and control information are associated with the logical connection.

A logical connection also allows for the use of sequencing, which means that each PDU is sequentially numbered. The end stations maintain a list of locally generated outgoing numbers and incoming numbers. Sequencing allows for ordered delivery, flow control, and error control. These concepts can be explained as follows:

- Ordered delivery—In a connection-oriented environment, because each PDU is identified by a connection identifier and sequence number, correct ordering of PDUs can be maintained. A unique sequential numbering scheme is determined during the connection establishment phase. The receiving station can use the sequential numbering scheme to easily reorder received PDUs, even if they arrive out of order.

- Flow control—With flow control, the transmitting station does not send data or information faster than the receiving station or any intermediate device can handle it. Again, with a connection-oriented protocol, the sequence numbers provide this function. The fundamental approach used with most protocols is a windowing technique in which the receiving station specifies how much buffer space is available for incoming PDUs. The sender sends that amount of data in PDUs and then waits to receive acknowledgment from the receiving station that it has received all or some of these PDUs and is ready to receive more.

- Error control—An end station detects damaged PDUs by performing a calculation on the bits received. If a PDU is damaged or lost, the end station requests retransmission of the affected PDU based on its record of sequence numbers.

The final phase of a connection-oriented operation is the termination of the connection. This can be initiated by any of the parties involved. Either of the end stations or the central authority, if one is involved, can send a termination request.

The following are examples of connection-oriented protocols:

- IEEE 802.2 (LLC) offers three types of service, one of which, Type 2, is connection oriented. LLC Type 2 (LLC2) is a connection-oriented OSI data link layer protocol that is widely used in local-area network (LAN) environments, particularly among IBM communication systems connected by Token Ring.

- ATM is a connection-oriented environment. All traffic to or from an ATM network is prefaced with a virtual path identifier (VPI) and virtual channel identifier (VCI). A VPI/VCI pair is considered a single virtual circuit (VC). Each VC is a private connection to another node on the ATM network. Each ATM node must establish a separate connection to every other node in the ATM network that it wants to communicate with.

- OSI offers a connection-oriented service sometimes called Connection-Mode Network Service (CMNS) as described in ISO 8208 and ISO 8878. (ISO 8208 is the X.25 packet-level protocol [PLP], sometimes referred to as Connection-Oriented Network Protocol [CONP]. ISO 8878 describes how to use ISO 8208 to provide OSI connection-oriented service.) OSI uses the X.25 packet-level protocol over IEEE 802 LANs for connection-oriented data movement and error indications.

  As with the OSI network layer, the OSI transport layer provides connection-oriented services. There are five connection-oriented OSI transport protocols: TP0, TP1, TP2, TP3, and TP4.

- In the TCP/IP protocol suite, TCP is a reliable, full-duplex, connection-oriented protocol that specifies the format of data and control packets that two computer systems exchange to transfer data.

- Novell's SPX is a connection-oriented NetWare transport protocol. Novell derived this protocol from the Xerox Network Systems (XNS) Sequenced Packet Protocol (SPP). As with TCP and many other transport protocols, SPX is a reliable, connection-oriented protocol that supplements the datagram service provided by Layer 3 protocols.

- AppleTalk supports several upper-layer protocols that are connection oriented. ATP is a popular transport-layer protocol that allows reliable request-response exchanges between two socket clients.

- DECnet's network layer uses the X.25 packet-level protocol, which is also known as X.25 Level 3, and CONP.

You will find that all protocol suites offer a combination of connection-oriented and connectionless services. If you spend most of your time learning one protocol, you will be pleasantly surprised to learn how fast you can pick up another protocol suite's connectionless and connection-oriented transport characteristics.

The next section discusses the OSI data link layer specifically. It's important to spend time focusing on your network's Layer 2 features in order to quickly recognize Layer 2 faults and misconfigurations.

OSI Layer 2 Characteristics

The OSI Layer 2, the data link layer, is responsible for arranging data into frames that are locally addressed. Specifically, this section covers LAN and WAN Layer 2 framing, such as Ethernet/IEEE 802.3, Token Ring/802.5, FDDI, and PPP.

Ethernet/IEEE 802.3

This section focuses on the most popular data link layer protocols: Ethernet/IEEE 802.3, Token Ring, FDDI, PPP, SDLC, X.25, Frame Relay, and ISDN.

Ethernet was developed by Xerox Corporation's Palo Alto Research Center (PARC) in the 1970s. Digital Equipment Corporation, Intel Corporation, and Xerox Corporation jointly developed and released an Ethernet specification (Version 2.0) that is substantially compatible with IEEE 802.3. IEEE 802.3 was first approved by the Institute of Electrical and Electronic Engineers (IEEE) board in 1983. Together, Ethernet and IEEE 802.3 currently maintain the greatest market share of any LAN protocol. Today, the term *Ethernet* is often used to refer to all carrier-sense multiple access collision detection (CSMA/CD) LANs that generally conform to Ethernet specifications, including IEEE 802.3.

Ethernet was developed to fill the middle ground between long-distance, low-speed networks and specialized computer-room networks carrying data at high speeds for very limited distances. Ethernet is well suited to applications where a local communication medium must carry bursty, occasionally heavy traffic at high peak data rates.

Ethernet and IEEE 802.3 specify similar technologies. Both are CSMA/CD LANs. Stations on a CSMA/CD LAN can access the network at any time. Before sending data, CSMA/CD stations listen to the network to see if it is already in use. If it is, the station that wants to transmit waits, in a sort of "deferral process." If the network is not in use, the station transmits. A collision occurs when two stations listen for network traffic, hear none and transmit simultaneously. In this case, both transmissions are damaged and the stations must retransmit later. A backoff algorithm determines when the colliding stations retransmit. CSMA/CD stations can detect collisions, so they know when they must retransmit.

Both Ethernet and IEEE 802.3 hubbed and repeated LANs are broadcast networks. In other words, all stations see all frames, regardless of whether they represent an intended destination. Each station must examine received frames to determine whether the station is a destination. If it is, the frame is passed to a higher protocol layer for appropriate processing. Layer 2 bridges and switches dynamically change this model by limiting unnecessary traffic propagation.

Differences between Ethernet and IEEE 802.3 LANs are subtle. Ethernet provides services corresponding to Layers 1 and 2 of the OSI reference model, and IEEE 802.3 specifies the physical layer (Layer 1) and only a portion of Layer 2. IEEE 802.2 specifies the remaining portion of Layer 2 (the LLC portion). Both Ethernet and IEEE 802.3 are implemented in hardware as either an interface card in a host computer or circuitry on a primary circuit board within a host computer.

IEEE 802.3 specifies several different physical layers, whereas Ethernet defines only one. Each IEEE 802.3 physical layer protocol has a name that summarizes its characteristics. The coded components of an IEEE 802.3 physical layer name are shown in Figure 2-9.

Figure 2-9   *The IEEE 802.3 physical layer name components describe its functionality.*

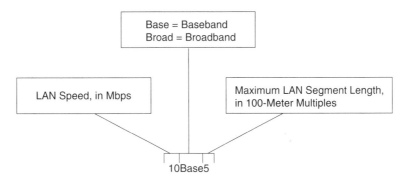

Table 2-1 is a summary of Ethernet Version 2 and IEEE 802.3 characteristics.

Table 2-1   *Ethernet Version 2 and IEEE 802.3 physical characteristics.*

Characteristic	Ethernet Value	802.3 Values					
		10Base5	10Base2	1Base5	10BaseT	100BaseT	10Broad36
Data rate (Mbps)	10	10	10	1	10	100	10
Signaling method	Baseband	Baseband	Baseband	Baseband	Baseband	Baseband	Broadband
Maximum segment length (m)	500	500	185	250	100	100	1800
Media	50-ohm coax (thick)	50-ohm coax (thick)	50-ohm coax (thin)	Unshielded twisted pair	Unshielded twisted pair	Unshielded twisted pair	75-ohm coax
Topology	Bus	Bus	Bus	Star	Star	Star	Bus

Ethernet is most similar to IEEE 802.3 10Base5. Both protocols specify a bus-topology network with a connecting cable between the end stations and the actual network medium. In the case of Ethernet, that cable is called a *transceiver cable*. The transceiver cable connects to a transceiver device attached to the physical network medium. The IEEE 802.3 configuration is similar, except that the connecting cable is referred to as an *attachment unit interface (AUI)*, and the transceiver is called a *medium attachment unit (MAU)*. In both cases, the connecting cable attaches to an interface board (or interface circuitry) within the end station. Figure 2-10 shows the Ethernet and IEEE 802.3 frame formats.

Figure 2-10 *The type and length fields differentiate Ethernet_II and IEEE 802.3 frame formats.*

Ethernet

7	1	6	6	2	46–1500	4
Preamble	S O F	Destination Address	Source Address	Type	Data	FCS

IEEE 802.3

7	1	6	6	2	46–1500	4
Preamble	S O F	Destination Address	Source Address	Length	802.2 Header and Data	FCS

SOF = Start-of-Frame Delimiter
FCS = Frame Check Sequence

Both Ethernet and IEEE 802.3 frames begin with an alternating pattern of ones and zeros called a *preamble*. The preamble tells receiving stations that a frame is coming.

The byte before the destination address in both an Ethernet and an IEEE 802.3 frame ends with two consecutive 1 bits, which synchronize the frame reception portions of all stations on the LAN. The IEEE 802.3 specification defines this as the start-of-frame delimiter (SFD), following a 7-byte preamble, whereas the Ethernet specifications simply include this pattern at the end of the 8-byte preamble.

Immediately following the preamble/SFD in both Ethernet and IEEE 802.3 frames are the destination and source address fields. Both Ethernet and IEEE 802.3 addresses are 6 bytes long. Addresses are contained in hardware on the Ethernet and IEEE 802.3 interface cards. The first 3 bytes of the addresses are specified by the IEEE as a vendor code, and the last 3 bytes are specified by the interface card vendor. The source address is always a unicast (that is, single-node) address, and the destination address can be unicast, multicast (group), or broadcast (all nodes).

In Ethernet frames, the 2-byte field following the source address is a type field. This field specifies the upper-layer protocol to receive the data after Ethernet processing is complete.

In IEEE 802.3 frames, the 2-byte field following the source address is a length field, which is a value in the range 0001 to 05DC (hexadecimal) and indicates the number of bytes of data that follow this field and precede the frame check sequence (FCS) field.

Following the type/length field is the actual data contained in the frame. After physical-layer and link-layer processing is complete, this data is eventually sent to an upper-layer protocol. In the case of Ethernet, the upper-layer protocol is identified in the type field. In the case of IEEE 802.3, the upper-layer protocol must be defined within the data portion of the frame. If data in the frame is insufficient to fill the frame to its minimum 64-byte size, padding bytes are inserted to ensure at least a 64-byte frame.

After the data field is a 4-byte FCS field that contains a cyclic redundancy check (CRC) value. The CRC is created by the sending device and recalculated by the receiving device to check for damage that might have occurred to the frame in transit.

Figure 2-11 shows the 802.2 header and data frame format. (This format is also referred to as the LLC PDU.)

Figure 2-11 *The 802.2 header and data frame format is also referred to as the LLC PDU.*

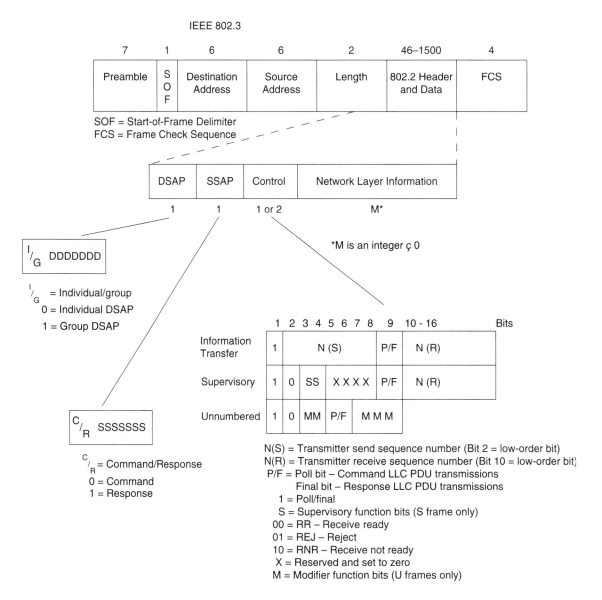

The 1-byte destination service access point (DSAP) and source service access point (SSAP) fields specify the destination and sending upper-layer protocols. The SAP fields have the same function as the type field in an Ethernet Version 2 frame.

The control field identifies the particular PDU and specifies various control functions. It is 1 or 2 bytes long, depending on the type of PDU. The PDU can be either a command or a response and is either an information transfer, a supervisory, or an unnumbered information PDU.

The network-layer information field carries the upper-layer protocol data.

An extension to the LLC was defined by the Internet community in RFC 1042, primarily to encapsulate IP datagrams and ARP requests and replies within IEEE 802.3, IEEE 802.4 (Token Bus), IEEE 802.5 (Token Ring), and FDDI networks. Doing this allows IP datagrams, which have historically been tied to Ethernet frames, to be transported across non-Ethernet networks through a Subnetwork Access Protocol (SNAP) mechanism. Figure 2-12 shows the SNAP frame format.

Figure 2-12 *SAP AA fields indicate a SNAP frame.*

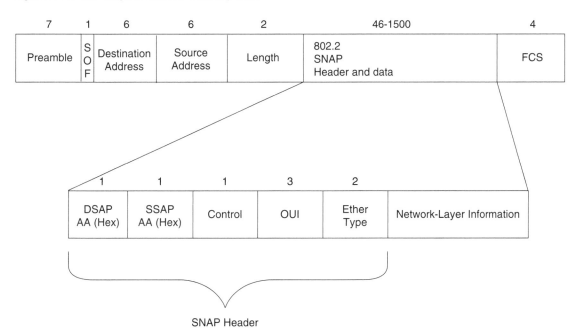

The first 3 bytes of the 802.2 portion of the frame are the same as for the LLC frame. The DSAP and SSAP fields have the special value AA (hex, indicating that this is a SNAP-format frame).

Following the control field is a 5-byte protocol identifier; the first 3 bytes represent the organizational unit identifier (OUI), a unique value that is assigned to an organization by the IEEE. The remaining 2 bytes contain information that is similar to the type field used in an Ethernet frame.

For more information on Ethernet, IEEE 802.3, or other network types, refer to Appendix C, "References and Recommended Reading."

Token Ring/IEEE 802.5

Token Ring was originally developed by IBM in the early 1980s. It is still IBM's primary LAN technology, and is second only to Ethernet/IEEE 802.3 in general LAN popularity. The IEEE 802.5 specification is almost identical to IBM's Token Ring network. In fact, the IEEE 802.5 specification was modeled after IBM Token Ring and continues to shadow IBM's Token Ring development. The term *Token Ring* is generally used to refer to both IBM's Token Ring networks and IEEE 802.5 networks.

Token Ring and IEEE 802.5 networks are compatible, although the specifications differ in relatively minor ways. IBM's Token Ring network specifies a star, with all end stations attached to a device called a multistation access unit (MSAU), whereas IEEE 802.5 does not specify a topology (although virtually all IEEE 802.5 implementations are also based on a star). There are other differences, including media type (IEEE 802.5 does not specify a media type, and IBM Token Ring networks primarily use twisted pair) and routing information field size. In some cases, the specifications are identical. Both IBM Token Ring and IEEE 802.5 specify the following:

- Baseband signaling
- Token passing
- Data rates of either 4 or 16 Mbps

Token Ring and IEEE 802.5 are the primary examples of token-passing networks. Token-passing networks move a small frame, called a *token*, around the network. Possession of the token grants the right to transmit. If a node receiving the token has no information to send, it simply passes the token to the next end station. Each station has a limitation on the amount of time that it can hold the token.

If a station that possesses the token has information to transmit, it alters 1 bit of the token (which turns the token into a start-of-frame sequence), appends the information it wants to transmit, performs a CRC calculation on the contents of the frame, and sends this information to the next station on the ring. While the information frame is circling the ring, there is no token on the network (unless the ring supports early token release), so other stations that want to transmit must wait. Therefore, collisions cannot occur in Token Ring networks. If early token release is supported, a new token can be released when frame transmission is completed. Although there may be multiple frames on the ring, there can be only one token on the ring at any time.

The information frame circulates the ring until it reaches the intended destination station, which copies the information for further processing. The information frame continues to circle the ring and is finally removed when it reaches the sending station. The sending station can check the returning frame to see whether the frame was seen and subsequently copied by the destination. The sending station is responsible for stripping the frame off the ring once it has returned.

Unlike CSMA/CD networks (such as Ethernet), token-passing networks are deterministic. In other words, it is possible to calculate the maximum time that will pass before any end station will be able to transmit. This feature and several reliability features make Token Ring networks ideal for applications where delay must be predictable, and robust network operation is important. Factory automation environments are examples of such applications.

Token Ring network stations are directly connected to MSAUs, which can be wired together to form one large ring (as shown in Figure 2-13). Patch cables connect MSAUs to adjacent MSAUs. Lobe cables connect MSAUs to stations. MSAUs include bypass relays for removing stations from the ring.

Figure 2-13   *Token Ring devices connect through MSAUs.*

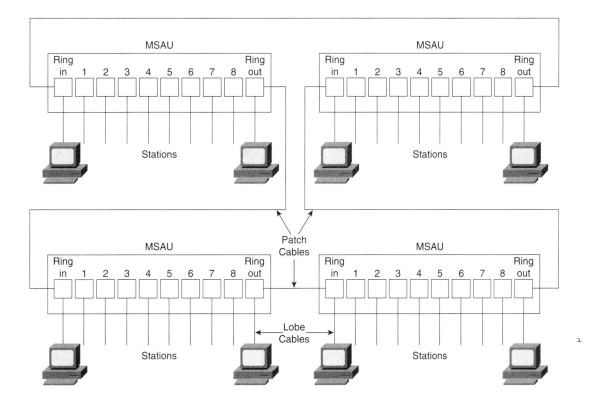

Token Ring networks use several mechanisms for detecting and compensating for network faults. For example, one station in the Token Ring network is selected to be the active monitor. This station, which can potentially be any station on the network, acts as a centralized source of timing information for other ring stations and performs a variety of ring maintenance functions. One of these functions is the removal of continuously circulating frames from the ring. When a sending device fails, its frame might continue to circle the ring. This can prevent other stations from transmitting their own frames and essentially lock up the network. The active monitor can detect such frames, remove them from the ring, and generate a new token.

The Token Ring network's star topology also contributes to overall network reliability. Because all information in a Token Ring network is seen by active MSAUs, intelligent versions of these devices can be programmed to check for problems and selectively remove stations from the ring if necessary.

A Token Ring process called *beaconing* detects and tries to repair certain network faults. Whenever a station detects a serious problem with the network (such as a cable break), it sends a beacon frame. The beacon frame defines a fault domain, which includes the station reporting the failure, its nearest active upstream neighbor (NAUN), and everything in between. Beaconing initiates a process called *autoreconfiguration*, where nodes within the fault domain automatically perform diagnostics in an attempt to reconfigure the network around the failed areas. Physically, the MSAU can accomplish this through electrical reconfiguration.

Token Ring networks support a sophisticated priority system that permits high-priority applications to use the network more frequently than lower-priority applications. Token Ring frames have two fields that control priority: the priority field and the reservation field.

Only stations with a priority equal to or higher than the priority value contained in a token can seize that token. After the token is seized and changed to an information frame, only stations with a priority value higher than that of the transmitting station can reserve the token for the next pass around the network. When the next token is generated, it includes the higher priority of the reserving station. Stations that raise a token's priority level must reinstate the previous priority after their transmission is complete.

Token Ring networks define two frame types: tokens and data/command frames. Figure 2-14 shows both formats.

Figure 2-14 *The IEEE 802.5 and IBM Token Ring frame formats are identical.*

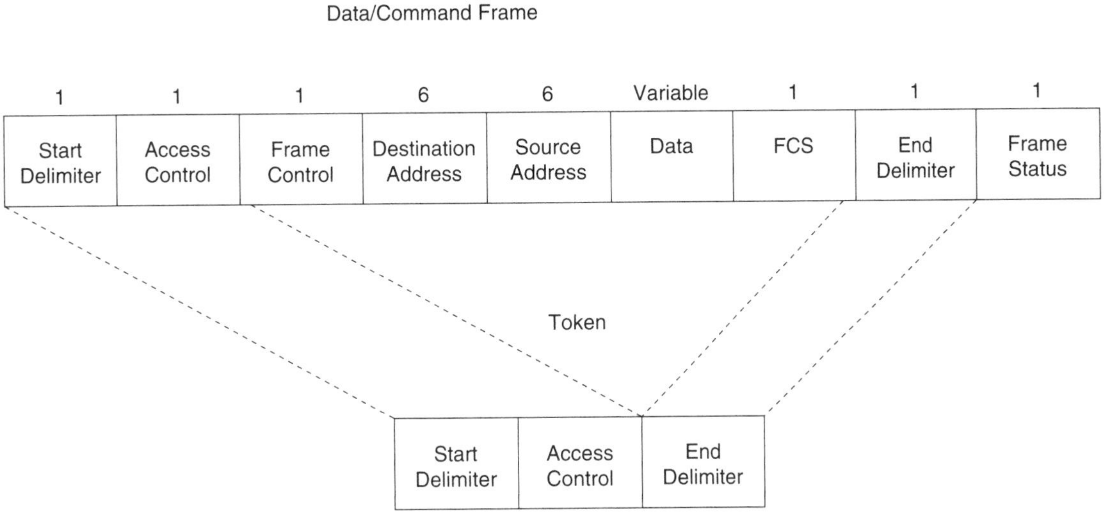

Data/Command Frame

1	1	1	6	6	Variable	1	1	1
Start Delimiter	Access Control	Frame Control	Destination Address	Source Address	Data	FCS	End Delimiter	Frame Status

Token

Start Delimiter	Access Control	End Delimiter

Tokens

A token is 3 bytes long and consists of a start delimiter, an access control byte, and an end delimiter.

The start delimiter alerts each station that a token (or data/command frame) has arrived. This field includes signals that distinguish the byte from the rest of the frame by violating the encoding scheme used elsewhere in the frame.

The access control byte contains the priority and reservation fields (used to allow some devices more frequent access to the token); a token bit (used to differentiate a token from a data/command frame); and a monitor bit (used by the active monitor to determine whether a frame is circling the ring endlessly).

Finally, the end delimiter signals the end of the token or data/command frame. It also contains bits to indicate a damaged frame and a frame that is the last in a logical sequence.

Data/Command Frames

Data/command frames vary in size, depending on the size of the data (information) field. Data frames carry information for upper-layer protocols; command frames contain control information and have no data for upper-layer protocols.

In data/command frames, a frame control byte follows the access control byte. The frame control byte indicates whether the frame contains data or control information. In control frames, this byte specifies the type of control information.

Following the frame control byte are the two address fields that identify the destination and source stations. As with IEEE 802.3, addresses are 6 bytes long.

The data field follows the address fields. The length of this field is limited by the token holding timer, which defines the maximum time a station can hold the token.

Following the data field is the FCS field. This field is filled by the source station with a calculated value dependent on the frame contents. The destination station recalculates the value to determine whether the frame was damaged in transit. If it was damaged, the frame is discarded.

As with the token, the end delimiter signifies the end of the data/command frame. However, unlike the token, the frame status byte follows the end delimiter in a data/command frame. The frame status field includes the address recognized and frame-copied indicators. The address recognized indicator allows the destination station to indicate that it recognized the destination address. The frame-copied indicator allows the destination station to indicate that it copied the frame data.

For more information on Token Ring technology, refer to Appendix C, "References and Recommended Reading."

FDDI

The FDDI standard was produced by the ANSI X3T9.5 standards committee in the mid-1980s. During this period, high-speed engineering workstations were beginning to tax the capabilities of existing LANs (primarily Ethernet and Token Ring). A new LAN technology was needed that could easily support these workstations and their new distributed applications. At the same time, network reliability was becoming an increasingly important issue as system managers began to migrate mission-critical applications from large computers to networks. FDDI was developed to fill these needs.

After completing the FDDI specification, American National Standards Institute (ANSI) submitted FDDI to the ISO. ISO has created an international version of FDDI that is completely compatible with the ANSI standard version.

FDDI has gained a substantial following that continues to increase as the cost of FDDI interfaces decreases. FDDI is frequently used as a backbone technology as well as a means to connect high-speed computers in a local area.

FDDI specifies a 100-Mbps, token-passing, dual-ring LAN using a fiber-optic transmission medium. It defines the physical layer and the media-access portion of the data link layer and is roughly analogous to IEEE 802.3 and IEEE 802.5 in its relationship to the OSI reference model.

FDDI is similar to Token Ring, although it operates at faster speeds. The two networks share many features, including topology (ring), media-access technique (token passing), and reliability features (beaconing, for example).

One of FDDI's most important characteristics is its use of optical fiber as a transmission medium. Optical fiber offers several advantages over traditional copper wiring:

- Security—Fiber does not emit electrical signals that can be tapped.
- Reliability—Fiber is immune to electrical interference.
- Speed—Fiber has much higher throughput potential than copper cable.

FDDI defines the use of two types of fiber: single mode (sometimes called monomode) and multimode. Modes can be thought of as bundles of light rays entering the fiber at a particular angle. Single-mode fiber allows only one mode of light to propagate through the fiber, and multimode fiber allows multiple modes of light to propagate through the fiber. Because multiple modes of light propagating through the fiber might travel different distances (depending on the entry angles), causing them to arrive at the destination at different times (a phenomenon called *modal dispersion*), single-mode fiber is capable of higher bandwidth and greater cable run distances than multimode fiber. Due to these characteristics, single-mode fiber is often used for campus backbones, and multimode fiber is often used for workgroup connectivity. Multimode fiber uses light-emitting diodes (LEDs) as the light-generating devices, and single-mode fiber generally uses lasers.

FDDI is defined by four separate specifications (see Figure 2-15).

Figure 2-15   *There are several FDDI standards for Layer 1 and 2 connectivity.*

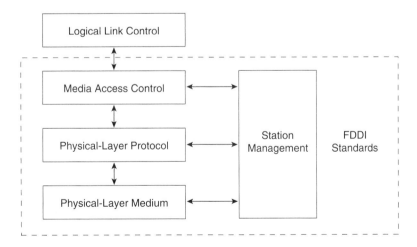

The following list explains these specifications in more detail:

- Physical-Layer Medium Dependent (PMD)—Defines the characteristics of the transmission medium, including the fiber-optic link, power levels, bit error rates, optical components, and connectors.
- Physical-Layer Protocol (PHY)—Defines data encoding/decoding procedures, clocking requirements, framing, and other functions.

- Media Access Control (MAC)—Defines how the medium is accessed, including frame format, token handling, addressing, calculating a cyclic redundancy check value, and recovering from errors.

- Station Management (SMT)—Defines the FDDI station configuration, ring configuration, and ring control features, including station insertion and removal, initialization, fault isolation and recovery, scheduling, and statistics collection.

FDDI specifies the use of dual rings. Traffic on these rings travels in opposite directions. Physically, the rings consist of two or more point-to-point connections between adjacent stations. One of the two FDDI rings is called the *primary ring*; the other is called the *secondary ring*. The primary ring is used for data transmission, and the secondary ring is generally used as a backup.

There are two classes that define device attachment to the FDDI network. Class B stations, or single attachment stations (SASs), attach to one ring; Class A stations, or dual attachment stations (DASs), attach to both rings. SASs are attached to the primary ring through a concentrator that provides connections for multiple SASs. The concentrator ensures that failure or power down of any given SAS does not interrupt the ring (see Figure 2-16). This is particularly useful when PCs or similar devices that power on and off frequently connect to the ring.

Figure 2-16 *A typical FDDI configuration with both DASs and SASs includes the FDDI node types DAS, SAS, and concentrator.*

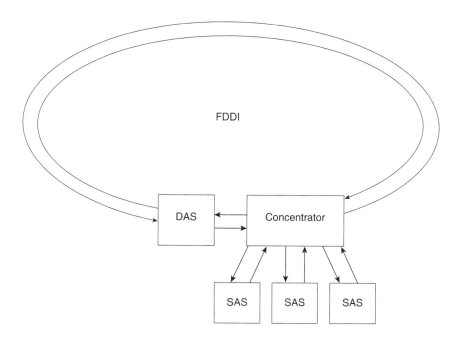

Each FDDI DAS has two ports designated A and B. These ports connect the station to the dual FDDI ring. Therefore, each port provides a connection for both the primary and the secondary ring, as Figure 2-17 shows.

Figure 2-17 *FDDI DASs connect Port A to Port B.*

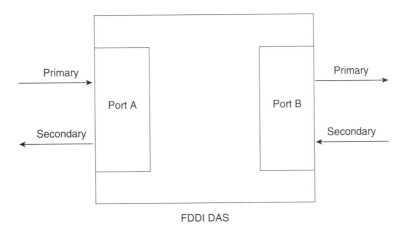

FDDI DAS

FDDI supports real-time allocation of network bandwidth, making it ideal for a variety of application types. FDDI provides this support by defining two types of traffic: synchronous and asynchronous. Synchronous traffic can consume a portion of the 100-Mbps total bandwidth of an FDDI network, and asynchronous traffic can consume the rest. Synchronous bandwidth is allocated to stations that require continuous transmission capability. This capability is useful for transmitting voice and video information, for example. Other stations use the remaining bandwidth asynchronously. FDDI's SMT specification defines a distributed bidding scheme to allocate FDDI bandwidth.

Asynchronous bandwidth is allocated using an eight-level priority scheme. Each application can be assigned an asynchronous priority level. FDDI also permits extended dialogues, where stations can temporarily use all asynchronous bandwidth by using a reserved token. FDDI's reserved token mechanism can essentially lock out stations that cannot use synchronous bandwidth.

FDDI provides several fault-tolerant features. The primary fault-tolerant feature is the dual ring. If a station on the dual ring fails or is powered down, or if the cable is damaged, the dual ring is automatically "wrapped" (that is, doubled back onto itself) into a single ring, as shown in Figure 2-18. In this figure, when Station 3 fails, the dual ring is automatically wrapped in Stations 2 and 4, forming a single ring. Although Station 3 is no longer on the ring, network operation continues for the remaining stations.

Figure 2-18   *FDDI station failures result in ring recovery via ring wrapping.*

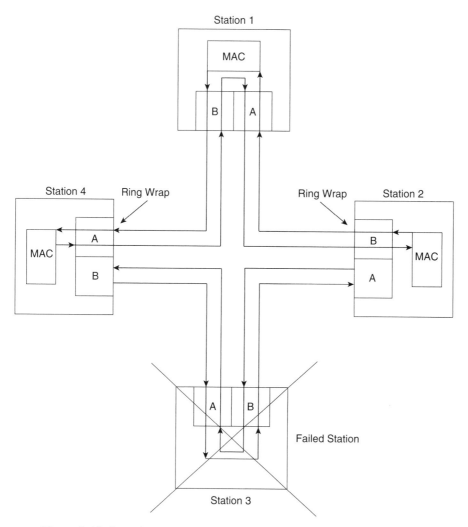

Figure 2-19 shows how FDDI compensates for a wiring failure. Stations 3 and 4 wrap the ring within themselves when wiring between them fails.

Figure 2-19 *Failed wiring also results in ring recovery via ring wrapping.*

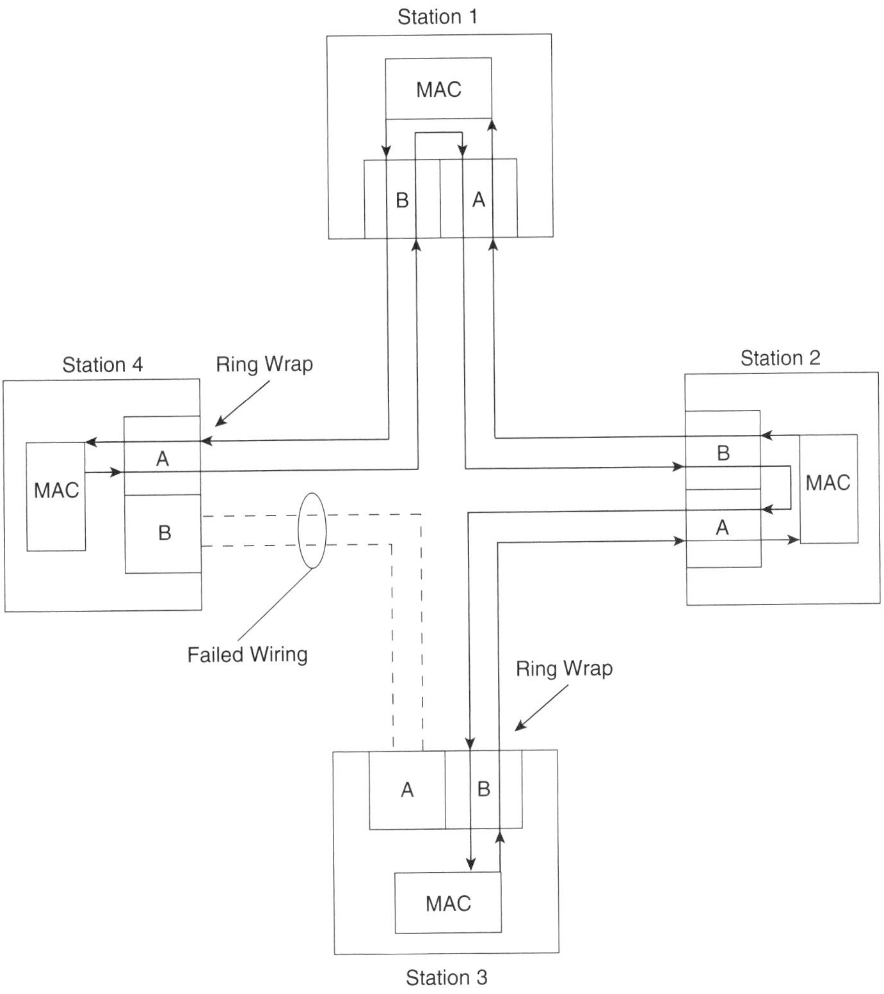

As FDDI networks grow, the possibility of multiple ring failures grows. When two ring failures occur, the ring is wrapped in both cases, which might segment the ring into two separate rings that cannot communicate with each other. Subsequent failures might cause additional ring segmentation.

Optical bypass switches can be used to prevent ring segmentation by eliminating failed stations from the ring. Figure 2-20 shows that station 1 has been completely removed from the ring.

Figure 2-20 *Optical bypass switches can be used for ring recovery.*

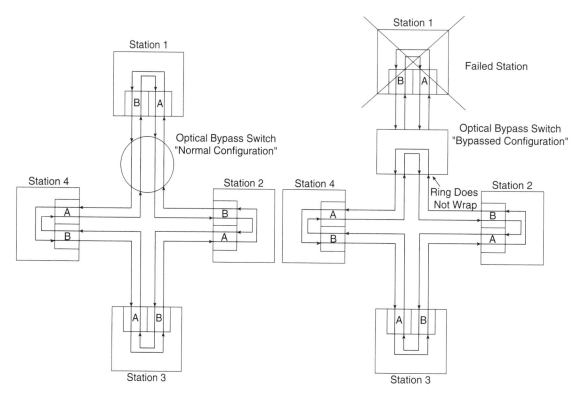

Critical devices such as routers or mainframe hosts can use another fault-tolerant technique called *dual homing* to provide additional redundancy and help guarantee operation. In dual-homing situations, the critical device is attached to two concentrators. One concentrator link is declared the active link; the other is declared passive. The passive link stays in backup mode until the primary link (or the concentrator to which it is attached) is determined to have failed. When this occurs, the passive link is automatically activated.

FDDI frame formats (shown in Figure 2-21) are similar to those of Token Ring.

Figure 2-21 *The FDDI frame format is similar to the Token Ring format.*

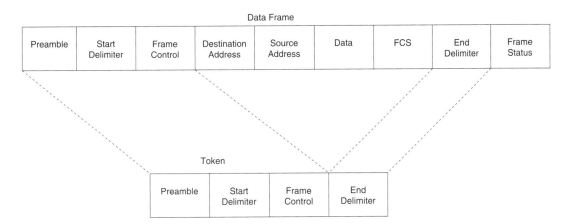

The preamble prepares each station for the upcoming frame. The start delimiter indicates the beginning of the frame. It consists of signaling patterns that differentiate it from the rest of the frame.

The frame control field indicates the size of the address fields, whether the frame contains asynchronous or synchronous data, and other control information.

As with Ethernet and Token Ring, FDDI addresses are 6 bytes. The destination address field can contain a unicast (singular), multicast (group), or broadcast (every station) address, and the source address identifies the single station that sent the frame.

The data field contains either information destined for an upper-layer protocol or control information.

As with Token Ring and Ethernet, the FCS field is filled by the source station with a calculated CRC value dependent on the frame contents. The destination station recalculates the value to determine whether the frame was damaged in transit. If it was damaged, the frame is discarded.

The end delimiter contains nondata symbols that indicate the end of the frame.

The frame status field allows the source station to determine if an error occurred and if the frame was recognized and copied by a receiving station.

For more information on FDDI, refer to Appendix C, "References and Recommended Reading."

PPP

In the late 1980s, the Internet began to experience explosive growth in the number of hosts supporting IP. The vast majority of these hosts were connected to LANs of various types, Ethernet being the most common. Most of the other hosts were connected through wide-area networks (WANs) such as X.25 public data networks (PDNs). Relatively few of these hosts were connected with simple point-to-point (that is, serial) links. Yet point-to-point links are among the oldest methods of data communications, and almost every host supports point-to-point connections.

One reason for the small number of point-to-point IP links was the lack of a standard Internet encapsulation protocol. PPP was designed to solve this problem. In addition to solving the problem of standardized Internet encapsulation of IP over point-to-point links, PPP was also designed to address other issues, including assignment and management of IP addresses, asynchronous (start/stop) and bit-oriented synchronous encapsulation, network protocol multiplexing, link configuration, link quality testing, error detection, and option negotiation for such capabilities as network-layer address negotiation and data compression negotiation. PPP addresses these issues by providing an extensible Link Control Protocol and a family of Network Control Protocols to negotiate optional configuration parameters and facilities. Today, PPP supports other protocols besides IP, including IPX and DECnet.

PPP provides a method for transmitting datagrams over serial point-to-point links. It has three main components:

- A method for encapsulating datagrams over serial links—PPP uses HDLC as a basis for encapsulating datagrams over point-to-point links.

- An extensible Link Control Protocol to establish, configure, and test the data-link connection.

- A family of Network Control Protocols for establishing and configuring different network-layer protocols. PPP is designed to allow the simultaneous use of multiple network-layer protocols.

In order to establish communications over a point-to-point link, the originating PPP station first sends LCP frames to configure and (optionally) test the data link. After the link has been established and optional facilities have been negotiated as needed by the LCP, the originating PPP sends Network Control Protocol frames to choose and configure one or more network-layer protocols. When each of the chosen network-layer protocols has been configured, packets from each network-layer protocol can be sent over the link. The link remains configured for communications until explicit LCP or NCP frames close the link or until some external event occurs (for example, an inactivity timer expires or a user intervenes).

PPP can operate across any data terminal equipment (DTE)/data circuit-terminating equipment (DCE) interface (for example, EIA/TIA-232, EIA/TIA-422, EIA/TIA-423, or ITU-T V.35). The only absolute requirement imposed by PPP is the provision of a duplex circuit, either dedicated or switched, that can operate in either an asynchronous or synchronous bit-serial mode, transparent to PPP link-layer frames. PPP does not impose any restrictions regarding transmission rate, other than those imposed by the particular DTE/DCE interface in use. Figure 2-22 shows the PPP frame format.

Figure 2-22 *The PPP frame format allows for both synchronous and asynchronous connections.*

1	1	1	2	Variable	2 or 4
Flag	Address	Control	Protocol	Data	FCS

The flag sequence is a single byte and indicates the beginning or end of a frame. The flag sequence consists of the binary sequence 01111110.

The address field is a single byte and contains the binary sequence 11111111, the standard broadcast address. PPP does not assign individual station addresses because it supports only a single connection between two devices.

The control field is a single byte and contains the binary sequence 00000011, which calls for transmission of user data in an unsequenced frame. A connectionless link service similar to that of LLC Type 1 is provided.

The protocol field is 2 bytes, and its value identifies the protocol encapsulated in the information field of the frame. The most up-to-date values of the protocol field are specified in the most recent assigned RFC numbers (RFC 1700).

NOTE   An up-to-date list of assigned numbers can be found at www.iana.org.

The data field is 0 or more bytes long and contains the datagram for the protocol specified in the protocol field. The end of the information field is found by locating the closing flag sequence and allowing 2 bytes for the FCS field. The default maximum length of the information field is 1,500 bytes. By prior agreement, consenting PPP implementations can use other values for the maximum information field length.

The FCS field is normally 2 bytes. By prior agreement, consenting PPP implementations can use a 4-byte FCS for improved error detection.

The LCP can negotiate modifications to the standard PPP frame structure. However, modified frames are always clearly distinguishable from standard frames.

The PPP LCP provides a method of establishing, configuring, maintaining and terminating the point-to-point connection. LCP goes through four distinct phases:

Step 1 Link establishment and configuration negotiation—Before any network-layer datagrams (for example, IP) can be exchanged, LCP must first open the connection and negotiate configuration parameters. This phase is complete when a configuration acknowledgment frame has been both sent and received.

Step 2 Link quality determination—LCP allows an optional link quality determination phase following the link establishment and configuration negotiation phase. In this phase, the link is tested to determine whether the link quality is sufficient to bring up network-layer protocols. This phase is optional. LCP can delay transmission of network-layer protocol information until this phase is completed.

Step 3 Network-layer protocol configuration negotiation—When LCP has finished the link quality determination phase, network-layer protocols can be separately configured by the appropriate NCP and can be brought up and taken down at any time. If LCP closes the link, it informs the network-layer protocols so that they can take appropriate action.

Step 4 Link termination—LCP can terminate the link at any time. This is usually done at the request of a user, but can happen because of a physical event such as the loss of carrier or the expiration of an idle-period timer.

There are three classes of LCP frames:

* Link establishment frames—Used to establish and configure a link.
* Link termination frames—Used to terminate a link.
* Link maintenance frames—Used to manage and debug a link.

These frames are used to accomplish the work of each of the LCP phases.

For more information on PPP, refer to Appendix C, "References and Recommended Reading."

SDLC and Derivatives

IBM developed the SDLC protocol in the mid-1970s for use in Systems Network Architecture (SNA) environments. SDLC was the first of an important new type of link-layer protocols based on synchronous, bit-oriented operation. Compared to synchronous character-oriented (for example, Bisync from IBM) and synchronous byte-count-oriented protocols (for example, Digital Data Communications Message Protocol [DDCMP] from Digital Equipment Corporation), bit-oriented synchronous protocols are more efficient, more flexible, and often faster.

After developing SDLC, IBM submitted it to various standards committees. The ISO modified SDLC to create the HDLC protocol. The Consultative Committee for International Telegraph and Telephone (CCITT), which is now the Telecommunication Standardization Sector of the ITU (the ITU-T), subsequently modified HDLC to create Link Access Procedure (LAP) and then Link Access Procedure, Balanced (LAPB). The IEEE modified HDLC to create IEEE 802.2. Each of these protocols has become important in its own domain. SDLC remains SNA's primary link-layer protocol for WAN links.

SDLC supports a variety of link types and topologies. It can be used with point-to-point and multipoint links, half-duplex and full-duplex transmission facilities, and circuit-switched and packet-switched networks.

SDLC identifies two types of network nodes:

- Primary—Controls the operation of other stations (called secondaries). The primary polls the secondaries in a predetermined order. Secondaries can then transmit if they have outgoing data. The primary also sets up and tears down links and manages the link while it is operational.

- Secondary—Secondaries are controlled by a primary. Secondaries can only exchange information with primary, but they cannot send unless the primary gives permission.

SDLC primaries and secondaries can be connected in four basic configurations:

- Point-to-point—Involves only two nodes, one primary and one secondary.

- Multipoint—Involves one primary and multiple secondaries.

- Loop—Involves a loop topology, with the primary connected to the first and last secondaries. Intermediate secondaries pass messages through one another as they respond to the primary's requests.

- Hub go-ahead—Involves an inbound and an outbound channel. The primary uses the outbound channel to communicate with the secondaries. The secondaries use the inbound channel to communicate with the primary. The inbound channel is daisy-chained back to the primary through each secondary.

Figure 2-23 shows the SDLC frame.

Figure 2-23 *SDLC frames are used for SNA connectivity.*

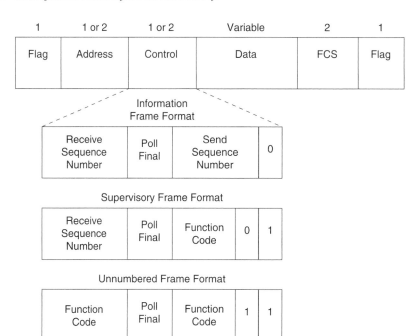

As Figure 2-23 shows, SDLC frames are bounded by flag fields that indicate the start and end of the SDLC frame. The address field always contains the address of the secondary involved in the current communication. Because the primary is either the communication source or destination, there is no need to include the primary's address—it is already known by all secondaries.

The control field uses three different formats, depending on the type of SDLC frame used. The three SDLC frames are described as follows:

- Information (I) frames—These frames carry upper-layer information and some control information. Send and receive sequence numbers and the poll final (P/F) bit perform flow and error control. The send sequence number refers to the number of the frame now being sent. The receive sequence number provides the number of the frame to be received next. Both the sender and the receiver maintain send and receive sequence numbers. The primary uses the P/F bit to tell the secondary whether it requires an immediate response. The secondary uses this bit to tell the primary whether the current frame is the last in its current response.

- Supervisory (S) frames—These frames provide control information. They request and suspend transmission, report on status, and acknowledge the receipt of I frames. They do not have a data field.

- Unnumbered (U) frames—These frames, as the name suggests, are not sequenced. They are used for control purposes. For example, they can specify either a 1- or 2-byte control field, initialize secondaries, and do other similar functions. They can have a data field.

The FCS precedes the ending flag delimiter. The FCS is usually a CRC calculation remainder. The CRC calculation is redone in the receiver. If the result differs from the value in the sender's frame, an error is assumed.

Figure 2-24 shows a typical SDLC-based network configuration. As illustrated, an IBM establishment controller (formerly called a *cluster controller*) in a remote site connects to dumb terminals and to a Token Ring network. In a local site, an IBM host connects (via channel attach techniques) to an IBM front-end processor (FEP), which can also have links to local Token Ring LANs and an SNA backbone. The two sites are connected through an SDLC-based 56-kbps leased line.

Figure 2-24 *Typical SDLC-based network configuration connects users to the data center.*

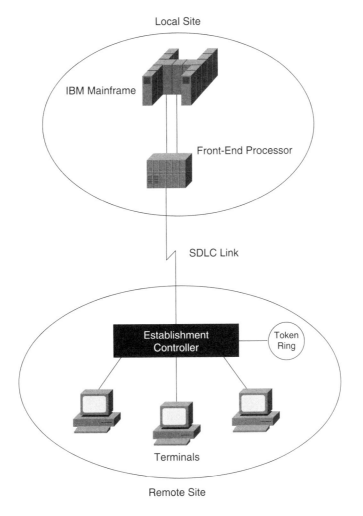

Although it omits several features used in SDLC, HDLC is generally considered to be a compatible superset of SDLC. LAP is a subset of HDLC. LAPB was created to ensure ongoing compatibility with HDLC, which was modified in the early 1980s. IEEE 802.2 is a modification of HDLC for LAN environments. Qualified Logical Link Control (QLLC) is a link-layer protocol defined by IBM that allows SNA data to be transported across X.25 networks.

HDLC

HDLC shares SDLC's frame format, and HDLC fields have the same purpose as those in SDLC. Also, like SDLC, HDLC supports synchronous, full-duplex operation.

HDLC differs from SDLC in several minor ways. First, HDLC has an option for a 4-byte checksum. Also, unlike SDLC, HDLC does not support the loop or hub go-ahead configurations.

Also, HDLC has a 2-byte control field, allowing for a 7-bit window size (128 values) rather than the 3-bit (8 values) that SDLC allows.

The major difference between HDLC and SDLC is that SDLC supports only one transfer mode, and HDLC supports three. The three HDLC transfer modes are as follows:

- Normal response mode (NRM)—This transfer mode is used by both HDLC and SDLC. In this mode, secondaries cannot communicate with a primary until the primary has given permission.

- Asynchronous response mode (ARM)—This transfer mode is used by HDLC only and allows secondaries to initiate communication with a primary without receiving permission.

- Asynchronous balanced mode (ABM)—ABM introduces the combined node. A combined node can act as a primary or a secondary, depending on the situation. All ABM communication is between multiple combined nodes. In ABM environments, any combined station can initiate data transmission without permission from any other.

LAPB

LAPB is best known for its presence in the X.25 protocol stack. LAPB shares the same frame format, frame types, and field functions as SDLC and HDLC. Unlike either of these, however, LAPB is restricted to the ABM transfer mode, and so is appropriate only for combined stations. Also, LAPB circuits can be established by either the DTE or the DCE. The station initiating the call is determined to be the primary, and the responding station is the secondary. Finally, LAPB use of the P/F bit is somewhat different from that of the other protocols.

IEEE 802.2

IEEE 802.2 is often referred to as LLC. It is extremely popular in LAN environments, where it interoperates with protocols such as IEEE 802.3, IEEE 802.4, and IEEE 802.5. IEEE 802.2

offers three types of service. Type 1 provides unacknowledged connectionless service, Type 2 provides connection-oriented service, and Type 3 provides acknowledged connectionless service.

As an unacknowledged connectionless service, LLC Type 1 does not confirm data transfers. Because many upper-layer protocols such as TCP offer reliable data transfer that can compensate for unreliable lower-layer protocols, Type 1 is a commonly used service.

LLC2 service establishes logical connections between sender and receiver, and is therefore connection oriented. LLC2 acknowledges data upon receipt. It is commonly found in IBM communication systems.

Although LLC Type 3 service supports acknowledged data transfer, it does not establish logical connections. As a compromise between the other two LLC services, LLC Type 3 is useful in factory automation environments where error detection is important (through acknowledgment) but virtual connection capability is extremely limited (due to memory constraints).

End stations can support multiple LLC service types. A Class I device supports only Type 1 service. A Class II device supports both Type 1 and Type 2 services. Class III devices support both Type 1 and Type 3 services, and Class IV devices support all three types of service.

Upper-layer processes use IEEE 802.2 services through service access points (SAPs). The IEEE 802.2 header begins with a DSAP field, which identifies the receiving upper-layer process. In other words, after the receiving node's IEEE 802.2 implementation completes its processing, the upper-layer process identified in the DSAP field receives the remaining data. Following the DSAP address is the SSAP address, which identifies the sending upper-layer process. As an example, the value 06 (hexadecimal) indicates the upper-layer process is IP. The value E0 (hexadecimal) represents IPX.

QLLC

QLLC provides the data link control capabilities that are required to transport SNA data across X.25 networks. Together, QLLC and X.25 replace SDLC in the SNA protocol stack.

QLLC uses the packet-level protocol (Layer 3) of the X.25 protocol stack. To indicate that a Layer 3 X.25 packet must be handled by QLLC, a special bit, called the qualifier bit, in the general format identifier (GFI) of the Layer 3 X.25 packet-level header is set to 1. The SNA data is carried as user data in Layer 3 X.25 packets.

ATM Switching

ATM is an ITU standard for cell relay wherein information for multiple service types, such as voice, video, or data, is conveyed in small, fixed-size cells. ATM networks are connection-oriented. This chapter provides summaries of ATM protocols, services, and operation. Figure 2-25 illustrates a private ATM network and a public ATM network carrying voice, video, and data traffic.

Figure 2-25 *A private ATM network and a public ATM network can both carry voice, video, and data traffic.*

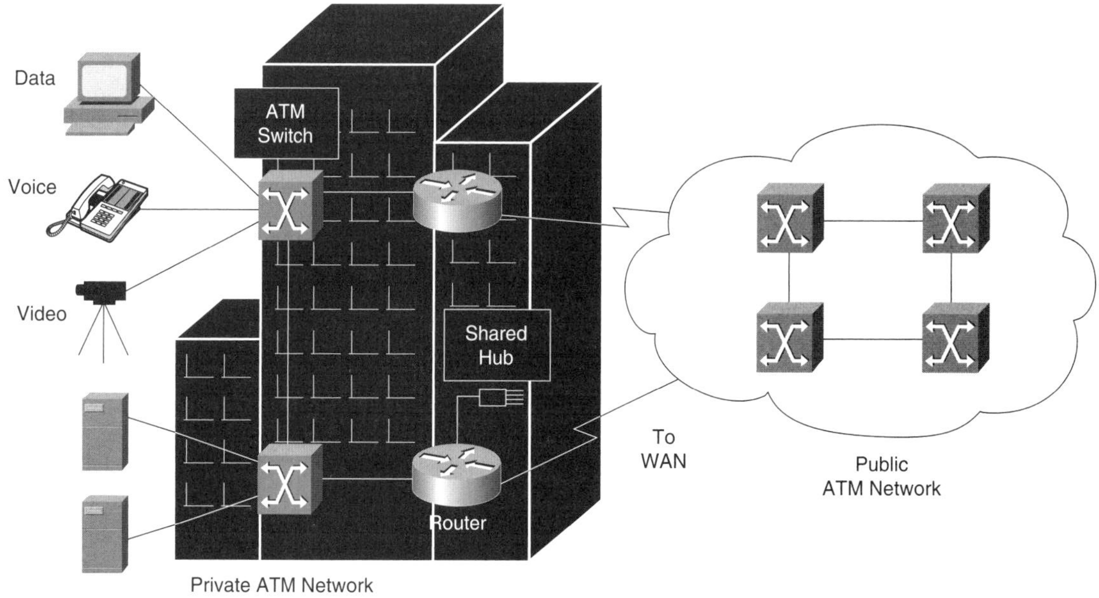

ATM combines the benefits of circuit switching (guaranteed capacity and constant transmission delay) with those of packet switching (flexibility and efficiency for intermittent traffic). It provides scalable bandwidth from a few megabits per second (Mbps) to many gigabits per second (Gbps). Because of its asynchronous nature, ATM is more efficient than synchronous technologies, such as time-division multiplexing (TDM).

With TDM, users are assigned to time slots, and no other station can send in that time slot. If a station has a lot of data to send, it can send only when its time slot comes up, even if all other time slots are empty. If, however, a station has nothing to transmit when its time slot comes up, the time slot gets sent empty and is wasted. Because ATM is asynchronous, time slots are available on demand with information identifying the source of the transmission contained in the header of each ATM cell.

ATM Devices

An ATM network is made up of an ATM switch and ATM endpoints. An ATM switch is responsible for cell transit through an ATM network. The job of an ATM switch is well defined: It accepts the incoming cell from an ATM endpoint or another ATM switch. It then reads and updates the cell-header information and quickly switches the cell to an output interface towards its destination. An ATM endpoint (or end system) contains an ATM network interface adapter. Examples of ATM endpoints are workstations, routers, data-service units (DSUs), LAN switches, and video coder-decoders (CODECs). Figure 2-26 illustrates an ATM network made up of ATM switches and ATM endpoints.

Figure 2-26 *An ATM network comprises ATM switches and endpoints.*

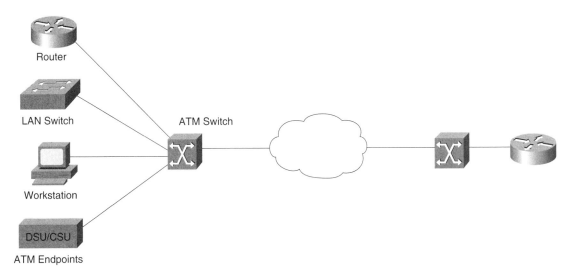

ATM Network Interfaces

An ATM network consists of a set of ATM switches interconnected by point-to-point ATM links or interfaces. ATM switches support two primary types of interfaces: User-Network Interface (UNI) and Network-to-Network Interface (NNI). The UNI connects ATM end-systems (such as hosts and routers) to an ATM switch. The NNI connects two ATM switches.

Depending on whether the switch is owned and located at the customer's premises or publicly owned and operated by the telephone company, UNI and NNI can be further subdivided into public and private UNIs and NNIs. A private UNI connects an ATM endpoint and a private ATM switch. Its public counterpart connects an ATM endpoint or private switch to a public switch. A private NNI connects two ATM switches within the same private organization. A public one connects two ATM switches within the same public organization.

Figure 2-27 illustrates the ATM interface specifications for private and public networks.

Figure 2-27 *ATM interface specifications differ for private and public networks.*

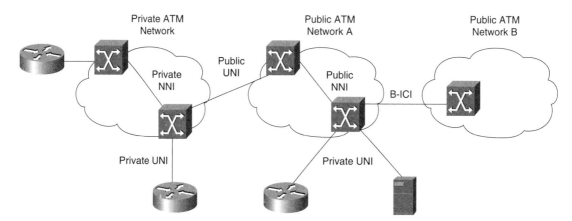

ATM Cell-Header Format

ATM transfers information in fixed-size units called *cells*. Each cell consists of 53 octets, or bytes. The first 5 bytes contain cell-header information, and the remaining 48 contain the "payload" (that is, the user information). Small fixed-length cells are well suited to transferring voice and video traffic because such traffic is intolerant of delays that result from having to wait for a large data packet to download, among other things.

An ATM cell header can be one of two formats: UNI or NNI. The UNI header is used for communication between ATM endpoints and ATM switches in private ATM networks. The NNI header is used for communication between ATM switches. Figure 2-28 depicts the basic ATM cell format, the ATM UNI cell-header format, and the ATM NNI cell-header format.

Unlike the UNI, the NNI header does not include the generic flow control (GFC) field. Additionally, the NNI header has a VPI field that occupies the first 12 bits, allowing for larger trunks between public ATM switches.

In addition to GFC and VPI header fields, several others are used in ATM cell-header fields. The following descriptions summarize the ATM cell-header fields illustrated in Figure 2-28:

- GFC—Provides local functions, such as identifying multiple stations that share a single ATM interface. This field is typically not used and is set to its default value.

- VPI—In conjunction with the VCI, identifies the next destination of a cell as it passes through a series of ATM switches on the way to its destination.

- VCI—In conjunction with the VPI, identifies the next destination of a cell as it passes through a series of ATM switches on the way to its destination.

- Payload type (PT)—Indicates in the first bit whether the cell contains user data or control data. If the cell contains user data, the second bit indicates congestion, and the third bit indicates whether the cell is the last in a series of cells that represent a single AAL5 frame.

- Congestion loss priority (CLP)—Indicates whether the cell should be discarded if it encounters extreme congestion as it moves through the network. If the CLP bit equals 1, the cell should be discarded in preference to cells with the CLP bit equal to zero.

- Header error control (HEC)—Calculates checksum only on the header itself.

Figure 2-28 *An ATM cell, ATM UNI cell, and ATM NNI cell header each contain 48 bytes of payload.*

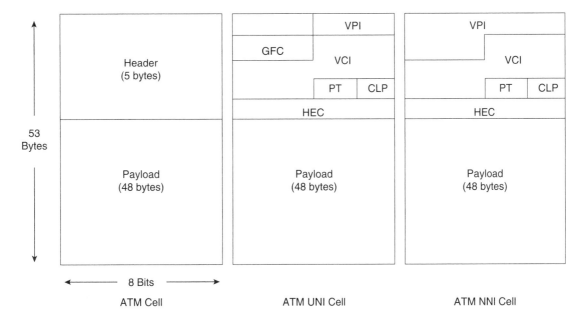

ATM Services

Three types of ATM services exist: permanent virtual circuits (PVCs), switched virtual circuits (SVCs), and connectionless service (which is similar to Switched Multimegabit Data Service [SMDS]).

A PVC allows direct connectivity between sites. In this way, a PVC is similar to a leased line. Among its advantages, a PVC guarantees availability of a connection and does not require call setup procedures between switches. Disadvantages of PVCs include static connectivity and manual setup.

An SVC is created and released dynamically and remains in use only as long as data is being transferred. In this sense, it is similar to a telephone call. Dynamic call control requires a signaling protocol between the ATM endpoint and the ATM switch. The advantages of SVCs include connection flexibility and call setup that can be handled automatically by a networking device. Disadvantages include the extra time and overhead required to set up the connection.

ATM networks are fundamentally connection-oriented, which means that a virtual channel must be set up across the ATM network prior to any data transfer. (A virtual channel is roughly equivalent to a virtual circuit.)

Two types of ATM connections exist: *virtual paths (VPs)*, which are identified by virtual path identifiers, and *virtual channels (VCs)*, which are identified by the combination of a VPI and a VCI.

A virtual path is a bundle of virtual channels, all of which are switched transparently across the ATM network on the basis of the common VPI. All VCIs and VPIs, however, have only local significance across a particular link and are remapped, as appropriate, at each switch.

A transmission path is a bundle of VPs. Figure 2-29 illustrates how VCs concatenate to create VPs, which, in turn, concatenate to create a transmission path.

Figure 2-29   *Multiple VCs are bundled together to create VPs.*

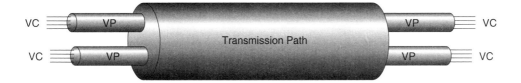

ATM Switching Operation

The basic operation of an ATM switch is straightforward: The cell is received across a link on a known VCI or VPI value. The switch looks up the connection value in a local translation table to determine the outgoing port (or ports) of the connection and the new VPI/VCI value of the connection on that link. The switch then retransmits the cell on that outgoing link with the appropriate connection identifiers. Because all VCIs and VPIs have only local significance across a particular link, these values are remapped, as necessary, at each switch.

The ATM Reference Model

The ATM architecture uses a logical model to describe the functionality it supports. ATM functionality corresponds to the physical layer and part of the data link layer of the OSI reference model.

The ATM reference model is composed of the following planes, which span all layers:

- Control—This plane is responsible for generating and managing signaling requests.

- User—This plane is responsible for managing the transfer of data.

- Management—This plane contains two components:

    — Layer management manages layer-specific functions, such as the detection of failures and protocol problems.

    — Plane management manages and coordinates functions related to the complete system.

The ATM reference model is composed of the following ATM layers:

- Physical layer—Analogous to the physical layer of the OSI reference model, the ATM physical layer manages the medium-dependent transmission.

- ATM layer—Combined with the ATM adaptation layer, the ATM layer is roughly analogous to the data link layer of the OSI reference model. The ATM layer is responsible for establishing connections and passing cells through the ATM network. To do this, it uses information in the header of each ATM cell.

- ATM adaptation layer (AAL)—Combined with the ATM layer, the AAL is roughly analogous to the data link layer of the OSI model. The AAL is responsible for isolating higher-layer protocols from the details of the ATM processes.

Finally, the higher layers residing above the AAL accept user data, arrange it into packets, and hand it to the AAL. Figure 2-30 illustrates the ATM reference model.

Figure 2-30 *The ATM reference model relates to the lowest two layers of the OSI reference model.*

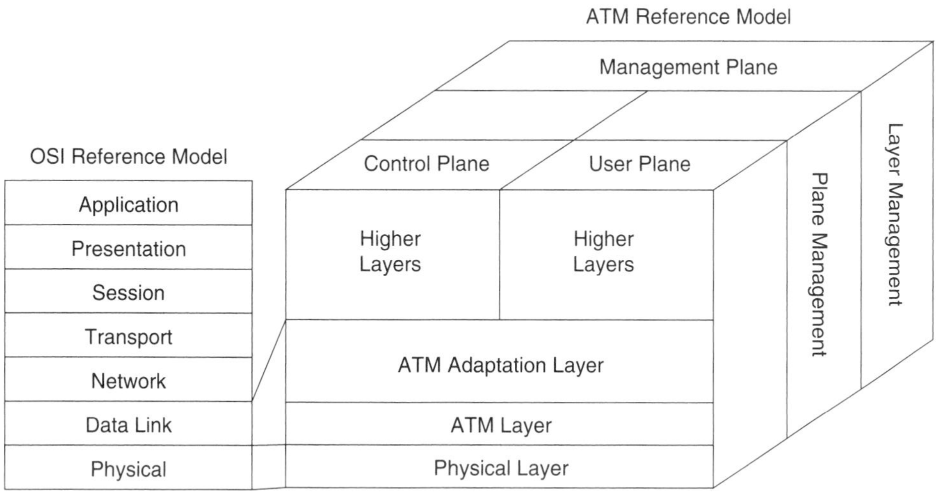

The ATM physical layer has four functions: Bits are converted into cells; the transmission and receipt of bits on the physical medium are controlled; ATM cell boundaries are tracked; and cells are packaged into the appropriate type of frame for the physical medium.

AAL1, a connection-oriented service, is suitable for handling circuit-emulation applications, such as voice and video conferencing. Circuit-emulation service also accommodates the attachment of equipment currently using leased lines to an ATM backbone network. AAL1 requires timing synchronization between the source and destination. For this reason, AAL1 depends on a medium, such as SONET, that supports clocking.

AAL3/4 supports both connection-oriented and connectionless data. It was designed for network service providers and is closely aligned with SMDS. AAL3/4 is used to transmit SMDS packets over an ATM network.

AAL5 is the primary AAL for data and supports both connection-oriented and connectionless data. It is used to transfer most non-SMDS data, such as classical IP over ATM and LAN Emulation (LANE).

ATM Addressing

The ITU-T standard is based on the use of E.164 addresses (similar to telephone numbers) for public ATM (BISDN) networks. The ATM Forum extended ATM addressing to include private networks. ITU-T decided on the subnetwork or overlay model of addressing, in which the ATM layer is responsible for mapping network-layer addresses to ATM addresses. This subnetwork model is an alternative to using network-layer protocol addresses (such as IP and IPX) and existing routing protocols (such as IGRP and RIP). The ATM Forum defined an address format based on the structure of the OSI network service access point (NSAP) addresses.

The Subnetwork Model of Addressing   The subnetwork model of addressing decouples the ATM layer from any existing higher-layer protocols, such as IP or IPX. As such, it requires an entirely new addressing scheme and routing protocol. All ATM systems must be assigned an ATM address, in addition to any higher-layer protocol addresses. This requires an ATM address resolution protocol (ATM_ARP) to map higher-layer addresses to their corresponding ATM addresses.

NSAP-Format ATM Addresses   The 20-byte NSAP-format ATM addresses are designed for use within private ATM networks, whereas public networks typically use E.164 addresses, which are formatted as defined by ITU-T. The ATM Forum did specify an NSAP encoding for E.164 addresses, which will be used for encoding E.164 addresses within private networks, but this address also can be used by some private networks.

Such private networks can base their own (NSAP format) addressing on the E.164 address of the public UNI to which they are connected and can take the address prefix from the E.164 number, identifying local nodes by the lower-order bits.

All NSAP-format ATM addresses consist of three components: the authority and format identifier (AFI), the initial domain identifier (IDI), and the domain-specific part (DSP). The AFI identifies the type and format of the IDI, which, in turn, identifies the address allocation and administrative authority. The DSP contains actual routing information.

Three formats of private ATM addressing differ by the nature of the AFI and IDI. In the NSAP-encoded E.164 format, the IDI is an E.164 number. In the DCC format, the IDI is a data country code (DCC), which identifies particular countries, as specified in ISO 3166. Such addresses are administered by the ISO National Member Body in each country. In the ICD format, the IDI is an international code designator (ICD), which is allocated by the ISO 6523 registration authority (the British Standards Institute). ICD codes identify particular international organizations.

The ATM Forum recommends that organizations or private-network service providers use either the DCC or ICD formats to form their own numbering plan.

Figure 2-31 illustrates the three formats of ATM addresses used for private networks.

Figure 2-31 *Three formats of ATM addresses are used for private networks: DCC and ICD ATM formats and NASP E.164.*

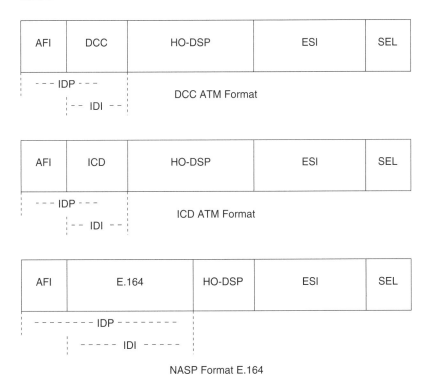

The following descriptions summarize the fields illustrated in Figure 2-31:

- AFI—Identifies the type and format of the address (E.164, ICD, or DCC).

- DCC—Identifies particular countries.

- High-order domain-specific part (HO-DSP)—Combines the Routing Domain (RD) and Area Identifier (AREA) of the NSAP addresses. The ATM Forum combined these fields to support a flexible, multi-level addressing hierarchy for prefix-based routing protocols.

- End system identifier (ESI)—Specifies the 48-bit MAC address, as administered by the IEEE.

- Selector (SEL)—Used for local multiplexing within end stations and has no network significance.

- ICD—Identifies particular international organizations.

- E.164—Indicates the BISDN E.164 address.

ATM Connections

ATM supports two types of connections: point-to-point and point-to-multipoint. Point-to-point connects two ATM end systems and can be unidirectional (one-way communication) or bidirectional (two-way communication). Point-to-multipoint connects a single-source end-system (known as the root node) to multiple destination end-systems (known as leaves). Such connections are unidirectional only. Root nodes can transmit to leaves, but leaves cannot transmit to the root or each other on the same connection. Cell replication is done within the ATM network by the ATM switches where the connection splits into two or more branches.

It would be desirable in ATM networks to have bidirectional multipoint-to-multipoint connections. Such connections are analogous to the broadcasting or multicasting capabilities of shared-medium LANs, such as Ethernet and Token Ring. A broadcasting capability is easy to implement in shared-medium LANs, where all nodes on a single LAN segment must process all packets sent on that segment. Unfortunately, a multipoint-to-multipoint capability cannot be implemented by using AAL5, which is the most common AAL to transmit data across an ATM network. Unlike AAL3/4, with its message identifier (MID) field, AAL5 does not provide a way within its cell format to interleave cells from different AAL5 packets on a single connection. This means that all AAL5 packets sent to a particular destination across a particular connection must be received in sequence; otherwise, the destination reassembly process will be unable to reconstruct the packets. This is why ATM AAL5 point-to-multipoint connections can be only unidirectional. If a leaf node were to transmit an AAL5 packet onto the connection, for example, it would be received by both the root node and all other leaf nodes. At these nodes, the packet sent by the leaf could be interleaved with packets sent by the root and possibly other leaf nodes, precluding the reassembly of any of the interleaved packets.

ATM QOS

ATM supports *quality of service* (QOS) guarantees comprising traffic contract, traffic shaping, and traffic policing.

A *traffic contract* specifies an envelope that describes the intended data flow. This envelope specifies values for peak bandwidth, average sustained bandwidth, and burst size, among others. When an ATM end system connects to an ATM network, it enters a "contract" with the network based on QOS parameters.

Traffic shaping is the use of queues to constrain data bursts, limit peak data rate, and smooth jitters so that traffic will fit within the promised envelope. ATM devices are responsible for adhering to the contract by means of traffic shaping. ATM switches can use methods known as traffic policing to enforce the contract. The switch can measure the actual traffic flow and compare it against the agreed-upon traffic envelope. If the switch finds that traffic is outside the agreed-upon parameters, it can set the cell-loss priority (CLP) bit of the offending cells. Setting the CLP bit makes the cell "discard eligible," which means that any switch handling the cell is allowed to drop the cell during periods of congestion.

LANE

LANE is a standard defined by the ATM Forum that provides to stations attached via ATM the same capabilities they normally obtain from legacy LANs, such as Ethernet and Token Ring. As the name suggests, the function of the LANE protocol is to emulate a LAN on top of an ATM network. Specifically, the LANE protocol defines mechanisms for emulating either an IEEE 802.3 Ethernet or an 802.5 Token Ring LAN. The current LANE protocol does not define a separate encapsulation for FDDI. (FDDI packets must be mapped into either Ethernet or Token Ring emulated LANs [ELANs] by using existing translational bridging techniques.) Fast Ethernet (100BaseT) and IEEE 802.12 (100VG-AnyLAN) both can be mapped unchanged because they use the same packet formats. Figure 2-32 compares a physical LAN and an ELAN.

The LANE protocol defines a service interface for higher-layer (that is, network-layer) protocols that is identical to that of existing LANs. Data sent across the ATM network is encapsulated in the appropriate LAN MAC packet format. Simply put, the LANE protocols make an ATM network look and behave like an Ethernet or Token Ring LAN—albeit one operating much faster than an actual Ethernet or Token Ring LAN network.

It is important to note that LANE does not attempt to emulate the actual MAC protocol of the specific LAN concerned (that is, CSMA/CD for Ethernet or token passing for IEEE 802.5). LANE requires no modifications to higher-layer protocols to enable their operation over an ATM network. Because the LANE service presents the same service interface of existing MAC protocols to network-layer drivers (such as an NDIS- or ODI-like driver interface), no changes are required in those drivers.

Figure 2-32 *An ATM network can emulate a physical LAN.*

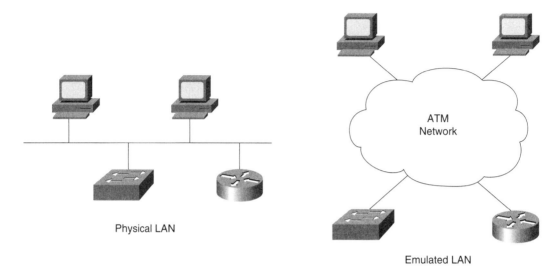

Physical LAN

Emulated LAN

LANE Protocol Architecture The basic function of the LANE protocol is to resolve MAC addresses to ATM addresses. The goal is to resolve such address mappings so that LANE end systems can set up direct connections between themselves and then forward data. The LANE protocol is deployed in two types of ATM-attached equipment: ATM network interface cards (NICs) and internetworking and LAN-switching equipment.

ATM NICs implement the LANE protocol and interface to the ATM network but present the current LAN service interface to the higher-level protocol drivers within the attached end system. The network-layer protocols on the end system continue to communicate as if they were on a known LAN, by using known procedures. However, they are able to use the vastly greater bandwidth of ATM networks.

The second class of network gear that implements LANE consists of ATM-attached LAN switches and routers. These devices, together with directly attached ATM hosts equipped with ATM NICs, are used to provide a virtual LAN (VLAN) service in which ports on the LAN switches will be assigned to particular VLANs independent of physical location. Figure 2-33 shows the LANE protocol architecture implemented in ATM network devices.

NOTE The LANE protocol does not directly affect ATM switches. LANE, as with most of the other ATM internetworking protocols, builds on the overlay model. As such, the LANE protocols operate transparently over and through ATM switches, using only standard ATM signaling procedures.

Figure 2-33 *LANE protocol architecture can be implemented in ATM network devices.*

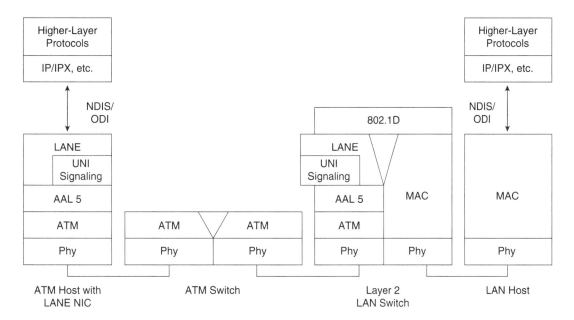

X.25

In the 1970s, a set of protocols was needed to provide users with WAN connectivity across PDNs. PDNs such as Telnet and Tymnet had achieved remarkable success, but it was thought that protocol standardization would increase subscription to PDNs by providing improved equipment compatibility and lower cost. The result of the ensuing development effort was a group of protocols, the most popular of which is X.25.

X.25 was developed by the common carriers (phone companies, essentially) rather than any single commercial enterprise. The specification is therefore designed to work well regardless of a user's system type or manufacturer. Users contract with the common carriers to use their packet-switched networks (PSNs) and are charged based on PSN use. Services offered and charges levied are regulated by the Federal Communications Commission (FCC) in the United States.

One of X.25's unique attributes is its international nature. X.25 and related protocols are administered by an agency of the United Nations called the ITU. The ITU-T carries out the functions of the former CCITT. Union members include the FCC, the European Postal Telephone and Telegraph organizations, the common carriers, and many computer and data communications companies. As a result, X.25 is truly a global standard.

NOTE   ITU can be reached at www.itu.ch.

X.25 defines a telephone network for data communications. To begin communication, one computer calls another to request a communication session. The called computer can accept or refuse the connection. If the call is accepted, the two systems can begin full-duplex information transfer. Either side can terminate the connection at any time.

The X.25 specification defines a point-to-point interaction between DTE and DCE. Terminals and hosts in the user's facilities connect to modems or packet switches generally located in the carrier's facilities, which connect to packet-switching exchanges (PSE) and other DCEs inside a PSN and, ultimately, to another DTE device. Figure 2-34 shows the relationship between the entities in an X.25 network.

Figure 2-34   *PSE and DCE devices make up the X.25 service cloud.*

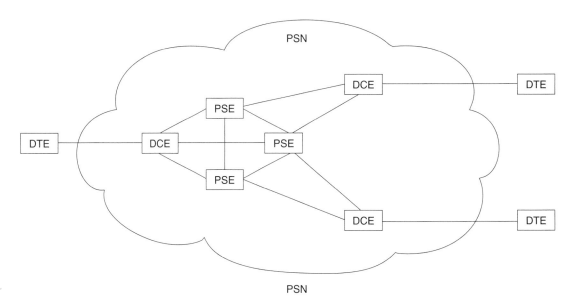

A DTE can be a terminal that does not implement the complete X.25 functionality. A DTE is connected to a DCE through a translation device called a packet assembler/disassembler (PAD). The operation of the terminal-to-PAD interface, the services offered by the PAD, and the interaction between the PAD and the host are defined by ITU-T Recommendations X.28, X.3, and X.29, respectively.

The X.25 specification maps to Layers 1 through 3 of the OSI reference model. Layer 3 X.25 describes packet formats and packet exchange procedures between peer Layer 3 entities. Layer 2 X.25 is implemented by LAPB. LAPB defines packet framing for the DTE/DCE link. Layer 1 X.25 defines the electrical and mechanical procedures for activating and deactivating the physical medium connecting the DTE and the DCE. This relationship is shown in Figure 2-35. Note that Layers 2 and 3 are also referred to as the ISO standards ISO 7776 (LAPB) and ISO 8208 (the X.25 packet layer).

Figure 2-35 *X.25 has references to the lower three layers of the OSI reference model.*

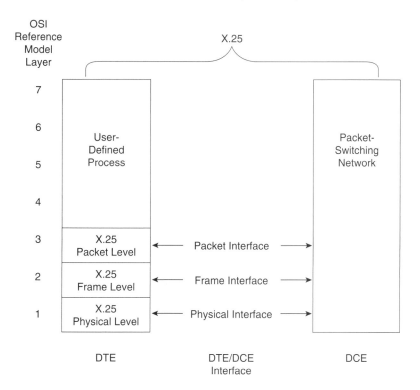

End-to-end communication between DTEs is accomplished through a bidirectional association called a virtual circuit. Virtual circuits permit communication between distinct network elements through any number of intermediate nodes without the dedication of portions of the physical medium that characterizes physical circuits. Virtual circuits can either be permanent or switched (temporary). Permanent virtual circuits are commonly called PVCs; switched virtual circuits are commonly called SVCs. PVCs are typically used for frequent data transfers, and SVCs are used for sporadic data transfers. Layer 3 X.25 is concerned with end-to-end communication involving both PVCs and SVCs.

After a virtual circuit is established, the DTE sends a packet to the other end of the connection by sending it to the DCE using the proper virtual circuit. The DCE looks at the virtual circuit number to determine how to route the packet through the X.25 network. The Layer 3 X.25 protocol multiplexes between all the DTEs served by the DCE on the destination side of the network, and the packet is delivered to the destination DTE.

An X.25 frame is composed of a series of fields, as shown in Figure 2-36. Layer 3 X.25 fields make up an X.25 packet and include a header and user data. Layer 2 X.25 (LAPB) fields include frame-level control and addressing fields, the embedded Layer 3 packet, and an FCS.

Figure 2-36 *X.25 frames contain control information for reliability and windowing.*

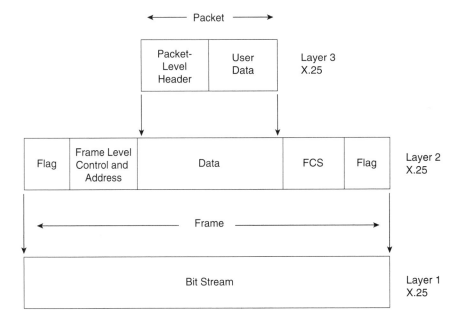

Layer 3 X.25

The Layer 3 X.25 header is made up of a GFI, a logical channel identifier (LCI), and a packet type identifier (PTI). The GFI is a 4-bit field that indicates the general format of the packet header. The LCI is a 12-bit field that identifies the virtual circuit. The LCI is locally significant at the DTE/DCE interface. In other words, the PDN connects two logical channels, each with an independent LCI, on two DTE/DCE interfaces to establish a virtual circuit. The PTI field identifies one of X.25's 17 packet types.

Addressing fields in call setup packets provide source and destination DTE addresses. These are used to establish the virtual circuits that constitute X.25 communication. ITU-T Recommendation X.121 specifies the source and destination address formats. X.121 addresses (also referred to as international data numbers, or IDNs) vary in length and can be up to 14 decimal digits long. Byte 4 in the call setup packet specifies the source DTE and destination DTE address lengths. The first four digits of an IDN are called the data network identification code (DNIC). The DNIC is divided into two parts: the first (three digits) specifying the country and the last specifying the PSN itself. The remaining digits are called the national terminal number (NTN) and are used to identify the specific DTE on the PSN. Figure 2-37 shows the X.121 address format.

Figure 2-37 *X.25 uses the X.121 address format.*

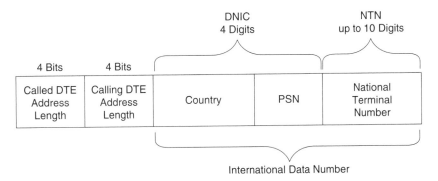

The addressing fields that make up the X.121 address are necessary only when an SVC is used, and then only during call setup. After the call is established, the PSN uses the LCI field of the data packet header to specify the particular virtual circuit to the remote DTE.

Layer 3 X.25 uses three virtual circuit operational procedures:

- Call setup
- Data transfer
- Call clearing

Execution of these procedures depends on the virtual circuit type being used. For a PVC, Layer 3 X.25 is always in data transfer mode because the circuit has been permanently established. If an SVC is used, all three procedures are used.

Data transfer is affected by data packets. Layer 3 X.25 segments and reassembles user messages if they are too long for the circuit's maximum packet size. Each data packet is given a sequence number so error and flow control can occur across the DTE/DCE interface.

Layer 2 X.25

Layer 2 X.25 is implemented by LAPB. LAPB allows both sides—the DTE and the DCE—to initiate communication with the other. During information transfer, LAPB checks that the frames arrive at the receiver in the correct sequence and error free.

As with similar link-layer protocols, LAPB uses three frame format types:

- Information (I) frame—These frames carry upper-layer information and some control information (necessary for full-duplex operation). Send and receive sequence numbers and the P/F bit perform flow control and error recovery. The send sequence number refers to the number of the current frame. The receive sequence number records the number of the frame to be received next. In full-duplex conversation, both the sender and the receiver keep send and receive sequence numbers. The poll bit is used to force a final bit message in response; this is used for error detection and recovery.

- Supervisory (S) frames—These frames provide control information. They request and suspend transmission, report on status, and acknowledge the receipt of I frames. They do not have an information field.

- Unnumbered (U) frames—These frames, as the name suggests, are not sequenced. They are used for control purposes. For example, they can initiate a connection using standard or extended windowing (modulo 8 versus 128), disconnect the link, report a protocol error, or perform other similar functions.

Figure 2-38 shows the LAPB frame.

Figure 2-38 *LAPB is used by X.25 for Layer 2 encapsulation.*

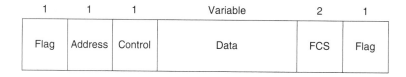

The flag fields delimit the LAPB frame. Bit stuffing is used to ensure that the flag pattern does not occur within the body of the frame.

The address field indicates whether the frame carries a command or a response.

The control field provides further qualifications of command and response frames, and also indicates the frame format (U, I, or S), frame function (for example, receiver ready or disconnect), and the send/receive sequence number.

The data field carries upper-layer data. Its size and format vary depending on the Layer 3 packet type. The maximum length of this field is set by agreement between a PSN administrator and the subscriber at subscription time. The FCS field ensures the integrity of the transmitted data.

Layer 1 X.25

Layer 1 X.25 uses the X.21bis physical layer protocol, which is roughly equivalent to EIA/TIA-232-C. The X.21bis protocol was derived from ITU-T Recommendations V.24 and V.28, which identify the interchange circuits and electrical characteristics (respectively) of a DTE-to-DCE interface. X.21 bis supports point-to-point connections, speeds of up to 19.2 kbps, and synchronous, full-duplex transmission over four-wire media (with speeds of up to 64 kbps). The maximum distance between DTE and DCE is 15 meters.

For more information on X.25, refer to Appendix C, "References and Recommended Reading."

Frame Relay

Frame Relay was originally conceived as a protocol for use over ISDN interfaces, and initial proposals to this effect were submitted to the CCITT in 1984. Work on Frame Relay was also undertaken in the ANSI-accredited T1S1 standards committee in the United States.

There was a major development in Frame Relay's history in 1990 when Cisco Systems, StrataCom, Northern Telecom, and Digital Equipment Corporation formed a consortium to focus Frame Relay technology development and accelerate the introduction of interoperable Frame Relay products. This consortium developed a specification conforming to the basic Frame Relay protocol being discussed in T1S1 and CCITT but extended it with features that provide additional capabilities for complex internetworking environments. These Frame Relay extensions are referred to collectively as the Local Management Interface (LMI).

Frame Relay exists at Layer 2 of the OSI model. It provides a packet-switching data communications capability that is used across the interface between user devices (for example, routers, bridges, host machines) and network equipment (for example, switching nodes). User devices are often referred to as DTEs, and network equipment that interfaces to a DTE is often referred to as a DCE. The network providing the Frame Relay interface can be either a carrier-provided public network or a network of privately owned equipment serving a single enterprise.

As an interface to a network, Frame Relay is the same type of protocol as X.25. However, Frame Relay differs significantly from X.25 in its functionality and format. In particular, Frame Relay is a more streamlined protocol, facilitating higher performance and greater efficiency.

As an interface between user and network equipment, Frame Relay provides a means for statistically multiplexing many logical data conversations (referred to as virtual circuits) over a single physical transmission link. This contrasts with systems that use only time-division multiplexing (TDM) techniques for supporting multiple data streams. Frame Relay's statistical multiplexing provides more flexible and efficient use of available bandwidth. It can be used without TDM techniques or on top of channels provided by TDM systems.

Another important characteristic of Frame Relay is that it exploits the recent advances in WAN transmission technology. Earlier WAN protocols such as X.25 were developed when analog transmission systems and copper media were predominant. These links are much less reliable than the fiber media/digital transmission links available today. Over links such as these, link-layer protocols can forego time-consuming error correction algorithms, leaving these to be performed at higher protocol layers. Greater performance and efficiency are therefore possible without sacrificing data integrity. Frame Relay is designed with this approach in mind. It includes a CRC algorithm for detecting corrupted bits (so the data can be discarded), but it does not include any protocol mechanisms for correcting bad data (for example, by retransmitting it at this level of protocol).

Another difference between Frame Relay and X.25 is the absence of explicit, per-virtual-circuit flow control in Frame Relay. Now that many upper-layer protocols are effectively executing their own flow control algorithms, the need for this functionality at the data link layer has diminished. Frame Relay, therefore, does not include explicit flow control procedures that duplicate those in higher layers. Instead, very simple congestion notification mechanisms are provided to allow a network to inform a user device that the network resources are close to a congested state. This notification can alert higher-layer protocols that flow control may be needed.

Frame Relay provides connection-oriented data link-layer communication. This service is implemented using virtual circuits. A Frame Relay virtual circuit is a logical connection created between two DTE devices across a Frame Relay PSN. Virtual circuits provide a bidirectional communications path from one DTE device to another. They are uniquely identified by the data link connection identifier (DLCI). A virtual circuit can pass through any number of intermediate DCE devices (switches) located within the Frame Relay PSN. A number of virtual circuits can be multiplexed into a single physical circuit for transmission across the network. Frame Relay virtual circuits can be either SVCs or PVCs.

In addition to the basic Frame Relay protocol functions for transferring data, the consortium Frame Relay specification includes LMI extensions that make supporting large, complex internetworks easier. Some LMI extensions are referred to as "common" and are expected to be implemented by everyone who adopts the specification. Other LMI functions are referred to as "optional." A summary of the LMI extensions follows:

- Virtual circuit status messages (common)—Provide communication and synchronization between the network and the user device, periodically reporting the existence of new PVCs and the deletion of already existing PVCs, and generally providing information about PVC integrity. Virtual circuit status messages prevent the sending of data into black holes, that is, over PVCs that no longer exist.

- Multicasting (optional)—Allows a sender to transmit a single frame but have it delivered by the network to multiple recipients. Thus, multicasting supports the efficient conveyance of routing protocol messages and address resolution procedures that typically must be sent to many destinations simultaneously.

- Global addressing (optional)—Gives connection identifiers global rather than local significance, allowing them to be used to identify a specific interface to the Frame Relay network. Global addressing makes the Frame Relay network resemble a LAN in terms of addressing; address resolution protocols therefore perform over Frame Relay exactly as they do over a LAN.

- Simple flow control (optional)—Provides for an XON/XOFF flow control mechanism that applies to the entire Frame Relay interface. It is intended for those devices whose higher layers cannot use the congestion notification bits and that need some level of flow control.

Figure 2-39 shows the Frame Relay frame. Flags delimit the frame's beginning and end. Following the leading flags are 2 bytes of address information. Ten bits of these 2 bytes make up the actual circuit ID (called the DLCI, or data link connection identifier).

Figure 2-39 *The Frame Relay frame format was defined by the Internet Engineering Task Force.*

1	1	Variable	2	1
Flags	Address	Data	FCS	Flags

The 10-bit DLCI value is the heart of the Frame Relay address field in the header. It identifies the logical connection that is multiplexed into the physical channel. In the basic (that is, not extended by the LMI) mode of addressing, DLCIs have local significance; that is, the end devices at two different ends of a connection may use a different DLCI to refer to that same connection. Figure 2-40 provides an example of the use of DLCIs in nonextended Frame Relay addressing.

Figure 2-40 *DLCIs are used for addressing PVCs in Frame Relay networks.*

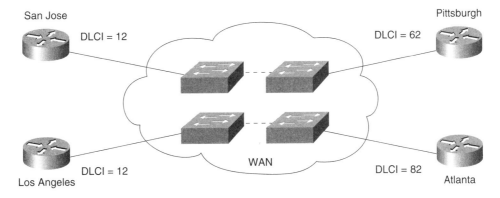

In Figure 2-40, assume that there are two PVCs, one between Atlanta and Los Angeles, and one between San Jose and Pittsburgh. Los Angeles may refer to its PVC with Atlanta using DLCI = 12, and Atlanta refers to the same PVC with DLCI = 82. Similarly, San Jose may refer to its PVC with Pittsburgh using DLCI = 12. The network uses internal proprietary mechanisms to keep the two locally significant PVC identifiers distinct.

At the end of each DLCI byte is an extended address (EA) bit. If this bit is 1, the current byte is the last DLCI byte. All implementations currently use a 2-byte DLCI, but the presence of the EA bits means that longer DLCIs may be agreed upon and used in the future.

Three bits in the 2-byte DLCI are fields related to congestion control. The forward explicit congestion notification (FECN) bit is set by the Frame Relay network in a frame to tell the DTE receiving that frame that congestion was experienced in the path from source to destination. The backward explicit congestion notification (BECN) bit is set by the Frame Relay network in frames traveling in the opposite direction from frames encountering a congested path. The notion behind both of these bits is that the FECN or BECN indication can be promoted to a higher-level protocol that can take flow control action as appropriate. (FECN bits are useful to higher-layer protocols that use receiver-controlled flow control, and BECN bits are significant to those that depend on "emitter controlled" flow control.)

The discard eligibility (DE) bit is set by the DTE to tell the Frame Relay network that a frame has lower importance than other frames and should be discarded before other frames if the network becomes short of resources. Thus, it represents a very simple priority mechanism. This bit is usually set only when the network is congested.

The previous section described the basic Frame Relay protocol format for carrying user data frames. The consortium's Frame Relay specification also includes the LMI procedures. LMI messages are sent in frames distinguished by an LMI-specific DLCI (defined in the consortium specification as DLCI = 1023). Figure 2-41 shows the LMI message format.

Figure 2-41 *LMI messages are used for signaling between Frame Relay switches and end devices.*

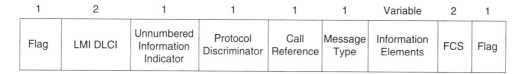

1	2	1	1	1	1	Variable	2	1
Flag	LMI DLCI	Unnumbered Information Indicator	Protocol Discriminator	Call Reference	Message Type	Information Elements	FCS	Flag

In LMI messages, the basic protocol header is the same as in normal data frames. The actual LMI message begins with four mandatory bytes, followed by a variable number of information elements (IEs). The format and encoding of LMI messages is based on the ANSI T1S1 standard.

The first of the mandatory bytes (unnumbered information indicator) has the same format as the LAPB unnumbered information (UI) frame indicator with the poll/final bit set to zero. The next byte is referred to as the protocol discriminator, which is set to a value that indicates LMI. The third mandatory byte (call reference) is always filled with zeros.

The final mandatory byte is the message type field. Two message types have been defined:

- Status-inquiry messages allow the user device to inquire about network status. Status messages respond to status-inquiry messages.

- Keepalives (messages sent through a connection to ensure that both sides will continue to regard the connection as active) and PVC status messages are examples of these messages and are the common LMI features that are expected to be a part of every implementation that conforms to the consortium specification.

Together, status and status-inquiry messages help verify the integrity of logical and physical links. This information is critical in a routing environment because routing algorithms make decisions based on link integrity.

Following the message type field is some number of IEs. Each IE consists of a single-byte IE identifier, an IE length field, and one or more bytes containing actual data.

Frame Relay Global Addressing

In addition to the common LMI features, several optional LMI extensions are useful in an internetworking environment. The first important optional LMI extension is global addressing. As noted earlier, the basic (nonextended) Frame Relay specification supports only values of the DLCI field that identify PVCs with local significance. In this case, there are no addresses that identify network interfaces or nodes attached to these interfaces. Because these addresses do not exist, they cannot be discovered by traditional address resolution and discovery techniques. This means that with normal Frame Relay addressing, static maps must be created to tell routers which DLCIs to use to find a remote device and its associated internetwork address.

The global addressing extension permits node identifiers. With this extension, the values inserted in the DLCI field of a frame are globally significant addresses of individual end-user devices (for example, routers). This is implemented as shown in Figure 2-42.

Figure 2-42 *Globally significant DLCIs must be unique across the network.*

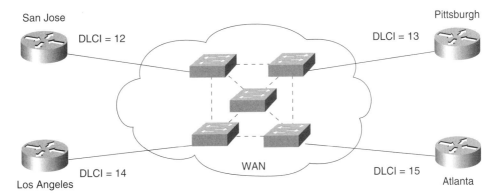

In Figure 2-42, note that each interface has its own identifier. Suppose Pittsburgh must send a frame to San Jose. San Jose's identifier is 12, so Pittsburgh places the value 12 in the DLCI field and sends the frame into the Frame Relay network. At the exit point, the DLCI field contents are changed by the network to 13 to reflect the frame's source node. As each router's interface has a distinct value as its node identifier, individual devices can be distinguished. This permits adaptive routing in complex environments.

Global addressing provides significant benefits in a large, complex internetwork. The Frame Relay network now appears to the routers on its periphery like a typical LAN. No changes to higher-layer protocols are needed to take full advantage of higher-layer protocol capabilities.

Frame Relay Multicasting

Multicasting is another valuable optional LMI feature. Multicast groups are designated by a series of four reserved DLCI values (1019 to 1022). Frames sent by a device using one of these reserved DLCIs are replicated by the network and sent to all exit points in the designated set. The multicasting extension also defines LMI messages that notify user devices of the addition, deletion, and presence of multicast groups.

In networks that take advantage of dynamic routing, routing information must be exchanged among many routers. Routing messages can be sent efficiently by using frames with a multicast DLCI. This allows messages to be sent to specific groups of routers.

Frame Relay can be used as an interface to either a publicly available carrier-provided service or to a network of privately owned equipment. A typical means of private network implementation is to equip traditional T1 multiplexers with Frame Relay interfaces for data devices, as well as non-Frame Relay interfaces for other applications such as voice and videoteleconferencing. Figure 2-43 shows this configuration.

A public Frame Relay service is deployed by putting Frame Relay switching equipment in the central offices of a telecommunications carrier. In this case, users can gain economic benefits from traffic-sensitive charging rates and are relieved from the work necessary to administer and maintain the network equipment and service.

In either type of network, the lines that connect user devices to the network equipment can operate at a speed selected from a broad range of data rates. Speeds between 56 kbps and 2 Mbps are typical, although Frame Relay can support lower and higher speeds.

ISDN

ISDN refers to a set of communication protocols implemented by telephone companies to permit telephone networks to carry digitized voice, data, text, graphics, music, and video to end users over existing telephone systems. ISDN services are offered by many carriers under tariff.

ISDN is generally viewed as an alternative to Frame Relay and T1 wide-area telephone services (WATS). In practical terms, ISDN has evolved into one of the leading technologies for facilitating telecommuting arrangements and internetworking small, remote offices into corporate campuses.

ISDN is addressed by a suite of ITU-T standards, spanning the physical, data link, and network layers of the seven-layer OSI reference model.

Figure 2-43 *Hybrid Frame Relay networks combine data, voice, and video services.*

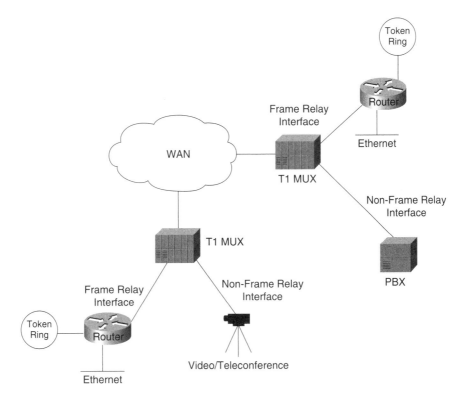

The ISDN BRI service provides two bearer channels and one data channel. The BRI B-channel service operates at 64 kbps and carries data, and the BRI D-channel service operates at 16 kbps and usually carries control and signaling information. The total bit rate is 144 kbps.

The ISDN Primary Rate Interface (PRI) service delivers 23 B channels and one 64-kbps D channel in North America and Japan for a total bit rate of up to 1.544 Mbps. In Europe, Australia, and other parts of the world, ISDN provides 30 B channels and one 64-kbps D channel, for a total bit rate of up to 2.048 Mbps.

There are three principal categories of ISDN network components:

- ISDN terminal equipment
- ISDN termination devices
- ISDN reference points

ISDN Terminal Equipment

ISDN specifies two basic terminal equipment types:

- Terminal Equipment Type 1 (TE1)—A TE1 is a specialized ISDN terminal, including computer equipment or telephones. It is used to connect to ISDN through a four-wire, twisted-pair digital link.

- Terminal Equipment Type 2 (TE2)—A TE2 is a non-ISDN terminal such as DTE that predates the ISDN standards. A TE2 connects to ISDN through a terminal adapter (TA). An ISDN TA can be either a standalone device or a board inside the TE2.

ISDN Network Termination Devices

ISDN specifies a type of intermediate equipment called a network termination (NT) device. NTs connect the four-wire subscriber wiring to two-wire local loops. There are three supported NT types:

- NT Type 1 (NT1) device—An NT1 device is treated as customer premises equipment (CPE) in North America, but is provided by carriers elsewhere.

- NT Type 2 (NT2) device—An NT2 device is typically found in digital private branch exchanges (PBXs). An NT2 performs Layer 2 and 3 protocol functions and concentration services.

- NT Type 1/2 (NT1/2) device—An NT1/2 device provides combined functions of separate NT1 and NT2 devices. An NT1/2 is compatible with NT1 and NT2 devices and is used to replace separate NT1 and NT2 devices.

ISDN Reference Points

ISDN reference points define logical interfaces. Four reference points are defined in ISDN:

- R reference point—Defines the reference point between non-ISDN equipment and a TA.
- S reference point—Defines the reference point between user terminals and an NT2.

- T reference point—Defines the reference point between NT1 and NT2 devices.
- U reference point—Defines the reference point between NT1 devices and line-termination equipment in a carrier network. (This is only in North America, where the NT1 function is not provided by the carrier network.)

The data link layer of the ISDN signaling protocol is Link Access Procedure on the D channel (LAPD). LAPD is similar to the HDLC and LAPB specifications. LAPD is used to ensure that control and signaling information flows and is received properly. The LAPD frame format uses supervisory, information, and unnumbered frames. Figure 2-44 illustrates the fields associated with the ISDN data link-layer frame.

Figure 2-44 *ISDN uses LAPD for data link-layer signaling.*

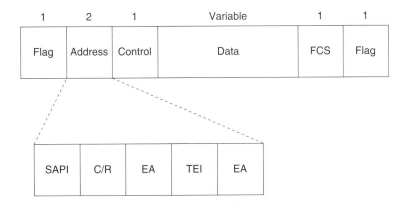

The LAPD flag, control, and FCS fields are identical to those of HDLC. The LAPD address field can be either 1 or 2 bytes long. If the EA bit of the first byte is set, the address is 1 byte; if it is not set, the address is 2 bytes. The first address field byte contains the service access point identifier (SAPI), which is a 6-bit field that identifies the point at which LAPD services are provided to Layer 3. The C/R bit indicates whether the frame contains a command or a response. The terminal endpoint identifier (TEI) field identifies either a single terminal or multiple terminals. A TEI of all ones indicates a broadcast.

For more information on ISDN, refer to Appendix C, "References and Recommended Reading."

OSI Layers 3 to 7 Characteristics—Routed Protocols and Routing Protocols

OSI Layers 3 through 7 (network, transport, session, presentation, and application layers) are defined as the *upper-layers* of the OSI reference model. This section covers the following protocol suites:

- TCP/IP
- NetWare
- AppleTalk

TCP/IP

In the mid-1970s, the Defense Advanced Research Projects Agency (DARPA) became interested in establishing a packet-switched network to provide communications between research institutions in the United States. DARPA and other government organizations understood the potential of packet-switched technology and were just beginning to face the problem virtually all companies with networks now have—communication between dissimilar computer systems.

With the goal of heterogeneous connectivity in mind, DARPA funded research by Stanford University and Bolt, Beranek, and Newman (BBN) to create a series of communication protocols. The result of this development effort, completed in the late 1970s, was the Internet protocol suite, of which TCP and IP are the two best known.

The Internet protocols can be used to communicate across any set of interconnected networks. They are equally well suited for LAN and WAN communications. The Internet suite includes not only lower-layer specifications (such as TCP and IP), but also specifications for such common applications as mail, terminal emulation, and file transfer. Figure 2-45 shows some of the most important Internet protocols and their relationship to the OSI reference model.

Creation and documentation of the Internet protocols closely resembles an academic research project. The protocols are specified in RFCs, which are published and then reviewed and analyzed by the Internet community. Protocol refinements are published in new RFCs. Taken together, the RFCs provide a colorful history of the people, companies, and trends that shaped the development of what is today the world's most popular open system protocol suite.

The TCP/IP Network Layer

IP is the primary Layer 3 protocol in the Internet suite. In addition to internetwork routing, IP provides fragmentation and reassembly of datagrams and error reporting. Along with TCP, IP represents the heart of the Internet protocol suite. Figure 2-46 shows the IP packet format.

Figure 2-45 *The TCP/IP stack combines the upper three layers of the OSI reference model into one application layer.*

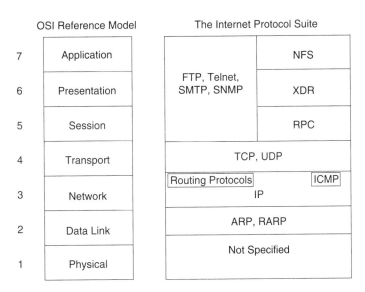

Figure 2-46 *The IP packet header includes the source and destination addresses required for routing IP packets.*

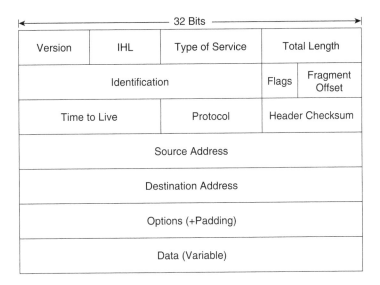

The IP header begins with a 4-bit version number, which indicates the version of IP currently used. The current version of IP is 4, so IP is sometimes called IPv4.

NOTE   IPv6 is the next generation of the IP protocol. (Actually, there is an entire set of protocols to support the version 6 protocol level.) The key changes seen in IPv6 are in the following areas:

- IP address—IPv6 addresses are 16 bytes long and are not class based.

- Configuration—IPv6 has many of the autoconfiguration characteristics of IPX.

- Security—IPv6 has added levels of security to fix some of the inadequacies of IPv4.

This section focuses on IPv4, not IPv6.

The 4-bit IP header length (IHL) field indicates the datagram header length in 32-bit words.

The type-of-service (TOS) field is an 8-bit field that specifies how a particular upper-layer protocol wants the current datagram to be handled. Datagrams can be assigned various levels of importance through this field.

The 16-bit total length field specifies the length of the entire IP packet, including data and header, in bytes.

The 16-bit identification field contains an integer that identifies the current datagram. This field is used to help piece together datagram fragments.

The flags field is a 3-bit field of which the low-order 2 bits control fragmentation. The high-order bit is set to 0. The first low-order bit specifies whether the packet can be fragmented (0 = may fragment, 1 = don't fragment); the second bit specifies whether the packet is the last fragment in a series of fragmented packets (0 = last fragment, 1 = more fragments).

The 13-bit fragment offset field indicates where in the entire datagram this fragment belongs and is measured in 64-bit units from the beginning of the datagram.

The 8-bit time-to-live field maintains a counter that gradually decrements down to zero, at which point the datagram is discarded. This keeps packets from looping endlessly.

The protocol field indicates which upper-layer protocol receives incoming packets after IP processing is complete. Examples include those listed in Table 2-2.

Table 2-2   *IP protocol field values.*

Decimal	Keyword	Description
1	ICMP	Internet Control Message Protocol
2	IGMP	Internet Group Management Protocol
6	TCP	Transmission Control Protocol
8	EGP	Exterior Gateway Protocol
9	IGRP	Interior Gateway Routing Protocol
16	CHAOS	Chaos
17	UDP	User Datagram Protocol
22	XNS-IDP	XNS Internetwork Datagram Protocol
29	ISO-TP4	ISO Transport Protocol Class 4
80	ISO-IP	ISO Internet Protocol
83	VINES	Virtual Integrated Network Service

The 16-bit header checksum field helps ensure IP header integrity.

The 32-bit source and destination address fields specify the IP address of sending and receiving hosts.

The variable-length options field allows IP to support options such as security and record route. The options field must end on a 32-bit boundary. Padding can be added to ensure this.

The data field contains upper-layer information.

TCP/IP Addressing

As with all network-layer protocols, IP's addressing scheme is integral to the process of routing IP datagrams through an internetwork. An IP address is 32 bits in length, divided into either two or three parts. The first part designates the network address, the second part (if present) designates the subnet address, and the final part designates the host address. Subnet addresses are only present if the network administrator has decided that the network should be divided into subnetworks. The lengths of the network, subnet, and host fields are all variable.

IP addressing supports five different network classes (the leftmost bits indicate the network class):

- Class A networks are intended mainly for use with a few very large networks, because they provide only 8 bits for the network address field.

- Class B networks allocate 16 bits for the network address field and 16 bits for the host address field. This address class offers a good compromise between network and host address space.

- Class C networks allocate 24 bits for the network address field. Class C networks provide only 8 bits for the host field, however, so the number of hosts per network may be a limiting factor.

- Class D addresses are reserved for multicast groups, as described formally in RFC 1112. In Class D addresses, the 4 highest-order bits are set to 1, 1, 1, and 0.

- Class E addresses are also defined by IP but are reserved for future use. In Class E addresses, the 4 highest-order bits are all set to 1.

IP addresses are written in dotted-decimal format—for example, 34.10.2.1. Figure 2-47 shows the address formats for Class A, B, and C IP networks.

Figure 2-47 *The leftmost bits of an IP address determine its class.*

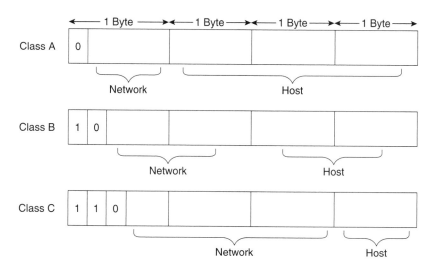

IP networks can also be divided into smaller units, called *subnets*. Subnets provide extra flexibility for network administrators. For example, assume that a network has been assigned a Class B address and all the nodes on the network currently conform to a Class B address format. Then, assume that the dotted-decimal representation of this network's address is 128.10.0.0 (all zeros in the host field of an address specifies the entire network). Rather than change all the addresses to some other basic network number, the administrator can subdivide the network by using subnetting. This is done by borrowing bits from the host portion of the address and using them as a subnet field, as shown in Figure 2-48.

Figure 2-48 *With subnetting, host bits are turned into subnet bits and become part of the subnet addresses.*

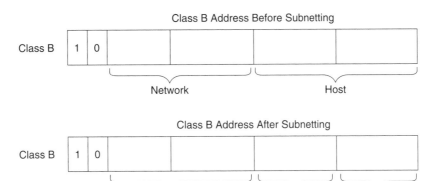

If a network administrator has chosen to use 8 bits of subnetting, the third octet of a Class B IP address provides the subnet number. In our example, address 128.10.1.0 refers to network 128.10, subnet 1; address 128.10.2.0 refers to network 128.10, subnet 2; and so on.

The number of bits borrowed for the subnet address is variable. To specify how many bits are used, IP provides the subnet mask. Subnet masks use the same format and representation technique as IP addresses. Subnet masks have ones in all bits except those bits that specify the host field. For example, the subnet mask that specifies 8 bits of subnetting for Class A address 34.0.0.0 is 255.255.0.0. The subnet mask that specifies 16 bits of subnetting for Class A address 34.0.0.0 is 255.255.255.0. Both of these subnet masks are shown in Figure 2-49.

Figure 2-49 *Ones in the subnet mask indicate the network portion of the address.*

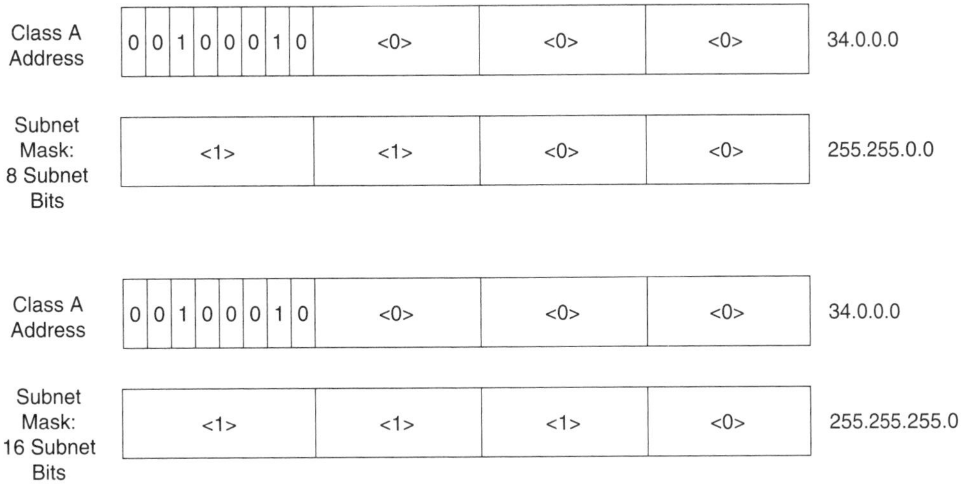

On some media (such as IEEE 802 LANs), media addresses and IP addresses are dynamically discovered through the use of two other members of the Internet protocol suite: ARP and RARP. ARP uses broadcast messages to determine the hardware MAC-layer address corresponding to a particular internetwork address. ARP is sufficiently generic to allow use of IP with virtually any type of underlying media-access mechanism. RARP uses broadcast messages to determine the Internet address associated with a particular hardware address. RARP is particularly important to diskless nodes, which may not know their internetwork address when they boot. Figure 2-50 shows the ARP/RARP packet structure.

Figure 2-50 *ARP/RARP packets are used for MAC/IP address resolution.*

Hardware Type		Protocol Type	
HA Length	PA Length	Operations	
Sender HA (Octets 0–3)*			
Sender HA (Octets 4–5)		Sender PA (Octets 0–1)	
Sender PA (Octets 2–3)		Target HA (Octets 0–1)	
Target HA (Octets 2–5)			
Target PA (Octets 0–3)			

*Field Lengths Assume HA = 6 Octets and PA = 4 Octets

HA = Hardware Address
PA = Protocol Address (IP Address)

The 16-bit hardware type field indicates the hardware type for which the request is being made. Examples include the following:

Value	Description
1	Ethernet (10 Mb)
4	Proteon ProNET Token Ring
6	IEEE 802 networks
7	ARCNET
11	LocalTalk

The 16-bit protocol type field is the protocol code or Ethertype. The hexadecimal value 0800 means IP.

The 8-bit hardware address (HA) length and protocol address (PA) length fields are the lengths (in octets), of the hardware and protocol addresses, respectively.

The 16-bit operation field indicates the operation code for this message:

Value	Description
1	ARP request
2	ARP reply
3	RARP request
4	RARP reply

The sender HA and target HA are the 48-bit (for Ethernet) hardware addresses, and the sender PA and target PA are the 32-bit (for IP) protocol addresses.

TCP/IP Internet Routing

Routing devices in the Internet have traditionally been called *gateways*—an unfortunate term because, elsewhere in the industry, the term applies to a device with somewhat different functionality. Gateways (which we call *routers* from this point on) within the Internet are organized hierarchically. Some routers are used to move information through one particular group of networks under the same administrative authority and control. A group of networks and routers under the same administrative control is called an *autonomous system (AS)*. Routers used for information exchange within autonomous systems are called *interior routers*, and they use a variety of IGPs to accomplish this purpose. Routers that move information between autonomous systems are called *exterior routers*, and they use an EGP for this purpose. Figure 2-51 shows the location of interior and exterior gateways.

Figure 2-51 *Exterior gateways are for routing between autonomous systems.*

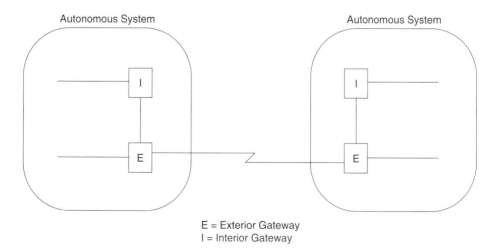

E = Exterior Gateway
I = Interior Gateway

IP routing protocols are dynamic. Dynamic routing calls for routes to be calculated at regular intervals by software in the routing devices. This contrasts with static routing, where routes are established by the network administrator and do not change until the network administrator changes them. An IP routing table consists of destination address/next hop pairs. A sample entry, shown in Figure 2-52, is interpreted as meaning "to get to Network 34.1.0.0 (Subnet 1 on Network 34), the next stop is the node at address 54.34.23.12."

Figure 2-52 *Routers store the next hops to destination networks in the IP routing table.*

Destination Address	Next Hop
34.1.0.0	54.34.23.12
78.2.0.0	54.34.23.12
147.9.5.0	.
17.12.0.0	.
.	54.32.12.10
.	54.32.12.10
.	.
.	

IP routing specifies that IP datagrams travel through internetworks one hop at a time. The entire route is not known at the outset of the journey. Instead, at each stop, the next destination is calculated by matching the destination address within the datagram with an entry in the current node's routing table. Each node's involvement in the routing process consists only of forwarding packets based on internal information, regardless of whether the packets get to their final destination. In other words, IP does not provide for error reporting back to the source when routing anomalies occur. This task is left to another Internet protocol, Internet Control Message Protocol (ICMP).

ICMP

ICMP performs a number of tasks within an IP internetwork. The principal reason it was created was for reporting routing failures back to the source. In addition, ICMP provides helpful messages such as the following:

- Echo and reply messages to test node reachability across an internetwork (via the **ping** command)
- Traceroute messages to test node reachability in a step-by-step fashion across an internetwork (via the **trace** command)
- Redirect messages to stimulate more efficient routing

- Time exceeded messages to inform sources that a datagram has exceeded its allocated time to exist within the internetwork

- Router advertisement and router solicitation messages to determine the addresses of routers on directly attached subnetworks

A more recent addition to ICMP provides a way for new nodes to discover the subnet mask currently used in an internetwork. All in all, ICMP is an integral part of any IP implementation, particularly those that run in routers.

NOTE   You can use ICMP as a diagnostic tool. By analyzing all ICMP traffic crossing the network, you can isolate routing faults, misconfigurations, security attacks, and more, so it's a good idea to learn ICMP in depth. Refer to RFC 792 for more details on ICMP.

IRDP

ICMP Router Discovery Protocol (IRDP) uses router advertisement and router solicitation messages to discover addresses of routers on directly attached subnets.

With IRDP, each router periodically multicasts router advertisement messages from each of its interfaces. Hosts discover the addresses of routers on the directly attached subnet by listening for these messages. Hosts can use router solicitation messages to request immediate advertisements, rather than wait for unsolicited messages.

IRDP offers several advantages over other methods of discovering addresses of neighboring routers. Primarily, it does not require hosts to recognize routing protocols, nor does it require manual configuration by an administrator.

Router advertisement messages allow hosts to discover the existence of neighboring routers, but not which router is best to reach a particular destination. If a host uses a poor first-hop router to reach a particular destination, it receives a redirect message identifying a better choice.

The TCP/IP Transport Layer

The Internet transport layer is implemented by TCP and UDP. TCP provides connection-oriented data transport, and UDP operation is connectionless. This section focuses on TCP first.

TCP   TCP provides full-duplex, acknowledged, and flow-controlled service to upper-layer protocols. It moves data in a continuous, unstructured byte stream where bytes are identified by sequence numbers. TCP can also support numerous simultaneous upper-layer conversations. Figure 2-53 shows the TCP packet format.

Figure 2-53 *The TCP segment header fields provide reliability, windowing, and connection orientation.*

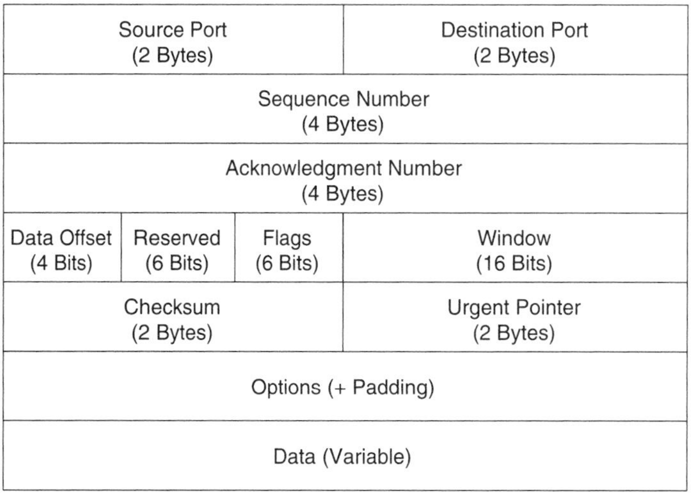

Source Port (2 Bytes)			Destination Port (2 Bytes)	
Sequence Number (4 Bytes)				
Acknowledgment Number (4 Bytes)				
Data Offset (4 Bits)	Reserved (6 Bits)	Flags (6 Bits)	Window (16 Bits)	
Checksum (2 Bytes)			Urgent Pointer (2 Bytes)	
Options (+ Padding)				
Data (Variable)				

The 16-bit source port and destination port fields identify the points at which upper-layer source and destination processes receive TCP services. Examples of TCP and UDP ports include those listed in Table 2-3.

Table 2-3 *TCP and UDP application port numbers.*

Decimal	Keyword	Description
7	ECHO	Echo
9	DISCARD	Discard
11	USERS	Active users
13	DAYTIME	Daytime
17	QUOTE	Quote
20	FTP-DATA	File transfer (data)
21	FTP	File transfer (control)
23	TELNET	Telnet
25	SMTP	Simple Mail Transfer Protocol
37	TIME	Time
42	NAMESERVER	Host name server
43	NICNAME	Who is

Table 2-3   *TCP and UDP application port numbers. (Continued)*

Decimal	Keyword	Description
53	DOMAIN	Domain name server
67	BOOTPS	BOOTP server/DHCP server
68	BOOTPC	BOOTP client/DHCP client
69	TFTP	Trivial File Transfer Protocol
79	FINGER	Finger
80	HTTP	Hypertext Transfer Protocol
102	ISO-TSAP	ISO-TSAP
103	X400	X400
111	SUNRPC	Sun remote-procedure call
137	NETBIOS—NS	NetBIOS name service
138	NETBIOS—DGM	NetBIOS datagram service
139	NETBIOS—SSSN	NetBIOS session service
146	ISO-TP0	ISO-TP0
147	ISO-IP	ISO-IP
161	SNMP	Simple Network Management Protocol
162	SNMPTRAP	SNMPTRAP
163	CMIP-Manage	CMIP/TCP manager
164	CMIP-Agent	CMIP/TCP agent
201	AT-RTMP	AppleTalk routing maintenance
202	AT-NBP	AppleTalk name binding
204	AT-ECHO	AppleTalk echo
206	AT-ZIS	AppleTalk zone information
520	RIP	Routing Information Protocol
524	NetWare over IP	NetWare 5's pure IP

The 32-bit sequence number field usually specifies the number assigned to the first byte of data in the current message. During session establishment, it can also be used to identify an initial sequence number to be used in the upcoming transmission.

The 32-bit acknowledgment number field contains the sequence number of the next byte of data the sender of the packet expects to receive.

The 4-bit data offset field indicates the number of 32-bit words in the TCP header.

The 6-bit reserved field is reserved for future use by protocol designers, and is set to 0.

The 6-bit flags field carries a variety of control information, such as the setup and termination of a session, expedited or urgent flow, or reset of a connection. The six flags, starting with the most significant bit, are as follows:

Flag	Description
URG	Urgent pointer field significant
ACK	Acknowledgment field significant
PSH	Push function
RST	Reset connection
SYN	Synchronize a new session
FIN	No more data from sender

The 16-bit window field specifies the size of the sender's receive window (that is, buffer space available for incoming data).

The 16-bit checksum field indicates whether the header or data was damaged in transit.

The 16-bit urgent pointer field points to the last byte of urgent data and allows the receiver to determine how much urgent data is coming. (In some implementations, the urgent pointer points to the byte following the last byte of urgent data.)

The variable-length options field specifies various TCP options. It must end on a 32-bit boundary. A padding field can be added to ensure this.

The data field contains upper-layer information.

UDP   UDP is a much simpler protocol than TCP and is useful in situations where TCP's powerful reliability mechanisms are not necessary. The UDP header (shown in Figure 2-54) has only four fields: 16-bit source port and destination port, 16-bit length, and 16-bit UDP checksum. The source and destination port fields serve the same functions as they do in the TCP header. The length field specifies the length of the UDP header and data, and the checksum field allows packet integrity checking. The UDP checksum is optional.

Figure 2-54 *The UDP header reflects the low overhead of connectionless services.*

Source Port (16 Bits)	Destination Port (16 Bits)
Length (16 Bits)	Checksum (16 Bits)
Data	

The 16-bit source port and destination port fields identify the points at which upper-layer source and destination processes receive UDP services. The source port value is optional, and when used, it specifies the port to which replies should be sent; if not used, it should be 0. Port numbers for UDP are the same as those for TCP (refer to Table 2-3).

The 16-bit length field contains a count of the total bytes in the UDP datagram, including the header and the user data.

The 16-bit checksum is optional; a value of 0 means that the checksum has not been computed.

TCP/IP Upper-Layer Protocols

The Internet Protocol suite includes many upper-layer protocols representing a wide variety of applications, including network management, file transfer, distributed file services, terminal emulation, and electronic mail. Table 2-4 maps the best-known Internet upper-layer protocols to the applications they support.

Table 2-4   *Internet protocol/application mapping.*

Application	Supported Protocols
File Transfer	File Transfer Protocol
Terminal emulation	Telnet, X Window system
Electronic mail	Simple Mail Transfer Protocol
Network management	Simple Network Management Protocol
Distributed file services	Network File System, external data representation, and remote-procedure call

FTP provides a way to move files between computer systems. Telnet allows virtual terminal emulation. The X Window system is a popular protocol that permits intelligent terminals to communicate with remote computers as if they were directly attached. Simple Mail Transfer Protocol (SMTP) provides an electronic mail transport mechanism. Simple Network Management Protocol (SNMP) is a network management protocol used for reporting anomalous network conditions and setting network threshold values. Network File System (NFS), external data representation (XDR), and remote-procedure call (RPC) combine to allow transparent access to remote network resources. These and other network applications use the services of TCP/IP and other lower-layer Internet protocols to provide users with basic network services.

RIP

RIP is a routing protocol originally designed for Xerox PARC Universal Protocol (where it was called GWINFO) and used in the XNS protocol suite. RIP became associated with both UNIX and TCP/IP in 1982, when the Berkeley Software Distribution (BSD) version of UNIX began shipping with a RIP implementation referred to as *routed* (pronounced "route-dee"). RIP, which is still a very popular routing protocol in the TCP/IP community, is formally defined in the XNS Internet Transport Protocols publication (1981) and in RFC 1058 (1988).

RIP has been widely adopted by PC manufacturers for use in networking products. For example, AppleTalk's routing protocol RTMP is a modified version of RIP. RIP was also the basis for the routing protocols of network architectures from Novell and Banyan.

Each entry in a RIP routing table provides a variety of information, including the ultimate destination, the next hop on the way to that destination, and a metric. The metric indicates the distance in number of hops to the destination. Other information can also be present in the routing table, including various timers associated with the route. Figure 2-55 shows a typical RIP routing table.

Figure 2-55 *RIP routing tables display distance information based on hop counts.*

Destination	Next hop	Distance	Timers	Flags
Network A	Router 1	3	t1, t2, t3	x, y
Network B	Router 2	5	t1, t2, t3	x, y
Network C	Router 1	2	t1, t2, t3	x, y
.	.	.	.	.
.	.	.	.	.
.	.	.	.	.

RIP maintains only the best route to a destination. When new information provides a better route, this information replaces old route information. Network topology changes can provoke changes to routes, causing, for example, a new route to become the best route to a particular destination. When network topology changes occur, they are reflected in routing update messages. For example, when a router detects a link failure or a router failure, it recalculates its routes and sends routing update messages. Each router that receives a routing update message that includes a change updates its tables and propagates the change.

Figure 2-56 shows the RIP packet format for IP implementations, as specified by RFC 1058.

Figure 2-56 *The RIP packets carry information on the networks advertised throughout the network.*

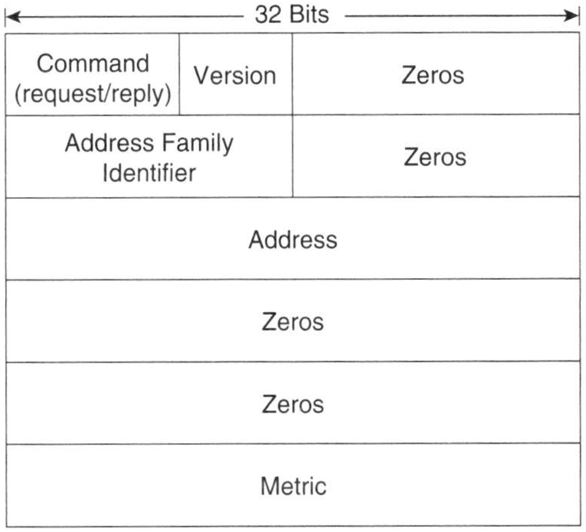

The first field in an IP RIP packet is the command field. This field carries an integer indicating either a request (value = 1) or a response (value = 2). The request command requests the responding system to send all or part of its routing table. Destinations for which a response is requested are listed later in the packet. The response command represents a reply to a request or, more frequently, an unsolicited regular routing update. In the response packet, a responding system includes all or part of its routing table. Regular routing update messages include the entire routing table.

The version number field specifies the RIP version being implemented (currently either 1 or 2). With the potential for many RIP implementations in an internetwork, this field can be used to signal different, potentially incompatible, implementations.

Following a 16-bit field of all zeros is the address family identifier field, which specifies the particular address family being used. This is typically IP (value = 2), but other network types can also be represented.

After another 16-bit field of zeros is a 32-bit address field. This field typically contains an IP address.

Following two more 32-bit fields of zeros is the RIP metric, which is a hop count. It indicates how many internetwork hops (routers) must be traversed before the destination can be reached.

Up to 25 occurrences of the address family identifier through metric fields are permitted to occur in any single IP RIP packet. In other words, up to 25 destinations can be listed in any single RIP packet. Multiple RIP packets are used to convey information from larger routing tables.

Like other routing protocols, RIP uses certain timers to regulate its performance. The RIP routing update timer is generally set to 30 seconds, ensuring that each router will send a complete copy of its routing table to all neighbors every 30 seconds. The route invalid timer determines how much time must expire without a router having heard about a particular route before that route is considered invalid. When a route is marked invalid, neighbors are notified of this fact. This notification must occur prior to expiration of the route flush timer, which indicates when the route is removed from the routing table. Typical initial values for these timers are 90 seconds for the route invalid timer and 270 seconds for the route flush timer.

RIP implementations can use several features to make operation more stable in the face of rapid network topology changes. These include a hop-count limit, holddowns, triggered updates, split horizon, and poison reverse updates.

RIP Hop-Count Limit   RIP permits a maximum hop count of 15. Any destination greater than 15 hops away is tagged as unreachable. RIP's maximum hop count greatly restricts its use in large internetworks but prevents a problem called count to infinity from causing endless network routing loops.

In Figure 2-57, consider what will happen if the link from Router 1 to Network A fails. Router 1 will remove the entry for Network A from its routing table, but in the meantime, Router 2 will advertise that it has a link to Network A. This will cause Router 1 to begin routing all traffic for Network A through Router 2. This creates a routing loop, because Router 2 has in its table that the next hop to Network A is Router 1, and Router 1 has in its table that the next hop to Network A is Router 2. A frame destined for Network A would continue to loop indefinitely except that the IP time-to-live field will finally decrement to 0, causing the frame to be stopped.

Figure 2-57 *Even small networks can experience routing loops.*

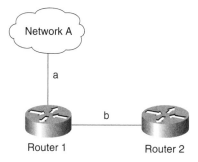

The looping frame is not the only problem. The other problem is that when Router 2 advertises a one-hop link to Network A, Router 1 changes its own routing table to show that it has a two-hop path to Network A. Router 1 advertises this path in its next update. This will cause Router 2 to advertise a three-hop path, and so on. This problem will continue indefinitely unless some external boundary condition is imposed. That boundary condition is RIP's hop-count maximum. When the hop count exceeds 15, the route is marked unreachable. Over time, the route is removed from the table.

RIP Holddowns and Triggered Updates   Holddowns can be used to prevent regular update messages from inappropriately reinstating a route that has gone bad. Holddowns tell routers to hold down any changes that might affect recently removed routes for some period of time. The hold-down period is usually calculated to be just greater than the period of time necessary to update the entire network with a routing change. Holddowns prevent the count-to-infinity problem.

When a route goes down, neighboring routers detect this. Triggered updates allow routers to inform their neighbors of the route change immediately, without waiting for a regular update period. Triggered updates cause a wave of routing updates that travel through the network.

Triggered updates do not instantly arrive at every network device. It is therefore possible that a device that has yet to be informed of a network failure may send a regular update message (indicating that a route that has just gone down is still good) to a device that has just been notified of the network failure. In this case, the latter device now contains (and potentially advertises) incorrect routing information. Holddowns prevent this.

RIP Split Horizon   The split-horizon rule derives from the fact that it is usually not useful to send information about a route back in the direction from which it came. For example, consider Figure 2-58.

Figure 2-58 *Split horizon prevents Router 2 from advertising Network A back to Router 1.*

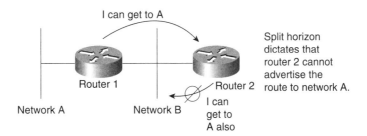

Router 1 initially advertises that it has a route to Network A. There is no reason for Router 2 to include this route in its update back to Router 1, because Router 1 is closer to Network A. The split-horizon rule says that Router 2 should strike this route from any updates it sends to Router 1.

The split-horizon rule helps prevent two-node routing loops. For example, consider the case discussed earlier, where Router 1's interface to Network A goes down. Without split horizon, Router 2 informs Router 1 that it can get to Network A. Router 1 picks up Router 2's route as an alternative to its failed direct connection, causing a routing loop. Although holddowns should prevent this, split horizon provides extra algorithm stability.

RIP Poison Reverse Updates   Poison reverse allows a router to include in its routing updates networks with a hop count set to infinity. This can be used for unreachable networks or another way of implementing split horizon. When used as an alternative to a split-horizon implementation, a router can include networks reachable via the link onto which the update is being sent but specify the hop count as infinity. This immediately kills two-node routing loops.

IGRP and Enhanced IGRP

Interior Gateway Routing Protocol (IGRP) is a routing protocol developed in the mid-1980s by Cisco Systems, Inc. Cisco's principal goal in creating IGRP was to provide a robust protocol for routing within an AS that has an arbitrarily complex topology and media with diverse bandwidth and delay characteristics. An AS is a collection of networks under common administration that share a common routing strategy.

In the mid-1980s, the most popular intra-AS routing protocol was RIP. Although RIP was quite useful for routing within small to moderate-sized, relatively homogeneous internetworks, its limits were being pushed by network growth. In particular, RIP's small hop-count limit (15) restricted the size of internetworks, and its single metric (hop count) did not allow for much routing flexibility in complex environments. The popularity of Cisco routers and the robustness of IGRP have encouraged many organizations with large internetworks to replace RIP with IGRP.

Cisco's initial IGRP implementation worked in IP networks. IGRP was designed to run in any network environment, however, and Cisco soon ported it to run in OSI CLNP networks.

Cisco developed Enhanced IGRP in the early 1990s to improve the operating efficiency of IGRP. Enhanced IGRP is discussed in detail later in this chapter.

IGRP is a distance-vector IGP. Distance-vector routing protocols call for each router to send all or a portion of its routing table in a routing update message at regular intervals to each of its neighboring routers. As routing information proliferates through the network, routers can calculate distances to all nodes within the internetwork.

Distance-vector routing protocols are often contrasted with link-state routing protocols, which send local connection information to all nodes in the internetwork.

IGRP uses a combination of metrics. Internetwork delay, bandwidth, reliability, and load are all factored in to the routing decision. Network administrators can set the weighting factors for each of these metrics. IGRP uses either the administrator-set or the default weightings to automatically calculate optimal routes.

IGRP provides a wide range for its metrics. For example, reliability and load can take on any value between 1 and 255, bandwidth can take on values reflecting speeds from 1,200 bps to 10 Gbps, and delay is measured in tens of microseconds and can take on any value from 1 to 2^{24}. Wide metric ranges allow satisfactory metric setting in internetworks with widely varying performance characteristics. Most importantly, the metric components are combined in a user-definable algorithm. As a result, network administrators can influence route selection in an intuitive fashion.

To provide additional flexibility, IGRP permits multipath routing. Dual equal-bandwidth lines may run a single stream of traffic in round-robin fashion, with automatic switchover to the second line if one line goes down. Also, multiple paths can be used even if the metrics for the paths are different. For example, if one path is three times better than another because its metric is three times lower, the better path will be used three times as often. Only routes with metrics that are within a certain range of the best route are used as multiple paths.

IGRP provides a number of features that are designed to enhance its stability. These include holddowns, split horizon, triggered updates, and poison reverse updates. These work in a similar fashion to the stability options discussed earlier in this chapter, in the section "RIP."

IGRP Holddowns and Triggered Updates   Holddowns are used to prevent regular update messages from inappropriately reinstating a route that may have gone bad. When a route goes down, neighboring routers detect this via the lack of regularly scheduled update messages. These routers then calculate new routes and send routing update messages to inform their neighbors of the route change. This activity begins a wave of triggered updates that filter through the network.

These triggered updates do not instantly arrive at every network device. It is therefore possible that a device that has yet to be informed of a network failure might send a regular update message (indicating that a route that has just gone down is still good) to a device that has just been notified of the network failure. In this case, the latter device would now contain (and potentially advertise) incorrect routing information.

Holddowns tell routers to hold down any changes that might affect routes for some period of time. The hold-down period is usually calculated to be just greater than the period of time necessary to update the entire network with a routing change.

IGRP Split Horizon   The split-horizon rule derives from the fact that it is usually not useful to send information about a route back in the direction from which it came. For example, consider Figure 2-59.

Figure 2-59 *Split horizon supplies the same benefit for IGRP as it does for RIP.*

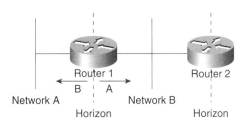

Router 1 initially advertises that it has a route to Network A. There is no reason for Router 2 to include this route in its update back to Router 1, because Router 1 is closer to Network A. The split-horizon rule says that Router 2 should strike this route from any updates it sends to Router 1.

The split-horizon rule helps prevent routing loops. For example, consider the case where the link from Router 1 to Network A goes down. Without split horizon, Router 2 informs Router 1 that it can get to Network A. If Router 1 does not have sufficient intelligence, it may actually pick up Router 2's route as an alternative to its failed direct connection, causing a routing loop. Although holddowns should prevent this, split horizon is implemented in IGRP because it provides extra algorithm stability.

IGRP Poison Reverse Updates   Whereas split horizon should prevent routing loops between adjacent routers, poison reverse updates are intended to defeat larger routing loops. Increases in routing metrics generally indicate routing loops. Poison reverse updates are sent to remove the route and place it in holddown. In Cisco's implementation of IGRP, poison reverse updates are sent if a route metric has increased by a factor of 1.1 or greater.

IGRP Timers   IGRP maintains a number of timers and variables containing time intervals. These include an update timer, an invalid timer, a hold-time period, and a flush timer. The update timer specifies how frequently routing update messages should be sent. The IGRP default for this variable is 90 seconds. The invalid timer specifies how long a router should wait, in the absence of routing update messages about a specific route, before declaring that route invalid. The IGRP default for this variable is three times the update period. The hold-time variable specifies the hold-down period. The IGRP default for this variable is three times the update timer period plus 10 seconds. Finally, the flush timer indicates how much time should pass before a route should be flushed from the routing table. The IGRP default is seven times the routing update period.

Enhanced IGRP   Enhanced IGRP combines the advantages of link-state protocols with the advantages of distance-vector protocols. Enhanced IGRP incorporates the Diffusing Update Algorithm (DUAL) developed at SRI International by Dr. J.J. Garcia-Luna-Aceves. Enhanced IGRP includes the following features:

- Fast convergence—Enhanced IGRP uses DUAL to achieve convergence quickly. A router running Enhanced IGRP stores all of its neighbors' routing tables so that it can quickly adapt to alternate routes. If no appropriate route exists, Enhanced IGRP queries its neighbors to discover an alternate route. These queries propagate until an alternate route is found.

- Variable-length subnet masks—Enhanced IGRP includes full support for variable length subnet masks. Subnet routes are automatically summarized on a network number boundary. In addition, Enhanced IGRP can be configured to summarize on any bit boundary at any interface.

- Partial, bounded updates—Enhanced IGRP does not make periodic updates. Instead, it sends partial updates only when the metric for a route changes. Propagation of partial updates is automatically bounded so that only those routers that need the information are updated. As a result of these two capabilities, Enhanced IGRP consumes significantly less bandwidth than IGRP.

- Multiple network-layer support—Enhanced IGRP includes support for AppleTalk, IP, and Novell NetWare. The AppleTalk implementation uses RTMP to redistribute routes. The IP implementation can use OSPF, RIP, Intermediate System-to-Intermediate System (IS-IS), EGP, or BGP to redistribute routes. The Novell implementation can use Novell RIP and Service Advertising Protocol (SAP) to redistribute routes.

Enhanced IGRP provides compatibility and seamless interoperation with IGRP routers. An automatic redistribution mechanism allows IGRP routes to be imported into Enhanced IGRP and Enhanced IGRP routes to be imported into IGRP, so it is possible to add Enhanced IGRP gradually into an existing IGRP network. Because the metrics for both protocols are directly translatable, they are as easily comparable as if they were routes that originated in their own ASs. In addition, Enhanced IGRP treats IGRP routes as external routes and provides a way for the network administrator to customize them.

Enhanced IGRP consists of the following components:

- Neighbor discovery/recovery
- Reliable Transport Protocol (RTP)
- DUAL finite state machine
- Protocol-dependent modules

Neighbor discovery/recovery is the process that routers use to dynamically learn about other routers on their directly attached networks. Routers must also discover when their neighbors become unreachable or inoperative. This process is achieved with low overhead by periodically sending small hello packets. As long as a router receives hello packets from a neighboring router, it assumes that the neighbor is functioning and that they can exchange routing information.

RTP is responsible for guaranteed, ordered delivery of Enhanced IGRP packets to all neighbors. It supports intermixed transmission of multicast or unicast packets. For efficiency, only certain Enhanced IGRP packets are transmitted reliably. For example, on a multiaccess network that has multicast capabilities, such as Ethernet, it is not necessary to send hello packets reliably to all neighbors individually. For that reason, Enhanced IGRP sends a single multicast hello packet containing an indicator that informs the receivers that the packet need not be acknowledged. Other types of packets, such as updates, indicate in the packet that acknowledgment is required. RTP has a provision for sending multicast packets quickly when unacknowledged packets are pending, which helps ensure that convergence time remains low in the presence of varying speed links.

The DUAL finite state machine embodies the decision process for all route computations. It tracks all routes advertised by all neighbors. DUAL uses distance information to select efficient, loop-free paths and selects routes for insertion in a routing table based on feasible successors. A feasible successor is a neighboring router used for packet forwarding that is a least-cost path to a destination guaranteed not to be part of a routing loop. When a neighbor changes a metric or when a topology change occurs, DUAL tests for feasible successors. If one is found, DUAL uses it to avoid recomputing the route unnecessarily. When there are no feasible successors but there are neighbors advertising the destination, a recomputation (also known as a diffusing computation) must occur to determine a new successor. Although recomputation is not processor intensive, it affects convergence time, so it is advantageous to avoid unnecessary recomputations.

The protocol-dependent modules are responsible for network-layer, protocol-specific requirements. For example, the IP Enhanced IGRP module is responsible for sending and receiving Enhanced IGRP packets that are encapsulated in IP. IP Enhanced IGRP is also responsible for parsing Enhanced IGRP packets and informing DUAL of the new information that has been received. IP Enhanced IGRP asks DUAL to make routing decisions, the results of which are stored in the IP routing table. IP Enhanced IGRP is responsible for redistributing routes learned by other IP routing protocols.

Enhanced IGRP Packet Types   Enhanced IGRP uses five packet types:

- Hello/acknowledgment
- Update
- Query
- Reply
- Request

Hello packets are multicast for neighbor discovery/recovery and do not require acknowledgment. An acknowledgment packet is a hello packet that has no data. Acknowledgment packets contain a nonzero acknowledgment number, and they are always sent using a unicast address.

Update packets are used to convey reachability of destinations. When a new neighbor is discovered, unicast update packets are sent so the neighbor can build up its topology table. In other cases, such as a link cost change, updates are multicast. Updates are always transmitted reliably.

Query and reply packets are sent when a destination has no feasible successors. Query packets are always multicast. Reply packets are sent in response to query packets to indicate to the originator that the originator does not need to recompute the route because there are feasible successors. Reply packets are unicast to the originator of the query. Both query and reply packets are transmitted reliably.

Request packets are used to get specific information from one or more neighbors. Request packets are used in route server applications and can be multicast or unicast. Request packets are transmitted unreliably.

Enhanced IGRP Neighbor Tables   When a router discovers a new neighbor, it records the neighbor's address and interface as an entry in the neighbor table. There is one neighbor table for each protocol-dependent module. When a neighbor sends a hello packet, it advertises a hold time, which is the amount of time a router treats a neighbor as reachable and operational. If a hello packet is not received within the hold time, the hold time expires and DUAL is informed of the topology change.

The neighbor table entry also includes information required by RTP. Sequence numbers are employed to match acknowledgments with data packets. The last sequence number received from the neighbor is recorded so that out-of-order packets can be detected. A transmission list is used to queue packets for possible retransmission on a per-neighbor basis. Round-trip timers are kept in the neighbor table entry to estimate an optimal retransmission interval.

Enhanced IGRP Topology Tables   The topology table contains all destinations advertised by neighboring routers. The protocol-dependent modules populate the table, and the table is acted on by the DUAL finite state machine. Each entry in the topology table includes the destination address and a list of neighbors that have advertised the destination. For each neighbor, the entry records the advertised metric, which the neighbor stores in its routing table. An important rule that distance-vector protocols must follow is that if the neighbor is advertising this destination, it must be using the route to forward packets.

The metric that the router uses to reach the destination is also associated with the destination. The metric that the router uses in the routing table and to advertise to other routers is the sum of the best advertised metric from all neighbors plus the link cost to the best neighbor.

Enhanced IGRP Route States   A topology table entry for a destination can be in one of two states: active or passive. A destination is in the passive state when the router is not performing a recomputation and in the active state when the router is performing a recomputation. If feasible successors are always available, a destination never has to go into the active state, thereby avoiding a recomputation.

A recomputation occurs when a destination has no feasible successors. The router initiates the recomputation by sending a query packet to each of its neighboring routers. The neighboring router can send a reply packet, indicating that it has a feasible successor for the destination, or it can send a query packet, indicating that it is participating in the recomputation. While a destination is in the active state, a router cannot change the destination's routing table information. Once the router has received a reply from each neighboring router, the topology table entry for the destination returns to the passive state and the router can select a successor.

Enhanced IGRP Route Tagging   Enhanced IGRP supports internal and external routes. Internal routes originate within an Enhanced IGRP AS. Therefore, a directly attached network that is configured to run Enhanced IGRP is considered an internal route and is propagated with this information throughout the Enhanced IGRP AS. External routes are learned by another routing protocol or reside in the routing table as static routes. These routes are tagged individually with the identity of their origin.

External routes are tagged with the following information:

- The router ID of the Enhanced IGRP router that redistributed the route
- The AS number of the destination
- A configurable administrator tag
- The ID of the external protocol
- The metric from the external protocol
- Bit flags for default routing

Route tagging allows the network administrator to customize routing and maintain flexible policy controls. Route tagging is particularly useful in transit ASs where Enhanced IGRP typically interacts with an interdomain routing protocol that implements global policies, resulting in scalable, policy-based routing.

OSPF

OSPF (Open Shortest Path First) is a routing protocol developed for IP networks by the IGP working group of the Internet Engineering Task Force (IETF). The working group was formed in 1988 to design an IGP based on the shortest path first (SPF) algorithm for use in the Internet. Like IGRP, OSPF was created because RIP was, in the mid-1980s, increasingly unable to serve large, heterogeneous internetworks.

OSPF was derived from several research efforts, including the following:

- BBN's SPF algorithm developed in 1978 for the ARPANET (a landmark packet-switching network developed in the early 1970s by BBN)
- Dr. Radia Perlman's research on fault-tolerant broadcasting of routing information (1988)
- BBN's work on area routing (1986)
- An early version of the OSI IS-IS routing protocol

As indicated by its abbreviation, OSPF has two primary characteristics. First, it is open, in that its specification is in the public domain and was originally described in RFC 1131. The most recent version, known as OSPF 2, is described in RFC 1583. Second, it is based on the SPF algorithm, which is sometimes referred to as the Dijkstra algorithm, named for the person credited with its creation.

OSPF is a link-state routing protocol. As such, it calls for the sending of link-state advertisements (LSAs) to all other routers within the same hierarchical area. Information on attached interfaces, metrics used, and other variables is included in OSPF LSAs. As OSPF routers accumulate link-state information, they use the SPF algorithm to calculate the shortest path to each node.

As a link-state algorithm, OSPF contrasts with RIP and IGRP, which are distance-vector routing protocols. Routers running the distance-vector algorithm send all or a portion of their routing tables in routing update messages, but only to their neighbors.

Unlike RIP, OSPF can operate within a hierarchy. The largest entity within the hierarchy is the AS. An AS is a collection of networks under a common administration, sharing a common routing strategy. OSPF is an intra-AS (interior gateway) routing protocol, although it is capable of receiving routes from and sending routes to other ASs.

An AS can be divided into a number of areas, which are groups of contiguous networks and attached hosts. Routers with multiple interfaces can participate in multiple areas. These routers, which are called *area border routers, maintain separate topological databases for each area.*

A topological database is essentially an overall picture of networks in relationship to routers. The topological database contains the collection of LSAs received from all routers in the same area. Because routers within the same area share the same information, they have identical topological databases.

The term *domain* is sometimes used to describe a portion of the network in which all routers have identical topological databases.

An area's topology is invisible to entities outside the area. By keeping area topologies separate, OSPF passes less routing traffic than it would if the AS were not partitioned.

Area partitioning creates two different types of OSPF routing, depending on whether the source and destination are in the same or different areas. *Intra-area routing* occurs when the source and destination are in the same area; *interarea routing* occurs when they are in different areas.

An OSPF backbone is responsible for distributing routing information between areas. It consists of all area border routers, networks not wholly contained in any area, and their attached routers. Figure 2-60 shows an example of an internetwork with several areas.

Figure 2-60 *OSPF uses hierarchical internetwork design to optimize routing.*

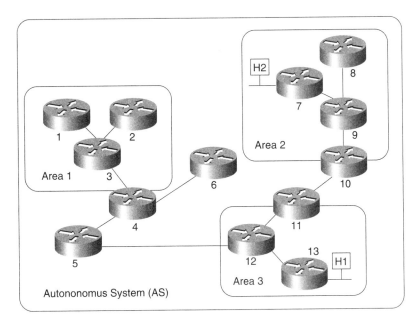

In Figure 2-60, Routers 4, 5, 6, 10, 11, and 12 make up the backbone. If Host 1 in Area 3 wants to send a packet to Host 2 in Area 2, the packet is sent to Router 13, which forwards the packet to Router 12, which sends the packet to Router 11. Router 11 forwards the packet along the backbone to area border router Router 10, which sends the packet through two intra-area routers (Router 9 and Router 7) to be forwarded to Host 2.

The backbone itself is an OSPF area (Area 0), so all backbone routers use the same procedures and algorithms to maintain routing information within the backbone that any area router would. The backbone topology is invisible to all intra-area routers, as are individual area topologies to the backbone.

AS border routers running OSPF learn about exterior routes through exterior gateway protocols such as EGP or BGP, or through configuration information.

The SPF Algorithm   The SPF routing algorithm is the basis for OSPF operations. When an SPF router is powered up, it initializes its routing protocol data structures and then waits for indications from lower-layer protocols that its interfaces are functional.

When a router is assured that its interfaces are functioning, it uses the OSPF Hello protocol to acquire neighbors, which are routers with interfaces to a common network. The router sends Hello packets to its neighbors and receives their Hello packets. In addition to helping acquire neighbors, Hello packets also act as keepalives to let routers know that other routers are still functional.

On multiaccess networks (that is, networks supporting more than two routers), the Hello protocol elects a designated router and a backup designated router. The designated router is responsible, among other things, for generating LSAs for the entire multiaccess network. Designated routers allow a reduction in network traffic and in the size of the topological database.

When the link-state databases of two neighboring routers are synchronized, the routers are said to be adjacent. On multiaccess networks, the designated router determines which routers should become adjacent. Topological databases are synchronized between pairs of adjacent routers. Adjacencies control the distribution of routing protocol packets. These packets are sent and received only on adjacencies.

Each router periodically sends an LSA. LSAs are also sent when a router's state changes. LSAs include information on a router's adjacencies. By comparing established adjacencies to link states, failed routers can be quickly detected and the network's topology altered appropriately. From the topological database generated from LSAs, each router calculates a shortest-path tree, with itself as root. The shortest-path tree, in turn, yields a routing table.

OSPF Packet Format   Figure 2-61 shows the OSPF packet header. The first field in the OSPF header is the OSPF version number. The version number identifies the particular OSPF implementation being used.

Figure 2-61 *Each OSPF packet begins with a 24-byte header.*

1	1	2	4	4	2	2	8	Variable
Version Number	Type	Packet Length	Router ID	Area ID	Checksum	Authentication type	Authentication	Data

Following the version number is the type field. There are five OSPF packet types:

- Hello—Establishes and maintains neighbor relationships. These messages are sent at regular intervals (typically every 10 seconds on a LAN).

- Database description—Describes the contents of the topological database. These messages are exchanged when an adjacency is being initialized.

- Link-state request—Requests pieces of the topological database from neighbor routers. These messages are exchanged after a router discovers (through examination of database description packets) that parts of its topological database are out of date.

- Link-state update—Responses to link-state request packets. These messages are also used for the regular dispersal of LSAs. Several LSAs can be included within a single link-state update packet.

- Link-state acknowledgment—Acknowledges link-state update packets. Link-state update packets must be explicitly acknowledged to ensure that link-state flooding throughout an area is a reliable process.

Each LSA in a link-state update packet contains a type field. There are four LSA types:

- Router-links advertisements (RLAs)—Describe the collected states of the router's links to a specific area. A router sends an RLA for each area to which it belongs. RLAs are flooded throughout the entire area, and no further.

- Network-links advertisements (NLAs)—Sent by the designated routers. They describe all the routers that are attached to a multiaccess network, and are flooded throughout the area containing the multiaccess network.

- Summary-links advertisements (SLAs)—Summarize routes to destinations outside an area, but within the AS. They are generated by area border routers, and are flooded throughout the area. Only intra-area routes are advertised into the backbone. Both intra-area and interarea routes are advertised into the other areas.

- AS external-links advertisements—Describe a route to a destination that is external to the AS. AS external-links advertisements are originated by AS boundary routers. This type of advertisement is the only type that is forwarded everywhere in the AS; all others are forwarded only within specific areas.

Following the OSPF packet header's type field is a packet length field, which provides the packet's length, including the OSPF header, in bytes.

The router ID field identifies the packet's source.

The area ID field identifies the area to which the packet belongs. All OSPF packets are associated with a single area.

A standard IP checksum field checks the entire packet contents for potential damage suffered in transit.

The authentication type field contains an authentication type. "Simple password" is an example of an authentication type. All OSPF protocol exchanges are authenticated. The authentication type is configurable on a per-area basis.

The authentication field is 64 bits in length and contains authentication information.

Additional OSPF Features   Additional OSPF features include equal-cost, multipath routing and routing based on upper-layer TOS requests. TOS-based routing supports upper-layer protocols that can specify particular types of service. For example, an application might specify that certain data is urgent. If OSPF has high-priority links at its disposal, these can be used to transport the urgent datagram.

OSPF supports one or more metrics. If only one metric is used, it is considered to be arbitrary, and TOS is not supported. If more than one metric is used, TOS is optionally supported through the use of a separate metric (and, therefore, a separate routing table) for each of the eight combinations created by the three IP TOS bits (the delay, throughput, and reliability bits). For example, if the IP TOS bits specify low delay, low throughput, and high reliability, OSPF calculates routes to all destinations based on this TOS designation.

IP subnet masks are included with each advertised destination, enabling variable-length subnet masks. With variable-length subnet masks, an IP network can be broken into many subnets of various sizes. This provides network administrators with extra network configuration flexibility.

EGP

EGP is an interdomain reachability protocol. EGP is documented in RFC 904, published in April 1984. As the first exterior gateway protocol to gain widespread acceptance in the Internet, EGP served a valuable purpose. EGP's weaknesses became more apparent as the Internet grew and matured. Because of these weaknesses, EGP is being phased out of the Internet, replaced mainly by BGP.

EGP was originally designed to communicate reachability to and from the ARPANET core routers. Information was passed from individual source nodes in distinct Internet ASs up to the core routers, which passed the information through the backbone until it could be passed down to the destination network within another AS. This relationship between EGP and other ARPANET components is shown in Figure 2-62.

Figure 2-62 *EGP was used for routing between autonomous systems in the ARPANET.*

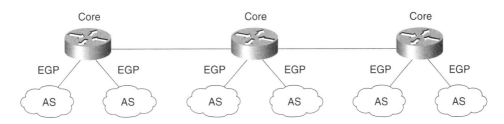

Although EGP is a dynamic routing protocol, it uses a very simple design. It does not use metrics and therefore cannot make intelligent routing decisions. EGP routing updates contain network reachability information. In other words, they specify that certain networks are reachable through certain routers.

EGP has three primary functions. First, routers running EGP establish a set of neighbors. These neighbors are simply routers with which an EGP router wishes to share reachability information; there is no implication of geographic proximity. Second, EGP routers poll their neighbors to see whether they are alive. Third, EGP routers send update messages containing information about the reachability of networks within their ASs.

EGP Packet Format   The EGP packet format is shown in Figure 2-63. The first field in the EGP packet header is the EGP version number field. This field identifies the current EGP version and is checked by recipients to determine whether there is a match between the sender and recipient version numbers.

Figure 2-63 *The EGP packet header consists of eight fields.*

1	1	2	1	2	2	2	Variable
EGP Version Number	Type	Code	Status	Checksum	Autonomous System Number	Sequence Number	Data

The code field distinguishes among message subtypes.

The status field contains message-dependent status information. Status codes include insufficient resources, parameter problem, and protocol violation.

The checksum field is used to detect possible problems that may have developed with the packet in transit.

The autonomous system number field identifies the AS to which the sending router belongs.

The sequence number field is the last field in the EGP packet header. This field allows two EGP routers exchanging messages to match requests with replies. The sequence number is initialized to zero when a neighbor is established and incremented by one with each request-response transaction.

EGP Message Types   Additional fields follow the EGP header. The contents of these fields vary depending on the message type (as specified by the type field):

- Neighbor acquisition—The neighbor acquisition message includes a hello interval field and a poll interval field. The hello interval field specifies the interval period for testing whether neighbors are alive. The poll interval field specifies the routing update frequency.

- Neighbor reachability—The neighbor reachability message adds no extra fields to the EGP header. These messages use the code field to indicate whether the message is a hello message or a response to a hello message. Separating the reachability assessment function from the routing update function reduces network traffic because network reachability changes usually occur more often than routing parameter changes. Only after a specified percentage of reachability messages have not been received does an EGP node declare a neighbor to be down.

- Poll—To provide correct routing between ASs, EGP must know the relative location of remote hosts. The poll message allows EGP routers to acquire reachability information about the networks on which these hosts reside. These messages only have one field beyond the common header—the IP source network field. This field specifies the network to be used as a reference point for the request.

- Routing update—Routing update messages provide a way for EGP routers to indicate the locations of various networks within their ASs. In addition to the common header, these messages include many additional fields. The number of interior gateways field indicates the number of interior gateways appearing in the message. The number of exterior gateways field indicates the number of exterior gateways appearing in the message. The IP source network field provides the IP address of the network from which reachability is measured. Following this field is a series of gateway blocks. Each gateway block provides the IP address of a gateway and a list of networks and distances associated with reaching those networks.

   Within the gateway block, EGP lists networks by distances. In other words, at distance three, there may be four networks. These networks are then listed by address. The next group of networks may be those that are distance four away, and so on.

   EGP does not interpret the distance metrics that are contained within the routing update messages. In essence, EGP uses the distance field to indicate whether a path exists; the distance value can only be used to compare paths if those paths exist wholly within a particular AS. For this reason, EGP is more a reachability protocol than a routing protocol. This restriction also places topology limitations on the structure of the Internet. Specifically, an EGP portion of the Internet must be a tree structure in which a core gateway is the root, and there are no loops among other ASs within the tree. This restriction is a primary limitation of EGP, and provides an impetus for its gradual replacement by other, more capable exterior gateway protocols.

- Error—Error messages identify various EGP error conditions. In addition to the common EGP header, EGP error messages provide a reason field, followed by an error message header. Typical EGP errors (reasons) include bad EGP header format, bad EGP data field format, excessive polling rate, and the unavailability of reachability information. The error message header consists of the first three 32-bit words of the EGP header.

BGP

BGP performs interdomain routing. BGP is an exterior gateway protocol, which means that it performs routing between multiple ASs and exchanges routing and reachability information with other BGP systems.

BGP was developed to replace its predecessor, EGP, as the standard exterior gateway routing protocol used in the global Internet. BGP solves serious problems with EGP and scales to Internet growth more efficiently.

BGP is specified in several RFCs:

- RFC 1771—This RFC describes BGP4, the current version of BGP.
- RFC 1654—This RFC describes the first BGP4 specification.
- RFC 1105, RFC 1163, and RFC 1267—These RFCs describe versions of BGP prior to BGP4.

Although BGP was designed as an inter-AS protocol, it can be used both within and between ASs. Two BGP neighbors communicating between ASs must reside on the same physical network. BGP routers within the same AS communicate with one another to ensure that they have a consistent view of the AS and to determine which BGP router within that AS will serve as the connection point to or from certain external ASs.

Some ASs are merely pass-through channels for network traffic. In other words, some ASs carry network traffic that did not originate within and is not destined for them. BGP must interact with whatever intra-AS routing protocols exist within these pass-through ASs.

BGP update messages consist of network number/AS path pairs. The AS path contains the string of ASs through which the specified network may be reached. These update messages are sent over the TCP transport mechanism to ensure reliable delivery.

The initial data exchange between two routers is the entire BGP routing table. Incremental updates are sent out as the routing tables change. Unlike some other routing protocols, BGP does not require periodic refresh of the entire routing table. Instead, routers running BGP retain the latest version of each peer routing table. Although BGP maintains a routing table with all feasible paths to a particular network, it only advertises the primary (optimal) path in its update messages.

The BGP metric is an arbitrary unit number specifying the degree of preference of a particular path. These metrics are typically assigned by the network administrator through configuration files. Degree of preference may be based on any number of criteria, including AS count (paths with a smaller AS count are generally better) and stability and speed of the link.

BGP Packet Format   The BGP packet format is shown in Figure 2-64.

Figure 2-64 *The BGP packet header consists of four fields.*

BGP packets have a common 19-byte header consisting of three fields:

- The marker field is 16 bytes long and contains a value that the receiver of the message can predict. This field is used for authentication.

- The length field contains the total length of the message, in bytes.

- The type field specifies the message type.

BGP Message Types   Four message types are specified in BGP:

- Open—After a transport protocol connection is established, the first message sent by each side is an open message. If the open message is acceptable to the recipient, a keepalive message confirming the open message is sent back. Upon successful confirmation of the open message, updates, keepalives, and notifications may be exchanged.

  In addition to the common BGP packet header, open messages define several fields. The version field provides a BGP version number and allows the recipient to check that it is running the same version as the sender. The autonomous system field provides the AS number of the sender. The hold-time field indicates the maximum number of seconds that may elapse without receipt of a message before the transmitter is assumed to be dead. The authentication code field indicates the authentication type being used (if any). The authentication data field contains actual authentication data (if any).

- Update—BGP update messages provide routing updates to other BGP systems. Information in these messages is used to construct a graph describing the relationships of the various ASs. In addition to the common BGP header, update messages have several additional fields. These fields provide routing information by listing path attributes corresponding to each network. BGP currently defines five attributes:

— Origin—Can take on one of three values: IGP, EGP, and incomplete. The IGP attribute means that the network is part of the AS. The EGP attribute means that the information was originally learned from the EGP. BGP implementations would be inclined to prefer IGP routes over EGP routes, since EGP fails in the presence of routing loops. The incomplete attribute is used to indicate that the network is known via some other means.

— AS path—Provides the actual list of ASs on the path to the destination.

— Next hop—Provides the IP address of the router that should be used as the next hop to the networks listed in the update message.

— Unreachable—If present, indicates that a route is no longer reachable.

— Inter-AS metric—Provides a way for a BGP router to advertise its cost to destinations within its own AS. This information can be used by routers external to the advertiser's AS to select an optimal route into the AS to a particular destination.

- Notification—Notification messages are sent when an error condition has been detected and one router wants to tell another why it is closing the connection between them. Aside from the common BGP header, notification messages have an error code field, an error subcode field, and error data. The error code field indicates the type of error, and can be one of the following:

— Message header error—Indicates a problem with the message header such as an unacceptable message length, an unacceptable marker field value, or an unacceptable message type.

— Open message error—Indicates a problem with an open message such as an unsupported version number, an unacceptable AS number or IP address, or an unsupported authentication code.

— Update message error—Indicates a problem with the update message. Examples include a malformed attribute list, an attribute list error, and an invalid next-hop attribute.

— Hold time expired—Indicates a hold-time expiration, after which a BGP node will be declared dead.

- Keepalive—Keepalive messages do not contain any additional fields beyond those in the common BGP header. These messages are sent often enough to keep the hold-time timer from expiring.

NetWare Protocols

NetWare is a network operating system (NOS) that provides transparent remote file access and numerous other distributed network services, including printer sharing, electronic mail transfer, and database access. Much of NetWare's networking technology was derived from XNS, a networking system created by Xerox Corporation in the late 1970s.

Novell introduced NetWare to the market in the early 1980s. By the early 1990s, NetWare's NOS market share had risen to between 50% and 75%. With more than 500,000 NetWare networks installed worldwide and an accelerating movement to connect networks to other networks, NetWare and its supporting protocols often coexist on the same physical channel with many other popular protocols, including TCP/IP and AppleTalk.

As a NOS environment, NetWare specifies the upper five layers of the OSI reference model. Like other NOSs such as NFS from Sun Microsystems, Inc., and NT from Microsoft Corporation, NetWare is based on a client/server architecture. In such architectures, clients (sometimes called workstations) request certain services such as file and printer access from servers.

Figure 2-65 illustrates a simplified view of NetWare's best-known protocols and their relationship to the OSI reference model. With appropriate drivers, NetWare can run on any media-access protocol. The figure lists the media-access protocols currently supported with NetWare drivers.

Figure 2-65 *The NetWare protocol suite maps to all OSI reference model layers.*

OSI Reference Model		NetWare				
7	Application	Application				
		NetBIOS Emulator	NetWare Shell (client)	NetWare Core Protocol (NCP)	Routing Information Protocol (RIP)	NetWare Link Services Protocol (NLSP)
6	Presentation					
5	Session		SPX			
4	Transport			IPX		
3	Network					
2	Data Link	Ethernet/ IEEE 802.3	Token Ring/ IEEE 802.5	FDDI	ARCnet	PPP
1	Physical					

NetWare also works over synchronous WAN links using PPP.

The NetWare Network Layer

IPX is Novell's network-layer protocol. When a device to be communicated with is located on a different network, IPX routes the information to the destination through any intermediate networks. Figure 2-66 shows the IPX packet format.

Figure 2-66   *IPX uses 32-bit network and 48-bit node addresses.*

Checksum (16 Bits)	
Packet Length (16 Bits)	
Transport Control (8 Bits)	Packet Type (8 Bits)
Destination Network (32 Bits)	
Destination Node (48 Bits)	
Destination Socket (16 Bits)	
Source Network (32 Bits)	
Source Node (48 Bits)	
Source Socket (16 Bits)	
Upper-Layer Data	

The IPX packet begins with a 16-bit checksum field that is set to ones by default. (FFFF in hexadecimal.) NetWare 4.x and 5.x enable you to turn on IPX checksumming.

A 16-bit packet length field specifies the length, in bytes, of the complete IPX datagram (including the IPX header and valid data, but excluding any data-link padding). IPX packets can be any length up to the media maximum transmission unit (MTU) size. There is no packet fragmentation in IPX.

The 8-bit transport control field indicates the number of routers the packet has passed through. This field is set to 0 by IPX before packet transmission and is incremented by each router that forwards the packet. When the value of this field reaches 15, the packet is discarded under the assumption that a routing loop might be occurring. This is always a silent discard—no discard notification process is available for IPX.

The 8-bit packet type field specifies the upper-layer protocol to receive the packet's information. Common values for this field are 0, which specifies unknown packet; 1, which specifies RIP; 5, which specifies SPX; and 17, which specifies NCP.

The destination network, destination node, and destination socket fields specify destination information. The source network, source node, and source socket fields specify source information.

The network number is a 32-bit number assigned by the network administrator, and the node number is a 48-bit number that identifies the LAN hardware address. The socket number is a 16-bit hexadecimal number that identifies the higher-layer process. Values are as follows:

Value	Description
0451	NetWare Core Protocol
0452	Service Advertising Protocol
0453	Routing Information Protocol
0455	NetBIOS
0456	Diagnostics
0457	Serialization
4000–8000	Dynamic sockets

The upper-layer data field contains information for upper-layer processes.

NetWare Encapsulation Types   *Encapsulation* is the process of packaging upper-layer protocol information and data into a frame. Novell supports multiple encapsulation schemes on Ethernet/802.3 networks. A Cisco router supports multiple encapsulation schemes on a single router interface, provided that multiple network numbers are assigned.

NetWare supports the Ethernet/IEEE 802.3 encapsulation schemes listed in Table 2-5 and shown in Figure 2-67.

Table 2-5   *NetWare Ethernet encapsulation types.*

Common Term	Novell Term	Cisco Term	Characteristics
Ethernet V. 2	ETHERNET_II	arpa	Includes Ethertype
IEEE 802.3	ETHERNET_802.2	sap	Includes 802.3 length and 802.2 SAPs
Novell 802.3 raw	ETHERNET_802.3	novell-ether	Includes 802.3 length with no 802.2 SAPs
SNAP	ETHERNET_SNAP	snap	Includes 802.2 SAPs and SNAP header

Figure 2-67 *There are four IPX encapsulation types for Ethernet LANs.*

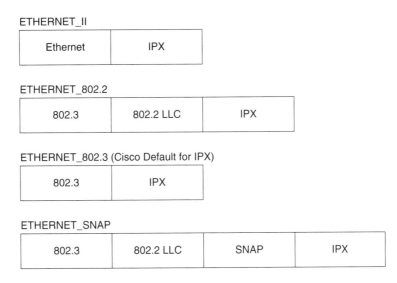

To route packets in an internetwork, IPX uses the dynamic routing protocol RIP. IPX RIP is similar but not identical to IP RIP. Figure 2-68 shows the IPX RIP packet format.

Figure 2-68 *Novell RIP uses ticks and hops as routing metrics.*

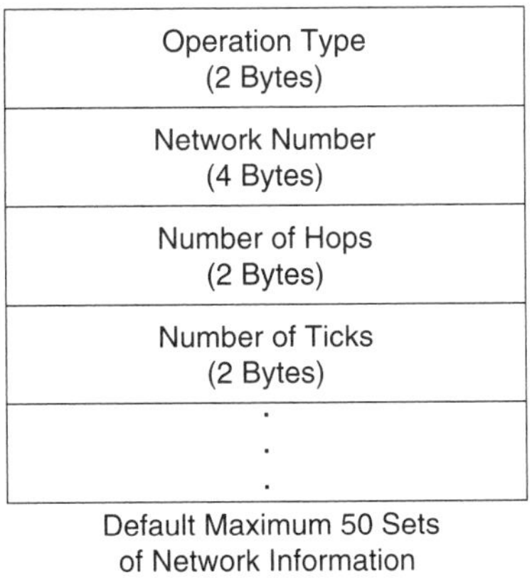

The operation field specifies the packet operation, with value 1 indicating RIP request and 2 indicating RIP response.

The network number is the 32-bit address of the specified network.

The hops field indicates the number of routers that must be passed through to reach the specified network.

The ticks field is a measure of time needed to reach the specified network (18.21 ticks/second).

Novell uses another protocol, Service Advertising Protocol (SAP), to broadcast and discover network services. SAP allows nodes that provide services (such as file servers and print servers) to advertise their addresses and the services they provide. Note that this is a completely different concept than an LLC service access point (SAP). Figure 2-69 shows the IPX SAP packet format.

Figure 2-69 *SAP packets are advertised every 60 seconds.*

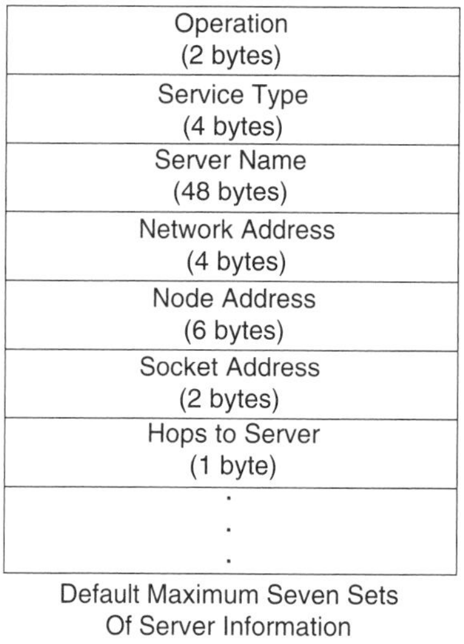

The operation field specifies the operation that the packet will perform:

Value	Description
1	General service request
2	General service reply
3	Nearest service request
4	Nearest service reply

NOTE   NetWare 5 also includes the ability to send SAP requests and include server names or addresses in the lookup (instead of just denoting the service type desired). This technology, called specific SAP technology, uses SAP types 12, 13, 14, and 15.

The service type field specifies the service performed. Values are given in hexadecimal and examples include the following:

Value	Description
0004	File Server
0007	Print Server
0047	Advertising Print Server
0107	NetWare Remote Console
0278	NDS Server

The server name is a 48-byte field containing the server's name. If the server name is shorter than 48 bytes, the field is zero-padded.

The network address and the node address contain the server's 32-bit network and 48-bit node numbers, respectively. The socket address field is the server's 16-bit socket number which identifies the source process (similar to a TCP/IP port number).

The hops field is the number of routers that must be passed through to reach the specified server.

NLSP   NetWare Link Services Protocol (NLSP) is a link-state routing protocol from Novell designed to overcome some of the limitations associated with IPX RIP and its companion protocol, SAP. Compared to RIP and SAP, NLSP provides better reliability, improved routing, reduced network overhead, and increased scalability.

NLSP facilitates improved routing decisions by specifying that NLSP-based routers store a complete map of the network instead of only next-hop information, which RIP-based routers store. Routing information is transmitted only when the topology has changed. (RIP sends routing information every 60 seconds, regardless of whether the topology has changed.) Additionally, NLSP-based routers send service information updates only when services change. (SAP sends service information every 60 seconds, regardless of whether there have been any changes.)

To further reduce the effects of network traffic, NLSP supports multicast addressing so that routing information is sent only to other NLSP routers. (RIP sends routing information to all devices.)

NLSP supports load balancing across parallel paths. If there are two or more equal-cost paths between two network nodes, the traffic is automatically divided among them to make efficient use of the internetwork. NLSP periodically checks links for connectivity and for the data integrity of routing information. If a link fails, NLSP switches to an alternate link and updates the network topology databases stored in each router in the routing area.

Other useful features of NLSP are its support for up to 127 hops (RIP supports only 15 hops) and its support for hierarchical addressing of network nodes, allowing networks to contain thousands of LANs and servers. NLSP is based on the OSI IS-IS protocol and is designed to be used in a hierarchical routing environment, where routing areas can be linked into routing domains and domains can be linked into a global internetwork. Hierarchical routing simplifies the process of enlarging a network by reducing the information that every router must store and process to route packets within and between areas and domains.

NLSP was designed to replace RIP, which is Novell's original routing protocol, designed when internetworks were local and relatively small. NLSP is better suited to today's large, global internetworks. NLSP-based routers are backward compatible with RIP-based routers. Any combination of NLSP-based and RIP-based routers can be used in the same internetwork during the migration from RIP to NLSP.

The NetWare Transport Layer

SPX is a commonly used NetWare transport protocol. Novell derived this protocol from XNS's SPP. As with TCP and many other transport protocols, SPX is a reliable, connection-oriented protocol that supplements the datagram service provided by Layer 3 protocols.

NOTE   With the release of NetWare 5, Novell began supporting NCP with TCP/IP (or UDP/IP) used for Layer 3 and Layer 4 protocol services as an alternative to IPX.

NetWare Upper-Layer Protocols

NetWare supports a wide variety of upper-layer protocols, but several are somewhat more popular than others. The NetWare client software runs in clients (often called *workstations* in the NetWare community) and intercepts application I/O calls to determine whether they require network access. If so, the NetWare client software packages the requests and sends them to lower-layer software for processing and network transmission. If not, they are simply passed to local I/O resources. Client applications are unaware of any network access required for completion of application calls.

NCP consists of a series of server routines designed to satisfy application requests coming from, for example, the NetWare client software. Services provided by NCP include file access, name management, accounting, security, and file synchronization.

NetWare also supports the Network Basic Input/Output System (NetBIOS) session-layer interface specification from IBM and Microsoft. NetWare's NetBIOS emulation software allows programs written to the industry-standard NetBIOS interface to run within the NetWare system.

NetWare application-layer services are most often provided through NetWare Loadable Modules (NLMs). NLMs are implemented as add-on modules that attach into the NetWare system. NLMs for alternate protocol stacks, communication services, database services, and many other services are currently available from Novell and third parties.

AppleTalk

In the early 1980s, as Apple Computer, Inc., was preparing to introduce the Macintosh computer, Apple engineers knew that networks would become a critical need. They wanted to ensure that a Macintosh-based network was a seamless extension of the revolutionary Macintosh user interface. With these two goals in mind, Apple decided to build a network interface into every Macintosh and to integrate that interface into the desktop environment. Apple's new network architecture was called AppleTalk.

The original implementation of AppleTalk, which was designed for local workgroups, is now commonly referred to as AppleTalk Phase 1. With the installation of more than 1.5 million Macintosh computers in the first five years of the product's life, however, Apple found that some large corporations were exceeding the built-in limits of AppleTalk Phase 1, so they enhanced the protocols. The new protocols, known as AppleTalk Phase 2, enhanced AppleTalk's routing capabilities and allowed AppleTalk to run successfully in larger networks.

AppleTalk was designed as a client/server distributed network system. In other words, users share network resources (such as files and printers) with other users. Computers supplying these network resources are called *servers*; computers using a server's network resources are called *clients*. Interaction with servers is essentially transparent to the user because the computer itself determines the location of the requested material and accesses it without further information from the user. In addition to their ease of use, distributed systems also enjoy an economic advantage over peer-to-peer systems because important materials can be located in a few, rather than many, locations.

AppleTalk corresponds relatively well to the OSI reference model. In Figure 2-70, AppleTalk protocols are shown adjacent to the OSI layers to which they map.

Figure 2-70 *The AppleTalk protocol suite maps to every layer of the OSI reference model.*

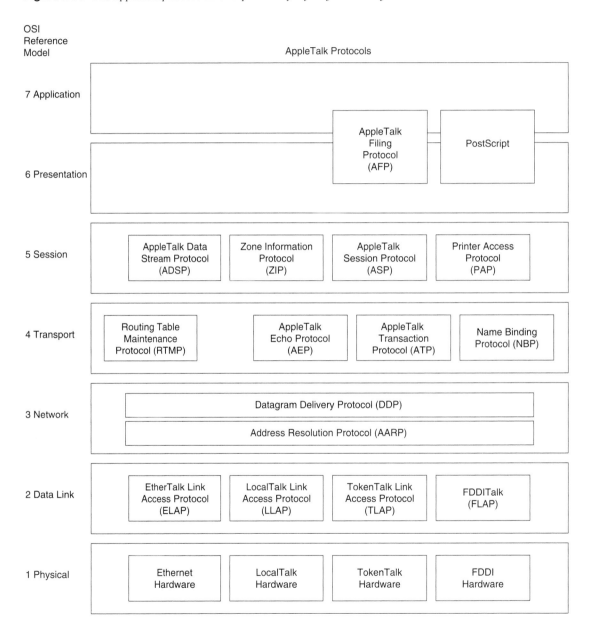

Apple constructed AppleTalk to be link-layer independent. In other words, it can theoretically run on top of any link-layer implementation. Apple supports a variety of link-layer implementations, including Ethernet, Token Ring, FDDI, and LocalTalk. Apple refers to AppleTalk over Ethernet as EtherTalk, to AppleTalk over Token Ring as TokenTalk, and to AppleTalk over FDDI as FDDITalk.

LocalTalk is Apple's proprietary media-access system. It is based on contention access, bus topology, and baseband signaling, and runs on shielded twisted-pair media at 230.4 kbps. The physical interface is EIA/TIA-422, a balanced electrical interface supported by EIA/TIA-449. LocalTalk segments can span up to 300 meters and support a maximum of 32 nodes.

The AppleTalk Network Layer

This section describes AppleTalk network-layer concepts and protocols. It includes discussion of protocol address assignment, network entities, and AppleTalk protocols that provide OSI reference model Layer 3 functionality.

AppleTalk Protocol Address Assignment   To ensure minimal network administrator overhead, AppleTalk node addresses are assigned dynamically. When a Macintosh running AppleTalk starts up, it chooses a protocol (that is, network-layer) address and checks to see whether that address is currently in use. If not, the new node has successfully assigned itself an address. If the address is currently in use, the node with the conflicting address sends a message indicating a problem, and the new node chooses another address and repeats the process. Figure 2-71 shows the AppleTalk address selection process.

Figure 2-71 *AppleTalk clients dynamically acquire network and node addresses.*

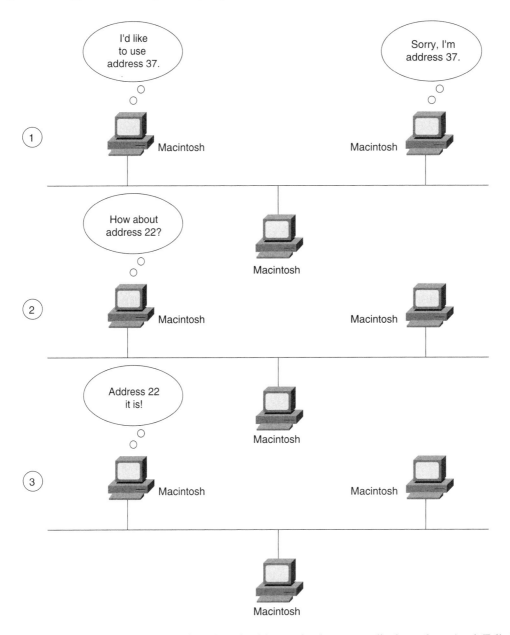

The actual mechanics of AppleTalk address selection are media dependent. AppleTalk Address Resolution Protocol (AARP) is used to associate AppleTalk addresses with particular media addresses. When AppleTalk must send a packet to another network node, the protocol address is passed to AARP. AARP first checks an address cache to see whether the relationship between the protocol and the hardware address is already known. If it is known, that relationship is passed up to the inquiring protocol stack. If it is not known, AARP initiates a broadcast or multicast message inquiring about the hardware address for the protocol address in question. If the broadcast reaches a node with the specified protocol address, that node replies with its hardware address. This information is passed up to the inquiring protocol stack, which uses the hardware address in communications with that node. Figure 2-72 shows the AARP packet format.

Figure 2-72 *AARP packets use SNAP encapsulation.*

Data Link Layer Header (Variable Length)	
SNAP Protocol Discriminator	
Hardware Type	
Protocol Type	
Hardware Address Length	Protocol Address Length
Function	
Source Hardware Address	
Source AppleTalk Address	
Destination Hardware Address	
Destination AppleTalk Address	

The SNAP protocol discriminator field defined for AARP is the hexadecimal value 80F3.

The hardware type field has either the value 1 indicating Ethernet or 2 indicating Token Ring as the data link.

The protocol type field indicates the AppleTalk protocol family and has the value 809B.

The 1-byte hardware address length, with the value 6, indicates the length in bytes of the field containing the Ethernet or Token Ring address.

The 1-byte protocol address length, with the value 4, indicates the length in bytes of the field containing the AppleTalk protocol address. (The high byte of the address field must be set to 0, followed by the 2-byte network number, and then the 1-byte node ID.)

The function field indicates the type of AARP packet, where 1 = request, 2 = response, and 3 = probe.

The remainder of the AARP packet contains the source and destination hardware and AppleTalk addresses, the latter always in a 4-byte field with the upper byte set to 0.

AppleTalk Network Entities   AppleTalk identifies several network entities. The most elemental is a *node*, which is any device connected to an AppleTalk network. The most common nodes are Macintosh computers and laser printers, but many other types of computers are also capable of AppleTalk communication, including IBM PCs, Digital Equipment Corporation VAX computers, and a variety of workstations.

The next entity defined by AppleTalk is the *network*. An AppleTalk network is a single logical cable. Although the logical cable is frequently a single physical cable, some sites use bridges to interconnect several physical cables.

Finally, an AppleTalk *zone* is a logical group of (possibly noncontiguous) nodes. Figure 2-73 shows these AppleTalk entities.

Figure 2-73   *An AppleTalk network consists of a hierarchy of components.*

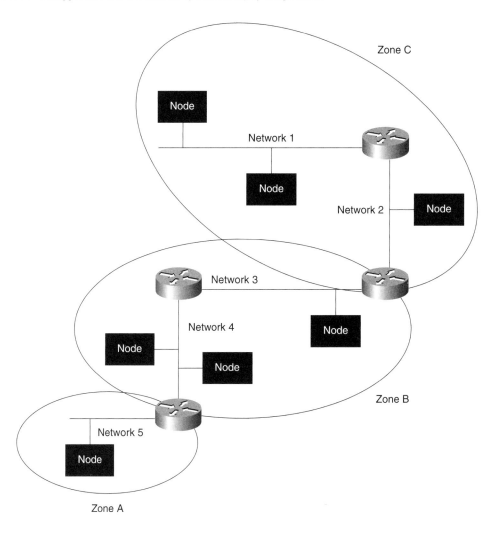

DDP   AppleTalk's primary network-layer protocol is Datagram Delivery Protocol (DDP). DDP provides connectionless service between network sockets. Sockets can be assigned either statically or dynamically.

AppleTalk addresses, which are administered by the DDP, consist of two components: a 16-bit network number and an 8-bit node number. The two components are usually written as decimal numbers, separated by a period (for example, 10.1 means network 10, node 1). When an 8-bit socket identifying a particular process is added to the network number and node number, a unique process on a network is specified.

AppleTalk Phase 2 distinguishes between nonextended and extended networks. In a nonextended network such as LocalTalk, each AppleTalk node number is unique. Nonextended networks were the sole network type defined in AppleTalk Phase 1. In an extended network such as EtherTalk or TokenTalk, each network number/node number combination is unique.

Zones are defined by the AppleTalk network manager during the router configuration process. Each node in an AppleTalk network belongs to a single specific zone. Extended networks can have multiple zones associated with them. Nodes on extended networks can belong to any single zone associated with the extended network.

Figure 2-74 shows the format of the short header DDP packet and the extended header DDP packet.

The short DDP header is used on nonextended networks when source and destination sockets have the same network number. The extended DDP header is used on extended networks. An extended DDP header is also used on nonextended networks between sockets with different network numbers.

The first 2 bytes contain the 10-bit datagram length field (length of the header plus data), with the most significant bits in the first byte. In the short DDP header, the upper 6 bits of the first byte are not significant and are set to 0. In the extended header, 4 of these bits are used for a hop count field. The source node of the datagram sets the hop count field to 0 before sending the datagram. Each intermediate router increments this field, up to a maximum of 15.

The following fields—DDP checksum, destination and source network numbers, and destination and source node IDs—are applicable to the extended header only. Calculation of the DDP checksum on the header and data is optional.

The DDP checksum is followed by 16-bit destination and source network numbers and 8-bit destination and source network node IDs.

In both the short and extended headers, the next two 8-bit fields are the destination and source socket numbers, respectively. Values of DDP sockets are 1 = RTMP, 2 = names information, 4 = echoer, and 6 = zone information.

The 8-bit DDP type values are 1 = RTMP response or data packet, 2 = NBP packet, 3 = ATP packet, 4 = AEP packet, 5 = RTMP request packet, 6 = ZIP packet, and 7 = ADSP packet.

Figure 2-74 *DDP is the Layer 3 routed protocol of the AppleTalk suite.*

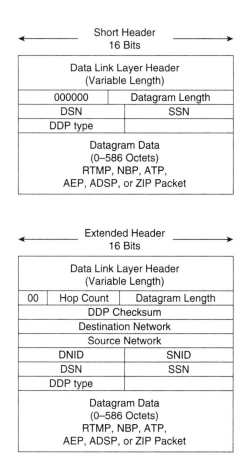

RTMP The protocol that establishes and maintains AppleTalk routing tables is called RTMP. An AppleTalk routing table contains an entry for each network that a datagram can reach. Each entry includes the router port that leads to the destination network, the node ID of the next router to receive the packet, the distance in hops to the destination network, and the current state of the entry (good, suspect, or bad). Periodic exchange of routing tables allows the routers in an internet to ensure that they supply current and consistent information. Figure 2-75 shows a sample routing table and the corresponding network architecture, and Figure 2-76 shows the RTMP packet format for both nonextended and extended networks.

Figure 2-75 *RTMP uses hop count as its routing metric.*

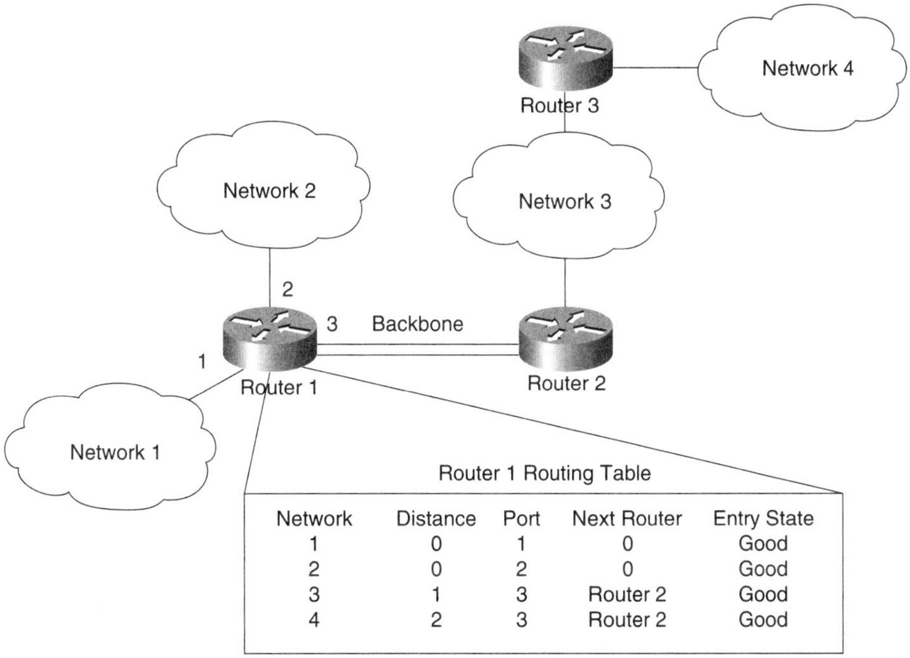

| Router 1 Routing Table | | | | |
Network	Distance	Port	Next Router	Entry State
1	0	1	0	Good
2	0	2	0	Good
3	1	3	Router 2	Good
4	2	3	Router 2	Good

The first 2-byte field is the router's network number, that is, the sender's network number.

The ID length is a 1-byte field that indicates the length of the sender's node address.

The 1-byte router's node ID field indicates the sender's node address.

Following the sender's node ID in a nonextended packet is a 3-byte field indicating the version number of the packet, with a hexadecimal value of 000082. The version number of a packet sent on an extended network is specified in the first tuple.

There are two types of routing tuples. Nonextended network tuples are of the form <network number (2-bytes), distance (1-byte)>, and extended tuples are of the form <network number range start (2-bytes), distance (1-byte), network number end range (2-bytes), unused byte (value = 82)>. An extended tuple is differentiated by having the high bit of its distance field set.

Figure 2-76 *RTMP uses tuples to advertise network addresses and metrics.*

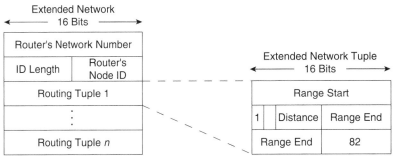

NBP AppleTalk's NBP associates AppleTalk names (expressed as network-visible entities, or NVEs) with addresses. An NVE is an AppleTalk network-addressable service, such as a socket. NVEs are associated with one or more entity names and attribute lists. Entity names are character strings such as printer@net1, and attribute lists specify NVE characteristics.

Named NVEs are associated with network addresses through the process of name binding. Name binding can be done when the user node is first started up, or dynamically, immediately before first use. NBP orchestrates the name binding process, which includes name registration, name confirmation, name deletion, and name lookup.

Figure 2-77 shows the NBP packet format.

Figure 2-77 *NBP packets carry information about network services.*

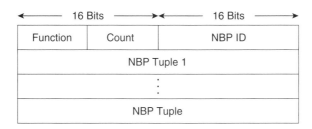

The high-order 4 bits of the first byte indicate the function of the type of NBP packet. The values are 1 = broadcast request (BrRq), 2 = lookup (LkUp), 3 = lookup reply (LkUp-Reply), and 4 = forward request (FwdReq).

The low-order 4 bits contain a count of the number of NBP tuples in that packet.

The NBP ID is used to associate LkUp-Reply packets with BrRq or LkUp packets.

The NBP tuples, the name/address pairs, consist of the entity's socket address, enumerator, and entity name.

Zones allow name lookup in a group of logically related nodes. To look up names within a zone, an NBP lookup request is sent to a local router, which sends a broadcast request to all networks that have nodes belonging to the target zone.

ZIP maintains network number to zone name mappings in zone information tables (ZITs). ZITs are stored in routers, which are the primary users of ZIP, but end nodes also use ZIP during the startup process to choose their zones and to acquire internetwork zone information. RTMP uses ZIP to maintain a list of zones for known networks. When RTMP learns of a new network it sends a ZIP query to request the zone names. Figure 2-78 shows a sample ZIT.

Figure 2-78 *The zone information table maps zone names to cable ranges.*

Network Number	Zone
1–1	My
2–2	Your
3–3	Marketing
4–4	Documentation
5–5	Sales

The AppleTalk Transport Layer

AppleTalk's transport layer is implemented by two primary Apple protocols: ATP and AppleTalk Data Stream Protocol (ADSP). ATP is transaction oriented, and ADSP is data-stream oriented.

ATP   ATP is one of AppleTalk's transport-layer protocols. ATP is suitable for transaction-based applications such as those found in banks or retail stores.

ATP transactions consist of requests (from clients) and replies (from servers). Each request/reply pair has a particular transaction ID. Transactions occur between two socket clients. ATP uses exactly once (XO) and at-least-once (ALO) transactions. XO transactions are required in situations where accidentally performing the transaction more than once is unacceptable. Bank transactions are examples of such nonidempotent situations (that is, situations where repeating a transaction causes problems by invalidating the data involved in the transaction).

ATP is capable of most important transport-layer functions, including data acknowledgment and retransmission, packet sequencing, and fragmentation and reassembly. ATP limits message segmentation to eight packets, and ATP packets cannot contain more than 578 data bytes.

ADSP   ADSP is another important AppleTalk transport-layer protocol. As its name implies, ADSP is data-stream oriented rather than transaction oriented. It establishes and maintains full-duplex data streams between two sockets in an AppleTalk internetwork.

ADSP is a reliable protocol in that it guarantees that data bytes will be delivered in the same order in which they were sent and that they are not duplicated. ADSP numbers each data byte to keep track of the individual elements of the data stream.

ADSP also specifies a flow-control mechanism. The destination can essentially slow source transmissions by reducing the size of its advertised receive window.

ADSP also provides an out-of-band control message mechanism. Attention packets are used as the vehicle for movement of out-of-band control messages between two AppleTalk entities. These packets use a separate sequence number stream to differentiate them from normal ADSP data packets.

AppleTalk Upper-Layer Protocols

AppleTalk supports several upper-layer protocols. AppleTalk Session Protocol (ASP) establishes and maintains sessions (logical conversations) between an AppleTalk client and a server. AppleTalk's PAP is a connection-oriented protocol that establishes and maintains connections between clients and print servers. AppleTalk Echo Protocol (AEP) is an extremely simple protocol that generates packets that can be used to test the reachability of various network nodes. Finally, AFP helps clients share server files across a network.

Summary

This chapter focuses on the most popular media access types, such as IEEE 802.3, IEEE 802.5, and FDDI, as well as the most popular protocol suites, such as TCP/IP, Novell's IPX/SPX, and AppleTalk. Knowing the basic technical details of these communication methods will help you understand how the network should function and recognize when the communication "rules" are being broken.

As you use your systematic method for troubleshooting network problems, narrow the scope of facts by knowing the targets that you pay closest attention to as possible problem causes.

If the problem has affected your users' ability to make a connection, the sequence of gathering facts and considering possibilities begins by targeting the physical-layer prerequisites.

The relevant hardware and physical connections must be working before it is meaningful to check for data-link problem causes. Also, if the problem has interrupted the transfer of data, check first to see if the physical connection has been broken.

Data-link checking on Cisco routers focuses on the direct connection linking network devices across an interface. The Cisco IOS software **show interface** commands provide facts relevant to problem-solving efforts. In particular, a quick output line to check is to see if the interface is up (for example, "Ethernet 0 is up") and to see if the data link is up (for example, "line protocol is up"). We will explore the **show interface** command in Chapter 3, "Cisco Routing and Switching Processes."

With the data link layer working, you can troubleshoot targets at the layers above the data link layer. Begin by checking the basic connection sequence for the protocol suite in question. Cisco IOS commands that focus on a specific protocol suite can help you check.

Various **show** commands available in the Cisco IOS software provide you with aggregate information about routed and routing protocols. Output from these commands may contain high-level facts that can point the way to other targets as you narrow the likely cause of the problem. These commands are introduced in later chapters.

You can augment your problem-solving resources by having handy access to the breakdown of explanations for the output fields and other related Cisco IOS commands that can provide further information.

One handy method is for you to have a copy of the Cisco IOS documentation available on a CD-ROM. Check the troubleshooting guides available over your CCO session or refer to your paper-based manuals. If necessary, extend your efforts by using a third-party protocol analyzer.

Chapter 3, "Cisco Routing and Switching Processes," focuses specifically on router processing and functionality.

Chapter 2 Test
Protocol Characteristics Overview

Estimated Time: 15 minutes

Complete all the exercises to test your knowledge of the materials contained in this chapter. Answers are listed in Appendix A, "Chapter Test Answer Key."

Use the information contained in this chapter to answer the following questions.

Question 2.1

Define the two types of protocols that are used to communicate between devices.

a. _____

b. _____

Question 2.2

List at least two connection-oriented protocols.

a. _____

b. _____

Question 2.3

Which OSI reference model layer defines flow-control functionality?

_____

Question 2.4

What field begins both Ethernet and 802.3 frame types?

_____

Question 2.5

What Token Ring technology supports multiple frames on the cable at one time?

_____

Question 2.6

What other media access type is FDDI similar to?

_____

Question 2.7

Differentiate the following types of 802.2 service from one another:

    a.   LLC1: _____

    b.   LLC2: _____

    c.   LLC3: _____

Question 2.8

What is the purpose of a Frame Relay DLCI?

Question 2.9

What TCP/IP protocol is used to obtain a hardware address for an IP device?

Question 2.10

What TCP/IP protocol set is Novell's IPX most closely related to?

Question 2.11

What are the link-state routing protocols used by TCP/IP and IPX/SPX?

Question 2.12

What is the service discovery mechanism used with AppleTalk?

Question 2.13

What are the three phases typically seen on connection-oriented communications?

    a. _____

    b. _____

    c. _____

Question 2.14

List at least two key advantages that connectionless protocols have over connection-oriented protocols:

a. _____

b. _____

Question 2.15

What connection-oriented and connectionless transport-layer protocols are used in TCP/IP communications?

a.   Connection-oriented: _____

b.   Connectionless: _____

Question 2.16

Match the following terms with their definitions:

a. Ethernet	**1.** 4- or 16-Mbps bandwidth
b. Token Ring	**2.** Similar to 802.3
c. FDDI	**3.** Contains DSAP/SSAP fields
d. 802.2	**4.** Dual-ring LAN

Question 2.17

Which fiber mode is capable of higher bandwidth and greater cable runs?

a.   Single mode

b.   Multimode

Question 2.18

What TCP/IP protocol reports routing errors back to the source of a communication?

_____

Question 2.19

What technologies help prevent the count-to-infinity problem?

_____

_____

Question 2.20

Is BGP an interior gateway protocol or an exterior gateway protocol?

_____

Question 2.21

List and define Novell's two routing protocols.

a. _____

b. _____

Question 2.22

Which three of the following attributes fit the definition of ATM networking?

a. Uses variable-length cells

b. Built to carry voice, video, and data traffic

c. Primarily a connection-oriented network

d. Uses efficient synchronous communications

e. Supports virtual paths and virtual channels

Cisco Routing and Switching Processes

In this chapter, you'll learn the technical details of Cisco's IOS routing and switching architecture. This foundational knowledge will help you understand and interpret the Cisco management tools and diagnostic commands covered in Part II, "Routing and Routed Protocol Troubleshooting."

There are several types of routing and switching processes. Although often Cisco devices are referred to as simply *routers*, they are much more functional than simple routers because all Cisco IOS platforms perform both routing and switching functions. Cisco commonly refers to this module in the router as the Route Switch Processor (RSP).

The routing, or forwarding, function comprises two interrelated processes to move information in the network:

- Making a routing decision based on Layer 3 information
- Moving packets to the next-hop destination by switching

First, we'll examine the routing and switching functions in more detail.

Routing

The routing process assesses the source and destination of traffic based on knowledge of network conditions. Routing protocols identify the best path to use for moving the traffic to the destination out one or more of the router interfaces. Link-state routing decisions are based on a variety of criteria such as link speed, topological distance, and protocol. Distance-vector routing decisions are based solely on topological distance. Each protocol maintains its own routing information, as shown in Figure 3-1.

Figure 3-1 *The router exchanges routing updates with all its neighbors.*

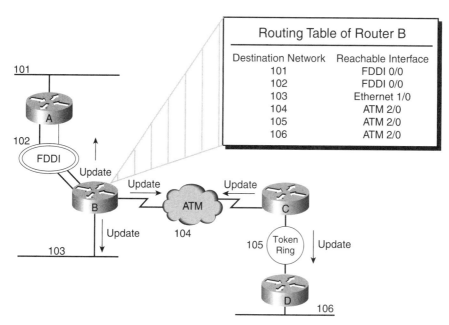

Routing is more processing intensive and has higher latency than switching because it determines path and next-hop by looking into each packet's Layer 3 information. This process also requires the router to strip off the old Media Access Control (MAC) header and build a new one before sending the packet. Switching involves only a MAC address lookup, which is considerably faster. The first packet routed requires a lookup in the routing table to determine the route. The route cache is populated after the first packet is routed by the route-table lookup. Subsequent traffic for the same destination is switched using the routing information stored in the route cache.

A router sends routing updates out each of its interfaces that are configured for a particular protocol, as shown in Figure 3-1. It also receives routing updates from other attached routers. From these received updates and its knowledge of attached networks, the router builds a map of the network topology for each configured protocol. Each table is independent of the others; the independence of the routing tables is sometimes called *ships in the night routing*.

Switching

Through the switching process, the router encapsulates the packet to be sent out the appropriate interface toward the destination address. Switching moves traffic from an input interface to one or more output interfaces. For example, an incoming Ethernet packet is switched to an outgoing FDDI interface.

Switching is optimized and has lower latency than routing because it can move packets, frames, or cells from buffer to buffer with relatively simple determination of the source and destination of the traffic. It saves resources because it does not involve extra lookups. Figure 3-2 illustrates the basic switching process.

Figure 3-2   *The switching process moves a packet from the Ethernet buffer to the FDDI buffer.*

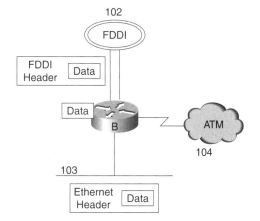

In Figure 3-2, packets are received on the Fast Ethernet interface and destined for the FDDI interface. Based on information in the packet header and destination information stored in the routing table, the router determines the destination interface. It looks in the protocol's routing table to discover the destination interface that services the destination address of the packet.

The destination MAC address is stored in tables such as Address Resolution Protocol (ARP) tables for IP and AppleTalk ARP (AARP) tables for AppleTalk. If there is no entry for the destination, the router discovers the destination address by using ARP. Layer 3 IP addressing information is mapped to the Layer 2 MAC address for the next hop. Figure 3-3 illustrates the mapping that occurs to determine the next hop.

Figure 3-3 *ARP maps Layer 3 addresses to Layer 2 addresses.*

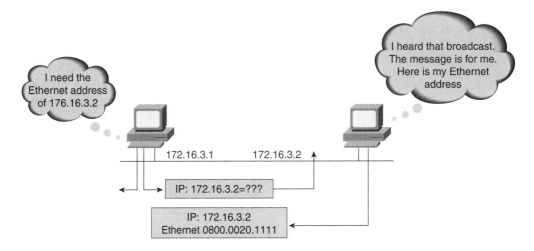

Basic Switching Paths

When a router receives a frame, there are many different paths it can take through the router's hardware. These paths are dependent on both hardware and IOS configuration. These paths, called *switching paths*, determine router hardware utilization as well as router throughput in terms of packets routed per second. The basic switching paths are

- Process switching
- Fast switching
- Silicon switching/autonomous switching
- Optimum switching
- Distributed switching
- NetFlow switching

The following sections define and differentiate each of these switching paths.

NOTE   All these different switching types are configured on a per-protocol, per-interface basis with the following syntax:

```
protocol route-cache switching type
```

NOTE   The type of switching performed (for example, silicon, autonomous, fast, or process) is determined by the configuration applied to the destination interface and by the revision of the Cisco IOS software. The switching mode used depends on the Cisco IOS version, network protocol, interface processor, configuration, and packet encapsulation. There are numerous combinations of these. To find out which protocols and configurations result in process switching, contact your technical support representative for specific data or refer to the information available at Cisco Connection Online (www.cisco.com) or on the Cisco documentation CD-ROM.

Process Switching

In process switching, the first packet is copied to the system buffer. The router looks up the Layer 3 network address in the routing table and initializes the fast-switching cache. The frame is rewritten with the destination address and sent to the exit interface that services that destination. Subsequent packets for that destination are sent by the same switching path. The route processor computes the cyclic redundancy check (CRC), which performs an error-checking mechanism on the contents of the packet. Process switching adds overhead by requiring CPU interrupts to process packets.

The following are some values indicating packets processed per second across Cisco router platforms based on a 64-byte IP packet:

Platform	Performance
Cisco 7500/RSP4	18000 pps
Cisco 7500/RSP2	8000 pps
Cisco 7200-150	5000 pps
Cisco 4500 and 4700	3500 and 4600 pps
Cisco 3620 and 3640	2000 and 4000 pps
Cisco 7000/7010 with SSP	2500 pps
Cisco 7000/7010 with SP	2000 pps
AGS+/CSC4	2000 pps
Cisco 4000	1800 pps
Cisco 3000/2500	900 pps

Fast Switching

When packets are fast switched, the first packet is copied to memory, and the destination network or host is found in the fast-switching cache. The frame is rewritten and sent to the exit interface that services the destination. Subsequent packets for the same destination use the same switching path. The interface processor computes the CRC for the outbound packets. Fast switching is the default switching mechanism for all protocols except IP.

The Cisco 4000, 3000, and 2500 series routers have shared memory space for all packet buffers and cache. The fast-switching cache resides in this shared memory. No silicon or autonomous switching is possible on these routers. The following are some values indicating packets processed per second across Cisco router platforms, based on a 64-byte IP packet:

Platform	Performance
Cisco 7500/RSP4	320,000–350,000 pps
Cisco 7500/RSP2	220,000–250,000 pps
Cisco 7200-150	150,000 pps
Cisco 4500 and 4700	45,000 and 75,000 pps
Cisco 3620 and 3640	16,000 and 40,000 pps
Cisco 7000/7010 with SSP	30,000 pps
Cisco 7000/7010 with SP	28,000 pps
AGS+/CSC4	6000–20,000 pps
Cisco 4000	14,000 pps
Cisco 2500	6000 pps

Silicon Switching/Autonomous Switching

Whether you perform silicon switching or autonomous switching depends on the hardware. In the Cisco 7000 series routers, the silicon-switching cache and the autonomous-switching cache reside on the Silicon Switch Processor (SSP) card. If the router is equipped with only a Switch Processor (SP) card but not an SSP, then no silicon switching can occur. The fast-switching cache resides on the Route Processor (RP).

The SSP (or SP) switches packets from source to destination. The RP builds the routing table for the routed protocols and sends routing protocol updates.

The RP is the processor module in the Cisco 7000 series routers that contains the CPU, system software, and most of the memory components that are used in the router. This processor is sometimes called a *supervisory processor*. The SP is a Cisco 7000 series processor module that acts as the administrator for all CxBus activities. This is sometimes called the *ciscoBus controller*.

Optimum Switching

Optimum switching is similar to fast switching, but it is faster. The first packet is copied to packet memory, and the destination network or host is found in the optimum-switching cache. The frame is rewritten and sent to the exit interface that services the destination. Subsequent packets for the same destination use the same switching path. The interface processor computes the CRC. Optimum switching is the default switching mechanism for TCP/IP traffic.

NOTE   Optimum switching is enabled by default on Cisco 7500 series routers; it is disabled for debugging. Debugging requires process switching.

Distributed Switching

Switching becomes more efficient the closer to the interface the function occurs. *Distributed switching* moves the process of getting a packet from one incoming interface to another outgoing interface down to the interface level.

On the Cisco 7500 routers, the interfaces are installed on cards called *blades* that are inserted into the slots of the 7500 chassis. Each blade has several interfaces on it (such as Ethernet, Fast Ethernet, Token Ring, and FDDI). Distributed switching enables switching between one blade and another interface on the same blade, without the necessity of forwarding the packet to the backplane.

The processor that enables distributed switching is called a Versatile Interface Processor (VIP). The VIP's RISC-based processor can receive any cache routing information from the route server in the RSP. Using this data, the VIP can make switching decisions locally, relieving the RSP of involvement and speeding overall throughput. Router throughput increases based on the number of VIP cards installed in the router.

Distributed switching uses the same technology that is used by Cisco Fusion technology. In the Cisco Fusion architecture, the route server can distribute routing information to multilayer switches in wiring closets.

Figure 3-4 illustrates the functional elements of the Cisco 7500 series router. These elements include an integrated RSP. The RSP in the Cisco 7500 series routers integrates the functions of the RP and the SP.

Figure 3-4 *Cisco 7500 series routers support both optimum switching and distributed switching with the use of VIP cards.*

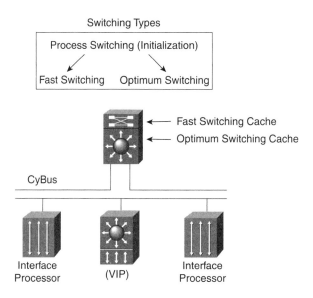

NetFlow Switching

NetFlow switching enables you to collect the data required for flexible and detailed accounting, billing, and chargeback for network and application resource utilization. Accounting data can be collected for both dedicated line and dial-access accounting. NetFlow switching over a foundation of VLAN technologies provides the benefits of both switching and routing, on the same platforms. NetFlow switching is supported over switched LAN or ATM backbones, allowing scalable inter-VLAN forwarding. NetFlow switching can be deployed at any location in the network as an extension to existing routing infrastructures.

NetFlow switching identifies traffic flows between hosts, and switches packets in these flows at the same time that it applies relevant services.

Traffic flows are unidirectional streams of packets between a given source and destination, defined by network-layer (that is, IP) address and transport-layer port number. In conventional network-layer switching, each incoming packet is handled on an individual basis.

The router performs a series of separate lookups for each packet and then sends (that is, switches) each packet to its destination. These lookups include checking to see whether a security access filter applies and updating traffic accounting records.

With NetFlow switching, the lookup process described previously occurs only with the first packet in a flow. When a network flow has been identified and services relevant to it determined, all subsequent packets are handled on a connection-oriented basis as part of this flow.

Packets are switched and services are applied to them in tandem by a single task. This streamlined way of handling packets increases performance for network services. On Cisco 7500 series routers, for example, NetFlow switching can take advantage of distributed switching and service capabilities provided by the new VIP cards.

By performing distributed NetFlow switching on each VIP, system performance of the Cisco 7513 can scale to more than one million packets per second. NetFlow Switching provides increased performance for Cisco IOS services relating to security, as well as quality of service (QoS) and traffic accounting. At the same time, NetFlow switching enables these services to be more efficiently applied on a per-user and per-application (that is, session) basis.

Sample Packet Flow

WARNING   This breakdown of tracing the flow of a packet is given for informational purposes only, as are the buffer and queue details in the upcoming sections. It is not a comprehensive explanation of the operation of the router's switching architecture, but is intended to help you gain a general understanding of the path a packet takes when switched through the router, and the buffers and queues involved. For details, consult Cisco Technical Assistance Center (TAC).

Consider what happens when the first packet of a particular protocol arrives at a 7000 router interface destined for a particular output interface. In Figures 3-5, 3-6, and 3-7, the packet arriving on the Ethernet interface is destined for the FDDI interface (this is based on the destination address in the packet header).

Figure 3-5   *A frame travels through the router's internal buffers and buses.*

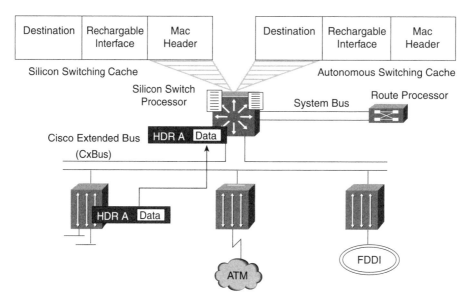

Figure 3-6   *For process switching, the entire packet must be sent across the system bus.*

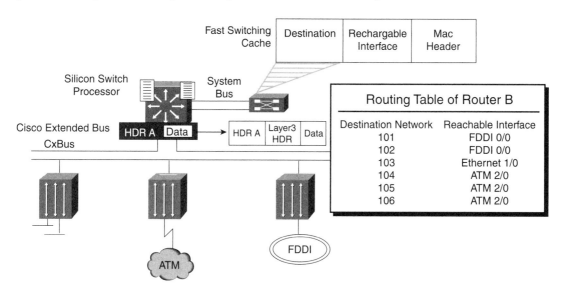

Figure 3-7   *The outbound packet traverses the same path in the opposite direction.*

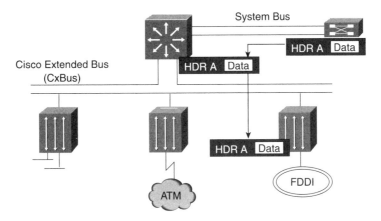

The packet is then processed as described in the following steps:

Step 1   The packet arrives at the hardware buffer on an interface processor (an Ethernet interface processor, in this case).

Step 2   The packet is copied across the CxBus to a packet buffer on the SSP.

Step 3   The silicon-switching cache is checked to see whether there is an entry for the destination. In this instance, because this is the first packet received for that particular destination, there is no entry.

Step 4   The autonomous-switching cache is checked to see whether there is an entry for the destination. In this instance, because this is the first packet received, there is no entry.

Step 5   Because there are no entries in the switching caches, the packet (Layer 3) header is copied across the system bus to RP memory.

Step 6   The optimum-switching cache (the default for TCP/IP traffic) or fast-switching cache (the default for all other protocols) is checked to see whether there is an entry for the destination. In this instance, because this is the first packet, there is again no entry.

Step 7   The complete packet is copied to the RP memory. (Just the packet header was copied before.)

Step 8   The RP looks for an entry for the destination network address in the appropriate routing table. (Recall that the routing table has been built from routing updates received from adjacent routers and by the RP's knowledge of directly attached networks.) If there is no entry in the routing table, or if the route entry indicates a route that is in a hold-down state, the packet is dropped and the source is informed of an unreachable destination (if the protocol offers this feature).

This procedure demonstrates why process switching is comparatively slow; it is necessary to interrupt the RP for the length of time it takes to copy the packet from the SP to the RP.

Step 9   The RP builds the encapsulation based on that of the destination interface. When this encapsulation has been built, the configuration for the particular destination interface is checked.

Step 10   If the interface has been configured for silicon switching for the protocol being considered, the encapsulation information is copied to the silicon-switching cache. If the interface has been configured for autonomous switching for the protocol being considered, the encapsulation information is copied to the autonomous-switching cache. If the destination interface has not been configured for either silicon or autonomous switching, the encapsulation information is copied to the fast-switching cache, unless for any particular reason the interface must be process switched (for example, it might have been configured for **no <protocol> route-cache** or for an uncommon protocol encapsulation).

Step 11   The RP moves the packet across the system bus to a packet buffer on the SP.

Step 12   The packet is copied across the CxBus to a hardware buffer on an interface processor (the FDDI Interface Processor).

Step 13   The packet is transmitted to the destination interface.

This initialization sequence is followed for the first packet of a particular protocol that is destined for a particular destination interface. The sequence is also followed for any packet that is to be process switched out of an interface.

Switching Features That Affect Performance

Router performance is affected by the switching mechanism you are using. Some Cisco IOS features require special handling and cannot be switched until the additional processing they require has been performed. This special handling is not processing that the interface processors can do. Because these features require additional processing, they affect switching performance. These features include

- Queuing
- Random early detection
- Compression
- Filtering (using access lists)
- Encryption
- Accounting

The following sections define each of these features.

Queuing

Queuing occurs because of network congestion. When traffic is moving well within the network, packets are sent as they arrive at the interface and queuing is not necessary.

Cisco IOS software implements four different queuing algorithms:

- First-in, first-out (FIFO) queuing—Packets are forwarded in the same order in which they arrive at the interface.

- Priority queuing—Packets are forwarded based on an assigned priority. You can create priority lists and groups to define rules for assigning packets to priority queues.

- Custom queuing—You can control a percentage of interface bandwidth for specified traffic by creating protocol queue lists and custom queue lists.

- Weighted fair queuing—Weighted fair queuing provides automatic traffic priority management. Low-bandwidth sessions have priority over high-bandwidth sessions, and high-bandwidth sessions are assigned weights. Weighted fair queuing is the default for interfaces slower than 2.048 Mbps.

Queuing mechanisms and configurations are covered in detail in *Advanced Cisco Router Configuration*.

Random Early Detection

Random early detection is designed for congestion avoidance. Traffic is prioritized based on type of service (ToS), or precedence. This feature is available on T3, OC-3, and ATM interfaces.

Compression

Depending on the protocol you are using, various compression options are available in Cisco IOS software. Refer to the Cisco IOS configuration guide for the protocol you are using to see what compression options you have.

Filtering

You can define access lists to control access to or from a router for a number of services. You could, for example, define an access list to prevent packets with a certain IP address from leaving a particular interface on a router. The way access lists are used depends on the protocol. For information on access lists, refer to *Advanced Cisco Router Configuration*.

Encryption

You can apply encryption algorithms to data to alter its appearance and make it incomprehensible to those who are not authorized to see it.

Accounting

You can configure accounting features to collect network data related to resource usage. The information you collect (in the form of statistics) can be used for billing, chargeback, and planning resource usage. Refer to the appropriate Cisco IOS configuration guide for the protocol you are using for information regarding accounting features you can use.

Process Switching

This chapter has focused on basic router functionality. You should be comfortable with the concept of packet flow used to increase routing performance. The next section of this chapter focuses on the IOS tools available to troubleshoot various router problems related to the internal buffering and busing of packets.

Figure 3-8   *The route processor handles broadcasts and overhead traffic.*

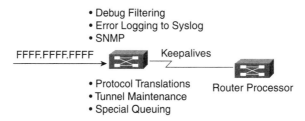

More activities are moved from process switching to faster switching modes with each new release of the Cisco IOS software. Depending on the version of the Cisco IOS software you are using, the following processes might still be handled by process switching:

- The FFFF.FFFF.FFFF MAC-layer broadcasts and frames related to maintaining routing tables
- Debug packet filtering and related processes
- Error logging (including sending errors to the syslog server)
- Simple Network Management Protocol (SNMP) processing
- Protocol translations, such as the following:
  - Source-route translational bridging (SR/TLB)
  - DEC address translation and LAT to Telnet conversion
  - SDLC conversion

- Tunneling, including the following:
    - X.25 remote switching
    - Generic routing encapsulation (GRE)
- Other overhead activities, including the following:
    - Custom and priority queuing
    - Sending and tracking keepalives
- Link compression

System Buffering and Queuing

The system buffers on the RP are part of system memory allocated to hold packets and are used for process switching. Although manual buffer tuning is possible on these buffers, it is only done in rare cases and has no effect on fast, autonomous, or silicon switching. The best way to improve performance is to use fast, autonomous, or silicon switching rather than process switching.

Process switching has one advantage over faster switching methods: A large pool of buffers can be allocated from the available system RAM. When a packet is hung on an input processor or an output processor queue, the system allocates the packet to a particular buffer pool, depending on the size of the packet or the protocol that is being switched. The types of buffers and their sizes are as follows:

Buffer	Size
Small buffers	104 bytes
Middle buffers	600 bytes
Big buffers	1524 bytes
Very big buffers	4520 bytes
Large buffers	5024 bytes
Huge buffers	18,024 bytes

At startup, the system allocates memory to these buffers based on the hardware configuration. Each buffer pool is allocated a certain number of buffers. The parameters that apply to each pool are as follows:

- *Permanent*—The number of permanent buffers that the system tries to allocate. Permanent buffers are normally not deallocated by the system.
- *Max-free*—The maximum number of free or unallocated buffers in a buffer pool.

- *Min-free*—The minimum number of free or unallocated buffers in a buffer pool.

- *Initial*—The number of additional temporary buffers that should be allocated when the system is reloaded. This parameter can be used to ensure that the system has the necessary buffers immediately after reloading in a high-traffic environment.

Adjustments can be made to the initial buffer pool settings and to the limits at which temporary buffers are created and destroyed. The RP allocates more buffers from processor RAM if required and if memory permits. The system creates more buffers when the number of buffers in the free-list falls below *Min-free*. The system deallocates buffers when the number of buffers in the free-list exceeds *Max-free*.

If a process-switched protocol is experiencing poor performance, you can use the **show buffers** command to look at the performance, as shown in Figure 3-9. A *buffer miss* occurs when there are no free buffers on the free list. A miss triggers the system to attempt to allocate more buffers so that the next time an attempt is made to get a buffer, one will be available. If the attempt to allocate more buffers is unsuccessful, a *failure* is generated. A large number of buffer misses for a particular buffer size indicates that the minimum number of buffers and the number of permanent buffers could be increased. Call your technical support representative before adjusting buffers.

Figure 3-9 *Cisco routers use six different buffer sizes for handling process-switched packets.*

```
Router# show buffers
Buffer elements:
     398 in free list (500 max allowed)
     1266 hits, 0 misses, 0 created

Public buffer pools:
Small buffers, 104 bytes (total 50, permanent 50):
     50 in free list (20 min, 150 max allowed)
     551 hits, 0 misses, 0 trims, 0 created
Middle buffers, 600 bytes (total 25, permanent 25):
     25 in free list (10 min, 150 max allowed)
     39 hits, 0 misses, 0 trims, 0 created
Big buffers, 1524 bytes (total 50, permanent 50):
     49 in free list (5 min, 150 max allowed)
     27 hits, 0 misses, 0 trims, 0 created
VeryBig buffers, 4520 bytes (total 10, permanent 10):
     10 in free list (0 min, 100 max allowed)
     0 hits, 0 misses, 0 trims, 0 created
Large buffers, 5024 bytes (total 0, permanent 0):
     0 in free list (0 min, 10 max allowed)
     0 hits, 0 misses, 0 trims, 0 created
Huge buffers, 18024 bytes (total 0, permanent 0):
     0 in free list (0 min, 4 max allowed)
     0 hits, 0 misses, 0 trims, 0 created

Interface buffer pools:
Ethernet0 buffers, 1524 bytes (total 64, permanent 64):
```

The system buffers are also used to store packets that the router itself generates, such as routing tables. System buffers are also used when the router is the source or destination of packets, as in the following examples:

- ICMP redirects
- Routing protocol updates
- ICMP responses (**ping** reply)
- SNMP query responses
- Novell IPX SAP updates

Input and Output Queues

Each interface has an input queue and an output queue, which are linked lists of processor buffers, as shown in Figure 3-10.

Figure 3-10 *The queues for each interface point to the system buffers.*

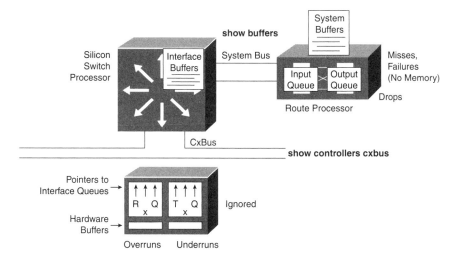

A queue may grow to a configured limit, or it may shrink to zero, as required. The queue can be composed of different-sized buffers. The appropriate-sized buffer is grabbed from the free buffer pool when a packet is queued. If the input queue limit is exceeded (that is, more packets arrive than can be processed by the processor), these packets are dropped and the result is an *input queue drop*. An input queue drop indicates that the CPU cannot process these packets in buffer memory and should cause you concern if it occurs frequently. Input queue drops are often associated with bursty traffic arriving on an interface. Similarly, *output queue drops* indicate that the output queue limit has been exceeded. This is equivalent to a busy signal from the router. A drop within Layer 3 protocols is normal and indicates a healthy slowing down of a protocol.

Interface hold queues are associated with process switching. Hold queues are not involved with fast, autonomous, or silicon switching.

By default, the input interface hold queue is 40 packets, and the output interface hold queue is 75 packets.

Interface Buffers

The interface buffers on the SP are used for buffering packets copied from the interface processors. The SP and SSP controllers have 512 KB available for packet buffering. Part of this memory is also used by the autonomous-switching cache. Packet buffers of the following sizes are allocated for interface processors by default:

Buffer Type	Size
FIP	44,709 bytes
HSSI	4470 bytes
FSIP	4470 bytes
EIP	1524 bytes
TRIP	4470 bytes
AIP	4470 bytes

The **show controllers cxbus** command shows the allocation of these buffers upon router startup. The numbers allocated depend on the number of interfaces installed on the router.

Changing these defaults may have a negative effect on switching performance.

If the interface hardware buffers are full, an *ignore* is registered, and the interface throttles very briefly. An *ignore* occurs if a high-speed interface is accepting frames at close to wire speed and the SP can't pull the frames out of the hardware buffers fast enough, or if the interface processor cannot get access to the CxBus because it is being used for other transfers. *Ignores* should happen rarely.

An *overrun* occurs when the receiver hardware is unable to hand received data to a hardware buffer because the input rate exceeded the receiver's ability to handle the data.

An *underrun* is when the transmitter has been running faster than the router can handle.

Because of a different hardware architecture, packets are buffered differently on Cisco 4000 and 2500 series routers. With the Cisco 4000 and 2500 series routers, all packets, buffers, and tables reside in one location—shared memory.

All packets are read directly from the interface hardware buffers into shared memory, and the processor operates on the packets in shared memory.

Because there is only one set of buffers, the packet is not copied between buffers; the processor just queues the packet for processing. When the destination interface has been determined, the buffer is queued for output.

Summary

This chapter explored the internal workings of Cisco routers and the various ways they can handle packets from both a processing and a buffering point of view. You have learned about several types of fast switching that routers can employ depending on their hardware configuration and IOS version. You have also followed a packet through the various switching engines and buffers on the router. This will better prepare you to understand the output of the various **show** and **debug** commands introduced in the chapters that follow.

Chapter 3 Test
Cisco Routing and Switching Processes

Estimated Time: 20 minutes

Complete all the exercises to test your knowledge of the materials contained in this chapter. Answers are listed in Appendix A, "Chapter Test Answer Key."

Use the information contained in this chapter to answer the following questions.

Question 3.1

What technology is used to get a packet from an incoming interface to an outgoing interface in the Cisco router?

_____

_____

_____

Question 3.2

What technology is used to determine the direction of the destination network defined by an incoming packet?

_____

_____

_____

Question 3.3

On a router with two Ethernet interfaces and two FDDI interfaces, which interfaces are routing updates sent on?

_____

_____

_____

Question 3.4

List at least three switching path types:

_____

_____

_____

Question 3.5

What is the default switching mechanism for IP traffic?

_____

_____

_____

Question 3.6

What switching mechanism is used to relieve the RSP of involvement and uses VIPs?

_____

_____

_____

Question 3.7

List at least four special features that affect performance.

_____

_____

_____

_____

General Troubleshooting Tools

This chapter presents an overview of the various tools that are available for troubleshooting networks that include Cisco internetworking devices. These tools include network management applications; third-party hardware tools such as digital test equipment, time domain reflectometers (TDRs), and digital interface testing tools; and software tools such as network monitors, protocol analyzers, and simulation/modeling tools.

Each of these tools has a specific purpose and works at specific OSI reference model layers. Understanding what each tool can do and which tool is appropriate for each troubleshooting task will help you become a more efficient network technician.

When troubleshooting, you should start at the physical layer. Use cable testers and other low-level testers to ensure that there are no problems with the media, such as noise, too much attenuation, improper cable lengths, improper connectors, and so forth. If the physical layer seems fine, then move up the layers to the data link layer. You can use a protocol analyzer to check for excessive collisions on Ethernet, beaconing on Token Ring or FDDI networks, excessive soft errors on Token Ring, and other link-layer issues. If the data link layer seems fine, check for routing errors or misconfigurations at the network layer, using a protocol analyzer and Cisco IOS commands. Finally, you can look for upper-layer problems such as misconfigurations, software bugs, and user errors.

Low-End Cable Test Equipment

At the low-technology end of the spectrum of test equipment are volt-ohm meters and digital multimeters. These devices measure parameters such as AC and DC voltage, current, resistance, capacitance, and cable continuity. They can be used to check physical connectivity.

Cable testers (that is, scanners) can also be used to check physical connectivity. Cable testers give users access to physical-layer information and are available for shielded twisted-pair (STP), unshielded twisted-pair (UTP), 10BaseT, and coaxial and twinax cables. These testers can test and report cable conditions including near-end crosstalk (NEXT), attenuation, and noise. Some of them also have TDR (Time Domain Reflectometer), traffic monitoring, and wire map functions. In addition, some handheld network testers display Media Access Control (MAC) layer information about LAN traffic, provide statistics such as network utilization and packet error rates, and perform limited protocol testing (for example, TCP/IP tests such as **ping**).

Similar testing equipment is available for fiber-optic cable. Due to the relatively high cost of fiber cable and its installation, it is recommended that fiber-optic cable be tested before installation (that is, on-the-reel testing) and after installation. Continuity testing of the fiber requires either a visible light source or a reflectometer. Light sources capable of providing light at the three predominant wavelengths—850 nm, 1300 nm, and 1550 nm—are used with power meters that can measure the same wavelengths and test attenuation and return loss in the fiber.

Figure 4-1 shows one of the cable scanners available from Microtest: the OMNI Scanner. The OMNI Scanner has the functionality to test cables complying with current and upcoming standards with an extremely wide dynamic range of 100 dB and the ability to support up to 300 MHz bandwidth. The OMNI Scanner can test all the way up to 300 MHz on Category 7 cables.

NOTE   Microtest, Inc., is located at 4747 N. 22nd St., Phoenix, AZ 85016-4708, and can be reached at 602-952-6400.

Figure 4-1   *Microtest's OMNI Scanner handheld cable scanners can test a wide range of cable.*

High-End Cable Testers

At the most technologically advanced end of the cable testing spectrum are TDRs. These devices can quickly locate opens, shorts, crimps, kinks, sharp bends, impedance mismatches, and other defects in metallic cables.

A TDR works by "bouncing" a signal off the end of the cable, much like radar. Opens, shorts, and other problems reflect the signal back at different amplitudes, depending on the problem. A TDR measures how much time it takes for the signal to reflect (that is, round-trip time) and uses the principle

Distance = Rate of propagation × Time to calculate the distance to a fault in the cable

When a signal reaches the end of a cable, it reflects at a very low amplitude, so TDRs can also be used to measure the length of a cable. Some TDRs can also calculate the propagation rate based on a configured cable length.

Fiber-optic measurement is performed by an optical TDR (OTDR). These devices can accurately measure the length of the fiber, locate cable breaks, measure the fiber attenuation, and measure splice or connector losses by measuring the reflections that occur. Pulse reflections that are generated at breaks or joints, and backscatter reflections that are generated uniformly throughout the cable, are used to measure the fiber attenuation. One way in which the OTDR can be put to good use is to take the signature of a particular installation, noting attenuation and splice losses. This baseline measurement can then be compared with future signatures when a problem in the system is suspected.

Figure 4-2 shows a TDR made by Biddle.

NOTE   For more information on this product, you can contact AVO International at www.avointl.com/contact/index.html.

Figure 4-2 *The Biddle 510B is a handheld TDR that can find trouble on twisted-pair, coaxial, and power cable.*

Digital Interface Testing Tools

Several test tools can be used to measure the discrete digital signals that are present at PCs, modems, printers, and other peripheral interfaces. Examples of this type of test equipment include breakout boxes, fox boxes, and bit/block error rate testers (BERTs/BLERTs). These devices can monitor data line conditions, analyze and trap data, and diagnose problems common to data communication systems. Traffic from data terminal equipment (DTE) through data communications equipment (DCE) can be examined to help eliminate problems, identify bit patterns, and ensure that the proper cabling has been installed.

Figure 4-3 shows the line-powered Blue Box 100 breakout box from IDS, Inc. The Blue Box 100 is a breakout box and cable tester that is compact, handheld, and fully 100 LED. It accesses and monitors all 25 conductors of the RS-232-C, EIA-232-D, CCITT, and V.24, and any other single-ended interface such as the Centronics parallel printer interface. One hundred red and green LEDs monitor and display high, low, off, and signal activity conditions for each of 25 conductors on the DTE and DCE sides of the interface.

NOTE   For more information on the Blue Box 100, contact IDS, Inc., at 800-IDS-DATA or 401-737-9900; e-mail sales@idsdata.com.

Figure 4-3   *The Blue Box 100 breakout box is a useful tool for troubleshooting serial cables and connections.*

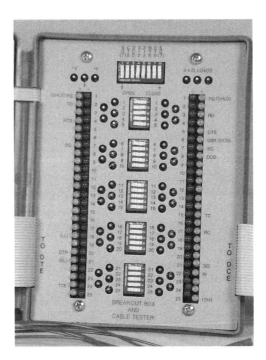

Network Monitors

Network monitors continuously track packets crossing a network, providing an accurate picture of network activity at any moment or a historical record of network activity over a period of time. Monitors collect information such as packet sizes, the number of packets, error packets, overall usage of a connection, the number of hosts and their MAC addresses, and details about communications between hosts and other devices. Correlation of this data allows network administrators to create profiles of their LAN traffic and find traffic overloads, plan for network expansion, detect intruders, establish baseline performance, and distribute traffic more efficiently.

Not only must the monitor collect information about frames, but it must also be able to warn users if any frames are dropped or flag users if certain events such as bad frames, protocol errors, or illegal addresses occur. Visible and audible alarms for the entire network or for individual stations can be set, allowing the network manager to be informed when certain parameters have exceeded predetermined thresholds.

The concept of baselining is becoming very important to network managers. To create a baseline, the activity on a network is sampled over a period of time, and averages, means, and other statistical calculations are used to establish a normal performance profile, or baseline. This baseline can then be used as a reference if any abnormal performance is noted in the network, or it can be used to plan expansion options.

Network monitors further enhance network management by gathering information from remote sites and sending it back to a central management location.

Apart from gathering the standard traffic information, many monitors implement Simple Network Management Protocol (SNMP), Remote Monitoring (RMON), and Management Information Bases (MIBs) to gather information for central management stations. CiscoWorks can also supply network monitoring functions.

Figure 4-4 shows some of the monitor screens on a Sniffer Pro product. These charts and graphs enable you to easily build graphical baseline reports on your network.

Figure 4-4   *The Sniffer Pro can provide network monitoring services.*

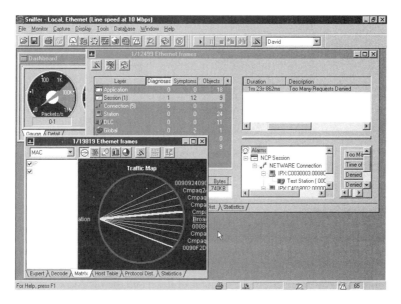

Protocol Analyzers

A protocol analyzer records, interprets, and analyzes how a communication protocol operates in a particular network architecture. It captures frames as they travel across the network. It then decodes the various layers of protocol in the recorded frame contents and presents them as readable abbreviations or summaries, detailing what layer is involved (physical, data link, and some protocol analyzers, right up to the application layer) and what function each byte or byte content serves. With LAN/WAN networks that involve multiple protocols, it is important that a protocol analyzer be able to detect and decode all the protocols used in the network environment.

In capture mode, filters can be set to record only traffic that meets certain criteria; for example, if a particular unit is suspected of inconsistent protocol behavior, then a filter can be configured that captures all traffic to and from that unit. The analyzer should have the capability to timestamp all the captured data. This can be extremely important when determining the effects of peak traffic periods and when analyzing network performance—for example, determining protocol response times by measuring the delta time between frames.

In display mode, an analyzer interprets the captured traffic, presenting the protocol layers in an easily readable form. Filters can be set to allow only those captured frames that meet certain criteria to be displayed.

It is also important that the analyzer be able to generate frames and transmit them onto the network in order to perform capacity planning or load testing of specific devices such as servers, bridges, routers, and switches. The analyzer should be able to send multiple captured frames in succession, as well as allow network managers to tailor the frames by being able to edit the frames prior to generation.

Figure 4-5 shows a packet that is decoded by the Sniffer Pro protocol analyzer. Sniffer Pro analyzers include the Expert System that identifies fault symptoms and provides a diagnosis of the network problems. Sniffer Pro provides decodes for more than 250 protocols.

NOTE   For more information on Sniffer Pro, see the Network Associates Web site at www.nai.com.

Figure 4-5   *The Sniffer Pro can decode frame and packet information.*

```
DLC: ----- DLC Header -----
DLC:
DLC: Frame 1 arrived at 15:05:33.389; frame size is 62 (003E hex) bytes.
DLC:  AC: Frame priority 0, Reservation priority 0, Monitor count 0
DLC: FC: LLC frame, PCF attention code: None
DLC: FS:   Addr recognized indicators: 00, Frame copied indicators: 00
DLC: Destination = Station cisco       A05903
DLC: Source  = Station IBM 0AE59
DLC:

LLC: ----- LLC Header -----
LLC:
LLC: DSAP = AA, SNAP = AA, C
LLC:

SNAP: ----- SNAP Header -----
SNAP:
SNAP: Type = 0800 (IP)
SNAP:
```

Summary	Delta	T	DST	SRC					
1			DCE	DTE	HDLC	SABM			P/F=1
2	0.0412		DTE	DCE	HDLC	UA			P/F=1
3	0.0492		DCE	DTE	HDLC	I	NR=0	NS=0	P/F=0
4	0.0408		DTE	DCE	HDLC	RR	NR=1		P/F=0
5	0.0438		DTE	DCE	HDLC	I	NR=1	NS=0	P/F=0
6	0.0287		DCE	DTE	HDLC	RR	NR=1		P/F=0
7	9.8700		DCE	DTE	HDLC	I	NR=1	NS=1	P/F=0
8	0.0379		DTE	DCE	HDLC	RR	NR=2		P/F=0
9	0.3000		DTE	DCE	HDLC	I	NR=2	NS=1	P/F=0

Portability of the analyzer is also an important factor because networks are not physically located in one place, and the analyzer must be moved from segment to segment as problems arise. Several manufacturers provide tools that allow for the remote gathering (and in some cases, analysis) of data and transmission back to a central console or master station.

The ability of the analyzer to use a set of rules and knowledge of the network operation to diagnose network problems is the emergent feature of an expert system. The expert system gleans its knowledge from theoretical databases (that is, from standards information), from network-specific databases (that is, topological information relating to the network), and from users' previous results and experience. From these repositories, the expert system generates a hypothesis about the problem it has detected and offers a plan of action to resolve it.

Protocol analyzers are generally available in three categories:

- Software-based analyzers are software packages that are installed on personal computers (usually portable notebook PCs) that are equipped with appropriate LAN interface adapters.

- General-purpose analyzers offer a wide range of uses, such as traffic monitoring, reasonably extensive protocol capture and decode support, and some network traffic modeling during the network design phase.

- High-end analyzers offer a range of advanced features and can typically capture traffic at higher rates and provide a more comprehensive protocol decode than can the other analyzers. They also support generate-and-capture capabilities, which means you can use them to stress-test parts of the network.

Network Management Systems

As networks grow larger and more complex, there is a greater chance of network failures that can disable the entire network or degrade performance to an unacceptable level. The complexity of such large networks makes the use of automated network management tools a critical factor in efficient management. It is important that the continued addition of users, interfaces, protocols, and vendor equipment to the network does not result in the network manager losing control of these resources and how they are used. It is also important that as network resources become more critical in an organization's operations, downtime be reduced. To ensure maximum network availability, network managers should include network management in their internetwork designs.

The International Organization for Standardization (ISO) has defined five key functional areas of network management: fault management, accounting management, configuration management, performance management, and security management.

The functions of fault, performance, and configuration management are most applicable to a troubleshooting environment. To achieve maximum network availability, all individual components of a network must be maintained in working order. A key ingredient to achieving this is having a mechanism in place that reports a fault immediately as it occurs. A fault can be defined as an abnormal network event, usually indicated by network components failing to operate correctly or causing excessive errors. It is therefore important to be able to do the following:

- Determine exactly where the fault has occurred.
- Isolate the failed area from the rest of the network so that the rest of the network can continue operating.
- Reconfigure or modify the network or its configuration to minimize the impact of operating without the failed component or affected portions of the network.
- Repair or replace the failed components to restore normal network operation.

Configuration management involves several functions. The network manager should be able to set up the network by initial configuration of the network components and interactively control these components by changing their configuration in response to performance evaluation or in response to network upgrades or fault recovery.

SNMP is an application-layer protocol that facilitates the exchange of management information between network devices. It is part of the TCP/IP protocol suite. SNMP enables network administrators to manage network performance, find and solve network problems, and plan for network growth. An SNMP network consists of SNMP agents (managed devices) and an SNMP management station (manager).

Figure 4-6 shows a typical SNMP design where an SNMP manager queries an SNMP agent on a router to obtain operational statistics from the agent.

Figure 4-6   *The SNMP manager sends queries to the SNMP agent in order to obtain management statistics.*

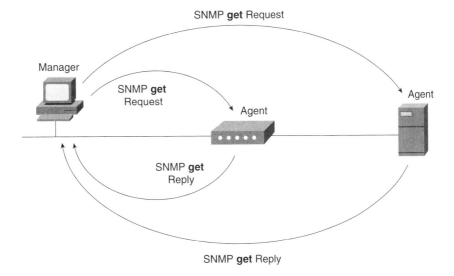

Simulation and Modeling Tools

Simulation/modeling software is useful for purposes such as initial network design, analysis of a network reconfiguration or redesign, and stress-testing a network.

This type of software usually uses object-oriented design to predict the performance of networks, ranging from departmental LANs up to complex, enterprisewide internetworks and WANs.

By selecting numerous objects that represent network topology, protocols in use, traffic, and routing algorithms, Netsys Baseliner attempts to simulate the operation of the network. Most types of LAN, MAN, and WAN technologies can be modeled by these tools. The output gives measures of the network performance such as response times; network throughput; node, link, and LAN utilization; packets dropped; and other performance data.

Many analyzer vendors offer the capability to export the data from their analyzers into the simulation/modeling tools, thus providing a source of real network data.

These simulation/modeling tools allow the network manager to see and test network performance before committing to proposed designs or changes.

Summary

In this chapter you have learned about several different troubleshooting tools that are used at various times when troubleshooting and managing internetworks.

Network modeling and simulation tools help you plan a new design or redesign. When implementing the design, you can use cable testers and other low-level testers to certify the installation of the cabling. You can use network management tools to simplify the configuration of routers, switches, and other devices.

When a network is operational, you can use network monitors and network management tools, including RMON-based applications, to monitor the network for errors and performance problems. When serious performance problems occur or when the network ceases to operate, you need low-level testers as well as a protocol analyzer or an RMON tool that lets you capture and display frames. Many problems can also be diagnosed by using the tools and commands built in to the Cisco Internetwork Operating System (IOS) software. We will talk more about these tools in Chapter 5, "Cisco Management and Diagnostic Tools."

Chapter 4 Test
General Troubleshooting Tools

Estimated Time: 15 minutes

Complete all the exercises to test your knowledge of the materials contained in this chapter. Answers are listed in Appendix A, "Chapter Test Answer Key."

Use the information contained in this chapter to answer the following questions.

Question 4.1

Match the most appropriate tool with the required task.

Answer	Task	Tool
_____	1. Analyze network design.	a. Cable testers
_____	2. Examine DTE-to-DCE communications.	b. BERT/BLERT testers
_____	3. Capture and decode packets.	c. Network monitors
_____	4. Locate crosstalk.	d. Modeling tools
_____	5. Bounce signal off end of cable to locate distance to fault.	e. TDRs
_____	6. Profile LAN traffic.	f. Protocol analyzers

Question 4.2

At which OSI reference model layer should troubleshooting start?

Question 4.3

You are concerned about broadcast overhead on the network. Which tool should you use to determine the current broadcast rate?

Question 4.4

You suspect that intermittent disconnections are due to a cable problem on your network. What tool would help you troubleshoot this most efficiently?

Question 4.5

You are designing a new campus LAN for a client. What tool can you use to review your design before implementing it?

Cisco Management and Diagnostic Tools

This chapter introduces Cisco's management tools and commands. It presents the output of router diagnostic commands from real-world environments with network problems. You will learn to recognize statistics that point to possible issues and concerns. Cisco management tools covered in this chapter include CiscoWorks, CiscoView, TrafficDirector, and VlanDirector.

This chapter also presents commands and functions such as core dumps that provide information you can give to Cisco or third-party support personnel when troubleshooting problems.

Cisco Management Tools

Cisco has developed a number of tools to manage and model network traffic flows. Each of the Cisco management tools has a distinct purpose. The following sections examine each of the following tools and their capabilities:

- CiscoWorks
- Netsys Network Management Suites
- TrafficDirector Remote Monitoring Software
- The VlanDirector Switch Management Application
- WAN Manager

Let's begin with the large family of management tools called CiscoWorks.

CiscoWorks

CiscoWorks is Cisco's flagship network management product line. It delivers device-level monitoring, configuration, and fault-management tools. CiscoWorks network management software lets you monitor complex internetworks that use Cisco routing devices and helps you plan, troubleshoot, and analyze your network. CiscoWorks uses Simple Network Management Protocol (SNMP) to monitor and control any SNMP device on the network.

CiscoWorks works directly with third-party SNMP network management platforms, allowing CiscoWorks applications to be integrated with the features and applications of these platforms. Supported management platforms include

- Hewlett-Packard OpenView on HP-UX
- SunNet Manager, Sun Solstice Site Manager, Domain Manager, and Enterprise Manager on Solaris
- Tivoli TME/10 NetView on AIX

The following is a brief list of CiscoWorks tools:

- **show** commands—You can display detailed router system and protocol information without needing to remember complex command-line languages or syntax.
- Configuration management—You can analyze or edit configuration files of local and remote Cisco Systems devices in your network. You can compare the contents of two configuration files in the database or compare the configuration currently running on the device and the configuration that represents the last time you performed a database-to-device command.
- Configuration snap-in manager—You can create and execute system commands on a device or group of devices at any time via the Global Command Scheduler application.
- Device management—You can create and maintain a database that holds a complete inventory of your network, including hardware, software, release levels of operation components, individuals responsible for maintaining the devices, and associated locations. You can enter or change data in the database tables for network devices, networks, interfaces, contacts, vendors, and so on.
- Device monitor—You can monitor your network devices for information about environmental and interface statistics. You can specify how often CiscoWorks should check this information and whether to log it in to the Log Manager application.
- Path tool—You can view and analyze the path between two devices. You can analyze on the path to collect utilization and error data.
- Security manager—You can set up authority-checking procedures to protect selected CiscoWorks applications and your network devices from unauthorized individuals by setting up your CiscoWorks environment to require a login to access applications.
- Software inventory manager—You can update the Sybase database to include current device software and hardware status. Device information is sorted according to platform and software image so that you can invoke Device Software Manager to update specific devices.

There are four versions of CiscoWorks products:

- CiscoWorks Blue—Designed to address the vast and complex networking requirements in integrated IBM SNA and IP environments.

- CiscoWorks Windows—An integrated PC-based network configuration and diagnostic tools for small to medium-sized networks or remote workgroups that use 5 to 50 Cisco devices.
- CiscoWorks Switched Internetwork Solutions (CWSI)—Delivers a management system specifically designed for increasing switched internetworks.
- CiscoWorks2000—A new family of Web-based and management platform-independent products for managing Cisco enterprise networks and devices.

CiscoWorks Windows creates a multilevel, hierarchical map that provides real-time status of individual routers, switches, hubs, and access servers by using color-coded icons.

CiscoView is the graphical device-management technology that is the standard for managing Cisco devices, providing back- and front-panel displays. These dynamic, color-coded graphical displays simplify device-status monitoring, device-specific component diagnostics, and application launching. CiscoView also provides additional applets that simplify the management of Cisco devices. It is bundled with the CiscoWorks software and is also available as a standalone product.

The CiscoView software graphically displays a physical view of Cisco devices, giving network managers a complete view of Cisco products without physically checking each device at remote sites. Additionally, this network management tool provides monitoring functions and offers basic troubleshooting.

CiscoView and the other parts of CiscoWorks are complemented by Cisco Resource Manager (CRM), a new suite of Web-based network management applications that enhance inventory and software distribution capabilities. The CRM suite consists of a Web server and four key management applications: Inventory Manager, Availability Manager, Syslog Analyzer, and Software Image Manager.

Together, these applications speed Cisco Internetwork Operating System (IOS) software deployment and provide network managers with a number of multi-device-management capabilities, including views of network change status, the ability to track device availability, and the ability to monitor, categorize, and analyze syslog messages. Cisco Resource Manager dynamically tracks Cisco and SNMP MIB II device information as well as Cisco software versions and Cisco device configuration information, automatically identifying changes.

CWSI can be integrated with popular SNMP management platforms, including the GUI environments of SunNet Manager, HP OpenView, and NetView.

CWSI includes comprehensive SNMP manageability, Cisco Discovery Protocol (CDP) for adjacent discovery, Virtual Trunk Protocol (VTP) for automated VLAN setup, and RMON for traffic analysis.

CWSI is a suite of campus LAN management applications that include VlanDirector, TrafficDirector, and CiscoView. These applications provide services such as topology mapping, VLAN management, device configuration management, and performance management of collected RMON traffic data.

Through an autodiscovery and topology mapping function, CWSI provides a campus view of interconnected Cisco switches and routers that administrators can use to learn connection relationships and to display logical VLAN topologies superimposed on the underlying physical network.

The Netsys Network Management Suites

Cisco Netsys connectivity tools are a series of simulation-based planning and problem-solving products for network managers, analysts, and designers. The Connectivity Tools assist network planners with problem solving, design, and planning activities focusing on network connectivity, route, and flow analysis.

The Netsys management suites are used to proactively check network designs to display, debug, and validate your network configuration. Netsys allows you to test configurations and changes offline before committing them to the live network.

There are two flavors of Netsys: Cisco Netsys Baseliner 4.0 for Windows NT and the Cisco Netsys Service-Level Management (SLM) Suite.

Cisco Netsys Baseliner 4.0 for Windows NT

Cisco Netsys Baseliner 4.0 for Windows NT creates a model of your network and checks for more than 100 common yet difficult-to-isolate configuration problems. You can graphically view your network as it is configured, not as it is planned or discovered. Baseliner gives you the big picture instantly, allowing you to visually navigate your network and gain a complete understanding of how it works. You can proactively monitor configuration changes; when problems occur, recent configuration changes are often to blame.

Building on the map created by the Connectivity Baseliner, planners can use the Connectivity Solver's analysis environment to study the impact of failed devices and links, varying access list configurations and other configuration changes before implementation in the production network.

Netsys collects actual Cisco router configuration files from the online network and processes the Cisco IOS commands to create an accurate offline model of the network. Netsys then analyzes the offline model for errors and generates graphical topology views and reports. At this point the user can submit proposed configuration changes or corrections to the offline model for reanalysis. This is often an iterative process as the user refines the network configuration. Users safely apply only fully tested changes to the online network.

Most network management tools provide only a topology view based on information manually entered or via an SNMP discovery process. Although these views are acceptable for some applications, they lack depth and miss critical elements such as routing protocols. By using the actual router configuration files, Baseliner can display all physical and logical relationships between routers on the network. The topologies are drawn automatically, so you don't have to spend hours manually linking interfaces and grouping objects. You can also generate views such as campus, virtual ring group, and Open Shortest Path First (OSPF) areas in an instant.

The Cisco Netsys SLM Suite

With the Cisco Netsys SLM suite, Cisco Systems is releasing the industry's first policy-based service-level management solution that enables network managers to define, monitor, and assess network connectivity, security, and performance policies, and to troubleshoot problems quickly when they occur.

Netsys SLM consists of the four modules:

- The Netsys Connectivity Service Manager—The Netsys Connectivity Service Manager monitors your actual network configuration data and uses built-in intelligence to verify the availability of key network services; it allows you to establish service-level policies for connectivity, reliability, and security services; and it uses the unique VISTA (View, Isolate, Solve, Test, Apply) troubleshooting methodology to automate the diagnosis and repair of problems.

- The Netsys Performance Service Manager—The Netsys Performance Service Manager complements the capabilities of the Connectivity Service Manager, allowing you to define, monitor, and optimize performance service levels; make the most efficient use of existing network resources; diagnose and solve network performance problems; tune existing networks; and plan network changes. By accurately modeling routing and flow transport over Cisco devices, you can analyze interactions between traffic flows, topologies, routing parameters, router configurations, and Cisco IOS software features.

- The Netsys LAN Service Manager—The Netsys LAN Service Manager complements the Connectivity Service Manager by adding LAN switching topology viewing and diagnostic capabilities. It gives you an integrated view of your router/LAN switching network and traffic paths, and checks the integrity of your LAN switch domain, improving your spanning-tree configuration.

- The Netsys WAN Service Manager—The Netsys WAN Service Manager adds integrated WAN switching analysis and troubleshooting capabilities to the SLM Suite. It provides integrated Layer 2/Layer 3 topologies, automated integrity checking, and path tracing via simulation of AutoRoute Layer 2 routing. It incorporates observed Layer 3 traffic to determine how your WAN is really being used, in comparison to the estimated loads it was designed to support. Similar to the Connectivity Service Manager, you can analyze what-if scenarios to determine the behavior of your WAN under failure or after configuration changes prior to implementing them online.

TrafficDirector Remote Monitoring Software

The TrafficDirector remote monitoring (RMON) console application analyzes traffic and enables proactive management of switched internetworks. Traffic Director works with both RMON and RMON2 extensions. TrafficDirector offers a common traffic analysis and performance application for managing the embedded RMON agents within the Catalyst switches and standalone Cisco SwitchProbe products. The powerful graphic capabilities within this application offer both real-time analysis of traffic behaviors and network usage information as well as proactive trending data for network planners and managers.

TrafficDirector software, operated in conjunction with the embedded RMON agents within the Catalyst switches, can quickly determine traffic utilization, broadcast levels, error rates, and the number of collisions on any selected port or group of ports. Additionally, network managers can set thresholds on Catalyst switch ports and direct traps to TrafficDirector software when these thresholds have been exceeded.

With its extensive network traffic views, TrafficDirector offers advanced monitoring and troubleshooting capabilities from RMON data collected by the SwitchProbe products. This traffic data can be used to profile network usage at the link, network, transport, and application layers.

Performance and fault management are simplified using TrafficDirector's multilayer traffic analysis, proactive alarms, and remote packet capture features. TrafficDirector can be used to remotely monitor enterprise networks from a central site. Primary uses for TrafficDirector include the following:

- Analyze network traffic patterns
- Troubleshoot protocol-related problems
- Report long-term trends
- Set up proactive alarms to detect problems before they affect users

The TrafficDirector software runs on Microsoft Windows/NT, SunOS, Solaris, HP/UX, and IBM-AIX.

TrafficDirector is a truly switch-aware traffic management application that includes complete support for Catalyst LAN switches with Cisco IOS embedded RMON agents. In TrafficDirector, a Catalyst switch is recognized as a special managed device with embedded mini-RMON (Statistics, History, Alarms, and Events) and a Switched Port Analyzer (SPAN) port. If a SwitchProbe device is connected to the SPAN port, TrafficDirector can seamlessly provide complete RMON and RMON2 support for any port on the switch. The TrafficDirector software can also recognize up to four SwitchProbes on Fast Ethernet trunk or server links and integrate this information in traffic displays for the switch.

The extended analysis features of a SwitchProbe device can be applied to any switch port simply by selecting the desired feature from a single menu. The TrafficDirector software then automatically configures the SPAN port to mirror traffic from the selected port to the external

SwitchProbe and begins using the more powerful SwitchProbe agent for the extended analysis being requested. Users need not concern themselves with this background activity and can simply use the systems as if each switch port and trunk link had an agent that supported all RMON and RMON2 groups.

NOTE   The first RMON standard, RFC 1271, defines two Ethernet-specific groups and seven other groups that apply to both Token Ring and Ethernet. The second standard, RFC 1513, defines Token Ring extensions to RMON.

TrafficDirector also provides virtual LAN (VLAN) monitoring, SQL-based trend reporting, seven-layer traffic analysis, distributed polling, threshold monitoring, protocol analysis, and proactive management capabilities.

VLAN Monitoring

The TrafficDirector analysis capabilities can be applied to analyze network activity on VLANs and trunk links as well as on all switch ports, LAN segments, and rings. TrafficDirector provides traffic statistics on a per-VLAN basis to allow monitoring of utilization, broadcast, multicast, and error rates for each VLAN on critical trunk links. VLANs are covered in more detail in Chapters 10, "Diagnosing and Correcting Catalyst Problems," and 11, "Troubleshooting VLANs on Routers and Switches."

The SQL-Based Trend Reporting Engine

TrafficDirector includes an enhanced SQL-based reporting engine that provides reports for analyzing long-term trends in network traffic patterns, determining overall network health, and identifying potential problem areas in the enterprise network. Data is polled from multiple RMON agents at user-specified intervals and logged in to a SQL database. Reports can then be generated for vital network statistics, host (that is, network-device-level) information, and interdevice conversation traffic profiling. Data can be exported in comma- or tab-separated variable (CSV or TSV) formats for custom reporting needs. UNIX versions of the TrafficDirector application include an embedded SQL database; Windows versions require the use of Microsoft's SQL server.

Complete Seven-Layer Traffic Analysis

The TrafficDirector advanced packet filters let users monitor all seven layers of network traffic. Using Cisco IOS embedded RMON agents and SwitchProbe standalone probes, managers can view enterprisewide network traffic from the link, network, transport, and application layers. The TrafficDirector multilayer traffic summary provides a quick, high-level assessment of network loading and protocol distributions. Managers can then "zoom in" on a specific segment, ring, switch port, or trunk link and apply real-time analysis and diagnostic tools to view hosts, conversations, and packet captures.

Distributed Polling and Threshold Monitoring

TrafficDirector also provides the powerful Resource Monitor tool, which, when used with a SwitchProbe device with the Resource Monitor option, provides distributed polling and SNMP threshold monitoring for remote sites and/or divisions within large enterprise networks. These distributed management tools let users proactively monitor the status of any remote device via a **ping** or by performing an SNMP Get to check any specified MIB object's value against a preset threshold.

Protocol Analysis

The TrafficDirector protocol analysis tool provides rapid, centralized troubleshooting for most protocol-related network problems. These packets can also be saved to a file in Sniffer format for additional analysis, by using an existing protocol analyzer, thus protecting and leveraging existing investments in network management tools. The TrafficDirector software supports full seven-layer decodes for the AppleTalk, DECnet, IP, ISO, Novell, SNA, Sun-NFS, Banyan VINES, and XNS protocol suites.

Proactive Management

TrafficDirector threshold monitoring enables users to implement a proactive management environment. First, thresholds for critical MIB variables are set within the RMON agent. When these thresholds are exceeded, traps are sent to the appropriate management station to notify the network administrator of an impending problem.

The VlanDirector Switch Management Application

VlanDirector is a graphically based, system-level VLAN management application for configuring, managing, and monitoring interconnected Cisco switches and routers. Integral components of VlanDirector include

- Graphical mapping utilities for viewing and configuring logically defined workgroups
- "Drag-and-drop" port-level configuration options for assigning users to VLANs
- Automated link assignment settings for managing VLANs campuswide
- Integration with common SNMP management platforms for consolidating system resources and detailed reporting functions for maintaining audit trails

These advanced VLAN management functions provide the keys for configuring and managing networks logically to reflect the way that workgroups typically communicate. VLANs substantially improve the overall flow of communications, deliver greater security and network segmentation, and reduce the administration expenses typically associated with managing shared LAN segments.

These VlanDirector features greatly reduce the configuration complexities of configuring VLANs and minimize much of the administrative detail typically associated with moves, additions, and changes.

Implementing VLANs on a network allows administrators to logically segment users based on their workflow, not on their physical locations. This capability enhances network performance by limiting broadcast traffic to logical workgroups and improves security by containing sensitive traffic within a VLAN.

VlanDirector simplifies the task of configuring, monitoring, and managing VLANs configured on the network. Administrators can configure VLANs with a simple drag-and-drop action. Inter-switch VLAN links are automatically configured, reducing the chance of misconfiguration.

WAN Manager

WAN Manager is an SNMP-based multiprotocol management software package designed specifically for wide-area multiservice networks. It provides integrated service management and process automation to simplify the management of even the most complex networks. WAN Manager allows you to easily monitor usage, provision connections, detect faults, configure devices, and track network statistics.

WAN Manager is designed to address the significant demands in managing and operating next-generation, wide-area, multiservice networks. The multiservice environment is complex and has a large number of connections and a wide variety of services, making the administration of the network a potentially impossible task without the right tools.

Based on a robust, scalable architecture, WAN Manager not only meets today's business requirements for control and operation, but also integrates with other Cisco network management products to provide end-to-end service management of wide-area multiservice networks.

NOTE   For more information on Cisco's management tools, see www.cisco.com. Product datasheets, customer profiles, and system requirements are readily available for each of the solutions defined herein. CCO is discussed in more detail in Appendix B, "Cisco Support Functions."

Cisco Diagnostic Commands

This section lists the Cisco diagnostic commands. These commands enable you to view the router's current configuration characteristics and operating statistics.

This section covers the following commands:

- **show** commands
- **debug** commands
- **ping** commands
- **trace** commands
- **cdp** commands
- **core dump** commands

In this chapter, you'll learn to identify and apply the Cisco-specific network troubleshooting tools that are built in to Cisco IOS and other operating software.

Although these troubleshooting tools are readily available from the same command-line interface as the one you use for your configuration tasks, you need to handle these tools— especially the **debug** commands—properly. Proper handling of tools is important because it is one thing to use **debug** to troubleshoot a design network that lacks end-user application traffic, and another thing to use **debug** on a production network that users depend on for data flow.

Nonetheless, with the proper, selective, and temporary use of these tools, you can easily obtain potentially useful information as you gather facts and consider possibilities. You can use these tools to narrow the set of possible causes while at the same time minimizing the impact of the tool on the sustained switching type that the router uses and on how much of the data flow the router has available for end-user traffic.

To help you become better able to interpret the output from these powerful troubleshooting tools, this chapter presents a description of some of the main architectural elements and operational processes performed in the router.

You will also find a description of how to selectively file the types of errors reported, how to direct **debug** and error message output, and how to interpret the output. You will see several of the command output details that help guide technical support troubleshooting for a problem call.

NOTE   See Chapter 2, "Protocol Characteristics Overview," for more extensive information on protocol technical characteristics.

Because your response to a production network problem must be rapid and effective, you need whatever tools can help you diagnose protocol behavior. The tools you apply must provide output about the network in a form that you can interpret.

As you interpret the output, you associate symptoms with router conditions. This association requires that you understand the router architecture and processes as well as the protocols that provide the technical context for diagnostic output. This is discussed in Chapters 2, "Protocol Characteristics Overview," 3, "Cisco Routing and Switching Processes," and 4, "General Troubleshooting Tools."

However, most diagnostic or control tools compete with other processing in the router or switch. In order to filter and display packet flow, the troubleshooting tool may need to slow down the operation of packet switching.

Because the problem condition is an abnormal situation, you might be willing to temporarily trade off switching efficiency for the opportunity to rapidly diagnose and correct the problem:

- You need to know about the details of the impact your troubleshooting tool has on router performance.

- You need to know about the most selective and focused use of the diagnostic tool.

- You need to know how you can minimize the impact of your troubleshooting in other processes competing for resources on the network device.

- You need to know how to stop the troubleshooting tool when you are finished diagnosing so that the router can resume its most efficient switching.

The **show** commands are among the most important tools for understanding the status of a router, detecting neighboring routers, monitoring the network in general, and isolating problems in an internetwork. The **show** commands are essential in almost any troubleshooting and monitoring situation.

The **debug** privileged EXEC commands can provide a wealth of information about the traffic being seen (or not seen) on an interface, error messages generated by nodes on the network, protocol-specific diagnostic packets, and other useful troubleshooting data.

WARNING   You risk router and network disruption if **debug** commands are enabled on a router in an internetwork that is experiencing heavy loads. **debug** commands cause great overhead traffic. When using **debug** commands, being as specific as possible with the command keywords can help with this problem. Buffering the output instead of logging it to the console can also help alleviate this.

The **ping** (ICMP echo request/response) command is available to test interconnectivity of TCP/IP. A **ping**-like test is also available for protocols such as ISO CLNS, AppleTalk, Novell NetWare, XNS, and Banyan VINES.

Finally, this section provides guidance on diagnostic steps that may be required when you contact Cisco technical support.

show Commands

The **show** commands are the most common set of commands that are used to troubleshoot the Cisco routed environment. The **show** commands covered in this section include

* **show buffers**
* **show interfaces**
* **show interfaces ethernet**
* **show interfaces tokenring**
* **show interfaces serial**
* **show interfaces fddi**
* **show interfaces atm**
* **show controllers**
* **show memory**
* **show processes**

The **show buffers** Command

You use the **show buffers** EXEC command to display statistics for the buffer pools on the router. Figure 5-1 shows the output from the **show buffers** command.

Figure 5-1   *The **show buffers** command lists hits, misses, and buffer sizes.*

```
Router# show buffers
Buffer elements:
     398 in free list (500 max allowed)
     1266 hits, 0 misses, 0 created

Public buffer pools:
Small buffers, 104 bytes (total 50, permanent 50):
     50 in free list (20 min, 150 max allowed)
     551 hits, 0 misses, 0 trims, 0 created
Middle buffers, 600 bytes (total 25, permanent 25):
     25 in free list (10 min, 150 max allowed)
     39 hits, 0 misses, 0 trims, 0 created
Big buffers, 1524 bytes (total 50, permanent 50):
     49 in free list (5 min, 150 max allowed)
     27 hits, 0 misses, 0 trims, 0 created
```

```
Very Big buffers, 4520 bytes (total 10, permanent 10):
    10 in free list (0 min, 100 max allowed)
    0 hits, 0 misses, 0 trims, 0 created
Large buffers, 5024 bytes (total 0, permanent 0):
    0 in free list (0 min, 10 max allowed)
    0 hits, 0 misses, 0 trims, 0 created
Huge buffers, 18024 bytes (total 0, permanent 0):
    0 in free list (0 min, 4 max allowed)
    0 hits, 0 misses, 0 trims, 0 created

    Interface buffer pools:
    Ethernet0 buffers, 1524 bytes (total 64, permanent 64):
```

A router has one pool of queuing elements and a set of pools of packet buffers of different sizes. For each pool, the router keeps counts of the number of buffers outstanding, the number of buffers in the free list, and the maximum number of buffers allowed in the free list.

The following significant fields shown in the display in Figure 5-1 are useful in a troubleshooting environment:

Field	Description
Buffer elements	Small structures used as placeholders for buffers in internal operating system queues. Buffer elements are used when a buffer may need to be on more than one queue.
Free list	Total number of the currently unallocated buffer elements.
Max allowed	Maximum number of buffers that are available for allocation.
Hits	Count of successful attempts to allocate a buffer when needed.
Misses	Count of buffer allocation attempts that resulted in increasing the buffer pool to allocate a buffer.
Created	Count of new buffers created to satisfy buffer allocation attempts when the available buffers in the pool have already been allocated.
Small buffers	Buffers that are 104 bytes long.
Middle buffers	Buffers that are 600 bytes long.
Big buffers	Buffers that are 1524 bytes long.
Very Big buffers	Buffers that are 4520 bytes long.
Large buffers	Buffers that are 5024 bytes long.
Huge buffers	Buffers that are 18,024 bytes long.
Total	Total number of this type of buffer.
Permanent	Number of these buffers that are permanent.

continues

Field	Description
Free list	Number of available or unallocated buffers in the buffer pool.
Min	Minimum number of free or unallocated buffers in the buffer pool.
Max allowed	Maximum number of free or unallocated buffers in the buffer pool.
Hits	Count of successful attempts to allocate a buffer when needed.
Misses	Count of buffer allocation attempts that resulted in increasing the buffer pool in order to allocate a buffer.
Trims	Count of buffers released to the system because they were not being used. This field is displayed only for dynamic buffer pools, not interface buffer pools, which are static.
Created	Count of new buffers created in response to misses. This field is displayed only for dynamic buffer pools, not interface buffer pools, which are static.

The network transfers data across the communications link between computers, routers, switches, and other devices. When problems occur (for example, when a connection is not possible, or when data transfer becomes too slow, or when the data itself is distorted), you must understand which data-link troubleshooting targets to consider.

The data-link control operation is limited to one individual link to an adjacent system on the data link. Among the data-link responsibilities are ensuring the systems on each side of the link that data has been transmitted without errors.

The basic physical and data-link connection in Cisco routers uses the router interfaces and, for some interfaces, the controller.

When network problems occur, data-link troubleshooting usually is only one of the indicators to check. Error checking and retransmission may also be provided by other higher-level processes.

These indicators can include routed and routing protocols as well as other processes. However, just as the data link layer depends on the physical layer working, so too do these high-level processes depend on the assumption of a properly functioning data link layer.

The data-link troubleshooting targets are interfaces. In this chapter, the router interfaces to check include Ethernet, Token Ring, serial, FDDI, and ATM.

You can go to the physical interface itself and examine the cable connection on the router or switch that links to the next adjacent router or switch in the path. The connection has two pieces—the physical or hardware portion and the logical or software portion.

The hardware portion comprises connectors, hardware signals, and cables. If the cable is not connected between devices, there can be no communication. An assumption before you do data-link troubleshooting is that the prerequisite physical-layer connection is functioning properly. To verify this assumption, use the output of the Cisco IOS commands, as well as hands-on checking, and as required, additional physical media test tools.

The software portion includes the messages being passed back and forth between the adjacent devices. These messages can be keepalive messages that let the device on the other end know that someone is still alive on the other end of the link.

The **show interfaces** Command

The **show interfaces** command displays statistics for the network interfaces, as shown in Figure 5-2.

Figure 5-2   *The* **show interfaces** *command displays the interface counters for Layer 2 troubleshooting.*

```
Router> show interfaces s 1

Serial1 is up, line protocol is up

    Hardware is cxBus Serial
    Description: 56Kb Line San Jose - MP
    Internet address is 150.136.190.203, subnet mask is 255.255.255.0
    MTU 1500 bytes, BW 56 Kbit, DLY 20000 usec, rely 255/255, load 1/255
    Encapsulation HDLC, loopback not set, keepalive set (10 sec)
    Last input 0:00:07, output 0:00:00, output hang never
    Last clearing of "show interface" counters 2w4d
    Output queue 0/40, 0 drops; input queue 0/75, 0 drops
    Five minute input rate 0 bits/sec, 0 packets/sec
    Five minute output rate 0 bits/sec, 0 packets/sec
        16263 packets input, 1347238 bytes, 0 no buffer
        Received 13983 broadcasts, 0 runts, 0 giants
        2 input errors, 0 CRC, 0 frame, 0 overrun, 0 ignored, 2 abort
        0 input packets with dribble condition detected
        22146 packets output, 2383680 bytes, 0 underruns
        0 output errors, 0 collisions, 2 interface resets, 0 restarts
        1 carrier transitions
```

The resulting display on the Cisco 7000 series shows the interface processors in slot order. If you use the **show interfaces** command on the Cisco 7000 series without the slot/port arguments, information for all interface types is shown. For example, if you type **show interfaces ethernet**, you will receive information for all Ethernet, serial, Token Ring, ATM, and FDDI interfaces. Only by adding the *type slot/port* argument can you specify a particular interface.

If you enter a **show interfaces** command for an interface type that has been removed from the router, interface statistics are displayed, accompanied by the text "Hardware has been removed."

If you shut an interface, the keepalives that cause the message "line protocol is up" are not received on the interface.

You will use the **show interfaces** command frequently while configuring and monitoring routers. Current information is important in network troubleshooting. If you suspect an interface problem (that is, in the physical or hardware portion and the logical or software portion), you need to gather facts so you can get more detailed information about what is happening on the interface. The router keeps statistical counters to help diagnose problems. These counters display when you enter the **show interfaces** command.

In Figure 5-2, there have been more than 22,000 packets transmitted. Until you know the duration of the tracking period, you cannot determine whether this is desirable performance. Notice in the first highlighted line that it has been two weeks and four days since the counters were last cleared. The information in these statistics is from many days in the past.

- To diagnose a new problem, use the **clear counters** command to reset these counters to zero.

- To see how long it has been since the counters have been cleared so that the count can renew, check for a line in the **show interfaces** output.

The **show interfaces ethernet** Command

You use the **show interfaces ethernet** command to display information about an Ethernet interface on the router, as shown in Figure 5-3.

Figure 5-3 *You should pay particular attention to the error counters displayed by the **show interfaces ethernet** command.*

```
Router# show interfaces ethernet 0

Ethernet 0 is up, line protocol is up
    Hardware is MCI Ethernet, address is aa00.0400.0134 (bia 0000.0c00.4369)
        Internet address is 131.108.1.1, subnet mask is 255.255.255.0
        MTU 1500 bytes, BW 10000 Kbit, DLY 1000 usec, rely 255/255, load 1/255
        Encapsulation ARPA, loopback not set, keepalive set (10 sec)
        ARP type: ARPA, PROBE, ARP Timeout 4:00:00
        Last input 0:00:00, output 0:00:00, output hang never
        Last clearing of "show interface" counters 0:56:40
        Output queue 0/40, 0 drops; input queue 0/75, 2 drops
        Five minute input rate 6100 bits/sec, 4 packets/sec
        Five minute output rate 1000 bits/sec, 2 packets/sec
            2295197 packets input, 305539992 bytes, 0 no buffer
            Received 1925500 broadcasts, 0 runts, 0 giants
            3 input errors, 3 CRC, 0 frame, 0 overrun, 0 ignored, 0 abort
            0 input packets with dribble condition detected
            3594664 packets output, 436549843 bytes, 0 underruns
            8 output errors, 1790 collisions, 10 interface resets, 0 restarts
```

The following are some significant fields shown in Figure 5-3 that are useful in a troubleshooting environment:

Field	Description
Ethernet...is {up | down | administratively down}	This field indicates whether the interface hardware is currently active and whether it has been taken down by an administrator.
line protocol is {up | down}	This field indicates whether the software processes that handle the line protocol consider the interface usable (that is, whether keepalives are successful). If the interface receivers miss three consecutive keepalives, the line protocol is marked as down. On the AGS+ and 7000-series routers, the output can show *disabled* if the router has received more than 5000 errors in a keepalive interval. Errors include input buffer drops and giants on the 7000. Other types of errors are included on the AGS+.
MTU	Maximum transmission unit of the interface.
BW	Bandwidth of the interface in kilobits per second. The bandwidth parameter is used to compute IGRP metrics only.
DLY	Delay of the interface in microseconds.
Rely	Reliability of the interface as a fraction of 255 (255/255 is 100% reliability), calculated as an exponential average over 5 minutes.
Load	Load on the interface as a fraction of 255 (255/255 is completely saturated), calculated as an exponential average over 5 minutes.
Keepalive	Indicates whether keepalives are set.
Last input	Number of hours, minutes, and seconds since the last packet was successfully received by an interface. Useful for knowing when a dead interface failed.
Output	Number of hours, minutes, and seconds since the last packet was successfully transmitted by an interface. Useful for knowing when a dead interface failed.
Last clearing	Time at which the counters that measure cumulative statistics shown in this report (such as number of bytes transmitted and received) were last reset to zero. Note that variables that might affect routing (for example, load and reliability) are not cleared when the counters are cleared. *** indicates that the elapsed time is too large to be displayed.
Output queue, input queue, drops	Number of packets in output and input queues. Each number is followed by a slash, the maximum size of the queue, and the number of packets dropped due to a full queue.
packets input	Total number of error-free packets received by the system.
bytes input	Total number of bytes, including data and MAC encapsulation, in the error-free packets received by the system.

continues

Field	Description
no buffers	Number of received packets discarded because there was no buffer space in the main system. Compare with ignored count. Broadcast storms on Ethernets are often responsible for no input buffer events.
Received…broadcasts	Total number of broadcast or multicast packets received by the interface. The number of broadcasts should be kept as low as practicable. An approximate threshold is less than 20% of the total number of input packets.
Runts	Number of packets that are discarded because they are smaller than the medium's minimum packet size. Any Ethernet packet that is less than 64 bytes is considered a runt. Runts are usually caused by collisions. More than one runt per million bytes received should be investigated.
Giants	Number of packets that are discarded because they exceed the medium's maximum packet size. Any Ethernet packet that is greater than 1518 bytes is considered a giant.
input error	Includes runts, giants, no buffer, cyclic redundancy check (CRC), frame, overrun, and ignored counts. Other input-related errors can also cause the input errors count to be increased, and some datagrams may have more than one error; therefore, this sum may not balance with the sum of enumerated input error counts.
CRC	CRC generated by the originating LAN station does not match the checksum calculated from the data received. On a LAN, this usually indicates noise or transmission problems on the LAN interface or the LAN bus itself. A large number of CRCs is usually the result of collisions or a station transmitting bad data. More than one CRC error per million bytes received should be investigated.
Frame	Number of packets received incorrectly with a CRC error and a non-integer number of octets. On a LAN, this is usually the result of collisions or a malfunctioning Ethernet device.
Overrun	Number of times the receiver hardware was unable to hand received data to a hardware buffer because the input rate exceeded the receiver's ability to handle the data.
Ignored	Number of received packets ignored by the interface because the interface hardware ran low on internal buffers. These buffers are different than the system buffers mentioned previously in the buffer description. Broadcast storms and bursts of noise can cause the ignored count to be increased.
Collisions	Number of messages retransmitted due to an Ethernet collision. Collisions are a normal part of Ethernet carrier-sense multiple access collision detection (CSMA/CD). Excessive collisions are usually the result of a malfunctioning network interface card somewhere on the Ethernet or an overextended LAN (for example, Ethernet or transceiver cable too long, more than two repeaters between stations, or too many cascaded multiport transceivers). The total number of collisions with respect to the total number of output packets should be around 0.1% or less. A packet that collides is counted only once in output packets.

interface resets	Number of times an interface has been completely reset. This can happen if packets queued for transmission were not sent within several seconds. Interface resets can also occur when an interface is looped back or shut down.
Restarts	Number of times a Type 2 Ethernet controller was restarted because of errors. The number shown here can be compared with the line "Restarts: …" in the **show controllers** command output.

The **show interfaces tokenring** Command

You use the **show interfaces tokenring** command to display information about a Token Ring interface and the state of source-route bridging, as shown in Figure 5-4.

Figure 5-4   *You can use the **show interfaces tokenring** command to identify Token Ring errors and functionality.*

```
Router# show interfaces tokenring

TokenRing 0 is up, line protocol is up
    Hardware is 16/4 Token Ring, address is 5500.2000.dc27 (bia 0000.3000.072b)
    Internet address is 150.136.230.203, subnet mask is 255.255.255.0
    MTU 8136 bytes, BW 16000 Kbit, DLY 630 usec, rely 255/255, load 1/255
    Encapsulation SNAP, loopback not set, keepalive set (10 sec)
    ARP type: SNAP, ARP Timeout 4:00:00
    Ring speed: 16 Mbps
    Single ring node, Source Route Bridge capable
    Group address: 0x00000000, Functional Address: 0x60840000
    Last input 0:00:01, output 0:00:01, output hang never
    Output queue 0/40, 0 drops; input queue 0/75, 0 drops
    Five minute input rate 0 bits/sec, 0 packets/sec
    Five minute output rate 0 bits/sec, 0 packets/sec
        16339 packets input, 1496515 bytes, 0 no buffer
        Received 9895 broadcasts, 0 runts, 0 giants
        0 input errors, 0 CRC, 0 frame, 0 overrun, 0 ignored, 0 abort
        32648 packets output, 9738303 bytes, 0 underruns
        0 output errors, 0 collisions, 2 interface resets, 0 restarts
        5 transitions
```

The following are some significant fields from Figure 5-4 that are useful in a troubleshooting environment:

Field	Description
Token Ring…is {up | down | administratively down}	Interface is either currently active and inserted into ring (up) or inactive and not inserted (down). If administratively down, then the hardware has been taken down by an administrator.
Token Ring is Reset	Hardware error has occurred.
Token Ring is initializing	Hardware is up, in the process of inserting into the ring.

continues

Field	Description
line protocol is {up | down}	Indicates whether the software processes that handle the line protocol believe the interface is usable (that is, whether keepalives are successful).
Ring speed:	Speed of Token Ring = 4 or 16 Mbps.
{Single ring/multiring node}	Indicates whether a node is enabled to collect and use source-routing information (RIF) for routable Token Ring protocols.
Group Address:	The interface's group address, if any. The group address is a multicast address; any number of interfaces on the ring can share the same group address. Each interface can have at most one group address.
interface resets	Number of times an interface has been reset. The interface may be reset by the administrator or automatically when an internal error occurs. If this value is increasing, a likely cause is a lobe cable failure.
transitions	Number of times the ring made a transition from up to down, or vice versa. A large number of transitions indicates a problem with the ring or the interface.

The **show interfaces serial** Command

The **show interfaces serial** command is useful for displaying information about a serial interface and normally gives good clues to serial-line problems, as shown in Figure 5-5.

Figure 5-5 *The **show interfaces serial** command lists carrier transitions, alarms, and other Layer 1 information.*

```
Router# show interfaces serial 2/3

Serial2/3 is up, line protocol is up
    Hardware is cxBus Serial
    Internet address is 150.136.190.203, subnet mask is 255.255.255.0
    MTU 1500 bytes, BW 1544 Kbit, DLY 20000 usec, rely 255/255, load 1/255
    Encapsulation HDLC, loopback not set, keepalive not set
    Last input 0:00:21, output 0:00:21, output hang never
    Last clearing of "show interface" counters 2w4d
    Output queue 0/40, 0 drops; input queue 0/75, 0 drops
    Five minute input rate 0 bits/sec, 0 packets/sec
    Five minute output rate 0 bits/sec, 0 packets/sec
        16263 packets input, 1347238 bytes, 0 no buffer
        Received 13983 broadcasts, 0 runts, 0 giants
        2 input errors, 2 CRC, 0 frame, 0 overrun, 0 ignored, 2 abort
        22146 packets output, 2383680 bytes, 0 underruns
        0 output errors, 0 collisions, 2 interface resets, 0 restarts
        1 carrier transitions
        2 alarm indications, 333 remote alarms, 332 rx LOF, 0 rx LOS
        RTS up, CTS up, DTR up, DCD up, DSR up
        BER inactive, NELR inactive, FELR inactive
```

The display shown in Figure 5-5 is a sample output from the **show interfaces serial** command for a synchronous serial interface. The following are some significant fields from this display that are useful in a troubleshooting environment:

Field	Description
Serial…is {up | down | administratively down}	Indicates whether the interface hardware is up (Carrier Detect [CD] is present), down (CD is not present), or if the interface hardware has been taken down by an administrator.
line protocol is {up | down}	Indicates whether the software processes that handle the line protocol consider the line usable (that is, whether keepalives are successful). On the AGS+ and 7000 series routers, the output can show *disabled* if the router has received more than 5,000 errors in a keepalive interval. Errors include input buffer drops and giants on the 7000. Other types of errors are included on the AGS+.
BW 1544 Kbit	Indicates the value of the bandwidth parameter that has been configured for the interface (in kilobits per second). The bandwidth parameter is used to compute IGRP metrics only. If the interface is attached to a serial line with a line speed that does not match the default (1536 or 1544 for T1 and 56 for a standard synchronous serial line), use the **bandwidth** command to specify the correct line speed for this serial line.
keepalive	Indicates whether keepalives are set.
packets input	Total number of error-free packets received by the system. For a serial line, this entry is very important; it is used with the number of input errors. For example, if there is no network clock or network master, or if there are two masters, then the total number of packets input will be low, if any, and the input error count will increase.
bytes input	Total number of bytes, including data and MAC encapsulation, in the error-free packets received by the system.
no buffers	Number of received packets discarded because there was no buffer space in the main system. Compare with ignored count. Bursts of noise on serial lines are often responsible for no input buffer events.
input error	Total number of no buffer, runts, giants, CRCs, frame, overrun, ignored, and abort counts. Other input-related errors can also increment the count, so this sum may not balance with the other counts.
ignored	Number of received packets ignored by the interface because the interface hardware ran low on internal buffers. Bursts of noise can cause this count to increase.
carrier transitions	Number of times the CD signal of a serial interface has changed state. For example, if Data Carrier Detect (DCD) goes down and comes up, the carrier transition counter will increment two times. Indicates modem or line problems if the CD line is changing state often.

continues

Field	Description
interface resets	Number of times an interface has been completely reset. This can happen if packets queued for transmission are not sent within several seconds. On a serial line, this can be caused by a malfunctioning modem that is not supplying the transmit clock signal or by a cable problem. If the system notices that the CD line of a serial interface is up but the line protocol is down, it periodically resets the interface in an effort to restart it. Interface resets can also occur when an interface is looped back or shut down.
alarm indications, remote alarms, rx LOF, rx LOS	Number of channel service unit/data service unit (CSU/DSU) alarms and number of occurrences of receive loss of frame and receive loss of signal.
BER inactive, NELR inactive, FELR inactive	Status of G.703-E1 counters for bit error rate (BER) alarm, near-end loop remote (NELR), and far-end loop remote (FELR). You cannot set the NELR or FELR.

The **show interfaces fddi** Command

You use the **show interfaces fddi** command to display information about an FDDI interface, as shown in Figure 5-6.

Figure 5-6   *The **show interfaces fddi** command lists the Physical A and Physical B states as well as the token rotation time.*

```
Router> show interfaces fddi 3/0

Fddi3/0 is up, line protocol is up
  Hardware is cxBus Fddi, address is 0000.0c02.adf1 (bia 0000.0c02.adf1)
  Internet address is 131.108.33.14, subnet mask is 255.255.255.0
  MTU 4470 bytes, BW 100000 Kbit, DLY 100 usec, rely 255/255, load 1/255
  Encapsulation SNAP, loopback not set, keepalive not set
  ARP type: SNAP, ARP Timeout 4:00:00
  Phy-A state is  active, neighbor is   B, cmt signal bits 008/20C, status ILS
  Phy-B state is  active, neighbor is   A, cmt signal bits 20C/008, status ILS
  ECM is in, CFM is thru, RMT is ring_op
  Token rotation 5000 usec, ring operational 21:32:34
  Upstream neighbor 0000.0c02.ba83, downstream neighbor 0000.0c02.ba83
  Last input 0:00:05, output 0:00:00, output hang never
  Last clearing of "show interface" counters 0:59:10
  Output queue 0/40, 0 drops; input queue 0/75, 0 drops
  Five minute input rate 69000 bits/sec, 44 packets/sec
  Five minute output rate 0 bits/sec, 1 packets/sec
     113157 packets input, 21622582 bytes, 0 no buffer
     Received 276 broadcasts, 0 runts, 0 giants
     0 input errors, 0 CRC, 0 frame, 0 overrun, 0 ignored, 0 abort
     4740 packets output, 487346 bytes, 0 underruns
     0 output errors, 0 collisions, 0 interface resets, 0 restarts
     0 transitions, 2 traces, 3 claims, 2 beacons
```

The following are some significant fields shown in Figure 5-6 that are useful in a troubleshooting environment:

Field	Description	
Phy-{A | B}	Lists the state the Physical A or Physical B connection is in. The state can be off, active, trace, connect, next, signal, join, verify, or break. The following states are defined by the FDDI standard:	
	Off	Indicates that CMT (Configuration Management) is not running on the physical sublayer. The state will be off if the interface has been shut down or if the **cmt disconnect** command has been issued for Physical A or Physical B.
	Brk	Break State is the entry point in the start of a PCM connection.
	Tra	Trace State localizes a stuck beacon condition.
	Con	Connect State is used to synchronize the ends of the connection for the signaling sequence.
	Nxt	Next State separates the signaling performed in the Signal State and transmits PDUs while MAC local loop is performed.
	Sig	Signal State is entered from the Next State when a bit is ready to be transmitted.
	Join	Join State is the first of three states in a unique sequence of transmitted symbol streams received as line states—the Halt Line State, Master Line State, and Idle Line State, or HLS-MLS-ILS—that leads to an active connection.
	Vfy	Verify State is the second state in the path to the Active State and will not be reached by a connection that is not synchronized.
	Act	Active State indicates that the CMT process has established communications with its physical neighbor.
neighbor	State of the neighbor. Can be one of the following:	
	A	Indicates that the CMT process has established a connection with its neighbor. The bits received during the CMT signaling process indicate that the neighbor is a Physical A type dual attachment station (DAS) or concentrator that attaches to the primary ring IN and the secondary ring OUT when attaching to the dual ring.
	S	Indicates that the CMT process has established a connection with its neighbor and that the bits received during the CMT signaling process show that the neighbor is one physical type in a single attachment station (SAS).

continues

Field	Description	
	B	Indicates that the CMT process has established a connection with its neighbor and that the bits received during the CMT signaling process show that the neighbor is a Physical B DAS or concentrator that attaches to the secondary ring IN and the primary ring OUT when attaching to the dual ring.
	M	Indicates that the CMT process has established a connection with its neighbor and that the bits received during the CMT signaling process indicate that the router's neighbor is a Physical M-type concentrator that serves as a Master to a connected station or concentrator.
	Unk	Indicates that the router has not completed the CMT process, and as a result, does not know about its neighbor.
cmt signal bits	Shows the transmitted/received CMT bits. The transmitted bits are 0x008 for a Physical A type and 0x20C for a Physical B type. The number after the slash (/) is the received signal bits. If the connection is not active, the received bits are zero (0); see the line beginning Phy-B earlier in the display.	
status	Status value displayed is the actual status on the fiber. The FDDI standard defines the following values:	
	LSU	Line state unknown—the criteria for entering or remaining in any other line state have not been met.
	NLS	Noise line state is entered upon the occurrence of 16 potential noise events without satisfying the criteria for entry into another line state.
	MLS	Master line state is entered upon the reception of eight or nine consecutive HQ or QH symbol pairs.
	ILS	Idle line state is entered upon receipt of four or five idle symbols.
	HLS	Halt line state is entered upon the receipt of 16 or 17 consecutive H symbols.
	QLS	Quiet line state is entered upon the receipt of 16 or 17 consecutive Q symbols or when CD goes low.
	ALS	Active line state is entered upon receipt of a JK symbol pair when CD is high.
	OVUF	Elasticity buffer overflow/underflow. The normal states for a connected physical type are ILS and ALS. If the report displays the QLS status, this indicates that the fiber is disconnected from Physical B, or that it is not connected to another physical type, or that the other station is not running.

ECM is...	ECM is the SMT entity coordination management, which overlooks the operation of CFM and PCM. The ECM state can be one of the following:	
	Out	The router is isolated from the network.
	In	The router is actively inserted in the network. This is the normal state for a connected router.
	Trace	The router is trying to localize a stuck beacon condition.
	Leave	The router is allowing time for all the connections to break before leaving the network.
	path_test	The router is testing its internal paths.
	Insert	The router is allowing time for the optical bypass to insert.
	Check	The router is making sure optical bypasses switched correctly.
	Deinsert	The router is allowing time for the optical bypass to deinsert.
CFM is...	Contains information about the current state of the MAC connection. The configuration management (CFM) state can be one of the following:	
	Isolated	The MAC is not attached to any physical type.
	wrap_a	The MAC is attached to Physical A. Data is received on Physical A and transmitted on Physical A.
	wrap_b	The MAC is attached to Physical B. Data is received on Physical B and transmitted on Physical B.
	wrap_s	The MAC is attached to Physical S. Data is received on Physical S and transmitted on Physical S. This is the normal mode for a SAS.
	Thru	The MAC is attached to Physical A and B. Data is received on Physical A and transmitted on Physical B. This is the normal mode for a DAS with one MAC.
RMT is...	RMT (ring management) is the SMT MAC-related state machine. The RMT state can be one of the following:	
	Isolated	The MAC is not trying to participate in the ring. This is the initial state.
	non_op	The MAC is participating in ring recovery and ring is not operational.
	ring_op	The MAC is participating in an operational ring. This is the normal state while the MAC is connected to the ring.
	Detect	The ring has been nonoperational for longer than normal. Duplicate address conditions are being checked.

continues

Field	Description
non_op_dup	Indications have been received that the address of the MAC is a duplicate of another MAC on the ring. Ring is not operational.
ring_op_dup	Indications have been received that the address of the MAC is a duplicate of another MAC on the ring. Ring is operational in this state.
Directed	The MAC is sending beacon frames notifying the ring of the stuck condition.
Trace	Trace has been initiated by this MAC, and the RMT state machine is waiting for its completion before starting an internal path test.
token rotation	Token rotation value is the default or configured rotation value as determined by the **fddi token-rotation-time** command. The default is 5000 microseconds. When the ring is operational, the displayed value is the negotiated token rotation time of all stations on the ring.
ring operational	Operational times are displayed by the number of hours, minutes, and seconds the ring has been up. If the ring is not operational, the message "ring not operational" is displayed.
upstream | downstream neighbor	Displays the canonical MAC address of outgoing upstream and downstream neighbors. If the address is unknown, the value is the FDDI unknown address (0x00 00 f8 00 00 00).

The **show interfaces atm** Command

You use the **show interfaces atm** command to display information about the ATM interface, as shown in Figure 5-7.

Figure 5-7 *The **show interfaces atm** command displays current and maximum virtual circuits (VCs).*

```
Router# show interfaces atm 4/0

ATM4/0 is up, line protocol is up
  Hardware is cxBus ATM
  Internet address is 131.108.97.165, subnet mask is 255.255.255.0
  MTU 4470 bytes, BW 100000 Kbit, DLY 100 usec, rely 255/255, load 1/255
  Encapsulation ATM, loopback not set, keepalive set (10 sec)
  Encapsulation(s): AAL5, PVC mode
  256 TX buffers, 256 RX buffers, 1024 Maximum VCs, 1 Current VCs
  Signalling vc = 1, vpi = 0, vci = 5
  ATM NSAP address: BC.CDEF.01.234567.890A.BCDE.F012.3456.7890.1234.13
  Last input 0:00:05, output 0:00:05, output hang never
  Last clearing of "show interface" counters never
  Output queue 0/40, 0 drops; input queue 0/75, 0 drops
  Five minute input rate 0 bits/sec, 0 packets/sec
  Five minute output rate 0 bits/sec, 0 packets/sec
```

```
144 packets input, 3148 bytes, 0 no buffer
Received 0 broadcasts, 0 runts, 0 giants
0 input errors, 0 CRC, 0 frame, 0 overrun, 0 ignored, 0 abort
154 packets output, 4228 bytes, 0 underruns
0 output errors, 0 collisions, 1 interface resets, 0 restarts
```

Some significant fields from Figure 5-7 that are useful in a troubleshooting environment follow:

Field	Description
ATM…is {up | down | administratively down}	Indicates whether the interface hardware is currently active and whether it has been taken down by an administrator.
line protocol is {up | down}	Indicates whether the software processes that handle the line protocol think the line is usable (that is, whether keepalives are successful).
Encapsulation(s)	AAL5, permanent virtual circuit (PVC), or switched virtual circuit (SVC) mode.
TX buffers	Number of buffers configured with the **atm txbuff** command.
RX buffers	Number of buffers configured with the **atm rxbuff** command.
Maximum VCs	Maximum number of virtual circuits.
Current VCs	Current number of virtual circuits.
Signaling vc, vpi, vci	Number of the signaling PVC, virtual path identifier, virtual channel identifier.
Last input/output	Number of hours, minutes, and seconds since the last packet was successfully received/transmitted by an interface.
output hang	Number of hours, minutes, and seconds (or never) since the interface was last reset because of a transmission that took too long.

The **show controllers** Command

To display information about memory management and error counters for interface cards, use the **show controllers** {**bri** \| **e1** \| **ethernet** \| **fddi** \| **lex** \| **mci** \| **pcbus** \| **serial** \| **token**} command. The output varies, depending on the card. Some of the output is proprietary and meaningful only to technical support personnel.

Figure 5-8 shows the output from the **show controllers token** command, which includes information relevant to troubleshooting. The output shows the number of Token Ring soft errors and hard errors, as well as reports on the number of times the following conditions have occurred:

Figure 5-8 *You can use the **show controllers token** command to display management and error statistics for an interface.*

```
Router> show controllers token
TR Unit 0 is board 0 - ring 0
  state 3, dev blk: 0x1D2EBC, mailbox: 0x2100010, sca: 0x2010000
    current address: 0000.3080.6f40, burned in address: 000.3080.6f40
    current TX ptr: 0xBA8, current RX ptr: 0x800
    Last Ring Status: none
  Stats: soft:0/0, hard:0/0, sig loss:0/0
         tx beacon: 0/0, wire fault 0/0, recovery: 0/0
         only station: 0/0, remote removal: 0/0
    Bridge: local 3330, bnum 1, target 3583
      max_hops 7, target idb: 0x0, not local
    Interface failures: 0 -- Bkgnd Ints: 0
    TX shorts 0, TX giants 0
    Monitor state: (active)
      flags 0xC0, state 0x0, test 0x0, code 0x0, reason 0x0
f/w ver: 1.0, chip f/w: '000000.ME31100', [bridge capable]
    SMT versions: 1.01 kernel, 4.02 fastmac
    ring mode: F00, internal enables: SRB REM RPS CRS/NetMgr
    internal functional: 0000011A (0000011A), group: 00000000 (00000000)
    if_state: 1, ints: 0/0, ghosts: 0/0, bad_states: 0/0
    t2m fifo purges: 0/0
    t2m fifo current: 0, t2m fifo max: 0/0, proto_errs: 0/0
    ring: 3330, bridge num: 1, target: 3583, max hops: 7
Packet counts:
    receive total: 298/6197, small: 298/6197, large 0/0
        runts: 0/0, giants: 0/0
        local: 298/6197, bridged: 0/0, promis: 0/0
      bad rif: 0/0, multiframe: 0/0
      ring num mismatch 0/0, spanning violations 0
    transmit total: 1/25, small: 1/25, large 0/0
        runts: 0/0, giants 0/0, errors 0/0
bad fs: 0/0, bad ac: 0
congested: 0/0, not present: 0/0
    Unexpected interrupts: 0/0, last unexp. int: 0
    Internal controller counts:
    line errors: 0/0, internal errors: 0/0
    burst errors: 0/0, ari/fci errors: 0/0
    abort errors: 0/0, lost frame: 0/0
    copy errors: 0/0, rcvr congestion: 0/0
    token errors: 0/0, frequency errors: 0/0
    dma bus errors: -/-, dma parity errors: -/-
    Internal controller smt state:
Adapter MAC:       0000.3080.6f40,  Physical drop:       00000000
NAUN Address:      0000.a6e0.11a6,  NAUN drop:           00000000
Last source:       0000.a6e0.11a6,  Last poll:           0000.3080.6f40
Last MVID:         0006,            Last attn code:      0006
Txmit priotity:    0006,            Auth Class:          7FFF
Monitor Error:     0000,            Interface Errors:    FFFF
Correlator:        0000,            Soft Error Timer:    00C8
Local Ring:        0000,            Ring Status:         0000
Beacon rcv type:   0000,            Beacon txmit type:   0000
Beacon type:       0000,            Beacon NAUN:         000.a6e0.11a6
```

- The station was the only one on the ring.
- The station was removed by a remote management application.
- The station transmitted a beacon frame to alert other stations that the ring is down.

A Token Ring algorithm called *beaconing* detects and tries to repair certain network faults. Whenever a station detects a serious problem with the network (such as a wire fault or signal loss), it sends a beacon frame.

In the example, soft: 0/0 means that no soft errors have occurred since the last time the command was entered as well as since the last reboot. The first number displays the number of times the error or condition has occurred since the last time the data was displayed. The second number displays the total number of times the error or condition has occurred since the last reboot (not counting the current number).

For the following line of output, an explanation of each entry follows:

```
f/w ver: 1.0 expr 0, chip f/w: '000000.ME31100', [bridge capable]
```

Field	Description
f/w ver: 1.0	Version of the Cisco firmware on the board.
chip f/w: '000000.ME31100'	Firmware on the chipset.
[bridge capable]	Interface has not been configured for bridging, but it has that capability.

ring num mismatch 0/0 is receiver-specific information that indicates whether a mismatch of the ring number has been detected by the controller.

The following output lines are provided by the controller chipset. They show the number of times the station has experienced soft errors. The first number shows the number of errors since the last time the command was entered; the second number shows the total (minus the current number).

These statistics can be helpful when troubleshooting Token Ring problems. For example, the command output line errors: 0/0 shows that there have not been any CRC errors.

indicator burst error: 0/0 means the router has not encountered a signaling problem (usually caused by noise or crosstalk) on the interface card.

A receive congested error (rcvrcongestion: 0/0) means that the station has not had a problem of not keeping up with traffic destined to it.

Line errors, burst errors, and receive congested errors are among the most common problems that occur on Token Ring networks.

You can use the output from the **show controllers token** command as well as a protocol analyzer to isolate the cause of excessive numbers of line errors, burst errors, and receive congested errors. The **show controllers token** command shows errors encountered by *this* station, as shown in Figure 5-8. The output from the **show controllers token** command includes the nearest active upstream neighbor (NAUN) address. This is the MAC address of this station's closest upstream network device that is still active. It will help you understand ring order and isolate a failure domain when problems occur.

Token Ring devices keep track of two types of soft errors—isolating soft errors and non-isolating soft errors. With isolating soft errors, the NAUN in the soft error report frame is relevant. The problem lies somewhere between the station reporting the problem and the NAUN (or with the station or NAUN). With non-isolating soft errors, the problem cannot be isolated to a station and the station's NAUN or the cabling between them.

Isolating soft errors include the following:

- Line error—Invalid bit in a frame or token (that is, a CRC error).

- Internal error—The station generating the error had a recoverable internal error. This can be used to detect a station in marginal operating condition.

- Burst error—The incoming signal is not correctly encoded, usually due to a physical-layer problem such as crosstalk or noise. This counter is incremented when a station detects the absence of transitions for five half-bit times (burst-five error). Note that only one station detects a burst-five error because the first station to detect it converts it to a burst-four.

- ARI/FCI error—The station generating the error received more than one Active Monitor Present or Standby Monitor Present frame with the address recognized and frame copied bits set to zero, indicating a problem with neighbor notification (ring poll). The NAUN may be causing this problem.

- Abort error—The station generating the error had a problem while transmitting.

Non-isolating soft errors include the following:

- Lost frame—The transmitter failed to receive its own frame back.

- Copy error—The station saw a frame addressed to itself with the address recognized bits already set. Though it is unlikely, it is possible that a station has joined the ring with this station's address. For example, if two bridged rings are joined into one ring while stations are active, two stations with the same address can end up on the same ring.

- Receive congested—The station generating the error has been unable to copy all the data sent to it. It may seem surprising that the receive congested error is non-isolating. It is isolating from the point of view that you can use this information to determine which station is congested. However, the NAUN may not be relevant in the frame. The station could be congested because of any other station sending it too much data.

- Token error—The active monitor generates this error whenever it needs to regenerate the token. This may be perfectly normal unless it occurs often. The token can get damaged when a new station enters the ring.

- Frequency error—The frequency of incoming signals is not correct. The active monitor should compensate for this. If this problem occurs often, temporarily remove the station that is acting as the active monitor so that another station becomes the active monitor.

The **show memory** Command

You use the **show memory** command to show statistics about the router's memory, including free pool statistics, as shown in Figure 5-9.

Figure 5-9   *The **show memory** command displays system memory allocation statistics.*

```
Router# show memory

              Head      Free Start    Total Bytes    Used Bytes    Free Bytes
SRAM          1000      7AE0          65538          27360         38178
Processor     20CFC4    23E178        2043964        282372        1761592
IO Memory     6000000   6132DA0       4194656        1471412       2723244

Address    Bytes    Prev.   Next    Ref    PrevF    NextF    Alloc PC    What
1000       2032     0       17F0    1                        3E73E       *Init*
17F0       2032     1000    1FE0    1                        3E73E       *Init*
1FE0       544      17F0    2200    1                        3276A       *Init*
2200       52       1FE0    2234    1                        31D68       *Init*
2234       52       2200    2268    1                        31DAA       *Init*
2268       52       2234    229C    1                        31DF2       *Init*
72F0       2032     6E5C    7AE0    1                        3E73E       Init
7AE0       38178    72F0    0       0      0        0        0
```

The first section of the display includes summary statistics about the activities of the system memory allocation. The **show memory** field descriptions are as follows:

Field	Description
Head	The hexadecimal address of the head of the memory allocation chain
Free Start	The hexadecimal address of the base of the free list
Total Bytes	The total amount of system memory
Used Bytes	The amount of memory in use
Free Bytes	The amount of memory not in use

NOTE   The **show memory** command on the Cisco 4000 series includes information about SRAM and I/O memory as well as information about the processor memory allocation. The **show memory** command on the Cisco 2500 series includes information about processor and I/O memory.

The second section of the display is a block-by-block listing of memory usage. Characteristics of each block of memory are as follows:

Field	Description
Address	Hexadecimal address of block
Bytes	Size of block in bytes
Prev	Address of the previous block (should match the Address on the previous line)
Next	Address of the next block (should match the address on the next line)
Free?	Tells if the block is free
Alloc PC	Address of the system call that allocated the block
What	Name of the process that owns the block

When you check this output, check the size of the largest block free, and compare whether the free amount number is rapidly going down or whether it is a very small number relative to your baseline free memory amount.

Some of the otherwise random router errors may relate to a condition where there is insufficient memory into which processes may expand as their need for memory increases.

The display of the **show memory free** command contains the same types of information as the **show memory** display, except that only free memory is displayed, and the information is displayed in order for each free list.

Other **show memory** commands that are useful for diagnosing memory problems are the following:

- The **show memory io** command displays the free I/O memory blocks. On the Cisco 4000, this command quickly shows how much unused I/O memory is available.

- The **show memory sram** command displays the free SRAM blocks. For the Cisco 4000, this command supports the high-speed static RAM pool to make it easier to debug or diagnose problems with allocation or freeing of such memory.

The **show processes** Command

You use the **show processes** command to display information about the active processes, as shown in Figure 5-10.

Figure 5-10 *The 5-minute utilization level is the most important field in the output of the* ***show processes*** *command.*

```
Router# show processes

CPU utilization for five seconds: 0%/0%; one minute: 0%; five minutes: 0%
PID  Q  T  PC      Runtime(ms) Invoked  uSecs  Stacks     TTY  Process
1    M  T  40FD4   1736        58       29931  910/1000   0    Check heaps
2    H  E  9B49C   68          585      116    790/900    0    IP Input
3    M  E  AD4E6   0           737      0      662/1000   0    TCP Timer
4    L  E  AEBB2   0           2        0      896/1000   0    TCP Protocols
5    M  E  A2F9A   0           1        0      852/1000   0    BOOTP Server
6    L  E  4D2A0   16          127      125    876/1000   0    ARP Input
7    L  E  50C76   0           1        0      936/1000   0    Probe Input
8    M  E  63DA0   0           7        0      888/1000   0    MOP Protocols
9    M  E  86802   0           2        0      1468/1500  0    Timers
10   M  E  7EBCC   692         64       10812  794/1000   0    Net Background
11   L  E  83BSS   0           5        0      870/1000   0    Logger
12   M  T  11C454  0           38       0      574/1000   0    BGP Open
13   H  E  7F0E0   0           1        0      446/500    0    Net Input
14   M  T  436EA   540         3435     157    737/1000   0    TTY Background
15   M  E  11BA9C  0           1        0      960/1000   0    BGP I/O
16   M  E  11553A  5100        1367     3730   1250/1500  0    IGRP Router
17   M  E  11B76C  88          4200     20     1394/1500  0    BGP Router
18   L  T  11BA64  152         14650    10     942/1000   0    BGP Scanner
19   M  *  0       192         80       2400   1714/2000  0    Exec
```

The first line of output shows CPU utilization for the last 5 seconds, 1 minute, and 5 minutes. The second part of the 5-second figure (0%/0%) is the percentage of the CPU used by interrupt routines.

NOTE

Because the router has a 4-millisecond clock resolution, run times are considered reliable only after a large number of invocations or a reasonable, measured run time.

Take snapshots of this command, about 1 minute apart, and compare the output line-by-line to see which processes are often invoked. The one that has been invoked the most is likely to be responsible for the CPU load.

Other parameters include the following:

Parameter	Description
Runtime (ms)	CPU time the process has used, in milliseconds.
Invoked	Number of times the process has been invoked.
Usecs	Microseconds of CPU time for each process invocation.

A high short-term CPU utilization value can indicate that there is a process (or processes) creating a load.

You can use the **cpu** optional keyword when invoking the **show processes** command to see the CPU utilization for each process. When the **cpu** optional keyword is provided, the output includes the following columns:

Column	Description
five seconds	CPU utilization by task, in the past 5 seconds. (Displayed in hundredths of seconds.)
one minute	CPU utilization by task in the past minute. (Displayed in hundredths of seconds.)
five minutes	CPU utilization by task in the past 5 minutes. (Displayed in hundredths of seconds.)

To make room for the extra columns, the following columns are *not* shown when the **cpu** optional keyword is used:

- Q—Process queue priority
    - H (high)
    - M (medium)
    - L (low)
- T—Scheduler test
    - * (currently running)
    - E (waiting for an event)
    - S (ready to run, voluntarily relinquished processor)
    - T (time, obsolete, not in 11.0)
    - rd (ready to run, wakeup conditions have occurred)
    - we (waiting for an event)
    - sa (sleeping until an absolute time)
    - si (sleeping for a time interval)
    - sp (sleeping for a time interval [alternate call])

— st (sleeping until a timer expires)

— hg (hung; the process will never execute again)

— xx (dead; the process has terminated, but has not yet been deleted)

- PC—Program counter

- Stacks—Low-water mark/total stack space available, shown in bytes

You use the **show processes memory** command to show memory utilization, as shown in Figure 5-11.

Figure 5-11 *The **show processes memory** command indicates memory currently used by each active process.*

```
Router# show processes memory

Total: 2416588, Used: 530908, Free: 1885680
PID     TTY     Allocated   Freed   Holding   Process
0       0       461708      2048    460660    *Init*
0       0       76          4328    4252      *Sched*
0       0       82732       33696   49036     *Dead*
1       0       2616        0       2616      Net Background
2       0       0           0       0         Logger
21      0       20156       40      20116     IGRP Router
4       0       104         0       104       BOOTP Server
5       0       0           0       0         IP Input
6       0       0           0       0         TCP Timer
7       0       360         0       360       TCP Protocols
8       0       0           0       0         ARP Input
9       0       0           0       0         Probe Input
10      0       0           0       0         MOP Protocols
11      0       0           0       0         Timers
12      0       0           0       0         Net Input
```

The Allocated column gives the sum of all memory that process has requested from the system.

debug Commands

The **debug** privileged EXEC commands can provide a wealth of information about the traffic being seen (or not seen) on an interface, error messages generated by nodes on the network, protocol-specific diagnostic packets, and other useful troubleshooting data, as shown in Figure 5-12. But be aware that these commands often generate data that is of little use for a specific problem.

Figure 5-12 *debug broadcast provides information on broadcast traffic for all protocols.*

```
router# debug broadcast

Ethernet0: Broadcast ARPA, src 0000.0c00.6fa4, dst ffff.ffff.ffff, type 0x0800,
data 4500002800000000FF11EA7B, len 60
Serial3: Broadcast HDLC, size 64, type 0x800, flags 0x8F00
Serial2: Broadcast PPP, size 128
Serial7: Broadcast FRAME-RELAY, size 174, type 0x800, DLCI 7a
```

You should use **debug** commands to isolate problems, not to monitor normal network operation. Because the high overhead of **debug** commands can disrupt router operation, you should use them only when you are looking for specific types of traffic or problems and have narrowed your problems to a likely subset of causes.

WARNING　The use of **debug** commands is suggested for obtaining information about network traffic and router status. Use these commands with great care. In general, it is recommended that these commands be used only under the direction of your router technical support representative when troubleshooting specific problems. Enabling debugging can disrupt operation of the router when internetworks experience high load conditions. Because debugging output is assigned high priority in the CPU process, it can render the system unusable; therefore, it is best to use **debug** commands during periods of low network traffic and few users. Debugging during these periods reduces the effect these commands have on other users on the system. When you finish using a **debug** command, remember to disable it with its specific **no debug** command or with the **no debug all** command.

As a router begins to switch packets to its interfaces, the process switching performed in memory initializes the other, faster-switching, caches. After initialization and determination of the destination interface packets (for example, end-user's application data flow) can occur without the involvement of the route processor.

However, when a problem is detected, a network administrator or engineer must be able to filter, capture, and display packets and router events to troubleshoot the situation. As mentioned previously, debugging, access lists, syslog maintenance, and other special processes that act on packets require functioning of the route processor.

Acting on packet data flow, a **debug** command uses process switching and interrupts the faster switching types for these data flows.

In some of the **debug** commands (covered later in this chapter) you must even enter a configuration command to turn off faster switching before issuing the **debug** command, which means that during the period of time when you are using these commands, you disrupt the fastest switching types. And the router CPU will give a higher priority to processing a **debug** and a lower priority to processing other packet data flow.

You need to know the specific demands and loading factors of your network to assess this trade-off—temporary slower switching during network troubleshooting—and be able to determine whether it is acceptable for the situation.

For example, enabling a **debug** privileged EXEC command can be disastrous in any environment experiencing excessively high traffic levels, perhaps even making the system unusable.

This potential risk being acknowledged, the **debug** tools can be very helpful when you use them properly. As you will see in the next several pages, proper debug handling can mitigate (or minimize) this impact.

When you interpret the information you need from the **debug** command and undo the **debug** (and any other related configuration setting), the router can resume its faster switching. You can resume your problem solving, create a better-targeted action plan, and be better able to take the action that fixes the network problem.

For troubleshooting, Cisco engineers recommend that you use the Cisco IOS **service timestamps** [*type*][*time-format*] command. This command puts a timestamp on a **debug** or log message that can provide valuable information about when debug elements occurred and the duration of time between events.

The timestamp *type* specifies the type of message (either **debug** or **log**). By default, the command shows date and time format. Alternatively, you can specify the *time-format* argument to show time in uptime since system boot (**uptime** keyword), milliseconds added to date and time (**msec** keyword), and local time zone (**localtime** keyword).

Do not use the command **debug all** because it may generate so much output that it can severely diminish the router's performance, or even render the router unusable. Instead, add one or more arguments to the command to narrow the focus of this powerful tool.

You can use the **terminal monitor** privileged EXEC command to copy **debug** command output and system error messages to your current terminal display—as well as to the console terminal.

terminal monitor permits you to establish a Telnet connection to the router and view **debug** command output remotely, without being connected through the console port.

Output formats vary with each **debug** command:

- Some generate a single line of output per packet; others generate multiple lines of output per packet.
- Some generate large amounts of output; others generate only occasional output.
- Some generate lines of text; others generate information in field format.

You will see more about the output of specific **debug** commands for various Layer 2 and 3 protocols in the chapters that follow.

To list and briefly describe all the debugging command options, enter the command **debug ?** in privileged EXEC mode on the command line.

Before invoking any **debug** commands, use the **cpu** optional keyword when invoking the **show processes** command. This command displays the CPU utilization for each process. If the values of CPU utilization are 50% or greater, consider debugging events, rather than debugging packets.

Just as you can set up an access list to filter packet traffic, you can also use an access list to constrain the focus of an IP **debug** command. This constraint on debug has several good results:

- The limited focus means that there will be less packet output information that the router needs to send to your terminal device.

- You will have an easier time identifying troubleshooting facts from the output because the output will not include extraneous output.

NOTE   Use **debug** commands with great care. If you are unsure about the impact of using a **debug** command, check CCO for details, consult with a technical support representative, or check when troubleshooting specific problems. Always remember to remove all debugging tools when you are finished with troubleshooting.

NOTE   No single tool works best in all cases. In some cases, third-party diagnostic tools can be more useful than integrated tools. For example, enabling a **debug** privileged EXEC command can be disastrous in any environment experiencing excessively high traffic levels. Attaching a network analyzer to the suspect network is less intrusive and more likely to yield applicable information without exacerbating load problems for a router.

If you intend to keep the output of the **debug** command, spool the output to a file on a syslog server.

Error Message Logging Priorities

By default, the router sends the output from **debug** commands and system error messages to the console terminal. These messages can also be redirected to other destinations. The commands used for redirecting error and debug messages are

- **logging console**
- **logging buffered**
- **logging monitor**
- **logging trap**
- **show logging**
- **terminal monitor**

All debug and system error messages are assigned one of eight levels of message logging, based on the severity of that message. The keywords listed under the heading Level Name in Figure 5-13 are used to assign the recorded message level.

Figure 5-13 *There are eight levels of errors.*

Level Name	Level	Description	Syslog Definition
emergencies	0	System unusable	LOG_EMERG
alerts	1	Immediate action needed	LOG_ALERT
critical	2	Critical conditions	LOG_CRIT
errors	3	Error conditions	LOG_ERR
warnings	4	Warning conditions	LOG_WARNING
notifications	5	Normal but significant condition	LOG_NOTICE
informational	6	Informational messages only	LOG_INFO
debugging	7	Debugging messages	LOG_DEBUG

Error Message Formats

Error messages begin with a percent sign and are structured as follows:

```
%FACILITY-SEVERITY-MNEMONIC: Message-text
```

The following are the fields in the error message format:

Field	Description
FACILITY	A code consisting of two or more uppercase letters that indicate the facility to which the message refers. A facility can be a hardware device, a protocol, or a module of the system software.
SEVERITY	A single-digit code from 0 to 7 that reflects the severity of the condition. The lower the number, the more serious the situation.
MNEMONIC	A code consisting of uppercase letters that uniquely identifies the error message.

continues

Field	Description
Message-text	A text string describing the condition. This portion of the message sometimes contains detailed information about the event being reported, including terminal port numbers, network addresses, or addresses that correspond to locations in the system's memory address space. Because the information in these variable fields changes from message to message, it is represented here by short strings enclosed in square brackets ([ ]). A decimal number, for example, is represented as [dec].

In the following, the Token Ring hardware is reporting a wire fault condition. This is an error condition (level 3):

```
%TR-3-WIREFAULT: Unit [0], wire fault: check the lobe cable MAU connection.
```

Check the cable connecting the router to the Token Ring MAU.

The following are notification messages only (level 5):

```
%SYS-5-RELOAD Reload requested
%SYS-5-RESTART System restarted
```

No action is required.

In the following, no other AppleTalk routers were found on the network attached to the port; this is an informational message (level 6):

```
%AT-6-ONLYROUTER: [Ethernet 0]: AppleTalk port enabled; no neighbors found
```

No action is required.

System Logging Commands

Figure 5-14 shows the commands that are used to enable message logging to different destinations.

Figure 5-14 *Error messages can be logged to the console, a buffer, a telnet session, or a syslog server.*

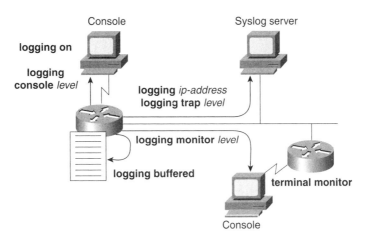

To control logging of error messages, use the global configuration command **logging on**. This command enables or disables message logging to all destinations except the console terminal. The **no logging on** command enables logging to the console terminal only.

NOTE   Be aware that the logging destination you use affects system overhead. Logging to the console produces very high overhead, whereas logging to a virtual terminal produces less overhead. Logging to a syslog server produces even less, and logging to an internal buffer produces the least overhead of any method.

To limit messages logged to the console based on severity, use this global configuration command:

```
logging console level
```

Specifying a level name causes messages at that level and numerically lower levels to be displayed at the console terminal. The **no logging console** command disables logging to the console terminal.

This command copies logging messages to an internal buffer instead of writing them to the console terminal:

```
logging buffered
```

The buffer is circular in nature, so newer messages overwrite older messages. The **no logging buffered** command cancels the use of the buffer and writes messages to the console terminal, which is the default.

To display the messages that are logged in the buffer, use the EXEC command **show logging**. The first message displayed is the oldest message in the buffer.

To limit messages logged to the terminal lines (monitors) based on severity, use this global configuration command:

```
logging monitor level
```

This command limits the logging messages displayed on terminal lines other than the console line to messages at that level and numerically lower levels. To display logging messages on a terminal, use the privileged EXEC command **terminal monitor**. The **no logging monitor** command disables logging to terminal lines other than the console line.

This command identifies a syslog server host to receive logging messages:

```
logging ip-address
```

The *ip-address* argument is the IP address of the host. By issuing this command more than once, you build a list of syslog servers that receive logging messages. The **no logging** *ip-address* command deletes the syslog server with the specified address from the list of syslogs.

This command limits the logging messages sent to syslog servers to messages at that level and numerically lower levels:

```
logging trap level
```

The default trap level is informational. The **no logging trap** command disables logging to syslog servers.

The IOS software generates four categories of syslog messages:

- Error messages about software or hardware malfunctions, displayed at the error level.
- Interface up/down transitions and system restart messages, displayed at the notification level.
- Reload requests and low-process stack messages, displayed at the informational level.
- Output from the **debug** commands, displayed at the debugging level.

The **show logging** command displays the state of syslog error and event logging, including host addresses and whether console logging is enabled, as shown in Figure 5-15.

Figure 5-15 *You can use the **show logging** command to view the current logging status.*

```
Router# show logging

Syslog logging: enabled
    Console logging: disabled
    Monitor logging: level debugging, 266 messages logged.
    Trap logging: level informational, 266 messages logged.
    Logging to 131.108.2.238

SNMP logging: disabled, retransmission after 30 seconds
    0 messages logged
```

This command also displays SNMP configuration parameters and protocol activity. The significant fields in this display are as follows:

Field	Description
Syslog logging	When enabled, system logging messages are sent to a UNIX host that acts as a syslog server; that is, it captures and saves the messages.
Console logging	If enabled, states the level; otherwise, this field displays disabled.
Monitor logging	Minimum level of severity required for a log message to be sent to a monitor terminal (not the console).
Trap logging	Minimum level of severity required for a log message to be sent to a syslog server.
SNMP logging	Shows whether SNMP logging is enabled and the number of messages logged, and the retransmission interval.

ping and trace Commands

As you apply your problem-solving method, you should test the reachability of some network target (for example, an interface address on another router across a data link, or across an internetwork). You might want to test reachability several times during the process—as you gather initial facts and consider possibilities, and then again as a way of testing the results of your problem-solving action plan, and if you iterate the process. **ping** and **trace** commands are extremely useful in determining host reachability and network connectivity.

ping (which stands for packet Internet groper) originated in the TCP/IP community as an application of the ICMP echo message and reply function. However, troubleshooters found that the same functionality would be useful for other protocols in addition to IP, so development engineers made this **ping** functionality available. In Cisco IOS privileged mode, **ping** functionality as a troubleshooting tool is extended in several ways (and also its potential for disrupting router efficiency if not handled properly).

trace tests the step-by-step paths that packets sent out a router interface follow when traveling to their destination. Again, this application originated in the TCP/IP community and in Cisco IOS privileged mode, has been added as a tool for other protocols as well.

The IP User **ping** Command

To check host reachability and network connectivity, use the **ping** user EXEC command, as shown in Figure 5-16. This command can be used to diagnose basic network connectivity on AppleTalk, CLNS, IP, Novell, Apollo, VINES, DECnet, or XNS networks.

Figure 5-16 *IP* ***ping*** *uses ICMP echo messages to test connectivity and round-trip time.*

```
Router> ping fred
   Type escape sequence to abort.
   Sending 5, 100-byte ICMP Echos to 192.31.7.27, timeout is 2 seconds:
   !!!!!
   Success rate is 100 percent, round-trip min/avg/max = 1/3/4 ms
Router> ping 192.45.3.1
   Type escape sequence to abort.
   Sending 5, 100-byte ICMP Echos to 192.45.3.1, timeout is 2 seconds:
   .U.U.
   Success rate is 0 percent (0/5)
```

For IP, the **ping** command sends ICMP echo messages. If a station receives an ICMP echo message, it sends an ICMP echo reply message to the source of the ICMP echo message.

The user **ping** feature provides a basic **ping** facility for IP users who do not have system privileges. This feature allows the router to perform the simple default **ping** functionality for the IP protocol. Only the nonverbose form of the **ping** command is supported for user **ping**s.

Figure 5-16 shows real output that was seen when the **ping** command was used to check the reachability to host fred and host 192.45.3.1.

The simple **ping** sends 5 100-byte packets with a 2-second timeout:

Output	Description
!!!!!	Each exclamation point (!) indicates receipt of a reply. A period (.) indicates that the router timed out while waiting for a reply. Other characters may appear in the **ping** output display, depending on the protocol type.
Success rate is100 percent	Percentage of packets successfully echoed back to the router. Anything less than 80% is usually considered problematic.
round-trip min/avg/max = 1/3/4 ms	Round-trip travel time intervals for the protocol echo packets, including minimum/average/maximum (in milliseconds).

In Figure 5-16 the first set of **ping**s had a success rate of 100%. The second set of **ping**s had a success rate of 0%. The destination 192.45.3.1 is unreachable (U). The router timed out waiting for the result of the first **ping** and displayed a period. On the second **ping**, the router received an ICMP destination unreachable message.

The first **ping** often times out. If a receiving station or router needs to send an ARP frame before replying, then too much time elapses, and the sending router times out.

Some routers, including Cisco routers, implement an ICMP throttle, which specifies that the router should not send too many ICMP messages in a time period. This might explain the timeout for the third and fifth **ping**s in Figure 5-16.

If the system cannot map an address for a host name, it returns an "%Unrecognized host or address" error message.

To terminate a **ping** session, type the escape sequence Ctrl-Shift-6 (this is done by simultaneously pressing the Ctrl, Shift, and 6 keys), or Ctrl-C.

The test characters that are displayed in IP **ping** responses are as follows:

Character	Description
!	Each exclamation point indicates receipt of a reply.
.	Each period indicates that the router timed out while waiting for a reply.
U	Destination unreachable.
N	Network unreachable.
P	Protocol unreachable.
Q	Source quench.
M	Could not fragment.
?	Unknown packet type.

Another useful command when using **ping** for IP is **debug ip icmp**. After you set up the **debug** command, have the other side **ping** your local target and then observe the **debug** output.

A useful sequence of **ping** commands can help isolate possible reachability problem locations. As you receive the characters that return from the **ping**, ask the question "What part of the network is sending this message?"

The AppleTalk and IPX User **ping** Command

The **ping appletalk** command sends Apple Echo Protocol (AEP) datagrams to other AppleTalk nodes to verify connectivity and measure round-trip times, as shown in Figure 5-17.

Figure 5-17 *Cisco supports AppleTalk and IPX ping processes.*

```
Router> ping appletalk 1024.128
Type escape sequence to abort.
Sending 5, 100-byte AppleTalk Echoes to 1024.128, timeout is 2 seconds:
!!!!!
Success rate is 100 percent, round-trip min/avg/max = 4/4/8 ms


Router> ping ipx 211.0000.0c01.f4cf
Type escape sequence to abort.
Sending 5, 100-byte Novell Echoes to 211.0000.0c01.f4cf, timeout is 2 seconds:
.....
Success rate is 0 percent (0/5)
```

Only an interface that supports hearing itself can respond to packets generated at a local console and directed to an interface on the same router. Cisco routers support this only on Ethernet.

The test characters that are displayed in the AppleTalk **ping** responses are as follows:

Character	Description
!	Each exclamation point indicates receipt of a reply.
.	Each period indicates that the router timed out while waiting for a reply.
B	A bad or malformed echo was received from the target address.
C	An echo with a bad DDP checksum was received.
E	Transmission of an echo packet to the target address failed.
R	Transmission of the echo packet to the target address failed due to lack of a route to the target address.

The **ping** (*ipx*) command works only on Cisco routers running IOS Release 8.2 or later. By default, the **ping** (*ipx*) command sends Cisco-proprietary **ping**s. (Cisco developed a **ping** before Novell did.) Novell IPX devices will not respond to this command.

To change to the new Novell **ping**, use the command **ipx ping-default novell**. Novell **ping**s conform to the definition in the Novell NetWare Link Services Protocol (NLSP) specification. You do not need to be running NLSP to use the Novell **ping**, however. IPXPING.NLM is included in the NetWare IPXRTR file.

You cannot **ping** (*ipx*) a router from itself except on Cisco 7000 routers.

The test characters that are displayed in the IPX **ping** responses are as follows:

Character	Description
!	Each exclamation point indicates receipt of a reply.
.	Each period indicates that the router timed out while waiting for a reply.
U	A destination unreachable error PDU was received.
C	A congestion experienced packet was received.
I	A user interrupted the test.
?	Unknown packet type.
&	Packet lifetime exceeded.

The Privileged IP **ping** Command

The extended command mode of **ping** allows you to specify the supported IP header options, as shown in Figure 5-18. This feature allows the router to perform a more extensive range of test options. To enter **ping** extended command mode, enter **yes** at the extended commands prompt of the **ping** command.

Figure 5-18 *The privileged ping command provides more options for advanced tests.*

```
Router# ping
Protocol [ip]:
Target IP address: fred
Repeat count [5]:
Datagram size [100]:
Timeout in seconds [2]
Extended commands [n]: y
Source address:
Type of service [0]:
Set DF bit in IP header? [no]:
Data pattern [0xABCD]:
Loose, Strict, Record, Timestamp, Verbose[none]: r
Number of hops [9]:
Loose, Strict, Record, Timestamp, Verbose[RV]:
Sweep range of sizes [n]:
Type escape sequence to abort.
Sending 5, 100-byte ICMP Echos to 131.108.1.115, timeout is 2 seconds:
Packet has IP options: Total option bytes=39, padded length=40
Record route: <*> 0.0.0.0 0.0.0.0 0.0.0.0 0.0.0.0
      0.0.0.0 0.0.0.0 0.0.0.0 0.0.0.0 0.0.0.0

The following display is a detail of the Echo packet section:

0 in 4 ms. Received packet has options
  Total option bytes= 40, padded length=40
  Record route: 160.89.80.31 131.108.6.10 131.108.1.7 131.108.1.115
      131.108.1.115 131.108.6.7 160.89.80.240 160.89.80.31 <*> 0.0.0.0
  End of list

1 in 8 ms. Received packet has options
  Total option bytes= 40, padded length=40
  Record route: 160.89.80.31 131.108.6.10 131.108.1.6 131.108.1.115
      131.108.1.115 131.108.6.7 160.89.80.240 160.89.80.31 <*> 0.0.0.0
End of list
                  :
                  :
2 in 4 ms. Received packet has options
  Total option bytes= 40, padded length=40
  Record route: 160.89.80.31 131.108.6.10 131.108.1.7 131.108.1.115
      131.108.1.115 131.108.6.7 160.89.80.240 160.89.80.31 <*> 0.0.0.0
End of list

Success rate is 100 percent, round-trip min/avg/max = 4/5/8 ms
```

The test characters that are displayed in **ping** responses are the same as those for the user **ping** feature described earlier.

The following are the significant fields shown in Figure 5-18:

Field	Description
Protocol [ip]:	The default is IP.
Target IP address:	Prompts for the IP address or host name of the destination node you plan to **ping**.
Repeat count [5]:	Number of **ping** packets that will be sent to the destination address. The default is 5.
Datagram size [100]:	Size of the **ping** packet (in bytes). The default is 100 bytes.
Timeout in seconds [2]:	Timeout interval. The default is 2 (seconds).
Extended commands [n]:	Specifies whether or not a series of additional commands appears. Many of the following displays and tables show and describe these commands. The default is no.
Source address:	IP address that appears in the **ping** packet as the source address.
Type of service [0]:	IP service quality selection. See RFC 791 for more information. The default is 0.
Set DF bit in IP header?	Don't Fragment. Specifies that if the packet encounters a node in its path that is configured for a smaller MTU than the packet's MTU, the packet is to be dropped and an error message is to be sent to the router at the packet's source address. If performance problems are encountered on the network, a node configured for a small MTU could be a contributing factor. This feature can be used to determine the smallest MTU in the path. The default is no.
Data pattern [0xABCD]:	Sets 16-bit hexadecimal data pattern. The default is 0xABCD. Varying the data pattern in this field (for example, to all ones or all zeros) can be useful when debugging data sensitivity problems on CSUs/DSUs or detecting cable-related problems such as crosstalk.
Loose, Strict, Record, Timestamp, Verbose [none]:	Supported IP header options. The router examines the header options to every packet that passes through it. If it finds a packet with an invalid option, the router sends an ICMP Parameter Problem message to the source of the packet and discards the packet. The IP header options follow: • Loose • Strict • Record • Timestamp • Verbose The default is none. For more information on these header options, see RFC 791.

Field	Description
Sweep range of sizes [n]:	Allows you to vary the sizes of the echo packets being sent. This capability is useful for determining the minimum sizes of the MTUs configured on the nodes along the path to the destination address. Packet fragmentation contributing to performance problems can then be reduced.
!!!!!	Each exclamation point (!) indicates receipt of a reply. A period (.) indicates that the router timed out while waiting for a reply. Other characters may appear in the **ping** output display, depending on the protocol type.
Success rate is 100 percent	Percentage of packets successfully echoed back to the router. Anything less than 80% is usually considered problematic.
round-trip min/avg/ max = 1/3/4 ms	Round-trip travel time intervals for the protocol echo packets, including minimum/average/maximum (in milliseconds).

In Figure 5-18, extended commands are used and the Record Route option is specified. The lines of **ping** output that are unique when the Record Route option is specified are described as follows:

- The following line of output allows you to specify the number of hops that will be recorded in the route:

```
Number of hops [9]:
```

The range is 1 through 9. The default is 9.

- The following lines of output indicate that the fields that will contain the IP addresses of the nodes in the routes have been zeroed out in the outgoing packets:

```
Record route: <*> 0.0.0.0 0.0.0.0 0.0.0.0 0.0.0.0
    0.0.0.0 0.0.0.0 0.0.0.0 0.0.0.0 0.0.0.0
```

- The following is a detail of the responses received to the echo packets, as shown in Figure 5-18. Five **ping** echo packets were sent to the destination address 131.108.1.115. The following lines of output display statistics for the first of the five echo packets sent:

```
0 in 4 ms. Received packet has options
Total option bytes = 40, padded length = 40
Record route: 160.89.80.31 131.108.6.10 131.108.1.7
131.108.1.115
    131.108.1.115 131.108.6.7 160.89.80.240 160.89.80.31 <*> 0.0.0.0
```

0 is the number assigned to this packet to indicate that it is the first in the series. 4 ms indicates the round-trip travel time for the packet.

- The following line of output indicates that four nodes were included in the packet's route, including the router at source address 160.89.80.31, two intermediate nodes at addresses 131.108.6.10 and 131.108.1.7, and the destination node at address 131.108.1.115:

```
Record route: 160.89.80.31 131.108.6.10 131.108.1.7 131.108.1.115
```

- The following line of output includes the addresses of the four nodes in the return path of the echo packet. The return route differs from the original route shown in the previous line of output:

```
131.108.1.115 131.108.6.7 160.89.80.240 160.89.80.31 <*> 0.0.0.0
```

The Privileged IPX **ping** Command

The privileged **ping** (IPX echo) command provides a complete **ping** facility for users who have system privileges, as shown in Figure 5-19.

Figure 5-19 *You can use the IPX **ping** in privileged mode to enable more **ping** options.*

```
Router# ping
Protocol [ip]: ipx
Target Novell Address: 211.0000.0c01.f4cf
Repeat count [5]:
Datagram Size [100]:
Timeout in seconds [2]:
Verbose [n]:
Novell Standard Echo [n]:
Type escape sequence to abort.
Sending 5 100-byte Novell echoes to 211.0000.0c01.f4cf, timeout is 2 seconds.
!!!!!
Success rate is 100%, round trip min/avg/max = 1/2/4 ms.
```

The **ping** command works only on Cisco routers running IOS Software Release 8.2 or later.

Novell IPX devices that support the echo function defined in version 1.0 of the NLSP specification respond to this command if you answer yes to the prompt "Novell Standard Echo" that is displayed when you use the **ping** command. If you answer no to this prompt, Novell IPX devices do not respond.

The Privileged AppleTalk **ping** Command

Figure 5-20 shows a sample AppleTalk **ping** session with verbose mode enabled.

Figure 5-20 *You can use the AppleTalk **ping** command in privileged mode to enable more **ping** options.*

```
Router# ping
Protocol [ip]: appletalk
Target AppleTalk address: 4.129
Repeat count [5]:
Datagram size [100]:
Timeout in seconds [2]:
Verbose [n]: y
Sweep range of sizes [n]:
Type escape sequence to abort.
Sending 5, 100-byte AppleTalk Echos to 4.129, timeout is 2 seconds:
0 in 4 ms from 4.129 via 1 hop
1 in 8 ms from 4.129 via 1 hop
```

Figure 5-20 *You can use the AppleTalk **ping** command in privileged mode to enable more **ping** options. (Continued)*

```
2 in 4 ms from 4.129 via 1 hop
3 in 8 ms from 4.129 via 1 hop
4 in 8 ms from 4.129 via 1 hop
Success rate is 100 percent, round trip min/avg/max = 4/6/8 ms
```

Fields in the verbose mode portion of the display are as follows:

Field	Meaning
0	Sequential number identifying the packet's relative position in the group of **ping** packets sent.
in 4 ms	Round-trip travel time of the **ping** packet, in milliseconds.
from 4.129	Source address of the **ping** packet.
via 1 hop	Number of hops the **ping** packet traveled to the destination.

The User IP **trace** Command

The **trace** user EXEC command discovers the routes the router's packets follow when traveling to their destinations, as shown in Figure 5-21. This command works by taking advantage of the error message generated by routers when a datagram exceeds its Time-To-Live (TTL) value.

Figure 5-21 *The **trace** command displays all routers used along the path to a device.*

```
Router# trace ip ABA.NYC.mil
Type escape sequence to abort.
Tracing the route to ABA.NYC.mil (26.0.0.73)
1 DEBRIS.CISCO.COM (131.108.1.6) 1000 msec 8 msec 4 msec
2 BARRNET-GW.CISCO.COM (131.108.16.2) 8 msec 8 msec 8 msec
3 EXTERNAL-A-GATEWAY.STANFORD.EDU (192.42.110.225) 8 msec 4 msec 4 msec
4 BB2.SU.BARRNET.NET (131.119.254.6) 8 msec 8 msec 8 msec
5 SU.ARC.BARRNET.NET (131.119.3.8) 12 msec 12 msec 8 msec
6 MOFFETT-FLD-MB.in.MIL (192.52.195.1) 216 msec 120 msec 132 msec
7 ABA.NYC.mil (26.0.0.73) 412 msec 628 msec 664 msec
```

The **trace** command starts by sending probe datagrams with a TTL value of 1. This causes the first router to discard the probe datagrams and send back "time exceeded" error messages. The **trace** command then sends several probes, and displays the round-trip time for each. After every third probe, the TTL is increased by 1.

Each outgoing packet can result in one of two error messages. A "time exceeded" error message indicates that an intermediate router has seen and discarded the probe. A "port unreachable" error message indicates that the destination node has received the probe and discarded it because it could not deliver the packet to an application. If the timer goes off before a response comes in, **trace** prints an asterisk (*).

The **trace** command terminates when the destination responds, when the maximum TTL is exceeded, or when the user interrupts the trace with the escape sequence.

Common Trace Problems

Because of bugs in the IP implementation of various hosts and routers, the IP **trace** command may behave in odd ways.

Not all destinations respond correctly to a probe message by sending back an ICMP port unreachable message. A long sequence of TTL levels with only asterisks, terminating only when the maximum TTL has been reached, might indicate that the destination does not send ICMP port unreachable messages.

NOTE   There is a known problem with the way some hosts handle an ICMP TTL exceeded message. Some hosts generate an ICMP message, but they reuse the TTL of the incoming packet. Because this is zero, the ICMP packets do not make it back. When you trace the path to such a host, you may see a set of TTL values with asterisks (*) before you finally see the response from the destination host.

The fields shown in Figure 5-21 are as follows:

Field	Description
1	Indicates the sequence number of the router in the path to the host
DEBRIS.CISCO.COM	Host name of this router
131.108.1.61	IP address of this router
1000 msec 8 msec 4 msec	Round-trip time for each of the three probes that are sent

The following describes the characters that can appear in **trace** outputs:

Field	Description
nn msec	For each node, the round-trip time in milliseconds for the specified number of probes
*	The probe timed out
?	Unknown packet type
Q	Source quench
P	Protocol unreachable
N	Network unreachable
U	Port unreachable
H	Host unreachable

The Privileged IP **trace** Command

The following describes the fields that are unique to the extended **trace** sequence, as shown in Figure 5-22:

Figure 5-22   *Using the **trace** command in privileged mode enables you to alter **trace** tests.*

```
Router# trace
Protocol [ip]:
Target IP address: mit.edu
Source address:
Numeric display [n]:
Timeout in seconds [3]:
Probe count [3]:
Minimum Time to Live [1]:
Maximum Time to Live [30]:
Port number[33434]:
Loose, Strict, Record, Timestamp, Verbose[none]:
Type escape sequence to abort.
Tracing the route to MIT.EDU (18.72.2.1)
  1 ICM-DC-2-V1.ICP.NET (192.108.209.17) 72 msec 72 msec 88 msec
  2 ICM-FIX-E-H0-T3.ICP.NET (192.157.65.122) 80 msec 128 msec 80 msec
  3 192.203.229.246 540 msec 88 msec 84 msec
  4 T3-2.WASHINGTON-DC-CNSS58.T3.ANS.NET (140.222.58.3) 84 msec 116 msec 88 msec
  5 T3-3.WASHINGTON-DC-CNSS56.T3.ANS.NET (140.222.56.4) 80 msec 132 msec 88 msec
  6 T3-0.NEW-YORK-CNSS32.T3.ANS.NET (140.222.32.1) 92 msec 132 msec 88 msec
  7 T3-0.HARTFORD-CNSS48.T3.ANS.NET (140.222.48.1) 88 msec 88 msec 88 msec
  8 T3-0.ENSS134.T3.ANS.NET (140.222.134.1) 92 msec 128 msec 92 msec
  9 W91-CISCO-EXTERNAL-FDDI.MIT.EDU (192.233.33.1) 92 msec 92 msec 112 msec
 10 E40-RTR-FDDI.MIT.EDU (18.168.0.2) 92 msec 120 msec 96 msec
 11 MIT.EDU (18.72.2.1) 96 msec 92 msec 96 msec
```

Field	Description
Target IP address	You must enter a host name or an IP address. There is no default.
Source address	One of the interface addresses of the router to use as a source address for the probes. If an address is not entered, the router picks the best source address to use.
Numeric display	The default is to have both symbolic (names) and numeric displays of IP addresses, but you can suppress the symbolic display by entering **yes** to the question about numeric display. IP addresses will be displayed as numbers only, with no names.
Timeout in seconds	The number of seconds to wait for a response to a probe packet. The default is 3 seconds.
Probe count	The number of probes to be sent at each TTL level. The default count is 3.
Minimum Time to Live [1]	The TTL value for the first probes. The default is 1, but it can be set to a higher value to suppress the display of known hops.

continues

Field	Description
Maximum Time to Live [30]	The largest TTL value that can be used. The default is 30. The **trace** command terminates when the destination is reached or when this value is reached.
Port Number	The destination port used by the UDP probe messages. The default is 33434.
Loose, Strict, Record, Timestamp, Verbose	IP header options. You can specify any combination. The **trace** command issues prompts for the required fields. **trace** places the requested options in each probe, but there is no guarantee that all routers (or end nodes) will process the options.
Loose Source Routing	Allows you to specify a list of nodes that must be traversed when going to the destination.
Strict Source Routing	Allows you to specify a list of nodes that must be the only nodes traversed when going to the destination.
Record	Allows you to specify the number of hops to leave room for.
Timestamp	Allows you to specify the number of timestamps to leave room for.
Verbose	If you select any option, the verbose mode is automatically selected and **trace** prints the contents of the option field in any incoming packets. You can prevent verbose mode by selecting verbose again, toggling its current setting.

The cdp Command

CDP is a media- and protocol-independent protocol that runs on all Cisco-manufactured equipment including routers, bridges, access servers, and switches. With CDP, network management applications can learn the device type and the SNMP agent address of neighboring devices. This enables applications to send SNMP queries to neighboring devices.

CDP runs on all media that support SNMP, including LANs, Frame Relay, and ATM networks. CDP runs over the data link layer only. Therefore, two systems that support different network-layer protocols can learn about each other.

CDP uses a small multicast packet to the common destination address 01-00-0C-CC-CC to send and receive periodic messages.

Each device advertises at least one address at which it can receive SNMP messages and a TTL that indicates the length of time a receiving device should hold CDP information before discarding it. By default, TTL is 180 seconds.

CDP packets are sent with a TTL value that is nonzero after an interface is enabled and with a TTL value of zero immediately before an interface is idled down, which provides for quick state discovery.

All Cisco devices receive CDP packets and cache the information in the packet. The cached information is available to network management through MIBs. Cisco devices never forward a CDP packet.

If any information changes from the last received packet, the new information is cached and the older information is discarded even if its TTL value has not yet expired. CDP is assigned the Cisco HDLC protocol type value 0x2000.

Cisco devices never forward CDP packets beyond the data-link-connected devices. In Figure 5-23, you can show CDP information for only the neighbors of the switch connected to the management terminal.

Figure 5-23 *A single command can summarize protocols and addresses on various Cisco devices.*

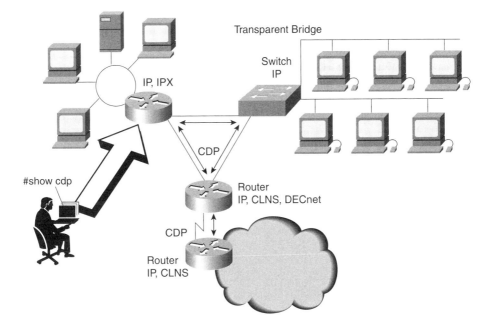

However, the administrator can use CDP to get the IP address of the neighboring router, Telnet to that router, and use **show cdp** again to see the router's directly connected neighbors.

By default, CDP is enabled at the global level and on all supported interfaces. It can, however, be configured for special functionality.

To configure CDP, perform the following tasks, which are described in the following sections:

Step 1 Set the CDP transmission timer and hold time.

Step 2 Disable and enable CDP.

Step 3 Disable and enable CDP on an interface.

Step 4 Monitor and maintain CDP.

NOTE	The **cdp enable**, **cdp timer**, and **cdp run** commands affect the operation of the IP on demand routing feature (that is, the **router odr** global configuration command). For more information on the **router odr** command, see *Introduction to Cisco Router Configuration* and *Advanced Cisco Router Configuration* from Cisco Press.

Setting the CDP Transmission Timer and Hold Time

To set the frequency of CDP transmissions and the hold time for CDP packets, use the following commands in global configuration mode:

Command	Task
cdp timer *seconds*	Specify frequency of transmission of CDP updates. The default is 60 seconds.
cdp holdtime *seconds*	Specify the amount of time a receiving device should hold the information sent by your device before discarding it. The default hold time is 180 seconds.

WARNING	Ensure that your **cdp timer** setting does not cause excessive network traffic by being set too low. The default, 60 seconds, should be sufficient for most networks.

CDP packets are sent with time-to-live, or hold time, that is nonzero after an interface is enabled and a hold time of 0 immediately before an interface is idled down. The CDP hold time must be set to a higher number of seconds than the time between CDP transmissions, which you set by using the **cdp timer** command.

Disabling and Enabling CDP Globally

CDP is enabled by default. To disable CDP and later reenable it, use the following commands in global configuration mode:

no cdp run

cdp run

Disabling and Enabling CDP on an Interface

CDP is enabled by default on the router and is also enabled by default on all supported interfaces to send and receive CDP information. To disable and later reenable CDP on an interface, use the following commands in interface configuration mode:

Command	Description
no cdp enable	Disable CDP on an interface.
cdp enable	Enable CDP on an interface.

Monitoring and Maintaining CDP

To monitor and maintain CDP on your device, use the following commands in privileged EXEC mode:

Command	Description
clear cdp counters	Reset the traffic counters to zero.
clear cdp table	Delete the CDP table of information about neighbors.
show cdp	Display global information such as frequency of transmissions and the hold time for packets being transmitted.
show cdp entry *entry-name* [**protocol** | **version**]	Display information about a specific neighbor. Display can be limited to protocol or version information.
show cdp interface	Display information about interfaces on which CDP is enabled.

You use the **show cdp neighbors** command to display information about the networks directly connected to the router, as shown in Figure 5-24.

Figure 5-24 *With the* **show cdp neighbors** *commands you can test Layer 2 connectivity between Cisco devices.*

```
routerA#show cdp neighbors
Capability Codes: R - Router, T - Trans Bridge,
          B - Source Route Bridge,
          S - Switch, H - Host, I - IGMP

Device ID       Local Intrfce  Holdtme  Capability Platform  Port ID
routerB.cisco.com   Eth 0       151       R T        AGS       Eth 0
routerB.cisco.com   Ser 0       165       R T        AGS       Ser 3

routerA#show cdp neighbors detail
-----------------------
Device ID: routerB.cisco.com
Entry address(es):
  IP address: 198.92.68.18
  CLNS address: 490001.1111.1111.1111.00
  Appletalk address: 10.1
Platform: AGS,  Capabilities: Router Trans-Bridge
Interface: Ethernet0,  Port ID (outgoing port): Ethernet0
Holdtime : 143 sec
```

The router at the bottom of Figure 5-22 is not directly connected to the router of the administrator's console. To obtain CDP information about this device, the administrator would need to Telnet to a router directly connected to this target.

Frames formed by CDP provide information about each CDP neighbor device. Notice that for each local port, the display shows the following:

- Neighbor's device ID
- Local port type and number
- Decremental hold time value in seconds
- Neighbor's device capability code
- Hardware platform of the neighbor
- Neighbor's remote port type and number

To see an additional display of the network-layer protocol information, you use the optional **show cdp neighbors detail** command. This can be a useful command for the initial fact gathering as you establish possible troubleshooting targets.

Figure 5-25 shows sample output from the **show cdp entry** command with no limits. Information about the neighbor device.cisco.com is displayed, including device ID, address and protocol, platform, interface, hold time, and version.

Figure 5-25 *If you know the host name of a neighbor, you can list its information exclusively.*

```
Router# show cdp entry device.cisco.com
------------------------
Device ID: device.cisco.com
Entry address(es):
  IP address: 192.168.68.18
  CLNS address: 490001.1111.1111.1111.00
  DECnet address: 10.1
Platform: cisco 4500, Capabilities: Router
Interface: Ethernet0/1, Port ID (outgoing port): Ethernet0
Holdtime : 125 sec
Version :
Cisco Internetwork Operating System Software
IOS (tm) 4500 Software (C4500-J-M), Version 11.2
Copyright  1986-1999 by cisco Systems, Inc.
Compiled Mon 07-Apr-98 19:51 by mregion
```

In Figure 5-26, the CDP table is cleared. The output of the **show cdp neighbors** command shows that all information has been deleted from the table.

Figure 5-26 *Clearing the CDP table can be useful for testing changes you've made to the network.*

```
Router# clear cdp table
CDP-AD: Deleted table entry for neon.cisco.com, interface Ethernet0
CDP-AD: Deleted table entry for neon.cisco.com, interface Serial0
Router# show cdp neighbors
Capability Codes: R - Router, T - Trans Bridge, B - Source Route Bridge
         S - Switch, H - Host, I - IGMP
Device ID    Local Intrfce   Holdtme  Capability Platform Port ID
```

The **show cdp** command, shown in Figure 5-27, displays the current CDP settings.

Figure 5-27 *You can use **show cdp** to view CDP timer values.*

```
Router# show cdp
Global CDP information:
    Sending CDP packets every 60 seconds
    Sending a holdtime value of 180 seconds
```

It's a good idea to practice with CDP on a live network to see how much information you can gather about the Cisco routers on the internetwork.

Working with Cisco Technical Support

When a problem arises that you cannot resolve, contact your router technical support representative. To analyze a problem, your technical support representative will need certain information about the situation and symptoms. It will speed the problem isolation process if you present this data when you contact your representative.

Before gathering any specific data, compile a list of all symptoms that users have reported on the internetwork (such as connections dropping or slow host responsiveness).

Next, gather specific information. Typical information needed to troubleshoot internetworking problems falls into two general categories: information required for any situation and information specific to the topology and problem.

Information always needed by technical support engineers includes the following:

- Configuration listing of all routers involved (obtained by the **show running-config** command, formerly the **write term** command)
- Complete specifications of all routers involved
- Version numbers of software (obtained with the **show version** command) and firmware (obtained with the **show controllers** command) on all routers
- Network topology map, including any suspected back doors
- List of hosts and servers (host and server type, number on network, description of host operating systems implemented)
- List of network layer protocols, versions, and vendors

Specific requirements vary depending on the situation:

- If the problem is a router crash or hang-up, the Cisco Support Engineer (CSE) may want you to provide output from the **show stacks** command. It may also be useful for some situations to provide a core dump—a copy of the output from **write core** or **exception dump**—that contains a full copy of the memory image of the router when it crashed or hung.
- If the problem is lost data or performance problems on the router, the CSE may ask for output from the **show** commands listed in Figure 5-28. Several of these commands have already been covered in this chapter. Examples of the others occur on the next several pages.

Figure 5-28 *CSEs use a variety of **show** commands when assisting you in troubleshooting your network.*

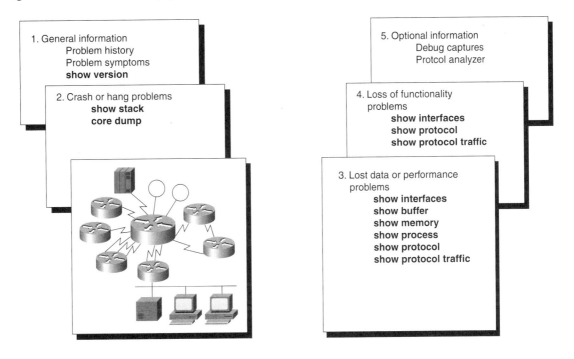

NOTE   Several of the commands of interest to Cisco's Technical Assistance Center (TAC) have
been combined so that they can be obtained when you enter a single privileged command
show tech-support.

- If the problem is loss of functionality—for example, an interface, protocol, or connection setup in a protocol does not operate properly—the CSE may ask for the output from **show** commands including those shown in Figure 5-28.

- For any of the previous situations, the CSE may ask for the output you captured with a Cisco IOS **debug** command or for the trace captured by a protocol analyzer.

Subsequent pages of this chapter present a description and example of many of these troubleshooting resources.

There are several ways of sending your IOS command output to TAC:

Step 1   Send data by electronic mail. Before trying this method, be sure to contact your router technical support representative, especially when transferring binary core dump files.

Step 2   Deliver information via the File Transfer Protocol (FTP) service over the Internet. If your environment supports FTP, you can place your file in the "incoming" directory on the host named ftp.cisco.com.

Step 3   Transfer data via a PC-based communications protocol, such as Kermit. Again, be sure to contact your technical support representative before attempting any transfer.

Step 4   Transfer data by disk or tape.

Step 5   Send information via hard-copy mail or fax.

The **show version** Command

You use the **show version** EXEC command to display the configuration of the system hardware, the software version, the names and sources of configuration files, and the boot images as shown in Figure 5-29.

Figure 5-29 *The **show version** command provides a summary of router IOS and hardware configuration.*

```
Router> show version
GS Software (GS7), Version 10.2
Copyright  1986-1994 by Cisco Systems, Inc.
Compiled Mon 11-Jan-94 14:44
System Bootstrap, Version 4.6(1)
Current date and time is Fri 8-26-1994 2:18:52
Boot date and time is Fri 9-22-1994 11:42:38
Router uptime is 3 weeks, 6 days, 14 hours, 36 minutes
System restarted by power-on
Running default software
Network configuration file is "Router", booted via tftp from 131.108.2.33
RP1 (68040) processor with 16384K bytes of memory.
X.25 software.
Bridging software.
1 Switch Processor.
1 TRIP controller (4 Token Ring).
4 Token Ring/IEEE 802.5 interface.
1 AIP controller (1(ATM))
1 ATM network interface
4096K bytes of flash memory on embedded flash (in RP1).
Configuration register is 0x0
```

The output of the **show version** EXEC command can also provide certain error messages, such as bus error messages. If such error messages appear, report the complete text of this message to your technical support specialist.

The following are significant fields from the output that are useful in a troubleshooting environment:

Field	Description
software version	Information identifying the software by name and version number, including the date and time it was compiled. Always specify the complete version number when reporting a possible software problem. In the sample output, the version number is 10.2.
System Bootstrap, Version	Bootstrap version string.
Current date and time Boot date and time Router uptime is	Current date and time, the date and time the system was last booted, and uptime (the amount of time the system has been up and running).
System restarted by power-on	Also displayed is a log of how the system was last booted, both as a result of normal system startup and of system error. For example, information can be displayed to indicate a bus error that is generally the result of an attempt to access a nonexistent address, as follows: System restarted by bus error at PC 0xC4CA, address 0x210C0C0.
Running default software	If the software was booted over the network, the IP address of the boot host is shown. If the software was loaded from onboard ROM, this line reads "running default software." In addition, the names and sources of the host and network configuration files are shown.
RP1...	The remaining output shows the hardware configuration and any nonstandard software options. The configuration register contents are displayed in hexadecimal notation.

The **show controllers cxbus** Command

You use the **show controllers cxbus** EXEC command to display information about the Switch Processor (SP) CxBus controller on the Cisco 7000 series as shown in Figure 5-30. This command displays information that is specific to the interface hardware and is generally useful for diagnostic tasks performed by technical support personnel only.

Figure 5-30 *You can use* **show controllers cxbus** *to display switch processor information.*

```
Router# show controllers cxbus

Switch Processor 5, hardware version 11.1, microcode version 172.6
  Microcode loaded from system
  512 Kbytes of main memory, 128 Kbytes cache memory
  75 1520 byte buffers, 86 4484 byte buffers
  Restarts: 0 line down, 0 hung output, 0 controller error
CIP 3, hardware version 1.1, microcode version 170.1
  Microcode loaded from system
  CPU utilization 7%, sram 145600/512K, dram 86688/2M
  Interface 24 - Channel 3/0
      43 buffer RX queue threshold, 61 buffer TX queue limit, buffer size 4484
      ift 0007, rql 32, tq 0000 0468, tql 61
      Transmitter delay is 0 microseconds
  Interface 25 - Channel 3/1
      43 buffer RX queue threshold, 61 buffer TX queue limit, buffer size 4484
      ift 0007, rql 34, tq 0000 0000, tql 61
      Transmitter delay is 0 microseconds
                       .
                       .
                       .
```

Some of the significant fields from Figure 5-30 that are useful in a troubleshooting environment are as follows:

Field	Description
hardware version	Version number of the controller.
microcode version	Version number of the controller's internal software (in read-only memory).
CPU utilization	Measure of how busy the CPU is during a given time interval.
Sram	The first value is the number of bytes of SRAM free (that is, not being used by code or data). The second value is the total bytes available of SRAM and is expressed in terms of kilobytes or megabytes. The SRAM is the high-speed static RAM that is used for running the operational code.
Dram	The first value is the number of bytes of DRAM free (that is, not being used by code or data). The second value is the total bytes available of DRAM and is expressed in terms of kilobytes or megabytes. The DRAM is normal dynamic RAM that is used for packet buffers, data, and so on.

The **show controllers cxbus** command on the AGS+ displays information about the ciscoBus controller. The command shows the capabilities of the card and reports controller-related failures.

The **show stacks** Command

The **show stacks** EXEC command is most important to capture facts that you pass along to TAC. When a Cisco router encounters a set of conditions it has not been programmed to handle (for example, during a hardware failure), it generates a stack trace. Stack traces can be displayed by executing the **show stacks** privileged command. The stack is a snapshot of the router that you may be able to capture before the router reload overwrites the stack contents.

The **show stacks** command monitors the stack utilization of processes and interrupt routines. Its display includes the reason for the last system reboot. If the system was reloaded because of a system failure, a saved system stack trace is displayed. This information helps engineers analyzing crashes in the field.

Also recall that the Stack Decoder is one of the tools on CCO that you can use for problem tracking and problem resolution. Stack Decoder decodes the stack trace and creates a symbol file and other information in the trace that usually provides enough information to isolate the cause.

Before Stack Decoder was available, you would send the **trace** to the TAC, which would decode the **trace**, analyze the related data, and compare the results to Cisco's bug tracking database, diagnostic rules, and hardware address information.

Figure 5-31 shows the output of the **show stacks** command.

Figure 5-31 *The **show stacks** command is good for troubleshooting IOS crashes.*

```
Router# show stacks
Minimum process stacks:
Free/Size  Name
 652/1000  Router Init
 726/1000  Init
 744/1000  BGP Open
 686/1200  Virtual Exec
Interrupt level stacks:
Level    Called Free/Size  Name
  1           0 1000/1000  env-flash
  3         738  900/1000  Multiport Communications Interfaces
  5         178  970/1000  Console UART
System was restarted by bus error at PC 0xAD1F4, address 0xD0D0D1A
GS Software (GS3), Version 9.1(0.16), BETA TEST SOFTWARE
Compiled Tue 11-Aug-92 13:27 by jthomas
Stack trace from system failure:
FP: 0x29C158, RA: 0xACFD4
FP: 0x29C184, RA: 0xAD20C
FP: 0x29C1B0, RA: 0xACFD4
FP: 0x29C1DC, RA: 0xAD304
FP: 0x29C1F8, RA: 0xAF774
FP: 0x29C214, RA: 0xAF83E
FP: 0x29C228, RA: 0x3E0CA
FP: 0x29C244, RA: 0x3BD3C
```

Some of the significant fields from the **display** that are useful in a troubleshooting environment are as follows:

Field	Description
System was restarted by…	Gives the reason for the last system reboot.
PC 0xAD1F4	Address at which the failure occurred. This address is also called the program counter (PC).
FP: 0x29C158	Stack frame pointer.
RA: 0xACFD4	Program counter of calling function saved in stack frame. This value is used to trace the flow of software function calls leading to the failure.

After you obtain the stack trace, use the **show version** command (when possible) to identify the software release and version number for reference by technical staff.

Core Dumps

When the router crashes, it can be very useful to obtain a full copy of the memory image (core dump) to analyze the cause of the crash. Core dumps generally are only useful to your router technical support representative.

NOTE   To obtain a core dump, the router must be running IOS Release 9.0 or later.

The **exception dump** global configuration command and **write core** EXEC command are among the most obscure (although useful) diagnostic commands available in your router toolkit. When a router's system software fails, using the **exception dump** command to obtain a core dump is sometimes the only way to determine what happened. The **write core** command is useful if the router is malfunctioning but has not crashed. The **exception dump** command sets up the router to obtain a core dump if and when the next crash occurs.

WARNING   Use the commands discussed here only in coordination with a qualified technical support representative. The resulting binary file must be directed to a specific TFTP server and subsequently interpreted by qualified technical personnel.

The core dump is written to a file named *hostname-core* on your TFTP server, where *hostname* is the name of the router, as assigned using the **hostname** global configuration command.

To obtain a core dump, use the **exception dump** *ip-address* global configuration command. *ip-address* is the address of your TFTP server.

This procedure cannot be guaranteed to work. It can fail if the system is malfunctioning too severely to perform the core dump or if the crash is serious.

If successful, the core dump file will be the size of the memory available on the processor (for example, 16 MB for a CSC/4). For very large size core dumps, you may need to use FTP rather than TFTP to dump the memory image.

Depending on your TFTP server, you may need to create a target file before the router can write to it. You can test this need by attempting to use the TFTP **put** command from a workstation.

Summary

In this chapter, you have been introduced to Cisco's management products and diagnostic tools. Understanding how to use these tools and interpret test results is a requirement for effective troubleshooting. In Chapter 6, "Troubleshooting Sample Exercises," you'll have an opportunity to test your troubleshooting interpretation of the output from these commands.

Chapter 5 Test
Cisco Management and Diagnostic Tools

Estimated Time: 15 minutes

Complete all the exercises to test your knowledge of the materials contained in this chapter. Answers are listed in Appendix A, "Chapter Test Answer Key."

Use the information contained in this chapter to answer the following questions.

Question 5.1

Match the Cisco management tool with the management requirements:

_____	1 TrafficDirector	**A** Need to perform protocol analysis and track utilization trends.
_____	2 VlanDirector	**B** Want to manage virtual network groupings to ensure the most efficient use of bandwidth.
_____	3 CiscoWorks	**C** Need an autodiscovered picture of the network layout.
_____	4 Netsys	**D** Want a graphical representation of what your network will look like once you deploy the new router configurations.

Question 5.2

What diagnostic command do you use to view the number of times a router buffer was available when it was needed?

Question 5.3

What command do you use to determine whether a serial interface is currently up?

Question 5.4

What command do you use to display memory management and error counters for interface cards?

Question 5.5

Where does the router automatically send the output from **debug** commands?

Question 5.6

List at least four commands you may need to use when requested by Cisco technical support.

_____

_____

_____

_____

CHAPTER 6

Troubleshooting Sample Exercises

This chapter presents three unique problems. The problems are not thoroughly defined at the beginning; you should look for any possible faults in these configurations. In each of these instances, you will be given the output from various router commands, each of which depicts typical problems that are encountered by Cisco engineers in the field.

Examine the listings and look for values that indicate potential network or router problems. The answers to this section can be found in Appendix A, "Chapter Test Answer Key."

Exercise 1: A Token Ring Network

Examine the output from the **show interfaces tokenring 0/0** and **show interfaces tokenring 0/1** commands for the Chicago router, looking for any indications of network or connectivity problems. Consider what the possible causes might be. The **show buffers** command output is also given.

```
Chicago# show interfaces tokenring 0/0
TokenRing0/0 is up, line protocol is up
 Hardware is cxBus Token Ring, address is 4000.0279.59f1 (bia 0000.30c0.95c3)
 MTU 4464 bytes, BW 16000 Kbit, DLY 630 usec, rely 255/255, load 1/255
 Encapsulation SNAP, loopback not set, keepalive set (10 sec)
 ARP type: SNAP, ARP Timeout 4:00:00
 Ring speed: 16 Mbps
 Multiring node, Source Route Transparent Bridge capable
 Source bridging enabled, srn 405 bn 1 trn 415 (ring group)
  proxy explorers disabled, spanning explorer enabled, NetBIOS cache disabled
 Group Address: 0x00000000, Functional Address: 0x0080011A
 Ethernet Transit OUI: 0x0000F8
 Last input 0:00:00, output 0:00:00, output hang never
 Last clearing of "show interface" counters 1d02
 Output queue 0/40, 0 drops; input queue 0/120, 1323 drops
 Five minute input rate 11000 bits/sec, 7 packets/sec
 Five minute output rate 8000 bits/sec, 9 packets/sec
    1196542 packets input, 281524050 bytes, 1323 no buffer
    Received 194383 broadcasts, 0 runts, 0 giants
    0 input errors, 0 CRC, 0 frame, 0 overrun, 0 ignored, 0 abor
 1093796 packets output, 183872185 bytes, 0 underruns
    0 output errors, 0 collisions, 0 interface resets, 0 restarts
    1 transitions
```

```
Chicago# show interfaces tokenring 0/1
TokenRing0/1 is up, line protocol is up
 Hardware is cxBus Token Ring, address is 4000.0279.69f1 (bia 0000.30c0.9523)
 MTU 4464 bytes, BW 16000 Kbit, DLY 630 usec, rely 255/255, load 1/255
 Encapsulation SNAP, loopback not set, keepalive set (10 sec)
 ARP type: SNAP, ARP Timeout 4:00:00
 Ring speed: 16 Mbps
 Multiring node, Source Route Transparent Bridge capable
 Source bridging enabled, srn 406 bn 1 trn 415 (ring group)
  proxy explorers disabled, spanning explorer enabled, NetBIOS cache disabled
 Group Address: 0x00000000, Functional Address: 0x0080011A
 Ethernet Transit OUI: 0x0000F8
 Last input 0:00:00, output 0:00:00, output hang never
 Last clearing of "show interface" counters 1d02
 Output queue 0/40, 0 drops; input queue 0/120, 1416 drops
 Five minute input rate 139000 bits/sec, 58 packets/sec
 Five minute output rate 65000 bits/sec, 57 packets/sec
    5391858 packets input, 1599029492 bytes, 1416 no buffer
    Received 208215 broadcasts, 0 runts, 0 giants
    0 input errors, 0 CRC, 0 frame, 0 overrun, 0 ignored, 0 abort
    5455949 packets output, 982243684 bytes, 0 underruns
    0 output errors, 0 collisions, 0 interface resets, 0 restarts
    1 transitions
Chicago# show buffers
Buffer elements:
    500 in free list (500 max allowed)
    18414674 hits, 0 misses, 0 created
Small buffers, 104 bytes (total 189, permanent 120):
    187 in free list (20 min, 250 max allowed)
    8417034 hits, 253 misses, 20 trims, 89 created
Middle buffers, 600 bytes (total 201, permanent 200):
    200 in free list (10 min, 200 max allowed)
    2518690 hits, 8695 misses, 8608 trims, 8609 created
Big buffers, 1524 bytes (total 90, permanent 90):
    90 in free list (5 min, 300 max allowed)
    336741 hits, 0 misses, 0 trims, 0 created
Large buffers, 5024 bytes (total 5, permanent 5):
    5 in free list (0 min, 30 max allowed)
    0 hits, 0 misses, 0 trims, 0 created
Huge buffers, 18024 bytes (total 0, permanent 0):
    0 in free list (0 min, 4 max allowed)
    0 hits, 0 misses, 0 trims, 0 created
8895 failures (0 no memory)
```

List your observations:

_____

_____

_____

_____

_____

_____

_____

_____

_____

List your suggested solutions:

_____

_____

_____

_____

_____

_____

_____

_____

Exercise 2: The Sydney Router

Examine the output of **show processes** commands for the Sydney router, looking for any indications of network or connectivity problems. Consider what the possible causes might be.

```
Sydney> show processes
  CPU utilization for five seconds: 21%; one minute: 55%; five minutes: 63%
   PID   Q  T  PC      Runtime (ms)  Invoked    uSecs   Stacks     TTY  Process
     1   M  E  56E30   4940          52197      94      862/1000   0    BOOTP Server
     2   H  E  4E76E   5259256       19741964   0       1622/2000  0    IPInput
     3   M  E  60E38   17468         656008     26      672/1000   0    TCPTimer
     4   L  E  62082   7688          262        29343   756/1000   0    TCP Protocols
     5   L  E  17FDA   449000        1207462    371     832/1000   0    ARP Input
     6   L  E  1B3F8   0             1          0       936/1000   0    Probe Input
     7   M  E  2C90C   4008          5592       716     840/1000   0    MOP Protocols
     8   M  E  2F0DE   37787184      47630985   0       410/1000   0    Timers
     9   M  E  129FC   2154856       108105     19000   620/1000   0    Net Background
    10   L  E  26406   208           156        1333    644/1000   0    Logger
   240   M  *  0       288           91         3164    1490/2000  2    Virtual Exec
    12   L  E  49EE    33884124      365760     92000   910/1000   0    Check heaps
    13   H  E  12EE0   364552        5212991    69      410/500    0    Net Input
    14   M  T  5216    8934368       3244124    2000    614/1000   0    TTY Background
    15   M  E  4B6CA   0             1          0       874/1000   0    Crash writer
    16   H  E  FCC4A   17333832      53039445   0       800/1000   0    Novell Input
    17   L  E  101816  267340528     15771771   16000   786/1000   0    Novell Router
    18   L  E  1016A6  110780        43660      771     806/1000   0    Novell Response
    19   L  E  1001B2  585201324     28847787   20000   794/1000   0    Novell SAP
    20   H  E  146722  21826772      47976525   0       1236/1500  0    CLNS Input
    21   L  E  14AEC2  3060904       3912386    0       1516/2000  0    ES-IS Routing
    27   M  E  D54C0   4186608       11358133   0       578/1000   0    OSPF Hello
    23   M  E  158B2E  18733152      20115491   0       2314/3000  0    IS-IS Adjacency
    24   M  E  15CB20  267922764     193611901  1000    2142/3000  0    IS-IS Update
    25   L  E  10E29A  1133544       543497     2000    680/1000   0    IP SNMP
    26   M  E  D5250   17722436      2414901    7000    1050/1500  0    OSPF Router
```

```
Sydney> show processes
  CPU utilization for five seconds: 24%; one minute: 53%; five minutes: 63%
    PID Q  T  PC       Runtime(ms)  Invoked    uSecs  Stacks      TTY  Process
    1   M  E  56E30    4940         52197      94     862/1000    0    BOOTP Server
    2   H  E  4E76E    5259280      19742060   0      1622/2000   0    IP Input
    3   M  E  60E38    17468        656012     26     672/1000    0    TCP Timer
    4   L  E  62082    7688         262        29343  756/1000    0    TCP Protocols
    5   L  E  17FDA    449000       1207466    371    832/1000    0    ARP Input
    6   L  E  1B3F8    0            1          0      936/1000    0    Probe Input
    7   M  E  2C90C    4008         5592       716    840/1000    0    MOP Protocols
    8   M  E  2F0DE    37787340     47631166   0      410/1000    0    Timers
    9   M  E  129FC    2154856      108105     19000  620/1000    0    Net Background
    10  L  E  26406    208          156        1333   644/1000    0    Logger
    240 M  *  0        348          102        3411   1490/2000   2    Virtual Exec
    12  L  E  49EE     33884124     365760     92000  910/1000    0    Check heaps
    13  H  E  12EE0    364552       5213010    69     410/500     0    Net Input
    14  M  T  5216     8934396      3244135    2000   614/1000    0    TTY Background
    15  M  E  4B6CA    0            1          0      874/1000    0    Crash writer
    16  H  E  FCC4A    17333896     53039638   0      800/1000    0    Novell Input
    17  L  E  101816   267340720    15771810   16000  786/1000    0    Novell Router
    18  L  E  1016A6   110780       143660     771    806/1000    0    Novell Response
    19  L  S  2960     585203692    28847955   20000  794/1000    0    Novell SAP
    20  H  E  146722   21826992     47976928   0      1236/1500   0    CLNS Input
    21  L  E  14AEC2   3060908      3912403    0      1516/2000   0    ES-IS Routing
    27  M  E  D54C0    4186628      11358172   0      578/1000    0    OSPF Hello
    23  M  E  158B2E   18733228     20115583   0      2314/3000   0    IS-IS Adjacency
    24  M  E  15CB20   267923420    193611946  1000   2142/3000   0    IS-IS Update
    25  L  E  10E29A   1133620      543532     2000   680/1000    0    IP SNMP
    26  M  E  D5250    17722448     2414905    7000   1050/1500   0    OSPF Router
Sydney> show processes
  CPU utilization for five seconds: 84%; one minute: 54%; five minutes: 63%
    PID Q  T  PC       Runtime(ms)  Invoked    uSecs  Stacks      TTY  Process
    1   M  E  56E30    4940         52197      94     862/1000    0    BOOTP Server
    2   H  E  4E76E    5259296      19742120   0      1622/2000   0    IP Input
    3   M  E  60E38    17468        656016     26     672/1000    0    TCP Timer
    4   L  E  62082    7688         262        29343  756/1000    0    TCP Protocols
    5   L  E  17FDA    449004       1207470    371    832/1000    0    ARP Input
    6   L  E  1B3F8    0            1          0      936/1000    0    Probe Input
    7   M  E  2C90C    4008         5592       716    840/1000    0    MOP Protocols
    8   M  E  2F0DE    37787536     47631338   0      410/1000    0    Timers
    9   M  E  129FC    2154888      108107     19000  620/1000    0    Net Background
    10  L  E  26406    208          156        1333   644/1000    0    Logger
    240 M  *  0        408          113        3610   1490/2000   2    Virtual Exec
    12  L  E  49EE     33884124     365760     92000  910/1000    0    Check heaps
    13  H  E  12EE0    364552       5213029    69     410/500     0    Net Input
    14  M  T  5216     8934424      3244146    2000   614/1000    0    TTY Background
    15  M  E  4B6CA    0            1          0      874/1000    0    Crash writer
    16  H  E  FCC4A    17333988     53039913   0      800/1000    0    Novell Input
    17  L  E  101816   267341536    15771891   16000  786/1000    0    Novell Router
    18  L  E  1016A6   110780       143660     771    806/1000    0    Novell Response
    19  L  E  1001B2   585208784    28848275   20000  794/1000    0    Novell SAP
    20  H  E  146722   21827152     47977247   0      1236/1500   0    CLNS Input
    21  L  E  14AEC2   3060928      3912429    0      1516/2000   0    ES-IS Routing
    27  M  E  D54C0    4186632      11358214   0      578/1000    0    OSPF Hello
    23  M  E  158B2E   18733296     20115673   0      2314/3000   0    IS-IS Adjacency
    24  M  E  15CB20   267924124    193611978  1000   2142/3000   0    IS-IS Update
    25  L  E  10E29A   1133620      543532     2000   680/1000    0    IP SNMP
    26  M  E  D5250    17722448     2414905    7000   1050/1500   0    OSPF Router
```

```
Sydney> show processes
CPU utilization for five seconds: 100%; one minute: 66%; five minutes: 73%
 PID  Q  T  PC      Runtime(ms)  Invoked     uSecs   Stacks      TTY  Process
   1  M  E  56E30   4944         52203       94      862/1000    0    BOOTP Server
   2  H  E  4E76E   5259892      19743976    0       1622/2000   0    IP Input
   3  M  E  60E38   17472        656088      26      672/1000    0    TCP Timer
   4  L  E  62082   7688         262         29343   756/1000    0    TCP Protocols
   5  L  E  17FDA   449044       1207596     371     832/1000    0    ARP Input
   6  L  E  1B3F8   0            1           0       936/1000    0    Probe Input
   7  M  E  2C90C   4008         5593        716     840/1000    0    MOP Protocols
   8  M  E  2F0DE   37793392     47636210    0       410/1000    0    Timers
   9  M  E  129FC   2155096      108119      19000   620/1000    0    Net Background
  10  L  E  26406   208          156         1333    644/1000    0    Logger
 240  M  *  0       472          123         3837    1490/2000   2    Virtual Exec
  12  L  E  49EE    33888616     365808      92000   910/1000    0    Check heaps
  13  H  E  12EE0   364612       5213580     69      410/500     0    Net Input
  14  M  T  5216    8935448      3244507     2000    614/1000    0    TTY Background
  15  M  E  4B6CA   0            1           0       874/1000    0    Crash writer
  16  H  E  FCC4A   17336000     53046263    0       800/1000    0    Novell Input
  17  L  E  101816  267413128    15776213    16000   786/1000    0    Novell Router
  18  L  E  1016A6  110784       143668      771     806/1000    0    Novell Response
  19  L  E  1001B2  585276184    28852139    20000   794/1000    0    Novell SAP
  20  H  E  146722  21834784     47986866    0       1236/1500   0    CLNS Input
  21  L  E  14AEC2  3061680      3912937     0       1516/2000   0    ES-IS Routing
  27  M  E  D54C0   4187112      11359382    0       578/1000    0    OSPF Hello
  23  M  E  158B2E  18735328     20117775    0       2314/3000   0    IS-IS Adjacency
  24  M  E  15CB20  267982552    193633767   1000    2142/3000   0    IS-IS Update
  25  L  E  10E29A  1133620      543532      2000    680/1000    0    IP SNMP
  26  M  E  D5250   17727576     2415165     7000    1050/1500   0    OSPF Router
```

List your observations:

_____

_____

_____

_____

_____

List your suggested solutions:

_____

_____

_____

_____

_____

Exercise 3: The Brussels Router

Examine the output of **show interfaces ethernet 0** commands for the Brussels router, looking for any indications of network or connectivity problems. The protocols that were running across this router are TCP/IP, Novell NetWare, and Banyan VINES.

```
Brussels# show interfaces ethernet 0
Ethernet 0 is up, line protocol is up
 Hardware is cBus Ethernet, address is 0000.0c06.3342 (bia 0000.0c06.3342)
 Description: Brussels  - San-Francisco
 Internet address is 156.144.204.36, subnet mask is 255.255.255.224
 MTU 1500 bytes, BW 10000 Kbit, DLY 1000 usec, rely 255/255, load 1/255
 Encapsulation ARPA, loopback not set, keepalive set (10 sec)
 ARP type: ARPA, ARP Timeout 4:00:00
 Last input 0:00:00, output 0:00:00, output hang never
 Last clearing of "show interface" counters 0:00:19
 Output queue 0/75, 0 drops; input queue 17/150, 22 drops
 Five minute input rate 97000 bits/sec, 39 packets/sec
 Five minute output rate 17000 bits/sec, 13 packets/sec
    790 packets input, 268110 bytes, 0 no buffer
    Received 365 broadcasts, 0 runts, 0 giants
    0 input errors, 0 CRC, 0 frame, 0 overrun, 0 ignored, 0 abort
    254 packets output, 40303 bytes, 0 underruns
    0 output errors, 3 collisions, 0 interface resets, 0 restarts

Brussels# show interfaces ethernet 0
Ethernet 0 is up, line protocol is up
 Hardware is cBus Ethernet, address is 0000.0c06.3342 (bia 0000.0c06.3342)
 Description: Brussels  - San-Francisco
 Internet address is 156.144.204.36, subnet mask is 255.255.255.224
 MTU 1500 bytes, BW 10000 Kbit, DLY 1000 usec, rely 255/255, load 1/255
 Encapsulation ARPA, loopback not set, keepalive set (10 sec)
 ARP type: ARPA, ARP Timeout 4:00:00
 Last input 0:00:00, output 0:00:00, output hang never
 Last clearing of "show interface" counters 0:00:29
 Output queue 0/75, 0 drops; input queue 19/150, 22 drops
 Five minute input rate 97000 bits/sec, 37 packets/sec
 Five minute output rate 17000 bits/sec, 13 packets/sec
    1157 packets input, 371851 bytes, 0 no buffer
    Received 496 broadcasts, 0 runts, 0 giants
    0 input errors, 0 CRC, 0 frame, 0 overrun, 0 ignored, 0 abort
    394 packets output, 67669 bytes, 0 underruns
    0 output errors, 5 collisions, 0 interface resets, 0 restarts

    Brussels# show interfaces ethernet 0
Ethernet 0 is up, line protocol is up
 Hardware is cBus Ethernet, address is 0000.0c06.3342 (bia 0000.0c06.3342)
```

```
Description: Brussels  - San-Francisco
Internet address is 156.144.204.36, subnet mask is 255.255.255.224
MTU 1500 bytes, BW 10000 Kbit, DLY 1000 usec, rely 255/255, load 1/255
Encapsulation ARPA, loopback not set, keepalive set (10 sec)
ARP type: ARPA, ARP Timeout 4:00:00
Last input 0:00:00, output 0:00:00, output hang never
Last clearing of "show interface" counters 0:00:39
Output queue 0/75, 0 drops; input queue 2/150, 22 drops
Five minute input rate 95000 bits/sec, 37 packets/sec
Five minute output rate 19000 bits/sec, 15 packets/sec
   1540 packets input, 464209 bytes, 0 no buffer
   Received 614 broadcasts, 0 runts, 0 giants
   0 input errors, 0 CRC, 0 frame, 0 overrun, 0 ignored, 0 abort
   545 packets output, 99222 bytes, 0 underruns
   0 output errors, 5 collisions, 0 interface resets, 0 restarts
```

Brussels# **show interfaces ethernet 0**
```
Ethernet 0 is up, line protocol is up
 Hardware is cBus Ethernet, address is 0000.0c06.3342 (bia 0000.0c06.3342)
 Description: Brussels  - San-Francisco
 Internet address is 156.144.204.36, subnet mask is 255.255.255.224
 MTU 1500 bytes, BW 10000 Kbit, DLY 1000 usec, rely 255/255, load 1/255
 Encapsulation ARPA, loopback not set, keepalive set (10 sec)
 ARP type: ARPA, ARP Timeout 4:00:00
 Last input 0:00:00, output 0:00:00, output hang never
 Last clearing of "show interface" counters 0:00:49
 Output queue 0/75, 0 drops; input queue 14/150, 46 drops
 Five minute input rate 97000 bits/sec, 39 packets/sec
 Five minute output rate 19000 bits/sec, 14 packets/sec
   2020 packets input, 658112 bytes, 0 no buffer
   Received 906 broadcasts, 0 runts, 0 giants
   0 input errors, 0 CRC, 0 frame, 0 overrun, 0 ignored, 0 abort
   687 packets output, 111868 bytes, 0 underruns
   0 output errors, 5 collisions, 0 interface resets, 0 restarts
```

Brussels# **show interfaces ethernet 0**
```
Ethernet 0 is up, line protocol is up
 Hardware is cBus Ethernet, address is 0000.0c06.3342 (bia 0000.0c06.3342)
 Description: Brussels  - San-Francisco
 Internet address is 156.144.204.36, subnet mask is 255.255.255.224
 MTU 1500 bytes, BW 10000 Kbit, DLY 1000 usec, rely 255/255, load 1/255
 Encapsulation ARPA, loopback not set, keepalive set (10 sec)
 ARP type: ARPA, ARP Timeout 4:00:00
 Last input 0:00:00, output 0:00:00, output hang never
 Last clearing of "show interface" counters 0:00:59
 Output queue 0/75, 0 drops; input queue 0/150, 46 drops
 Five minute input rate 95000 bits/sec, 39 packets/sec
 Five minute output rate 19000 bits/sec, 16 packets/sec
   2343 packets input, 738939 bytes, 0 no buffer
   Received 1009 broadcasts, 0 runts, 0 giants
   0 input errors, 0 CRC, 0 frame, 0 overrun, 0 ignored, 0 abort
   829 packets output, 137889 bytes, 0 underruns
   0 output errors, 5 collisions, 0 interface resets, 0 restarts
```

```
Brussels# show interfaces ethernet 0
Ethernet 0 is up, line protocol is up
 Hardware is cBus Ethernet, address is 0000.0c06.3342 (bia 0000.0c06.3342)
 Description: Brussels  - San-Francisco
 Internet address is 156.144.204.36, subnet mask is 255.255.255.224
 MTU 1500 bytes, BW 10000 Kbit, DLY 1000 usec, rely 255/255, load 1/255
 Encapsulation ARPA, loopback not set, keepalive set (10 sec)
 ARP type: ARPA, ARP Timeout 4:00:00
 Last input 0:00:00, output 0:00:01, output hang never
 Last clearing of "show interface" counters 0:01:09
 Output queue 0/75, 0 drops; input queue 15/150, 46 drops
 Five minute input rate 92000 bits/sec, 37 packets/sec
 Five minute output rate 21000 bits/sec, 16 packets/sec
    2695 packets input, 822049 bytes, 0 no buffer
    Received 1105 broadcasts, 0 runts, 0 giants
    0 input errors, 0 CRC, 0 frame, 0 overrun, 0 ignored, 0 abort
    991 packets output, 170540 bytes, 0 underruns
    0 output errors, 5 collisions, 0 interface resets, 0 restarts

Brussels# show interfaces ethernet 0
Ethernet 0 is up, line protocol is up
 Hardware is cBus Ethernet, address is 0000.0c06.3342 (bia 0000.0c06.3342)
 Description: Brussels  - San-Francisco
 Internet address is 156.144.204.36, subnet mask is 255.255.255.224
 MTU 1500 bytes, BW 10000 Kbit, DLY 1000 usec, rely 255/255, load 1/255
 Encapsulation ARPA, loopback not set, keepalive set (10 sec)
 ARP type: ARPA, ARP Timeout 4:00:00
 Last input 0:00:00, output 0:00:00, output hang never
 Last clearing of "show interface" counters 0:01:19
 Output queue 0/75, 0 drops; input queue 25/150, 46 drops
 Five minute input rate 94000 bits/sec, 37 packets/sec
 Five minute output rate 19000 bits/sec, 14 packets/sec
    3199 packets input, 1018909 bytes, 0 no buffer
    Received 1392 broadcasts, 0 runts, 0 giants
    0 input errors, 0 CRC, 0 frame, 0 overrun, 0 ignored, 0 abort
    1125 packets output, 183119 bytes, 0 underruns
    0 output errors, 7 collisions, 0 interface resets, 0 restarts

Brussels# show interfaces ethernet 0
Ethernet 0 is up, line protocol is up
 Hardware is cBus Ethernet, address is 0000.0c06.3342 (bia 0000.0c06.3342)
 Description: Brussels  - San-Francisco
 Internet address is 156.144.204.36, subnet mask is 255.255.255.224
 MTU 1500 bytes, BW 10000 Kbit, DLY 1000 usec, rely 255/255, load 1/255
 Encapsulation ARPA, loopback not set, keepalive set (10 sec)
 ARP type: ARPA, ARP Timeout 4:00:00
 Last input 0:00:00, output 0:00:00, output hang never
 Last clearing of "show interface" counters 0:01:30
 Output queue 0/75, 0 drops; input queue 147/150, 48 drops
 Five minute input rate 92000 bits/sec, 36 packets/sec
 Five minute output rate 19000 bits/sec, 15 packets/sec
    3676 packets input, 1124803 bytes, 0 no buffer
    Received 1663 broadcasts, 0 runts, 0 giants, throttled
    0 input errors, 0 CRC, 0 frame, 0 overrun, 0 ignored, 0 abort
    1286 packets output, 211034 bytes, 0 underruns
    0 output errors, 7 collisions, 0 interface resets, 0 restarts
```

```
Brussels# show interfaces ethernet 0
Ethernet 0 is up, line protocol is up
 Hardware is cBus Ethernet, address is 0000.0c06.3342 (bia 0000.0c06.3342)
 Description: Brussels  - San-Francisco
 Internet address is 156.144.204.36, subnet mask is 255.255.255.224
 MTU 1500 bytes, BW 10000 Kbit, DLY 1000 usec, rely 255/255, load 1/255
 Encapsulation ARPA, loopback not set, keepalive set (10 sec)
 ARP type: ARPA, ARP Timeout 4:00:00
 Last input 0:00:00, output 0:00:00, output hang never
 Last clearing of "show interface" counters 0:01:42
 Output queue 0/75, 0 drops; input queue 79/150, 50 drops
 Five minute input rate 91000 bits/sec, 38 packets/sec
 Five minute output rate 22000 bits/sec, 14 packets/sec
    4110 packets input, 1246502 bytes, 0 no buffer
    Received 1950 broadcasts, 0 runts, 0 giants
    0 input errors, 0 CRC, 0 frame, 0 overrun, 0 ignored, 0 abort
    1449 packets output, 251003 bytes, 0 underruns
    0 output errors, 7 collisions, 0 interface resets, 0 restarts

Brussels# show interfaces ethernet 0
Ethernet 0 is up, line protocol is up
 Hardware is cBus Ethernet, address is 0000.0c06.3342 (bia 0000.0c06.3342)
 Description: Brussels  - San-Francisco
 Internet address is 156.144.204.36, subnet mask is 255.255.255.224
 MTU 1500 bytes, BW 10000 Kbit, DLY 1000 usec, rely 255/255, load 1/255
 Encapsulation ARPA, loopback not set, keepalive set (10 sec)
 ARP type: ARPA, ARP Timeout 4:00:00
 Last input 0:00:00, output 0:00:00, output hang never
 Last clearing of "show interface" counters 0:01:49
 Output queue 0/75, 0 drops; input queue 84/150, 94 drops
 Five minute input rate 90000 bits/sec, 37 packets/sec
 Five minute output rate 21000 bits/sec, 13 packets/sec
    4308 packets input, 1311511 bytes, 0 no buffer
    Received 2065 broadcasts, 0 runts, 0 giants
    0 input errors, 0 CRC, 0 frame, 0 overrun, 0 ignored, 0 abort
    1526 packets output, 264900 bytes, 0 underruns
    0 output errors, 9 collisions, 0 interface resets, 0 restarts

Brussels# show interfaces ethernet 0
Ethernet 0 is up, line protocol is up
 Hardware is cBus Ethernet, address is 0000.0c06.3342 (bia 0000.0c06.3342)
 Description: Brussels  - San-Francisco
 Internet address is 156.144.204.36, subnet mask is 255.255.255.224
 MTU 1500 bytes, BW 10000 Kbit, DLY 1000 usec, rely 255/255, load 1/255
 Encapsulation ARPA, loopback not set, keepalive set (10 sec)
 ARP type: ARPA, ARP Timeout 4:00:00
 Last input 0:00:00, output 0:00:00, output hang never
 Last clearing of "show interface" counters 0:01:59
 Output queue 0/75, 0 drops; input queue 69/150, 94 drops
 Five minute input rate 88000 bits/sec, 35 packets/sec
 Five minute output rate 19000 bits/sec, 13 packets/sec
    4580 packets input, 1421235 bytes, 0 no buffer
    Received 2151 broadcasts, 0 runts, 0 giants
    0 input errors, 0 CRC, 0 frame, 0 overrun, 0 ignored, 0 abort
    1650 packets output, 277728 bytes, 0 underruns
    0 output errors, 14 collisions, 0 interface resets, 0 restarts
```

```
Brussels# show interfaces ethernet 0
Ethernet 0 is up, line protocol is up
 Hardware is cBus Ethernet, address is 0000.0c06.3342 (bia 0000.0c06.3342)
 Description: Brussels  - San-Francisco
 Internet address is 156.144.204.36, subnet mask is 255.255.255.224
 MTU 1500 bytes, BW 10000 Kbit, DLY 1000 usec, rely 255/255, load 1/255
 Encapsulation ARPA, loopback not set, keepalive set (10 sec)
 ARP type: ARPA, ARP Timeout 4:00:00
 Last input 0:00:00, output 0:00:01, output hang never
 Last clearing of "show interface" counters 0:02:09
 Output queue 0/75, 0 drops; input queue 18/150, 94 drops
 Five minute input rate 88000 bits/sec, 35 packets/sec
 Five minute output rate 19000 bits/sec, 13 packets/sec
    4930 packets input, 1543839 bytes, 0 no buffer
    Received 2296 broadcasts, 0 runts, 0 giants
    0 input errors, 0 CRC, 0 frame, 0 overrun, 0 ignored, 0 abort
    1789 packets output, 302572 bytes, 0 underruns
    0 output errors, 17 collisions, 0 interface resets, 0 restarts

Brussels# show interfaces ethernet 0
Ethernet 0 is up, line protocol is up
 Hardware is cBus Ethernet, address is 0000.0c06.3342 (bia 0000.0c06.3342)
 Description: Brussels  - San-Francisco
 Internet address is 156.144.204.36, subnet mask is 255.255.255.224
 MTU 1500 bytes, BW 10000 Kbit, DLY 1000 usec, rely 255/255, load 1/255
 Encapsulation ARPA, loopback not set, keepalive set (10 sec)
 ARP type: ARPA, ARP Timeout 4:00:00
 Last input 0:00:00, output 0:00:01, output hang never
 Last clearing of "show interface" counters 0:02:19
 Output queue 0/75, 0 drops; input queue 24/150, 94 drops
 Five minute input rate 89000 bits/sec, 37 packets/sec
 Five minute output rate 21000 bits/sec, 15 packets/sec
    5472 packets input, 1701308 bytes, 0 no buffer
    Received 2587 broadcasts, 0 runts, 0 giants
    0 input errors, 0 CRC, 0 frame, 0 overrun, 0 ignored, 0 abort
    1961 packets output, 337388 bytes, 0 underruns
    0 output errors, 17 collisions, 0 interface resets, 0 restarts

Brussels# show interfaces ethernet 0
Ethernet 0 is up, line protocol is up
 Hardware is cBus Ethernet, address is 0000.0c06.3342 (bia 0000.0c06.3342)
 Description: Brussels  - San-Francisco
 Internet address is 156.144.204.36, subnet mask is 255.255.255.224
 MTU 1500 bytes, BW 10000 Kbit, DLY 1000 usec, rely 255/255, load 1/255
 Encapsulation ARPA, loopback not set, keepalive set (10 sec)
 ARP type: ARPA, ARP Timeout 4:00:00
 Last input 0:00:00, output 0:00:00, output hang never
 Last clearing of "show interface" counters 0:02:32
 Output queue 0/75, 0 drops; input queue 24/150, 94 drops
 Five minute input rate 89000 bits/sec, 35 packets/sec
 Five minute output rate 19000 bits/sec, 13 packets/sec
    5940 packets input, 1872552 bytes, 0 no buffer
    Received 2762 broadcasts, 0 runts, 0 giants
    0 input errors, 0 CRC, 0 frame, 0 overrun, 0 ignored, 0 abort
    2150 packets output, 359783 bytes, 0 underruns
    0 output errors, 17 collisions, 0 interface resets, 0 restarts
```

```
Brussels# show interfaces ethernet 0
Ethernet 0 is up, line protocol is up
 Hardware is cBus Ethernet, address is 0000.0c06.3342 (bia 0000.0c06.3342)
 Description: Brussels  - San-Francisco
 Internet address is 156.144.204.36, subnet mask is 255.255.255.224
 MTU 1500 bytes, BW 10000 Kbit, DLY 1000 usec, rely 255/255, load 1/255
 Encapsulation ARPA, loopback not set, keepalive set (10 sec)
 ARP type: ARPA, ARP Timeout 4:00:00
 Last input 0:00:00, output 0:00:01, output hang never
 Last clearing of "show interface" counters 0:02:40
 Output queue 0/75, 0 drops; input queue 10/150, 94 drops
 Five minute input rate 89000 bits/sec, 35 packets/sec
 Five minute output rate 19000 bits/sec, 13 packets/sec
    6215 packets input, 1956056 bytes, 0 no buffer
    Received 2891 broadcasts, 0 runts, 0 giants
    0 input errors, 0 CRC, 0 frame, 0 overrun, 0 ignored, 0 abort
    2247 packets output, 384565 bytes, 0 underruns
    0 output errors, 18 collisions, 0 interface resets, 0 restarts

Brussels# show interfaces ethernet 0
Ethernet 0 is up, line protocol is up
 Hardware is cBus Ethernet, address is 0000.0c06.3342 (bia 0000.0c06.3342)
 Description: Brussels  - San-Francisco
 Internet address is 156.144.204.36, subnet mask is 255.255.255.224
 MTU 1500 bytes, BW 10000 Kbit, DLY 1000 usec, rely 255/255, load 1/255
 Encapsulation ARPA, loopback not set, keepalive set (10 sec)
 ARP type: ARPA, ARP Timeout 4:00:00
 Last input 0:00:00, output 0:00:00, output hang never
 Last clearing of "show interface" counters 0:02:49
 Output queue 0/75, 0 drops; input queue 9/150, 108 drops
 Five minute input rate 91000 bits/sec, 37 packets/sec
 Five minute output rate 21000 bits/sec, 11 packets/sec
    6754 packets input, 2114110 bytes, 0 no buffer
    Received 3213 broadcasts, 0 runts, 0 giants
    0 input errors, 0 CRC, 0 frame, 0 overrun, 0 ignored, 0 abort
    2367 packets output, 414671 bytes, 0 underruns
    0 output errors, 18 collisions, 0 interface resets, 0 restarts

Brussels# show interfaces ethernet 0
Ethernet 0 is up, line protocol is up
 Hardware is cBus Ethernet, address is 0000.0c06.3342 (bia 0000.0c06.3342)
 Description: Brussels  - San-Francisco
 Internet address is 156.144.204.36, subnet mask is 255.255.255.224
 MTU 1500 bytes, BW 10000 Kbit, DLY 1000 usec, rely 255/255, load 1/255
 Encapsulation ARPA, loopback not set, keepalive set (10 sec)
 ARP type: ARPA, ARP Timeout 4:00:00
 Last input 0:00:00, output 0:00:01, output hang never
 Last clearing of "show interface" counters 0:02:59
 Output queue 0/75, 0 drops; input queue 1/150, 108 drops
 Five minute input rate 91000 bits/sec, 37 packets/sec
 Five minute output rate 20000 bits/sec, 11 packets/sec
    7107 packets input, 2229593 bytes, 0 no buffer
    Received 3320 broadcasts, 0 runts, 0 giants
    0 input errors, 0 CRC, 0 frame, 0 overrun, 0 ignored, 0 abort
    2511 packets output, 430238 bytes, 0 underruns
    0 output errors, 20 collisions, 0 interface resets, 0 restarts
```

```
Brussels# show interfaces ethernet 0
Ethernet 0 is up, line protocol is up
 Hardware is cBus Ethernet, address is 0000.0c06.3342 (bia 0000.0c06.3342)
 Description: Brussels  - San-Francisco
 Internet address is 156.144.204.36, subnet mask is 255.255.255.224
 MTU 1500 bytes, BW 10000 Kbit, DLY 1000 usec, rely 255/255, load 1/255
 Encapsulation ARPA, loopback not set, keepalive set (10 sec)
 ARP type: ARPA, ARP Timeout 4:00:00
 Last input 0:00:00, output 0:00:01, output hang never
 Last clearing of "show interface" counters 0:03:09
 Output queue 0/75, 0 drops; input queue 0/150, 108 drops
 Five minute input rate 91000 bits/sec, 37 packets/sec
 Five minute output rate 20000 bits/sec, 13 packets/sec
    7473 packets input, 2325272 bytes, 0 no buffer
    Received 3396 broadcasts, 0 runts, 0 giants
    0 input errors, 0 CRC, 0 frame, 0 overrun, 0 ignored, 0 abort
    2678 packets output, 457850 bytes, 0 underruns
    0 output errors, 20 collisions, 0 interface resets, 0 restarts

Brussels# show interfaces ethernet 0
Ethernet 0 is up, line protocol is up
 Hardware is cBus Ethernet, address is 0000.0c06.3342 (bia 0000.0c06.3342)
 Description: Brussels  - San-Francisco
 Internet address is 156.144.204.36, subnet mask is 255.255.255.224
 MTU 1500 bytes, BW 10000 Kbit, DLY 1000 usec, rely 255/255, load 1/255
 Encapsulation ARPA, loopback not set, keepalive set (10 sec)
 ARP type: ARPA, ARP Timeout 4:00:00
 Last input 0:00:00, output 0:00:00, output hang never
 Last clearing of "show interface" counters 0:03:19
 Output queue 0/75, 0 drops; input queue 0/150, 114 drops
 Five minute input rate 92000 bits/sec, 39 packets/sec
 Five minute output rate 22000 bits/sec, 13 packets/sec
    7997 packets input, 2477386 bytes, 0 no buffer
    Received 3699 broadcasts, 0 runts, 0 giants
    0 input errors, 0 CRC, 0 frame, 0 overrun, 0 ignored, 0 abort
    2809 packets output, 488524 bytes, 0 underruns
    0 output errors, 20 collisions, 0 interface resets, 0 restarts

Brussels# show interfaces ethernet 0
Ethernet 0 is up, line protocol is up
 Hardware is cBus Ethernet, address is 0000.0c06.3342 (bia 0000.0c06.3342)
 Description: Brussels  - San-Francisco
 Internet address is 156.144.204.36, subnet mask is 255.255.255.224
 MTU 1500 bytes, BW 10000 Kbit, DLY 1000 usec, rely 255/255, load 1/255
 Encapsulation ARPA, loopback not set, keepalive set (10 sec)
 ARP type: ARPA, ARP Timeout 4:00:00
 Last input 0:00:00, output 0:00:00, output hang never
 Last clearing of "show interface" counters 0:03:30
 Output queue 0/75, 0 drops; input queue 13/150, 114 drops
 Five minute input rate 90000 bits/sec, 37 packets/sec
 Five minute output rate 22000 bits/sec, 13 packets/sec
    8348 packets input, 2595028 bytes, 0 no buffer
    Received 3814 broadcasts, 0 runts, 0 giants
    0 input errors, 0 CRC, 0 frame, 0 overrun, 0 ignored, 0 abort
    2989 packets output, 513535 bytes, 0 underruns
    0 output errors, 21 collisions, 0 interface resets, 0 restarts
```

```
Brussels# show interfaces ethernet 0
Ethernet 0 is up, line protocol is up
 Hardware is cBus Ethernet, address is 0000.0c06.3342 (bia 0000.0c06.3342)
 Description: Brussels  - San-Francisco
 Internet address is 156.144.204.36, subnet mask is 255.255.255.224
 MTU 1500 bytes, BW 10000 Kbit, DLY 1000 usec, rely 255/255, load 1/255
 Encapsulation ARPA, loopback not set, keepalive set (10 sec)
 ARP type: ARPA, ARP Timeout 4:00:00
 Last input 0:00:00, output 0:00:00, output hang never
 Last clearing of "show interface" counters 0:03:39
 Output queue 0/75, 0 drops; input queue 1/150, 114 drops
 Five minute input rate 92000 bits/sec, 35 packets/sec
 Five minute output rate 21000 bits/sec, 15 packets/sec
   8681 packets input, 2714096 bytes, 0 no buffer
   Received 3950 broadcasts, 0 runts, 0 giants
   0 input errors, 0 CRC, 0 frame, 0 overrun, 0 ignored, 0 abort
   3129 packets output, 535835 bytes, 0 underruns
   0 output errors, 21 collisions, 0 interface resets, 0 restarts
```

List your observations:

_____

_____

_____

_____

_____

_____

_____

_____

_____

_____

_____

_____

_____

_____

_____

_____

List your suggested solutions:

_____

_____

_____

_____

_____

Summary

These three examples should give you some practice on how to spot unusual output from a router. Take your time and go through each of these exercises thoroughly. If you are uncertain of what the possible problem may be, just make suggestions and write them down so that you can refer to them to see where you were headed with the troubleshooting after you check the answers. The answers are contained in Appendix A.

The next part of this book, Part II, "Routing and Routed Protocol Troubleshooting," will give you more experience in troubleshooting internetworks that use TCP/IP, NetWare IPX/SPX, and AppleTalk communications. You will also get some additional help on WAN connectivity troubleshooting.

Routing and Routed Protocol Troubleshooting

Troubleshooting TCP/IP Connectivity

The purpose of this chapter is to discuss troubleshooting tips and techniques specific to the TCP/IP protocol suite. The goal is to help you prepare for real-world troubleshooting on the job.

Much of the troubleshooting for networks that use Windows NT/95/98 involves a variety of protocols that may need to work together. You will be better able to perform troubleshooting tasks as you become familiar with these internetworks.

This chapter focuses on TCP/IP operations on the Cisco router. Microsoft protocols that are beyond the scope of this course are covered in Microsoft Resource Kits, MCSE training offerings, and books from various publishers.

TCP/IP Router Diagnostic Tools

Four main diagnostic commands are used on Cisco routers for troubleshooting TCP/IP networks:

- **ping**
- **trace**
- **show**
- **debug**

We begin with a quick look at how to use each of these commands to identify the source of TCP/IP network problems.

The TCP/IP ping Command

The **ping** utility is used as a connectivity test. An IP **ping** packet is actually an Internet Control Message Protocol (ICMP) echo test packet. An IP device that receives an ICMP echo test packet addressed to it responds by echoing back the packet to the source.

NOTE	A loopback **ping** test is one of the first **ping** tests you should perform when connectivity is in question. A loopback **ping** is addressed to 127.0.0.1 (the loopback address) to check the local TCP/IP stack integrity.

NOTE	To abort a **ping** session, you type the escape sequence; the escape sequence is Ctrl-Shift-6, which means you simultaneously press the Ctrl, Shift, and 6 keys.

There are two versions of the **ping** command: the user EXEC **ping** command and the privileged EXEC **ping** command. In the following sections, you'll learn the differences between the two versions.

The User EXEC **ping** Command

To perform a basic check of host reachability and network connectivity, use the **ping** user EXEC command, which has the following syntax:

```
ping [protocol] {host | address}
```

The following are the details of this syntax:

Parameter	Description
protocol (Optional)	Identifies the **ping** protocol to use. The default is IP. Other supported protocols are IPX, AppleTalk, CLNS, DECnet, VINES, and XNS.
host	The host name of the system to **ping**—uses Domain Name System (DNS) lookup to locate the IP address.
address	The IP address of the system to **ping**.

As mentioned earlier, **ping** sends ICMP echo messages. If the communication server receives an ICMP echo message, it sends an ICMP echo reply message to the source of the ICMP echo message.

The user EXEC **ping** feature provides a basic **ping** facility for IP users who do not have system privileges. This feature allows you to perform the simple default **ping** functionality for IP. Only the nonverbose form of the **ping** command is supported for user **ping**s.

If the system cannot map an address for a host name, it returns an "%Unrecognized host or address" error message.

Table 7-1 describes the test characters that the **ping** facility sends.

Table 7-1   *ping test characters.*

Character	Description
!	Receipt of a reply
.	Network server timed out while waiting for a reply
U	Destination unreachable
N	Network unreachable
P	Protocol unreachable
Q	Source quench
M	Could not fragment
?	Unknown packet type

Figure 7-1 shows sample **ping** output when you **ping** a host named fred. Notice that the router resolves the name Fred to the IP address 192.31.7.27.

Figure 7-1   *A successful **ping** confirms Layer 3 connectivity.*

```
cs> ping fred
Type escape sequence to abort.
Sending 5, 100-byte ICMP Echos to 192.31.7.27, timeout is 2 seconds:
!!!!!
Success rate is 100 percent, round-trip min/avg/max = 1/3/4 ms
```

Figure 7-2 shows the **ping** output you get when you **ping** the broadcast address 255.255.255.255.

Figure 7-2   *A local broadcast **ping** receives responses from all directly connected IP devices.*

```
cs> ping 255.255.255.255
Type escape sequence to abort.
Sending 5, 100-byte ICMP Echos to 255.255.255.255, timeout is 2 seconds:
Reply to request 0 from 160.89.48.15 (4 ms)
Reply to request 0 from 160.89.48.10 (4 ms)
Reply to request 0 from 160.89.48.19 (4 ms)
Reply to request 0 from 160.89.49.15 (4 ms)
Reply to request 1 from 160.89.48.15 (4 ms)
Reply to request 1 from 160.89.48.10 (4 ms)
Reply to request 1 from 160.89.48.19 (4 ms)
Reply to request 1 from 160.89.49.15 (4 ms)
Reply to request 2 from 160.89.48.15 (4 ms)
Reply to request 2 from 160.89.48.10 (4 ms)
Reply to request 2 from 160.89.48.19 (4 ms)
Reply to request 2 from 160.89.49.15 (4 ms)
Reply to request 3 from 160.89.48.15 (4 ms)
Reply to request 3 from 160.89.48.10 (4 ms)
Reply to request 3 from 160.89.48.19 (4 ms)
Reply to request 3 from 160.89.49.15 (4 ms)
```

continues

Figure 7-2   *A local broadcast **ping** receives responses from all directly connected IP devices. (Continued)*

```
Reply to request 4 from 160.89.48.15 (4 ms)
Reply to request 4 from 160.89.48.10 (4 ms)
Reply to request 4 from 160.89.48.19 (4 ms)
Reply to request 4 from 160.89.49.15 (4 ms)
```

The Privileged EXEC **ping** Command

To perform a more advanced check of host reachability and network connectivity, you use the **ping** privileged EXEC command. To use this feature, enter **ping** at the command line, and you are prompted for the following fields:

Field	Description
Protocol [ip]:	The default is IP.
Target IP address:	Prompts for the IP address or host name of the destination node.
Repeat count [5]:	The number of **ping** packets to send to the destination address. The default is 5.
Datagram size [100]:	The size of the **ping** packet (in bytes). The default is 100 bytes.
Timeout in seconds [2]:	The timeout interval. The default is 2 (seconds).
Extended commands [n]:	Specifies whether a series of additional commands appears. Many of the following displays and tables show and describe these commands. The default is no.
Source address:	The IP address that appears in the **ping** packet as the source address.
Type of service [0]:	The Internet service quality selection. See RFC 791. The default is 0.
Set DF bit in IP header?	Don't fragment. Specifies that if the packet encounters a node in its path that is configured for a smaller maximum transmission unit (MTU) than the packet's MTU, the packet is to be dropped and an error message is to be sent to the communication server at the packet's source address. If performance problems are encountered on the network, a node configured for a small MTU could be a contributing factor. This feature can be used to determine the smallest MTU in the path. The default is no.
Data pattern [0xABCD]:	Sets a 16-bit hexadecimal data pattern. Default: 0xABCD. Varying the data pattern in this field (to all ones or all zeros, for example) can be useful when you're debugging data sensitivity problems on channel service units/data service units (CSUs/DSUs), or when you're detecting cable-related problems such as crosstalk.

Field	Description
Loose, Strict, Record, Timestamp, Verbose [none]:	Supported Internet header options. The communication server examines the header options to every packet that passes through it. If it finds a packet with an invalid option, the communication server sends an ICMP problem message to the source of the packet and discards the packet. The Internet header options are • Loose • Strict • Record • Timestamp • Verbose The default is none. For more information on these header options, see RFC 791.
Sweep range of sizes [n]:	Allows you to vary the sizes of the echo packets being sent. This capability is useful for determining the minimum sizes of the MTUs configured on the nodes along the path to the destination address. Packet fragmentation contributing to performance problems can then be reduced.
!!!!!	Each exclamation point (!) indicates receipt of a reply. A period (.) indicates that the network server timed out while waiting for a reply. Other characters may appear in the **ping** output display, depending on the protocol type.
Success rate is 100 percent	The percentage of packets successfully echoed back to the communication server. Anything less than 80% is usually considered problematic.
round-trip min/avg/max = 1/3/4 ms	Round-trip travel time intervals for the protocol echo packets, including minimum/average/maximum (in milliseconds).

You can use the extended command mode of the **ping** command to specify the supported Internet header options, as shown in Figure 7-3.

To enter **ping** extended command mode, enter **yes** at the extended commands prompt of the **ping** command. Figure 7-3 shows a sample **ping** extended command sequence.

Figure 7-3 *The extended **ping** gives network administrators more troubleshooting options.*

```
cs# ping
Protocol [ip]:
Target IP address: 192.31.7.27
Repeat count [5]:
Datagram size [100]:
```

continues

Figure 7-3   *The extended **ping** gives network administrators more troubleshooting options. (Continued)*

```
Timeout in seconds [2]:
Extended commands [n]: y
Source address: 131.108.1.1
Type of service [0]:
Set DF bit in IP header? [no]:
Data pattern [0xABCD]:
Loose, Strict, Record, Timestamp, Verbose[none]:
Sweep range of sizes [n]:
Type escape sequence to abort.
Sending 5, 100-byte ICMP Echos to 192.31.7.27, timeout is 2 seconds:
!!!!!
Success rate is 100 percent, round-trip min/avg/max = 1/3/4 ms
```

The TCP/IP trace Command

Another privileged mode command for IP connectivity testing is the **trace** command. **trace** is used to trace the path between two devices by sending a packet with a Time-To-Live (TTL) value of 1 to start. A host can identify the local router, which must discard this "old" packet and send an ICMP time exceeded message back to the source. The source sends additional packets with a gradually increasing TTL value. This should eventually yield a list of routers along the path as well as the round-trip time to reach those routers.

The syntax for the **trace** command is simple:

> **trace** [*destination*]

where

Field	Description
destination	The destination address or host name on the command line. The default parameters for the appropriate protocol are assumed, and the tracing action begins.

The **trace** command works by taking advantage of the error messages generated by communication servers when a datagram exceeds its TTL value. The **trace** command sends out one probe at a time. Each outgoing packet may result in one or two error messages. A time exceeded error message indicates that an intermediate communication server has seen and discarded the probe. A destination unreachable error message indicates that the destination node has received the probe and discarded it because it could not deliver the packet. If the timer goes off before a response comes in, **trace** prints an asterisk (*).

The **trace** command terminates when the destination responds, when the maximum TTL is exceeded, or when the user interrupts the **trace** with the escape sequence. By default, to invoke the escape sequence, you type Ctrl-Shift-6, which means you simultaneously press the Ctrl, Shift, and 6 keys.

To discover the routes the packets follow when traveling to their destinations from the router, use the **trace** privileged EXEC command.

NOTE	There is a known problem with the way some hosts handle an ICMP TTL exceeded message. Some hosts generate an ICMP message but they reuse the TTL of the incoming packet. Because this is zero, the ICMP packets do not make it back. When you trace the path to such a host, you may see a set of TTL values with asterisks (*). Eventually the TTL gets high enough that the ICMP message can get back. For example, if the host is six hops away, **trace** will time out on responses 6 through 11.

Figure 7-4 shows sample **trace** output when a destination host name has been specified.

Figure 7-4 *The **trace** command output shows step-by-step what path through the network is being used to reach a specific destination.*

```
cs# trace ip ABA.NYC.mil
Type escape sequence to abort.
Tracing the route to ABA.NYC.mil (26.0.0.73)
    1 DEBRIS.CISCO.COM (131.108.1.6) 1000 msec 8 msec 4 msec
    2 BARRNET-GW.CISCO.COM (131.108.16.2) 8 msec 8 msec 8 msec
    3 EXTERNAL-A-GATEWAY.STANFORD.EDU (192.42.110.225) 8 msec 4 msec 4 msec
    4 BB2.SU.BARRNET.NET (131.119.254.6) 8 msec 8 msec 8 msec
    5 SU.ARC.BARRNET.NET (131.119.3.8) 12 msec 12 msec 8 msec
    6 MOFFETT-FLD-MB.in.MIL (192.52.195.1) 216 msec 120 msec 132 msec
    7 ABA.NYC.mil (26.0.0.73) 412 msec 628 msec 664 msec
```

The following are the fields shown in Figure 7-4:

Field	Description
1	The sequence number of the communication server in the path to the host.
DEBRIS.CISCO.COM	The host name of this communication server.
131.108.1.61	The Internet address of this communication server.
1000 msec 8 msec 4 msec	The round-trip time for each of the three probes that are sent.

TCP/IP show Commands

The **show** commands provide essential information about interface conditions, protocol status, neighbor reachability, and traffic.

The following sections describe some of the ways these **show** commands can be used to troubleshoot a TCP/IP network:

- **show ip access-list**
- **show ip arp**
- **show ip interface**
- **show ip ospf database**
- **show ip ospf interface**
- **show ip protocols**
- **show ip route**
- s**how ip traffic**

The **show ip access-list** Command

The **show ip access-list** command displays the contents of all current IP access lists. This can help you debug problems that occur due to access or security settings. The command shows the access list number or name, the permit and deny source and destination addresses and wildcard masks, the port or protocol arguments, and packets that the router which matched each of the access list entries displayed in the output from the **show access-lists** command. Figure 7-5 shows sample output from the **show ip access-list** command.

Figure 7-5 *Access list 101 permits TFTP, DNS, and all other non-UDP traffic.*

```
Router# show ip access-list

Extended IP access list 101
        deny udp any any eq ntp
        permit tcp any any
        permit udp any any eq tftp
        permit icmp any any
        permit udp any any eq domain
```

The **show ip arp** Command

The **show ip arp** command displays the entries in the ARP cache for the router. Sometimes you can solve intermittent problems by clearing the ARP cache (using **clear arp-cache**). Figure 7-6 shows sample output from the **show ip arp** command.

Figure 7-6   *The ARP table maps IP addresses to MAC addresses.*

```
Router# show ip arp

Protocol     Address          Age(min)    Hardware Addr    Type    Interface
Internet     171.69.233.22    9           0000.0c59.f892   ARPA    Ethernet0/0
Internet     171.69.233.21    8           0000.0c07.ac00   ARPA    Ethernet0/0
Internet     171.69.233.19    -           0000.0c63.1300   ARPA    Ethernet0/0
Internet     171.69.233.30    9           0000.0c36.6965   ARPA    Ethernet0/0
Internet     172.19.168.11    -           0000.0c63.1300   ARPA    Ethernet0/0
Internet     172.19.168.25    9           0000.0c36.6965   ARPA    Ethernet0/0
```

The following are the significant fields shown in Figure 7-6:

Field	Description
Protocol	Protocol for network address in the Address field.
Address	The network address that corresponds to Hardware Address.
Age (min)	Age, in minutes, of the cache entry. A hyphen (-) means the address is local.
Hardware Addr	LAN hardware address that corresponds to a network address.
Type	Type of encapsulation: • ARPA—Ethernet • SNAP—RFC 1042 • SAP—IEEE 802.3
Interface	Interface to which this address mapping has been assigned.

The **show ip interface** Command

The **show ip interface** command displays the usability status of interfaces. Among other things, this can help you make sure the router interface or subinterface is up and configured with the correct address and subnet mask, to check for routes that may have been learned from the wrong interface or protocol (for example, due to disabled split horizon on a LAN). Figure 7-7 shows sample output from the **show ip interface** command.

Figure 7-7   *The **show ip interface** command gives detailed information on each interface's IP configuration.*

```
Router# show ip interface

Ethernet0 is up, line protocol is up
   Internet address is 192.195.78.24, subnet mask is 255.255.255.240
   Broadcast address is 255.255.255.255
   Address determined by non-volatile memory
   MTU is 1500 bytes
   Helper address is not set
   Secondary address 131.192.115.2, subnet mask 255.255.255.0
   Directed broadcast forwarding is enabled
   Multicast groups joined: 224.0.0.1 224.0.0.2
   Outgoing access list is not set
   Inbound  access list is not set
   Proxy ARP is enabled
   Security level is default
   Split horizon is enabled
   ICMP redirects are always sent
   ICMP unreachables are always sent
   ICMP mask replies are never sent
   IP fast switching is enabled
   IP fast switching on the same interface is disabled
   IP SSE switching is disabled
   Router Discovery is disabled
   IP output packet accounting is disabled
   IP access violation accounting is disabled
   TCP/IP header compression is disabled
   Probe proxy name replies are disabled
```

The following are the fields shown in Figure 7-7:

Field	Description
Ethernet0 is up	If the interface hardware is usable, the interface is marked *up*. For an interface to be usable, both the interface hardware and line protocol must be up.
line protocol is up	If the interface can provide two-way communication, the line protocol is marked *up*. For an interface to be usable, both the interface hardware and line protocol must be up.
Internet address and subnet mask	IP Internet address and subnet mask of the interface.
Broadcast address	Shows the broadcast address.
Address determined by …	Indicates how the IP address of the interface was determined.
MTU	Shows the MTU value set on the interface.
Helper address	Shows a helper address, if one has been set.

Field	Description
Secondary address	Shows a secondary address, if one has been set.
Directed broadcast forwarding	Indicates whether directed broadcast forwarding is enabled.
Multicast groups joined	Indicates the multicast groups of which this interface is a member.
Outgoing access list	Indicates whether the interface has an outgoing access list set.
Inbound access list	Indicates whether the interface has an incoming access list set.
Proxy ARP	Indicates whether proxy ARP is enabled for the interface.
Security level	Specifies the IPSO security level set for this interface.
Split horizon	Indicates split horizon is enabled.
ICMP redirects	Specifies whether redirects will be sent on this interface.
ICMP unreachables	Specifies whether unreachable messages will be sent on this interface.
ICMP mask replies	Specifies whether mask replies will be sent on this interface.
IP fast switching	Specifies whether fast switching has been enabled for this interface. It is generally enabled on serial interfaces, such as this one.
IP SSE switching	Specifies whether IP SSE switching is enabled.
Router Discovery	Specifies whether the discovery process has been enabled for this interface. It is generally disabled on serial interfaces.
IP output packet accounting	Specifies whether IP accounting is enabled for this interface and specifies the threshold (maximum number of entries).
TCP/IP header compression	Indicates whether compression is enabled or disabled.
Probe proxy name	Indicates whether HP probe proxy name replies are generated.

The **show ip ospf database** Command

The **show ip ospf database** command displays detailed Open Shortest Path First (OSPF) information depending on the optional keywords. For example, the **router** keyword displays information about router link states. The **network** keyword displays information about network link states. The **asbr-summary** keyword displays information about autonomous system boundary router link states. The following are some of the most useful keyword variations:

```
show ip ospf [process-id area-id] database [asbr-summary] [link-state-id]
show ip ospf [process-id area-id] database [database-summary]
show ip ospf [process-id] database [external] [link-state-id]
show ip ospf [process-id area-id] database [network][link-state-id]
show ip ospf [process-id area-id] database [router] [link-state-id]
show ip ospf [process-id area-id] database [summary] [link-state-id]
```

Figure 7-8 shows sample output from the **show ip ospf database** command.

Figure 7-8 *The **show ip ospf database** command is useful for verifying that link state updates are being received.*

```
Router# show ip ospf database

OSPF Router with id(190.20.239.66) (Process ID 300)
                Displaying Router Link States(Area 0.0.0.0)
    Link ID        ADV Router      Age     Seq#        Checksum    Link count
 155.187.21.6     155.187.21.6     1731    0x80002CFB   0x69BC      8
 155.187.21.5     155.187.21.5     1112    0x800009D2   0xA2B8      5
 155.187.1.2      155.187.1.2      1662    0x80000A98   0x4CB6      9
 155.187.1.1      155.187.1.1      1115    0x800009B6   0x5F2C      1
 155.187.1.5      155.187.1.5      1691    0x80002BC    0x2A1A      5
 155.187.65.6     155.187.65.6     1395    0x80001947   0xEEE1      4
 155.187.241.5    155.187.241.5    1161    0x8000007C   0x7C70      1
 155.187.27.6     155.187.27.6     1723    0x80000548   0x8641      4
 155.187.70.6     155.187.70.6     1485    0x80000B97   0xEB84      6
                Displaying Net Link States(Area 0.0.0.0)
    Link ID        ADV Router      Age     Seq#        Checksum
 155.187.1.3      192.20.239.66    1245    0x800000EC   0x82E
                Displaying Summary Net Link States(Area 0.0.0.0)
    Link ID        ADV Router      Age     Seq#        Checksum
 155.187.240.0    155.187.241.5    1152    0x80000077   0x7A05
 155.187.241.0    155.187.241.5    1152    0x80000070   0xAEB7
 155.187.244.0    155.187.241.5    1152    0x80000071   0x95CB
```

The following are the fields shown in Figure 7-8:

Field	Description
Ethernet0 is up	If the interface hardware is usable, the interface is marked *up*. For an interface to be usable, both the interface hardware and line protocol must be up.
line protocol is up	If the interface can provide two-way communication, the line protocol is marked *up*. For an interface to be usable, both the interface hardware and line protocol must be up.

Field	Description
Internet address and subnet mask	IP Internet address and subnet mask of the interface.
Broadcast address	Shows the broadcast address.
Address determined by...	Indicates how the IP address of the interface was determined.
MTU	Shows the MTU value set on the interface.
Helper address	Shows a helper address, if one has been set.
Secondary address	Shows a secondary address, if one has been set.
Directed broadcast forwarding	Indicates whether directed broadcast forwarding is enabled.
Multicast groups joined	Indicates the multicast groups of which this interface is a member.
Outgoing access list	Indicates whether the interface has an outgoing access list set.
Inbound access list	Indicates whether the interface has an incoming access list set.
Proxy ARP	Indicates whether proxy ARP is enabled for the interface.
Security level	Specifies the IPSO security level set for this interface.
Split horizon	Indicates split horizon is enabled.
ICMP redirects	Specifies whether redirects will be sent on this interface.
ICMP unreachables	Specifies whether unreachable messages will be sent on this interface.
ICMP mask replies	Specifies whether mask replies will be sent on this interface.
IP fast switching	Specifies whether fast switching has been enabled for this interface. It is generally enabled on serial interfaces, such as this one.
IP SSE switching	Specifies whether IP SSE switching is enabled.
Router Discovery	Specifies whether the discovery process has been enabled for this interface. It is generally disabled on serial interfaces.

continues

Field	Description
IP output packet accounting	Specifies whether IP accounting is enabled for this interface and specifies the threshold (maximum number of entries).
TCP/IP header compression	Indicates whether compression is enabled or disabled.
Probe proxy name	Indicates whether HP probe proxy name replies are generated.

The **show ip ospf interface** Command

The **show ip ospf interface** command displays summary OSPF interface information. Figure 7-9 shows sample output from the **show ip ospf interface** command.

Figure 7-9 *Neighbor information should match on directly connected routers.*

```
Router# show ip ospf interface ethernet 0

Ethernet 0 is up, line protocol is up
Internet Address 131.119.254.202, Mask 255.255.255.0, Area 0.0.0.0
AS 201, Router ID 192.77.99.1, Network Type BROADCAST, Cost: 10
Transmit Delay is 1 sec, State OTHER, Priority 1
Designated Router id 131.119.254.10, Interface address 131.119.254.10
Backup Designated router id 131.119.254.28, Interface addr 131.119.254.28
Timer intervals configured, Hello 10, Dead 60, Wait 40, Retransmit 5
Hello due in 0:00:05
Neighbor Count is 8, Adjacent neighbor count is 2
    Adjacent with neighbor 131.119.254.28  (Backup Designated Router)
    Adjacent with neighbor 131.119.254.10  (Designated Router)
```

The following are the significant fields shown in Figure 7-9:

Field	Description
Ethernet	Status of physical link and operational status of protocol.
Internet Address	Interface IP address, subnet mask, and area address.
AS	Autonomous system number (OSPF process ID), router ID, network type, and link state cost.
Transmit Delay	Transmit delay, interface state, and router priority.
Designated Router	Designated router ID and respective interface IP address.

Field	Description
Backup Designated router	Backup designated router ID and respective interface IP address.
Timer intervals configured	Configuration of timer intervals.
Hello	Number of seconds until next hello packet is sent out this interface.
Neighbor Count	Count of network neighbors and list of adjacent neighbors.

The **show ip protocols** Command

The **show ip protocols** command displays the parameters and current state of the active routing protocol process. This command can help you debug problems with many IP protocols (including Interior Gateway Routing Protocol [IGRP] and Enhanced IGRP), check on update and administrative distance issues, determine whether access lists or routing redistribution is in effect, and identify which routing information sources were used by the router. Figure 7-10 shows sample output from the **show ip protocols** command.

Figure 7-10 *The **show ip protocols** command is useful for verifying routing protocol configuration.*

```
Router# show ip protocols

Routing Protocol is "igrp 109"
  Sending updates every 90 seconds, next due in 44 seconds
  Invalid after 270 seconds, hold down 280, flushed after 630
  Outgoing update filter list for all interfaces is not set
  Incoming update filter list for all interfaces is not set
  Default networks flagged in outgoing updates
  Default networks accepted from incoming updates
  IGRP metric weight K1=1, K2=0, K3=1, K4=0, K5=0
  IGRP maximum hopcount 100
  IGRP maximum metric variance 1
  Redistributing: igrp 109
  Routing for Networks:
    198.92.72.0
  Routing Information Sources:
    Gateway         Distance     Last Update
    198.92.72.18         100     0:56:41
    198.92.72.19         100     6d19
    198.92.72.22         100     0:55:41
    198.92.72.20         100     0:01:04
    198.92.72.30         100     0:01:29
  Distance: (default is 100)
```

continues

Figure 7-10 *show ip protocols is useful for verifying routing protocol configuration. (Continued)*

```
Routing Protocol is "bgp 1878"
  Sending updates every 60 seconds, next due in 0 seconds
  Outgoing update filter list for all interfaces is 1
  Incoming update filter list for all interfaces is not set
  Redistributing: igrp 109
  IGP synchronization is disabled
  Automatic route summarization is enabled
  Neighbor(s):
    Address            FiltIn FiltOut DistIn DistOut Weight RouteMap
    192.108.211.17            1
    192.108.213.89            1
    198.6.255.13             1
    198.92.72.18             1
    198.92.72.19
    198.92.84.17             1
  Routing for Networks:
    192.108.209.0
    192.108.211.0
    198.6.254.0
  Routing Information Sources:
    Gateway         Distance      Last Update
    198.92.72.19         20       0:05:28
  Distance: external 20 internal 200 local 200
```

The following are the significant fields shown in Figure 7-10:

Field	Description
Routing Protocol is "igrp 109"	Specifies the routing protocol used.
Sending updates every 90 seconds	Specifies the time between sending updates.
next due in 44 seconds	Precisely when the next update is due to be sent.
Invalid after 270 seconds	Specifies the value of the invalid parameter.
hold down for 280	Specifies the current value of the hold-down parameter.
flushed after 630	Specifies the time in seconds after which the individual routing information will be thrown (flushed) out.
Outgoing update...	Specifies whether the outgoing filtering list has been set.
Incoming update...	Specifies whether the incoming filtering list has been set.
Default networks	Specifies how these networks will be handled in both incoming and outgoing updates.
IGRP metric	Specifies the value of the K0–K5 metrics, as well as the maximum hop count.
Redistributing	Lists the protocol that is being redistributed.

Field	Description
Routing	Specifies the networks for which the routing process is currently injecting routes.
Routing Information Sources	Lists all the routing sources the Cisco IOS software is using to build its routing table. For each source, you see the following displayed: • IP address • Administrative distance • Time the last update was received from this source

The **show ip route** Command

The **show ip route** command displays the entries in the routing table. You can use this command to determine whether routes appear in the routing table. This can help you determine whether IP routing is running (and able to populate the routing table with entries) and whether the routing protocol is misconfigured on one or several of the routers in the network. This might be the cause of host access problems (for example, if you see the message "host or destination unreachable").

You can include the optional **address** keyword to limit the display to only information about that address. You can include a protocol keyword (**bgp**, **egp**, **eigrp**, **igrp**, **isis**, **ospf**, **rip**, **static**, or **connected**) to limit the display to information about only that routing protocol. To limit the output, use the **summary** keyword, which displays counts of networks but not the whole table. Figure 7-11 shows sample output from the **show ip route** command.

Figure 7-11 *All known routes in the network should be listed in the routing table.*

```
Router# show ip route

Codes: I - IGRP derived, R - RIP derived, O - OSPF derived
       C - connected, S - static, E - EGP derived, B - BGP derived
       * - candidate default route, IA - OSPF inter area route
       E1 - OSPF external type 1 route, E2 - OSPF external type 2 route
Gateway of last resort is 131.119.254.240 to network 129.140.0.0
O E2 150.150.0.0 [160/5] via 131.119.254.6, 0:01:00, Ethernet2
E    192.67.131.0 [200/128] via 131.119.254.244, 0:02:22, Ethernet2
O E2 192.68.132.0 [160/5] via 131.119.254.6, 0:00:59, Ethernet2
O E2 130.130.0.0 [160/5] via 131.119.254.6, 0:00:59, Ethernet2
E    128.128.0.0 [200/128] via 131.119.254.244, 0:02:22, Ethernet2
E    129.129.0.0 [200/129] via 131.119.254.240, 0:02:22, Ethernet2
E    192.65.129.0 [200/128] via 131.119.254.244, 0:02:22, Ethernet2
E    131.131.0.0 [200/128] via 131.119.254.244, 0:02:22, Ethernet2
E    192.75.139.0 [200/129] via 131.119.254.240, 0:02:23, Ethernet2
E    192.16.208.0 [200/128] via 131.119.254.244, 0:02:22, Ethernet2
E    192.84.148.0 [200/129] via 131.119.254.240, 0:02:23, Ethernet2
E    192.31.223.0 [200/128] via 131.119.254.244, 0:02:22, Ethernet2
```

continues

Figure 7-11 *All known routes in the network should be listed in the routing table. (Continued)*

```
E    192.44.236.0 [200/129] via 131.119.254.240, 0:02:23, Ethernet2
E    140.141.0.0 [200/129] via 131.119.254.240, 0:02:22, Ethernet2
E    141.140.0.0 [200/129] via 131.119.254.240, 0:02:23, Ethernet2
```

The following are the significant fields shown in Figure 7-11:

Field	Description
O	Indicates protocol that derived the route. Possible values include the following: • I—IGRP derived • R—RIP derived • O—OSPF derived • C—Connected • S—Static • E—EGP derived • B—BGP derived • i—IS-IS derived
E2	Non-fast-switched packets. However, it does not indicate what path will be used next when forwarding a non-fast-switched packet, except when the paths are equal cost: • IA—OSPF inter-area route • E1—OSPF external type 1 route • E2—OSPF external type 2 route • L1—IS-IS Level 1 route • L2—IS-IS Level 2 route
150.150.0.0	Indicates the address of the remote network.
[160/5]	The first number in the brackets is the administrative distance of the information source; the second number is the metric for the route.
via 131.119.254.6	Specifies the address of the next router to the remote network.
0:01:00	Specifies the last time the route was updated in hours:minutes:seconds format.
Ethernet2	Specifies the interface through which the specified network can be reached.

The **show ip traffic** Command

The **show ip traffic** command displays the statistics that the router has gathered about its IP protocol processes. This includes packets received and sent, and in some cases, the broadcasts and error counts. Included in the error statistics that can help you with debugging are format errors, bad hop count, failed encapsulations, and packets discarded due to no route.

Figure 7-12 shows sample output from the **show ip traffic** command.

Figure 7-12 *The **show ip traffic** command provides a summary of IP overhead traffic on the router.*

```
Router# show ip traffic

IP statistics:
    Rcvd:    98 total, 98 local destination
                   0 format errors, 0 checksum errors, 0 bad hop count
                   0 unknown protocol, 0 not a gateway
                   0 security failures, 0 bad options
          Frags:  0 reassembled, 0 timeouts, 0 too big
                   0 fragmented, 0 couldn't fragment
    Bcast:  38 received, 52 sent
    Sent:  44 generated, 0 forwarded
                   0 encapsulation failed, 0 no route
    ICMP statistics:
    Rcvd:    0 format errors, 0 checksum errors, 0 redirects, 0 unreachable
                   0 echo, 0 echo reply, 0 mask requests, 0 mask replies, 0 quench
                   0 parameter, 0 timestamp, 0 info request, 0 other
    Sent:   0 redirects, 3 unreachable, 0 echo, 0 echo reply
                   0 mask requests, 0 mask replies, 0 quench, 0 timestamp
                   0 info reply, 0 time exceeded, 0 parameter problem
    UDP statistics:
    Rcvd:    56 total, 0 checksum errors, 55 no port
    Sent:    18 total, 0 forwarded broadcasts
    TCP statistics:
        Rcvd:        0 total, 0 checksum errors, 0 no port
    Sent:    0 total
    EGP statistics:
    Rcvd:    0 total, 0 format errors, 0 checksum errors, 0 no listener
        Sent:        0 total
    IGRP statistics:
    Rcvd:    73 total, 0 checksum errors
        Sent:        26 total
    HELLO statistics:
    Rcvd:    0 total, 0 checksum errors
    Sent:    0 total
    ARP statistics:
    Rcvd:    20 requests, 17 replies, 0 reverse, 0 other
    Sent:    0 requests, 9 replies (0 proxy), 0 reverse
    Probe statistics:
    Rcvd:   6 address requests, 0 address replies
    0 proxy name requests, 0 other
    Sent:    0 address requests, 4 address replies (0 proxy)
                           0 proxy name replies
```

The following are the significant fields shown in Figure 7-12:

Field	Description
format errors	A gross error in the packet format, such as an impossible Internet header length.
bad hop count	Occurs when a packet is discarded because its TTL field was decremented to zero.
encapsulation failed	Usually indicates that the router had no ARP request entry and therefore did not send a datagram.
no route	Counted when the Cisco IOS software discards a datagram it did not know how to route.
proxy name reply	Counted when the Cisco IOS software sends an ARP or probe reply on behalf of another host. The display shows the number of probe proxy requests that have been received and the number of responses that have been sent.

TCP/IP debug Commands

The **debug** commands should be used carefully because some of them generate a lot of output for each IP packet processed. Careful consideration should be given in production networks.

The following sections describe these **debug** commands, which can be used to troubleshoot TCP/IP networks:

- **debug ip eigrp**
- **debug ip icmp**
- **debug ip igrp events**
- **debug ip ospf events**
- **debug ip packet**
- **debug ip rip**
- **debug arp**

The **debug ip eigrp** Command

The **debug ip eigrp** command helps you analyze Enhanced IGRP packets sent and received on an interface. Figure 7-13 shows sample output from the **debug ip eigrp** command.

Figure 7-13 *Routing updates are displayed in real-time.*

```
Router# debug ip eigrp

IP-EIGRP: Processing incoming UPDATE packet
IP-EIGRP: Ext 192.168.3.0 255.255.255.0 M 386560 - 256000 130560 SM 360960 - 256000
104960
IP-EIGRP: Ext 192.168.0.0 255.255.255.0 M 386560 - 256000 130560 SM 360960 - 256000
104960
IP-EIGRP: Ext 192.168.3.0 255.255.255.0 M 386560 - 256000 130560 SM 360960 - 256000
104960
IP-EIGRP: 172.24.43.0 255.255.255.0, - do advertise out Ethernet0/1
IP-EIGRP: Ext 172.24.43.0 255.255.255.0 metric 371200 - 256000 115200
IP-EIGRP: 192.135.246.0 255.255.255.0, - do advertise out Ethernet0/1
IP-EIGRP: Ext 192.135.246.0 255.255.255.0 metric 46310656 - 45714176 596480
IP-EIGRP: 172.24.40.0 255.255.255.0, - do advertise out Ethernet0/1
IP-EIGRP: Ext 172.24.40.0 255.255.255.0 metric 2272256 - 1657856 614400
IP-EIGRP: 192.135.245.0 255.255.255.0, - do advertise out Ethernet0/1
IP-EIGRP: Ext 192.135.245.0 255.255.255.0 metric 40622080 - 40000000 622080
IP-EIGRP: 192.135.244.0 255.255.255.0, - do advertise out Ethernet0/1
```

The following are the significant fields shown in Figure 7-13:

Field	Description
IP-EIGRP:	Indicates that this is an IP Enhanced IGRP packet.
Ext	Indicates that the following address is an external destination rather than an internal destination, which would be labeled as Int.
M	Shows the computed metric, which includes SM and the cost between this router and the neighbor. The first number is the composite metric. The next two numbers are the inverse bandwidth and the delay, respectively.
SM	Shows the metric as reported by the neighbor.

The **debug ip icmp** Command

The **debug ip icmp** command helps you determine whether the router is sending or receiving ICMP messages, such as redirect or network unreachable messages. You can use this command when you are troubleshooting an end-to-end connection problem. Figure 7-14 shows sample output from the **debug ip icmp** command.

Figure 7-14 *The **debug ip icmp** command is a useful tool for tracking down problems with failed **ping**s.*

```
Router# debug ip icmp

ICMP: rcvd type 3, code 1, from 10.95.192.4
ICMP: src 10.56.0.202, dst 172.16.16.1, echo reply
ICMP: dst (10.120.1.0) port unreachable rcv from 10.120.1.15
ICMP: src 172.16.12.35, dst 172.16.20.7, echo reply
ICMP: dst (255.255.255.255) protocol unreachable rcv from 10.31.7.21
ICMP: dst (10.120.1.0) port unreachable rcv from 10.120.1.15
ICMP: dst (255.255.255.255) protocol unreachable rcv from 10.31.7.21
ICMP: dst (10.120.1.0) port unreachable rcv from 10.120.1.15
ICMP: src 10.56.0.202, dst 172.16.16.1, echo reply
ICMP: dst (10.120.1.0) port unreachable rcv from 10.120.1.15
ICMP: dst (255.255.255.255) protocol unreachable rcv from 10.31.7.21
ICMP: dst (10.120.1.0) port unreachable rcv from 10.120.1.15
```

The following are the significant fields shown in Figure 7-14:

Field	Description
ICMP:	Indicates that this message describes an ICMP packet.
rcvd type 3	The type field can be one of the following:
	• 0—Echo reply
	• 3—Destination unreachable
	• 4—Source quench
	• 5—Redirect
	• 8—Echo
	• 9—Router Discovery Protocol advertisement
	• 10—Router Discovery Protocol solicitations
	• 11—Time exceeded
	• 12—Parameter problem
	• 13—Timestamp
	• 14—Timestamp reply
	• 15—Information request
	• 16—Information reply
	• 17—Mask request
	• 18—Mask reply

Field	Description
code 1	This field is a code. The meaning of the code depends upon the type field value:

This field is a code. The meaning of the code depends upon the type field value:

- Echo and Echo Reply—The code field is always zero.

- Destination Unreachable—The code field can have the following values:
  - 0—Network unreachable
  - 1—Host unreachable
  - 2—Protocol unreachable
  - 3—Port unreachable
  - 4—Fragmentation needed and DF bit set
  - 5—Source route failed

- Source Quench—The code field is always 0.

- Redirect—The code field can have the following values:
  - 0—Redirect datagrams for the network
  - 1—Redirect datagrams for the host
  - 2—Redirect datagrams for the command mode of service and network
  - 3—Redirect datagrams for the command mode of service and host

- Router Discovery Protocol Advertisements and Solicitations—The code field is always zero.

- Time Exceeded—The code field can have the following values:
  - 0—Time to live exceeded in transit
  - 1—Fragment reassembly time exceeded

- Parameter Problem—The code field can have the following values:
  - 0—General problem
  - 1—Option is missing
  - 2—Option missing, no room to add

- Timestamp and Timestamp Reply—The code field is always zero.

- Information Request and Information Reply—The code field is always zero.

- Mask Request and Mask Reply—The code field is always zero.

continues

Field	Description
from 10.95.192.4	Source address of the ICMP packet.
ICMP:	Indicates that this message describes an ICMP packet.
src 10.5610.120.0.202	The address of the sender of the echo.
dst 172.16.16.1	The address of the receiving router.
echo reply	Indication the router received an echo reply.

The **debug ip igrp** events Command

The **debug ip igrp events** command displays summary information about IGRP routing messages, such as the source and destination of each update, and the number of routes in each update. This command is useful when there are many networks in your routing table and the router is very busy. To avoid flooding the console, use this command instead of the **debug ip igrp transactions** command. Figure 7-15 shows sample output from the **debug ip igrp transactions** command.

Figure 7-15 *You can use the **debug ip igrp transactions** command to display routing update contents.*

```
Router# debug ip igrp transactions
IGRP: received update from 160.89.80.240 on Ethernet
subnet 160.89.66.0, metric 1300 (neighbor 1200)
subnet 160.89.56.0, metric 8676 (neighbor 8576)
subnet 160.89.48.0, metric 1200 (neighbor 1100)
subnet 160.89.50.0, metric 1300 (neighbor 1200)
subnet 160.89.40.0, metric 8676 (neighbor 8576)
network 192.82.152.0, metric 158550 (neighbor 158450)
network 192.68.151.0, metric 1115511 (neighbor 1115411)
network 150.136.0.0, metric 16777215 (inaccessible)
exterior network 129.140.0.0, metric 9676 (neighbor 9576)
exterior network 140.222.0.0, metric 9676 (neighbor 9576)
IGRP: received update from 160.89.80.28 on Ethernet
subnet 160.89.95.0, metric 180671 (neighbor 180571)
subnet 160.89.81.0, metric 1200 (neighbor 1100)
subnet 160.89.15.0, metric 16777215 (inaccessible)
IGRP: sending update to 255.255.255.255 via Ethernet0 (160.89.64.31)
subnet 160.89.94.0, metric=847
IGRP: sending update to 255.255.255.255 via Serial1 (160.89.94.31)
subnet 160.89.80.0, metric=16777215
subnet 160.89.64.0, metric=1100
```

The output shows that the router being debugged has received updates from two other routers on the network. The router at source address 160.89.80.240 sent information about 10 destinations in the update; the router at source address 160.89.80.28 sent information about 3 destinations in its update. The router being debugged also sent updates—in both cases to the broadcast address 255.255.255.255 as the destination address. On the second line the first field refers to the type of destination information: subnet (interior), network (system), or exterior

(exterior). The second field is the Internet address of the destination network. The third field is the metric stored in the routing table and the metric advertised by the neighbor sending the information. An *inaccessible* metric usually means that the neighbor router has put the destination in holddown. The entries show that the router is sending updates that are similar, except that the numbers in parentheses are the source addresses used in the IP header. A metric of 16777215 is inaccessible.

The **debug ip ospf events** Command

The **debug ip ospf events** command displays information about OSPF-related events, such as adjacencies, flooding information, designated router selection, and shortest path first (SPF) calculations. If a router configured for OSPF routing is not seeing an OSPF neighbor on an attached network, you can use this command to make sure this router's OSPF hello and dead intervals and its IP subnet mask match those configured for the neighbor. Figure 7-16 shows sample output from the **debug ip ospf events** command.

Figure 7-16 *Verifying hello packets being received is useful for solving neighbor problems with directly connected routers.*

```
Router# debug ip ospf events

OSPF:hello with invalid timers on interface Ethernet0
hello interval received 10 configured 10
net mask received 255.255.255.0 configured 255.255.255.0
dead interval received 40 configured 30
```

The **debug ip packet** Command

The **debug ip packet** command displays general IP debugging information and IP security option transactions. You can use this command to analyze messages traveling between local and remote hosts when troubleshooting an end-to-end connection problem. IP debugging information includes packets received, generated, and forwarded. Fast-switched packets do not generate messages. An optional *access-list-number* argument lets you limit the scope (and resulting load on the router) caused by this debugging command. You can use this command to analyze messages traveling between local and remote hosts when troubleshooting an end-to-end connection problem. IP debugging information includes packets received, generated, and forwarded. Fast-switched packets do not generate messages. Figure 7-17 shows sample output from the **debug ip packet** command.

Figure 7-17 *The output shows two types of messages that the **debug ip packet** command can produce.*

```
Router# debug ip packet

IP: s=172.16.13.44 (Fddi0), d=10.125.254.1 (Serial2), g=172.16.16.2, forward
IP: s=172.16.1.57 (Ethernet4), d=10.36.125.2 (Serial2), g=172.16.16.2, forward
IP: s=172.16.1.6 (Ethernet4), d=255.255.255.255, rcvd 2
IP: s=172.16.1.55 (Ethernet4), d=172.16.2.42 (Fddi0), g=172.16.13.6, forward
```

continues

Figure 7-17 *The output shows two types of messages that the **debug ip packet** command can produce. (Continued)*

```
IP: s=172.16.89.33 (Ethernet2), d=10.130.2.156 (Serial2), g=172.16.16.2, forward
IP: s=172.16.1.27 (Ethernet4), d=172.16.43.126 (Fddi1), g=172.16.23.5, forward
IP: s=172.16.1.27 (Ethernet4), d=172.16.43.126 (Fddi0), g=172.16.13.6, forward
IP: s=172.16.20.32 (Ethernet2), d=255.255.255.255, rcvd 2
IP: s=172.16.1.57 (Ethernet4), d=10.36.125.2 (Serial2), g=172.16.16.2, access denied
```

The first line of output describes an IP packet that the router forwards, and the third line of output describes a packet that is destined for the router. In the third line of output, rcvd 2 indicates that the router decided to receive the packet.

The following are the fields shown in Figure 7-17:

Field	Description
IP:	Indicates that this is an IP packet.
s = 172.16.13.44 (Fddi0)	Indicates the source address of the packet and the name of the interface that received the packet.
d = 10.125.254.1 (Serial2)	Indicates the destination address of the packet and the name of the interface (in this case, S2) through which the packet is being sent out on the network.
g = 172.16.16.2	Indicates the address of the next-hop gateway.
forward	Indicates that the router is forwarding the packet. If a filter denies a packet, *access denied* replaces *forward*, as shown in the last line of output.

The **debug ip rip** Command

The **debug ip rip** command displays information about Routing Information Protocol (RIP) routing transactions, such as routing table updates sent and received on an interface. Figure 7-18 shows sample output from the **debug ip rip** command.

Figure 7-18 *The **debug ip rip** command displays routing update contents sent and received by the router.*

```
router# debug ip rip
RIP: received update from 160.89.80.28 on Ethernet0
160.89.95.0 in 1 hops
160.89.81.0 in 1 hops
160.89.66.0 in 2 hops
131.108.0.0 in 16 hops (inaccessible)
0.0.0.0 in 7 hop
RIP: sending update to 255.255.255.255 via Ethernet0 (160.89.64.31)
subnet 160.89.94.0, metric 1
131.108.0.0 in 16 hops (inaccessible)
RIP: sending update to 255.255.255.255 via Serial1 (160.89.94.31)
subnet 160.89.64.0, metric 1
subnet 160.89.66.0, metric 3
131.108.0.0 in 16 hops (inaccessible)
default 0.0.0.0, metric 8
```

The output shows that the router being debugged has received updates from one router at source address 160.89.80.28. That router sent information about five destinations in the routing table update. Notice that the fourth destination address in the update—131.108.0.0—is inaccessible because it is more than 15 hops away from the router sending the update. The router being debugged also sent updates, in both cases to broadcast address 255.255.255.255 as the destination. The second line is an example of a routing table update. It shows how many hops a given Internet address is from the router.

The **debug arp** Command

You use the **debug arp** command to check the flow of information on Address Resolution Protocol (ARP) transactions. You use it for problems in which some nodes on a TCP/IP network respond but other nodes do not respond. **debug arp** checks whether the router is sending and receiving ARP requests and replies.

Figure 7-19 shows output from the **debug arp** command. Each line of output represents an ARP packet that the router sent or received.

Figure 7-19 *The fourth output line indicates a problem—the router received an ARP reply for its own address!*

```
router# debug arp
IP ARP: sent req src 131.108.22.7 0000.0c01.e117, dst 131.108.22.96 0000.0000.0000
IP ARP: rcvd rep src 131.108.22.96 0800.2010.b908, dst 131.108.22.7
IP ARP: rcvd req src 131.108.6.10 0000.0c00.6fa2, dst 131.108.6.62
IP ARP: rep filtered src 131.108.22.7 080.5a36.a4 56, dst 255.255.255.255
ffff.ffff.ffff
```

The first line of the output indicates that the router at IP address 131.108.22.7 and MAC address 0000.0c01.e117 sent an ARP request for the MAC address of the host at 131.108.22.96. The series of zeros (0000.0000.0000) following this address indicates that the router is currently unaware of the MAC address.

The second line of the output indicates that the router at IP address 131.108.22.7 received a reply from the host at 131.108.22.96, and the host's MAC address is 0800.2010.b908.

The third line of output indicates that the router received an ARP request from the host at 131.108.6.10 requesting the MAC address for the host at 131.108.6.62.

The fourth line of the output indicates that another host on the network attempted to send the router an ARP reply for the router's address. The router filters meaningless replies. Usually, meaningless replies are caused by a configuration problem. Another station might be incorrectly configured with the router's IP address. This can cause serious internetworking problems and should be investigated.

From this output, you can tell that the router filters improper replies but displays them when the **debug arp** command is issued. You can use the information displayed to troubleshoot.

It's important to use **debug** commands appropriately because, as mentioned earlier, some of them can generate a substantial amount of output for every IP packet processed. For example, on a production network, you should use **debug** when traffic on the IP network is low so other activity on the system is not adversely affected.

To avoid problems, use commands that generate only summary information, for example, **debug ip igrp events**. Remember to turn off the **debug** when you are done with your troubleshooting. You can use **no debug all** as a safe way to turn off all debugging on a router.

Problem Isolation in TCP/IP Networks

Usually, everything does not break at once. Therefore, you can typically troubleshoot by working outward from an operational node to the cause of failure.

Figure 7-20 illustrates steps that can help you isolate the source of a connection problem between a local host and a remote host.

Figure 7-20   *Troubleshooting steps to isolate a connection problem between a local and remote host.*

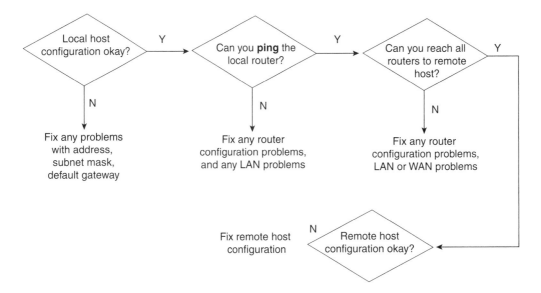

The following list explains these steps in more detail:

Step 1   Check the configuration of the local host.

Does it have a correct address, subnet mask, and default gateway?

Step 2   Use **ping** or **trace** to verify the communication path to the remote host:

— Start with the most local router and then progressively "**ping** out" through the internetwork.

— Use IP addresses, not names, to rule out problems with the DNS.

Step 3   When you discover a router that does not respond to **pings**:

— Examine the router's configuration (by using **show** commands to determine the router state)

— Examine the router's routing table (by using **show ip route** to make sure a path to the remote host is in the table)

— Examine ARP tables (by using **show ip arp** to make sure a node that can reach the remote host is in the table)

— Examine the router's fast-switching route cache (by using **show ip cache** to look for anomalies)

— Check the router's interfaces for any signs of LAN or WAN errors.

— Use protocol analyzers, time domain reflectometers (TDRs) and bit error rate testers (BERTs) to isolate the cause of errors.

Step 4   Check the configuration of the remote host you are trying to reach. Check its address, subnet mask, default gateway, and DNS name.

The following sections describe some real-life IP troubleshooting examples.

Symptom: Users Can Access Some Hosts but Not Others

Many problems in IP environments are caused by addressing and subnet mask problems. In this example, as shown in Figure 7-21, the symptoms are that users can access some hosts but not others. Also, the router and hosts cannot reach certain parts of their own networks.

Figure 7-21 *The network experiences connectivity problems.*

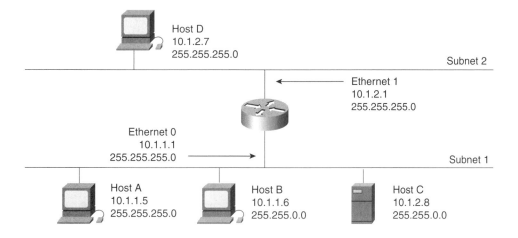

An inexperienced network administrator moved Host C from Subnet 2 to Subnet 1 and changed the subnet mask rather than change the address. The network administrator tested the change by sending a **ping** frame from Host B to Host C. This solution worked; however, will it allow Host A to connect to Host C?

This is a real-life example of IP addressing mistakes found on a Cisco customer's IP network. The Cisco router was correctly configured, but some of the hosts were not. The main symptom was that users could access some hosts, but not others. Also, routers and hosts could not reach certain parts of their own network. (These symptoms are included in Table 7-3, later in this chapter.)

An inexperienced network administrator moved Host C from the top network in the drawing to the bottom network and changed Host C's subnet mask rather than its IP address. The network administrator tested the change by sending a **ping** frame from Host B to Host C, which worked because Host B had a misconfigured subnet mask already. No one had reported problems with Host B because users at Host B did not need to access offnet hosts.

The network administrator was able to successfully send a **ping** frame from Host B to Host C because Host B assumed that Host C was on the same subnet. The significant bits in Host B's address are the same as those in Host C's address. (The subnet mask specifies which bits are significant.) Host B sent an ARP frame, received a reply, and then sent the **ping** frame (that is, ICMP echo) directly to Host C (not via the router).

However, Host A probably cannot connect to Host C. Host A assumes that Host C is on a different network segment because the significant bits in their addresses are different. Host A sends frames destined for Host C to the router. The router, which is correctly configured, sends frames for Host C to Subnet 2. Unfortunately, Host C is no longer physically located on Subnet 2. (Some hosts send ARP frames for remote hosts. If Host A sends an ARP frame for Host C, and Host C responds before the router responds, then Host A will be able to communicate with Host C.)

Host A can connect to Host B and vice versa, even though Host B has an incorrect subnet mask. The incorrect mask does not matter in this case because the third octet of both addresses is the same.

Host D cannot connect to Host C. Host D assumes that Host C is local and sends an ARP frame but does not receive a reply.

Ask yourself the following questions:

- Can Host C reach Host A?

    The answer is yes if by *reach* you mean send an ARP request and receive an ARP reply. Because of the mistake in the subnet mask, Host C will send an ARP request for Host A. Host A will see the ARP request because it is on the same network segment and will respond.

However, can Host C reach Host A by using **ping**? Host C can successfully send a **ping** frame to Host A, but Host A's response will go to the router, so the answer is no. (Actually, one caveat is that some implementations simply reverse source and destination addresses without looking at IP routing tables or comparing IP addresses. If this is the case, then Host A would respond to Host C, which would make troubleshooting more difficult because the results would be confusing!)

- Can Host D reach Host B and vice versa?

  Although Host D can reach Host B, Host B cannot respond (with the caveat just mentioned).

Symptom: Users Cannot Connect When One Redundant Path Is Down

Let's look at another problem scenario. In Figure 7-22, if Serial Z is lost, traffic cannot traverse from Net C1 to Net C2 through Router B1. Major Network Net C becomes a discontiguous network because Router B1 is separating the two Net C subnets (Net C1 and Net C2). Traffic between Router C1 and Router C2 will not get through Router B1 because Router B1 assumes that Net C1 and Net C2 are directly connected.

Figure 7-22 *The redundant path appears to directly affect general communications.*

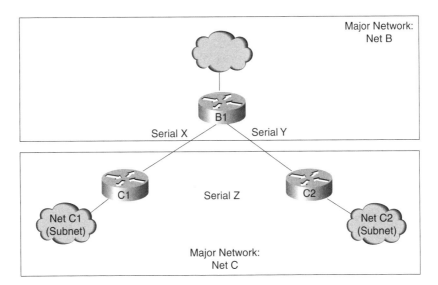

As an alternative, you can use a secondary IP address configuration to ensure that all interfaces are included in the same major network. Another alternative would be to configure a classless routing protocol such as OSPF or Enhanced IGRP.

Troubleshooting IP Internetworking with Windows NT

When you configure with Cisco IOS software, the commands you use depend on which type of traffic requirements on both the Windows NT server and the NT client configurations will pass through your Cisco routers. Table 7-2 shows five variations.

Table 7-2   *Windows NT networking options.*

Traffic Requirement	Router Setup
NetBEUI traffic	Transparent bridging or source-route bridging (SRB)
Transparent bridging or SRB	Data-link switching (DLSw) or remote source-route bridging (RSRB)
Novell type 20 NetBIOS traffic	**ipx type-20-propagation**
A Microsoft WINS server is configured on the segment	Native IP. No special configuration is needed on the router.
UDP encapsulated NetBIOS broadcasts via IP	**ip helper-address** and **ip forward-protocol udp**

Basic troubleshooting for TCP/IP on Windows NT/95/98 combines facts gathered from both a Cisco router (or switch) perspective and facts gathered from a Windows client and server perspective.

Many of the same Cisco IOS tools that you use for diagnosing and correcting any TCP/IP problems can apply to a network containing Microsoft Windows NT/95/98 systems.

The same system that you use as a router console also provides Telnet access so that you can use the command-line TCP/IP tools included with Windows NT/95/98 client or server computers. We will now discuss some of these tools and how they can be used.

Check the local host configuration. Enter a DOS window on the Windows NT/98 host and enter the **ipconfig /all** command. Those using Windows 95 can use the command **wini pcfg** from a DOS window or the run dialog. The results of this command show your TCP/IP address configuration, including the address of the DNS server. Figure 7-23 shows a sample display when this command is issued on a Windows NT workstation.

Figure 7-23   *Output of the IP Config/All command.*

```
C:\TEMP>ipconfig /all

Windows NT IP Configuration

        Host Name . . . . . . . . . : test.rtr.net.test.com.au
        DNS Servers . . . . . . . . : 11.209.24.250
                                      11.209.24.99
        Node Type . . . . . . . . . : Hybrid
        NetBIOS Scope ID. . . . . . :
        IP Routing Enabled. . . . . : No
        WINS Proxy Enabled. . . . . : No
        NetBIOS Resolution Uses DNS : Yes
```

Figure 7-23 *Windows NT servers can be configured for IP RIP routing. (Continued)*

```
Ethernet adapter IBMC1:

        Physical Address. . . . . . : 00-04-AC-90-52-D2
        DHCP Enabled. . . . . . . . : No
        IP Address. . . . . . . . . : 10.72.128.45
        Subnet Mask . . . . . . . . : 255.255.255.0
        Default Gateway . . . . . . : 10.72.128.1
        Primary WINS Server . . . . : 110.2.130.15
        Secondary WINS Server . . . : 110.72.1.4
```

If any IP addresses are incorrect or if no IP address is displayed, determine the correct IP address and edit it or enter it for the local host.

Most incorrect IP address or subnet mask errors appear in Event Viewer. Examine the Event Viewer system log and look for any entry with TCP/IP or Dynamic Host Configuration Protocol (DHCP) as the source.

Read the appropriate entries by double-clicking them. Because DHCP configures TCP/IP remotely, DHCP errors cannot be corrected from the local computer.

Check the router configuration. The commands to use for checking the router configuration with Cisco IOS software are covered elsewhere in this chapter and in Chapters 4, "General Troubleshooting Tools," and 5, "Cisco Management and Diagnostic Tools."

Check whether you can connect by using IP addresses. Use an IP address as a target for the standard TCP/IP commands such as **ping**, **trace** (and **tracert**), and **telnet**.

Check the configurations on the NT server. If you can connect by using an IP address but are unable to connect with one of the legacy Microsoft network target entities, then try to isolate a problem on the Windows NT server configuration.

Other problem areas include NetBIOS support, and a variety of mechanisms to resolve non-IP entities into IP addresses. You can check for these non-IP problems by using the **nbstat** command.

Browsing Problems

To access other devices within the network, Microsoft uses a process called *browsing*. When you browse on a Microsoft NT/95/98 network, you are searching for icon representations of the resources that are available on the network. To use the browsing functions in the NT version 4.0 desktop, or in a Windows 95/98 environment, double-click on the desktop icon for the Network Neighborhood. This opens a graphical user interface (GUI) window that uses a tree structure to display the icons for available domains or workgroups.

Users can click to view the subordinate list of all the network resources that they can access or manipulate. These resources include network-connected servers and specific resources on the servers such as disks, subdirectories, printers, and other shares.

Browsing problems are among the most frequently encountered in NT networks. The browsing problems usually involve resources that have been added, removed, or changed; this alteration of the network's resources is not accurately indicated when the user browses to see the list of what (or who) is currently on the network.

Nonetheless, if the user is unable to browse an NT resource, he or she may still be able to connect to it with some other process or network application.

Although Microsoft intends that NT networks self-administer browsing and that resources add themselves in a "plug and play" manner, administrators tend to focus much of their troubleshooting attention on browsing.

Several of the possible causes of browsing problems are

- Incorrect configuration introduced as the network grows beyond a simple LAN. An organization may find that domain security or some other function of a campus network scale requires reconfiguration on the LAN.

- Inaccurate or incomplete resolution of non-IP entities into IP addresses. Name resolution on Windows NT/95/98 requires proper functioning of the LMHOSTS and HOSTS files as well as the WINS and DNS servers.

- Inappropriate sources for browser update information on the network. A conflict can arise when several NT systems are set up as master browsers and send inconsistent update information that hinders convergence.

Check the Microsoft Web site (www.microsoft.com) for more information and technical support on troubleshooting with Windows.

TCP/IP Symptoms and Problems

Table 7-3 shows common TCP/IP symptoms and possible problems. Using this table, you can identify possible problems and make a plan to verify problem causes and fix the causes. Note that the problem list says "misconfigured access list." Be aware that the access list might be configured correctly. It might be intentional that users can access some hosts or networks, but not others. When troubleshooting possible misconfigured access lists or other filters, use the **show ip route** command to check routing tables. Use the appropriate **debug** commands or a protocol analyzer to check protocol exchanges. Look for information concerning the network with which you are unable to communicate.

Table 7-3   *Common TCP/IP symptoms and possible problems.*

Symptom	Possible Problem
Host cannot access offnet hosts through router.	• No default gateway specified on local host • Misconfigured subnet mask on local host • Router between hosts is down
Host cannot access certain networks through router.	• No default gateway specified on local host • Misconfigured access list • Discontiguous network due to poor design or link failure
Users can access some hosts, but not others.	• Misconfigured subnet mask or address on hosts or router • Misconfigured access list • No default gateway specified on remote host
Some services are available, but others are not.	• Misconfigured extended access list
Users cannot connect when one redundant path is down.	• Discontiguous network due to link failure • Routing has not converged • Misconfigured access list or other routing filters
Router sees duplicate routing updates and packets.	• Bridge or repeater in parallel with router
Certain protocols are being routed, but others are not.	• Misconfigured access list
Router or host cannot reach certain parts of its own network.	• Subnet mask configuration mismatch between router and host • Misconfigured access list • No default gateway specified
Routing is not working when redistribution is used.	• Missing **redistribute** or **default-metric** command • Problem with default administrative distance

TCP/IP Problems and Action Plans

Table 7-4 provides a list of possible problems and some suggested action plans to help isolate the sources of the problems.

Table 7-4   *Suggested action plans.*

Problem	Action Plan
No default gateway specified on local or remote host	• Check routing table of host by using the **netstat -rn** command.
	• If there is no default, use the **route add default** *address* **1** command, where *address* is the IP address of default gateway.
	• To boot with the default gateway already configured, specify the default gateway IP address in host **files/etc/defaultrouter**.
Misconfigured subnet mask on local or remote host or router	• Check hosts files/etc/netmasks and /etc/rc.local.
	• Check host configuration by using **ifconfig -a**.
	• Check router configuration by using **show ip interface**.
Router between hosts is down	• **ping** outward until problem area is isolated.
	• Check and fix router configurations.
	• Check and fix intermediate LAN or WAN problems.
Misconfigured access list or other filter	• **ping** and **trace** to isolate router with misconfigured list.
	• Check routing table by using **show ip route**.
	• Check protocol exchanges (for example, by using **debug ip rip**).
	• Temporarily disable access lists by using **no ip access-group**.
	• Debug access lists that cause problems.
Discontiguous network due to poor design or link failure	• Check routes and how they are learned by using **show ip route**.
	• **trace** or **ping** to determine where traffic stops.
	• Fix topology or reassign addressing (assign segments to same major network).
	• If backup path exists, assign secondary address.
	• If discontiguous network due to link failure, fix link.

Table 7-4   *Suggested action plans. (Continued)*

Problem	Action Plan
Routing has not converged	• Check for problems by using **show ip route**.
Discontiguous network due to poor design or link failure	• Check routes and how they are learned by using **show ip route**. • **trace** or **ping** to determine where traffic stops. • Fix topology or reassign addressing (assign segments to same major network). • If backup path exists, assign secondary address. • If discontiguous network due to link failure, fix link.
Routing has not converged	• Check for problems by using **show ip route**.

To determine whether a default gateway is included in the routing table of a UNIX host, use the **netstat -rn** UNIX command. Look at the output of this command for a default gateway specification. If the default gateway specification is incorrect, or if it is not present, you can change or add a default gateway by using the **route add default** *address* **1** command at the local host. (*address* is the IP address of the default gateway; the value **1** indicates that the specified node is one hop away.) You might need to reboot the host for this change to take effect.

To automate this as part of the boot process, specify the default IP address of the gateway in the /etc/defaultrouter UNIX host file. This filename may be different for your particular version of UNIX. If you are working with a PC or a Macintosh, consult the corresponding documentation to determine how to set the default gateway.

When troubleshooting possible misconfigured access lists or other filters, use the **show ip route** command to check routing tables. Use the appropriate **debug** commands or a protocol analyzer to check protocol exchanges. Look for information concerning the network with which you are unable to communicate. Check the use of access lists on the routers in the path and make sure that a **distribute-list** or **distance** router configuration command does not filter out the route. Temporarily remove **ip access-group** interface configuration commands to disable access lists, and use the **trace** or **ping** command with the Record Route option to determine whether traffic can get through when the access list is removed. After you have determined which access lists are causing the problems, debug the access lists, reapply them, and test to make sure the problems have been solved.

If you suspect that your routing problems are temporary due to slow router convergence, examine routing tables for routes listed as "possibly down," meaning that the routing protocol has not converged. Some routing protocols take a long time to converge. For example, IGRP generally converges more quickly than RIP.

If a router sees duplicate routing updates on different interfaces, and network users experience loss of connections and poor performance, a bridge or repeater may have been placed in parallel with the router such that the router sees other routers on multiple interfaces. You can use the **show ip route** command to examine routes for each interface. Look for paths to the same networks with the same cost on multiple interfaces. Use **debug** commands such as **debug ip igrp events** to examine routing updates, which identifies the source of the routing update and the inbound interface. If you determine that there is a parallel bridge, disable the bridge or configure bridge filters that block routing updates.

When redistributing routes from a routing protocol used in one domain to a routing protocol used in a different domain, problems can arise because the metrics of one routing protocol do not necessarily translate into the metrics of another. For example, the RIP metric is a hop count and the IGRP metric is a combination of five quantities. The **default-metric** or **redistribute** *protocol* **metric** router configuration command can be used to assign an IGRP metric (or other routing protocol metric) to all RIP-derived routes (or routes derived from other protocols).

Because of this unavoidable tampering with dynamic information, carelessly exchanging routing information between different routing protocols can create routing loops, which can seriously degrade network operation. Also, problems can occur when a particular route is, by default, trusted less than another but is actually the preferred route. You should determine the policy for identifying how much you trust routes derived from different domains and use the **distance** router configuration command to vary the level of trust associated with specific routing information, as necessary.

If NT hosts cannot browse offnet hosts through a router, the problem may be that the non-IP target is not resolved correctly to an IP address.

For example, incorrect setup of the network domains can hinder a nonrouted protocol such as NetBEUI when NetBEUI cannot use the broadcasting it requires on the entire network.

By default, a router in the network does not permit the broadcasts of browse lists and other information. The same problems can occur if the Internet separates Windows NT/95/98 domain controllers on a bridged network.

Microsoft offers several resolution functions to address these problems. These functions must be correctly used and can be order dependent. You might find a better overall solution by switching your enterprise network to TCP/IP if it is practical to do so on your internetwork.

NOTE   Much of the troubleshooting information in the rest of this chapter derives from procedures on Microsoft's Technical Support Web site. Refer to www.microsoft.com/support/ for updates and other details.

When you cannot connect to a specified IP target on a network with Windows NT hosts, try to isolate the problem with **ping** tests. Use the **ipconfig /all** DOS command on the other computer to determine current IP address settings.

pinging Your Loopback and Local IP Addresses

The loopback **ping** test checks whether TCP/IP itself is working properly:

```
C:\>ping 127.0.0.1
```

An error at this point would indicate that TCP/IP is not properly installed.

If the loopback **ping** returns successful echoes, try **ping**ing your own host address. Target the local IP address you have obtained from the NT host control panel or **ipconfig** output. An error at this point indicates a possible problem interfacing with the network adapter.

pinging Your Cisco Router

You need to determine whether you can reach a router. You can use a console connection or Telnet to get the router IP interface addresses. Target the address of the Cisco router on the same subnet as the NT host. Then to check routing, target a different IP address (for example, the IP address on a different router interface).

pinging the DNS Server, Default Gateway, and WINS Server

To test whether you are able to communicate with the server, **ping** the DNS server's address that is listed as output from the **ipconfig** command. **ipconfig** also returns the default gateway and the WINS server in use (if any). Check this information, and verify that the listed address for each of these servers is correct.

If you cannot **ping** the address of your server or gateway, the server or gateway either does not exist or has the wrong address entered.

If you cannot connect to a server by using the machine name, you might be having a problem connecting to your WINS server to provide NetBIOS name resolution, or the WINS server may not be resolving names. To determine whether you can communicate with the WINS server, **ping** the server's address.

To change or add a valid IP address, you can edit the TCP/IP properties in Network properties as follows:

Step 1 In the Control Panel, double-click Network.

Step 2 On the Protocols tab, click the TCP/IP protocol, and then click Properties.

Step 3 Click the tab for the appropriate server.

Step 4 If you are adding a server or gateway, click Add. If you are editing an existing server or gateway, click the appropriate server or gateway address, and then click Edit.

Step 5 Type the new server or gateway IP address, and then click OK.

Step 6 Click OK again, and then click Close. You may need to reboot the computer after this step.

Step 7 Retest connectivity to the IP address of the server or gateway by using **ping**.

pinging the Remote Target IP Address

You should try to **ping** the computer you are having trouble connecting to. If you cannot **ping** the computer, the problem might be caused by an incorrect target address or subnet mask. You might need to contact the target system's network administrator or the owner of the computer you are trying to connect to in order to obtain the correct IP address.

Similarly, you might need to verify that other appropriate services are running on the target computer. For example, if you are attempting to Telnet to the remote computer, make sure that the Telnet server service is running on the target computer. To do this, attempt to connect to the remote computer from another host, preferably one on the same subnet as the target computer.

The tracert Tool

The **tracert** tool on an NT host reports each connection a TCP/IP packet crosses on its way to a destination. The syntax for the **tracert** command is

```
tracert [-d] [-h maximum-hops] [-j host-list] [-w timeout] target-name
```

Its parameters are as follows:

Parameter	Description
-d	Specifies to not resolve addresses to host names.
-h *maximum-hops*	Specifies the maximum number of hops to take in searching for the target.

Parameter	Description
-j *host-list*	Specifies a loose source route along the host list.
-w *timeout*	Waits the number of milliseconds specified by *timeout* for each reply.
target-name	The name or IP address of the target host.

Errors that may occur include the asterisk (*) and a message that the request timed out. This message indicates a problem with the router (either the router the packet passed or the first one to return a timeout) or elsewhere on the network.

Another common error is a report that a destination network is unreachable. This error might indicate that there is a proxy or a firewall between your computer and the computer you are targeting as your **tracert** destination.

Checking the Routing Table on a Windows NT System

To verify the routing table on a Windows NT system, type the **route print** command at a command prompt. In this example, the local IP address is 192.1.1.3, and the default gateway is 192.1.1.254. The response should be similar to that shown in Table 7-5.

Table 7-5   *A Windows NT routing table.*

Network Address	Netmask	Gateway Address	Interface	Metric
0.0.0.0	0.0.0.0	192.1.1.254	192.1.1.3	1
192.1.0.0	255.255.0.0	192.1.1.3	192.1.1.3	1
192.1.1.3	255.255.255.255	127.0.0.1	127.0.0.1	1
192.255.255.255	255.255.255.255	192.1.1.3	192.1.1.3	1
127.0.0.1	255.0.0.0	127.0.0.1	127.0.0.1	1
224.0.0.0	224.0.0.0	192.1.1.3	192.1.1.3	1
255.255.255.255	255.255.255.255	192.1.1.3	192.1.1.3	1

Starting from the top of Table 7-5, the entries are

- Default gateway
- Local network
- Local host
- Network broadcast

- Loopback
- Multicast address
- Limited broadcast

Note that the order of the entries in your routing table may vary. If you have TCP/IP bound to more than one network card in your computer, you will have additional entries in your table.

Make sure that one of the table entries is not pointing to an incorrect gateway for the computer you are attempting to target with your connection attempt. To remove an entry in the routing table, type

```
route delete [destination-ip] mask [subnet-mask] [gateway]
```

where *destination-ip* is the IP address of the entry, *subnet-mask* is the subnet mask, and *gateway* is the gateway.

Clearing the Windows NT System ARP Cache

You should try to fix an address problem by clearing the ARP cache. The ARP cache is a list of recently resolved IP address-to-MAC address mappings. If an entry in the ARP cache is incorrect, the TCP/IP packet is sent to the wrong computer. Figure 7-24 shows output from the **arp -a** command, which displays the cache.

Figure 7-24   *The **arp –a** command displays all entries from a Windows NT ARP cache.*

```
C:\>arp -a
Interface: 192.1.1.3 on Interface 2
Internet Address      Physical Address      Type
192.1.1.1             08-00-02-06-ed-20     dynamic
192.1.1.2             08-00-02-0a-a3-10     dynamic
```

To remove entries, use the command **arp -d** [*ip-address*], where *ip-address* is the IP address of the incorrect entry.

If you are using TCP/IP in your network and have verified that the IP settings are correct, the sequence of how to resolve non-IP entities begins with NBT—NetBEUI over TCP/IP. This approach includes checking DNS configuration as well as the HOSTS and LMHOSTS files.

DNS Configuration

If you can connect to the server by using the IP address only, you may be having trouble with your DNS service. If you do not have a DNS server address configured, you cannot communicate on the network via domain names. You need to contact your network administrator to obtain a valid DNS server address. When you have a valid DNS address, you need to update your TCP/IP settings or Dial-Up Networking phone book entry.

The HOSTS File

You should check the HOSTS file for an improper entry. The HOSTS file is usually located in the Winnt\System32\Drivers\Etc folder. The HOSTS file is a text file that you can edit with any text editor (such as Notepad).

Search the file for the host name you are attempting to connect to, and verify that any entries are correct. Remove or correct any improper entries. Make sure that there is a carriage return after the last entry. If not, it will be ignored.

The LMHOSTS File

The LMHOSTS file is usually located in the Winnt\System32\Drivers\Etc folder. The LMHOSTS file is a text file that you can edit with any text editor (such as Notepad). Check the LMHOSTS file for an improper entry. Search the file for the host name you are attempting to connect to, and verify that any entries are correct.

Microsoft recommends that if there are any #include entries, you should temporarily remove them; also, remove any #BEGIN_ALTERNATE to #END_ALTERNATE blocks.

If removing lines in the LMHOSTS file corrects the problem, add back one line at a time until the problem recurs, and then search the appropriate LMHOSTS files pointed to by the line most recently added. This process of elimination may provide a way to isolate the cause of the problem.

Winsock Proxy Problems

The NT system might be configured to use a proxy agent for connections to remote hosts. This use of a proxy can cause problems when the NT system tries to connect to hosts that should not have to go through the proxy.

To determine a Winsock proxy setting, check for a WSP icon in Control Panel. If one exists, try disabling it by clearing the Enable Winsock Proxy. Check the Client check box. After rebooting the NT system, try connecting again.

If the check box was already cleared, click on it to select it. You might need to contact your system administrator for the name of the proxy server or you may be able to examine a computer that can connect and copy its WSP information.

Many Web browsers have built-in support for proxies. If you are attempting to connect with HTTP to a remote Web site, you might need to disable or enable proxy support on the NT system.

Check the documentation provided with your Web browser software for information concerning proxies. For example, if you are using Netscape's rather than Microsoft's browser, check the Web site home.netscape.com.

NOTE   If you must use a NetBEUI environment, the search sequence to resolve an entity is different than if you are using TCP/IP. The NetBEUI approach includes the following sequence of searching for resolution sources: the local HOSTS file, then WINS, then the LMHOSTS file, and finally, any DNS.

Summary

When something goes wrong with your TCP/IP network, you need to use a systematic method to isolate whether the problem is with the software, the hardware, or the network.

Cisco routers have a very rich set of built-in tools to help you. First, try the extended **ping** command, the **trace** command, the **show** commands, and the **debug** commands. You will probably have an easier time with your troubleshooting efforts if you partition the scope of your action plans.

As needed, check that the TCP/IP configurations on the Windows NT/95/98 hosts are working properly. There are supplementary tools to check the network from the vantage of the host.

If TCP/IP configurations are correct, then proceed to check the various resolution functions such as the HOSTS and LMHOSTS file entries. Also check servers such as the WINS and DNS servers.

As you gather the facts, be aware of the problems that can originate from combining Microsoft's nonroutable NetBEUI with the TCP/IP routing protocols.

Often, these problems (such as inaccurate browsing lists) occur as the Windows NT/95/98 network grows and needs more complex security or domain configurations.

An additional problem may come from end users who misconfigure their workstations in a way that conflicts with the addressing, subnet masks, and server roles set up by the network administrator.

If you want to find out more about Windows NT/95/98 networking problems, several books and classes, some offered by Microsoft itself, can supplement the information contained in this chapter. For details see www.microsoft.com.

Chapter 7 Test
Troubleshooting TCP/IP Connectivity

Estimated Time: 15 minutes

Complete all the exercises to test your knowledge of the materials contained in this chapter. Answers are listed in Appendix A, "Chapter Test Answer Key."

Use the information contained in this chapter to answer the following questions.

Question 7.1

What four commands are used to troubleshoot most TCP/IP problems?

a. _____

b. _____

c. _____

d. _____

Question 7.2

Enter the command syntax required to perform the following tasks:

a. Display OSPF information

_____

b. Display usability of an interface

_____

c. Display the count of networks in the IP routing tables

_____

d. Determine whether the router is sending network unreachable messages

_____

e. Display the router's OSPF hello interval setting

_____

Question 7.3

List five ways for Windows networking traffic to be carried across a Cisco router.

_____

_____

_____

_____

_____

Question 7.4

On a Windows NT system, list the commands to

    a.   Display the routing table.

_____

    b.   Clear the ARP cache of all entries.

_____

Troubleshooting Novell Connectivity

This chapter discusses troubleshooting tips and techniques specific to the Novell NetWare protocol suite. The goal is to help you prepare for real-world troubleshooting on the job.

NOTE   This chapter focuses specifically on Novell networks based on Internetwork Packet Exchange (IPX)/Sequenced Packet Exchange (SPX) communications. If you are working on a NetWare 5 network that supports Pure IP (that is, NetWare commands native over Transmission Control Protocol/Internet Protocol [TCP/IP] instead of IPX), refer to Chapter 7, "Troubleshooting TCP/IP Connectivity."

Novell NetWare Router Diagnostic Tools

Three diagnostic commands are primarily used to troubleshoot Novell networks:

- **ping**
- **show**
- **debug**

The following sections focus on the Novell-specific parameters that can be used with these commands.

The IPX ping Command

The IPX **ping** command works only on Cisco routers running Cisco IOS 8.2 or later. By default, the IPX **ping** command sends Cisco-proprietary pings. Novell IPX devices do not respond to this command. To change to the new Novell **ping**, use the **ping-default novell** command. Novell **ping**s conform to the definition in the NetWare Link Services Protocol (NLSP) specification. You do not need to run NLSP to use the Novell **ping**, however. IPXPING.NLM is included in the IPXRTx upgrade for NetWare 3.x and 4.x servers. Figure 8-1 shows sample output from the Novell **ping** command.

Figure 8-1   *Novell **ping**s are useful tools for Layer 3 testing.*

```
Router# ping
Protocol [ip]: ipx
Target IPX address: 211.0000.0c01.f4cf
Repeat count [5]:
Datagram size [100]:
Timeout in seconds [2]:
Verbose [n]:
Novell Standard Echo [n]:y
Type escape sequence to abort.
Sending 5 100-byte IPX echoes to 211.0000.0c01.f4cf, timeout is 2 seconds.
!!!!!
Success rate is 100 percent (0/5)
```

The IPX show Commands

Some of the most common **show** commands used when troubleshooting IPX networks on Cisco routers are

- **show ipx eigrp topology**
- **show ipx interface**
- **show ipx nlsp database**
- **show ipx route**
- **show ipx servers**
- **show ipx traffic**

The **show** commands provide essential information about interface conditions, protocol status, neighbor reachability, and traffic. You can use the commands described in the following sections when troubleshooting IPX networks.

NOTE   More details on these commands can be found in *Cisco IOS Command Reference*.

The **show ipx eigrp topology** Command

The **show ipx eigrp topology** command displays the IPX Enhanced Interior Gateway Routing Protocol (Enhanced IGRP) topology table. A related command is **show ipx eigrp neighbors**, which displays the neighbors discovered by Enhanced IGRP. Figure 8-2 shows sample output from the **show ipx eigrp topology** command.

Figure 8-2   *The EIGRP topology table shows information about successors determined using the feasible distance.*

```
Router# show ipx eigrp topology
IPX EIGRP Topology Table for process 109
Codes: P - Passive, A - Active, U - Update, Q - Query, R - Reply,
r - Reply status
P 42, 1 successors, FD is 0
   via 160.0000.0c00.8ea9 (345088/319488), Ethernet0
P 160, 1 successor via Connected, Ethernet
   via 160.0000.0c00.8ea9 (307200/281600), Ethernet0
P 165, 1 successors, FD is 307200
   via Redistributed (287744/0)
   via 160.0000.0c00.8ea9 (313344/287744), Ethernet0
P 164, 1 successors, flags: U, FD is 200
   via 160.0000.0c00.8ea9 (307200/281600), Ethernet1
   via 160.0000.0c01.2b71 (332800/307200), Ethernet1
P A112, 1 successors, FD is 0
   via Connected, Ethernet2
   via 160.0000.0c00.8ea9 (332800/307200), Ethernet0
P AAABBB, 1 successors, FD is 10003
   via Redistributed (287744/0),
   via 160.0000.0c00.8ea9 (313344/287744), Ethernet0
A A112, 0 successors, 1 replies, state: 0, FD is 0
   via 160.0000.0c01.2b71 (307200/281600), Ethernet1
   via 160.0000.0c00.8ea9 (332800/307200), r, Ethernet1
```

The following are the fields shown in Figure 8-2:

Field	Description	
Codes	State of this topology table entry. Passive and Active refer to the Enhanced IGRP state with respect to this destination; Update, Query, and Reply refer to the type of packet that is being sent:	
	P—Passive	No Enhanced IGRP computations are being performed for this destination.
	A—Active	Enhanced IGRP computations are being performed for this destination.
	U—Update	Indicates that an update packet was sent to this destination.
	Q—Query	Indicates that a query packet was sent to this destination.
	R—Reply	Indicates that a reply packet was sent to this destination.
	r—Reply status	Flag that is set after the Cisco IOS software has sent a query and is waiting for a reply.
42, 160, and so on	Destination IPX network number.	

continues

Field	Description
successors	Number of successors. This number corresponds to the number of next hops in the IPX routing table.
FD	Feasible distance. This value is used in the feasibility condition check. If the neighbor's reported distance (the metric after the slash) is less than the feasible distance, the feasibility condition is met and that path is a feasible successor. When the router determines that it has a feasible successor, it does not have to send a query for that destination.
replies	Number of replies that are still outstanding (that is, have not been received) with respect to this destination. This information appears only when the destination is in Active state.
state	Exact Enhanced IGRP state that this destination is in. It can be the number 0, 1, 2, or 3. This information appears only when the destination is Active.
via	IPX address of the peer who told the Cisco IOS software about this destination. The first *n* of these entries, where *n* is the number of successors, are the current successors. The remaining entries on the list are feasible successors.
(345088/319488)	The first number is the Enhanced IGRP metric that represents the cost to the destination. The second number is the Enhanced IGRP metric that this peer advertised.
Ethernet0	The interface from which this information was learned.

The **show ipx interface** Command

The **show ipx interface** command displays the configured parameters and status of IPX interfaces. Figure 8-3 shows sample output from the **show ipx interface** command.

Figure 8-3 *The **show ipx interface** command provides useful information for verifying and troubleshooting interface configuration problems.*

```
Router# show ipx interface ethernet 1

Ethernet1 is up, line protocol is up
  IPX address is C03.0000.0c05.6030, NOVELL-ETHER [up] line-up, RIPPQ: 0, SAPPQ : 0
  Delay of this Novell network, in ticks is 1
  IPXWAN processing not enabled on this interface.
  IPX SAP update interval is 1 minute(s)
  IPX type 20 propagation packet forwarding is disabled
  Outgoing access list is not set
  IPX Helper access list is not set
  SAP Input filter list is not set
  SAP Output filter list is not set
  SAP Router filter list is not set
  SAP GNS output filter list is not set
```

Figure 8-3 *The **show ipx interface** command provides useful information for verifying and troubleshooting interface configuration problems.(Continued)*

```
Input filter list is not set
Output filter list is not set
Router filter list is not set
Netbios Input host access list is not set
Netbios Input bytes access list is not set
Netbios Output host access list is not set
Netbios Output bytes access list is not set
Update time is 60 seconds
IPX accounting is enabled
IPX fast switching is configured (enabled)
IPX SSE switching is disabled
```

The following are the fields shown in Figure 8-3:

Field	Description
Ethernet1 is…, line protocol is…	Type of interface and whether it is currently active and inserted into the network (up) or inactive and not inserted (down).
IPX address is…	Network and node address of the local router interface, followed by the type of encapsulation configured on the interface and the interface's status.
NOVELL-ETHER	Type of encapsulation being used on the interface, if any.
[up] line-up	Indicates whether IPX routing is enabled or disabled on the interface. *line-up* indicates that IPX routing has been enabled with the **ipx routing** command. *line-down* indicates that it is not enabled. The word in square brackets provides more detail about the status of IPX routing when it is in the process of being enabled or disabled.
RIPPQ	Number of packets in the RIP queue.
SAPPQ	Number of packets in the SAP queue.
Secondary address is …	Address of a secondary network configured on this interface, if any, followed by the type of encapsulation configured on the interface and the interface's status. This line is displayed only if you have configured a secondary address.
Delay of this IPX network, in ticks, …	Value of the ticks field (configured with the **ipx delay** command).

continues

Field	Description
Throughput	Throughput of the interface (configured with the **ipx spx-idle-time** interface configuration command).
link delay	Link delay of the interface (configured with the **ipx link-delay** interface configuration command).
IPXWAN processing...	Indicates whether IPXWAN processing has been enabled on this interface with the **ipx ipxwan** command.
IPX SAP update interval	Indicates the frequency of outgoing SAP updates (configured with the **ipx update interval** command).
IPX type 20 propagation packet forwarding...	Indicates whether forwarding of IPX type 20 propagation packets (used by NetBIOS) is enabled or disabled on this interface, as configured with the **ipx type-20-propagation** command.
Outgoing access list	Indicates whether an access list has been enabled with the **ipx access-group** command.
IPX Helper access list	Number of the broadcast helper list applied to the interface with the **ipx helper-list** command.
SAP Input filter list	Number of the input SAP filter applied to the interface with the **ipx input-sap-filter** command.
SAP Output filter list	Number of the output SAP filter applied to the interface with the **ipx output-sap-filter** command.
SAP Router filter list	Number of the router SAP filter applied to the interface with the **ipx router-sap-filter** command.
SAP GNS output filter list	Number of the Get Nearest Server (GNS) response filter applied to the interface with the **ipx output-gns-filter** command.
Input filter list	Number of the input filter applied to the interface with the **ipx input-network-filter** command.
Output filter list	Number of the output filter applied to the interface with the **ipx output-network-filter** command.

Field	Description
Router filter list	Number of the router entry filter applied to the interface with the **ipx router-filter** command.
Netbios Input host access list	Name of the IPX NetBIOS input host filter applied to the interface with the **ipx netbios input-access-filter host** command.
Netbios Input bytes access list	Name of the IPX NetBIOS input bytes filter applied to the interface with the **ipx netbios input-access-filter bytes** command.
Netbios Output host access list	Name of the IPX NetBIOS output host filter applied to the interface with the **ipx netbios input-access-filter host** command.
Netbios Output bytes access list	Name of the IPX NetBIOS output bytes filter applied to the interface with the **ipx netbios input-access-filter bytes** command.
Update time	How often the Cisco IOS software sends RIP updates, as configured with the **ipx update sap-after-rip** command.
Watchdog spoofing …	Indicates whether watchdog spoofing is enabled or disabled for this interface, as configured with the **ipx watchdog-spoof** command. This information is displayed only on serial interfaces.
IPX accounting	Indicates whether IPX accounting has been enabled with the **ipx accounting** command.
IPX SSE switching	Indicates whether IPX SSE switching is enabled for this interface, as configured with the **ipx route-cache sse** command.

The **show ipx nlsp database** Command

The **show ipx nlsp database** command displays the entries in the link-state database. A related command is **show ipx nlsp neighbors**, which shows the router's NLSP neighbors and their states. Figure 8-4 shows sample output from the **show ipx nlsp database** command.

Figure 8-4   *You can use the **show ipx nlsp database** command to verify NLSP operation.*

```
LSPID                   LSP Seq Num   LSP Checksum   LSP Holdtime   ATT/P/OL
0000.0C00.3097.00-00*  0x00000042    0xC512         699            0/0/0
0000.0C00.3097.06-00*  0x00000027    0x0C27         698            0/0/0
0000.0C02.7471.00-00   0x0000003A    0x4A0F         702            0/0/0
0000.0C02.7471.08-00   0x00000027    0x0AF0         702            0/0/0
0000.0C02.747D.00-00   0x0000002E    0xC489         715            0/0/0
0000.0C02.747D.06-00   0x00000027    0xEEFE         716            0/0/0
```

continues

Figure 8-4 *You can use the **show ipx nlsp database** command to verify NLSP operation. (Continued)*

```
0000.0C02.747D.0A-00   0x00000027   0xFE38      716           0/0/0
0000.0C02.74AB.00-00   0x00000035   0xE4AF      1059          0/0/0
0000.0C02.74AB.0A-00   0x00000027   0x34A4      705           0/0/0
0000.0C06.FBEE.00-00   0x00000038   0x3838      1056          0/0/0
0000.0C06.FBEE.0D-00   0x0000002C   0xD248      1056          0/0/0
0000.0C06.FBEE.0E-00   0x0000002D   0x7DD2      1056          0/0/0
0000.0C06.FBEE.17-00   0x00000029   0x32FB      1056          0/0/0
0000.0C00.AECC.00-00*  0x000000B6   0x62A8      7497          0/0/0
   IPX Area Address: 00000000 00000000
   IPX Mgmt Info 87.0000.0000.0001  Ver 1   Name oscar
   Metric: 45 Lnk 0000.0C00.AECC.06  MTU 1500  Dly 8000  Thru 64K   PPP
   Metric: 20 Lnk 0000.0C00.AECC.02  MTU 1500  Dly 1000  Thru 10000K  802.3 Raw
   Metric: 20 Lnk 0000.0C01.EF90.0C  MTU 1500  Dly 1000  Thru 10000K  802.3 Raw
0000.0C00.AECC.02-00*  0x00000002   0xDA74      3118          0/0/0
   IPX Mgmt Info E0.0000.0c00.aecc  Ver 1   Name Ethernet0
   Metric: 0  Lnk 0000.0C00.AECC.00  MTU 0  Dly 0  Thru 0K  802.3 Raw
0000.0C00.AECC.06-00*  0x00000002   0x5DB9      7494          0/0/0
   IPX Mgmt Info 0.0000.0000.0000  Ver 1   Name Serial0
   Metric: 0  Lnk 0000.0C00.AECC.00  MTU 0  Dly 0  Thru 0K  PPP
   Metric: 1  IPX Ext D001  Ticks 0
   Metric: 1  IPX SVC Second-floor-printer  D001.0000.0000.0001  Sock 1  Type 4
```

The following fields are shown in Figure 8-4:

Field	Description
LSPID	System ID (network number), pseudonode circuit identifier, and fragment number.
LSP Seq Num	Sequence number of this link-state packet (LSP).
LSP Checksum	Checksum of this LSP.
LSP Holdtime	Time until this LSP expires, in hours or seconds.
ATT/P/OL	Indicates which of 3 bits are set. 1 means the bit is set, and 0 means it is not set. ATT is the L2-attached bit. OL is the overload bit. P is the partition repair bit. This bit is not used in NLSP.
IPX Area Address:	Area address of the router advertising the LSP.
IPX Mgmt Info	Management information. For nonpseudonode LSPs, the internal network number is advertised in this field. For pseudonode LSPs, the network number of the associated interface is advertised.
Ver	NLSP version running on the advertising router.
Name	For nonpseudonode LSPs, the name of the router. For pseudonode LSPs, the name (or description, if configured) of the associated interface.

continues

Field	Description
Link Information	Information about the link.
Metric:	NLSP metric (cost) for the link. Links from a pseudonode to real nodes have a cost of 0 so that this link cost is not counted twice.
Lnk	System ID of the adjacent node.
MTU	MTU of the link in bytes. For pseudonode LSPs, the value in this field is always 0.
Dly	Delay of the link in microseconds. For pseudonode LSPs, the value in this field is always 0.
Thru	Throughput of the link in bits per second. For pseudonode LSPs, the value in this field is always 0.
802.3 Raw, Generic LAN	Link media type.
External (RIP) Networks	Information about an external (RIP) network.
Metric:	Received RIP hop count.
IPX Ext	IPX network number.
Ticks	Received RIP tick count.
SAP Services	Information about SAP services.
Metric:	Received SAP hop count.
IPX SVC	Name of the IPX service.
D001.000.0000.0001	IPX address of the server advertising this service.
Sock	Socket number of the service.
Type	Type of service.

The **show ipx route** Command

The **show ipx route** command displays the contents of the IPX routing table. You can enter a network number option to limit the display to just the routing table entry for that network. Figure 8-5 shows sample output from the **show ipx route** command.

Figure 8-5 *All known networks should be listed in the IPX routing table.*

```
Router# show ipx route

Codes: C - Connected primary network,    c - Connected secondary network
             S - Static, F - Floating static, L - Local (internal), W - IPXWAN
             R - RIP, E - EIGRP, N - NLSP, X - External, A - Aggregate
             s - seconds, u - uses
8 Total IPX routes. Up to 1 parallel paths and 16 hops allowed.
No default route known.
L       D40 is the internal network
C       100 (NOVELL-ETHER), Et1
C      7000 (TUNNEL),       Tu1
S       200 via     7000.0000.0c05.6023,         Tu1
R       300 [02/01] via     100.0260.8c8d.e748,   19s, Et1
S      2008 via     7000.0000.0c05.6023,         Tu1
R    CC0001 [02/01] via     100.0260.8c8d.e748,   19s, Et1
```

The following are the fields shown in Figure 8-5:

Field	Description	
Codes	Codes defining how the route was learned:	
	L—Local	Internal network number.
	C—Connected primary network	Directly connected primary network.
	c—connected secondary network	Directly connected secondary network.
	S—Static	Statically defined route via the **ipx route** command.
	R—RIP	Route learned from a RIP update.
	E—EIGRP	Route learned from an Enhanced IGRP update.
	W—IPXWAN	Directly connected route determined via IPXWAN.
8 Total IPX routes	Number of routes in the IPX routing table.	
No parallel paths allowed	Maximum number of parallel paths for which the Cisco IOS software has been configured with the **ipx maximum-paths** command.	
Novell routing algorithm variant in use	Indicates whether the Cisco IOS software is using the IPX-compliant routing algorithms (default).	
Net 1	Network to which the route goes.	

continues

Field	Description
[3/2]	Delay/Metric. Delay is the number of IBM clock ticks (each tick is 1/18 second) reported to the destination network. Metric is the number of hops reported to the same network. Delay is used as the primary routing metric, and the metric (hop count) is used as a tie-breaker.
via network.node	Address of a router that is the next hop to the remote network.
Age	Amount of time (in hours, minutes, and seconds) that has elapsed since information about this network was last received.
Uses	Number of times this network has been looked up in the route table. This field is incremented when a packet is process-switched, even if the packet is eventually filtered and not sent. As such, this field represents a fair estimate of the number of times a route is used.
Ethernet0	Interface through which packets to the remote network will be sent.
(NOVELL-ETHER)	Encapsulation (frame) type. This is shown only for directly connected networks.
is directly connected	Indicates that the network is directly connected to the router.

The **show ipx servers** Command

The **show ipx servers** command displays the IPX servers discovered through Service Advertising Protocol (SAP) advertisements. Figure 8-6 shows sample output from the **show ipx servers** command when NLSP is enabled.

Figure 8-6   *All non-filtered SAPs should be listed in the SAP table.*

```
Router# show ipx servers

Codes: S - Static, P - Periodic, E - EIGRP, N - NLSP, H - Holddown, + = detail
9 Total IPX Servers
Table ordering is based on routing and server info
TypeName                          Net Address                Port   Route Hops   Itf
N+  4 MERLIN1-VIA-E03             E03E03.0002.0004.0006:0451  4/03       4        Et0
N+  4 merlin                      E03E03.0002.0004.0006:0451  4/03       3        Et0
N+  4 merlin 123456789012345      E03E03.0002.0004.0006:0451  4/03       3        Et0
S   4 WIZARD1--VIA-E0             E0.0002.0004.0006:0451      none       2        Eto
N+  4 dtp-15-AB                   E002.0002.0004.0006:0451    none       4        Et0
N+  4 dtp-15-ABC                  E002.0002.0004.0006:0451    none       4        Et0
N+  4 dtp-15-ABCD                 E002.0002.0004.0006:0451    none       4        Et0
N+  4 merlin                      E03E03.0002.0004.0006:0451  4/03       3        Et0
N+  4 dtp-15-ABC                  E002.0002.0004.0006:0451    none       4        Et0
```

The following fields are shown in Figure 8-6:

Field	Description	
Codes:	Codes defining how the service was learned:	
	S—Static	Statically defined service via the **ipx sap** command.
	P—Periodic	Service learned via a SAP update.
	E—EIGRP	Service learned via Enhanced IGRP.
	N—NLSP	Service learned via NLSP.
	H—Holddown	Indicates that the entry is in holddown mode and is not reachable.
	+—detail	Indicates that multiple paths to the server exist. Use the **show ipx servers** detailed EXEC command to display more detailed information about the paths.
Type	Contains codes from Codes field to indicates how service was learned.	
Name	Name of server.	
Net	Network on which server is located.	
Address	Network address of server.	
Port	Source socket number.	
Route	Ticks/hops (from the routing table).	
Hops	Hops (from the SAP protocol).	
Itf	Interface through which to reach server.	

The **show ipx traffic** Command

The **show ipx traffic** command displays information about the number and type of IPX packets transmitted and received by the router. Figure 8-7 shows sample output from the **show ipx traffic** command.

Figure 8-7   *The **show ipx traffic** command provides a summary of overhead traffic on the router.*

```
Router> show ipx traffic

Rcvd:   593135 total, 38792 format errors, 0 checksum errors, 0 bad hop count,
        21542 packets pitched, 295493 local destination, 0 multicast
Bcast:  295465 received, 346725 sent
```

Figure 8-7 *The **show ipx traffic** command provides a summary of overhead traffic on the router. (Continued)*

```
Sent:    429393 generated, 276100 forwarded
         0 encapsulation failed, 0 no route
SAP:     124 Total SAP requests, 124 Total SAP replies, 4 servers
         5 SAP general requests, 5 replies
         110 SAP Get Nearest Server requests, 110 replies
                5 SAP Nearest Name requests, 5 replies
          4 SAP General Name requests, 4 replies
          27 SAP advertisements received, 103 sent
          4 SAP flash updates sent, 0 SAP format errors
RIP:     4676 RIP requests, 336 RIP replies, 18 routes
         87274 RIP advertisements received, 69438 sent
         74 RIP flash updates sent, 0 RIP format errors
Echo:    Rcvd 0 requests, 0 replies
         Sent 0 requests, 0 replies
         7648 unknown: 0 no socket, 0 filtered, 7648 no helper
         0 SAPs throttled, freed NDB len 0
Watchdog:
         0 packets received, 0 replies spoofed
Queue lengths:
         IPX input: 0, SAP 0, RIP 0, GNS 0
         SAP throttling length: 0/(no limit), 0 nets pending lost route reply
         Delayed process creation: 0
EIGRP:   Total received 0, sent 0
         Updates received 0, sent 0
         Queries received 0, sent 0
         Replies received 0, sent 0
         SAPs received 0, sent 0
NLSP:    Level-1 Hellos received 0, sent 0
         PTP Hello received 0, sent 0
         Level-1 LSPs received 0, sent 0
                LSP Retransmissions: 0
         LSP checksum errors received: 0
         LSP HT=0 checksum errors received: 0
         Level-1 CSNPs received 0, sent 0
         Level-1 PSNPs received 0, sent 0
         Level-1 DR Elections: 0
         Level-1 SPF Calculations: 0
         Level-1 Partial Route Calculations: 0
```

The following are the fields shown in Figure 8-7:

Field	Description
593135 total	Total number of packets received.
38792 format errors	Number of bad packets discarded (for example, packets with a corrupted header). Includes IPX packets received in an encapsulation for which this interface is not configured.
0 checksum errors	Number of packets containing a checksum error. This number should always be 0 because IPX rarely uses a checksum.

continues

Field	Description
0 bad hop count	Number of packets discarded because their hop count exceeded 16.
21542 packets pitched	Number of times the device received its own broadcast packet.
295493 local destination	Number of packets sent to the local broadcast address or specifically to the router.
0 multicast	Number of packets received that were addressed to an IPX multicast address.
Bcast:	Description of the broadcast packets the router has received and sent.
295465 received	Number of broadcast packets received.
346725 sent	Number of broadcast packets sent. It includes broadcast packets the router is either forwarding or has generated.
Sent:	Description of those packets that the software generated and then sent, and also those the software has received and then routed to other destinations.
429393 generated	Number of packets transmitted that it generated itself.
276100 forwarded	Number of packets transmitted that it forwarded from other sources.
0 encapsulation failed	Number of packets the software was unable to encapsulate.
0 no route	Number of times the software could not locate a route to the destination in the routing table.
SAP:	Description of the SAP packets sent and received.
124 SAP requests	Cumulative sum of SAP requests received—SAP general requests and SAP Get Nearest Server requests.
124 SAP replies	Cumulative sum of all SAP replies—SAP general replies, SAP GNS replies, SAP Nearest Name replies, and SAP General Name replies.
4 servers	Number of servers in the SAP table.
5 SAP general requests 5 replies	Number of general SAP requests and replies. This field applies to Cisco IOS Release 11.2.
110 SAP Get Nearest Server requests 110 replies	Number of GNS requests and replies. This field applies to Cisco IOS Release 11.2.
5 SAP Nearest Name requests 5 replies	Number of SAP Nearest Name requests and replies. This field applies to Cisco IOS Release 11.2.
4 SAP General Name requests 4 replies	Number of SAP General Name requests and replies. This field applies to Cisco IOS Release 11.2.

Field	Description
27 SAP advertisements received 103 sent	Number of SAP advertisements generated and then sent as a result of a change in its routing or service tables.
4 SAP flash updates sent	Number of SAP flash updates generated and then sent as a result of a change in its routing or service tables.
0 SAP format errors	Number of SAP advertisements received that were incorrectly formatted.
RIP:	Description of the RIP packets sent and received.
4676 RIP requests	Number of RIP requests received.
336 RIP replies	Number of RIP replies sent in response to RIP requests.
18 routes	Number of RIP routes in the current routing table.
87274 RIP advertisements received	Number of RIP advertisements received from another router.
69438 sent	Number of RIP advertisements generated and then sent.
74 RIP flash updates sent	Number of RIP advertisements generated and then sent as a result of a change in its routing table.
0 RIP format errors	Number of RIP packets received that were incorrectly formatted.
freed NDB length	Number of Network Descriptor Blocks (NDBs) that have been removed from the network but still need to be removed from the router's routing table.
Echo:	Description of the **ping** replies and requests sent and received.
Rcvd 55 requests, 0 replies	Number of **ping** requests and replies received.
Sent 0 requests, 0 replies	Number of **ping** requests and replies sent.
7648 unknown	Number of packets received on socket that are not supported.
0 SAPs throttled	Number of SAP packets discarded because they exceeded buffer capacity.
Watchdog:	Description of the watchdog packets the software has handled.
0 packets received	Number of watchdog packets received from IPX servers on the local network.
0 replies spoofed	Number of times the software has responded to a watchdog packet on behalf of the remote client.
Queue lengths	Description of outgoing packets currently in buffers that are waiting to be processed.
IPX input	Number of incoming packets waiting to be processed.
SAP	Number of outgoing SAP packets waiting to be processed.
RIP	Number of outgoing RIP packets waiting to be processed.

continues

Field	Description
GNS	Number of outgoing GNS packets waiting to be processed.
SAP throttling length	Maximum number of outgoing SAP packets allowed in the buffer. Any packets received beyond this number are discarded.
EIGRP totals:	Description of the Enhanced IGRP packets the router has sent and received.
Updates received	Number of Enhanced IGRP updates sent and received.
Queries received	Number of Enhanced IGRP queries sent and received.
Replies received	Number of Enhanced IGRP replies sent and received.
SAPs received	Number of SAP packets sent to and received from Enhanced IGRP neighbors.
0 unknown: 0 socket, 0 filtered, 0 no helper	Number of packets the software was unable to forward, for example, because of a misconfigured helper address or because no route was available.
NLSP:	Description of the NLSP packets the router has sent and received.
Level-1 Hellos	Number of LAN hello packets sent and received.
PTP Hello	Number of point-to-point packets sent and received.
Level-1 LSPs	Number of LSPs sent and received.
Level-1 CSNPs	Number of complete sequence number PDU (CSNP) packets sent and received.
Level-1 PSNPs	Number of partial sequence number PDU (PSNP) packets sent and received.
Level-1 DR Elections	Number of times the software has calculated its designated router election priority.
Level-1 SPF Calculations	Number of times the software has performed the shortest path first (SPF) calculation.
Level-1 Partial Route Calculations	Number of times the software has recalculated routes without running SPF.

The IPX debug Commands

You should use **debug** commands carefully because some of them generate a lot of output for each IPX packet processed. (For more information on which commands generate a lot of output, see the *Debug Command Reference*.) Also, use **debug** commands only when traffic on the IPX network is low so other activity on the system is not adversely affected. For example, in a large IPX network with many SAPs on a low-speed WAN link, you would use **debug ipx sap activity | events** instead of debugging the IPX SAP advertisements.

You can use the **debug** commands described in the following sections to isolate Novell problems:

- **debug ipx ipxwan**
- **debug ipx packet**
- **debug ipx routing**
- **debug ipx sap**

The **debug ipx ipxwan** Command

The **debug ipx ipxwan** command displays debug information for interfaces configured to use IPXWAN. You can use this command to verify the startup negotiations between two routers running the IPX protocol through a WAN. It produces output only during state changes or startup. During normal operations, no output is produced. Figure 8-8 shows sample output from the **debug ipx ipxwan** command during link startup.

Figure 8-8   *You can use **debug ipxwan** when starting up serial links to test IPXWAN operation.*

```
Router# debug ipx ipxwan

%LINEPROTO-5-UPDOWN: Line protocol on Interface Serial1, changed state to up
IPXWAN: state (Disconnect -> Sending Timer Requests) [Serial1/6666:200 (IPX line
  state brought up)]
IPXWAN: state (Sending Timer Requests -> Disconnect) [Serial1/6666:200 (IPX line
  state brought down)]
IPXWAN: state (Disconnect -> Sending Timer Requests) [Serial1/6666:200 (IPX line
  state brought up)]
IPXWAN: Send TIMER_REQ [seq 0] out Serial1/6666:200
IPXWAN: Send TIMER_REQ [seq 1] out Serial1/6666:200
IPXWAN: Send TIMER_REQ [seq 2] out Serial1/6666:200
IPXWAN: Send TIMER_REQ [seq 0] out Serial1/6666:200
IPXWAN: Rcv TIMER_REQ on Serial1/6666:200, NodeID 1234, Seq 1
IPXWAN: Send TIMER_REQ [seq 1] out Serial1/6666:200
IPXWAN: Rcv TIMER_RSP on Serial1/6666:200, NodeID 1234, Seq 1, Del 6
IPXWAN: state (Sending Timer Requests -> Master: Sent RIP/SAP) [Serial1/6666:200
  (Received Timer Response as master)]
IPXWAN: Send RIPSAP_INFO_REQ [seq 0] out Serial1/6666:200
IPXWAN: Rcv RIPSAP_INFO_RSP from Serial1/6666:200, NodeID 1234, Seq 0
IPXWAN: state (Master: Sent RIP/SAP -> Master: Connect) [Serial1/6666:200 (Received
Router Info Rsp as Master)]
```

The following line indicates that the interface has initialized:

```
%LINEPROTO-5-UPDOWN: Line protocol on Interface Serial1, changed state to up
```

The following lines indicate that the startup process failed to receive a timer response, brought the link down, and then brought the link up and tried again with a new timer set:

```
IPXWAN: state (Sending Timer Requests -> Disconnect) [Serial1/6666:200 (IPX line
state brought down)]
IPXWAN: state (Disconnect -> Sending Timer Requests) [Serial1/6666:200 (IPX line
state brought up)]
```

The following lines indicate that the interface is sending timer requests and waiting on timer response:

```
IPXWAN: Send TIMER_REQ [seq 0] out Serial1/6666:200
IPXWAN: Send TIMER_REQ [seq 1] out Serial1/6666:200
```

The following lines indicate that the interface has received a timer request from the other end of the link and has sent a timer response. The fourth line shows that the interface has come up as the master on the link:

```
IPXWAN: Rcv TIMER_REQ on Serial1/6666:200, NodeID 1234, Seq 1
IPXWAN: Send TIMER_REQ [seq 1] out Serial1/6666:200
IPXWAN: Rcv TIMER_RSP on Serial1/6666:200, NodeID 1234, Seq 1, Del 6
IPXWAN: state (Sending Timer Requests -> Master: Sent RIP/SAP) [Serial1/6666:200
(Received Timer Response as master)]
```

The following lines indicate that the interface is sending RIP/SAP requests:

```
IPXWAN: Send RIPSAP_INFO_REQ [seq 0] out Serial1/6666:200
IPXWAN: Rcv RIPSAP_INFO_RSP from Serial1/6666:200, NodeID 1234, Seq 0
IPXWAN: state (Master: Sent RIP/SAP -> Master: Connect) [Serial1/6666:200
(Received Router Info Rsp as Master)]
```

The **debug ipx packet** Command

The **debug ipx packet** command displays information about packets received, transmitted, and forwarded. To generate **debug ipx packet** information on all IPX traffic traveling through the router, you must first configure the router so that fast switching is disabled. Use the **no ipx route-cache** command on all interfaces on which you want to observe traffic. If the router is configured for IPX fast switching, only non-fast-switched packets will produce output. When the IPX cache is invalidated or cleared, one packet for each destination is displayed as the cache is repopulated. Figure 8-9 shows sample output from the **debug ipx packet** command.

Figure 8-9   *Packet debugging provides details on all packets traversing the router.*

```
Router# debug ipx packet

IPX: src=160.0260.8c4c.4f22, dst=1.0000.0000.0001, packet received
IPX: src=160.0260.8c4c.4f22, dst=1.0000.0000.0001,gw=183.0000.0c01.5d85,
sending packet
```

The first line indicates that the router receives a packet from a Novell station (address 160.0260.8c4c.4f 22); this trace does not indicate the address of the immediate router sending the packet to this router. In the second line, the router forwards the packet toward the Novell server (address 1.0000.0000.0001) through an immediate router (183.0000.0c01.5d85).

The following are the fields shown in Figure 8-9:

Field	Description
IPX	Indication that this is an IPX packet.
src = 160.0260.8c4c.4f22	Source address of the IPX packet. The Novell network number is 160. Its Media Access Control (MAC) address is 0260.8c4c.4f22.
dst = 1.0000.0000.0001	Destination address for the IPX packet. The address 0000.0000.0001 is an internal MAC address, and the network number 1 is the internal network number of a Novell 3.11 server.
packet received	Indicates that the router received this packet from a Novell station, possibly through an intermediate router.
gw = 183.0000.0c01.5d85	Indicates that the router is sending the packet over to the next hop router; its address of 183.0000.0c01.5d85 was learned from the IPX routing table.
sending packet	Indicates that the router is attempting to send this packet.

The **debug ipx routing** Command

The **debug ipx routing** command displays information about IPX routing packets that the router sends and receives. Figure 8-10 shows sample output from the **debug ipx routing** command.

Figure 8-10 *Routing updates are being sent and received every 60 seconds.*

```
Router# debug ipx routing

IPXRIP: update from 9999.0260.8c6a.1733
        110801 in 1 hops, delay 2
IPXRIP: sending update to 12FF02:ffff.ffff.ffff via Ethernet 1
        network 555, metric 2, delay 3
        network 1234, metric 3, delay 4
```

The following are the fields shown in Figure 8-10:

Field	Description
IPXRIP	This is an IPX RIP packet.
update from 9999.0260.8c6a.1733	This packet is a routing update from an IPX server at address 9999.0260.8c6a.1733.
110801 in 1 hops	Network 110801 is one hop away from the router at address 9999.0260.8c6a.1733.
delay 2	Delay is a time measurement (1/18 second) that the NetWare shell uses to estimate how long to wait for a response from a file server. Also known as ticks.
sending update to 12FF02:ffff.ffff.ffff via Ethernet 1	The router is sending this IPX routing update packet to address 12FF02:ffff.ffff.ffff through its Ethernet 1 interface.
network 555	The packet includes routing update information for network 555.
metric 2	Network 555 is two metrics (or hops) away from the router.
delay 3	Network 555 is a delay of 3 away from the router. Delay is a measurement that the NetWare shell uses to estimate how long to wait for a response from a file server. Also known as ticks.

The **debug ipx sap** Command

The **debug ipx sap** command displays information about IPX SAP packets that the router sends and receives. To access more detailed output of SAP packets, including displays of services in SAP packets, use the **activity** keyword. To reduce the amount of output for the **debug ipx sap** command, use the **events** keyword. Figure 8-11 shows sample output from the **debug ipx sap** command.

Figure 8-11 *SAP updates are being sent and received every 60 seconds.*

```
Router# debug ipx sap

IPXSAP: at 0023F778:
I SAP Response type 0x2 len 160 src:160.0000.0c00.070d dest:160.ffff.ffff.ffff(452)
   type 0x4, "Hello2", 199.0002.0004.0006 (451), 2 hops
   type 0x4, "Hello1", 199.0002.0004.0008 (451), 2 hops
IPXSAP: sending update to 160
IPXSAP: at 00169080:
  O SAP Update type 0x2 len 96 ssoc:0x452 dest:160.ffff.ffff.ffff(452)
IPX: type 0x4, "Magnolia", 42.0000.0000.0001 (451), 2hops
```

The **debug ipx sap** command generates multiple lines of output for each SAP packet—a packet summary message and a service detail message.

The first line displays the internal router memory address of the packet. The technical support staff may use this information in problem debugging:

```
IPXSAP: at 0023F778:
```

The following are the fields shown in Figure 8-11:

Field	Description
I	Indicates whether the router received the SAP packet as input (I) or is sending it as output (O).
SAP Response type 0x2	Packet type. Format is 0xn; possible values for n include • 1—General query • 2—General response • 3—GNS request • 4—GNS response
len 160	Length of this packet (in bytes).
src: 160.000.0c00.070d	Source address of the packet.
dest:160.ffff.ffff.ffff	The IPX network number and broadcast address of the destination IPX network for which the message is intended.
(452)	IPX socket number of the process sending the packet at the source address. This number is always 452, which is the socket number for the SAP process.
type 0x4	Indicates the type of service the server sending the packet provides. Format is 0xn. Some of the values for n are proprietary to Novell. Those values for n that have been published include • 0—Unknown • 1—User • 2—User group • 3—Print queue • 4—File server • 5—Job server • 6—Gateway • 7—Print server • 8—Archive queue • 9—Archive server • A—Job queue • B—Administration

continues

Field	Description
type 0x4	• 21—NAS SNA gateway
	• 24—Remote bridge server
	• 2D—Time Synchronization VAP
	• 2E—Dynamic SAP
	• 47—Advertising print server
	• 4B—Btrieve VAP 5.0
	• 4C—SQL VAP
	• 7A—TES—NetWare for VMS
	• 98—NetWare access server
	• 9A—Named Pipes server
	• 9E—Portable NetWare—UNIX
	• 111—Test server
	• 166—NetWare management
	• 233—NetWare management agent
	• 237—NetExplorer NLM
	• 239—HMI hub
	• 23A—NetWare LANalyzer agent
	• 26A—NMS management
	• FFFF—Wildcard (any SAP service)
	Contact Novell for more information.
"HELLO2"	Name of the server being advertised.
199.0002.0004.0006 (451)	Indicates the network number and address (and socket) of the server generating the SAP packet.
2 hops	Number of hops to the server from the router.
ssoc:0x452	Indicates the IPX socket number of the process sending the packet at the source address. Possible values include
	• 451—Network Core Protocol
	• 452—Service Advertising Protocol
	• 453—Routing Information Protocol
	• 455—NetBIOS
	• 456—Diagnostics
	• 4000 to 6000—Ephemeral sockets used for interaction with file servers and other network communications

The fifth line of output indicates that the router sent a SAP update to network 160:

```
IPXSAP: sending update to 160
```

The format for **debug ipx sap** output describing a SAP update the router sends is similar to that describing a SAP update the router receives, except that the ssoc: field replaces the src: field, as the following line of output indicates:

```
O SAP Update type 0x2 len 96 ssoc:0x452 dest:160.ffff.ffff.ffff(452)
```

Problem Isolation in NetWare Networks

You can isolate connection problems between NetWare clients and servers. Figure 8-12 illustrates the steps to follow.

Figure 8-12 *Following these steps can help you isolate connection problems between NetWare clients and servers.*

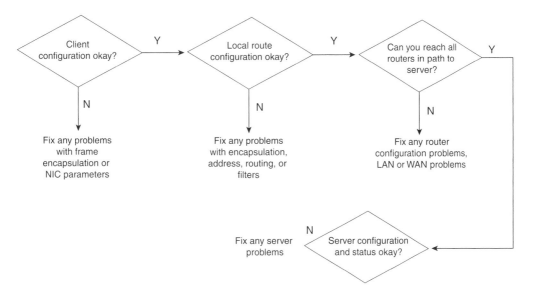

The following list explains these steps in more detail:

1 Check the configuration of the client:

— Is it using the correct frame encapsulation?

— Has the client for NetWare been installed, and has the user logged in?

— Are there any problems with the parameters for the network interface card (NIC)?

2 Check the local router's configuration:

— Use **show** commands to determine the router's configuration and state.

3 From the local router, progressively "**ping** out" through the internetwork. When you discover a router that does not respond to IPX **ping**s:

— Examine the routing table by using **show ipx route** to make sure a path to the server is in the table.

— Check network number specifications for duplication or other misconfigurations.

— Make sure IPX routing is running and that SAP and RIP packets are being sent.

4 Check the configuration and status of the server you are trying to reach for the following:

— Internal and external addresses

— Name

— Encapsulation

— Number of users signed on and number of users allowed

— CPU utilization

— Hard disk space available

— Memory usage

— Number of requests that are serviced from the memory cache as opposed to the hard disk

This book concentrates on router configuration problems. Nonetheless, you might need to solve Novell networking problems that have other symptoms. You should consider the following NetWare server problems as well:

- Assigning an external network number that does not agree with other servers and routers on that network segment

- Assigning two servers the same internal network number

- Assigning two servers the same name

- Forgetting to bind a protocol to an NIC

- Not fixing any interrupt or Direct Memory Access conflicts with NICs

- Using the wrong frame encapsulation type

- Letting the server run out of memory (which may cause an abnormal end)

- Letting the server's hard disk run out of space

- Letting the server CPU utilization get very high—it's best to keep the server CPU utilization below 65%

- Not allocating enough memory to the server's memory cache—server cache hits should be at least 90%

- Running out of available connections (beyond the number specified in the user license)

- Deleting the login directory

- Shutting down without issuing the proper **shutdown** command at the console—using the proper command updates file allocation tables, clears the cache, and alerts any applications so that they can clean up the database or other files

To conform to Novell specifications, Cisco has modified the behavior of GNS responses. The router responds only if there are no servers on the local segment.

In Cisco IOS Release 9.1(13), the default value of the **ipx gns-response-delay** command became zero milliseconds (ms). Prior software releases had a default delay of 500 ms (half a second). The 500-ms value was assigned to fix a problem in NetWare 2.x associated with dual-connected servers running in parallel with a Cisco router. The implemented delay prevented the parallel Cisco router from replying to a GNS request before the server itself.

If you are still running software prior to Release 9.1(13) and you do not have 2.x servers, you might need to manually decrease the GNS response delay, depending on your network topology, to improve response time when a Novell client starts up. Conversely, if you are using software Release 9.1(13) or later, you might need to manually increase the GNS response delay to compensate for a client that has a very slow processor and network interface card, causing it to miss the quick response from the router.

As of Cisco IOS software Release 9.21, the router can be configured to respond to GNS queries in a round-robin fashion if several equidistant servers are in the SAP table. Use the **ipx gns-round-robin** command to rotate using a round-robin selection method through a set of eligible servers when responding to GNS requests. If this round-robin selection method is not configured, the router responds with the first server in its SAP table by default. This can overwhelm some servers.

Access lists can also be used for limiting which servers can be reached by which clients. Cisco IOS software supports both the filtering of SAP advertisements between routers and the filtering of GNS responses to Novell clients. Static SAP entries, created with the **ipx sap** command, can be used to cause the router to always send users to a specific server. Refer to *Advanced Cisco Router Configuration* (Chappell, 1999) for more details on IPX traffic management.

NetWare Symptoms and Problems

Table 8-1 shows common NetWare symptoms and possible problems. Using this table, you can identify possible problems and make a plan to verify and fix problem causes.

Table 8-1   *NetWare symptoms and possible problems.*

Symptom	Possible Problem
Client cannot communicate with local server.	• Client or server is not on the network. • Client is not configured for correct frame encapsulation.

Symptom	Possible Problem
Client cannot communicate with remote server.	• Router interface is not functional. • Configuration mismatch. • Duplicate network numbers. • Misconfigured access list or other filter. • Backdoor bridge between segments. • Client or router is not configured for correct frame encapsulation. • GNS reply from router too quick for slow client.
SAP updates are not being propagated by router.	• Server is not sending SAP updates. • Misconfigured access list or other filter. • Configuration mismatch. • Duplicate network numbers. • Server cannot keep up with SAPs from router. • SAP or RIP timers mismatch.

Configuration mismatch refers to a common mistake made in NetWare networks where the external network number assigned on a server or router does not agree with the external network number for other servers or routers on that same segment. A similar mistake is to use a duplicate network number for an internal or external network number. In this case, the same network number is used to identify different parts of an internetwork. These mistakes are the result of not maintaining control of router and server configurations and not keeping updated documentation and network maps.

Troubleshooting Encapsulation Mismatches

A client and server (or router) that need to communicate on the same network segment must agree on the IPX encapsulation type. Because so many encapsulations exist for Ethernet networks, this is a typical problem area. A Cisco router defaults to novell-ether for IPX encapsulation. The encapsulations shown in Table 8-2 can be configured.

Table 8-2   *Ethernet encapsulation types for IPX networks.*

Common Term	Novell Term	Cisco Term	Characteristics
Ethernet V. 2	ETHERNET_II	arpa	Includes Ethertype
IEEE 802.3	ETHERNET_802.2	sap or iso1	Includes 802.3 length and 802.2 SAPs
Novell 802.3 raw	ETHERNET_802.3	novell-ether	Includes 802.3 length with no 802.2 SAPs
SNAP	ETHERNET_SNAP	snap	Includes 802.2 SAPs and SNAP header

The **ipx internal-network** command establishes the number you specify as a primary network number for the router. You must select a number for this entry that is unique across your internetwork. NLSP and IPXWAN advertise and accept packets for this internal network number out all the router interfaces. The NLSP process adds the host address 01. This means that you can use the combined address *network-number*.01 as a **ping** target when troubleshooting.

If you have selected NLSP as your routing protocol, you should enter the **ipx router nlsp** global configuration command. Note that the routing protocol RIP also runs by default unless you include the command **no ipx router rip**.

On each interface or subinterface, start the NLSP routing process by entering the **ipx nlsp enable** interface configuration command.

NetWare Problems and Action Plans

Table 8-3 provides a list of problems and some suggested action plans to help isolate the source of problems.

Table 8-3   *NetWare problems and action plans.*

Problem	Suggested Action Plan
Client or server is not on network.	• Attach a protocol analyzer to the network to which the client and server are connected. Look for the source addresses of both. • Look for an excessive number of collisions or other lower-layer errors. • Check NIC configuration parameters.
Client or router is not configured for correct frame encapsulation.	• Check client configuration files. • On the router, use the **show running-config** command to check the IPX encapsulation.

continues

Table 8-3   *NetWare problems and action plans. (Continued)*

Problem	Suggested Action Plan
Router interface is not functional.	• Check the operation of the router by using the **show interfaces** command. • Check the cable connections from the router.
Configuration mismatch.	• Check the router configuration. Verify that the network number agrees with other routers or servers on this segment by using the **show ipx interface** command.
Duplicate network numbers.	• Use the **show ipx servers** and **show ipx interface** commands to look for duplicate network numbers. Modify the server or router configuration if duplicates are found.
Misconfigured access list or other filter.	• Use **ping** to isolate a router with a misconfigured list. • Check the routing table by using the **show ipx route** command. • Check protocol exchanges (for example, by using the **debug ipx sap** command). • Temporarily disable access lists one at a time and test them. Debug access lists that cause connectivity problems.
Backdoor bridge between segments.	• Look for "bad hop count" by using the **show ipx traffic** command. • Use a protocol analyzer to look for packet loops. • Look for known remote network devices that show up on the local network with remote MAC addresses.
Server is not sending SAP updates.	• Check for SAP updates by using a protocol analyzer. • Check frame encapsulation for SAP updates.
Server cannot keep up with SAPs from router.	• Look for missing services by using the **show ipx servers** command on the router and **slist** on clients. • Use the **ipx output-sap-delay** command to specify the delay between packets in a multipacket SAP update.
SAP or RIP timers mismatch.	• Bring the timer values on servers and routers within three minutes of each other.

When a client cannot reach a server on the other side of a router, use the **show interfaces** command to check the operation of the router. Verify that the status line indicates that the interface and line protocol are up. If the interface is administratively down, add the **no shutdown** interface configuration command to the configuration for the interface. If the interface or line protocol is down, check the cable connections from the router. On serial interfaces, check for proper WAN encapsulation configuration.

If the interface and line protocol are up, make sure the interface is configured for the right type of frame encapsulation. The router defaults to novell-ether (ETHERNET_802.3) on Ethernet. If you are using NLSP, check for the **ipx nlsp enable** command on each interface.

After checking the interface, check the router configuration to see whether Novell IPX routing is enabled. If it is not, add the **ipx routing** global configuration command and related commands as necessary.

If you suspect that you have duplicate network numbers, use the **show ipx servers** command to look for duplicates. This command generates a list of servers by type, name, network number, MAC address, hop count, and interface. If you see duplicate network numbers, modify server or router configurations to eliminate duplicate network numbers from your internetwork.

To check for misconfigured filters, temporarily disable any filters with the **no ipx access-group** command. Be sure to disable any SAP-specific access lists by using **no ipx input-sap-filter** and **no ipx output-sap-filter** commands as appropriate.

Use the **display servers** command on the server or the **show ipx servers** command on the router or the **slist** command on the client to verify that the server is advertising services. Use the **debug ipx sap activity** router command to look for server name, network number, and MAC address. Revise access lists or filter statements as necessary and apply them individually to ensure that updates are being distributed appropriately.

If you suspect that a server is not sending SAP updates, use a protocol analyzer to look for SAP updates from the server. If the server is not sending SAP updates, make sure the server is attached to the network. In Ethernet environments, if the server is sending SAP updates, check the encapsulation type. The encapsulation type must match the encapsulation type used by routers and clients on that segment that need to communicate with the server.

Certain third-party NLMs are available that allow SAP updates to be disabled entirely. If you are using such software on your servers, make certain that the necessary SAP updates are being sent. Consult your third-party documentation for more information.

SAP and RIP timer values can be changed on servers running NetWare 4.x or later. Examine the configuration of the server and the routers to determine whether the timer values are the same. If the timer value configured on the server is more than three minutes greater than that configured on the router, the router will remove the server from the IPX servers table. This will result in clients being unable to see the services available on that server. You should bring the timer values within three minutes of each other to ensure that the router does not remove the server from its IPX servers table.

If Novell NetBIOS clients cannot reach a server through a router, use the **debug ipx packet** command or a protocol analyzer to look for Novell packets of type 20. Use the **show running-config** command to check for an **ipx type-20-propagation** command configured for the incoming *and* outgoing interface. If the command is not present, add it.

NOTE   Beginning in Cisco IOS Release 12.0, the **show running-config** command has been replaced with the **show system:running-config** command.

If Novell clients cannot connect to remote Novell servers across a Frame Relay network that has a hub-and-spokes topology, the problem might be related to the default split-horizon behavior for RIP and SAP. If you are running Cisco IOS Release 9.21 or later, configure subinterfaces on the Frame Relay interface of the hub router. Assign a subinterface to each spoke site. The hub router treats each subinterface as a physical interface, allowing it to advertise RIPs and SAPs without violating split horizon. For specific information on configuring subinterfaces, see the Cisco IOS configuration guides and command references. Another potential problem in Frame Relay networks is that Frame Relay is a nonbroadcast multi-access medium. The router must be configured to support broadcast traffic mimicking. This is done by using the **broadcast** keyword with the **frame-relay map** command. For example, **frame-relay map ipx 10.1234.5678.abcd 100 broadcast.** This command maps the next-hop IPX address 10.1234.5678.abcd to Frame Relay DLCI number 100 with broadcast mimicking enabled.

In Frame Relay networks, make sure the router and the switch agree on the Local Management Interface (LMI) type, which can be either ansi, cisco (default), or q933a.

In WAN environments make sure SAP updates are not being dropped due to a slow serial line. You can use the **show interfaces serial** command to examine the value indicated in the output queue "drops" field. A large number of dropped packets may indicate that SAP updates are not reaching clients across the serial link. Re-evaluate implemented SAP filtering. Eliminate the forwarding of any SAP updates that are not absolutely necessary, and increase the available bandwidth if possible.

For WAN point-to-point connections, make sure that the routers agree on the encapsulation type. If an encapsulation command is not present in the configuration, the default is High-Level Data Link Control (HDLC) encapsulation. For IPXWAN, the encapsulation should be Point-to-Point Protocol (PPP).

Summary

This chapter focuses on the diagnostic commands that can be used on a NetWare IPX/SPX network. Remember that NetWare 5 supports NetWare over TCP/IP. In Chapter 9, "Troubleshooting AppleTalk Connectivity," you'll learn techniques for troubleshooting AppleTalk communications.

Chapter 8 Test
Troubleshooting Novell Connectivity

Estimated Time: 15 minutes

Complete all the exercises to test your knowledge of the materials contained in this chapter. Answers are listed in Appendix A, "Chapter Test Answer Key."

Use the information contained in this chapter to answer the following questions:

Question 8.1

What three common commands can be used to effectively troubleshoot a NetWare IPX/SPX network?

a. _____

b. _____

c. _____

Question 8.2

Which commands can be used to perform the following tasks:

a. Display IPX interface statistics

_____

b. Display discovered IPX servers

_____

c. Display link state database entries

_____

d. Verify IPX WAN router negotiations

_____

e. Send a ping packet to a Novell 4.x server

_____

Question 8.3

What is the main cause of excessive overhead in Novell networks? List three ways of dealing with this problem on Cisco routers.

a. _____

b. _____

c. _____

Question 8.4

For two routers to share Novell updates, what three things must they agree on in their configuration?

a. _____

b. _____

c. _____

Question 8.5

T   F   For Enhanced IGRP, neighboring routers must use the same autonomous system number.

Question 8.6

T   F   For NLSP, neighboring routers must use the same internal network number.

Troubleshooting AppleTalk Connectivity

The purpose of this chapter is to discuss troubleshooting tips and techniques specific to the AppleTalk protocol suite. The goal is to help you prepare for real-world troubleshooting on the job. AppleTalk networks are still common in today's networks. The ease of implementation on the client means that troubleshooting is a little more difficult on the network side.

AppleTalk Router Diagnostic Commands

The following three commands can be used to isolate problems on an AppleTalk network:

- **show**
- **test appletalk**
- **debug**

The following sections provide details on AppleTalk-specific parameters that can be used with these commands.

AppleTalk show Commands

You can use the following **show** commands for troubleshooting AppleTalk networks:

- **show appletalk access-lists**
- **show appletalk adjacent-routes**
- **show appletalk arp**
- **show appletalk globals**
- **show appletalk interface**
- **show appletalk name-cache**
- **show appletalk route**
- **show appletalk traffic**
- **show appletalk zone**

These commands are discussed in more detail in the following sections.

The **show appletalk access-lists** Command

The **show appletalk access-lists** command displays the contents of all current AppleTalk access lists. Figure 9-1 shows sample output from the **show appletalk access-lists** command.

Figure 9-1 *Misconfigured access lists can be a cause of problems for AppleTalk networks.*

```
Router> show appletalk access-lists
AppleTalk access list 601:
        permit zone ZoneA
        permit zone ZoneB
        deny additional-zones
        permit network 55
        permit network 500
        permit cable-range 900-950
        deny includes 970-990
        permit within 991-995
        deny other-access
```

The following are the fields shown in the output in Figure 9-1:

Field	Description
AppleTalk access list 601:	Number of AppleTalk access lists.
permit zone deny zone	Indicates whether access to an AppleTalk zone has been explicitly permitted or denied with the **access-list zone** command.
permit additional-zones deny additional-zones	Indicates whether additional zones have been permitted or denied with the **access-list additional-zones** command.
permit network deny network	Indicates whether access to an AppleTalk network has been explicitly permitted or denied with the **access-list network** command.
permit cable-range deny cable-range	Indicates the cable ranges to which access has been permitted or denied with the **access-list cable-range** command.
permit includes deny includes	Indicates the cable ranges to which access has been permitted or denied with the **access-list includes** command.
permit within deny within	Indicates the additional cable ranges to which access has been permitted or denied with the **access-list within** command.
permit other-access deny other-access	Indicates whether additional networks or cable ranges have been permitted or denied with the **access-list other-access** command.

The **show appletalk adjacent-routes** Command

The **show appletalk adjacent-routes** command displays routes to networks that are directly connected or that are one hop away. Figure 9-2 shows sample output from the **show appletalk adjacent-routes** command.

Figure 9-2   *You can use the **show appletalk adjacent-routes** command to verify directly connected networks.*

```
Router# show appletalk adjacent-routes
Codes: R - RTMP derived, E - EIGRP derived, C - connected,
    S - static, P - proxy, 67 routes in internet
R Net 29-29 [1/G] via gatekeeper, 0 sec, Ethernet0, zone Engineering
C Net 2501-2501 directly connected, Ethernet1, no zone set
C Net 4160-4160 directly connected, Ethernet0, zone Low End SW Lab
C Net 4172-4172 directly connected, TokenRing0, zone Low End SW Lab
R Net 6160 [1/G] via urk, 0 sec, TokenRing0, zone Low End SW Lab
```

The following are the fields shown in the output in Figure 9-2:

Field	Description	
Codes:	Codes defining source of route:	
	R—RTMP derived	Route derived from an RTMP update.
	E—Enhanced IGRP derived	Route derived from an Enhanced IGRP.
	C—Connected	Directly connected network RTMP update.
	S—Static	Static route.
	P—Proxy	Proxy route.
67 routes in internet	Total number of known routes in the AppleTalk network.	
Net 29-29	Cable range or network to which the route goes.	
[1/G]	Hop count, followed by the state of the route. Possible values for state include the following: • G—Good (update has been received within the past 10 seconds) • S—Suspect (update has been received more than 10 seconds ago but less than 20 seconds ago) • B—Bad (update was received more than 20 seconds ago)	
via	NBP registered name or address of the router that sent the routing information.	
0 sec	Time, in seconds, since information about this network cable range was last received.	
directly connected	Indicates that the network or cable range is directly connected to the router.	

continues

Field	Description
Ethernet0	Possible interface through which updates to this NBP registered name or address will be sent.
zone	Zone name assigned to the network or cable range sending this update.

The **show appletalk arp** Command

The **show appletalk arp** command displays the contents of the AppleTalk Address Resolution Protocol (ARP) cache. Figure 9-3 shows sample output from the **show appletalk arp** command.

Figure 9-3   *All directly connected AppleTalk devices can be found in the **show appletalk arp** command output.*

```
Router# show appletalk arp
Address       Age (min)  Type      Hardware Addr   Encap    Interface
2000.1            -      Hardware  0000.0c04.1111  SNAP     Ethernet1
2000.2            0      Dynamic   0000.0c04.2222  SNAP     Ethernet1
2000.3            0      Dynamic   0000.0c04.3333  SNAP     Ethernet3
2000.4            -      Hardware  0000.0c04.4444  SNAP     Ethernet3
```

The following are the fields shown in the output in Figure 9-3:

Field	Description
Address	AppleTalk network address of the interface.
Age	Time, in minutes, that this entry has been in the ARP table. Entries are purged after they have been in the table for 240 minutes (4 hours). A hyphen indicates that this is a new entry.
Type	• Dynamic—Entry was learned via AARP. • Hardware—Entry was learned from an adapter in the router. • Pending—Entry for a destination for which the router does not yet know the address. When a packet requests to be sent to an address for which the router does not yet have the MAC-level address, the Cisco IOS software creates an AARP entry for that AppleTalk address, then sends an AARP Resolve packet to get the MAC-level address for that node. When the software gets the response, the entry is marked Dynamic. A pending AARP entry times out after 1 minute.
Hardware Addr	MAC address of this interface.

Field	Description
Encap	Encapsulation type. It can be one of the following: • ARPA • Ethernet-type encapsulation • Subnetwork Access Protocol (SNAP) • IEEE 802.3 encapsulation
Interface	Type and number of the interface

The **show appletalk globals** Command

The **show appletalk globals** command displays information about settings and parameters for the router's AppleTalk configuration. Figure 9-4 shows sample output from the **show appletalk globals** command.

Figure 9-4   *The **show appletalk globals** command provides a summary of AppleTalk overhead traffic on the router.*

```
Router# show appletalk globals
AppleTalk global information:
      The router is a domain router.
      Internet is compatible with older, AT Phase1, routers.
      There are 67 routes in the internet.
      There are 25 zones defined.
      All significant events will be logged.
      ZIP resends queries every 10 seconds.
      RTMP updates are sent every 10 seconds.
      RTMP entries are considered BAD after 20 seconds.
      RTMP entries are discarded after 60 seconds.
      AARP probe retransmit count: 10, interval: 200.
      AARP request retransmit count: 5, interval: 1000.
      DDP datagrams will be checksummed.
      RTMP datagrams will be strictly checked.
      RTMP routes may not be propagated without zones.
      Alternate node address format will not be displayed.
```

The following are the fields shown in the output in Figure 9-4:

Field	Description
AppleTalk global information:	Heading for the command output.
The router is a domain router.	Indicates whether this router is a domain router.
Internet is compatible with older, AT Phase1 routers.	Indicates whether the AppleTalk internetwork meets the criteria for interoperation with Phase 1 routers.
There are 67 routes in the internet.	Total number of routes in the AppleTalk internetwork from which this router has heard in routing updates.

continues

Field	Description
There are 25 zones defined.	Total number of valid zones in the current AppleTalk internetwork configuration.
All significant events will be logged.	Indicates whether the router has been configured with the **appletalk event-logging** command.
ZIP resends queries every 10 seconds.	Interval, in seconds, at which zone name queries are retried.
RTMP updates are sent every 10 seconds.	Interval, in seconds, at which the Cisco IOS software sends routing updates.
RTMP entries are considered BAD after 20 seconds.	Time after which routes for which the software has not received an update will be marked as candidates for being deleted from the routing table.
RTMP entries are discarded after 60 seconds.	Time after which routes for which the software has not received an update will be deleted from the routing table.
AARP probe retransmit count: 10, interval: 200	Number of AARP probe retransmissions that will be done before abandoning address negotiations and instead using the selected AppleTalk address, followed by the time, in milliseconds, between retransmission of ARP probe packets. You set these values with the **appletalk arp retransmit-count** and **appletalk arp interval** commands, respectively.
AARP request retransmit count: 5, interval: 1000.	Number of AARP request retransmissions that will be done before abandoning address negotiations and using the selected AppleTalk address, followed by the time, in milliseconds, between retransmission of ARP request packets. You set these values with the **appletalk arp retransmit-count** and **appletalk arp interval** commands, respectively.
DDP datagrams will be checksummed.	Indicates whether the **appletalk checksum** configuration command is enabled. When it is enabled, the software discards DDP packets when the checksum is incorrect and when the router is the final destination for the packet.
RTMP datagrams will be strictly checked.	Indicates whether **the appletalk strict-rtmp-checking** configuration command is enabled. When it is enabled, RTMP packets arriving from routers that are not directly connected to the router performing the check are discarded.

Field	Description
RTMP routes may not be propagated without zones.	Indicates whether the **appletalk require-route-zones** configuration command is enabled. When enabled, the Cisco IOS software does not advertise a route to its neighboring routers until it has obtained a network/zone association for that route.
Alternate node address format will not be displayed.	Indicates whether AppleTalk addresses will be printed in numeric or name form. You configure this with the **appletalk lookup-type** and **appletalk name-lookup-interval** commands.

The **show appletalk interface** Command

The **show appletalk interface** command displays the status of the AppleTalk interfaces configured in the router and the parameters configured on each interface. Figure 9-5 shows sample output from the **show appletalk interface** command.

Figure 9-5   *The **show appletalk interface** command is useful for debugging interface configuration errors.*

```
Router# show appletalk interface fddi 0
Fddi0 is up, line protocol is up
    AppleTalk cable range is 4199-4199
    AppleTalk address is 4199.82, Valid
    AppleTalk zone is "Low End SW Lab"
    AppleTalk address gleaning is disabled
    AppleTalk route cache is enabled
    Interface will not perform pre-FDDITalk compatibility
```

NOTE   The **show appletalk interface** command can show a node name in addition to the address, depending on how the software has been configured with the **appletalk lookup-type** and **appletalk name-lookup-interval** commands.

The following are the fields shown in the display as well as some fields not shown but that also may be displayed:

Field	Description
FDDI is…	Type of interface and whether it is currently active and inserted into the network (up) or inactive and not inserted (down).

continues

Field	Description
line protocol	Indicates whether the software processes that handle the line protocol believe the interface is usable (that is, whether keepalives are successful).
AppleTalk node	Indicates whether the node is up or down in the network.
AppleTalk cable range	Cable range of the interface.
AppleTalk address is …, Valid	Address of the interface, and whether the address conflicts with any other address on the network ("Valid" means it does not).
AppleTalk zone	Name of the zone that this interface is in.
AppleTalk port configuration verified…	When the access server implementation comes up on an interface, if there are other routers detected and the interface you are bringing up is not in discovery mode, our access server confirms the configuration with the routers that are already on the cable. The address printed in this field is that of the router with which the local router has verified that the interface configuration matches that on the running network.
AppleTalk discarded…packets due to input errors	Number of packets the interface discarded because of input errors. These errors are usually incorrect encapsulations (that is, the packet has a malformed header format).
AppleTalk address gleaning	Indicates whether the interface is automatically deriving ARP table entries from incoming packets (referred to as gleaning).
AppleTalk route cache	Indicates whether fast switching is enabled on the interface.
Interface will…	Indicates that the AppleTalk interface will check whether AppleTalk packets sent on the FDDI ring from routers running Cisco software releases prior to Release 9.0(3) or 9.1(2) are recognized.
AppleTalk domain	AppleTalk domain of which this interface is a member.

The **show appletalk name-cache** Command

The **show appletalk name-cache** command displays the router's cache of local names and services. To configure the service types for which the router will query and keep names, use the **appletalk lookup-type** and **appletalk name-lookup-interval** commands. Figure 9-6 shows sample output from the **show appletalk name-cache** command.

Figure 9-6   *The **show appletalk name-cache** command is useful for verifying NBP operations.*

```
Router# show appletalk name-cache
AppleTalk Name Cache:
Net    Adr  Skt  Name               Type           Zone
4160   19   8    gatekeeper         SNMP Agent     Underworld
4160   19   254  gatekeeper.Ether4  ciscoRouter    Underworld
4160   86   8    bones              SNMP Agent     Underworld
4160   86   72   131.108.160.78     IPADDRESS      Underworld
4160   86   254  bones.Ethernet0    IPGATEWAY      Underworld
```

The following are the fields shown in the output in Figure 9-6:

Field	Description
Net	AppleTalk network number or cable range.
Adr	Node address.
Skt	DDP socket number.
Name	Name of the service.
Type	Device type. The possible types vary, depending on the service. The following are the Cisco server types: • Cisco Router—Server is a Cisco router. • SNMP Agent—Server is an SNMP agent. • IPGATEWAY—Active MacIP server names. • IPADDRESS—Active MacIP server addresses.
Zone	Name of the AppleTalk zone to which this address belongs.

The **show appletalk route** Command

The **show appletalk route** command displays all entries or specified entries in the AppleTalk routing table. Figure 9-7 shows sample output from the **show appletalk route** command.

Figure 9-7   *All known networks should be displayed in the AppleTalk routing table.*

```
Router# show appletalk route
Codes: R - RTMP derived, E - EIGRP derived, C - connected, A - AURP
P - proxy, S - static
5 routes in internet
E Net 10000 -10000 [1/G] via 300.199, 275 sec, Ethernet2, zone France
R Net 890 [2/G] via 4.129, 1 sec, Ethernet0, zone release lab
R Net 901 [2/G] via 4.129, 1 sec, Ethernet0, zone Dave's House
C Net 999-999 directly connected, Serial3, zone Magnolia Estates
R Net 2003 [4/G] via 80.129, 6 sec, Ethernet4, zone Bldg-13
```

NOTE	Depending on the configuration of the global configuration commands **appletalk lookup-type** and **appletalk name-lookup-interval**, a node name may appear in this display instead of a node address.

The following are the fields shown in the display as well as some fields not shown, but that also may be displayed:

Field	Description	
Codes:	Codes defining how the route was learned:	
	R—RTMP derived	Route learned from an RTMP update.
	E—Enhanced IGRP derived	Route learned from an Enhanced IGRP update.
	C—Connected	Directly connected network.
	A—AURP	Route learned from an AURP update.
	S—Static	Statically defined route.
	P—Proxy	Proxy route. Proxy routes are included in outgoing RTMP updates as if they were directly connected routes (although they are not really directly connected), because they are not associated with any interface. Whenever an NBQ BrRq for the zone in question is generated by anyone anywhere in the internetwork, an NBP FwdReq is directed to any router connected to the proxy route. The Phase 2 router (which is the only router directly connected) converts the FwdReq to LkUps, which are understood by Phase 1 routers, and sends them to every network in the zone.
routes	Number of routes in the table.	
Net	Network to which the route goes.	
Net 999-999	Cable range to which the route goes.	
directly connected	Indicates that the network is directly connected to the router.	
uses	Fair estimate of the number of times a route gets used. It actually indicates the number of times the route has been selected for use prior to operations such as access list filtering.	
Ethernet	Possible interface through which updates to the remote network will be sent.	
zone	Name of zone of which the destination network is a member.	

Field	Description
[1/G]	Number of hops to this network, followed by the state of the link to that network. The state can be one of the following letters: • G—Link is good. • S—Link is suspect. • B—Link is bad. The state is determined from the routing updates that occur at 10-second intervals. A separate and nonsynchronized event occurs at 20-second intervals, checking and flushing the ratings for particular routes that have not been updated. For each 20-second period that passes with no new routing information, a rating changes from G to S and then from S to B. After 1 minute with no updates, that route is flushed. Every time the Cisco IOS software receives a useful update, the status of the route in question is reset to G. Useful updates are those advertising a route that is as good or better than the one currently in the table. When an AppleTalk route is poisoned by another router, its metric gets changed to poisoned (that is, 31 hops). The software then will age this route normally during a holddown period, during which the route will still be visible in the routing table.
via 258.179	Address of a router that is the next hop to the remote network.
via gatekeeper	Node name of a router that is the next hop to the remote network.
sec	Number of seconds that have elapsed since an RMTP update about this network was last received.

The **show appletalk traffic** Command

The **show appletalk traffic** command displays statistics about AppleTalk traffic. Figure 9-8 shows sample output from the **show appletalk traffic** command.

Figure 9-8   *You can use the **show appletalk traffic** command to get summary information for AppleTalk overhead.*

```
Router# show appletalk traffic
AppleTalk statistics:
  Rcvd:  357471 total, 0 checksum errors, 264 bad hop count
         321006 local destination, 0 access denied
         0 for MacIP, 0 bad MacIP, 0 no client
         13510 port disabled, 2437 no listener
         0 ignored, 0 martians
  Bcast: 191881 received, 270406 sent
  Sent:  550293 generated, 66495 forwarded, 1840 fast forwarded, 0 loopback
         0 forwarded from MacIP, 0 MacIP failures
         436 encapsulation failed, 0 no route, 0 no source
  DDP:   387265 long, 0 short, 0 macip, 0 bad size
  NBP:   302779 received, 0 invalid, 0 proxies
         57875 replies sent, 59947 forwards, 418674 lookups, 432 failures
  RTMP:  108454 received, 0 requests, 0 invalid, 40189 ignored
         90170 sent, 0 replies
```

continues

Figure 9-8   *You can use the* **show appletalk traffic** *command to get summary information for AppleTalk overhead. (Continued)*

```
   EIGRP: 0 received, 0 hellos, 0 updates, 0 replies, 0 queries
          0 sent,     0 hellos, 0 updates, 0 replies, 0 queries
          0 invalid, 0 ignored
   AURP: 0 Open Requests, 0 Router Downs
         0 Routing Information sent, 0 Routing Information received
         0 Zone Information sent, 0 Zone Information received
         0 Get Zone Nets sent, 0 Get Zone Nets received
         0 Get Domain Zone List sent, 0 Get Domain Zone List received
AppleTalk statistics:
         0 bad sequence
   ATP:   0 received
   ZIP:   13619 received, 33633 sent, 32 netinfo
   Echo:  0 received, 0 discarded, 0 illegal
          0 generated, 0 replies sent
   Responder:  0 received, 0 illegal, 0 unknown
          0 replies sent, 0 failures
   AARP:  85 requests, 149 replies, 100 probes
          84 martians, 0 bad encapsulation, 0 unknown
          278 sent, 0 failures, 29 delays, 315 drops
   Lost: 0 no buffers
   Unknown: 0 packets
   Discarded: 130475 wrong encapsulation, 0 bad SNAP discriminator
```

The following are the fields shown in the output in Figure 9-8:

Field	Description
Rcvd:	This section describes the packets received.
357741 total	Total number of packets received.
0 checksum errors	Number of packets that were discarded because their DDP checksum was incorrect. The DDP checksum is verified for packets that are directed to the router. It is not verified for forwarded packets.
264 bad hop count	Number of packets discarded because they had traveled too many hops.
321006 local destination	Number of packets addressed to the local router.
0 access denied	Number of packets discarded because they were denied by an access list.
0 for MacIP	Number of AppleTalk packets the Cisco IOS software received that were encapsulated within an IP packet.
0 bad MacIP	Number of bad MacIP packets the software received and discarded. These packets may have been malformed or may not have included a destination address.

Field	Description
0 no client	Number of packets discarded because they were directed to a nonexistent MacIP client.
13510 port disabled	Number of packets discarded because routing was disabled for that port (extended AppleTalk only). This is the result of a configuration error or a packet's being received while the software is in verification/discovery mode.
2437 no listener	Number of packets discarded because they were directed to a socket that had no services associated with it.
0 ignored	Number of routing update packets ignored because they were from a misconfigured neighbor or because routing was disabled.
0 martians	Number of packets discarded because they contained bogus information in the DDP header. What distinguishes this error from the others is that the data in the header is never valid as opposed to not being valid at a given point in time.
Bcast:	Number of broadcast packets sent and received.
191881 received	Number of broadcast packets received.
270406 sent	Number of broadcast packets sent.
Sent:	Number of packets transmitted.
550293 generated	Number of packets generated.
66495 forwarded	Number of packets forwarded using routes derived from process switching.
1840 fast forwarded	Number of packets sent using routes from the fast-switching cache.
0 loopback	Number of packets that were broadcast out an interface on the router for which the device simulated reception of the packet because the interface does not support sending a broadcast packet to itself. The count is cumulative for all interfaces on the device.
0 forwarded from MacIP	Number of IP packets forwarded that were encapsulated within an AppleTalk DDP packet.
0 MacIP failures	Number of MacIP packets sent that were corrupted during the MacIP encapsulation process.

continues

Field	Description
436 encapsulation failed	Number of packets the router could not send because encapsulation failed. This can happen because encapsulation of the DDP packet failed or because AARP address resolution failed.
0 no route	Number of packets the router could not send because it knew of no route to the destination.
0 no source	Number of packets the router sent when it did not know its own address. This should happen only if something is seriously wrong with the router or network configuration.
DDP:	This section describes DDP packets seen.
387265 long	Number of DDP long packets.
0 short	Number of DDP short packets.
0 macip	Number of IP packets encapsulated in an AppleTalk DDP packet that the router sent.
0 bad size	Number of packets whose physical packet length and claimed length differed.
NBP:	This section describes NBP packets.
302779 received	Total number of NBP packets received.
0 invalid	Number of invalid NBP packets received. Causes include invalid op code and invalid packet type.
0 proxies	Number of NBP proxy lookup requests received by the router when it was configured for NBP proxy transition usage.
57875 replies sent	Number of NBP replies sent.
59947 forwards	Number of NBP forward requests received or sent.
418674 lookups	Number of NBP lookups received.
432 failures	Generic counter that increments any time the NBP process experiences a problem.
RTMP:	This section describes RTMP packets.
108454 received	Total number of RTMP packets received.
0 requests	Number of RTMP requests received.
0 invalid	Number of invalid RTMP packets received. Causes include invalid op code and invalid packet type.

Field	Description
40189 ignored	Number of RTMP packets ignored. One reason for this is that the interface is still in discovery mode and is not yet initialized.
90170 sent	Number of RTMP packets sent.
0 replies	Number of RTMP replies sent.
Enhanced IGRP:	This section describes Enhanced IGRP packets.
0 received	Number of Enhanced IGRP packets received.
0 hellos	Number of Enhanced IGRP hello packets received.
0 updates	Number of Enhanced IGRP update packets received.
0 replies	Number of Enhanced IGRP reply packets received.
0 queries	Number of Enhanced IGRP query packets received.
0 sent	Number of Enhanced IGRP packets sent.
0 hellos	Number of Enhanced IGRP hello packets sent.
0 updates	Number of Enhanced IGRP update packets sent.
0 replies	Number of Enhanced IGRP reply packets sent.
0 queries	Number of Enhanced IGRP query packets sent.
0 invalid	Number of invalid Enhanced IGRP packets sent.
0 ignored	Number of packets ignored as a result of invalid IEGRP packets received.
ATP:	This section describes ATP packets.
0 received	Number of ATP packets the router received.
ZIP:	This section describes ZIP packets.
13619 received	Number of ZIP packets the router received.
33633 sent	Number of ZIP packets the router sent.
32 netinfo	Number of packets that requested port configuration via ZIP GetNetInfo requests. These are commonly used during node startup and are occasionally used by some AppleTalk network management software packages.
Echo:	A description of AEP packets.

continues

Field	Description
0 received	Number of AEP packets the router received.
0 discarded	Number of AEP packets the router discarded.
0 illegal	Number of illegal AEP packets the router received.
0 generated	Number of AEP packets the router generated.
0 replies sent	Number of AEP replies the router sent.
Responder:	This section describes Responder Request packets.
0 received	Number of Responder Request packets the router received.
0 illegal	Number of illegal Responder Request packets the router received.
0 unknown	Number of Responder Request packets the router received that it did not recognize.
0 replies sent	Number of Responder Request replies the router sent.
0 failures	Number of Responder Request replies the router could not send.
AARP:	This section describes AARP packets.
85 requests	Number of AARP requests the router received.
149 replies	Number of AARP replies the router received.
100 probes	Number of AARP probe packets the router received.
84 martians	Number of AARP packets the router did not recognize. If you start seeing an inordinate number of martians on an interface, check whether a bridge has been inserted into the network. When a bridge is starting up, it floods the network with AARP packets.
0 bad encapsulation	Number of AARP packets received that had an unrecognizable encapsulation.
0 unknown	Number of AARP packets the router did not recognize.
278 sent	Number of AARP packets the router sent.
0 failures	Number of AARP packets the router could not send.

Field	Description
29 delays	Number of AppleTalk packets delayed while waiting for the results of an AARP request.
315 drops	Number of AppleTalk packets dropped because an AARP request failed.
Lost: 0 no buffers	Number of packets lost because of lack of buffer space.
Unknown: 0 packets	Number of packets whose protocol could not be determined.
Discarded:	This section describes the number of packets that were discarded.
130475 wrong encapsulation	Number of packets discarded because they had the wrong encapsulation. That is, nonextended AppleTalk packets were on an extended AppleTalk network, or vice versa.
0 bad SNAP discrimination	Number of packets discarded because they had the wrong SNAP discriminator. This occurs when another AppleTalk device has implemented an obsolete or incorrect packet format.
AURP:	This section describes AppleTalk Update Routing Protocol packets.
0 open requests	Total number of open requests.
0 router downs	Number of router down packets received.
0 routing information sent	Number of routing information packets sent.
0 routing information received	Number of routing information packets received.
0 zone information sent	Number of ZIP packets sent.
0 zone information received	Number of ZIP packets received.
0 get zone nets sent	Number of get zone network packets sent requesting zone information.
0 get zone nets received	Number of get zone network packets received requesting zone information.
0 get domain zone list sent	Number of get domain zone list packets sent requesting domain zone list information.
0 get domain zone list received	Number of get domain zone list packets received requesting domain zone list information.
0 bad sequence	Number of AURP packets received out of sequence.

The **show appletalk zone** Command

The **show appletalk zone** command displays all entries or specified entries in the zone information table. Figure 9-9 shows sample output from the **show appletalk zone** command.

Figure 9-9 *All nonfiltered zones should be listed in the AppleTalk zone table.*

```
Router# show appletalk zone
Name                    Network(s)
Gates of Hell           666-666
Engineering             3 29-29 4042-4042
customer eng            19-19
CISCO IP                4140-4140
Dave's House            3876 3924 5007
Narrow Beam             4013-4013 4023-4023 4037-4037 4038-4038
Low End SW Lab          6160 4172-4172 9555-9555 4160-4160
Tir'n na'Og             199-199
Mt. View 1              7010-7010 7122 7142 7020-7020 7040-7040 7060-7060
Mt. View 2              7152 7050-7050
UDP                     1112-12
Empty Guf               69-69
Light                   80
europe                  2010 3010 3034 5004
Bldg-13                 4032 5026 61669 3012 3025 3032 5025 5027
Bldg-17                 3004 3024 5002 5006
```

The following are the fields shown in the output in Figure 9-9:

Field	Description
AppleTalk Zone Information	Name of the zone.
Valid for nets: 4140-4140	Cable range(s) or network numbers assigned to this zone.
Not associated with any interface.	Interfaces that have been assigned to this zone.
Not associated with any access list.	Access lists that have been defined for this zone.

NBP Testing

The **show appletalk nbp** command identifies Name Binding Protocol (NBP) services registered by the router. Configuring the router to use the service-name display feature aids in troubleshooting. Network administrators recognize AppleTalk names, but often not addresses, especially because AppleTalk addresses are dynamic.

The privileged **ping** command with the **nbp** option is known as **nbptest** facility, which is an interactive, menu-driven facility. This troubleshooting tool is available in Cisco IOS Release 11.0 and earlier; you can use the **nbptest** facility to search for NBP entities in a specific zone, display the router's current zone list, and poll all devices in all zones.

The following keywords to the **nbp** option summarize the **nbptest** tests you can perform:

- **lookup**—Searches for NBP entities in a specific zone.
- **parms**—Sets the parameters used in subsequent lookup and poll tests.
- **zones**—Displays the router's current zone list (equivalent to the **show appletalk zone** command).
- **poll**—Searches for all devices in all zones (use with caution).
- **help** or **?**—Displays the list of **nbptest** tests.
- **quit**—Exits the **nbptest** facility.

In Cisco IOS Release 11.1, a new command, **test appletalk**, replaces the **nbptest** facility. You can use the **test appletalk** command with the **nbp** options to perform informational lookups of NBP-registered entities. You can use the **nbp** options when AppleTalk zones are listed in the Chooser but services in these zones are unavailable.

Many of the options to the **test appletalk** command are undocumented features used by Cisco engineers. However, the **nbp** options are useful for troubleshooting. They include the following:

- **confirm**—Sends an NBP confirm packet to the specified entity.
- **lookup**—Prompts for name, type, and zone, and then looks up a network visible entity (NVE).
- **parameters**—Sets the parameters used in subsequent lookup and poll tests.
- **poll**—Searches for all devices in all zones.
- **?**—Displays the list of tests.
- **end**—Exits the test facility.

AppleTalk names are not case sensitive and are in the form *object:type@zone*. For example, the Sydney router in the Australia zone is specified as Sydney:CiscoRouter@Australia. For the object and type fields, you can use an equal sign (=) to signify all possible values. You can use a nonprinting character by entering a three-character string that is the hexadecimal equivalent of the character. For example, you type **:c5** to specify the truncation wildcard.

When running the **test appletalk** facility, you use the confirm option to check that a name of a specified type is registered on a device. For example, **nbp confirm 24279.173 my-mac:AFPServer@engineering** confirms that the name my-mac is registered on the device 24279.173 in the engineering zone. The object type is AFPServer.

You use the **lookup** and **poll** commands to search for objects. For example, **nbp lookup =:CiscoRouter@engineering** looks for all objects of type CiscoRouter in the engineering zone. The command **nbp lookup =:Macintosh:c5@engineering** looks for all objects whose type identifier starts with **Macintosh** in the engineering zone. This would find all Macintoshes, regardless of whether they are Macintosh IIs, Macintosh SEs, and so on.

AppleTalk debug Commands

You should use **debug** commands only when traffic on the AppleTalk network is low, so other activity on the system is not adversely affected.

Some of the **debug** commands can generate a significant amount of output for every AppleTalk packet processed. To avoid problems, use commands that generate summary information, such as **debug apple events**.

For more information on which commands generate a lot of output, see the *Debug Command Reference*. Among the key **debug** commands are

- **debug apple arp**
- **debug apple errors**
- **debug apple events**
- **debug apple nbp**
- **debug apple packet**
- **debug apple routing**
- **debug apple zip**

These commands are discussed in more detail in the following sections.

The **debug apple arp** Command

The **debug apple arp** command is helpful when you experience problems communicating with a node on a local network. If the output indicates that the router is receiving AppleTalk Address Resolution Protocol (AARP) replies, you can assume that the problem is not at the physical layer. Figure 9-10 shows sample output from the **debug apple arp** command.

Figure 9-10 *You can verify AppleTalk dynamic address acquisition by using the **debug apple arp** command.*

```
Router# debug apple arp
Ether0: AARP: Sent resolve for 4160.26
Ether0: AARP: Reply from 4160.26(0000.0c00.0453) for 4160.154(0000.0c00.8ea9)
Ether0: AARP: Resolved waiting request for 4160.26(0000.0c00.0453)
Ether0: AARP: Reply from 4160.19(0000.0c00.0082) for 4160.154(0000.0c00.8ea9)
Ether0: AARP: Resolved waiting request for 4160.19(0000.0c00.0082)
Ether0: AARP: Reply from 4160.19(0000.0c00.0082) for 4160.154(0000.0c00.8ea9)
```

Explanations for representative lines of output in Figure 9-10 follow.

The following line indicates that the router has requested the hardware MAC address of the host at network address 4160.26:

```
Ether0: AARP: Sent resolve for 4160.26
```

The following line indicates that the host at network address 4160.26 has replied, giving its MAC address (0000.0c00.0453). For completeness, the message also shows the network address to which the reply was sent and its hardware MAC address (also in parentheses).

```
Ether0: AARP: Reply from 4160.26(0000.0c00.0453) for 4160.154(0000.0c00.8ea9)
```

The following line indicates that the MAC address request is complete:

```
Ether0: AARP: Resolved waiting request for 4160.26(0000.0c00.0453)
```

The **debug apple errors** Command

The **debug apple errors** command displays errors such as configuration mismatch problems, wrong encapsulation, invalid echo packet, unsolicited echo reply, unknown echo function, invalid **ping** packet, unknown **ping** function, bad responder packet type, and NetInfoReply errors. Figure 9-11 shows sample output from the **debug apple errors** command.

Figure 9-11 *The **debug apple errors** command provides useful information for troubleshooting interface configuration errors.*

```
Router# debug apple errors
%AT-3-ZONEDISAGREES: Ethernet0: AppleTalk port disabled; zone list
incompatible with 4160.19
%AT-3-ZONEDISAGREES: Ethernet0: AppleTalk port disabled; zone list
incompatible with 4160.19
%AT-3-ZONEDISAGREES: Ethernet0: AppleTalk port disabled; zone list
incompatible with 4160.19
```

As Figure 9-11 suggests, a single error message indicates zone list incompatibility; this message is sent out periodically until the condition is corrected or **debug apple errors** is turned off.

Most of the other messages that **debug apple errors** can generate are obscure or indicate a serious problem with the AppleTalk network. Some of these other messages follow.

In the following message, RTMPRsp, RTMPReq, ATP, AEP, ZIP, ADSP, or SNMP could replace NBP, and *llap dest not for us* could replace wrong encapsulation:

```
Packet discarded, src 4160.12-254,dst 4160.19-254,NBP,wrong encapsulation
```

In the following message, in addition to invalid echo packet, other possible errors are unsolicited AEP echo reply, unknown echo function, invalid **ping** packet, unknown **ping** function, and bad responder packet type:

```
Ethernet0: AppleTalk packet error; no source address available
AT: pak_reply: dubious reply creation, dst 4160.19
AT: Unable to get a buffer for reply to 4160.19
Processing error, src 4160.12-254,dst 4160.19-254,AEP, invalid echo packet
```

The **debug apple errors** command can print out additional messages when other debugging commands are also turned on. When you turn on both **debug apple errors** and **debug apple events**, the following message can be generated:

```
Proc err, src 4160.12-254,dst 4160.19-254,ZIP,NetInfo Reply format is invalid
```

In the preceding message, in addition to NetInfo Reply format is invalid, other possible errors are NetInfoReply not for me, NetInfoReply ignored, NetInfoReply for operational net ignored, NetInfoReply from invalid port, unexpected NetInfoReply ignored, cannot establish primary zone, no primary has been set up, primary zone invalid, net information mismatch, multicast mismatch, and zones disagree.

When you turn on both **debug apple errors** and **debug apple nbp**, the following message can be generated:

```
Processing error,...,NBP,NBP name invalid
```

In the preceding message, in addition to NBP name invalid, other possible errors are NBP type invalid, NBP zone invalid, not operational, error handling brrq, error handling proxy, NBP fwdreq unexpected, No route to srcnet, Proxy to * zone, Zone * from extended net, No zone info for *, and NBP zone unknown.

When you turn on both **debug apple errors** and **debug apple routing**, the following message can be generated:

```
Processing error,...,RTMPReq, unknown RTMP request
```

In the preceding message, in addition to unknown RTMP request, other possible errors are RTMP packet header bad, RTMP cable mismatch, routed RTMP data, RTMP bad tuple, and Not Req or Rsp.

The **debug apple events** Command

The **debug apple events** command displays information about AppleTalk special events, neighbors becoming reachable or unreachable, and interfaces going up or down. Only significant events are logged. When configuring or making changes, you can enable **debug apple events** to track state changes or any errors that might result. You can also use this command periodically when you suspect problems.

In a stable network, the **debug apple events** command does not return any information. To monitor the internetwork for configuration and status changes, you can continuously log the output from this command to a syslog daemon on a UNIX host by using the **appletalk event-logging** command.

The **debug apple events** command is useful in tracking state changes when a new interface is brought up. When no problems are encountered, the state changes progress as follows:

Step 1   Line down

Step 2   Restarting

Step 3   Probing (for its own address using AARP)

Step 4   Acquiring (sending out GetNetInfo requests)

Step 5   Requesting zones (the list of zones for its cable)

Step 6   Verifying (that the router's configuration is correct; if it is not, a port configuration mismatch is declared)

Step 7   Checking zones (to make sure its list of zones is correct)

Step 8   Operational (participating in routing)

Figure 9-12 shows sample output from the **debug apple events** command.

Figure 9-12   *The **debug apple events** command reports on all AppleTalk packets being received or sent.*

```
Router# debug apple events
Ether0: AT: Resetting interface address filters
%AT-5-INTRESTART: Ether0: AppleTalk port restarting; protocol restarted
Ether0: AppleTalk state changed; unknown -> restarting
Ether0: AppleTalk state changed; restarting -> probing
%AT-6-ADDRUSED: Ether0: AppleTalk node up; using address 65401.148
Ether0: AppleTalk state changed; probing -> acquiring
AT: Sent GetNetInfo request broadcast on Ether0
AT: Sent GetNetInfo request broadcast on Ether0
AT: Sent GetNetInfo request broadcast on Ether0
AT: Sent GetNetInfo request broadcast on Ether0
AT: Sent GetNetInfo request broadcast on Ether0
```

When you attempt to bring up a non-seed router without a seed router on the wire, it never becomes operational; instead, it hangs in the acquiring mode and continues to send out periodic GetNetInfo requests.

The **debug apple nbp** Command

The **debug apple nbp** command displays debugging output from the NBP routines. To determine whether the router is receiving NBP lookups from a node on the AppleTalk network, you can enable **debug apple nbp** at each node between the router and the node in question to determine where the problem lies. Figure 9-13 shows sample output from the **debug apple nbp** command.

Figure 9-13   *You can view NBP lookups by using the **debug apple nbp** command.*

```
Router# debug apple nbp
AT: NBP ctrl = LkUp, ntuples = 1, id = 77
AT: 4160.19, skt 2, enum 0, name: =:ciscoRouter@Low End SW Lab
AT: LkUp =:ciscoRouter@Low End SW Lab
AT: NBP ctrl = LkUp-Reply, ntuples = 1, id = 77
AT: 4160.154, skt 254, enum 1, name: lestat.Ether0:ciscoRouter@Low End SW Lab
AT: NBP ctrl = LkUp, ntuples = 1, id = 78
```

continues

Figure 9-13 *You can view NBP lookups by using the **debug apple nbp** command. (Continued)*

```
AT: 4160.19, skt 2, enum 0, name: =:IPADDRESS@Low End SW Lab
AT: NBP ctrl = LkUp, ntuples = 1, id = 79
AT: 4160.19, skt 2, enum 0, name: =:IPGATEWAY@Low End SW Lab
AT: NBP ctrl = LkUp, ntuples = 1, id = 83
AT: 4160.19, skt 2, enum 0, name: =:ciscoRouter@Low End SW Lab
AT: LkUp =:ciscoRouter@Low End SW Lab
AT: NBP ctrl = LkUp, ntuples = 1, id = 84
AT: 4160.19, skt 2, enum 0, name: =:IPADDRESS@Low End SW Lab
AT: NBP ctrl = LkUp, ntuples = 1, id = 85
AT: 4160.19, skt 2, enum 0, name: =:IPGATEWAY@Low End SW Lab
AT: NBP ctrl = LkUp, ntuples = 1, id = 85
AT: 4160.19, skt 2, enum 0, name: =:IPGATEWAY@Low End SW Lab
```

The first three lines in Figure 9-13 describe an NBP lookup request:

```
AT: NBP ctrl = LkUp, ntuples = 1, id = 77
AT: 4160.19, skt 2, enum 0, name: =:ciscoRouter@Low End SW Lab
AT: LkUp =:ciscoRouter@Low End SW Lab
```

The following are the fields shown in the output in Figure 9-13:

Field	Description
AT: NBP	Indicates that this message describes an AppleTalk NBP packet.
ctrl = LkUp	Identifies the type of NBP packet. Possible values include • LkUp—NBP lookup request. • LkUp-Reply—NBP lookup reply.
ntuples = 1	Indicates the number of name-address pairs in the lookup request packet. The range is 1–31 tuples.
id = 77	Identifies an NBP lookup request value.
AT:	Indicates that this message describes an AppleTalk packet.
4160.19	Indicates the network address of the requester.
skt 2	Indicates the internet socket address of the requester. The responder will send the NBP lookup reply to this socket address.
enum 0	Indicates the enumerator field. Used to identify multiple names registered on a single socket. Each tuple is assigned its own enumerator, incrementing from 0 for the first tuple.

Field	Description
name: =:ciscoRouter@Low End SW Lab	Indicates the entity name for which a network address has been requested. The AppleTalk entity name includes three components:
	• Object (in this case, a wildcard character [=], indicating that the requester is requesting name–address pairs for all objects of the specified type in the specified zone)
	• Type (in this case, ciscoRouter)
	• Zone (in this case, Low End SW Lab)

The third line in Figure 9-13 essentially reiterates the information in the two lines above it, indicating that a lookup request has been made regarding name-address pairs for all objects of the ciscoRouter type in the Low End SW Lab zone.

Because the router is defined as an object of type ciscoRouter in zone Low End SW Lab, the router sends an NBP lookup reply in response to this NBP lookup request. The following two lines of output from Figure 9-13 show the router's response:

```
AT: NBP ctrl = LkUp-Reply, ntuples = 1, id = 77
AT: 4160.154, skt 254, enum 1, name: lestat.Ether0:ciscoRouter@Low End SW Lab
```

In the first line, ctrl = LkUp-Reply identifies this NBP packet as an NBP lookup request. The same value in the id field (id = 77) associates this lookup reply with the previous lookup request. The second line indicates that the network address associated with the router's entity name (lestat.Ether0:ciscoRouter@Low End SW Lab) is 4160.154. The fact that no other entity name/network address is listed indicates that the responder only knows about itself as an object of type ciscoRouter in zone Low End SW Lab.

The **debug apple packet** Command

The **debug apple packet** command displays at least one line of debugging output per AppleTalk packet. The **debug apple packet** command displays at least one line of debugging output per AppleTalk packet processed. Although it should only be used if CPU utilization on the router is less than 50%, it is often helpful for troubleshooting when used with other commands, as in the following examples:

- When used with the **debug apple routing**, **debug apple zip**, and **debug apple nbp** commands, the **debug apple packet** command adds protocol processing information in addition to generic packet details.

- When used with the **debug apple errors** command, the **debug apple packet** command reports packet-level problems, such as those concerning encapsulation.

Figure 9-14 shows sample output from the **debug apple packet** command.

Figure 9-14   *The **debug apple packet** command provides details on every AppleTalk packet.*

```
Router# debug apple packet
Ether0: AppleTalk packet: enctype SNAP, size 60, encaps00000000000000000000000000
AT: src=Ethernet0:4160.47, dst=4160-4160, size=10, 2 rtes, RTMP pkt sent
AT: ZIP Extended reply rcvd from 4160.19
AT: ZIP Extended reply rcvd from 4160.19
AT: src=Ethernet0:4160.47, dst=4160-4160, size=10, 2 rtes, RTMP pkt sent
Ether0: AppleTalk packet: enctype SNAP, size 60, encaps00000000000000000000000000
Ether0: AppleTalk packet: enctype SNAP, size 60, encaps00000000000000000000000000
```

The following are the fields shown in the output in Figure 9-14:

Field	Description
Ether0:	Name of the interface through which the router received the packet.
AppleTalk packet	Indicates that this is an AppleTalk packet.
Enctype SNAP	Encapsulation type for the packet.
size 60	Size of the packet (in bytes).
encaps00000000000000000000000000	Encapsulation.
AT:	Indicates that this is an AppleTalk packet.
Src = Ethernet0:4160.47	Name of the interface sending the packet and its AppleTalk address.
dst = 4160-4160	Cable range of the packet's destination.
size = 10	Size of the packet (in bytes).
2 rtes	Indicates that two routes in the routing table link these two addresses.
RTMP pkt sent	The type of packet sent

The third line in Figure 9-14 indicates the type of packet received and its source AppleTalk address. This message is repeated in the fourth line because AppleTalk hosts can send multiple replies to a given GetNetInfo request.

The **debug apple routing** Command

The **debug apple routing** command displays output from Routing Table Maintenance Protocol (RTMP) routines. This command can be used to monitor acquisition of routes, aging of routing table entries, and advertisement of known routes. It also reports conflicting network numbers on the same network if the network is misconfigured. Figure 9-15 shows sample output from the **debug apple routing** command.

Figure 9-15 *RTMP updates are sent and received every 10 seconds by the router.*

```
Router# debug apple routing
AT: src=Ethernet0:4160.41, dst=4160-4160, size=19, 2 rtes, RTMP pkt sent
AT: src=Ethernet1:41069.25, dst=41069, size=427, 96 rtes, RTMP pkt sent
AT: src=Ethernet2:4161.23, dst=4161-4161, size=427, 96 rtes, RTMP pkt sent
AT: Route ager starting (97 routes)
AT: Route ager finished (97 routes)
AT: RTMP from 4160.19 (new 0,old 94,bad 0,ign 0, dwn 0)
AT: RTMP from 4160.250 (new 0,old 0,bad 0,ign 2, dwn 0)
AT: RTMP from 4161.236 (new 0,old 94,bad 0,ign 1, dwn 0)
AT: src=Ethernet0:4160.41, dst=4160-4160, size=19, 2 rtes, RTMP pkt sent
```

NOTE   Because the **debug apple routing** command can generate a substantial number of messages, you should use it only when router CPU utilization is less than 50%.

The following are the fields in the first line of the sample **debug apple routing** output:

Field	Description
AT:	Indicates that this is AppleTalk debugging output.
src = Ethernet0:4160.41	Indicates the source router interface and network address for the RTMP update packet.
dst = 4160-4160	Indicates the destination network address for the RTMP update packet.
size = 19	Shows the size of this RTMP packet (in bytes).
2 rtes	Indicates that this RTMP update packet includes information on two routes.
RTMP pkt sent	Indicates that this type of message describes an RTMP update packet that the router has sent (rather than one that it has received).

The following two messages indicate that the ager has started and finished the aging process for the routing table and that this table contains 97 entries:

```
AT: Route ager starting (97 routes)
AT: Route ager finished (97 routes)
```

The following are the fields in the following line of **debug apple routing** output:

```
AT: RTMP from 4160.19 (new 0,old 94,bad 0,ign 0, dwn 0)
```

Field	Description
AT:	Indicates that this is AppleTalk debugging output.
RTMP from 4160	Indicates the source address of the RTMP update the router received.
new 0	Shows the number of routes in this RTMP update packet that the router did not already know about.
old 94	Shows the number of routes in this RTMP update packet that the router already knew about.
bad 0	Shows the number of routes the other router indicates have gone bad.
ign 0	Shows the number of routes the other router ignores.
dwn 0	Shows the number of poisoned tuples included in this packet.

The **debug apple zip** Command

The **debug apple zip** command reports significant Zone Information Protocol (ZIP) events such as the discovery of new zones and zone list queries. Figure 9-16 shows sample output from the **debug apple zip** command.

Figure 9-16 *You can monitor zone information exchanges by using the **debug apple zip** command.*

```
Router# debug apple zip
AT: Sent GetNetInfo request broadcast on Ether0
AT: Recvd ZIP cmd 6 from 4160.19-6
AT: 3 query packets sent to neighbor 4160.19
AT: 1 zones for 31902, ZIP XReply, src 4160.19
AT: net 31902, zonelen 10, name US-Florida
```

Explanations of the lines of output shown in Figure 9-16 follow.

The first line indicates that the router has received an RTMP update that includes a new network number and is now requesting zone information:

```
AT: Sent GetNetInfo request broadcast on Ether0
```

The second line indicates that the neighbor at address 4160.19 replies to the zone request with a default zone:

```
AT: Recvd ZIP cmd 6 from 4160.19-6
```

The third line indicates that the router responds with three queries to the neighbor at network address 4160.19 for other zones on the network:

```
AT: 3 query packets sent to neighbor 4160.19
```

The fourth line indicates that the neighbor at network address 4160.19 responds with a ZIP extended reply, indicating that one zone has been assigned to network 31902:

```
AT: 1 zones for 31902, ZIP XReply, src 4160.19
```

The fifth line indicates that the router responds that the zone name of network 31902 is US-Florida, and the zone length of that zone name is 10:

```
AT: net 31902, zonelen 10, name US-Florida
```

Problem Isolation in AppleTalk Networks

The steps illustrated in the flowchart shown in Figure 9-17 help when you're isolating the source of a problem in which zones do not appear in the Chooser window on a user's Macintosh.

Figure 9-17 *You can isolate connection problems between AppleTalk clients and servers by using these steps.*

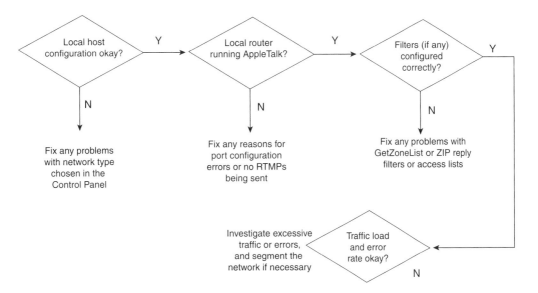

Let's take a closer look at these steps:

Step 1   Check the configuration of the local Macintosh. Pull down the Network Control Panel and make sure EtherTalk is selected if this is an Ethernet network, LocalTalk if this is a LocalTalk network, TokenTalk if this is a Token Ring network, or Remote Only if this is an AppleTalk Remote Access (ARA) connection.

Step 2 Check the local router's configuration. Make sure AppleTalk is running and that the interface port has not been disabled due to a configuration error, usually caused by the router disagreeing with another router on the segment about what the network cable range or zone names should be. If local zones are visible but not remote zones, check for duplicate or overlapping cable ranges in the internetwork.

Step 3 Check for filters that might cause the Macintosh not to see zone names. Check the following:

— AppleTalk access lists (numbered 600 to 699)

— GetZoneList filter, which hides specific zones from users on specific networks but not from routers

— ZIP reply filter, which hides zones in ZIP replies sent to routers

Step 4 Check the traffic load and error rate for the network. Use router tools and a protocol analyzer to check for excessive ZIP traffic, broadcast traffic, Ethernet collisions, retransmissions, and other errors.

When troubleshooting a problem in which zones do not appear in a user's Chooser window, keep in mind that the user's Macintosh gets the zone list from a local router.

An error might be preventing the user's Macintosh from retrieving the zone names. The error is probably either a user error or a problem with the network or router. The most common error that users make is to select the wrong type of network in the Network Control Panel.

Network problems might be physical-layer or link-layer problems. Some AppleTalk network devices are sensitive to excessive traffic on a network, especially third-party LocalTalk/EtherTalk routers with slow CPUs and very little memory.

NOTE   EtherTalk is AppleTalk's terminology for Ethernet.

AppleTalk Symptoms and Problems

Table 9-1 shows common AppleTalk symptoms and possible problems. Using this table, you can identify possible problems and make a plan to verify problem causes and fix the causes.

Table 9-1   *AppleTalk symptoms and problems.*

Symptoms	Possible Problems
Users cannot see zones and services on remote networks.	• Configuration mismatch • Phase 1/Phase 2 incompatibility

continues

Table 9-1   *AppleTalk symptoms and problems. (Continued)*

Symptoms	Possible Problems
Services in a network are not visible outside that network.	• Duplicate network numbers • Phase 1/Phase 2 incompatibility • Configuration mismatch • Misconfigured access list or other filters
Zones are missing from Chooser.	• User's Macintosh set for LocalTalk instead of EtherTalk • Misconfigured access list or other filters • Configuration mismatch • ZIP storm • Unstable routes • Routing has not converged
Services are not always available.	• Duplicate network numbers • ZIP storm • Unstable routes • Overloaded network
Services are visible, but users cannot connect.	• Duplicate network numbers • ZIP storm • Misconfigured access list
Zone list changes each time the Chooser is opened.	• Unstable routes • Configuration mismatch
Connection to services drops.	• Unstable routes • ZIP storm
Port seems stuck in restarting or acquiring mode.	• Configuration mismatch • No seed router
Old zone names appear in Chooser.	• Multiple serial lines between routers are inadvertently crossed • Incorrect process used to change zone names

There are two common problems in an AppleTalk network:

- Configuration mismatch—Routers on a segment do not agree on the cable range and list of zones.
- Duplicate network numbers—Network segments in different parts of the internetwork are assigned the same or an overlapping cable range.

Apple Computer, Inc., started shipping AppleTalk Phase 2 in 1989. Most installations have completely upgraded their internetworks to AppleTalk Phase 2, but there are still a few Phase 1 networks in existence. Merging a Phase 1 network with a Phase 2 network is possible if the Phase 2 network supports only unary cable ranges and one zone per network. A unary cable range (a cable range of length 1) is a range where both numbers are the same, for example, 5–5. This has the benefit of conserving address space by associating only one network address with the link.

Because AppleTalk is "plug and play," inexperienced users can configure routers. For example, it is very easy to configure an AppleTalk Internet Router (AIR). Unfortunately, it is also very easy to misconfigure an AIR.

Because AppleTalk network management is often handled by users rather than experienced network administrators, some installations are not documented correctly, making troubleshooting time-consuming and difficult.

For example, users in the marketing department might use the same network numbers as users in the sales department, without checking any global configuration plan.

A ZIP storm is a pathological problem on AppleTalk networks, where ZIP queries sent to discover zone names for new networks become so frequent that AppleTalk routers cannot keep up with them. Sometimes the ZIP storms cause so much traffic that nonrouters and non-AppleTalk devices are also affected. Fortunately, ZIP storms do not occur very often. Table 9-2 gives more details about ZIP storms.

Another cause for excessive traffic on AppleTalk networks is too many AARP broadcast frames. AARP has two purposes:

- AppleTalk devices use AARP to find other devices (similar to IP ARP).
- A new AppleTalk device uses AARP to select a unique address.

When a new AppleTalk device joins the network, it sends AARP probe frames to verify that its address is unique. An AppleTalk workstation sends 10 AARP broadcasts on Ethernet and Token Ring, and 640 broadcasts on LocalTalk. If the workstation receives a response, then it must try again. If you use unary cable ranges and you already have almost 254 nodes on a segment, then an AppleTalk device might need to try many times. To avoid excessive AARP probes, use generous cable ranges when possible and limit the number of stations on each segment.

AppleTalk Problems and Action Plans

Table 9-2 provides a list of possible problems and some suggested action plans to help isolate the source of AppleTalk problems.

Table 9-2   *AppleTalk problems and action plans.*

Problem	Action Plans
Configuration mismatch	• Check configurations (**show running-config**) and **show appletalk interface**. • Clear interface. • Use AppleTalk discovery mode.
Phase 1/Phase 2 incompatibility	• Use **show appletalk globals** to check for compatibility mode. • Use **show appletalk neighbors** to determine which neighbors are visible. • Use unary cable ranges and only one zone per network.
Duplicate network numbers	• Disable AppleTalk on suspect interface and use **show appletalk route** on a different router to determine if network number still exists. • Check and fix router configuration.
User's Macintosh set for LocalTalk instead of EtherTalk	• Check user's configuration in the Control Panel.
ZIP storm	• Use **show appletalk traffic** to check for increasing ZIP requests.
Unstable routes	• Use **show appletalk route** to look for missing networks. • Use **debug apple events** to make sure routes are being added and aged correctly. • Use the **appletalk timers** command to ensure consistent timer values throughout the internetwork.
Routing has not converged	• Check for problems with **show appletalk route**.
Overloaded network	• Use the **show interfaces** command and a protocol analyzer to check load. • Segment the network.
Multiple serial lines between routers inadvertently crossed	• Physically check wiring and check for errors with the **show interfaces** command.
No seed router	• Use **no appletalk discovery** to make port a seed port.

continues

Table 9-2   *AppleTalk problems and action plans. (Continued)*

Problem	Action Plans
Incorrect process used to change zone names	• When changing zones, make sure you change all affected routers and wait 10 minutes before re-enabling routers.

A common mistake users make in AppleTalk networks is to use a different cable range and list of zones on routers connected to the same network segment. To determine whether you have a configuration mismatch problem, use the **show appletalk interface** command to check for port configuration errors. Also, you can use the **clear interface** command to recover from temporary problems caused by configuration mismatches. The interfaces should be cleared after the configuration errors are fixed. It takes AppleTalk interfaces about a minute or so to verify connectivity and become fully operational.

To avoid problems with mismatches in configuration, a router can be configured as a non-seed or soft-seed router. A *non-seed router* has a cable range of 0–0 (**appletalk cable-range 0-0**). The router must learn the cable range from another router. A soft-seed configuration includes a cable range, but if the router discovers another router advertising a different cable range, the router disables the AppleTalk interface. Soft seed is the recommended configuration. A soft-seed configuration can include the statement **appletalk discovery** with the cable range. In this case, if the router hears a different cable range advertised for the network, then the router keeps AppleTalk enabled and changes its configuration to match the advertised cable range. Discovery is useful during initial setup and for troubleshooting. Soft seed without discovery mode is the recommended configuration when a router is stable.

A *hard-seed* router is configured with a cable range and with the statement **appletalk ignore-verify-errors**. Using a hard-seed router runs the risk of having configuration errors go unreported, but sometimes may be necessary as a last resort when troubleshooting. In certain situations, you might need to force an interface to come up despite the fact that its zone list conflicts with that of another router on the network.

If you still have networks that are running AppleTalk Phase 1, you should consider upgrading them to avoid potential problems and to increase the number of nodes and clients you can have per physical wire. If this is not possible, then cable ranges must not span more than one network number, and you can only assign one zone per network number. The **show appletalk globals** command lets you determine whether your router can support both AppleTalk Phases 1 and 2.

Another common mistake made in AppleTalk networks is using the same cable range or overlapping cable ranges for different network segments in different areas of the internetwork. AppleTalk does not recover gracefully from this error. To determine whether this is your problem, temporarily disable an interface that you suspect has a duplicate network number. Then show the AppleTalk routes and determine whether that network number still exists (because a different router is advertising it). If this is the case, re-enter the zones and a new network number for the suspect interface.

When bringing up an interface on an existing cable where a long zone list is defined, the following actions will help you avoid mistakes and save effort:

Step 1 Bring up the interface in discovery mode (by using the **appletalk discovery** interface configuration command). The **debug apple events** command lets you know when the process is complete by displaying an "operational" message.

Step 2 After discovery is complete and while in interface configuration mode, enter the **no appletalk discovery** interface configuration command for the specific AppleTalk interface being initialized. This action allows the acquired information to be saved and requires that the configuration be validated at port startup.

Step 3 The router exits discovery mode for normal operation and becomes a soft-seed, no-discovery router. (It is recommended that discovery mode be used only when initially configuring networks or when troubleshooting problems.)

Step 4 Issue the **copy running-config startup-config** command to save the acquired information to nonvolatile RAM.

Step 5 Verify the configuration with the **show startup-config** command.

ZIP storms are a serious problem on AppleTalk networks because they cause excessive traffic. Many ZIP packets are sent when a router advertises a new network number and all the other routers react by sending a ZIP query to find out the zone names for the new network. If this happens infrequently, it is not a problem, but sometimes due to misconfigurations or software bugs, a router continually advertises new network numbers. ZIP storms can spread quickly if each router learns about the new networks and includes them in the next routing table update (which happens within 10 seconds on AppleTalk networks). Cisco routers reduce the spread of ZIP storms by not including a new network until a zone name is known for it. To check for a ZIP storm on your internetwork, use the **show appletalk traffic** command. Wait 30 seconds, and enter the command again. If ZIP requests are increasing rapidly, a storm might be occurring. Use a protocol analyzer to confirm this.

Unstable routes can occur if routers do not agree on how often routing tables should be sent (10 seconds by default), how long a routing entry should be considered valid (20 seconds by default), and how quickly an invalid routing entry should be removed from the routing table (60 seconds by default). Use the **appletalk timers** command to change these values.

Excessive load on internetworks that have many routers can prevent some routers from sending RTMP updates every 10 seconds as they should. Because routes begin to be aged out after the loss of two successive RTMP updates, the failure of RTMP updates to arrive results in unnecessary route changes.

Zones might fade in and out of the Chooser or exhibit other unpredictable behavior. Existing connections might get dropped. Route instability associated with load problems is known as *route flapping*. Use the **debug apple events** command to check for route flapping. On a stable network with no route flapping, **debug apple events** displays nothing. On an unstable network, it displays information about bad, discarded, and added routes.

To address the problem of route flapping, adjust the AppleTalk timers by using the **appletalk timers** command. This may be necessary for compatibility with non-Cisco AppleTalk routers.

Set timers consistently to the same value throughout the internetwork, or at a minimum, throughout the backbone of the internetwork. Check with a qualified technical support representative before changing AppleTalk timer values.

AppleTalk does not provide a way to update ZIP tables when changing the mapping of zone names to cable ranges. For example, if the zone name for network 200–201 is Twilight Zone, but you decide to change the zone to No Parking Zone, the zone name on the interface can be changed, and the new zone name takes effect locally. However, unless you keep network 200–201 off the internetwork long enough for it to be completely aged out of the routing tables, some routers might continue to use the old zone name (called "ghost" zones). It takes about 10 minutes for the old zones to age out.

AppleTalk Internetworking Configuration Tips

Consider the following tips when designing your AppleTalk network:

- In most cases, you do not want the zone names for all backbone or WAN connections to appear in the Chooser. These zones usually do not have services on them. If you make the zone name of all the WAN links the same, only that entry appears in the Chooser. Having the zone name start with Z and not look user-friendly will discourage users from trying to find services on the backbone and WAN connections, which would cause NBP traffic to spread throughout the internetwork.

- Design your network with special attention to the direction in which traffic will flow in order to minimize NBP traffic. This is especially important for serial links that are tariffed based on traffic. Use Enhanced Interior Gateway Routing Protocol (Enhanced IGRP) or the AppleTalk Update-Based Routing Protocol (AURP) if you are concerned about too much routing overhead on your WAN links. These protocols save bandwidth because they send routing updates only when changes occur. Remember that Enhanced IGRP for AppleTalk works only in clientless environments.

- Control the number of zones used so that the user's Chooser window does not fill up. In addition, many routers have limits on the number of routes and zones they can handle. These limits usually result from memory constraints. If you exceed such a limit on one of these devices, zones can come and go unpredictably. Cisco routers do not impose fixed limits. However, for compatibility with other routers, you need to limit the number of zones.

- Name zones for the convenience of end users and not for diagnostic purposes. Do not use zones as cable labels. Do not identify one zone per cable with names such as Bld2 S/W Serial T1. In general, a mixture of location and departmental naming conventions works best—for example, Bldg 13 Engineering. In some cases physical location is important—for example, users trying to find printers based on the printer name and zone name.

- Networks should be numbered for convenience of troubleshooters, not of end users. For example, a building number and floor number can be encoded into the cable range. For example, Building 3, Floor 4 could be 3410–3420. Use generous cable ranges to avoid excessive AARP probes.

Summary

This chapter focused on the diagnostic commands that can be used on AppleTalk networks.

Chapter 9 Test
Troubleshooting AppleTalk Connectivity

Estimated Time: 15 minutes

Complete all the exercises to test your knowledge of the materials contained in this chapter. Answers are listed in Appendix A, "Chapter Test Answer Key."

Use the information contained in this chapter to answer the following questions.

Question 9.1

What three commands/tasks can be used to effectively troubleshoot an AppleTalk network?

a. _____

b. _____

c. _____

Question 9.2

Which commands can be used to complete the following tasks:

a.   Display the router's cache of local names and services

b.   Display the AppleTalk routing tables

c.   Perform informational lookups of NBP-registered entities

d.   Check that a name of a specified type is registered

e.   Display zone list query events

Question 9.3

T   F   When you're configuring Enhanced IGRP for AppleTalk, all routers must use the same ID number.

Question 9.4

T   F   Enhanced IGRP can be used only for WAN links or clientless environments.

Question 9.5

For two routers to share AppleTalk routing information, what 3 configuration parameters must they agree on?

_____

_____

_____

PART III

Campus Switch and VLAN Troubleshooting

Diagnosing and Correcting Catalyst Problems

LANs are increasingly forced to deal with applications that require more bandwidth and have lower-latency performance between the workstations on campus LANs.

Part of the demand for more network bandwidth is a result of the surge in the number of installed workstations: Many organizations have nearly one PC for every worker, and many of the hard-copy processes formerly used to run the enterprise have migrated to online, networked forms.

Part of the demand for more bandwidth is due to the applications themselves: Many applications require massive file transfers, and much of the interaction between networked workers formerly limited to alphanumeric text now have multimedia over more interactive forms. For example, consider multimedia whiteboard applications, which require a tremendous amount of bandwidth.

This chapter reviews the operations of the most commonly used Catalyst LAN switches. The technology review provides the context and meaning to help you understand the symptoms of problems.

The problems covered in this chapter are not due to routing issues. The high-speed, Layer 2 switched Ethernet that provides a high-bandwidth, low-latency backbone for campus LANs uses a switching process that closely relates to bridging. Layer 3 switching, however, is similar to routing because routing tables are computed on a hardware level. Some issues covered in this chapter deal with the computation of those routing tables.

The organization of the user PCs and their applications on the backbone segments the network into virtual LANs (VLANs). The VLANs establish a broadcast domain between localized switched-media devices in the various workgroups on the backbone.

Catalyst Series Overview

The Catalyst switch series includes (but is not limited to) the four major products shown in Figure 10-1.

Figure 10-1 *Catalyst switches are differentiated by slots, modularity, forwarding capabilities, and more.*

Product	Slots	PS Fixed PS	Mpps (max.)	Modular interfaces	Sups	LS1010 RSM
2900	2	1 Y	4	N	1	N N
5002	2	2 Y	4	Y	1	N N
5000	5	2 N	15	Y	1	N Y
5500/5505	13	2 N	36	Y	2	Y Y

Legend

PS = Power supply

Mpps = Millions of packets per second forwarded across all switching modules

Sups = Number of supervisor modules

LS1010 = Integrated LightStream ATM; RSM = Integrated Route Switch Module (4500)

At the lower end, the Catalyst 2900 switch offers users a fixed-configuration Fast Ethernet switch for 10/100BaseTX (Catalyst 2901) or 100BaseFX (Catalyst 2902).

At the high end, the Catalyst 5500 is a 13-slot modular switching platform that integrates existing Catalyst 5000 and LightStream 1010 interface modules. The Catalyst 5500 allows the enterprise to scale its LAN with Fast Ethernet, FDDI, or ATM switching and, in the future, Gigabit switching.

This book focuses on the midlevels of the Catalyst switch series: the Catalyst 5002 and the Catalyst 5000.

The Catalyst 5002 switch is a Catalyst 5000 in a compact chassis. The Catalyst 5002 is a modular switch with two slots and is intended for the network periphery. The Catalyst 5002 can be configured with any current or future Catalyst 5000 family modules.

The Catalyst 5000 modular switch is a larger chassis than the 5002 and offers five slots for modules. The Catalyst 5000 is intended for board closet and data center applications.

The Catalyst 5000 series provides virtual LAN networking and optional multilayer switching with Cisco IOS software functionality.

The modular design of the Catalyst 5000 series switches allows users to dedicate 10-Mbps Ethernet and 100-Mbps Fast Ethernet connections to existing LAN segments or high-performance workstations and servers, using unshielded twisted-pair (UTP), shielded twisted-pair (STP), and fiber-optic cable.

The switch architecture includes a single integrated 1.2 Gbps data switching backbone that supports wire-speed switched Ethernet and Fast Ethernet users across a wide range of backbone interfaces, including Fast Ethernet, Fiber Distributed Data Interface (FDDI), Copper Distributed Data Interface (CDDI), and Asynchronous Transfer Mode (ATM).

Catalyst 5000 Internal Architecture

To help you become better able to interpret what you see as output from the Catalyst troubleshooting tools, the next few pages present a description of some of the main architectural elements and operational protocols performed in the switch.

By knowing some of the fundamental aspects of Catalyst switch processes, you will be better able to interpret the output of the diagnostic commands that can help with your troubleshooting tasks.

The switching process basically moves the traffic received from an input port on a line-switching module, as shown in Figure 10-2, to a switching bus so that the traffic is sent out one or more output ports on a line switching module.

Figure 10-2 *Switching processes move data from an input port on one line-switching module to the output port on another line-switching module.*

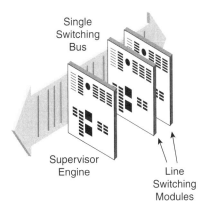

Switching is less processing intensive and has lower latency than routing because a switch can use a simpler determination of the source and destination for the traffic.

The Catalyst 5000 uses a single switching bus architecture, the simplest type of bus for switching up to 10 Gbps. Application-specific integrated circuits (ASICs) on the bus and on the ports arbitrate how to access the backplane and control the destination of packet transfers.

If the bus is oversubscribed, access to the bus is blocked. Unlike the Catalyst 5000, the Catalyst 5500 switch uses crossbar switching. Crossbar switching does not use bus arbitration and has a more complex process to control blocking.

Store-and-forward switching, provided by the Catalyst 5000, stores the entire frame before making a switching decision. This is appropriate for applications on a campus LAN backbone where buffering and error control occur. Other forwarding techniques include cut-through switching (in which frame forwarding begins immediately on receipt of the destination information at the start of the frame) and fragment-free switching (in which forwarding does not start until the switch has received 64 bytes of the frame, thereby ensuring that the packet was not a fragment).

The Catalyst 5000 uses input/output queuing and shared buffers, which avoids the head-of-the-line blocking problem that can occur when packets are stored in queues associated with incoming ports.

A packet is transmitted when all other packets earlier in the queue have been successfully transmitted. As a result, a single packet that cannot be transmitted because of a busy destination port can block all packets in the queue behind it, even if other destination ports are free.

With the input/output queuing and shared buffer in the Catalyst 5000, the switch is able to offer the highest throughput with the fewest number of buffers, and it also avoids the head-of-the-line blocking problem.

Figure 10-3 shows the central bus arbiter attached to the switch's single data bus. This central bus arbiter works with the local arbiter in each line card as required to set the queuing for each port.

Figure 10-3 *The Catalyst 5000/5002 internal architecture supports buffering on the backbone module.*

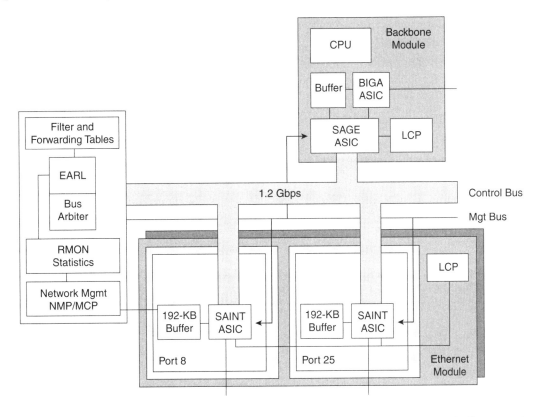

Input/output buffering is done on the backbone module and on the 192-KB buffers associated with each port. This architecture supports multiple levels of data prioritization, with each interface separately user-configurable as high or low priority. The 192-KB buffer for each port provides 160 KB for outbound traffic and 24 KB for inbound traffic. The ports are controlled by ASICs that have fast table add and lookup algorithms. Each Ethernet port interface comprises a custom ASIC, called the SAINT (Synergy Advanced Interface and Network Termination), with an integrated 10/100 Ethernet Media Access Control (MAC) controller and Direct Memory Access (DMA) engine that connects the 192-KB buffer to the data bus.

Other media ports make use of a second custom ASIC, called the SAGE (Synergy Advanced Gate-Array Engine), an ASIC without an integrated Ethernet MAC.

Catalyst 5000 memory contains a central address table in DRAM that contains the filter and forwarding tables. An ASIC called Enhanced Address Recognition Logic (EARL) works with bus arbitration to govern access to the data switching bus and control the destination of packet transfers.

The Network Management Processor/Master Control Processor (NMP/MCP) is the aggregation point for management information about the switch and its role in the network. This information includes data from Simple Network Management Protocol (SNMP) and remote monitoring (RMON).

The NMP also contains information about spanning-tree configuration details, Cisco Discovery Protocol (CDP) neighbors, and the VLAN Trunking Protocol (VTP). (These protocols are covered later in this chapter.) The NMP uses the management bus that operates at 761 kbps.

The BIGA (built-in gate array) connects the NMP to the 1.2-Gbps bus. The LCP is the line-module communication processor.

Self-diagnostics at startup occur during the power-up self-test, which checks the switch internal hardware components.

Power-up self-test output should resemble that shown in Figure 10-4.

Figure 10-4 *The power-up self-test checks LEDs, memory, and address recognition logic.*

```
ROM Power Up Diagnostics of January 27, 1999
Init NVRAM Log
LED Test   .................. done
ROM Checksum  .............. passed
Dual Port RAM r/w Test  ..... passed
ID PROM   ................... passed
System DRAM Size (Mb)  ....... 16
DRAM Data Bus Test  ........ passed
DRAM Address Test  ......... passed
DRAM Byte/Word Access Test .. passed
EARL Test  ................. passed
BOOTROM, Dated January 27, 1999 11:46:24
```

NOTE   While the Catalyst switch is running, you can get details about this (and other) information by using the Catalyst commands show system and show test. These and other show commands are covered in more detail later in this chapter.

Catalyst Switching Technology

First, it's important to learn the difference between bridging and switching.

A *bridge* is a device that connects and passes packets between two network segments that use the same communications protocol. Bridges operate at the data link layer (Layer 2) of the OSI reference model. In general, a bridge filters, forwards, or floods an incoming frame based on the MAC address of that frame.

A bridge uses a software-based process to set up and maintain a filtering database consisting of static entries. Each static entry equates a MAC destination address with a port that can receive frames with this MAC destination address and a set of ports on which the frames can be transmitted.

To avoid loops, a bridge uses the spanning-tree algorithm with one spanning-tree instance per physical port and a maximum of eight spanning trees on a microsegmented bridge, which usually has up to 16 ports. The bridge usually addresses a LAN overload condition by separating the LAN's traffic into segments.

Although a *switch* essentially performs a bridging function (the Catalyst 5000 series uses IEEE 802.1D Spanning-Tree Protocol), it is primarily hardware based, with ASICs and a high-capacity switching bus. Switches are much faster than bridges.

There can be many spanning-tree instances per port, especially if the port acts as a trunk that supports multiple VLANs. There should be one spanning tree for every VLAN, with up to 1,024 VLANs allowed on a Catalyst 5000.

Ports connect directly to end users and offer switched rather than shared Ethernet to provide greater access to bandwidth. Switches also connect to other switches and use advanced protocols to speed up configuration and convergence information flow across the network. A Catalyst 5000 can have 100 or more ports, depending on the line cards used.

Despite greater functionality, speed, and capacity, switch problems are easier to debug than the legacy bridges. Bridges were often meant to operate without much management, and problem causes (not the problems themselves) were often invisible. By contrast, switch debugging can use a full set of troubleshooting tools, including those covered in this chapter.

Table 10-1 provides a comparison between bridging and switching.

Table 10-1   *Legacy bridging versus LAN switching.*

Legacy Bridging	LAN Switching
Software based (slow)	Primarily hardware based (faster)
One to eight spanning trees on a segmented bridge	Supports as many spanning trees as there are VLANs
Connects overloaded LAN segments	Connects directly to other switches or to end users
Usually up to 16 ports	100 or more ports per switch

Spanning-Tree Review

The Spanning-Tree Protocol provides bridged networks with multiple link paths that ensure connectivity between all bridged nodes and loop-free paths throughout the network:

- When loops occur, packets travel from the source toward the destination (if known) and then loop around again and again.

- When the segment that contains the destination address is not yet learned, packets are sent as broadcasts, or multicasts. These packets can travel around the loop in both directions from a bridge again and again.

- When there are several bridges in the network, the bridges combine ports for many possible paths with multiple loops. Packets can be replicated out all the ports of each successive bridge's ports and exponentially loop around again and again.

Figure 10-5, for example, shows a network that contains two loops. Without a network-layer function, a bridged network lacks a Time To Live (TTL) mechanism. Without this decremental scheme at Layer 2 to eventually put an end to looping packets, even temporary transition loops are dangerous. Therefore, the main advantage of the Spanning-Tree Protocol is that it avoids loops.

Figure 10-5 *Network loops are often created when redundant paths are established.*

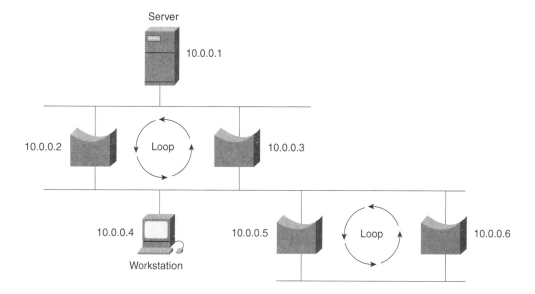

A broadcast storm of looping packets can quickly clog the network with unneeded traffic and prevent needed packet switching. With failures in the spanning-tree mechanisms, you might see a steady high switch load on the supervisor engine module LED, while the throughput you or your users experience is extremely sluggish or stalled.

To avoid loops, bridges and switches build a spanning tree that contains loop detection and avoidance mechanisms. These bridges and switches are designated points of continuity and continuously multicast membership (peer) identity to each other. There are two bridge types:

- A root bridge, which is a unique point of reference for the spanning tree that can be elected by tree members. A root bridge calculates the shortest-path distance from these other members to itself. This process is performed by adding up the cost to each other member and organizing the possible paths in order of lowest to highest cost. The root bridge becomes the timer master for slaved members of the tree, and validates topology changes on the tree.

- One or several designated bridges that elect the root bridge and then determine their hierarchical-cost path(s) to the root based on a "cost" parameter. Cost is a function of the bandwidth of each path, can be changed by a switch port, and is a summation value that represents accumulated path costs to the root bridge.

The ports contained in these bridges can be in one of several states and can make the transition through the states when they change from nonforwarding to forwarding. These port states are

- Blocking—The port is in a nonforwarding state because of a loop detection. These are nondesignated ports.

- Listening—The port is in a preforwarding state, able to check for bridge protocol data units (BPDUs) about the spanning tree.

- Learning—The port is in a preforwarding state, able to determine the topology details that indicate a path to the root bridge.

- Forwarding—Allows for output packets, which are designated ports that receive and send packets.

- Disabled—The port is not enabled for Spanning-Tree Protocol or has been administratively disabled.

- Cisco special port-fast and uplink-fast modes—The port has no timing clock constraints and is moved to a forwarding state more rapidly than a normal Spanning-Tree Protocol transition. Port-fast is for LAN traffic such as Novell IPX; uplink-fast is for dialup traffic.

These faster modes are useful for user traffic that cannot tolerate the typical Spanning-Tree Protocol transition, which could take 20 seconds from blocking to listening, plus 15 seconds from listening to learning, plus 15 seconds from learning to forwarding.

Figure 10-6 shows a network that has had its loops resolved by the Spanning-Tree Protocol. By blocking the redundant ports, two loops have been removed.

Figure 10-6 *Ports are blocked to resolve loops.*

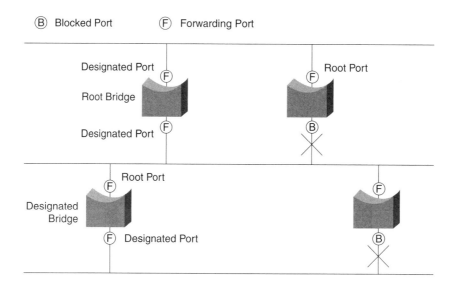

TIP	Each Catalyst 5000 VLAN has a unique bridge ID. A physical port that is a trunk may be part of more than one spanning tree. Loops on one spanning tree may affect other spanning trees if they share a topology.

To distribute the load on parallel VLAN Inter-Switch Links (ISLs), you can change the port priority per VLAN. To increase the chances of being a root port, lower the bridge priority to make the bridge ID numerically lower.

When you set up fast-mode devices, the setup processes bypass part of the spanning-tree learning transitions. Make sure you do not introduce spanning-tree loops.

VLAN Frame Tagging with ISL

ISL is used over point-to-point connections to interconnect two VLAN-capable Cisco products, such as the Catalyst 5000 and 3000 series switches, and the Cisco 4000 and 7000 series routers.

ISL is generally used on Fast Ethernet using full- or half-duplex 100-Mbps links; ISL can also run on 10-Mbps links, but this is not as common. The ISL specification also allows for the ISL frame to contain Token Ring frames, as well.

The 802.10 ISL protocol is a packet-tagging protocol that contains a standard Ethernet frame and the VLAN information associated with that frame. Think of it as a virtual topology going across a physical topology.

The ISL has three primary fields: the header, the original packet, and the frame check sequence (FCS) at the end. The header is further divided into fields as shown in Figure 10-7.

Figure 10-7   *The ISL frame encapsulation is added and removed by the VLAN switches at the start and end of the ISL path.*

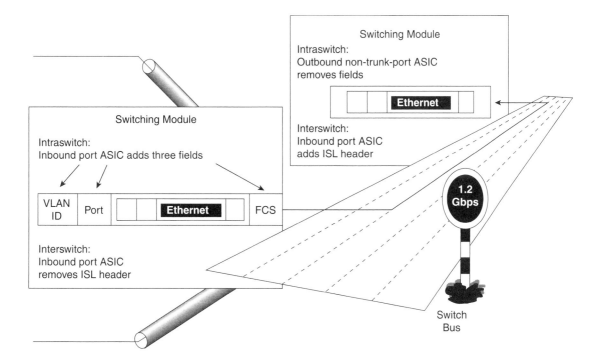

As a frame enters the switching module, it is stored in the port's frame buffer. In Figure 10-7, the SAINT ASICs on each port perform an encapsulation or de-encapsulation on the frame.

If a Catalyst port is on a switch trunk, the port will handle interswitch traffic between switches. An ASIC on the switching module that receives frames from the trunk de-encapsulates ISL frames.

The ASIC removes the 30 bytes of information used by ISL: 26 bytes of header information and a 4-byte FCS. This FCS is checked at the port receiving the frame from the trunk.

On the outgoing switching module, the ASIC adds ISL encapsulation before the module sends the frame to the trunk.

If a Catalyst port is not on a switch trunk, the port may handle intraswitch traffic between switching ports in the same switch. The ASIC encapsulates the frame that the inbound port on the network receives.

In Figure 10-7, an Ethernet frame is encapsulated with 30 bytes of information. The 30 bytes are used in three fields to indicate VLAN ID, the port of origin for the frame, and an FCS. This FCS is checked at the port receiving the frame from the switching bus.

For non-Ethernet frames, the SAGE ASIC provides the encapsulation. It is used for non-Ethernet applications, such as the FDDI module, the ATM LANE module, Token Ring, and the NMP on the supervisor engine.

The same type of ASIC on each outbound port also strips off that encapsulated information and extracts the Ethernet frame before sending it out destination ports.

The switching bus is a backplane that has 1.2-Gbps capacity for switching frames. The supervisor engine and all line modules have access to this switching bus.

Figure 10-8 shows the ISL frame tagging format.

Figure 10-8 *ISL framing encapsulates the existing Layer 2 frame.*

DDDDDDDD	DDDDDDDD	DDDDDDDD	DDDDDDDD	DDDDDDDD	TTTTUUUU
SSSSSSSS	SSSSSSSS	SSSSSSSS	SSSSSSSS	SSSSSSSS	SSSSSSSS
LLLLLLLL	LLLLLLLL	10101010	10101010	00000011	HHHHHHHH
HHHHHHHH	HHHHHHHH	VVVVVVVV	VVVVVVVB	IIIIIIII	IIIIIIII
RRRRRRRR	RRRRRRRR	Original frame, including original CRC Ethernet, Token Ring, FDDI			
CCCCCCCC	CCCCCCCC	CCCCCCCC	CCCCCCCC		

ISL Frame Details

The ISL frame encapsulation is 30 bytes and contains the following fields:

- D—Destination address, which is a 40-bit ISL multicast address that is currently set to 01000C0000.

- T—Type of frame that is encapsulated. The following TYPE codes have been defined: 0000 for Ethernet, 0001 for Token Ring, 0010 for FDDI, and 0011 for ATM.

- U—User-defined bits (TYPE extension) used to extend the meaning of the TYPE field. For example, for Ethernet frames, the user field bit 0 indicates the priority of the packet as it passes through the Catalyst 5000. 0000 means normal priority, 0001 means priority 1, 0010 means priority 2, and 0011 means high priority.

- S—Source address of the ISL packet. It should be set to the 48-bit 802.3 MAC address of the MAC transmitting the frame.

- L—Length field, a 16-bit value that indicates length of the packet in bytes, excluding the D, T, U, S, L, and CRC fields. The total length of the excluded fields is 18 bytes, so the L field is the total length minus 18 bytes.

- 1 and 0 expression—This value is AAAA03 to indicate that the ISL frames uses a Subnetwork Access Protocol (SNAP) Logical Link Control (LLC).

- H—High bits of source address. This field is the upper 3 bytes, the manufacturer's ID portion, of the source address field, also known as the organization unique identifier (OUI).

- V—VLAN ID of the packet, a 15-bit value that is used to distinguish frames on different VLANs. This field is often referred to as the "*color*" of the packet. Cisco devices use the lower 10 bits of this field to support 1,024 VLANs.

- B—BPDU/CDP/VTP indicator. The BPDU bit is set for all BPDUs that are encapsulated by the ISL packet. The spanning tree uses BPDUs for information about the topology of the network. This bit is also set for CDP and VTP packet encapsulation. This bit allows packets to get through on the ingress switch.

- I—Index field, which indicates the port index of the source of the packet as it comes out from the Catalyst switch. It is used for diagnostic purposes only and may be set to any value by other devices.

- R—Reserved field, which is used when Token Ring or FDDI packets are encapsulated with an ISL packet. In the case of Token Ring frames, the AC and FC fields are placed here. In the case of FDDI, the FC field is placed in the least significant bit of this field (e.g., an FC of 0x12 would have a RESERVED field of 0x0012). For Ethernet packets, the RESERVED field should be set to all zeros.

- Original Encapsulated Frame—This field is the encapsulated frame, including its own CRC value, completely unmodified. The internal frame must have a CRC value that is valid when the ISL encapsulation fields are removed. The length of this field can be from 1 to 24,575 bytes to accommodate Ethernet, Token Ring, and FDDI frames.

- C—The new CRC. This CRC is a standard 32-bit value calculated on the entire encapsulated frame from the D field to the Original Encapsulated Frame field. The receiving MAC checks this CRC and can discard packets that do not have a valid CRC on them. Note that this CRC is in addition to the one at the end of the Original Encapsulated Frame field.

Inter-Switch Trunk Links carry the packets for one or more VLANs. Network administrators need a VLAN mapping function to maintain VLAN configuration consistency throughout the switch fabric of the network.

In the switch fabric shown in Figure 10-9, VLAN information about VLAN 1 must traverse several ISL trunks using Fast Ethernet and FDDI.

Figure 10-9 *VTP is used to propagate VLAN information more efficiently.*

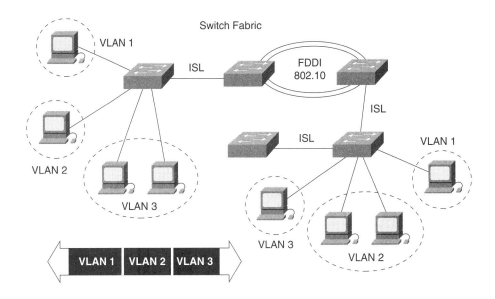

VTP

VTP is a Layer 2 multicast messaging protocol that allows VLAN classification done once at the ingress to the trunk to traverse the entire management domain, rather than requiring VLAN classifications on a hop-by-hop basis. This tremendously reduces latency, allowing intermediate switches to work at nearly wire speed.

VLANs across multiple LAN types are mapped by VTP to provide unique names and internal index associations. Trunk ports can forward all VLAN traffic within the domain.

VTP manages the addition, deletion, and renaming of VLANs at the system level without requiring manual intervention at each switch, which greatly reduces the device-level administration required and the potential for inconsistent names.

VTP keeps track of VLAN changes and multicasts periodic advertisements to communicate with other switches in the network. VTP provides globally consistent VLAN configuration information for the VTP domain.

A VTP domain comprises a group of one or more interconnected devices that share the same VTP domain name. A switch may be configured to be in only one VTP domain.

When you configure the VTP domain name, make sure the name is consistent throughout the network management domain. Use the command **set vtp domain admin-1**.

In Figure 10-10, VTP advertisements occur on a reserved VLAN trunk port across the ISL.

Figure 10-10 *The VTP server and client exchange VTP advertisements.*

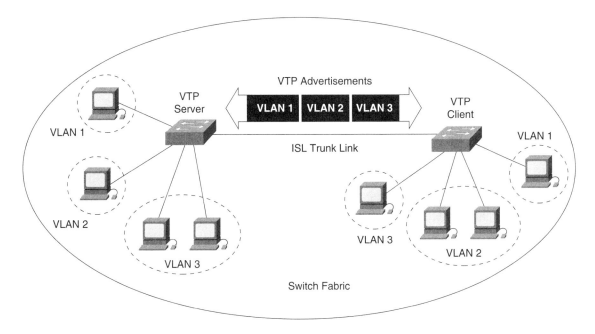

A VTP-capable switch can be configured in three modes: as a VTP server, as a VTP client, or in VTP transparent mode.

Servers and clients maintain the full list of all VLANs within the VTP domain (which defines the boundary of the defined VLANs). They also transmit and receive advertisements of known VLAN information.

A VTP server maintains its VLAN information in a nonvolatile store or TFTP device. You can modify the global VLAN information in a VTP server through the Catalyst command-line interface (CLI) using the VTP Management Information Base (MIB).

When a client or server detects the addition of a VLAN, it prepares to receive traffic with the newly defined VLAN ID on its trunk ports.

Another mode of operation, called *transparent mode*, is for switches that do not wish to participate in the automatic trunk configuration of VTP-created VLANs. However, transparent mode switches continue to forward VTP advertisements that they receive on one trunk port to other trunk ports.

VTP advertisements (called *adverts*) take place on a reserved VLAN on a trunk port. The VLAN number for VPT is set up automatically and varies depending on the media type of the trunk. The reserved VLAN for VTP cannot be deleted or changed.

Clients check advertisements for a configuration revision number. This number increments for successive VLAN change updates. When a client is presented with several advertisements, the advertisement with the highest revision number prevails as the source of VLAN information.

The last updater is a record of the IP address of the last switch (a VTP client or server) that sent a VLAN advertisement.

Troubleshooting VTP

There are some basic rules for troubleshooting VTP:

- Configure switches for transparent mode if they do not need to use VTP. If the proper operation of the switch can occur with a hard-coded setup of VLANs and has no productive use for advertisements about VLAN additions, deletions, and changes, transparent mode offers the simplest approach and easiest troubleshooting.

- A VLAN set up for a transparent-mode switch has local significance only. However, switches in transparent mode continue to relay VTP adverts from other switches configured as VTP servers or clients.

- If you will be using VTP clients and servers, the easiest topology to troubleshoot is one in which you have centralized VTP servers with the spanning-tree root bridge.

- The VTP server is the preferred mode for Catalyst switches. You need at least one VTP server in the VTP management domain.

- Do not configure VTP servers offline. When you configure a VTP server offline and then connect it to the network, you run the risk of an inconsistency when the server presents a VTP advert revision that does not accurately reflect the domain. Other switches that come online may use the inaccurate VTP information, and VLANs on the network may disappear.

- Configure other wiring closet switches as VTP clients, which can reduce the number of switches to consider as you troubleshoot VTP configuration problems because the client cannot create global VLANs.

- The VPT client role is best suited for devices that do not have sufficient nonvolatile memory to store the information about the global VLANs that a server learns through VTP adverts.

- Clients do not preserve the information about global VLANs when they restart, but instead depend on an update of VLAN information from VPT adverts that they get from servers.

- VTP does not work if there is no trunk port or no VLAN1. When troubleshooting, make sure that these essential requirements for VTP have been configured properly.

- For CiscoWorks for Switched Internetworks (CWSI) network management, VTP is required. If you will be using a network management application such as VlanDirector, there must be a VTP server.

To troubleshoot ISL, the first facts to check are that the interswitch physical characteristics—port speed, port duplex, and for optical links, fiber type—match.

In the core of your network make sure you hard-code trunks to be on. If you find that trunks are not on, you can correct the problem with the following command:

```
set trunk [slot/port] on
```

Make sure that the switch's VTP domain name is consistent for the ISL devices. To check VTP domain name, use the following command:

```
show vtp domain
```

Make sure your VLANs match on both sides of a trunk. To check that VLANs match, use one of the following commands on both switches on a link:

```
show trunk
```

or

```
show vlan
```

If you are unable to identify the cause of the ISL problem, you may need to apply additional tools to your troubleshooting efforts. For instance, use a Fast Ethernet analyzer (for example, SwitchProbe) if it is necessary to see frames decoded.

Catalyst 5000 Troubleshooting Tools

Catalyst 5000 troubleshooting begins with the supervisor engine module. The Catalyst 5000 and 5002 switches require a supervisor engine module in the top slot of the chassis. The other slots are for interface modules (for example, the remaining four slots of the Catalyst 5000 switch).

NOTE   Three supervisor engines are available (I, II, and III). Supervisor Engines I and II support fixed Fast Ethernet ports (either 100BaseTx or 100BaseFx). Supervisor Engine III is available with modular or fixed uplink ports and includes advanced functionality such as EARL. Refer to www.cisco.com for more configuration descriptions.

If slot 1 does not contain a supervisor engine module, the system will not boot up. The supervisor engine enables Layer 2 switching and network management. This module contains a console port and two Fast Ethernet interfaces network connections that can connect to workstations, servers, switches, and routers, as shown in Figure 10-11.

Figure 10-11 *The supervisor engine module includes an auxiliary port and LED indicators.*

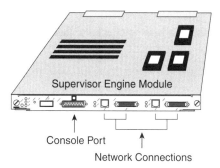

You can troubleshoot Catalyst 5000 series switches using a broad variety of tools:

- CWSI
- An embedded RMON agent and SwitchProbe
- Check switch LEDs and power-up test output
- TCP/IP **ping** and **telnet** utilities
- CDP
- Catalyst Switched Port Analyzer (SPAN)
- Catalyst commands (especially **show** commands)

For tools like CWSI or a network manager using the embedded RMON agent, you can use an in-band network connection, which can be on the supervisor engine or on one of the other modules.

SwitchProbe is a Fast Ethernet analyzer that can connect to an out-of-band network manager.

The console terminal port provides network administrators the CLI to ASCII text. This out-of-band connection requires no special applications to operate CDP or Catalyst commands. Use the CLI for TCP/IP utilities such as **ping** and **telnet**.

The remainder of the chapter offers additional details about each of these troubleshooting tools. The most emphasis is on LEDs, CDP, SPAN, and the available Catalyst **show** commands.

CWSI

CWSI is a specialized version of CiscoWorks that provides a network management application that uses a graphical user interface (GUI).

CWSI can be installed as a self-sufficient, standalone tool on a PC running Windows NT or on UNIX with support for Solaris, HP-UNIX, and AIX. Or CWSI can be installed as an SNMP element management application with HP OpenView, SunNet Manager, and NetView/AIX.

CWSI includes several management applications that can provide information that may help you identify the baseline performance of your switched network, recognizing possible problem facts, and troubleshooting:

- CiscoView provides a GUI that supports chassis physical view, configuration, performance monitoring, and minor troubleshooting.

- VlanDirector provides a GUI for adding new users, moving users between wiring closets, and changing users' VLAN associations.

- TrafficDirector provides a GUI for RMON console application tools for analyzing a united view of network activity on multiple switch ports and trunk links.

- The AtmDirector management application is a GUI that simplifies the installation and administration of ATM in switched internetworks.

- User Tracking utilities are used for setting up dynamic VLANs and tracking station locations within the network.

NOTE   For more details about CWSI, see www.cisco.com.

The Embedded RMON Agent and SwitchProbe

Catalyst software offers monitoring and network control capabilities through the switch via an integrated RMON agent, as shown in Figure 10-12. RMON became a standard for Ethernet in 1992 (as described in RFC 1271). The RMON specification offers network fault diagnosis, planning, and performance-tuning information as information organized into nine groups of monitoring elements.

Figure 10-12 *Statistics and event information are gathered by the RMON agents and reported to the network manager.*

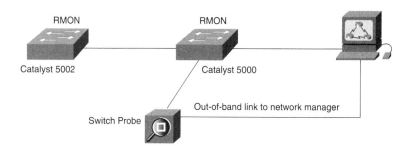

The Catalyst 5000 embedded RMON agent supports four groups in the RMON specification (as described in RFC 1757). RMON capabilities have been embedded into a high-performance switching platform for both 10BaseT and 100BaseT (Fast Ethernet), providing proactive network management access to the RMON statistics, history, alarms, and events groups. These four RMON groups have the most interest for LAN troubleshooting, including

- Packet traps to provide network alarms
- Packet capture for network traffic decoding and analysis
- Events and statistics as source data for network accounting/billing

With the SPAN feature, network managers can access the other five RMON groups, as well as the information provided by RMON2.

Cisco offers standalone RMON probes for monitoring any segment, ring, or switch link in an enterprise network. These SwitchProbe devices can monitor FDDI, CDDI, Token Ring, Ethernet, or Fast Ethernet network segments.

Troubleshooting Catalyst Switch LEDs

Part of a complete troubleshooting scenario includes checking for normal hardware status by looking at the front-panel LEDs on the supervisor module, line cards, and the power supply(ies).

Onboard hardware diagnostics and LEDs confirm module operation and enable easy visual troubleshooting. The status LED on each module shows successful completion and minor and major failure of power-up diagnostics.

The CWSI CiscoView application allows you to check these LEDs remotely. LEDs are represented as graphical objects. The following modules are manageable through CWSI:

- Supervisor engine module

  Check the various LEDs on the supervisor engine module, including the NMP, which acts as an aggregation point for switch management information.

Remote (out-of-band) management through SNMP sets or Telnet (client) connection occurs on any switched or ATM interface.

Local (in-band) management occurs on the Console port (female DCE EIA/TIA-232) for console terminal or modem connection. The Catalyst 5000 and 5002 switch supervisor engine module includes the following:

— A 25-MHz 68EC040 network management processor with 8-MB DRAM, 4-MB Flash EPROM for downloadable microcode and software upgrades, and 256-KB NVRAM; the supervisor engine is connected to a high-performance, low-latency, 1.2-Gbps switching backplane.

— Two Fast Ethernet interfaces (full- or half-duplex), which can be ISL trunks. Users can choose dual 100BaseTX (Category 5 UTP), dual multimode 100BaseFX, or dual single-mode 100BaseFX uplinks. Further, with Cisco's Fast EtherChannel technology, the two ports can be configured as a single, 400-Mbps, full-duplex fault-tolerant connection.

If CWSI autodiscovery terminates, check the supervisor engine module LEDs System Status light and Power Supplies indicators. With CWSI Release 1.2, a redundant power supply not turned on may terminate the autodiscovery process.

The supervisor engine module LEDs that show switch load are important indicators of normal and abnormal switch backplane activity. If the load indicators indicate a high load (80% to 100% steady), chances are good that a broadcast storm may be in progress. Use this LED indicator to check into possible causes for this condition.

- Line card modules

Check the power-up LED sequence on the line card switching modules. LEDs flash during startup and turn green when a successful initialization is completed. A red LED indicates a failure. An orange LED can also indicate a problem on some modules.

If the switch is running, check for normal LED status in all the installed modules. A line card that is not fully inserted can appear to be a hardware failure. Check the position of the extractor levers. A red status LED is an indication that the module is not in the slot.

The autosensing for a switching module port indicates the speed in operation on the port. If the 100-Mbps LED is off, that port is either not in use or is being used at 10 Mbps. Is this what you expect for the port? If not, troubleshoot further:

— Check whether a 10/100-Mbps connection is connected at 10 Mbps instead of 100 Mbps.

— Severe bends in a Category 5 cable can cause a 10/100-Mbps interface to run at 10 Mbps.

— Extreme temperatures may also cause intermittent failures.

— Some devices do not handle autonegotiation correctly.

The most common network problems can be traced to cable problems. See Table 10-2 for the distance limit specifications for each of the switch cable types.

Table 10-2   *Cable distance limitations.*

Module Type		Half-Duplex (e.g., a Hub)	Full-Duplex (with Adapter)
Copper Category 3	10BaseT	100 m	100 m
Copper Category 5	100BaseTX	100 m	100 m
Multimode fiber (MMF)	10BaseFL	2 km	2 km
	100BaseFX	400 m	2 km
Single-mode fiber (SMF)	100BaseFX	10 km	10 km

The fiber-optic cables MMF and SMF are used for ATM and FDDI. As you troubleshoot problems with fiber-optic cables, an important consideration is asymmetric connectivity problems, in which one side of a transmit and receive cable pair fails, but the remaining cable nonetheless forwards frames. This asymmetric connectivity can impair spanning-tree loop avoidance.

The answers to the following questions help determine whether there is a copper UTP cable problem:

- Are the cables the correct type for this installation? Category 3 is for 10BaseT and 10BaseT4 *only*. Was a Category 3 cable installed instead of a Category 5?

- If Category 5 cable is used, was the cable installed correctly? Were the connectors installed properly?

- Is the cable a crossover or straight-through? Which type should it be? Compare the RJ-45 connector wiring at both ends of the cable if you're not sure.

- Is there a broken wire at either end of the cable? Cables that are installed too tightly or bundled together tightly with a tie wrap may have broken wires in the connector. Cables that are pulled through a plenum can have broken wires and exhibit intermittent open circuit conditions.

- Is the cable longer than the 100-meter specification? A time domain reflectometer (TDR) can display the length of the cable, including all wiring closet connections.

- Is the punchdown wiring correct? Are there missing, loose, or broken wires on the punchdown block?

The following are some questions to ask related to end-user device connections:

- Is the network adapter card/interface port at the user end functioning properly?
- Is the device connected to the correct port? Is the port active?

One way to test installed cabling is to replace the entire cable run with an external cable. If you have a known good segment of Category 5 cable, run the cable between the two devices to test connectivity. This test will eliminate any uncertainties about plant cables or punchdown connections.

The following test equipment can be used to troubleshoot a wide variety of network and network cabling problems:

- TDR—Measure cable length and impedance by sending a signal down the cable and examining the reflection.
- Protocol analyzers—Capture and display protocol information by tapping into the network and decoding protocol information into a readable format.
- Cable testers—Scanners for STP, UTP, or fiber.
- Network monitors—Continuously monitor network traffic through SNMP agents.

Catalyst 5000 Switch Diagnostic Tools: ping

One of the most useful and important troubleshooting aids is the **ping** command, which provides a simple echo test. If you **ping** a destination device, do you get a response? If **ping** does not respond, ask the following questions:

- Is there a cable problem?
- Can the testing terminal (or workstation) communicate with any other devices?
- Can any other devices communicate with the switch?
- Are there port errors on the switch? (Check with the **show port** command.)
- Is there normal port traffic? (Check with the **show mac** command.)
- Are the port and interface sc0 in the same VLAN? (Check with the **show port** and **show interface** commands.)

CDP

CDP is a media- and protocol-independent device discovery protocol that runs on all Cisco manufactured equipment (routers, bridges, communication servers, and switches).

Cisco devices discover each other in a protocol-/media-independent way so that a network administrator or network management applications can dynamically discover Cisco devices that are neighbors of already-known devices.

CDP runs on various media that support SNAP, including LANs, Frame Relay, and ATM media. CDP runs over the data link layer only; therefore, two systems that support different network-layer protocols can learn about each other.

CDP uses a small multicast packet to the common destination address 01-00-0C-CC-CC to send and receive periodic messages.

Each device advertises at least one address at which it can receive SNMP messages and a TTL that indicates the length of time a receiving device should hold CDP information before discarding it. By default, TTL is 180 seconds.

CDP packets are sent with a TTL value that is nonzero after an interface is enabled and with a TTL value of zero immediately before an interface is idled down, which provides for quick state discovery.

All Cisco devices receive CDP packets and cache the information in the packet. The cached information is available to network management through MIBs. Cisco devices never forward a CDP packet.

If any information changes from the last received packet, the new information is cached and the older information is discarded, even if its TTL value has not yet expired. CDP is assigned the Cisco HDLC protocol type value 0x2000.

Cisco devices never forward CDP packets beyond the data-link-connected devices. In Figure 10-13, the network administrator can show CDP information for only the neighbors of the switch connected to the management terminal. However, the administrator can use CDP to get the IP address of the neighboring router, Telnet to that router, and use **show cdp** again to see the router's directly connected neighbors.

Figure 10-13 *Cisco devices use CDP to discover each other.*

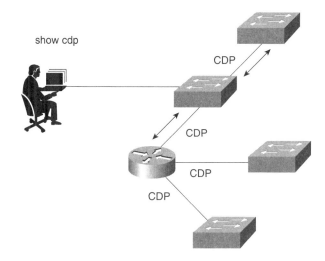

CDP provides a graphic similar to the information shown in Figure 10-14. The fields and their meaning follow:

Figure 10-14 *You use the CDP* **show cdp neighbor detail** *command to view the IP address of neighbor switches.*

```
show cdp neighbor detail
Device-ID: 003292129(MEKONG5K) ─────────── Name setup on switch
Device Addresses:
IP Address: 192.206.196.44 ───────── Sc0 port on the other switch
Holdtime: 154 sec
Capabilities: TRANSPARENT_BRIDGE SWITCH
Version:
 WS-C5000 Software, Version McpSW: 2.1(6) NmpSW: 2.1(6)
 Copyright (c) 1995,1996 by Cisco Systems
Platform: WS-C5000
Port-ID (Port on Device): 1/1
Port (Our Port): 1/1
```

Field	Description
Device-ID	Identifies the particular neighbor
IP Address	Identifies network-layer protocol addresses that are configured on the interface
Holdtime	Identifies how long this device should store this neighbor's information
Capabilities	Identifies the neighbor's capabilities (e.g., routing, bridging [SRB or TB], switch host, IGMP conditional filtering)
Version	Identifies the version of software that the neighbor is running
Platform	Identifies the platform (e.g., Cisco 7000 or Catalyst)
Port on Device	Identifies the interface on which CDP got information about the neighbor device
Our Port	Identifies the port (interface) to which the neighbor is connected

SPAN

SPAN is the Catalyst 5000 series switched port analyzer function on a Catalyst switch. When you use SPAN, the flow of data from a source and a destination port is mirrored to the port designated at the SPAN port, as shown in Figure 10-15.

Figure 10-15   *By mirroring module 2/port 8 to module 3/port 12, you can analyze that traffic.*

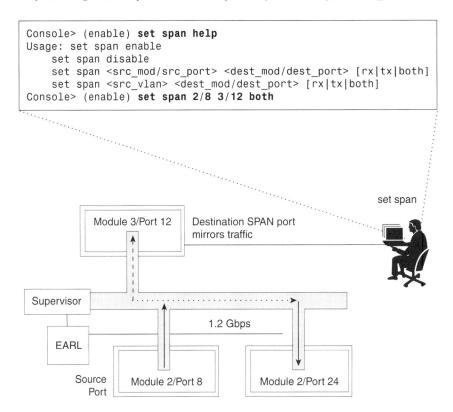

```
Console> (enable) set span help
Usage: set span enable
    set span disable
    set span <src_mod/src_port> <dest_mod/dest_port> [rx|tx|both]
    set span <src_vlan> <dest_mod/dest_port> [rx|tx|both]
Console> (enable) set span 2/8 3/12 both
```

Port mirroring enables the switch to make an extra copy of the data moving through one port (the SPAN monitored port) and transfer that data to another port (the SPAN destination).

A SPAN port does not behave as a regular switch port. Spanning-Tree Protocol is disabled, and you cannot change the VLAN identifier of a SPAN port.

Using SPAN, an external probe can capture and analyze frames as if it were on the same segment as the SPAN source port. This capability is sometimes referred to as *roving RMON*—that is, pointing an RMON agent at any traffic source on an as-needed basis.

SPAN mirrors traffic from any single port, trunk, or VLAN. Frames from a specified SPAN port can output to an external network analyzer, such as SwitchProbe. You use SPAN with an external analyzer to see additional RMON groups beyond the RFC 1757 groups (statistics, history, alarms, and events) available by default.

To initiate the SPAN function for mirrored data captures to the selected SPAN port, enter a command to direct certain port traffic to another. For example, you can direct all Port 3 traffic to Port 8 (where your analyzer is connected). With SPAN, ATM and FDDI can be source ports but not destination ports.

If you use SPAN on a trunk port, keep in mind that a trunk port must be designated as either a source port or as a destination port. If a destination port is a trunk port, all outgoing packets through SPAN carry an ISL header.

The SPAN command syntax shown in Figure 10-15 indicates the arguments you need to specify what you want to monitor, and where you want the SPAN port to be.

You can span a selected port or you can span a VLAN, as long as the source and destination ports are the same VLAN type.

Following is an example of the command to use for setting up SPAN to enable monitoring of VLAN 1 transmit/receive traffic by port 3/12. If SPAN is enabled to monitor VLAN traffic, you cannot select a trunk port as a monitored port:

```
Console> (enable) set span 1 3/12 both
Console> (enable) show span
Source      Destination     Direction         Status
------      ------------    --------------    --------
VLAN 1      Port 3/10       transmit/receive  enabled
```

Following is a second example of a command to use for setting up SPAN. The example enables monitoring of port 2/8 transmit/receive traffic by port 3/12:

```
Console> (enable) set span 2/8 3/12 both
Console> (enable) show span
Source      Destination     Direction         Status
------      ------------    --------------    --------
Port 2/8    Port 3/12       transmit/receive  enabled
```

NOTE   Automated procedures in TrafficDirector Version 4.1.3 and later simplify the setup, data capture, and analysis of SPAN traffic in Catalyst switches.

After you designate a port as a port that you want SPAN to monitor, the ASIC for that port tags packets for SPAN before they reach the switching bus and both the destination port and the mirrored SPAN port.

At the SPAN port, the mirrored packet capture is available for interpretation by a CWSI application or by some other protocol analyzer with a suitable decode capability.

Catalyst Commands

The four most useful commands for Catalyst switching are

- **set**—Establish switch parameters.
- **clear set**—Erase switch parameters or overwrite switch parameters.

- **show**—Check or verify parameters.
- **syslog**—Generate log messages.

The **show** commands are the focus of this section.

NOTE   A useful technique to help you identify the argument usages for a given Catalyst command is the enabled-mode **help** command, which uses the command followed by the argument, followed by the word **help** (alternatively you can use a **?**). The example that follows uses this technique to see the arguments for the **set span** command group:

```
Console> (enable) set span help
Usage: set span enable
       set span disable
       set span <src_mod/src_port> <dest_mod/dest_port> [rx|tx|both]
       set span <src_vlan> <dest_mod/dest_port> [rx|tx|both]
```

The **show** commands provide essential information about the Catalyst system settings, interfaces, and counters.

show Commands for System Settings

You use the following **show** commands for system settings:

- **show system**
- **show test**
- **show interface**
- **show log**
- **show mac**
- **show module**
- **show port**

These commands are described in more detail in the following sections.

show system

You use the **show system** command to display Catalyst system information, including the following:

- Status that corresponds to system LED status: power supplies (ok, fan failed, faulty, or none), fan (ok, faulty, or other), temperature alarm (off or on), and system status (ok or faulty).

- Uptime, the amount of time after which an idle session will be logged out, part number of all power supplies, modem status (enable or disable), baud rate to which the modem is set.

- Current traffic percentage, peak percentage of traffic on the backplane, and time stamp when this peak percentage was recorded.

- Any system name, location, and system contact information entered by the switch system administrator.

show test

You use the **show test** command to display the results of diagnostic tests. Optionally, you can specify a module number to show the test on that module. If no number is specified, test statistics are given for the general system as well as for module 1 (the supervisor engine). Information includes

- Environmental status for system test results that apply to the general system (any power supply, temperature, and fans test)

- Module 1 test results apply to module 1, the module type (NMP), test results for memory on the switch including ROM, Flash EEPROM, serial EEPROM, NVRAM

- EARL status, including several tests (NewLearnTest, IndexLearnTest, DontForwardTest, MonitorTest, DontLearn, FlushPacket, ConditionalLearn, EarlLearnDiscard, and EarlTrapTest)

- LCP Diag Status for module 1, including test results for the CPU, serial PROM, boot ROM checksum, archive Flash checksum, RAM, local target logic, VLAN color blocking logic, dual-port RAM, SAMBA chip, SAINT chips, packet buffers, repeater module, flash, and MII5 ports

- Whether there is a loopback in place and an active console

show interface

You use the **show interface** command to display information on network interface flags and addressing, which includes the following information:

- Whether there is any SLIP interface, and if there is, the IP address of the SLIP interface and the IP address of the SLIP destination

- Flags indicating the interface state (UP, DOWN, BROADCAST, LOOPBACK, POINTOPOINT, or RUNNING)

- VLAN information of the SC0 interface, also known as the management VLAN

- Sc0, the in-band interface, its IP address and network mask, and the broadcast address

show log

You use the **show log** command to display the error log for the system or a specific module. Information includes

- The active NPM log, including reset count, resets, bootup history, and failure counts
- NVRAM logs
- Module logs, including any resets that have occurred

show mac

You use the **show mac** command to display MAC information, including

- Module and port identifier and the frame traffic for the port
- The total transmit frames aborted due to excessive deferral or when MTU size was exceeded
- The number of incoming frames discarded because the frame did not need to be switched
- The number of content-addressable memory entries discarded due to page full in EARL
- The number of incoming or outgoing frames lost before being forwarded (due to insufficient buffer space)
- Token Ring and FDDI values
- Date and time of the last **clear counters** command

show module

You use the **show module** command to display module status and information. If you do not specify a module number, the command outputs information for all modules. This information includes

- The module number and name of the module, the number of ports on the module, its module type (such as 10BaseT Ethernet), model number, and serial number
- The status of the module (possible status strings are ok, disable, faulty, other, standby, or error)
- Any MAC address or MAC address range for the module
- The module's hardware version, firmware version, and software version
- Token Ring and FDDI values

Sometimes the **show module** command indicates that the status LED of an Ethernet module is green, even if some module ports fail the PMD loopback test during power up; the status LED of an Ethernet module is orange or red only when all the module ports fail the PMD loopback test.

To correct this error, use the **show test** command to view PMD loopback test results for a module and then reset the module by using the **reset** *mod_num* command; if the failure persists, replace the module.

show port

You use the **show port** command to display port status and counters. You have the option of specifying a specific module and port number. Information output from this command includes

- The module and port number, and any name (if configured) of the port
- The status of the port (connected, not connected, connecting, standby, faulty, inactive, shutdown, disabled, or monitor)
- Any VLAN(s) to which the port belongs
- Any level setting for the port (normal or high)
- Any duplex setting for the port (auto, full, half, a-half, or a-full), and port speed setting (auto, 10, 100, 155, a-10, or a-100)
- The port type (10BaseT, 10BaseFL MM, 100BaseTX, 100BaseT4, 100BaseFX MM, 100BaseFX SM, 10/100BaseTX, FDDI, CDDI, MLT3 CDDI, SDDI, SMF-FDDI, PreStd CDDI, SCF FDDI, OC3 MMF ATM, OC3 SMF ATM, OC3 UTP ATM, or Route Switch)
- Security enabled or disabled (if enabled, the secure MAC address for the security enabled port) and whether the port was shut down because of security
- The source MAC address of the last packet received by the port
- Whether the port trap is enabled or disabled
- Broadcast information, including the broadcast threshold configured for the port and the number of broadcast/multicast packets dropped because the broadcast limit for the port was exceeded
- Port errors, including the number of frames with alignment errors (frames that do not end with an even number of octets and have a bad CRC1) received on the port, the number of FCS errors that occurred on the port, the number of transmit or receive errors that occurred on the port (indicating that the internal transmit or receive buffer is full), the number of frames received that are less than 64 octets long (but are otherwise well formed)
- Collision information, including how many times one collision occurred before the port successfully transmitted a frame to the media, how many times multiple collisions occurred before the port successfully transmitted a frame to the media, the number of late collisions (collisions outside the collision domain), and the number of excessive collisions that occurred on the port (indicating that a frame encountered 16 collisions and was discarded)

- Any runts (frames that are smaller than the minimum IEEE 802.3 frame size) or giants (frames that exceed the maximum IEEE 802.3 frame size) received on the port

- The connection entity status and connection state of the port, as follows:

    — Disabled—The port has no line module, or it has been disabled by the user.

    — Connecting—The port is attempting to connect or is disabled.

    — Standby—The connection is withheld or is the inactive port of a dual homing concentrator.

    — Active—The port has made connection.

    — Other—The concentrator is unable to determine the connection state.

- Link error rate (LER) conditions, including an estimated LER, the LER-alarm threshold, and LER-cutoff value (the LER at which a link connection is flagged as faulty)

- Link error monitor (LEM) conditions, including the number of LEM errors received on the port and the number of times a connection was rejected because of excessive LEM errors

- The last time the port counters were cleared

show Commands for Switch Configuration

You use the following **show** commands to provide information about the Catalyst configuration, network entities such as VLANs, and neighbors:

- **show config**
- **show span**
- **show trunk**
- **show flash**
- **show spantree**
- **show vtp domain**
- **show cdp neighbor**

These commands are described in more detail in the following sections.

show config

You use the **show config** command to display the current system configuration. This command is comparable to the Cisco IOS **show running config** command. The command output includes

- Catalyst password, system, and contact information
- SNMP settings, TCP/IP addressing, and DNS server details

- Any TACACS+ configurations
- Bridging, VTP, Spanning-Tree Protocol, and syslog settings
- Information about switch modules and the ports

show span

You use the **show span** command to display information about the Catalyst 5000 series switched port analyzer function setting. Information includes

- Whether SPAN is enabled or disabled, and if SPAN is enabled, the source port or VLAN for SPAN to monitor and the destination port to direct mirrored SPAN information
- Whether transmit, receive, or transmit/receive information is monitored

show trunk

You use the **show trunk** command to display trunking information for the switch. You have the option of specifying a module and port number. Information output from this command includes

- The module and port number(s), administrative status of the port (on, off, auto, or desirable), and port status (trunking or not-trunking)
- VLAN information, including the range of VLANs allowed to go on the trunk (default is 1 to 1000), the VLANs allowed and active in the management domain within the allowed range, if the VLANS are in spanning-tree forwarding state and not pruned, the range of VLANs that actually go on the trunk with Spanning-Tree Protocol forwarding state

Figure 10-16 shows an example of using the **show trunk** command for troubleshooting information and action planning.

Figure 10-16 *The **show trunk** command displays active VLANs on this trunk.*

```
show trunk 1/1
Port    Mode        Status
1/1     auto        not-trunking
Port        Vlans allowed
1/1         1-2,10-15,200,254
Port        Vlans active
1/1         1
```

For the port 1/1 shown as nontrunking, try setting the trunk mode to on with the following command:

```
set trunk 1/1 on
```

All the VLANs for the trunk must show up as an entry for the **show trunk** command in order for the VLAN to be active. All working VLANs or VLANs added by VTP will show up as entries.

Make sure that at least one VLAN is configured for this trunk. To configure a VLAN for the trunk, use the following command:

```
set trunk 1/1 [vlans]
```

One important troubleshooting check is to make sure that both sides of the link agree on the VLANs that can use the trunk. If you need to remove a VAN from the trunk, use the following command:

```
clear trunk 1/1 [vlans]
```

NOTE   When you use the commands shown, replace the port number **1/1** with the correct port number for your switch.

NOTE   By default, the switch sends the output from **debug** commands and system error messages to the console terminal. Use the **show log** command to display the error log for the system or a specific module. These messages can also be redirected to other destinations.

Syslog error and event logging generate SNMP log messages that show configuration parameters and protocol activity. When enabled, system logging messages are typically sent to a UNIX host or other network management server that acts as a syslog server.

You can set up syslog as part of your preparation for switch management and troubleshooting so that the syslogd daemon will capture and save log messages that you can analyze later.

show flash

You use the **show flash** command to list Flash information, including file code names, version numbers, and sizes.

show spantree [vlan]

You use the **show spantree** [*vlan*] command to display spanning-tree information for a VLAN. You have the option of specifying the number of the VLAN (the default is VLAN1) and the number of the module and port on the module to narrow the display. Information from this command includes the following:

- The VLAN for which spanning-tree information is shown; whether Spanning-Tree Protocol is enabled or disabled, and if enabled, the MAC address of the designated spanning-tree root bridge; the priority of the designated root bridge; the total path cost to reach the root; the port through which the root bridge can be reached (shown only on nonroot bridges)

- BPDU information, including the amount of time a BPDU packet should be considered valid, how often the root-bridge sends BPDUs, and how much time the port should spend in listening or learning mode

- Bridge information, including the bridge MAC address, priority, maximum age, Hello time, and forward delay

- The port number and VLAN to which the port belongs

- The spanning-tree port state (disabled, inactive, not-connected, blocking, listening, learning, forwarding, bridging)

- The cost and priority associated with the port

- Whether the port is configured to use the fast-start feature

show spantree statistics

You use the **show spantree statistics** command to decode and interpret the Spanning-Tree Protocol BPDU communications, as shown in Figure 10-17.

Figure 10-17 *You can view BPDU communications with* **show spantree statistics***.*

```
show spantree statistics
Spanning tree enabled

Designated Root                 00-60-47-8f-9a-00
Designated Root Priority   1
Designated Root Cost       10
Designated Root Port       1/1
Root Max Age   20 sec    Hello Time 2  sec    Forward Delay 15 sec


Bridge ID MAC ADDR              00-60-83-4e-d6-00
Bridge ID Priority              32768
Bridge Max Age 6 sec    Hello Time 1  sec    Forward Delay 4 sec


Port      Vlan  Port-State      Cost    Priority  Fast-Start
--------  ----  -------------   -----   --------  ----------
1/1        1    forwarding        10      32       disabled
```

You can either specify a VLAN as in Figure 10-17, or you can get output about all the VLANs known to the switch. Spanning tree is enabled by default.

The following details are about VLAN 1:

Parameter	Description
Designated Root 00-60-47-8f-9a-00	Another Catalyst 5000 is root
Designated Root Priority 1	Priority of root bridge
Designated Root Cost 10	Shortest cost to root bridge
Designated Root Port 1/1	Connected to root through 1/1
Root Max Age 20 sec Hello Time 2 sec Forward Delay 15 sec	Max Age, Hello, Forward Delay—All from root bridge; all switches must use the values heard from root

The following details are about switch parameters:

Parameter	Description
Bridge ID MAC ADDR 00-60-83-4e-d6-00	Bridge ID for switch
Bridge ID Priority 32768	Bridge priority for switch obtained from the command **set spantree priority 1 32768** The lowest-priority bridge is the default root
Bridge Max Age 6 sec Hello Time 1 sec Forward Delay 4 sec	When the switch is the root, you can set these parameters using the following commands: **set spantree maxage 6 1** **set spantree hello 1 1** **set spantree fwddelay 4 1**

The following details are about port parameters:

Port	Vlan	Port-State	Cost	Priority	Fast-Start
1/1	1	Forwarding	10	32	disabled
1/2	1	not-connected	10	32	disabled

The following are descriptions of the port parameters:

Parameter	Description
Port	Keep in mind that a port may show up in more than one VLAN. To see all spanning trees on a trunk, use the command **show spantree** *slot/port*
VLAN	One spanning tree per VLAN
Port-State	Forwarding, listening, learning, blocking, not-connected
Cost	To set the cost, use the command **set spantree portcost** *slot/port cost*
Priority	To set the spanning-tree port priority for parallel interswitch links, use one of these commands: **set spantree portpri** *slot/port priority* or **set spantree portvlanpri** *slot/port priority* [*vlan*]
Fast-Start	To allow a port that is connected to a single workstation or PC to start more quickly when it is connected, use the following command: **set spantree portfast** *slot/port* {**enable**	**disable**}

Figure 10-18 shows the command to display details about the spanning tree for a specified VLAN. You may also enter an alternative argument for a specific port/slot.

Figure 10-18 *You use the **show spantree** command to view spanning-tree details.*

```
show spantree 5
VLAN 5
Spanning tree enabled
Designated Root              00-60-47-ca-ff-04
Designated Root Priority     32768
Designated Root Cost         0
Designated Root Port         1/0
Root Max Age   20 sec    Hello Time 2  sec   Forward Delay 15 sec
Bridge ID MAC ADDR           00-60-47-ca-ff-04
Bridge ID Priority           32768
Bridge Max Age 20 sec    Hello Time 2  sec   Forward Delay 15 sec
Port      Vlan  Port-State      Cost    Priority  Fast-Start
--------  ----  --------------  -----   --------  ----------
  3/9      5    not-connected    10        32      disabled
  3/10     5    not-connected    10        32      disabled
  3/11     5    not-connected    10        32      disabled
  3/12     5    not-connected    10        32      disabled
```

The following is a brief description of the elements shown in Figure 10-18:

Field	Description
VLAN	VLAN for which spanning-tree information is shown
Spanning tree enabled	Indicates whether Spanning-Tree Protocol is enabled or disabled
Designated Root	MAC address of the designated spanning-tree root bridge

continues

Field	Description
Designated Root Priority	Priority of the designated root bridge
Designated Root Cost	Indicates the total path cost to reach the root
Designated Root Port	Port through which the root bridge can be reached (shown only on non-root bridges)
Root Max Age	Amount of time a BPDU1 packet should be considered valid
Hello Time	Shows how often the root-bridge sends BPDUs
Forward Delay	Shows how much time the port should spend in listening or learning mode
Bridge ID MAC ADDR	Bridge MAC address
Bridge ID Priority	Bridge priority
Bridge Max Age	Bridge maximum age
Hello Time	Bridge Hello time
Forward Delay	Bridge forward delay
Port	Port number
Vlan	VLAN to which the port belongs
Port-State	Disabled, inactive, not-connected, blocking, listening, learning, forwarding, or bridging
Cost	Cost associated with the port
Priority	Priority associated with the port
Fast-Start	Indicates whether the port is configured to use the fast-start feature

show vtp domain

You use the **show vtp domain** command to display VTP domain information, which includes

- The name and index number of the VTP domain, and the VTP version number

- The local VTP mode (server, client, or transparent)

- The total number of VLANs in the domain and maximum number of VLANs allowed on the device

- The VTP revision number, used to exchange VLAN information, whether notification to SNMP is enabled or disabled, and the IP address through which VTP was last updated

- Whether VTP pruning is enabled or disabled and if enabled, the VLANs on which pruning is allowed

show cdp neighbors

You use the **show cdp neighbors** command to display CDP information about all Cisco products connected to the switch. Information includes neighbor device ID and addressing, capabilities, software version, hardware platform, module and port identifier on the neighbor device, and devices on this side of the data link.

Problem Isolation in Catalyst Networks

Typically, a general approach for troubleshooting problems like the approach shown in Figure 10-19 can systematically isolate a problem with a Catalyst switch network.

Figure 10-19 *You can use this Catalyst problem isolation flowchart to streamline troubleshooting procedures.*

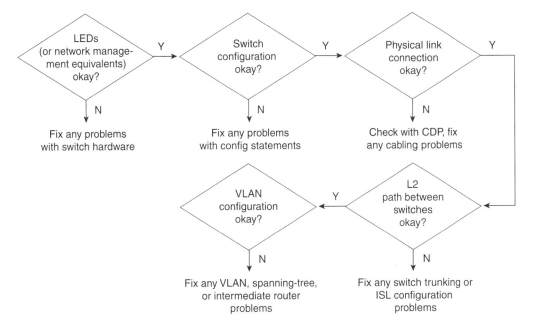

You proceed in the following order:

1 Check the physical indications of LEDs or their equivalents.

2 Work outward from a single switch configuration.

3 Check the Layer 1 link to another switch.

4 Check the Layer 2 link to the other switch.

5 Troubleshoot the VLAN that contains several switches.

As you troubleshoot, check to see whether the problem is a chronic one rather than an isolated fault. Some chronic problems are due to a growth of demand for services by desktop ports that outpaces the configuration, ISL trunking, or capacity to access server resources.

The use of Web technologies and traditional applications (such as file transfer, e-mail, and network backup) may be causing growth in the traffic that enterprise networks must handle.

Many campus LANs face unpredictable network traffic patterns that result from the combination of intranet traffic, fewer centralized campus server locations, and the increasing use of multicast applications.

The old 80/20 rule, which states that only 20% of network traffic goes over the backbone, has been scrapped. Internal Web browsing now enables users to locate and access information anywhere on the corporate intranet.

Traffic patterns are dictated by where the servers with the most valuable pages are, and not by the physical workgroup configurations with which they happen to be grouped.

If your network frequently experiences bottleneck symptoms such as excessive overflows, dropped frames, and retransmissions, check to see whether too many desktop ports egress a single trunk. Also check to see whether there are too many demand nodes for the link to global resources and the server.

If the majority of your traffic will traverse the backbone, and any-to-any access becomes common as users point and click their way through the corporate portfolio of Web-based resources and demanding multimedia applications, you may need to consider increasing your network resources to meet this growing demand.

Catalyst Symptoms and Problems

Table 10-3 shows high-level Catalyst problem facts or symptoms and the possibilities and action plans that may help you solve the problems.

Table 10-3   *Catalyst symptoms, possible problems, and action plans.*

Symptom	Possible Problems and Action Plans
Switch cannot communicate with local devices	? Power supply problem. Check LED and fuse.
	? Hardware problem. Check module LED and check whether module is properly seated in switch.
	? Cabling problem. Check connected LED and check for correct cable properly attached. Swap cable with cable known to be good.

Table 10-3   *Catalyst symptoms, possible problems, and action plans. (Continued)*

Symptom	Possible Problems and Action Plans
Terminal or modem connection cannot communicate with switch	? Misconfigured terminal and console port. Check that baud rate and character format match.
	? If terminal never worked before, check for incorrect cable:
	? Null-modem for direct attachment.
	? Straight-through for modem connect.
Server cannot communicate with remote devices on another LAN	? Misconfigured IP addressing or mask. Check with CDP.
	? Default gateway not specified or incorrect. Check switch, servers, and clients.
	? VLAN misconfigured. Check port assignments, eliminate unnecessary connections between VLANs if a port belongs to multiple VLANs.
	? VLAN inconsistency problem. Make sure VLANs match on both sides of a trunk.
	? ISL problem. Make sure there is proper trunking, use VLAN1, and make sure that no invalid VTP server information update has occurred.

Summary

In this chapter, you have acquired a basic knowledge about Catalyst 5000 data flows that can help you understand symptoms. You have learned that CWSI applications and RMON can help you with remote LAN management and that LEDs on the NMP supervisor module and the switching interface modules can show the first symptoms of a problem. You have learned how to use the Catalyst troubleshooting tools (**ping**, **telnet**, and the **show** commands, and CDP) for debugging, focusing on basic inactivity; the link; and then operation of spanning tree, VLANs, and ISL.

In Chapter 11, "Troubleshooting VLANs on Routers and Switches," you will learn VLAN troubleshooting techniques.

Chapter 10 Test
Diagnosing and Correcting Catalyst Problems

Estimated Time: 15 minutes

Complete all the exercises to test your knowledge of the materials contained in this chapter. Answers are listed in Appendix A, "Chapter Test Answer Key."

Use the information contained in this chapter to answer the following questions.

Question 10.1

T   F   Input/output buffering is done on the backbone module and on buffers associated with each port.

Question 10.2

T   F   Catalyst 5000 series devices are fixed-configuration Fast Ethernet switches.

Question 10.3

T   F   Bridges operate at Layer 2 of the OSI reference model.

Question 10.4

T   F   Spanning tree can only resolve loops that include links of a single media type.

Question 10.5

T   F   ISL can connect a non-VLAN-capable product with a VLAN-capable product.

Question 10.6

T   F   CWSI can use an in-band network connection.

Question 10.7

T   F   The **show** command can be used to view port, module, and trunk statistics.

Troubleshooting VLANs on Routers and Switches

Cisco routers and switches work together to configure logical topologies on top of the physical network infrastructure. This "virtual networking" allows any arbitrary collection of LAN segments within a network to be combined into an autonomous user group, appearing as a single LAN. For example, perhaps you are working on one IP network (10.0.0.0) but your data flows and network usage fall into three separate unique categories:

- The accounting department uses the accounting servers and six local printers.

- The management group accesses the corporate network servers and uses local printers only.

- The sales and marketing force accesses two database servers, the Internet, and the local printers only.

You can group together these devices into virtual networks that are based on this usage pattern. Traffic that is related to the users' needs is forwarded to them. Unrelated traffic is filtered out. You have one physical network and three separate virtual, or logical, networks.

For more information on switch and router functionality, refer to Chapter 3, "Cisco Routing and Switching Processes."

Virtual LAN (VLAN) technology functions by logically segmenting the network into different broadcast domains so that packets are only switched between ports that are designated for the same VLAN.

Switched virtual networks help reduce unnecessary network overhead by containing traffic originating on a particular LAN only to other LANs in the same VLAN. For example, consider a network that consists of both IP and IPX devices. The IPX broadcasts would be propagated throughout the network and heard by the IP devices. By separating this one network into separate VLANs, we can ensure that only relevant broadcasts are seen by the devices. These switched virtual networks thereby avoid wasting bandwidth, which is a drawback inherent in traditional bridged and switched networks, where packets are often forwarded to LANs that don't need them.

The role of the router has evolved beyond the traditional role of firewalls and broadcast suppression to become the focal device for policy-based control, broadcast management, and route processing and distribution.

Routers contribute to switched architectures configured as VLANs because they provide the communication between logically defined workgroups (that is, VLANs). Remember that a VLAN is a virtual network. The traditional role of a router is to connect networks together. Therefore, we use routers to connect VLANs together, enabling some traffic to cross VLAN boundaries.

Routers also provide VLAN access to shared resources such as servers and hosts, and they connect to other parts of the network that are either logically segmented with the more traditional subnet approach or require access to remote sites across wide-area links.

Cisco IOS VLAN services provide a powerful combination of multiprotocol routed and switched VLAN opportunities to improve performance.

Routers help with integration across Cisco's switching product family/partner products, and they bring scalability and flexibility to VLAN networks. In this chapter you will learn how VLANs are implemented on Cisco routers and what precautions you should take when configuring VLANs that work on routers together with switches.

VLANs on Routed and Switched Networks

Figure 11-1 shows a network that supports VLANs at the router and switches. The router connects the Group 1 and Group 2 VLANs.

Figure 11-1 *Multiple VLANs use packet tagging and Inter-Switch Link (ISL) for router and switch.*

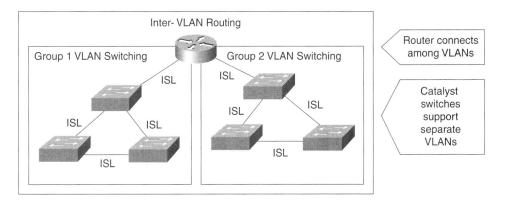

For a typical switched VLAN, traffic is only switched between LAN interfaces that belong to the same VLAN. Typically, the criterion for VLAN membership is departmental function. Users could, however, be grouped into VLANs based on a common protocol or subnet address. Your VLAN memberships should depend on a solid understanding of your data flow and resource usage.

Cisco offers ISL on Cisco 4000 and 7000 series routers and on Catalyst 5000 LAN series switches.

The ISL trunk protocol identifies traffic as belonging to a particular VLAN by using *frame tagging* as packets are switched onto the shared backbone network.

Receiving switches use ISL to make intelligent forwarding decisions and switch the packets to only those interfaces that are members of the same VLAN.

When combining LANs into a VLAN, a Spanning-Tree Protocol algorithm is used to eliminate the possibility of loops and to determine the best path through the network. Each VLAN in the switch has a unique bridge ID, and the Spanning-Tree Protocol algorithm runs separately for each VLAN. Each VLAN operates autonomously; its data flow need not be interrupted by physical changes or spanning-tree recomputations that go on elsewhere in the network topology.

Also, supporting a separate spanning tree for each VLAN enables optimal path determination for each VLAN and extends the diameter of the network. A physical port on a router or switch may be part of more than one spanning tree if it is a trunk. A *trunk* is a point-to-point link that transmits and receives traffic between switches or between switches and routers.

For routing or switching of inter-VLAN traffic, the router aggregates inter-VLAN routing for multiple VLAN switches. Traffic between VLANs can be switched autonomously on-card or between cards rather than via the central Route Switch Processor (RSP) on a Cisco 7000 series router.

Routers offer additional functionality such as access lists. Access lists enable a network administrator to implement the permit and deny policy of the organization.

VLAN Switching, Translation, and Routing

A Cisco router can bridge ISL and IEEE 802.10 VLANs (that is, where the VLAN encapsulating header is preserved) on the main/first interface.

In a Layer 2 VLAN switch, the Cisco IOS software runs an IEEE 802.1 spanning tree for each Layer 2 VLAN to enhance scalability and prevent topology changes in one switched VLAN domain from affecting a different VLAN.

A switched VLAN domain corresponds to a routed subnet/network number and is represented in the Cisco IOS software by a VLAN subinterface.

Layer 2 VLAN translation is the ability of the Cisco IOS software to "interpret" between different VLANs (which use the same or different VLAN protocols), or between VLAN and non-VLAN encapsulating interfaces at Layer 2.

Figure 11-2 depicts the differences between VLAN switching, translation, and routing.

Figure 11-2 *There are differences between VLAN switching, translation, and routing.*

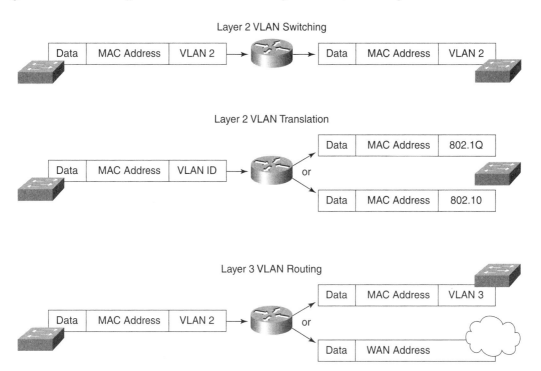

VLAN translation functionality is typically used for selective inter-VLAN switching of nonroutable protocols such as Maintenance Operation Protocol (MOP) and local-area transport (LAT) and to extend a single VLAN topology across hybrid (mixed 802.1Q and 802.10 networks) switching environments. VLAN translation was introduced in Cisco IOS Release 11.1 and is fast switched (route cache is used to expedite packet switching through a router).

The router can also perform Layer 3 routing between VLANs, which provides connectivity between different VLANs, and between VLANs and non-VLAN network interfaces, such as those that connect to WAN services or to the Internet.

As the router provides Layer 3 VLAN services, the router continues providing standard routing attributes such as network advertisements, secondary addresses, and helper addresses. VLAN routing is fast switched.

Another feature of routers is Hot Standby Router Protocol (HSRP), which provides automatic router backup by establishing a virtual router. HSRP allows two or more HSRP-configured routers to use the MAC address and IP network address of a virtual router. The virtual router does not physically exist; instead, it represents the common target for routers that are configured to provide backup to each other.

HSRP allows Cisco IOS routers to monitor each other's operational status and very quickly assume packet-forwarding responsibility if the current forwarder in the HSRP group fails or is taken down for maintenance. This mechanism remains transparent to the attached hosts and can be deployed on any LAN or VLAN type.

The Router's Layer 2 Translation Function

By definition VLANs perform network partitioning and traffic separation at Layer 2. Communication between different VLANs requires a Layer 3 routing or a Layer 2 translation function.

The Cisco IOS software platform incorporates full support for routing and translation between VLANs and between VLAN trunking and non-VLAN interfaces.

The integrated solution of high-speed, scalable VLAN switching of local traffic and efficient routing and switching of inter-VLAN traffic is becoming increasingly attractive in large networks.

Cisco routers address this requirement with their ability to address many different VLAN needs:

- ISL over Fast Ethernet.
- IEEE 802.1Q standards (especially for packet tagging as a common VLAN exchange mechanism between switches, routers, and server devices).
- IEEE 802.10 (especially for FDDI backbones). With IEEE 802.10–based VLANs, it is also possible to use High-Level Data Link Control (HDLC) serial links as VLAN trunks to extend a virtual topology beyond a LAN backbone.
- ATM LAN Emulation (LANE) VLANs.

The router also enables connectivity between VLANs and non-VLAN interfaces such as those that connect the campus LANs to the WAN and to the Internet. Cisco routers address this requirement with their ability to connect the following:

- WAN Layer 2 protocols such as HDLC, Point-to-Point Protocol (PPP), and Frame Relay
- Internet services, including those that use TCP/IP, Novell IPX, AppleTalk, DECnet, Banyan VINES, and several other protocols

Cisco IOS Fast Ethernet Troubleshooting

To troubleshoot the operation of router Fast Ethernet connections to Catalyst switches, you need to make sure that the Cisco IOS interface configuration is complete and correct:

- Do not configure an IP address on the main Fast Ethernet. Instead, configure an IP address for each subinterface that you specify as a connection to a VLAN.

- The media-type MII (Media-Independent Interface) may be on some Fast Ethernet interface modules (for example, the VIP card). If you will be using this interface rather than the default Category 5 cabling, enter this configuration statement only for the main interface.

- The full-duplex configuration can be a source of problems if the settings on both sides of the Fast Ethernet data link do not match. Use the **set port duplex** *mod num/port num* **full|half** command with caution; when in doubt, explicitly check that the router's (on the other side of the link) configuration setting on the Catalyst switch matches the duplex setting on the router.

- When the Cisco IOS VLAN switching code receives a VLAN packet, it first extracts the VLAN ID from the packet header (10-bit ISL VLAN ID) and then demultiplexes on this value into a subinterface of the receiving port.

- Figure 11-3 shows that VLAN 3 will traverse the ISL trunk for IP and for IPX. The network numbers on the router side and the switch side must match.

Figure 11-3   *In ISL VLAN setup on a router, the network numbers must match on the router and switch sides.*

```
Router A#(config-if)interface fastethernet 2/1.2
    ip address 192.168.20.40 255.255.255.0
    ipx network ace12
    encapsulation isl 2
    bridge-group 50
!
int fa 2/1.3
    ip address 192.168.30.50 255.255.255.0
    ipx network fad13
    encap isl 3
    bridge-group 50
...
router igrp 10
    network 192.168.20.0
    network 192.168.30.0

    bridge 50 protocol ieee
```

```
SWBlu_192.168.20.41>(enable)set trunk 1/2 on 1-1000
```

```
SWYel_192.168.30.51>(enable)set trunk 1/3 on 1-1000

SWYel_192.168.30.51>(enable)clear trunk -10
```

Trunks to router can handle traffic from
VLANs in range 1–1000 except
VLAN 10 on SWYel

- If the Cisco IOS code cannot resolve the VLAN identity into a subinterface, the Cisco IOS software may transparently bridge the received packet if the router is configured to bridge on the subinterface.

- VLAN packets received are then classified by protocol type. If the subinterface is assigned to a bridge group, then nonrouted packets are de-encapsulated before being bridged (this is called *fall-back bridging*) and fast switched.

Figure 11-3 shows the explicit configuration used to set up ISL VLANs on a router, along with the comparable configuration on the router's Catalyst 5000 neighbor.

ISL is available on the Catalyst 5000 line cards that offer 100Base media. ISL VLAN trunking is defined only on 100BaseTX/FX Fast Ethernet interfaces on the 7000 and 4500 series platforms. The design leverages the subinterface (or virtual interface) mechanism to view ISL as an encapsulation type.

You can map a router Fast Ethernet subinterface to the particular VLAN color (that is, ISL value) embedded within the VLAN header. This mapping determines which VLAN traffic is routed/bridged outside its own VLAN domain and allows for full Cisco IOS functionality to be applied on a subinterface basis. Also, in the VLAN routing paradigm, a switched VLAN corresponds to a single routed subnet, and the Layer 3 address is assigned to the subinterface.

Routing between VLANs is currently permitted only to IP and Novell-Ethernet IPX encapsulations on ISL. Integrated routing and bridging (IRB) enables routing and bridging between VLANs and includes support for IPX with SNAP and SAP encapsulations as well as for AppleTalk.

In the example shown in Figure 11-3, IP traffic is routed from ISL VLANs 2 and 3, as is the IPX traffic. The Fast Ethernet subinterfaces 2/1.3 and 2/1.3 are both in bridge group 50, so all the other nonrouted ISL traffic can be bridged between these two subinterfaces.

On the two switches, use the Catalyst 5000 **set trunk** command for the Fast Ethernet trunk that connects to the router. When you set the trunk on and enable the range of VLANs 1 through 1000, any VLANs set up on the switched network can traverse the ISL on the router.

To exclude a VLAN from traversing the ISL trunk and router, use the Catalyst 5000 **clear trunk** command for the Fast Ethernet trunk that connects to the router and specify the VLAN ID that you do not want to use on the router's ISL trunk.

NOTE   IRB is a feature of Cisco IOS Release 11.2. IRB was designed to enhance concurrent routing and bridging (CRB), a feature of Cisco IOS Release 11.0. In the past, Cisco routers could route or bridge a protocol, but not both.

CRB enables a user to both route and bridge a protocol on separate interfaces within a single router. However, the routed traffic is confined to the routed interfaces, and bridged traffic is confined to the bridged interfaces; for any given protocol, the traffic may be either routed or bridged on a given interface, but not both.

With IRB, a protocol can be routed either between both routed interfaces and bridged interfaces or between different bridge groups internal to the router. Note that you can run either IRB or CRB, but not both.

Refer to www.cisco.com/Mkt/cmc/cc/cisco/mkt/ios/rel/112/irb_dg.htm for a white paper titled *Using Integrated Routing and Bridging with Virtual LANs.*

VLAN Troubleshooting Issues

This section focuses on the following VLAN troubleshooting aspects:

- VLAN design
- The router's functionality in a switched network
- Cisco Discovery Protocol (CDP)
- Telnet

VLAN Design Issues

Several VLAN metrics are design considerations to set up, operate, and manage the extended router/switch network:

- As a general rule, the network diameter should have a maximum hop count of seven bridges (routers and switches). The network diameter influences the amount of temporary loss of connectivity during spanning-tree recomputations. During the listening phase of this period, data packets are discarded.

- A bridge protocol data unit (BPDU) age metric specifies how periodically the network device expects to receive (or will drop) BPDU messages at the point when the change occurred. This metric setting also influences the speed of convergence and the ensuing flooding of BPDUs.

- The values for the BPDU age, BPDU hello time, and forward delay (for that VLAN) set on the root bridge are imposed on all other switches in the root bridge's VLAN topology.

Table 11-1 shows the ISL VLAN ID numbers used by default for the various media types. The table also shows the 802.10 ID defaults for an 802.10 header packet outer header element called the Security Association Identifier (SAID).

Table 11-1   *Default ISL VLAN ID numbers.*

VLAN Name	Type	MTU	ISL VLAN-id	802.10 SAID
default	ethernet	1500	0001	1
fddi-default	fddi	4352	1002	101002
token-ring—default	token-ring	2048	1003	101003
fddinet—default	fddi-net	4352	1004	101004
trnet—default	tr-net	2048	1005	101005

For VLAN assignment, you can use VLAN numbers in the range of 1 through 1000. When you configure for the router/switch extended network VLANs, make sure that

- The media type and maximum transmission unit (MTU) are consistent on both sides of the link.

- If possible, the default Ethernet VLAN ID 1 should be used for management and troubleshooting only. Use the other numbers in the range (2 through 1000) for VLANs that will carry user traffic.

Router Functionality in a Switched Network

As you gather facts and consider possibilities for troubleshooting, remember several factors about the role of a router working with VLANs and switches:

- If you are using the router to bridge between ISL subinterfaces, the spanning trees of the associated VLANs will combine into a single spanning tree. This combination can make the router the best point of connectivity, and the router could become the root bridge.

- Avoid turning on multiple subinterfaces if you do not want the Spanning-Tree Protocol to merge the VLANs on each router subinterface bridged in a single tree.

- Check that the Spanning-Tree Protocol encapsulation set on the extended router/switch network is consistent. In other words, use IEEE Spanning-Tree Protocol everywhere in the network or use Digital Spanning-Tree Protocol everywhere in the network. Do not use both IEEE and Digital bridging.

A case study later in this chapter describes the serious problems that occur with incompatible Spanning-Tree Protocol domains. These problems include BPDUs and other packets dropped, loops, and broadcast storms.

The following list guides you through Spanning-Tree Protocol network troubleshooting:

- For the most effective troubleshooting to proceed, you need to know the location of the root bridge in your extended router/switch network. The **show** commands on both the router and the switches can display root bridge information.

- The root bridge is where you can configure the timers that set parameters such as forwarding delay and the maximum age for Spanning-Tree Protocol information. You also have the option of hard-coding a device that you want to establish as the root bridge.

- If the extended router/switch network encounters a period of instability, you might want to reduce the frequency of Spanning-Tree Protocol processes between devices because those processes may make matters worse.

- If you want to reduce BPDU traffic, set the timers on the root bridge at their maximum values. Specifically, set the forward delay parameter to the maximum of 30 seconds and set the maximum age parameter to the maximum of 40 seconds. However, this increases the amount of time it takes the network to converge, or learn about, network topology changes.

- A physical port on a router or switch may be part of more than one spanning tree if it is a trunk. As of Cisco IOS Release 11.2, Cisco's VLAN Trunking Protocol (VTP, a Layer 2 multicast messaging protocol) runs on Catalyst switches but not on routers.

- Until VTP is supported on the Cisco routers as well, it may be advisable (but is not required) to configure the Catalyst switch that is the router's neighbor to operate in VTP transparent mode.

CDP

Cisco's CDP runs on all Cisco routers that have Cisco IOS software Release 10.3 or later and on all Catalyst switches. Therefore, CDP is a useful tool to use when you begin troubleshooting; it is a medium-independent and protocol-independent utility.

CDP provides the capability to verify that the directly connected neighbor device indeed has the capabilities, protocols, and addressing that you expect. Many times, a discrepancy in these areas can be a very rapid way to find and fix a connectivity problem with a protocol.

Although CDP runs automatically on the router, you must explicitly enable CDP for the Fast Ethernet interface connecting the router to the switch. The CDP function automatically sends out a small (approximately 8 KB) multicast packet to the address 01-00-0C-CC-CC to begin sending and receiving hello-type updates about neighbor fundamentals.

You can display these neighbor fundamentals by using the Cisco IOS software **show cdp neighbors** command. If you need to get a target address to use for Telnet, CDP can provide this address for you.

Using Telnet to a Switch on a Different Subnet

When you use Telnet on a router, be aware that the switched environment using Spanning-Tree Protocol bridging has a single subnetwork for each VLAN. The Telnet connection on the router may be on a network that is different from the targeted switch and the switch does not have a routing table to resolve different network addresses.

To work around this obstacle when you troubleshoot, one option is to use Cisco IOS software to set a static IP route to the switch's IP address for its sc0, as shown in Figure 11-4.

Figure 11-4 *You can use **telnet** to reach another subnet.*

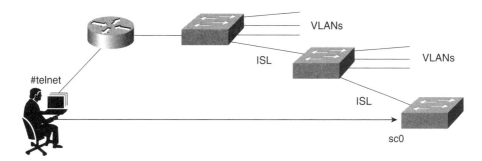

Although CDP itself displays only the information about the directly connected neighbor devices, you can repeat a sequence of steps to determine IP addresses and use Telnet across the switched network:

Step 1   Telnet to the neighbor switch and run the **show cdp neighbors** command on the Catalyst switch to determine the switch's neighbor's IP address.

Step 2   Telnet to a target address on the neighbor of the switch that you got with step 1.

Step 3   Repeat steps 1 and 2 as often as you need to for checking the extended router/ switch network.

This process somewhat resembles the iterations that occur in the IP trace process.

Router VLAN show Commands

The **show** commands provide essential information about the router system, interfaces, and counters. You will probably use some of the following commands when troubleshooting:

- **show vlans**—Use this command to display router VLAN information, including the identifier, trunk interface, protocols configured, network address, and packets count.

- **show span**—Use this command to display spanning-tree information, including the topology known to the router and whether any LAT code filtering is in effect.

NOTE   The Cisco IOS command **show span** does not show the information about the SPAN port settings on the Catalyst switch as does the Catalyst **show span** command. On the Catalyst, use the **show spantree** command to display spanning-tree information.

- **show bridge vlan**—Use this command to display information about the router as a VLAN bridge, including any bridge group, the VLAN trunk interface, the protocol for the VLAN, the VLAN ID, and spanning-tree port state for the interface.

- **show interfaces fastethernet**—Use this command to display router Fast Ethernet information.

NOTE	There are two flavors of the **show interface** command. The IOS version is **show interfaces** (plural), and the Catalyst version is **show interface** (singular). However, with these commands, a user only needs to type enough of the command to make it unique. For example, a user can type **sho int** and be successful in issuing the command in both situations.

- **show arp**—Use this command to display router address resolution information.

- **show cdp neighbors**—Use this command to display router VLAN neighbor fundamentals, including the neighbor device ID, address entries, platform capabilities, and software version.

The show vlan Command

You use the **show vlan** command to display VLAN information. As shown in Figure 11-5, you can specify a VLAN number to display information about that VLAN.

Figure 11-5 *You can use **show vlan** output to check basic VLAN parameters.*

```
router# show vlan 3

Virtual LAN ID:  3 (Inter Switch Link Encapsulation)

  vLAN Trunk Interface:    Fast Ethernet0/0.3

Protocols Configured:          Address:          Received:       Transmitted:
       IP                 192.168.30.50                32                101
       IPX          fad13.0060.5c82.6f00                 0                  2
```

Output from the **show vlan** command includes

- The VLAN ID
- The router subinterface for the VLAN
- Protocol information, including protocol type, address, and traffic displayed in number of packets

Figure 11-5 provides sample output from the **show vlan** command.

The show span Command

Use the **show span** privileged EXEC command to display the spanning-tree topology known to the router. As shown in Figure 11-6, you can use this command to get a display of the Spanning-Tree Protocol settings that the router is using as it participates in the router/switch network as a spanning-tree bridge.

Figure 11-6 *You can use **show span** output to create a bridged network map.*

```
router# show span 1

Bridge Group 1 is executing the IEEE compatible Spanning Tree protocol
  Bridge Identifier has priority 32768, address 0060.5c82.6f00
  Configured hello time 2, Max age 20, forward delay 15
  We are the root of the spanning tree
  Topology change flag not set, detected flag not set
  Times:  hold 1, topology change 30, notification 30
          hello 2, Max age 20, forward delay 15, aging 300
  Timers: hello 2, topology change 0, notification 0
Port 29 (FastEthernet0/0.3 ISL) of bridge group 1 is forwarding
  Port path cost 10, Port priority 128
  Designated root has priority 32768, address 0060.5c82.6f00
  Designated bridge has priority 32768, address 0060.5c82.6f00
  Designated port is 29, path cost 0
  Timers: message age 0, forward delay 0, hold
```

In Figure 11-6, the fields include the following:

- Bridge identifier—The spanning-tree priority and Media Access Control (MAC) address of the bridging node for which the **show span** EXEC command was executed. 0060.5c82.6f00 is the MAC address that the router uses as its bridge address.

- Root bridge identifier—The spanning-tree priority and MAC address of the known root bridge; this information appears in two places: with global information and with port-specific information. The router has been elected as the root bridge. This election can occur if the router is a juncture point between two VLANs that link to the router from Catalyst switches.

- Timers—The timer values are shown in seconds, and the timers are set to reasonable defaults. The maximum age is 40 seconds, and the maximum forward delay is 30 seconds.

- Root port—The spanning tree port on the bridge being examined through which the root bridge for the internetwork is found.

- Spanning-tree state—When a port is in forwarding mode, it is actively able to pass traffic over the link; when a port is in blocking mode, the link is an online backup that is not forwarding bridge traffic. Other possible modes are down, listening, and learning. Traffic is forwarded over the link only when the port is in forwarding mode.

- Designated bridge—The spanning-tree designated bridge MAC address for the port or interface. If the designated bridge does not match the bridge identifier, and the port is in the forwarding state, the port is a root port. If the designated bridge matches the bridge identifier, the port is in the forwarding state or is down.

- Designated port—The spanning-tree port associated with the designated bridge.

You can use some of the key information from the **show span** command to derive a map that reflects your Spanning-Tree Protocol network. A network map is an important part of the troubleshooting problem-solving model as you gather facts and consider possibilities.

You build a network map by identifying the addressing, root bridge information, and designated bridge ports to the neighbors of the router in the spanning tree. Your map can include the following important information:

- The name of the router or switch acting as a spanning-tree bridge

- The bridge priority for each device

- The bridge MAC address

- The root status, and if the device is not the root, the root port interface

For each interface acting as a spanning-tree port, your map can include the following important information:

- The subinterface ID

- The MAC address of the designated bridge

- The port to that designated bridge

- The port status (that is, listening, learning, forwarding, blocking, or disabled)

Creating a network map is a relatively simple, iterative process that consists of the following steps:

Step 1 Obtain the **show span** EXEC command output for each Cisco bridging node and make note of the values of the key fields.

Step 2   For each nonroot bridge, determine the direction, in terms of the relevant interface and port, to the root bridge.

Step 3   Draw your map as you identify the links.

The following rules apply when you're using spanning-tree information to create a network map:

- When the MAC address of the designated bridge is the same as the MAC address of the root bridge, the port or interface of the bridge being examined and the root bridge are attached to the same network.

- When the MAC address of the designated bridge is different from the MAC address of the bridge being examined, the designated bridge is in the path to the root bridge.

- When the MAC address of the designated bridge is the same as the bridge identifier of the bridge being examined, the port or interface points away from the root bridge.

- The designated port value specified for a particular port belongs to the bridge associated with the designated bridge shown in the port listing.

Router VLAN debug Commands

When you are troubleshooting a campus network that has both routers and switches, the two commands **debug vlan packet** and **debug span** can help you get a close-to-real-time perspective of VLAN problems and a status of the spanning tree from the router's perspective.

Although these troubleshooting tools are readily available from the same command-line interface as the one you use for your configuration tasks, these **debug** commands require that you handle them properly, especially if you use **debug** on a production network that users depend on for data flow.

Nonetheless, with the proper, selective, and temporary use of these tools, you can easily obtain potentially useful information as you gather facts and consider possibilities.

NOTE   Several of the precautions and issues for the proper use of **debug** are covered in Chapter 5, "Cisco Management and Diagnostic Tools."

The debug vlan packet Command

Use the **debug vlan packet** EXEC command to display general information on VLAN packets that the router received, but is not configured to support.

The **debug vlan packet** command displays only packets with a VLAN identifier that the router is not configured to support. This command allows you to identify other VLAN traffic on the network.

VLAN packets that the router is configured to route or switch are counted and indicated when you use the **show vlans** command.

Figure 11-7 shows a sample **debug vlan packet** output:

Figure 11-7 *The **debug vlan packet** output indicates that the router cannot identify the protocol of an incoming ISL packet.*

```
router# debug vlan packet

vLAN: Received ISL encapsulated UNKNOWN packet bearing color ID 4
     on interface FastEthernet0/0.4 which is not configured to
     route or bridge this packet type.
vLAN: ISL packet received bearing color ID 1 on FastEthernet0/0
     which has no sub-interface configured to route or bridge ID 1.
```

- In the first entry in the graphic sample output, the router received an ISL packet for VLAN 4 but could not determine the packet's protocol, and had no addressing established to determine how to route or bridge the packet.

- In the second entry, the router received an ISL packet on its main interface but had no subinterface configured for routing or bridging the packet for VLAN 1. The router could not handle this inadvertently received packet, so the router generated a **debug** entry.

In both these cases, the router simply drops the packet. If a dropped packet is a problem, look to the router's configuration statements and make sure that there is a legal protocol address, ISL encapsulation for the VLAN, or bridge group.

Alternately, the **debug vlan packet** output may simply reflect that packets traversed the ISL trunk between the router and its neighbor switch as part of a broadcast or multicast from a VLAN that is within the legal range of VLANs (1 through 1000).

You can prevent traffic from specific VLANs from traversing the ISL link to the router by entering the Catalyst **clear trunk** command and including an argument for the VLAN ID that has traffic you want to keep away from the router.

Always remember to turn off debugging when you no longer need it by using the **no debug vlan packet** command.

The debug span Command

You use the **debug span** EXEC command to display information on changes in the spanning-tree topology when debugging a transparent bridge. The **no** form of this command (that is, **no debug span**) disables debugging output.

After you get past the initial reaction of overload from the long string of characters, as shown in Figure 11-8, this command is useful for tracking and verifying that the Spanning-Tree Protocol is operating correctly.

Figure 11-8 *The **debug span** command displays spanning-tree topology changes.*

```
router# debug span

PST: Ether 0000000000000A080002A02D6700000000000A080002A02D6780010000140002000F00
           |A|B|C&D| E  |    F    |  G  |H|    I    |J|K| L  | M | O | P |

PST:                  Indication that this is a spanning-tree packet.
Ether                 Interface receiving the packet.
(A) 0000              Indication that this is an IEEE BPDU packet.
(B) 00                Version.
(C) 00                Command mode:
                      00 indicates Config BPDU.
                      80 indicates the Topology Change Notification (TCN) BPDU.
(D) 00                Topology change acknowledgment:
                      00 indicates no change.
                      80 indicates a change notification.
(E) 000A              Root priority.
(F) 080002A02D67      Root ID.
(G) 00000000          Root path cost (0 means the sender of this BPDU packet is the root
bridge).
(H) 000A              Bridge priority.
(I) 080002A02D67      Bridge ID.
(J) 80                Port priority.
(K) 01                Port No. 1.
(L) 0000              Message age in 256ths of a second (0 seconds, in this case).
(M) 1400              Maximum age in 256ths of a second (20 seconds, in this case).
(N) 0200               Hello time in 256ths of a second (2 seconds, in this case).
(O) 0F00              Forward delay in 256ths of a second (15 seconds, in this case).
```

You can see the router's perspective in the spanning-tree packets that the router receives. By counting out the digits and aligning the fields, you can get all the fields of data used for Spanning-Tree Protocol.

You can combine this information with what is available from the Catalyst **show span** command to get a close-to-real-time filtering of the Spanning-Tree Protocol BPDU messaging process.

NOTE   Figure 11-8 shows Spanning-Tree Protocol with IEEE encapsulation set. For Spanning-Tree Protocol with Digital encapsulation, refer to www.cisco.com.

Problem Isolation in Router/Switch VLAN Networks

A general troubleshooting approach like the flow of steps for problem isolation on a router/switch VLAN network is useful as you solve any problem (or problems) in a systematic way. Proceed in the order shown in Figure 11-9:

Step 1 Check the physical link connections between the router and the switch's connection to it over the Fast Ethernet.

Step 2 Look into any router and switch configuration problems, including inconsistent entries from one side or the other.

Step 3 Check the trunking and fix any problems you find with ISL (for example, wrong or missing statements).

Step 4 Troubleshoot any problem with a VLAN, its Spanning-Tree Protocol operations, and any problems that occur from the router connecting multiple VLANs.

Figure 11-9 *The VLAN problem isolation flowchart shows a general approach for troubleshooting VLANs.*

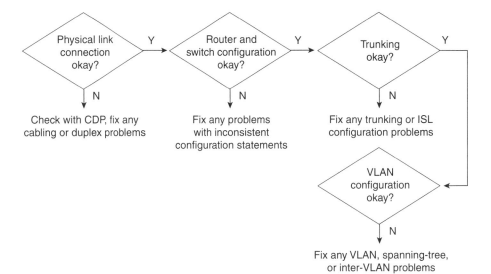

Troubleshooting Example: Dropped Packets and Loops

Spanning-tree bridges (that is, the switches and routers in Figure 11-10) use topology change notification BPDUs to notify other bridges of a change in the spanning-tree topology of the network.

Figure 11-10 *Different and incompatible spanning-tree versions cause problems.*

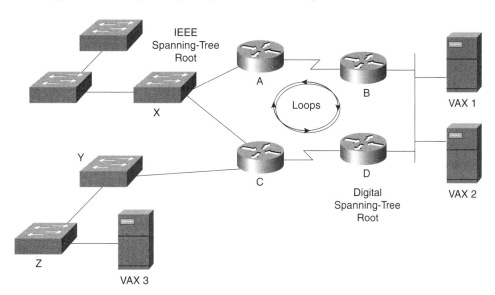

Bridges send these topology change notification BPDUs any time a port makes a transition to or from a forwarding state and you have other ports in the same bridge group (that is, VLAN). These BPDUs move toward the root bridge.

There can be only one root bridge per bridged network. After an election process to determine the root bridge, the root determines values for configuration messages (that is, BPDU) and sets the other bridge's timers.

Other designated bridges determine the shortest path to the root bridge and are responsible for advertising BPDUs to other bridges out designated ports. A bridge should have ports in blocking state if there is a physical/logical loop.

Problems can arise for internetworks in which both IEEE and Digital spanning-tree algorithms are used by bridging nodes. These problems are caused by differences in the way the bridging nodes handle spanning-tree BPDU packets (or hello packets) and in the way they handle data.

In the scenario shown in Figure 11-10, Router A, Router B, and Router C are running the IEEE spanning-tree algorithm, and Router D is inadvertently misconfigured to use the Digital spanning-tree version.

Router A claims to be the IEEE root, and Router D claims to be the Digital root. Router B and Router C propagate root information on all interfaces for IEEE spanning tree. However, Router D drops IEEE spanning-tree information. Similarly, the other routers drop Router D's claim to be the root.

The result is that none of the bridges in this internetwork believes that there is a loop. When a broadcast packet is sent on the network, a broadcast storm results over the entire internetwork, including the Switches X and Y and beyond.

To resolve this problem, reconfigure Router D for IEEE. Although a configuration change is necessary, it might not be sufficient to reestablish connectivity.

Assume that in this case connectivity is not restored, even when all bridging nodes are reconfigured to use the same spanning-tree algorithm. There will be a reconvergence delay as devices exchange BPDUs and recompute a spanning tree for the network.

Router VLAN Symptoms and Problems

Table 11-2 shows high-level VLAN problems that can occur with a router or switch. The problem facts or symptoms and the possibilities and action plans may help you identify and solve the problems.

Table 11-2 *Router VLAN symptoms, problems, and action plans.*

Symptom	Possible Problems and Action Plans
Performance on the VLAN is slow or unreliable	• Bad adapter in a device. Check hardware. • Full-duplex or half-duplex Ethernet settings incorrect. • Cabling problem. Check connected LED. Check for correct cable properly attached and if length exceeds maximum cable distance.
Attached terminal or modem connection cannot communicate with a router or with a switch	• Misconfigured terminal and console port. Check that baud rate and character format match. • Determine whether a default route is needed on a router to reach the switch on a different subnet.
Local VLAN device cannot communicate with remote devices on a VLAN beyond the router	• Misconfigured IP addressing or mask. Check with **cdp** and **show interface** commands. • Default gateway not specified or incorrect. Check router, switch, servers, and clients. • VLAN misconfigured. Check port assignments and eliminate unnecessary connections between VLANs if a port belongs to multiple VLANs. • VLAN inconsistency problem. Make sure VLANs match on both sides of a trunk. • ISL problem. Make sure there is proper trunking, use VLAN 1, and make sure that no invalid VTP server information update has occurred.

When faced with poor throughput problems, check to see what type of errors exist. There could be a bad adapter card. Combinations of FCS and alignment errors and runts generally point to a duplex mismatch—the usual culprit is the autonegotiation between devices or a mismatched setting between the two sides of a link.

NOTE	There is a myth that switched Ethernet eliminates collisions. The fact is that switches minimize the collision domain, but if you're running in half duplex, the collisions will still occur because two devices can always attempt to communicate at the same time. An example is a news server that has many clients attempting to communicate at the same time. The traffic comes through the router and switch to the directly connected server. At the same time, the server is attempting to communicate back to these clients. So as the server is answering one client, another client sends a request and there is a potential for collision. The only cure to collisions on Ethernet is to run in full duplex.

Is the problem on the local side or remote side of the link? Remember that a minimum of switch ports are involved in a link. What path is the packet taking—is it going across trunks or other switches?

If you see that the collisions count on output from a **show interface** command is increasing rapidly, the problem may be an overloaded link.

Summary

This chapter defined the router's role as VLAN switch, VLAN Layer 2 translator, and Layer 3 router between VLANs. It also provided the basic troubleshooting steps and commands for these types of networks.

Chapter 11 Test
Troubleshooting VLANs on Routers and Switches

Estimated Time: 15 minutes

Complete all the exercises to test your knowledge of the materials contained in this chapter. Answers are listed in Appendix A, "Chapter Test Answer Key."

Use the information contained in this chapter to answer the following questions.

Question 11.1

T   F   Combining IEEE and Digital spanning-tree protocols will create a single autonomous tree.

Question 11.2

T   F   Efficient troubleshooting of spanning-tree requires that you locate the root bridge.

Question 11.3

T   F   CDP uses broadcasts and should be used sparingly.

Question 11.4

T   F   You can use the **show span** command to build a map based on your spanning-tree protocol network.

Question 11.5

T   F   A **debug** command is automatically disabled after 100 lines of screen output.

PART IV

WAN Troubleshooting

Diagnosing and Correcting Frame Relay Problems

Frame Relay networks have become the WAN solution of choice wherever a suitable digital facility infrastructure permits Frame Relay's streamlined data transfer capacity. Although some testing is occurring with switched virtual circuits (SVCs), almost all production traffic for Frame Relay uses permanent virtual circuits (PVCs). PVCs are permanently established circuits configured in advance that eliminate dynamic circuit establishment and teardown—a key area for WAN troubleshooting.

The purpose of this chapter is to discuss troubleshooting tips specific to Frame Relay PVC networking on Cisco serial interfaces.

Troubleshooting Frame Relay

Although Frame Relay is a Layer 2 data-link protocol, when Frame Relay problems occur, you should first check the lower-layer hardware interface (physical layer). For example, check to see if a V.35 cable to a channel service unit/data service unit (CSU/DSU) is connected and working properly. Figure 12-1 shows the various elements of the physical Frame Relay connection.

Figure 12-1 *The physical Frame Relay connection consists of several elements.*

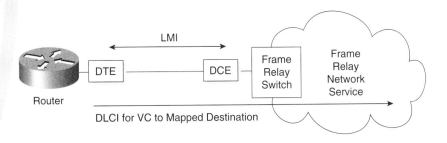

When you have determined that the hardware is working properly, proceed to Layer 2. The encapsulation (either Frame Relay or IETF) must match on the near- and far-end data terminal equipment (DTE).

The Local Management Interface (LMI) type configured must match on the DTE and on the data circuit-terminating equipment (DCE). For Frame Relay, the options are Cisco, ANSI, or q933a (ITU-T). The router autosenses which LMI is in use (for Cisco IOS 11.2 and later versions), and the LMI provides the keepalives that you can check when you troubleshoot. Use the command **frame-relay lmi-type** {ansi | cisco | q933a} to change the LMI type if necessary.

A Frame Relay service provider specifies the data-link connection identifier (DLCI) to use, and this identifier is significant locally only. As part of the configuration process, the DLCI maps to the destination Layer 3 address for that PVC. Often, a useful troubleshooting test is to verify the details and effects of this configuration process.

The framing fields for High-Level Data Link Control (HDLC) are streamlined for Frame Relay. One key field is the DLCI, which is represented as a 6-bit high-order and a 4-bit low-order part of the address octets, as shown in Figure 12-2. The 10-bit DLCI value is the heart of the Frame Relay header. It identifies the logical connection that is multiplexed into the physical channel.

Figure 12-2 *The most significant portion of the frame, the DLCI portion, determines the destination of the frame.*

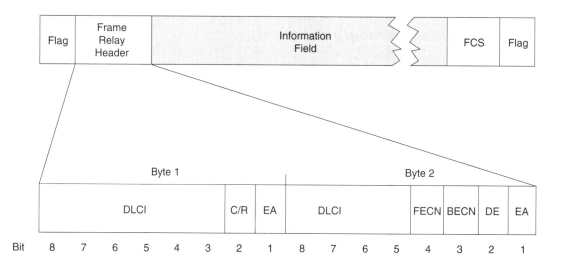

DCLI = Data-link connection identifier
C/R = Command/response field bit (application specific—not modified by network)
FECN = Forward explicit congestion notification
BECN = Backward explicit congestion notification
DE = Discard eligibility indicator
EA = Extension bit (allows indication of 3- or 4-byte header)

Frame Relay Frame Format

In the basic LMI addressing, DLCIs have local significance; that is, the end devices at two different ends of a connection may use different DLCIs to refer to that same connection. LMI is the connection status mechanism used by Frame Relay. There are three LMI specifications offered by Cisco, as defined earlier in this chapter.

Use of different DLCIs can be a source of problems if either DTE misinterprets or misapplies the DLCI number specified by the service provider. Typically, however, this problem is isolated and resolved during the testing phase.

Congestion-related bit positions in the frame are

- FECN—Forward explicit congestion notification, set by a Frame Relay network to inform the DTE receiving the frame that congestion was experienced in the path from source to destination.

  The Cisco router passes FECN along so that the DTE receiving frames with the FECN bit set can request that higher-level protocols take flow-control action as appropriate.

- BECN—Backward explicit congestion notification, set by a Frame Relay network in frames traveling in the opposite direction of frames encountering a congested path.

  Again, the router passes BECN along so that the DTE receiving frames with the BECN bit set can request that higher-level protocols take flow-control action as appropriate.

- DE—Discard eligibility, set by the DTE to tell the Frame Relay network that a frame has lower importance than other frames and should be discarded before other frames if the network becomes short of resources. Thus, it represents a simple priority mechanism.

You use the Cisco IOS **show frame-relay pvc** command and the **debug frame-relay** commands (covered later in this chapter) to see the current values in these frame fields.

Problem Isolation in Frame Relay WANs

The flowchart shown in Figure 12-3 provides the basic steps for problem isolation in a Frame Relay network. The tools available to check each element are covered in greater detail later in this chapter.

Figure 12-3 *You can use the Frame Relay problem isolation flowchart to troubleshoot more efficiently.*

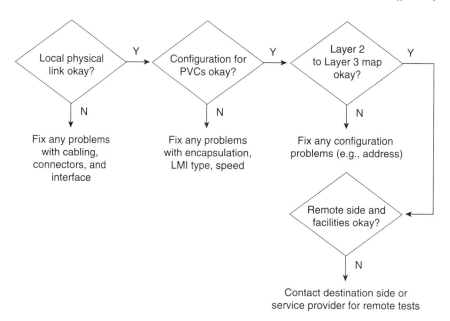

Let's examine the typical symptoms and problems that may occur on a WAN. Table 12-1 lists serial link problems, and Table 12-2 lists Frame Relay problems.

Table 12-1 *Generic serial link symptoms and possible problems.*

Symptom	Possible Problems
Intermittent connectivity	• Faulty router interface card or cable • Faulty CSU/DSU • Timing problem • Congested/overutilized serial line
Connection fails as load increases	• Dirty serial line • Congested/overutilized serial line
Connections fail at a particular time of day	• Congested/overutilized serial line
Connections fail after some period of normal operation	• Unshielded cable runs too close to EMI sources • Hardware in serial link failed • Incorrect routing tables (flapping links) • Buffer misses or other software problems
Connection has never worked	• Serial facility not provisioned or has failed

Table 12-1 *Generic serial link symptoms and possible problems. (Continued)*

Faulty router interface card or cable	• Use the **show interfaces serial** command to check for errors and swap card or cable if necessary
	• Use **show controllers** command to check microcode level; upgrade if the version is old
Faulty CSU/DSU	• Check for input errors with the **show interfaces serial** command and replace CSU/DSU if necessary
Timing problem	• Verify that serial clock transmit external (SCTE) terminal timing is enabled on CSU/DSU
	• Verify that the correct device is generating the system clock
	• Check cable length
	• Lower the line speed
Congested/overutilized serial line	• Reduce broadcast traffic
	• Use protocol analyzer to check application behavior (for example, very large file transfers during peak hours)
	• Implement priority queuing
	• Adjust hold queue and buffer sizes with help from a technical support representative
	• Add bandwidth, consider using dial backup
Dirty serial line	• Look for increasing input errors by using **show interfaces serial**
Unshielded cable runs too close to EMI sources	• Look for increasing input errors by using **show interfaces serial**
	• Inspect cables and relocate or shield cables if necessary
Hardware in serial link failed	• Confirm that link is down by using **show interfaces serial**
	• Use loopback tests and protocol analyzer to isolate problem
Incorrect routing tables	• Check routes by using the appropriate **show protocol route**
	• Look for source of bad routes by checking configuration and using a protocol analyzer
Buffer misses or other software problems	• Evaluate buffer status by using **show buffers**
	• With help from a technical support representative, modify buffers to prevent dropped connections

Table 12-2 *Frame Relay symptoms and possible problems*

Symptom	Possible Problems
Frame Relay switch is misconfigured	• Make sure LMI updates are being received by using **show interfaces serial** • Use the **debug frame-relay lmi** command to confirm that the DLCI numbers provided by your vendor match the PVC output
Router is misconfigured for Frame Relay	• Make sure the LMI type matches that of the switch • Examine output from the **show frame-relay map** command to make sure the remote networks have been learned
Users cannot connect to resources over a new Frame Relay link	• Faulty router interface card or cable • Frame Relay switch is misconfigured • Router is misconfigured for Frame Relay

Overview of Troubleshooting Commands

Figure 12-4 shows a summary of the commands covered in this chapter and the extent of troubleshooting coverage provided by each command.

Figure 12-4 *These Frame Relay troubleshooting commands are covered in this chapter.*

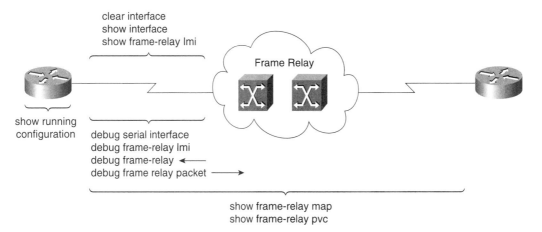

As you can see, each command listed can check a specific portion of the communication.

In the next section, you'll learn about the various diagnostic tools available to troubleshoot these WAN problems.

WAN and Frame Relay Diagnostic Tools

If traffic that uses Frame Relay is not working properly, a good initial test is whether it ever worked. If it never did, then the likely place to look for possible causes is in configuration of the PVCs. The **show** and **debug** commands are designed to help locate problems. Loopback tests are also valuable in troubleshooting.

The Frame Relay show Commands

The **show** commands provide information about the interface conditions, protocol status, and how the LMI and configuration are performing. The following **show** commands are covered in more detail in the following sections:

- **show interfaces serial**
- **show frame-relay lmi**
- **show frame-relay map**
- **show frame-relay pvc**

The **show interfaces serial** Command

In the **show interfaces serial** command example shown in Figure 12-5, the first highlighted line conveys information that is crucial for Frame Relay troubleshooting the Layer 1 hardware and Layer 2 keepalive conditions. Keepalives, which are LMI messages like those shown in Figure 12-5, are sent automatically from the router. Later in this chapter you'll find a description of the most important interpretations of this highlighted line.

Figure 12-5 *You can use the **show interfaces serial** command to troubleshoot Layer 1 and Layer 2 functions.*

```
Router#show interfaces serial 1
Serial1 is up, line protocol is down
  Hardware is MCI Serial
  Internet address is 131.108.174.48, subnet mask is 255.255.255.0
  MTU 1500 bytes, BW 1544 Kbit, DLY 20000 usec, rely 246/255, load 1/255
  Encapsulation FRAME-RELAY, loopback not set, keepalive set (10 sec)
  LMI enq sent  2, LMI stat recvd 0, LMI upd recvd 0, DTE LMI down
  LMI enq recvd 266, LMI stat sent  264, LMI upd sent  0
  LMI DLCI 1023  LMI type is CISCO  frame relay DTE
  Last input 0:00:04, output 0:00:02, output hang never
  Last clearing of "show interface" counters 0:44:32
  Output queue 0/40, 0 drops; input queue 0/75, 0 drops
  Five minute input rate 0 bits/sec, 0 packets/sec
  Five minute output rate 0 bits/sec, 0 packets/sec
     307 packets input, 6615 bytes, 0 no buffer
     Received 0 broadcasts, 0 runts, 0 giants
     0 input errors, 0 CRC, 0 frame, 0 overrun, 0 ignored, 0 abort
     0 input packets with dribble condition detected
     266 packets output, 3810 bytes, 0 underruns
     0 output errors, 0 collisions, 2 interface resets, 0 restarts
     178 carrier transitions
```

A key area to check is to determine whether the proper encapsulation has been set. Encapsulation must be configured consistently on both sides of the data link. In the case of a Frame Relay PVC, both routers need to have the same encapsulation or whatever the frame provider is using. In this case, the encapsulation must be **frame-relay**.

Another key area to check is that the LMI type configured is correct. Figure 12-5 shows that this is the Cisco LMI, which uses DLCI 1023 as its PVC.

Interface resets are key indicators for you to check when troubleshooting. The interface reset output indicates the number of times that the serial interface has been completely reset. Interface resets can happen if

- Packets queued for transmission are not sent within several seconds
- There is a hardware problem with the interface, cable, or CSU/DSU
- A problem exists with the clocking signals
- A problem exists with the carrier line
- An interface is looped or shut down
- The router is periodically trying to restart the interface, with line protocol down

You may have to reset the interface manually with the **clear int s 1 command**.

In Figure 12-6, the first highlighted line, which is the first line of the output, shows that the line protocol is down. Possible reasons are covered later in the chapter, along with suggested actions.

Figure 12-6 *This output from the **show interfaces serial 1** command indicates that the protocol is down.*

```
Router#show interfaces serial 1
Serial1 is up, line protocol is down
  Hardware is MCI Serial
  Internet address is 131.108.174.48, subnet mask is 255.255.255.0
  MTU 1500 bytes, BW 1544 Kbit, DLY 20000 usec, rely 249/255, load 1/255
  Encapsulation FRAME-RELAY, loopback not set, keepalive set (10 sec)
  LMI enq sent  4, LMI stat recvd 0, LMI upd recvd 0, DTE LMI down
  LMI enq recvd 268, LMI stat sent  264, LMI upd sent  0
  LMI DLCI 0  LMI type is ANSI Annex D  frame relay DTE
  Last input 0:00:09, output 0:00:07, output hang never
  Last clearing of "show interface" counters 0:44:57
  Output queue 0/40, 0 drops; input queue 0/75, 0 drops
  Five minute input rate 0 bits/sec, 0 packets/sec
  Five minute output rate 0 bits/sec, 0 packets/sec
     309 packets input, 6641 bytes, 0 no buffer
     Received 0 broadcasts, 0 runts, 0 giants
     0 input errors, 0 CRC, 0 frame, 0 overrun, 0 ignored, 0 abort
     0 input packets with dribble condition detected
     268 packets output, 3836 bytes, 0 underruns
     0 output errors, 0 collisions, 2 interface resets, 0 restarts
     180 carrier transitions
```

The LMI setting in this example occurs on DLCI 0 for LMI type ANSI Annex D; the other type of LMI is ITU-T for Q.933 Annex A. The router autosenses which LMI is in use (for Cisco IOS 11.2 and later versions). On Cisco IOS 11.1 and earlier, the default LMI type is Cisco.

For an indication of activity on the interface, check the number of packets input and output. Error counts beyond the baseline can be an important troubleshooting fact to check.

Another key indicator to check for is carrier transitions. This indicator counts the number of times that the Data Carrier Detect (DCD) signal has changed state. Some transitions are normal. But if you see a count that is much higher than what you expect as baseline, it may reflect the stability of the carrier's facility. When a transition occurs, the line may be dropped and reset.

When the first line of the **show interfaces serial** command output shows that the interface is down, the line protocol that depends on the interface must also be down.

Reasons why the serial interface is down include the following:

- Disconnected, faulty, or incorrect cabling.
- Telephone company problem (line down or not connected to CSU/DSU).
- Hardware failure (CSU/DSU or router serial card).
- The interface was configured incorrectly.

If you suspect that one or more of these problems is the cause of the downed serial line, appropriate actions to try include the following:

- Verify that you are using the proper cable and interface.
- Check the LEDs on the CSU/DSU to see if Carrier Detect (CD) is active.
- Insert a breakout box and check all control leads.
- Check your configuration to see whether you can generate keepalive packets between routers.
- Swap hardware used (e.g., try another cable or interface).
- Contact your leased-line or other carrier service.

When the first line of the **show interfaces serial** command output shows that the interface is up but the line protocol on the interface is down, reasons why the serial interface Layer 2 is down include the following:

- Keepalives are not being sent by the remote router. (By default, keepalives are sent every 10 seconds.)
- The local or remote router is misconfigured.
- There is a leased-line or other carrier service problem (e.g., noisy line, misconfigured or failed switch).
- There is a timing problem on the facility.
- There has been a router hardware failure (local or remote).
- The local or remote CSU/DSU has failed.

If you suspect that one or more of these problems is the cause of the line protocol being down, appropriate actions to try include the following:

- Check the data link for Frame Relay—the DTE-to-DCE interface.

- Check the link from CSU to CSU to eliminate link and hardware problems.

- Perform loopback tests to determine which parts of Layer 2 (if any) are active and which are not.

The **show frame-relay lmi** Command

The **show frame-relay lmi** command can help you troubleshoot by providing LMI statistics that may indicate a problem.

To set a starting point for getting statistics, use the **clear counters serial** *number* command. This command resets the interface counters that will be used with this **show** command and others.

In Figure 12-7, one key element to check is what role and keepalive type are being used for the Frame Relay interface. Here it is acting as a DTE on a User-Network Interface (UNI); it could also act as a Network-to-Network Interface (NNI).

Figure 12-7 *You can use the **show frame-relay lmi** command to check LMI statistics.*

```
Router#show frame-relay lmi
LMI Statistics for interface Serial1 (Frame Relay DTE) LMI TYPE = ANSI
  Invalid Unnumbered info 0          Invalid Prot Disc 0
  Invalid dummy Call Ref 0           Invalid Msg Type 0
  Invalid Status Message 0           Invalid Lock Shift 0
  Invalid Information ID 0           Invalid Report IE Len 0
  Invalid Report Request 0          Invalid Keep IE Len 0
  Num Status Enq. Sent 9            Num Status msgs Rcvd 0
  Num Update Status Rcvd 0          Num Status Timeouts 9
```

You should look for nonzero invalid LMI items accumulated in the counters. The explicit decodes of a protocol analyzer are required to see the information elements.

Also check Num Status Timeouts, which is the number of times the status message was not received within the keepalive timer. Num Status Enq. Timeouts is the number of times the status inquiry message was not received within the T392 DCE timer.

The **show frame-relay map** Command

You use the **show frame-relay map** command to troubleshoot the current DLCI to Layer 3 map entries and to check information about the connections. Output includes end-to-end information about the mapping of the locally significant DLCI to the far-end destination.

In Figure 12-8, the Frame Relay interface has been shut and has a PVC to the IP destination shown. The DLCI to reach this interface is

- 177 decimal
- B1 hexadecimal
- 2C10, as it appears on the facility

An upper-layer protocol process uses a broadcast if it does not know about the DLCIs configured on the interface.

Figure 12-8 *The Frame Relay interface is shut and has a PVC to an IP destination.*

```
Router#show frame-relay map
Serial 1 (administratively down): ip 131.108.177.177
dlci 177 (0xB1,0x2C10), static,
broadcast,
CISCO
TCP/IP Header Compression (inherited), passive (inherited)
```

Compression is inherited from the interface rather than from an explicit configuration statement.

The **show frame-relay pvc** Command

This **show frame-relay pvc** command provides the LMI status of each DLCI, as shown in Figure 12-9; or you can specify a given DLCI to check that PVC only.

Figure 12-9 *You can use the **show frame-relay pvc** command to check PVCs.*

```
Router#show frame-relay pvc
   PVC Statistics for interface Serial1 (Frame Relay DCE)
   DLCI = 100, DLCI USAGE = LOCAL, PVC STATUS = ACTIVE
      input pkts 0          output pkts 0         in bytes 0
      out bytes 0           dropped pkts 0        in FECN pkts 0
      in BECN pkts 0        out FECN pkts 0       out BECN pkts 0
      in DE pkts 0          out DE pkts 0
      pvc create time 0:03:03 last time pvc status changed 0:03:03
      Num Pkts Switched 0

   DLCI = 101, DLCI USAGE = LOCAL, PVC STATUS = INACTIVE
      input pkts 0          output pkts 0         in bytes 0
      out bytes 0           dropped pkts 0        in FECN pkts 0
      in BECN pkts 0        out FECN pkts 0       out BECN pkts 0
      in DE pkts 0          out DE pkts 0
      pvc create time 0:02:58 last time pvc status changed 0:02:58
      Num Pkts Switched 0
```

DLCI usage can be local DTE or SWITCHED (meaning that the router is acting as a switch). As DCE, the status refers to outgoing interfaces (up or down) and the status of the outgoing PVC.

PVCs terminated on a DCE interface use the status of the interface to set the PVC STATUS. If the usage is LOCAL, it indicated that the PVC was created with a configuration command on the router. You can troubleshoot by checking whether this configuration is correct. The PVC status can be active, inactive, or deleted. You should also check for the time when change occurred to associate the change with some other cause you are testing.

Finally, you should check for dropped frames, congestion notifications, and discard eligibles beyond baseline. The Frame Relay switch passes FECN bits, BECN bits, and DE bits unchanged from ingress to egress points in the network.

The Frame Relay debug Commands

The **debug** commands provide an ongoing display of Frame Relay details that include a captured flow of selected packet fields, events, and status.

On a production network supporting user traffic, you must be careful when you use some **debug** commands:

- Be as specific as possible with arguments to the command and consider using an access list to focus the **debug**.

- Know your network load so that you do not worsen a heavily loaded network with the additional processing and output of the **debug**.

- Always use the **no debug** or **undebug** command as soon as you have no further need for the debug tools.

The Cisco IOS software **debug** commands featured in this chapter are

- **debug serial interface**—Displays information about the Frame Relay or HDLC keepalive messages and other data-link messages.

- **debug frame-relay lmi**—Displays packet fields to determine whether the router and the Frame Relay switch are sending and receiving LMI packets properly.

- **debug frame-relay events**—Displays debugging information about the packets that are received on a Frame Relay interface.

- **debug frame-relay packet**—Displays debugging information about the packets that are sent out of a Frame Relay interface.

The **debug serial interface** Command

If the **show interfaces serial** command shows that the line and protocol are down, you can use the **debug serial interface** command to isolate a timing problem as the cause of a connection failure, as shown in Figure 12-10.

Figure 12-10 *HDLC keepalive myseq numbers increment, but one mineseen keepalive sequence number does not increment.*

```
Router# debug serial interface
Serial1: HDLC myseq 636127, mineseen 636127, yourseen 515040, line up
Serial1: HDLC myseq 636128, mineseen 636127, yourseen 515041, line up
Serial1: HDLC myseq 636129, mineseen 636129, yourseen 515042, line up


Serial1: HDLC myseq 636130, mineseen 636130, yourseen 515043, line up
Serial1: HDLC myseq 636131, mineseen 636130, yourseen 515044, line up
Serial1: HDLC myseq 636132, mineseen 636130, yourseen 515045, line up
Serial1: HDLC myseq 636133, mineseen 636130, yourseen 515046, line down
....
Illegal serial link type code xxx
```

The output of the **debug serial interface** command can vary, depending on the type of WAN configured for an interface: Frame Relay or HDLC (other interfaces are HSSI, SMDS, and X.25).

The output also can vary depending on the type of encapsulation configured for that interface. The hardware platform also can affect the output of the **debug serial interface** command.

For troubleshooting a Frame Relay data link, many engineers temporarily set the encapsulation to HDLC as shown in Figure 12-10 to see what keepalive traffic is present. They use this approach because if the LMI is down for Frame Relay, the interface with Frame Relay encapsulation will not be able to generate the keepalive values.

If the keepalive values are not incrementing in each subsequent line of output, there is a timing or line problem at one end of the connection. The field values are

- mineseq—The keepalive sent by the local side
- yourseen—The keepalive sent by the other side
- mineseen—The local keepalive seen by the other side

Figure 12-10 shows that the remote router is not receiving all the keepalives that the local router is sending. The DTE sends out a sequence number and expects the same sequence number back on a valid packet from the remote end.

When the difference in the values in the myseq and mineseen fields exceeds the values of two of six consecutive keepalive events (e.g., 636130 was the last mineseen but 636131 through 636133 were not seen), the line goes down and the interface is reset. The line protocol then goes down and any Layer 3 protocol will not consider the line to be available. Frame Relay LMI continues to try to reestablish a valid keepalive dialog. If the LMI gets three consecutive myseq/ mineseen indicators, it brings the line back up. The yourseen values that are sequenced from the remote end (e.g., 515040 through 515046) are incrementing appropriately. Frame flow from the remote side to the local side is working; the problem to check further is frame flow from this side to the other side.

The illegal serial link message is displayed if the encapsulation is Frame Relay (or HDLC) and the router attempts to send a packet containing an unknown packet type.

You will learn more on Frame Relay operations with the **debug frame-relay events** and **debug frame-relay packet** commands later in this chapter.

The **debug frame-relay lmi** Command

You can check LMI exchanges by using the **debug frame-relay lmi** command. The first four lines of output in Figure 12-11 describe an LMI exchange. The first line describes the LMI request the router has sent to the switch. The second line describes the LMI reply the router has received from the switch.

Figure 12-11 *You can use the **debug frame-relay lmi** command to check LMI exchanges.*

```
Router#debug frame-relay lmi
Serial 1 (out): StEnq, clock 20212760, myseq 206, mineseen 205, yourseen 136, DTE up
Serial 1 (in): Status, clock 20212764, myseq 206
RT IE 1, length 1, type 1
KA IE 3, length 2, yourseq 138, myseq 206
....
Serial 1 (out): StEnq, clock 20252760, myseq 210, mineseen 209, yourseen 144, DTE up
Serial 1 (in): Status, clock 20252764, myseq 210
RT IE 1, length 1, type 1
KA IE 3, length 2, yourseq 146, myseq 210
 PVC IE 0x7, length 0x6, dlci 400, status 0, bw 56000
 PVC IE 0x7, length 0x6, dlci 401, status 0, bw 56000
```

The (out) StEnq is an LMI status enquiry sent by the router and the (in) Status is the reply from the Frame Relay switch. The mineseen is the number of the last keepalive accepted as good by the switch.

The third and fourth lines describe the response to this request from the switch. The RT IE is a report type information element for keepalives with seq and seen values numbering the keepalives.

You use the clock to check elapsed milliseconds of system clock between messages or events.

The first four lines are an LMI exchange, the last six lines (after the ....) are a full LMI status message with PVC information. PVC information elements include DLCI, status 0 (added/ inactive), and committed info rate (CIR) of 56 kbps.

Because the **debug frame-relay lmi** command does not generate much output, you can use it at any time, even during periods of heavy traffic, without adversely affecting other users on the system.

The **debug frame-relay events** Command

The **debug frame-relay events** command helps you analyze the packets that have been received. However, because the **debug frame-relay events** command generates a lot of output, you should only use it when traffic on the Frame Relay network is lighter than 25 packets per second.

Output from the **debug frame-relay events** command can help you troubleshoot the inbound traffic and determine which application is using a DLCI. In Figure 12-12, all the packets on serial0 and serial1 are incoming (indicated by i).

Figure 12-12 *You can use the **debug frame-relay events** command on a network with traffic lighter than 25 packets per second due to the **debug** command's processing and output generation costs.*

```
router#debug frame-relay events
Serial0(i): dlci 500(0x7C41), pkt type 0x800,  datagramsize 24
Serial1(i): dlci 1023(0xFCF1), pkt type 0x309, datagramsize 13
Serial0(i): dlci 500(0x7C41), pkt type 0x800,  datagramsize 24
Serial1(i): dlci 1023(0xFCF1), pkt type 0x309, datagramsize 13
Serial0(i): dlci 500(0x7C41), pkt type 0x800,  datagramsize 24
```

As highlighted in Figure 12-12, the Frame Relay packets received on serial 0 DLCI 500 are type IP on 10-Mbps nets with 24-byte datagram size. Also highlighted in Figure 12-12, you can see that the Frame Relay packets received on serial 1 DLCI 1023 are ANSI LMI messages with 13-byte size. There are many other packet type codes. Cisco routers may also use the Ethernet type coded in the pkt type field.

Possible packet type values for signaling are

- 0x308—Signaling message; valid only with a DLCI of 0
- 0x309—LMI message; valid only with a DLCI of 1023

Possible Ethernet-type codes include the following:

- 0x0201—IP on 3-MB network
- 0xCC—RFC 1294 (only for IP)
- 0x0800—IP on 10-MB network
- 0x0806—IP ARP
- 0x0808—Frame Relay ARP
- 0x8035—RARP
- 0x8038—Digital spanning tree
- 0x809b—Apple EtherTalk
- 0x80f3—AppleTalk ARP
- 0x8137—IPX
- 0x9000—Ethernet loopback packet IP pkt type

Possible HDLC packet type codes are as follows:

- 0x1A58—IPX, standard form
- 0xFEFE—CLNS
- 0xEFEF—ES-IS
- 0x1998—Uncompressed TCP
- 0x1999—Compressed TCP
- 0x6558—Serial line bridging

The **debug frame-relay packet** Command

The **debug frame-relay packet** command helps you analyze the packets that have been sent, as shown in Figure 12-13. However, because the **debug frame-relay packet** command generates a lot of output, you should use it only when traffic on the Frame Relay network is lighter than 25 packets per second.

Figure 12-13 *The debug frame-relay packet command details packets sent.*

```
router#debug frame-relay packet
Serial0: broadcast = 1, link 809B, addr 65535.255
Serial0(o): dlci 500 type 800 size 24
Serial0: broadcast = 0, link 809B, addr 10.2
Serial0(o): dlci 100 type 809B size 104
Serial0: broadcast search
Serial0(o): dlci 300 type 809B size 24
Serial0(o): dlci 400 type 809B size 24
```

The Frame Relay packets sent on serial 0 DLCI 500 are type AppleTalk with 24-byte size. The addresses (addr) are from AppleTalk.

If the A broadcast value is 1, then the value is a broadcast address. If the broadcast value is 0, then the address is for a particular destination (that is, is not a broadcast). A broadcast search looks for a protocol map list entry for any address that has the keyword *broadcast*.

The type field uses the same packet type codes that are used with the **debug frame-relay** command.

Frame Relay Loopback Tests

Loopback tests can help you define the extent of a Frame Relay Layer 2 connectivity problem. You can gather some facts before you contact the leased line or Frame Relay service provider.

Usually, unless you have a clear indication of where the problem is, you should test loopbacks in the following sequence (use Figure 12-14 as a reference):

1 Do the local loopback test with LMI (Router A side).

2 Try the local test on the other-side LMI (Router B side).

3 If LMIs come up (e.g., 1023 for Cisco LMI), but you cannot get a non-LMI DLCI to the remote interface to carry other traffic, contact the service provider.

4 The Frame Relay service can perform remote loop tests and will be more willing to do so if you have already eliminated the local loops as a possible cause of the problem.

Figure 12-14 *There are several points where Frame Relay loopback tests can be used.*

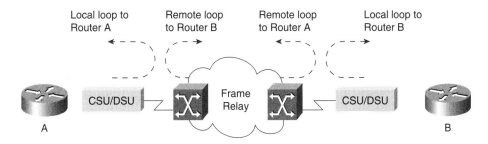

Summary

This chapter provides an overview of possible serial and Frame Relay link problems. It also covers **show** and **debug** commands and loopback test usage for isolating these problems.

Chapter 12 Test
Diagnosing and Correcting Frame Relay Problems

Estimated Time: 15 minutes

Complete all the exercises to test your knowledge of the materials contained in this chapter. Answers are listed in Appendix A, "Chapter Test Answer Key."

Use the information contained in this chapter to answer the following questions.

Question 12.1

T   F   Frame Relay is a Layer 2 data-link protocol.

Question 12.2

T   F   The LMI type options available are Cisco, IETF, and ANSI.

Question 12.3

T   F   End devices at two different ends of a connection must use the same DLCI.

Question 12.4

T   F   FECN is set to inform the DTE receiving the frame that congestion was experienced in the path.

Question 12.5

T   F   Discard eligibility represents a simple priority mechanism.

Question 12.6

List at least three **show** commands that can be useful in troubleshooting WAN and Frame Relay links.

_____

_____

_____

Diagnosing and Correcting ISDN BRI Problems

Integrated Services Digital Network (ISDN) services are rapidly establishing footholds in the networking and communications arenas. More network environments are turning to ISDN to solve a variety of wide-area networking connectivity problems. In particular, ISDN is rapidly gaining acceptance for telecommuting applications, high-speed file transfer, and video conferencing.

The purpose of this chapter is to discuss troubleshooting tips specific to ISDN Basic Rate Interface (BRI) networking on Cisco router interfaces. Another variation of the ISDN service is Primary Rate Interface (PRI), which offers 23 B channels and 1 D channel in North America and Japan, yielding a total bit rate of 1.544 Mbps (the PRI D channel runs at 64 kbps). ISDN PRI in Europe, Australia, and other parts of the world provides 30 B plus 1 64-kbps D channel, and a total interface rate of 2.048 Mbps.

Problem Isolation in ISDN BRI Networks

Figure 13-1 shows a flowchart for isolating problems on an ISDN BRI wide-area network (WAN) link. As you can see, troubleshooting starts at the physical layer and moves up.

Figure 13-1 *You can use this ISDN troubleshooting flowchart to streamline your problem resolution process.*

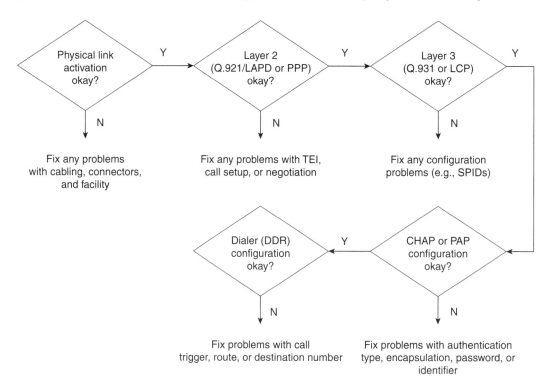

Table 13-1 lists generic serial problems and their symptoms. Table 13-2 lists problems specific to ISDN BRI links, and Table 13-3 lists possible solutions to ISDN BRI problems.

Table 13-1 *Generic serial symptoms and possible problems.*

Symptom	Possible Problems
Intermittent connectivity	• Faulty router interface card or cable
	• Faulty NT1 or facility
	• Timing problem
	• Congested/overutilized serial line
Connection fails as load increases	• Dirty serial line
	• Congested/overutilized serial line
Connection fails at a particular time of day	• Congested/overutilized serial line

Table 13-1   *Generic serial symptoms and possible problems. (Continued)*

Symptom	Possible Problems
Connection fails after some period of normal operation	• Unshielded cable runs too close to EMI sources • Hardware in the serial link failed • Incorrect routing tables (flapping links) • Buffer misses or other software problems
Connection has never worked	• Serial facility not provisioned or has failed
Faulty router interface card or cable	• Use the **show interfaces serial** command to check for errors and swap card or cable if necessary. • Use the **show controllers** command to check cable used and physically check that cable is properly installed.
Faulty NT1 or facility	• Check for input errors by using the **show interfaces serial** command and replace NT1 if necessary; contact service provider.
Timing problem	• Verify that the correct device is generating the system clock. • Check the cable length. • Lower the line speed.
Congested/overutilized serial line	• Reduce broadcast traffic. • Use protocol analyzer to check application behavior (for example, very large file transfers during peak hours). • Implement priority queuing. • Adjust hold queue and buffers sizes with help from a technical support representative. • Add bandwidth and consider using a dial backup.

Table 13-2   *ISDN BRI symptoms and possible problems.*

Symptom	Possible Problems
ISDN router does not dial.	• No ISDN switch specified or no route exists • Bad service profile identifier (SPID) or calling or called number • Incorrect dial-on-demand routing (DDR) statement (e.g., **dialer-list**, **dialer-group**, **dialer map**, or **dialer string**)
Users cannot connect.	• Faulty router interface card or cable. • Switch is misconfigured. • Router is misconfigured.

continues

Table 13-2   *ISDN BRI symptoms and possible problems. (Continued)*

Symptom	Possible Problems
ISDN call from router does not go through.	• Faulty router interface card or cable. • ISDN cables are not connected properly. • Requested facility not subscribed.
ISDN local router cannot **ping** remote router.	• CHAP problem. • Router is misconfigured for ISDN (dialer map is not pointing to remote interface or DDR is misconfigured). • Incorrect routing tables.
Second ISDN B channel will not come up.	• Problem with ISDN load threshold. • Router is misconfigured for second ISDN B channel.

Table 13-3   *ISDN BRI problems and possible solutions.*

Problem	Possible Solution
Router misconfigured for ISDN	• Use the **show running-config** command to check for the **no shutdown** command and use **dialer-list** to define which packets cause dialing. • Check the next-hop address with the **dialer map** command and fix if necessary. In Cisco IOS Release 12.0, this command was replaced with the **show system running-config** command.
ISDN cables not connected properly	• Ensure that the S-bus is terminated correctly.
Requested facility not subscribed	• Verify SPIDs, phone number, configuration, and switch type with service provider.
CHAP problem	• Check the username and password statements.
Problem with ISDN load threshold	• Make sure the **dialer load-threshold** command is in the configuration. • If necessary, lower the dialer load threshold to a value that will activate the second B channel.

Overview of Troubleshooting Commands

Figure 13-2 shows a summary of the commands covered in this chapter and the general extent of troubleshooting coverage provided by each command.

Figure 13-2 *The most appropriate command is determined by the element of the link that you are troubleshooting.*

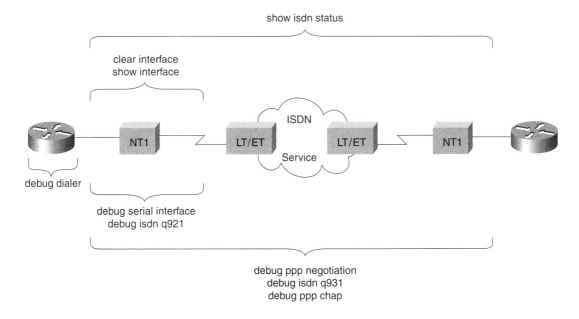

These commands are defined in detail in the following section.

ISDN BRI Diagnostic Tools

In this section, you'll learn how to use the **show** and **debug** commands to identify ISDN problems.

ISDN BRI show Commands

As a first test for troubleshooting ISDN BRI, try to **ping** the remote ISDN destination. This tests the call triggering of DDR and then tests the ability to use the BRI facility.

If **ping** does not show success, continue with other troubleshooting methods. The **show** commands provide information about the interface conditions, protocol status, and how the dialer (DDR process) initiates an ISDN call. You can also use **traceroute** to check the path between IP devices.

You can use the following commands to isolate ISDN problems:

- **clear interface bri** *number*—Resets the hardware logic on a BRI interface where *number* is the port number (or slot/port number). Use this command to reset the counters to zero if you want to restart the counters you are checking.

- **show interfaces bri** *number*—Displays information about the BRI D channel for the interface selected by the *number* argument.

- **show interfaces bri** *number* **1 2**—For the interface selected by the *number* argument, displays the information about the BRI B channels 1 and 2.

- **show controllers bri**—Displays information about the BRI controller, including activation status for Layer 1.

- **show isdn status**—Displays information about which ISDN switch is used and the status of Layers 1, 2, and 3 for BRI calls.

- **show dialer interface bri** *number*—Displays information about the DDR dial string, call status, and timer settings.

- **show ppp multilink**—Displays information about bundles of BRI B channels using an extended variation of Point-to-Point Protocol (PPP) encapsulation.

NOTE   For WAN troubleshooting, Cisco engineers recommend that you use the Cisco IOS **service timestamps** command. This command puts a timestamp on a debug or log message and can provide valuable information about when debug elements occurred and the duration of time between events. You can specify that the time measure be for debug type or log message type events. You can request that the display refer to uptime (that is, how long after the system was rebooted) or datetime (that is, a date and time indicator). And you can request that Cisco IOS software include millisecond or local time zone elements in the timestamp.

The following are other examples of this command:

- **service timestamps debug uptime**—Logs time with debug output by using the system clock, which may be external, such as Network Time Protocol (NTP).

- **service timestamps log datetime msec**—Logs with **datetime** and in **msec**.

Output and interpretation of some of the key content of the output of these commands appears in the following sections.

The **show interfaces bri** Command

BRI offers 144 kbps for use at small data concentration points. The interface creates the channels. Each BRI interface delivers two 64-kbps data channels (B channels) and one 16-kbps signaling channel (D channel), as shown in Figure 13-3. The BRI service is commonly referred to as 2B+D.

Figure 13-3 *The ISDN B channel is 64 kbps, and the D channel is 16 kbps.*

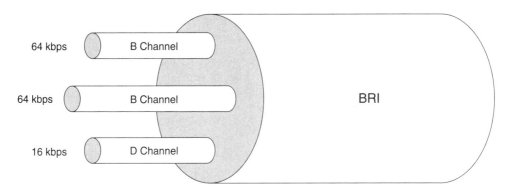

Pipe size defines the maximum amount of data that can be transmitted at one time. In many cases, the pipe size is less crucial than how the user application fills the pipe (for example, bursty traffic compared to a more consistent flow of data). The combined B channels do not necessarily provide the same capacity as one 128-kbps channel because the transfer rate is not proportional for packets sent.

When you are troubleshooting, you can focus on these specific components of BRI services as well as the 48 kbps of overhead bits that are also sent in the 48-bit BRI frame.

In Figure 13-4, which depicts the output from the **show interfaces bri** command, the message "Line protocol is up (spoofing)" is D channel information that the interface alleges to be up.

Figure 13-4 *"Line protocol is up (spoofing)" is D channel information.*

```
router# show interface bri 0
BRI0 is up, line protocol is up (spoofing)
Hardware is BRI
Internet address is 1.1.2.1, subnet mask is 255.255.255.0
MTU 1500 bytes, BW 56179 Kbit, DLY 20000 usec, rely 255/255,  load 1/255
Encapsulation PPP, loopback not set
Last input never, output 0:00:09, output hang never
Last clearing of "show interface" counters never
Output queue 0/40, 0 drops; input queue 0/75, 0 drops
Five minute input rate 0 bits/sec, 0 packets/sec
Five minute output rate 0 bits/sec, 0 packets/sec
1948 packets input, 11442 bytes, 0 no buffer
 Received 392 broadcasts, 0 runts, 0 giants
 0 input errors, 0 CRC, 0 frame, 0 overrun, 0 ignored, 0 abort
1961 packets output, 12249 bytes, 0 underruns
0 output errors, 0 collisions, 33 interface resets, 0 restarts
24 carrier transitions
```

Spoofing does not necessarily mean that the D channel is up. In fact, there may be no line on the interface. What spoofing does is "lie" to Layer 3 DDR so that a routing entry will be maintained in the router. Having this routing entry enables DDR to wake up and trigger a call to the ISDN network when user traffic requires the connection.

The router in the example just came up. For a router that has been operational for a long period, use the **clear interface bri 0** command to reset the counters for the interface. This clear counter condition allows you to set the starting time for many of the output fields in the **show interfaces** command.

The **show interfaces bri number 1 2** Command

When you use the variation of the **show interfaces bri** command that specifies the channel number, you can see output about one or both B channels on the BRI, as shown in Figure 13-5.

Figure 13-5 *The command argument 1 refers to BRI channel B1.*

```
router# show int bri 0 1
BRI0: B-Channel 1 is down, line protocol is down
Hardware is BRI
MTU 1500 bytes, BW 64 Kbit, DLY 20000 usec, rely 255/255, load 1/255
Encapsulation PPP, loopback not set, keepalive set (10 sec)
Last input never, output never, output hang never
Last clearing of "show interface" counters never
Output queue 0/40, 0 drops; input queue 0/75, 0 drops
Five minute input rate 0 bits/sec, 0 packets/sec
Five minute output rate 0 bits/sec, 0 packets/sec
0 packets input, 0 bytes, 0 no buffer
Received 0 broadcasts, 0 runts, 0 giants
1 input errors, 0 CRC, 0 frame, 0 overrun, 0 ignored, 1 abort
0 packets output, 0 bytes, 0 underruns
0 output errors, 0 collisions, 39 interface resets, 0 restart
7 carrier transitions
```

Possible causes for channel down include

- The protocol is down.
- The interface is not active.
- The cabling is incorrect.
- There is a telephone company problem (line down or not connected to switch).
- There is a hardware failure (e.g., router port/card).

The **show controllers bri** and **show isdn status** Commands

The **show controllers bri** and **show isdn status** commands provide troubleshooting information about the Layer 1 startup activation process of an ISDN line.

First, let's examine Layer 1 elements and functionality.

Standard ISDN BRI Roles and Interface Reference Points

You should focus your ISDN network troubleshooting efforts on the local loop. The ISDN central office (CO) is considered the network side of the ISDN local loop. The line termination/exchange termination (LT/ET) handles termination of the local loop and switching functions. Figure 13-6 shows all these elements.

Figure 13-6 *The ISDN local loop is the key focus for troubleshooting.*

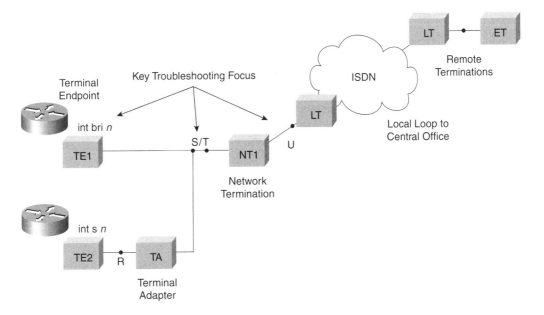

At the customer site, the ISDN local loop is terminated using a network termination type 1 (NT1). The NT1's responsibilities include line performance monitoring, timing, physical signaling protocol conversion, power transfer, and multiplexing of the B and D channels.

There are two other notable ISDN devices: terminal equipment (TE) and terminal adapters (TAs). TE refers to end-user devices such as digital telephones or workstations:

- Native ISDN terminals are referred to as terminal equipment type 1 (TE1). TE1s connect to the ISDN network through a four-wire, twisted-pair digital link.

- Non-ISDN terminals such as DTE that predate the ISDN standards are referred to as terminal equipment type 2 (TE2). TE2s connect to the ISDN network through terminal adapters. The ISDN TA can either be a standalone device or a board inside the TE2.

  If the TE2 is implemented as a standalone device, it connects to the TA via a standard physical-layer interface. Examples include EIA/TIA-232-C, V.24, and V.35. The TA performs the necessary protocol conversion to allow non-ISDN (TE2) equipment to access the ISDN network.

Reference points provide for a common term usage when troubleshooting a component of the local loop part of the network. Vendors and providers of ISDN use the reference points R, S, T, and U, as shown in Figure 13-6:

- R reference point—The interface between non-ISDN terminal equipment (TE2) and a TA. The TA allows the TE2 to appear to the network as an ISDN device. There is no standard for the R reference point. Vendors can choose a variety of different physical connections and communication schemes.

- S reference point—The interface between ISDN user equipment, either the TE1 or TA and the NT2 or NT1.

- T reference point—The interface between the customer site switching equipment (NT2) and the local loop termination (NT1).

  The International Telecommunications Union (ITU; formerly International Telegraph and Telephone Consultative Committee [CCITT]) specifically addresses protocols for the S and T reference points.

  In the absence of NT2 equipment, the User-Network Interface (UNI) is usually called the *S/T reference point*. The S/T interface is a key focus of the troubleshooting efforts covered in this chapter.

  Normally, the S/T interface is a four-wire facility that reuses the existing wire plant. This facility uses a transmit pair and a receive pair of pins.

- U reference point—The interface where transmission between the NT1 and the LE occurs.

  Normally, the U interface is a two-wire facility to reduce wiring costs. This facility uses a frequency division multiplexing technique and echo cancellation for a ping-pong operation of fast half duplex that simulates full duplex.

Both the S/T and the U interfaces achieve full-duplex communications.

Troubleshooting the Layer 1 S/T Interface

As shown in Figure 13-7, the four-wire service at the S/T interface uses an RJ-45 cable and connector.

Figure 13-7 *ISDN uses RJ-45 connectors (ISO 8877).*

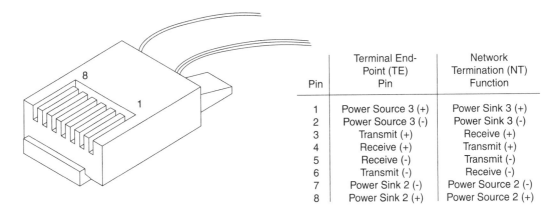

Pin	Terminal End-Point (TE) Pin	Network Termination (NT) Function
1	Power Source 3 (+)	Power Sink 3 (+)
2	Power Source 3 (-)	Power Sink 3 (-)
3	Transmit (+)	Receive (+)
4	Receive (+)	Transmit (+)
5	Receive (-)	Transmit (-)
6	Transmit (-)	Receive (-)
7	Power Sink 2 (-)	Power Source 2 (-)
8	Power Sink 2 (+)	Power Source 2 (+)

The mechanical specifications for the ISDN connector are specified by the ISO 8877 standard. Pins 3, 4, 5, and 6 are the key pins used for ISDN. When you troubleshoot, make sure that your cable and connector are correct for BRI. Also look for visible evidence of broken casing or wires.

ISDN uses the electrical specification for alternate mark inversion (AMI) line coding. The polarity indications in the table for transmit and receive circuits are the polarity of the framing pulses.

BRI Line Framing on the S/T Interface

From the local loop perspective, ISDN carries digital signals between two points. ISDN physical-layer (Layer 1) frame formats differ depending on whether the frame is outbound (from terminal to network) or inbound (from network to terminal), as shown in Figure 13-8. The frames are 48 bits long, and 36 bits of them represent data. The TE that will start sending frames has a 2-bit offset compared to the frames it receives from the NT.

Figure 13-8 *ISDN uses different Layer 1 frame formats for inbound and outbound traffic.*

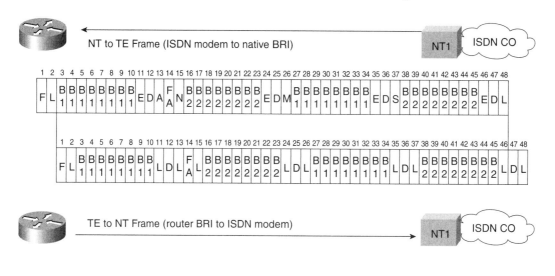

Bit Type	Role of Bit in BRI Time-Division Multiplexed Frame
F, FA, N	Synchronization bits
B1	Bearer Channel 1
B2	Bearer Channel 2
D	Data Channel (control)
A	Activation Indicator
L	DC Line Balancing
E, S, M	Collision Avoidance

The ISDN service comprises several logical channels for signaling and user data. The logical channels coexist using time-division multiplexing (TDM). With TDM, each channel has a dedicated time slot on the link. Transmission is an aggregate of the time slots:

- ISDN's TDM uses the B1, B2, and D bits.

- The synchronization mechanism uses line code violations with the F, FA, and N bits.

- Collision avoidance for up to eight TEs on the BRI subaddresses uses the echo channel with the E, S, and M bits.

- Electrical balancing for 0 volts DC uses the L bit for even and odd numbers of preceding bits.

- Line startup indication for the physical layer uses the A bit.

BRI Activation Process on the S/T Interface

Problems with the startup sequence for BRI physical-layer synchronization and activation are more serious than a transmission fault problem: A transmission fault affects only one channel, but a synchronization problem affects all the channels on the facility.

The startup activation sequence has five steps, as shown in Figure 13-9:

Figure 13-9 *The BRI activation process requires five steps.*

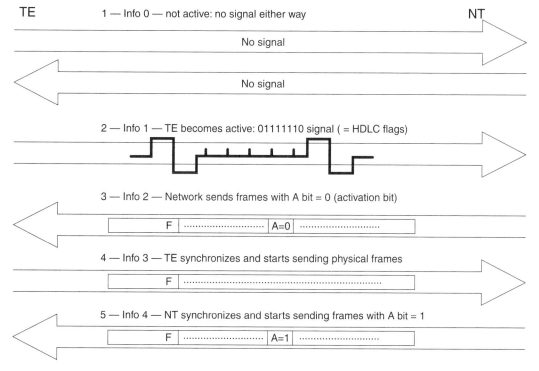

Step 1   First, there is no signal and the line is not active in either direction (TE to NT and NT to TE).

Step 2   A TE becomes active by signaling 01111110 (the 7E High-Level Data Link Control [HDLC] flag).

Step 3   The network side sends frames with the A bit (activation bit) set to 0 (not activated).

Step 4   The TE synchronizes on three successive pairs of line code violations (that is, the F and FA bits) and starts sending physical frames.

Step 5   The NT also synchronizes by using line code violations (the F and the FA or N bits) and starts sending frames with A bit = 1 (activated).

At this point, Layer 1 is up. As soon as no valid pair of line code violations is detected in either direction in two successive ISDN Layer 1 frames, synchronization is lost.

Checking Activation with the **show controllers bri** and **show isdn status** Commands

Figure 13-10 shows the output of the **show controllers bri** command. This shows the BRI D channel information and many other internal controller values.

Figure 13-10 *You can use the **show controllers bri** command to view D channel information.*

```
router#show controller bri
BRI unit 0
D Chan Info:
Layer 1 is ACTIVATED
idb 0x9F6E8, ds 0xA56F8, reset_mask 0x8
buffer size 1524
RX ring with 2 entries at 0x2101600 : Rxhead 0
00 pak=0x0AB0A4 ds=0x40CE70 status=D000 pak_size=0
(...)
```

Figure 13-11 shows the output of the **show isdn status** command. This shows a very useful status summary of each of the three ISDN layers. Engineers frequently use this command during troubleshooting to get the quickest snapshot of the switch type and interface status.

Figure 13-11 *You can use the **show isdn status** command to get a summary of information about Layers 1–3.*

```
router#show isdn status
The current ISDN Switchtype = basic-net3
ISDN BRI0 interface
    Layer 1 Status:
            DEACTIVATED
    Layer 2 Status:
            Layer 2 NOT Activated
    Layer 3 Status:
            No Active Layer 3 Call(s)
    Activated dsl 0 CCBs are 0, Allocated = 0
```

The **show dialer** Command

The trigger for an ISDN call is DDR. As shown in Figure 13-12, the command **show dialer bri n** provides information on the process whereby a Cisco router automatically initiates (and later closes) a circuit-switched session as transmitting stations demand.

Figure 13-12 *For an indication of remote failure, you can use the **show dialer** command to make sure the remote router is properly configured.*

```
router#show dialer
Dial String       Successes   Failures    Last called   Last status
        4155551212          1          0      00:00:00      successful
        4155551213          1          0      00:00:00      successful
        0 incoming call(s) have been screened.
        BRI0: B-Channel 1
        Idle timer (300 secs), Fast idle timer (20 secs)
        Wait for carrier (30 secs), Re-enable (15 secs)
        BRI0: B-Channel 2
        Idle timer (300 secs), Fast idle timer (20 secs)
        Wait for carrier (30 secs), Re-enable (15 secs)
```

The router spoofs keepalives so that end stations treat the session as active. DDR permits routing over ISDN or telephone lines using an external ISDN terminal adapter or modem beyond the BRI interface that you specify.

For an indication of errors in the dialer configuration, check the router configuration, specifically checking the following configuration commands:

- **dialer-list** command
- **dialer-group** command
- **dialer map/dialer string** command

The **show ppp multilink** Command

When you troubleshoot BRIs that use Multilink PPP (MLP) or Multilink Multichassis PPP (MMP), begin with the same command: **show ppp multilink**. The output contains summary and configuration information about the bundle or stack groups that have been set up.

BRI channels can aggregate into an MLP bundle for inverse multiplexing, as shown in Figure 13-13. MLP is designed to work over single or multiple interfaces that are configured to support both dial-on-demand rotary groups and PPP encapsulation.

Figure 13-13 *Multilink bundles are handled as a virtual PPP session.*

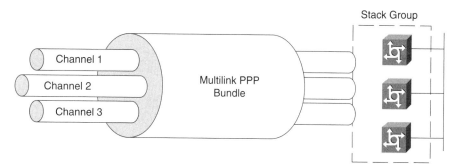

As shown in Figure 13-14, you use the **show interfaces bri0** command to examine the status of the multilink bundle.

Figure 13-14 *You can use the **show interfaces bri0** command to view the multilink bundle status.*

```
Router# show interfaces bri0
BRI0:2 is up, line protocol is up
  Hardware is BRI
  MTU 1500 bytes, BW 64 Kbit, DLY 20000 usec, rely 255/255, load 1/255
  Encapsulation PPP, loopback not set, keepalive set (10 sec)
  LCP Open, multilink Open
---Relevant information
  Last input 00:00:00, output 00:00:04, output hang never
  Last clearing of "show interface" counters never
  Queueing strategy: fifo
  Output queue 0/40, 0 drops; input queue 0/75, 0 drops
  5 minute input rate 0 bits/sec, 0 packets/sec
  5 minute output rate 0 bits/sec, 0 packets/sec
     371 packets input, 26644 bytes, 0 no buffer
     Received 371 broadcasts, 0 runts, 0 giants, 0 throttles
     0 input errors, 0 CRC, 0 frame, 0 overrun, 0 ignored, 0 abort
     314 packets output, 14612 bytes, 0 underruns
     0 output errors, 0 collisions, 13 interface resets
     0 output buffer failures, 0 output buffers swapped out
     394 carrier transitions
```

PPP Multilink also provides the ability to segment data packets before encapsulation to improve resequencing/reassembly performance. Data is encapsulated within a virtual PPP session bundle, and the datagram is given a sequence number. The receiving router uses the sequence number to recreate the original stream.

Cisco's MMP permits MLP links from a single client to terminate on different access servers. These access servers or routers are grouped into a stack group that operates like a rotary group that users can access from a single number.

From an ISDN troubleshooting perspective, you can use the same **show interfaces bri0** command to get information about these options for the PPP encapsulation.

Figure 13-15 shows a single MLP bundle (named rudder) with three members.

Figure 13-15 *A stack group member has a Virtual-Access bundle interface and two child interfaces.*

```
system# show ppp multilink
Bundle rudder, 3 members, first link is BRI0: B-channel 1
0 lost fragments, 8 reordered, 0 unassigned, sequence 0x1E/0x1E rcvd/sent
......
systema# show ppp multilink
Bundle hansolo 2 members, Master link is Virtual-Access4
0 lost fragments, 0 reordered, 0 unassigned, 100/255 load
0 discarded,  0 lost received, sequence 40/66 rcvd/sent
members 2
 Serial0:4
 systemb:Virtual-Access6    (1.1.1.1)
```

The next lines in Figure 13-15 show an MMP example: Router systema is a stack group member with hansolo as bundle interface Virtual-Access4. Two child interfaces are Serial 0:4 (a local PRI channel) and an interface from stack group member systemb.

Problems reported or indicated that involve MLP or MMP require additional checking of the multilink PPP configuration statements, and other protocols, such as Stack Group Bidding Protocol (SGBP) that are beyond the scope of this chapter.

ISDN BRI debug Commands

The **debug** commands provide an ongoing display that includes a captured flow of selected packet fields, setup and negotiation events, and status details. The output of **debug** commands for ISDN and related protocols can allow you to check Layers 1, 2, and 3 in a systematic manner as you gather facts and consider possibilities for your action plan.

You must be careful when you use some of the **debug** commands:

- Be as specific as possible with arguments to the command and indicate a specific interface.
- Consider using an access list to focus the debug.
- Know your network load so that you do not worsen a heavily loaded network with the additional processing and output of the debug.
- Add a **service timestamps** command so that the debug output will show when output events occurred (in the command, show milliseconds). This timestamp provides better identification and improves communications, and the time duration between output events may enable you to isolate problems.
- Always use the **no debug all** or **undebug all** command as soon as you have no further need for the debug tools.

The Cisco IOS software **debug** commands featured in this chapter are

- **debug bri**—Displays information about whether the ISDN code is enabling and disabling the B channels when you attempt an outgoing call. This command may show intensive Layer 1 information.

- **debug isdn q921**—Displays data link layer (Layer 2) access procedures that are taking place at the router on the D channel (Link Access Procedure on the D channel, or LAPD) of its interface.

- **debug ppp negotiation**—Shows information on traffic and exchanges in an internetwork implementing PPP by displaying fields from packets transmitted during startup, where PPP options are negotiated.

- **debug isdn q931**—Displays information about call setup and teardown of ISDN network connections (Layer 3) between the local router (that is, the user side) and the network.

- **debug ppp authentication**—Causes the **debug ppp** command to display authentication protocol messages, including Challenge Handshake Authentication Protocol (CHAP) packet exchanges and Password Authentication Protocol (PAP) exchanges.

Output and interpretation of some of the key content of the output of these commands appears in the following sections.

The **debug bri** Command

As shown in Figure 13-16, the **debug bri** command generates a significant amount of output and should be used only if the router is having trouble communicating with the ISDN switch or if traffic on the IP network is low, so other activity on the system is not adversely affected.

Figure 13-16 *The **debug bri** command can have lots of data in the output, so use it sparingly.*

```
router# debug bri
BRI: write_sid: wrote 20 for subunit 0, slot 1.
BRI: Starting Power Up timer for unit = 0.
BRI: write_sid: wrote 3 for subunit 0, slot 1.
BRI: Starting T3 timer after expiry of PUP timeout for unit = 0, current state is
F4.
BRI: write_sid: wrote FF for subunit 0, slot 1.
BRI: Activation for unit = 0, current state is F7.
BRI: enable channel B1
BRI: write_sid: wrote 14 for subunit 0, slot 1.
%LINK-3-UPDOWN: Interface BRI0: B-Channel 1, changed state to up
%LINK-5-CHANGED: Interface BRI0: B-Channel 1, changed state to up.!!!
BRI: disable channel B1
BRI: write_sid: wrote 15 for subunit 0, slot 1.
%LINK-3-UPDOWN: Interface BRI0: B-Channel 1, changed state to down
%LINK-5-CHANGED: Interface BRI0: B-Channel 1, changed state to down
%LINEPROTO-5-UPDOWN: Line protocol on Interface BRI0: B-Channel 1, changed
state to down
```

In the output shown in Figure 13-16, write_sid is an internal command written to the interface controller subunit identifier. The T3 timer is how long to wait for activation (generally 1 to 2 seconds). It occurs in the example after the power-up (PUP) timeout. If T3 expires, the expired state is F2. The %LINK messages indicate that the channel or the protocol on the interface changed state: Note that BRI 0 channel 1 came up briefly and then went back down.

When troubleshooting causes a quick change of state from up to down, check to see whether the cable is unplugged or whether the interface is shut.

Troubleshooting ISDN Layer 2 Q.921

After you have determined that the hardware is working properly, you can proceed to troubleshooting Layer 2 to ensure error-free communication for end stations over the physical link.

Layer 2 defines the logical connection between the user TE (that is, the router) and the local network termination (to the local ISDN switch), as shown in Figure 13-17.

Figure 13-17 *Layer 2 is between the TE (router) and the ET (local ISDN switch).*

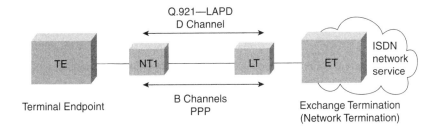

The ISDN signaling protocol is Link Access Procedure, D channel, also known as LAPD. The LAPD protocol is formally specified in ITU-T Q.920 and ITU-T Q.921.

The ISDN data carrying protocol is PPP or HDLC. Serial, synchronous, full-duplex transmission across either point-to-point or point-to-multipoint physical connections is supported.

LAPD operates with framing that is much like HDLC, as shown in Figure 13-18. The LAPD frame format has several fields in the address. One of these fields needed before Layer 2 setup is the terminal endpoint identifier (TEI).

Figure 13-18 *The ISDN frame format starts and ends with identical flag fields.*

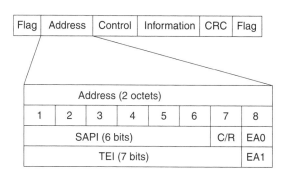

The following list briefly describes the fields contained in the ISDN frame shown in Figure 13-18:

- Flag (1 octet)—This is always 0x7E.

- SAPI (service access point identifier)—6 bits that identify the point where Layer 2 provides a service to Layer 3 (for example, SAPI 0 = call control procedures, SAPI 1 = Packet Mode using Q.931 call procedures, and SAPI 16 = Packet Mode communications procedures).

- C/R (Command/Response) bit—Indicates whether the frame is a command or a response.

- EA0 (Address Extension) bit—Indicates whether this is the final octet of the address.

- TEI—A 7-bit device identifier.

- EA1 (Address Extension) bit—Same as EA0.

- Control (2 octets)—The frame-level control field indicates the frame type (Information, Supervisory, or Unnumbered) and sequence numbers as required.

- Information—Layer 3 protocol information and data.

- CRC (2 octets)—Cyclic redundancy check, which is a low-level test for bit errors on the user data.

- Flag (1 octet)—This is always 0x7E.

A TEI uniquely identifies a terminal. You use the TEI to identify which terminal you are checking. The TEIs 64 through 126 are reserved for dynamic assignment during Layer 2 activation, and TEI 128 is used for a broadcast.

Several switches (5ESS, DMS-100, and National ISDN) do not remove assigned TEIs if an error occurs due to Layer 1 problems. If you want to remove a call's TEI, reload the router. When the router loads, it forces a negotiation for the ISDN TEI to occur with the first call so that incoming and outgoing calls can cause activation.

The service access point identifier (SAPI) is another key field in the LAPD address. The SAPI defines the message type. Key SAPIs to look for while troubleshooting are

- SAPI 63—Layer 2 management used for processes including TEI assignment

- SAPI 64—Used for call control

- SAPI 0—Indication that the message type is Layer 3 signaling (from Q.931, covered later in this chapter)

For Cisco routers, the troubleshooting view of Layer 2 comes primarily from the **debug isdn q921** command.

The LAPD frame format is very similar to that of HDLC. Like HDLC, LAPD uses supervisory, information, and unnumbered frames. In the frame, the control field indicates which type of LAPD (HDLC) message is in use. You can associate one or more of these message types with an ISDN process as you troubleshoot:

- A TEI process uses an unnumbered information frame (UI shown as 0x03) with SAPI 63 and TEI 127 (all ones).

- When a terminal has a TEI, it proceeds to call setup with set asynchronous balanced mode extended (SABME) that gets an unnumbered acknowledge (UA) if successful or a disconnect mode (DM) if unsuccessful.

- In user data transfer mode, look for information (INFO) with receiver ready (RR) or reject (REJ) or receiver not ready (RNR) as key troubleshooting message types to check when necessary.

The **debug isdn q921** Command

Figure 13-19 shows TEI assignment messages from the **debug isdn q921** command. TEI 64 is assigned by the switch when the router powers up.

Figure 13-19 *You can use the **debug isdn q921** command to view TEI assignment information.*

```
router# debug isdn-q921
2656.612 TX ->  IDREQ  ri = 14613  ai = 127
2656.648 RX <-  IDASSN ri = 14613  ai = 64
....
2424.920 TX ->  IDREQ  ri = 63529  ai = 127
2426.924 TX ->  IDREQ  ri = 31418  ai = 127
2428.928 TX ->  IDREQ  ri = 9819  ai = 127
```

In the first two lines of the output, the TE sends ID REQ, and the switch answers with ASSN ID (AI). An IDREQ indicates the identity request message type sent from the local router to the network during the automatic TEI assignment procedure. This message is sent in an unnumbered information command frame. AI = 127 asks for any TEI; AI = 64 means TEI 64 is assigned.

In the second group of messages, the IDREQ does not get a TEI, so the TE retransmits the IDREQ, each with a different reference indicator (ri).

Message types to check for during TEI identification are

- ID Request (1)
- ID Assigned (2)
- ID Denied (3)
- ID Check Request(4)
- ID Check Response (5)
- ID Remove (6)
- ID Verify (7)

Figure 13-20 continues the **debug isdn q921** command output. The switch uses an ID check request (IDCKRQ) to verify the TEIs assigned are still in use.

Figure 13-20 *The switch uses an ID check to find active and duplicate TEIs.*

```
11239.364 RX <-  IDCKRQ  ri = 0  ai = 127
11239.372 TX ->  IDCKRP  ri = 52714  ai = 115
11240.364 RX <-  IDCKRQ  ri = 0  ai = 127
11240.372 TX ->  IDCKRP  ri = 44171  ai = 115
...
2339.745 RX <-  IDREM  ri = 0  ai = 73
2340.524 RX <-  IDREM  ri = 0  ai = 73
2341.972 TX ->  IDREQ  ri = 25733  ai = 127
```

The active station answers with an ID check response (IDCKRP). Any TEIs that do not reply are removed by the network by using two ID remove (IDREM) commands. Two messages are used to overcome any problems with the UI message on the facility.

The switch also uses the IDCKRQ to determine whether duplicate TEIs are in use. The switch removes the TEI for both TE devices that use the duplicate TEI.

Any station that receives an IDREM must begin requesting a new TEI by using SAPI 63 and the all-ones broadcast TEI 127. However, the 5ESS, DMS-100, and National ISDN switches always keep Layer 2 active and do not remove Layer 2 TEIs if an error or Layer 1 failure occurs. To avoid confusion, the router also tries to keep the same TEI(s) for use. The only way to remove a TEI at the router is to reload the router.

The reloaded router boot code forces the isdn tei first-call flag to be set, regardless of what the configuration shows. This first call affects all switch types, but the process still allows incoming and outgoing calls to activate the BRI interface.

After ISDN Layer 2 has established the TEIs for end stations, the process continues with the SABME request, using the signaling SAPI 0.

For custom DMS-100 and National ISDN switch types, the router continuously attempts to bring up Layer 2 by sending out SABMEs, then an ID_Verify message, and finally SABMEs again, as shown in Figure 13-21. This sequence alternates between the SABMEs until the link comes up. The custom 5ESS sends only the SABMEs because the ID_Verify is not valid for the 5ESS custom.

Figure 13-21 *When the data-link connection is established, the data link sends INFO frames.*

```
2656.612 TX ->  IDREQ  ri = 14613   ai = 127
2656.648 RX <-  IDASSN ri = 14613   ai = 64
2656.652 TX ->  SABMEp  sapi = 0  tei = 64
2656.676 RX <-  UAf  sapi = 0  tei = 64
2658.360 RX <-  INFOc  sapi = 0  tei = 64  ns = 0  nr = 0
2658.368 TX ->  RRr  sapi = 0  tei = 64  nr = 1
2658.372 TX ->  INFOc  sapi = 0  tei = 64  ns = 0  nr = 1
```

As you troubleshoot, check whether the SABME fails with a disconnect mode (DM) response. If this is the case, there is no further call setup at Layer 3 and you need to find out why the SABME was unsuccessful.

If the SABME request succeeds, the response indicated is an unnumbered acknowledgment (UA). At this point, the Layer 2 connection is up. If a problem persists, you can move on to check Layer 3 or some other upper-layer protocol.

ISDN can move to the information transfer phase, and the TE can begin to transmit INFO frames. Acknowledgments for these INFO frames occur in either RR or other INFO frames.

The RR is used to verify the status of the data link when there are no INFO frames to transmit or receive. The indication nr refers to the number received. The indications p and f refer to poll and final, with the switch often more active as the polling side forcing a final reply from the router.

Either side can end the data link by issuing a disconnect (DISC). For troubleshooting, you can usually assume that the trouble occurs at the side of the data link that sent the DISC. In Figure 13-22, the local router received the DISC from the local switch. The I = indication has Layer 3 values from Q.931.

Figure 13-22 *Any side can disconnect the data link by sending a DISC frame.*

```
180484 RX <-  RRp  sapi = 0  tei = 80  nr = 5
180488 TX ->  RRf  sapi = 0  tei = 80  nr = 4
190484 RX <-  RRp  sapi = 0  tei = 80  nr = 5
190488 TX ->  RRf  sapi = 0  tei = 80  nr = 4
...
23:59:52: RX <-  INFOc  dsl = 0 sapi = 0  tei = 70  ns = 0  nr = 1
i = 0x0801895A08028183
23:59:52: TX ->  RRr  dsl = 0 sapi = 0  tei = 70  nr = 1.....
0:00:02: RX <-  DISCp  dsl = 0 sapi = 0  tei = 70
0:00:02: TX ->  UAf  dsl = 0 sapi = 0  tei = 70
0:00:09: RX <-  UI  dsl = 0 sapi = 0  tei = 127 i = 0x450003C06C0480323037
```

After a DISC, the TE and ET must go through the activation and Layer 2 reestablishment procedures again.

The **debug ppp negotiation** Command

For B channels on an interface, the BRI interface supports HDLC, PPP, X.25, and Frame Relay encapsulations. Unless there is a need for a particular encapsulation, PPP encapsulation is recommended, with CHAP authentication for added security.

The protocol field indicates the upper layer carried in the information field. Examples of protocol field values are

- 0021—IP
- 0029—AT
- 002B—IPX
- 003D—multilink
- 0201—802.1d hellos
- 0203—SRB BPDU
- 8021—IPCP
- 8029—ATCP
- 802B—IPXCP
- C021—LCP
- C023—PAP
- C025—LQR (link quality report)
- C223—CHAP

The LCP establishes and maintains the B-channel data links and provides a mechanism for negotiating PPP options. The number types and options that can be negotiated are

- Maximum Receive Unit (MRU)—The MTU size (default 1500 bytes). Not used by Cisco.
- Async Control Character Map—The control and escape characters on async links.
- Authentication Protocol—PAP (0xC023) or CHAP (0xC223) with the default on routers being no authentication.
- Quality Protocol—The process for data-link monitoring.
- Magic-Number—The technique used for detection of loopback links.
- Reserved (not currently used).
- Protocol Field Compression—The compression of the PPP protocol field.
- Address and Control Field Compression—The compression of the PPP address and control field.

The commands available with **debug ppp** allow you to see information for troubleshooting.

The negotiation of PPP options begins with the LCP at the local TE sending a configuration request (CONFREQ). If the options are acceptable to the remote TE, it sends back a configure acknowledge (CONFACK). In Figure 13-23, the authentication type CHAP is requested and acknowledged.

Figure 13-23 *An LCP configuration request begins a negotiation.*

```
router#debug ppp negotiation
PPP BRI0: B-Channel 1: LCP CONFREQ(1) id 2 (4)
PPP BRI0: B-Channel 1: LCP CONFACK(2) id 2 (4)
ppp: sending CONFREQ, type = 3 (CI_AUTHTYPE), value C223/0
ppp: config ACK  received, type = 3 (CI_AUTHTYPE), value C223/0
...
PPP BRI0: B-Channel 1:  LCP CONFREQ(1) id E4  MAGICNUMBER (6) 0 129 37 28
PPP BRI0: B-Channel 1: LCP CONFNAK(3) id E4 (6) MAGICNUMBER (6)
...
PPP BRI0: B-Channel 1: LCP CONFREQ(1) id 1 (1C) MRU (4) 6 174
   ASYNCMAP (6) 0 0 0
   AUTHTYPE (4) 192 35
   MAGICNUMBER (6) 178 72 127 10
   PCOMPRESSION (2)
   ACCOMPRESSION (2)
PPP BRI0: B-Channel 1: LCP CONFREJ(4) id 1 (1C) MRU (4) 6 174
```

If the remote TE recognizes but does not accept the option, the remote TE sends back a configure negative acknowledge (CONFNAK). In Figure 13-23, this CONFNAK occurs for the magic number option.

If the remote TE gets a request for an option that is unrecognizable or unacceptable, it sends back a configure reject (CONFREJ) like the example involving MRU (not supported on Cisco routers).

You can use the command **show interfaces bri 0 1** (covered previously in this chapter) to see if the PPP LCP state is open and which options and protocols have been negotiated.

The **debug ppp authentication** Command

Figure 13-24 shows the output from the **debug ppp authentication** command.

Figure 13-24 *You can use the **debug ppp chap authentication** command to view call setup procedures.*

```
router# debug ppp chap authentication
ISDN Event: Connected to 2823680 on B1 at 64 Kb/s.
BRI0: B-Channel 1: PPP AUTH CHAP input code = 1 id = 10 len = 14
BRI0: B-Channel 1: PPP AUTH CHAP input code = 2 id = 16 len = 26
BRI0: B-Channel 1: remote passed CHAP authentication.
```

continues

Figure 13-24 *You can use the **debug ppp chap authentication** command to view call setup procedures. (Continued)*

```
BRI0: B-Channel 1: PPP AUTH CHAP input code = 3 id = 10 len = 4
BRI0: B-Channel 1: Passed CHAP authentication with remote
...
BRI0: B-Channel 1: Unable to authenticate. No name received from peer
BRI0: B-Channel 1: Unable to validate CHAP response. USERNAME bomartin not found.
BRI0: B-Channel 1: Unable to validate CHAP response. No password defined for
USERNAME bomartin
BRI0: B-Channel 1: Failed CHAP authentication with remote.
Remote message is Unknown name
BRI0: B-Channel 1: remote passed CHAP authentication.
BRI0: B-Channel 1: Passed CHAP authentication with remote.
BRI0: B-Channel 1: CHAP input code = 4 id = 3 len = 48
```

Authenticating an ISDN call can be a key part of Layer 2 B-channel setup for you to troubleshoot. CHAP is the preferred selection because it provides superior authentication to the alternative, PAP. CHAP uses a three-way handshake:

1 The local TE station sends a challenge message to the remote peer TE (code 1, challenge).

2 The remote CHAP peer replies with a value using the one-way hash function (code 2, response).

3 If this value matches the local station's own calculation, authentication is given a code of 3 (success). If there is no match, the authentication is given a code of 4 (failure).

When you troubleshoot you must make sure that

- The passwords configured on both the local and remote TEs are identical.

- The router name of the remote TE that you configure on the local router is identical to the remote TE name.

The **debug isdn q931** Command

You use the **debug isdn q931** command to troubleshoot ISDN Layer 3 Q.931.

First, let's examine Layer 3 elements. Two Layer 3 specifications are used for ISDN signaling between the TE and the ET:

- ITU-T I.450 (also known as ITU-T Q.930)

- ITU-T I.451 (also known as ITU-T Q.931)

Together, these protocols support user-to-user, circuit-switched, and packet-switched connections for the local link's D channel, as shown in Figure 13-25. These protocols are not for B channels and do not operate end-to-end.

Figure 13-25 *The D channel uses Q.931 (specified in I.451 and Q.931/Q.932).*

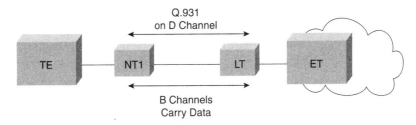

A variety of call establishment, call termination, information, and miscellaneous messages are available to help you troubleshoot, including SETUP, CONNECT, RELEASE, USER INFORMATION, CANCEL, STATUS, and DISCONNECT. These messages are functionally similar to those provided by the X.25 Layer 3 protocol.

One problem is that many ISDN switch vendors developed products before the specifications became final. This variety affects the bit interpretations used in Layer 3 framing.

The router configuration must accurately reflect the switch type used at the ISDN ET. This troubleshooting check can help you verify that the Q.931 exchanges sent between the router and the switch will be properly interpreted at each end of the Layer 3 link.

As shown in Table 13-4, the variety of switches primarily reflects the geographic location of the ISDN service and the vendor whose switch is used by the service provider or PTT (post, telephone, and telegraph). The table is not complete. For example, another switch type used in Australia is the basic-ts013.

Table 13-4 *Switch types.*

Switch Type	Description
basic-1tr6	1TR6 switch type for Germany
basic-5ess	AT&T 5ESS switch type for the U.S.
basic-dms100	Northern DMS-100 switch type
basic-net3	NET3 switch type for UK and Europe
basic-ni1	National ISDN-1 switch type
basic-nwnet3	NET3 switch type for Norway
basic-nznet3	NET3 switch type for New Zealand
basic-ts013	TS013 switch type for Australia
ntt	NTT switch type for Japan
vn2	VN2 switch type for France
vn3	VN3 and VN4 switch types for France

You use the **isdn switch-type ?** command to view the possible switch type settings.

One common indication of a misconfigured switch type selection is the symptom of a TE making a call at 56 kbps, but the ET announcing the call as a 64-kbps call.

When you use the command **debug isdn q931** to troubleshoot Layer 3 for the ISDN D channel, the command output interprets information from Q.931 frame values, as shown in Figure 13-26.

Figure 13-26 *The call reference flag in the Q.931 frame format is set to 0 for source and 1 for destination.*

```
Bit 8   Bit 7   Bit 6   Bit 5   Bit 4   Bit 3   Bit 2   Bit 1

┌─────────────────────────────────────────────────────────────┐
│                  Protocol Discriminator                      │
├─────────────────────────┬───────────────────────────────────┤
│                         │            Call Reference          │
│      0    0    0    0   │              Length                │
├──────┬──────────────────┴───────────────────────────────────┤
│ Flag │                 Call Reference                        │
├──────┼───────────────────────────────────────────────────────┤
│  0   │                 Message Type                          │
├──────┴───────────────────────────────────────────────────────┤
│                  Information Elements                        │
└─────────────────────────────────────────────────────────────┘
```

One aspect to keep in mind as you check the debug output is the call reference flag:

- 0—From call originator
- 1—To call originator (destination)

The message types values include

- 0x05—Q.931 setup
- 0x45—Disconnect
- 0x7D—Status

The Q.931 parameters are called information elements (IEs), and they include

- 0x04—Bearer capability
- 0x2C—Keypad facility (used to send on 5ESS and NI-1 switches)
- 0x6C—Calling party number
- 0x70—Called party number
- 0x3A—SPID

You can use call reference (CR) to distinguish different calls in your **debug** output. To interpret the CR, be aware of the following:

- The same reference number is used on an incoming and an outgoing call on the same subscriber line, except that the number reflects the flag bit value.

- The call reference flag is 0 if the message is sent from the side that originates the call. For example, the originator may use a reference of 0x02 (00000010).

- The call reference flag is 1 if the message is sent to the side that originates the call.

Note that in Figure 13-27, RX and TX messages that belong to the same call use a different CR because of the flag.

Figure 13-27 *You can check call reference numbers by using the **debug isdn q931** command.*

```
router# debug isdn q931
0:03:10:  190.680 TX ->  SETUP pd = 8  callref = 0x01
0:03:10:          Bearer Capability i = 0x8890
0:03:10:          Channel ID i = 0x83
0:03:10:          Called Party Number i = 0x80, '4839625'
...
   248236 TX ->  INFOc  sapi = 0  tei = 80  ns = 6  nr = 6
     SETUP pd = 8  callref = 0x02
         Bearer Capability i = 0x8890
         Channel ID i = 0x83
         Called Party Number i = 0x80, '372756'
   248392 RX <-  INFOc  sapi = 0  tei = 80  ns = 6  nr = 7
     CALL_PROC pd = 8  callref = 0x82
         Channel ID i = 0x89
```

Q.931 call setup passes information elements about the bearer capability. When you troubleshoot the bearer capability, you are checking problems with the type of service expected from the network as interpreted by the ISDN switches:

- Information transfer capability

- Unrestricted or restricted digital information

- Speech

- 3.1-kHz audio or 7-kHz audio

- Video

- Mode—Circuit mode or packet mode

- Rate—The default is 64 kbps, but the bearer capability can specify that the call is a 56-kbps call with rate adaptation

In Figure 13-27, the bearer code 0x8890 is a 64-kbps unrestricted data call in circuit mode—the most common traffic seen on the router.

The Q.931 call establishment messages specified for the typical stages of an ISDN circuit-switched call are shown in Figure 13-28.

Figure 13-28 *The Q.931 call setup exchanges all necessary information enabling the call to be set up successfully.*

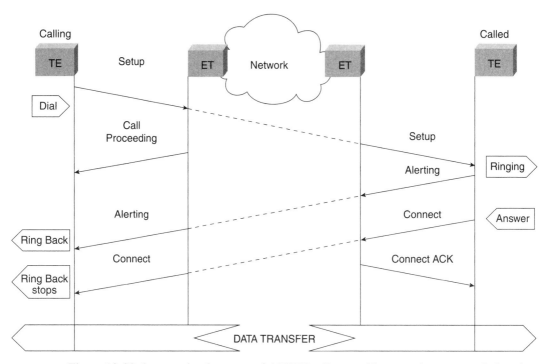

Figure 13-28 shows a simple, successful ISDN call setup. There can be many variations in the exchanges needed by specific ISDN switches or in cases where additional negotiation is required.

Figure 13-29 shows output of the **debug isdn q931** command, including exchanged Q.931 setup messages.

Figure 13-29 *The outgoing call setup from the calling TE shows SETUP, CALL_PROC, and CONNECT.*

```
routerA#debug isdn q931
248236 TX ->  INFOc  sapi = 0  tei = 80  ns = 6  nr = 6
   SETUP pd = 8  callref = 0x02
        Bearer Capability i = 0x8890
        Channel ID i = 0x83
        Called Party Number i = 0x80, '372756'
248392 RX <-  INFOc  sapi = 0  tei = 80  ns = 6  nr = 7
   CALL_PROC pd = 8  callref = 0x82
        Channel ID i = 0x89
249460 RX <-  INFOc  sapi = 0  tei = 80  ns = 7  nr = 7
    CONNECT pd = 8  callref = 0x82
```

In Figure 13-29, the outgoing call setup from the calling TE shows

- SETUP, with information elements that indicate capability, identifier, and called party

- CALL_PROC (for *call proceeding*), with a channel ID number that indicates this is a BRI and will use channel 1

- CONNECT, from the remote side to the originating side

Figure 13-29 shows a baseline exchange for a successful call setup at the call origination side.

Figure 13-30 shows output of the **debug isdn q931** command, where the incoming call setup from the called TE shows

- SETUP, with information elements that indicate capability, identifier, and calling party identification

- CONNECT

- CONNECT ACK

Figure 13-30 *The incoming call setup to the called TE shows SETUP, CONNECT, and CONNECT ACK.*

```
routerB #debug isdn q931
251076 RX <- UI  sapi = 0  tei = 127
    SETUP pd = 8  callref = 0x45
        Bearer Capability i = 0x8890
        Channel ID i = 0x8A
        Calling Party Number i = 0x0083, '372500'
        Calling Party SubAddr i = 0x80, 'P2902'
        Called Party Number i = 0x
251564 TX -> INFOc  sapi = 0  tei = 80  ns = 8  nr = 8
    CONNECT pd = 8  callref = 0xC5
251996 RX <- INFOc  sapi = 0  tei = 80  ns = 8  nr = 9
    CONNECT_ACK pd = 8  callref = 0x45
```

Figure 13-30 shows the baseline exchange for a successful call setup at the called side.

NOTE Figure 13-30 shows the timestamps available when you use the Cisco IOS **service timestamps debug datetime msec** command. Cisco engineers recommend that you set a timestamp when debugging WAN problems because it provides information about how quickly events occur and helps when you are working with other troubleshooting resources (e.g., Cisco TAC).

In Figure 13-31, the **debug** output shows an incoming call rejected, and the called TE clears the call.

Figure 13-31 *An incoming call is rejected, and the called TE clears the call.*

```
0:03:10:   190.680 TX ->  SETUP pd = 8  callref = 0x01
0:03:10:           Bearer Capability i = 0x8890
0:03:10:           Channel ID i = 0x83
0:03:10:           Called Party Number i = 0x80, '4839625'
0:03:10:   190.756 RX <-  RELEASE_COMP pd = 8  callref = 0x81
0:03:10:           Cause i = 0x8295 - Call rejected

312.900 RX <-  INFOc  sapi = 0  tei = 96  ns = 1  nr = 2
   DISCONNECT pd = 8  callref = 0x81
       Cause i = 0x82D8
       Signal i = 0x03
312.912 TX ->  RRr  sapi = 0  tei = 96  nr = 2 received HOST_DISCONNECT_ACK
312.920 TX ->  INFOc  sapi = 0  tei = 96  ns = 2  nr = 2
   RELEASE pd = 8  callref = 0x01
       Cause i = 0x8090
312.948 RX <-  RRr  sapi = 0  tei = 96  nr = 3
313.220 RX <-  INFOc  sapi = 0  tei = 96  ns = 2  nr = 3
   RELEASE_COMP pd = 8  callref = 0x81
```

As shown at the top of Figure 13-31, you can check how rapidly the release occurred to determine whether it came from the local side or the far side of the circuit (which often takes longer for the release). For instance, if the far side is set up with call screening, the resulting release will be slower than other causes.

ISDN call setup can be refused for various reasons, and either side can clear a call with DISCONNECT. The bottom of Figure 13-31 shows a DISCONNECT. Cause information from Cisco routers is usually "normal call clearing" 0x8090.

However, for problems, a release cause number and description may help identify the reason of the call clearing or call failure. Some causes reflect problems such as remote router call screening, out of channels, or bad SPID.

Consult your service provider to determine whether SPIDs are needed. A considerable amount of troubleshooting involving BRI needs this identifier. Provided by North American ISDN carriers, the SPID identifies the line configuration of the BRI service. Depending on the ISDN switch and the software version that the switch is running, SPIDs may be required.

If the switch is a DMS-100 or a National ISDN-1 (NI-1) switch, SPIDs are required. The AT&T 5ESS switch may also require SPIDs, depending on the version of software that the 5ESS is running. You use the **show running-config** privileged EXEC command (or **show system:running-config** in IOS 12.0) or **configure terminal** to view the router configuration. Verify that the SPID number shown is that assigned to you by your service provider.

Each SPID points to line setup and configuration information. The absence or presence of the second SPID in the router's configuration dictates whether the second B channel can be used for data or voice. Figure 13-32 shows the output from the **configure terminal** command.

Figure 13-32 *You can use the **configure terminal** command to get SPID information.*

```
router#configure terminal
isdn spid1 415555836201 5558362
isdn spid2 415555837002 5558370
```

- spid number is usually 10-digit telephone number with extra digits:

    415: area code

    555: exchange

    8362 and 8370: station ID

    01 and 02 : terminal identifier

- ldn local directory number for incoming calls on the second B channel:

    555: exchange

    8362 and 8370: station ID

If a SPID is necessary but not configured on the device, the device fails the D-channel Layer 3 initialization and calls cannot be placed. For troubleshooting, make sure that the SPID entered as a Cisco IOS configuration argument matches exactly the value provided by the ISDN service.

The SPID enables the TE to register the profile it wants, using a number that the service provider provisions for the local facility. SPIDS are validated by the switch after power up with a local handshake between the TE and local ISDN switch.

When a device is plugged in to the ISDN network, it performs a D-channel Layer 2 initialization process whereby an endpoint ID (EID) is assigned to the device. The device then attempts D-channel Layer 3 initialization. A valid SPID is acknowledged with an EID.

The router is able to answer calls based on EID if an incoming call is addressed to an EID instead of a local directory number (LDN). The EID is assigned during the SPID initialization.

Figure 13-33 provides a baseline of SPIDs working correctly for BRI call setup.

Figure 13-33 *SPIDs are validated by the switch after power up with a local handshake between the TE and the local ISDN switch.*

```
router# debug isdn q931
11438.776 TX -> INFORMATION pd = 8  callref = (null)
        SPID Information i = 0x363133373835323631323030
11438.872 RX <- INFORMATION pd = 8  callref = (null)
        ENDPOINT IDent i = 0xF180
11443.848 TX -> INFORMATION pd = 8  callref = (null)
        SPID Information i = 0x363133373835323631333030
11443.972 RX <- INFORMATION pd = 8  callref = (null)
        ENDPOINT IDent i = 0xF080
```

continues

Figure 13-33 *SPIDs are validated by the switch after power up with a local handshake between the TE and the local ISDN switch. (Continued)*

```
11438.776 TX ->  INFORMATION pd = 8  callref = (null)
        SPID Information i = 0x363133373835323631323030
11438.872 RX <-  INFORMATION pd = 8  callref = (null)
        ENDPOINT IDent i = 0xF180
ISDN Event: incoming ces value = 1
received HOST_TERM_REGISTER_ACK - received eid
        ENDPOINT IDent i = 0xF180
11443.848 TX ->  INFORMATION pd = 8  callref = (null)
        SPID Information i = 0x363133373835323631333030
11443.972 RX <-  INFORMATION pd = 8  callref = (null)
        ENDPOINT IDent i = 0xF080
ISDN Event: incoming ces value = 2
received HOST_TERM_REGISTER_ACK - received eid
        ENDPOINT IDent i = 0xF080
```

The output from the **debug isdn q931** command shown in Figure 13-34 gives an example of an invalid SPID. Indications of an invalid SPID include a cause statement that you can use to troubleshoot. The HOST_TERM_REGISTER_NACK provides additional cause information, as shown by the "invalid EID/SPID or TEI not assigned" message.

Figure 13-34 *HOST_TERM_REGISTER_NACK provides additional cause information.*

```
11678.060 TX ->  INFORMATION pd = 8  callref = (null)
        SPID Information i = 0x31323334353536373736
11678.164 RX <-  INFORMATION pd = 8  callref = (null)
        Cause i = 0x82E43A - Invalid IE contents
11678.060 TX ->  INFORMATION pd = 8  callref = (null)
        SPID Information i = 0x31323334353536373736
11678.164 RX <-  INFORMATION pd = 8  callref = (null)
        Cause i = 0x82E43A - Invalid IE contents
ISDN Event: incoming ces value = 1
received HOST_TERM_REGISTER_NACK - invalid EID/SPID or TEI not assigned
        Cause i = 0x8082 - No route to specified network
```

NOTE   You can also troubleshoot by using the **show isdn status** command. You may see SPID NACK records accumulated in the output. The **show isdn status** command displays the SPID information for 5ESS, NI-1, and DMS-100 switches if a SPID is configured. Output from the command shows whether a SPID is valid and whether the LDN is configured, and it shows the EID assigned by the switch. EIDs are applicable only on the NI-1 and DMS-100 switch types.

When you troubleshoot, make sure that an incoming call has an EID and the called party number exactly matches the LDN of the router ISDN SPID configuration. If these numbers do not match, the call is ignored.

Normally, the router accepts incoming calls to any number. However, when several (data) devices share the same BRI, you use a number to identify each device. You might want to specify that the router should verify a called party number or subaddress number in the incoming setup message for ISDN BRI calls, if the number is delivered by the switch. You can do so by configuring the number that is allowed. To set this up, configure Cisco IOS software using the **isdn answer1** and **isdn answer2** commands.

The router only accepts calls to the specified address (or subaddress). When a call is made that does not result in a connect, the use of a called address can be one possible cause for the call reject.

In a mismatch, the number set on the called router with the **isdn answer** command does not match the called party number sent by the calling router.

Figure 13-35 shows a keypad facility used on 5ESS and NI-1 switches to set call parameter variations in the octets of the called party number. The keypad IE is now ASCII decoded in the debugs. The keypad and the SPID info are decoded as ASCII.

Figure 13-35 *The Answer1 LDN number does not match the called party number.*

```
router#config t
interface bri 1
isdn answer1 375121200


router#debug isdn q931
251076 RX <-  UI   sapi = 0   tei = 127
    SETUP pd = 8   callref = 0x45
        Bearer Capability i = 0x8890
        Channel ID i = 0x8A
        Calling Party Number i = 0x0083, '372500'
        Calling Party SubAddr i = 0x80, 'P2902'
        Called Party Number i = 0x80, '372256'
251564 TX ->  INFOc  sapi = 0   tei = 80   ns = 8   nr = 8
    CONNECT pd = 8   callref = 0xC5
251996 RX <-  INFOc  sapi = 0   tei = 80   ns = 8   nr = 9
    CONNECT_ACK pd = 8   callref = 0x45
312.616 TX ->  INFOc  sapi = 0   tei = 96   ns = 1   nr = 0
    SETUP pd = 8   callref = 0x01
        Bearer Capability i = 0x8890
        Channel ID i = 0x83
        Keypad Facility i = 0x3939303439303530
```

A Cisco router that has one or more BRI (or PRI) may be configured to use an added level of security by using calling line identification (CLI, also called caller ID) screening to screen incoming calls.

By using the Cisco IOS **isdn caller** command, you can set up the router to verify that the calling line ID is from an expected origin. CLI screening requires a local switch that can deliver the CLI to the router. Figure 13-36 shows the configuration match allowing the call.

Figure 13-36 *The number for the ISDN caller matches the Calling Party Number.*

```
router#config t
interface bri 0
isdn caller 3725002902
```

```
router#debug isdn q931
251076 RX <- UI sapi= 0 tei= 127
    SETUP pd = 8 callref= 0x45
       Bearer Capability i= 0x8890
       ChannelID i= 0x8A
       Calling Party Number i= 0x0083, '372500'
       Calling Party SubA ddri= 0x80, 'P2902'
       Calling Party Number i= 0x80, '372756'
```

The calling ISDN address or subaddress originates the call, and normally the router accepts incoming calls from any address. However, if the call does not result in a connection, one thing to check is whether the router has a configuration with the ISDN caller. If it does, the following may occur:

- The router only accepts calls from the specified address(es).

- If caller ID screening is configured and the local switch does not deliver caller IDs, the router rejects all calls.

The **debug dialer** Command

ISDN, as a circuit-switched technology, makes calls only when there is a need to communicate. Cisco uses DDR to determine when a connection needs to be made between two sites.

With DDR, packets are classified as either "interesting" or "uninteresting" based on protocol-specific access lists and dialer lists or with the use of dialer profiles. The DDR protocol configuration establishes which traffic on the router should trigger an ISDN call.

When troubleshooting for a call that has never come up, check whether the access list tests are too restrictive to allow the **dialer-list** statement to bring up the line.

You can use the **show dialer** command on the calling router to see the current status of the dial string, DDR timers, and connection status. Use the **debug dialer** command to troubleshoot the DDR problems.

The dialer map specifies where DDR should dial (for example, an IP address on the called router that can be reached using a dial string). In Figure 13-37, the access list test permitted DDR to trigger a call, but the BRI 0 interface cannot perform the dialing operation because there is no dialer string defined.

Figure 13-37 *You can use **debug dialer** to check configuration for the DDR statements (for example, the dialer string).*

```
router#debug dialer
BRI0: Dialing cause: BRI0: ip PERMIT
        BRI0: No dialer string defined.  Dialing cannot occur..
        BRI0: Dialing cause: BRI0: ip PERMIT
        BRI0: No dialer string defined.  Dialing cannot occur..
        BRI0: Dialing cause: BRI0: ip PERMIT
        BRI0: No dialer string defined.  Dialing cannot occur..
        BRI0: Dialing cause: BRI0: ip PERMIT
        BRI0: No dialer string defined.  Dialing cannot occur..
        BRI0: Dialing cause: BRI0: ip PERMIT
        BRI0: No dialer string defined.  Dialing cannot occur..
```

Often a configuration has more than one map per destination or several destinations. You should troubleshoot to make sure that a string is defined and accurately refers to the ISDN destination.

Summary

This chapter focused on how to check the physical connection and line activation and how to verify that DDR is triggering an ISDN call. This chapter also depicted how to use **clear**, **show**, and **debug** commands.

You have learned to check the D channel Q.921 and the B channel's PPP at Layer 2. You have learned to check the D channel Q.931 and verify the information elements at Layer 3. You also know that misconfigured SPIDs can prevent call setup.

Chapter 13 Test
Diagnosing and Correcting ISDN BRI Problems

Estimated Time: 15 minutes

Complete all the exercises to test your knowledge of the materials contained in this chapter. Answers are listed in Appendix A, "Chapter Test Answer Key."

Use the information contained in this chapter to answer the following questions.

Question 13.1

T   F   Layer 1 and 2 tests check for local loop to the ISDN switch.

Question 13.2

T   F   Layer 3 tests check connectivity end-to-end.

Question 13.3

T   F   The **clear all** command resets the hardware logic.

Question 13.4

T   F   BRI offers a 16-kbps pipe.

Question 13.5

T   F   "Spoofing" indicates that a D channel is up.

Question 13.6

T   F   The Layer 1 S/T interface uses an RJ-45 cable and connector.

Question 13.7

T   F   Layer 1 frame formats differ depending on whether they are incoming or outgoing.

PART V

Appendixes

Chapter Test Answer Key

Chapter 1: "Troubleshooting Methodology"

1.1   Downtime cost calculations are based on

- Annual gross revenue for an organization or a department
- Total downtime hours experienced or anticipated
- Average user's annual salary
- Total number of users affected by the downtime

1.2   The eight-step problem-solving model shown in this chapter includes these steps:

Step 1   Define the problem.

Step 2   Gather the facts.

Step 3   Consider possibilities based on the facts.

Step 4   Create an action plan.

Step 5   Implement an action plan.

Step 6   Observe results.

Step 7   Repeat the process

Step 8   Resolve the problem.

1.3   You can gather facts from users; network administrators, managers; and any other key people involved with the network, network management systems, protocol analyzer traces, output from router diagnostic commands such as **debug** privileged EXEC commands and **show** EXEC commands, or software release notes.

1.4   Undo the changes that failed to solve the problem and restore the network to its original condition.

1.5   Be sure that your action plan does not change network security or management policies.

Chapter 2: "Protocol Characteristics Overview"

2.1   a. Connection-oriented

       b. Connectionless

2.2   a. TCP

       b. SPX

       c. NCP

       d. ATP

2.3   The transport layer

2.4   The preamble field

2.5   Early token release

2.6   Token Ring

2.7   a. LLC1: connectionless

       b. LLC2: connection-oriented, acknowledged

       c. LLC3: connectionless, acknowledged

2.8   The 10-bit DLCI identifies the logical connection that is multiplexed into a physical channel. This is in the heart of the Frame Relay address field in the packet header.

2.9   ARP

2.10   UDP/IP

2.11   OSPF for IP, and NLSP for IPX

2.12   NBP lookups are flooded in the appropriate zone to locate network services.

2.13   a. Connection establishment

       b. Data transfer

       c. Connection teardown

2.14   a. Efficiency

       b. Simple implementation

       c. Low network overhead

2.15   a. Connection-oriented: TCP

       b. Connectionless: UDP

2.16   a. 2

      b. 1

      c. 4

      d. 3

2.17   a. Single mode

2.18   ICMP

2.19   Hop-count limits, hold-downs, triggered updates, split horizon, and poison reverse updates

2.20   Exterior gateway protocol

2.21   a. RIP is a distance-vector routing protocol similar to IP RIP.

      b. NLSP is a link state protocol similar to OSI IS-IS and TCP/IP's OSPF.

2.22   b. built to carry voice, video, and data traffic

      c. Primarily a connection-oriented network

      e. Supports virtual paths and virtual channels

Chapter 3: "Cisco Routing and Switching Processes"

3.1   Switching technology is used to get a packet from an incoming interface to an outgoing interface in the Cisco router.

3.2   Routing technology is used to determine the direction of the destination network defined by an incoming packet.

3.3   Router updates are sent on all interfaces that are configured for that routing protocol.

3.4   The switching path types are

- Process switching
- Fast switching
- Optimum switching
- Distributed switching
- NetFlow switching

3.5   Fast switching is the default switching mechanism for IP traffic.

3.6   Distributed switching is a mechanism used to relieve the route/switch processor of involvement and uses VIPs.

3.7   The following special features can affect performance:

- Queuing
- Random early detection
- Compression
- Filtering (using access lists)
- Encryption
- Accounting
- Debugging

Chapter 4: "General Troubleshooting Tools"

4.1   a. 4

      b. 2

      c. 6

      d. 1

      e. 5

      f. 3

4.2   Troubleshooting should start at the physical layer.

4.3   Network monitors and protocol analyzers

4.4   Cable testers

4.5   Netsys or other modeling tools

Chapter 5: "Cisco Management and Diagnostic Tools"

5.1   a. 1

      b. 2

      c. 3

      d. 4

Chapter 6: "Troubleshooting Sample Exercises"

Exercise 1: Token Ring Network

Observations:

- There are nontrivial input queue drops.
- At the same time, the number of "no buffers" equals the number of input queue.
- Drops—this does not point to input queue problems, but to a problem with buffer availability.
- A look at the **show buffers** command output shows a significant number of hits, misses, trims, and created buffers.

Solutions:

- There are obviously problems with the number of middle buffers available. More data should be gathered to make sure that this is a trend and not an isolated incident. A protocol analyzer should be used to determine the reason for a large number of middle-sized frames. Determine whether the middle-sized frames can be reduced by a configuration change on servers, clients, or routers. If this is not the case, then you might need to tune your middle buffers.

- Possible values might be
  - buffers middle permanent 300
  - buffers middle max-free 400
- Call your technical support representative for help with tuning buffers.

Exercise 2: Sydney Network

Observations:

- CPU utilization is relatively high, with the short-term (5-second) value hitting 100%.
- Check which processes are using the most CPU resources (greatest runtime, in ms).
- These appear to be the IS-IS update, Novell router, and Novell SAP processes.

Solutions:

- Upgrade software to 9.21 or above, if the router was equipped with an earlier revision. This will provide a better granularity of control because wildcard characters can be specified in the SAP filters. With well-structured sap names, wildcard filters will reduce the length of SAP filters and the resulting CPU load.
- Increasing RIP/SAP update timers would help a bit, but would result in slower routing convergence.
- Moving the routing protocol to Enhanced IGRP for IPX would reduce the majority of the periodic RIP/SAP updates, thereby reducing CPU utilization. Using NLSP would also reduce the periodic RIP/SAP updates.

Exercise 3: Brussels Network

Observations:

- Input queue drops are incrementing.
- 0 no buffer, so buffer sizes are okay.
- 0 ignored, so ciscoBus complex is okay.
- Input queue hits 147/150, indicating that the input queue of pointers is being overrun by incoming frames. The first parameter of this queue parameter is an instantaneous value, and it is regularly showing a nontrivial entry. (The **show** command has been executed approximately every 10 seconds to try to capture these values.)
- Most drops seem to occur approximately every 60 seconds (look at "last clearing of **show interface** counters").

- Because Novell is running on this network, and with the regular flooding occurring every 60 seconds, this could be caused by RIP or SAP updates. (This network was receiving 4×1300 saps and 4×3000 Novell routes every 60 seconds!)

Solutions:

- In the long term, try to reduce SAP traffic (maybe by using a routing protocol such as Enhanced IGRP for IPX or NLSP) or spread the traffic in time (by using an **output-sap-delay**).
- In the short term, work with your technical support representative to increase the input hold queue size.

Chapter 7: "Troubleshooting TCP/IP Connectivity"

7.1   a. **ping**

b. **trace**

c. **show**

d. **debug**

7.2   a. **show ip ospf interface**, **show ip ospf database**, and **show ip ospf**

b. **show ip interface**

c. **show ip route summary**

d. **debug ip icmp**

e. **debug ip ospf events**, **show ip ospf interface**

7.3   The table shows the five variations:

Traffic Requirements	Router Setup
NetBEUI traffic	Transparent bridging or source-route bridging
Transparent bridging or SRB	Data-Link switching or remote source-route bridging
Novell type 20 NetBIOS traffic	**ipx type-20-propagation**
A Microsoft WINS server is configured on the segment	Native IP. No special configuration is needed on the router.
UDP encapsulated NetBIOS broadcasts via IP	**ip helper address** and **ip forward-protocol udp**

7.4   a. **route print**

b. **arp -d**

Chapter 8: "Troubleshooting Novell Connectivity"

8.1   a. **show**

b. **debug**

c. **ping ipx**

8.2   a. **show ipx interface**

b. **show ipx server**

c. **show ipx nlsp database**

d. **debug ipx ipxwan**

e. **ipx ping-default novell**

8.3   SAP traffic is the one cause of excessive overhead problems. There are three ways to deal with it:

a. SAP filters

b. Change update intervals

c. Use Enhanced IGRP for IPX on WAN links

8.4   a. Encapsulation type

b. Network number

c. Routing protocol

8.5   True

8.6   False—all internal network numbers must be unique IPX addresses.

Chapter 9: "Troubleshooting AppleTalk Connectivity"

9.1   a. **ping appletalk**

b. **show**

c. **debug**

d. **test appletalk**

9.2   a.   **show appletalk name-cache, show appletalk nbp**

  b.   **show appletalk route**

  c.   **test appletalk nbp**, then **nbp poll** or **nbp lookup**

  d.   **test appletalk nbp**, then **nbp confirm**

  e.   **debug apple zip or debug apple events**

9.3   False—each router must have a unique router ID.

9.4   True

9.5   a. Cable range

  b. Zone name

  c. Routing protocol

Chapter 10: "Diagnosing and Correcting Catalyst Problems"

10.1   True

10.2   False—they are fully modular.

10.3   True

10.4   False—spanning tree works for environments that contain both Ethernet and Fast Ethernet links.

10.5   False—ISL is a Cisco-proprietary protocol that works only on VLAN trunks.

10.6   True

10.7   True

Chapter 11: "Troubleshooting VLANs on Routers and Switches"

11.1   False—IEEE and DEC spanning tree protocols are not compatible in a single switched/ bridged environment.

11.2   True

11.3   False—CDP uses multicasts and is a very useful troubleshooting tool.

11.4   True for the router **show span** command. False for the Catalyst switch **show span** command. On the switch, this command gives statistics on port mirroring.

11.5   False—**debug** commands stay on until they are turned off with the **no debug** or **undebug** commands.

Chapter 12: "Diagnosing and Correcting Frame Relay Problems"

12.1   True

12.2   False—the LMI types available are Cisco, ANSI, and the ITU's q933a.

12.3   False—DLCIs are locally significant only.

12.4   True

12.5   True

12.6   **show interface serial [n]**

      show frame-relay lmi

      show frame-relay map

      show frame-relay pvc

Chapter 13: "Diagnosing and Correcting ISDN BRI Problems"

13.1   True

13.2   True

13.3   False—**clear all** is not a valid IOS command.

13.4   False—BRI ISDN offers two 64-KB B channels and one 16-KB D channel, for a total bandwidth of 144 KB.

13.5   True

13.6   True

13.7   True

Cisco Support Functions

Cisco offers an amazingly comprehensive set of support options, including its Web site, Cisco Connection Online (CCO). CCO is the umbrella for Cisco's online support channel. It is located at www.cisco.com (see Figure B-1) and includes the following support elements:

- Cisco documentation
- Cisco Press titles
- The Cisco software center
- The Cisco marketplace and technical tools
- Cisco training information

NOTE You must have a CCO password to enter some areas of CCO. You must be a CCIE, holder of a Cisco Service Contract, Cisco reseller, Premier Certified Partner, Cisco employee or badged contractor, customer of a Cisco partner, distributor, or reseller to obtain a CCO account and password. You can register through www.cisco.com/register.

Figure B-1   *Cisco Connection Online home page.*

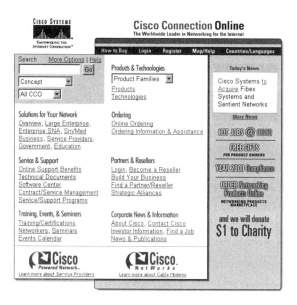

NOTE	In December 1998 Cisco Connection Online won the 1998 HotShots Award for Best Electronic Commerce Enabled Site sponsored by the Information Industry Association (IIA).

CCO is an award-winning example of doing business using electronic media and the networked environment of the Internet. You already use the network as an information-sharing tool. CCO can help you link many resources for your internetwork operations and troubleshooting efforts.

Because networks are complex and crucial, Cisco developed CCO as a scalable online resource to provide immediate access to resources, information, and systems. CCO is a worldwide intranet accessible over the Internet. Globalization features of CCO improve access to critical information and resources on a global scale.

CCO provides users with two levels of access:

- Guest access for the general public—Guest users have access to general company and product information.

- Registered access for customers that have either purchased a support contract from Cisco or have been sponsored by a Cisco-authorized partner—Registered users have access to all information at the guest level, plus additional in-depth information and advanced online applications and services.

The information on CCO can greatly help with your troubleshooting efforts. CCO has CD-based and Web-based tools that can help you prevent problems—including resources on how to design, order, configure, support, and provide for spares of Cisco products—and correct problems—including how to detect, identify, track, and resolve bugs and problems.

You can access the CCO infrastructure with your Web browser. Translated versions of the Cisco Web CCO English-language home page and many other key CCO pages are now available in many languages, including Chinese, Danish, Dutch, Finnish, French, German, Italian, Japanese, Korean, Norwegian, Portuguese, Russian, Spanish, and Swedish.

The major CCO support centers are in San Jose, California; Raleigh, North Carolina; Brussels, Belgium; and Sydney, Australia. Cisco also has installed CCO remote distribution servers with local points of presence (POPs) in countries throughout the world. Users can now access all CCO guest services—including product information, documentation, and technical tips— through dedicated links in Australia, China, France, Hong Kong, Japan, the Netherlands, and South Korea. Additional POPs will continue to open.

Selecting a server and clicking on Go will take you to that regional server, where you can access up-to-date guest information and services. The CCO home page is initially presented in English, but you can select a local language from the same globalization interface to view translated content. If you are a registered user and log in, you are taken to the main CCO server in San Jose, California.

At the entrance to the Cisco intranet, a firewall provides Cisco a secure transaction pipe between Web servers outside Cisco's corporate firewall (the public Internet) and Cisco's internal information systems and databases. This firewall includes Secure Transport Architecture (STA), a complex system of commercial products and custom-built applications.

Using CCO to Prevent Problems

Among the CCO resources that help you prevent problems are the following tools:

- The Documentation CD-ROM is an interactive library of technical product information that can help you design and configure your network correctly. You can use the CD-ROM to find out how to avoid many of the causes of network problems.

- Cisco Press publishes a library of resources for learning about all aspects of Cisco networks. Topics range from troubleshooting to network design to IOS configuration.

- CCO MarketPlace, through the Internetworking Products Center (IPC), allows you to purchase software products over the Internet. It uses agent application programs to help you with online commerce and to give you access to status information.

- The CCO Software Center is the new version of the Software Library service that lets you obtain upgrades and learn more about Cisco's broad and growing range of software products. You can also get maintenance releases and code patches.

Let's take a closer look at these tools that help you prevent problems.

Cisco Documentation

The Documentation CD-ROM is an interactive library of technical product information. After you install it on your system, the Documentation CD-ROM provides a series of interconnected documents that you navigate by clicking on hypertext links and using the navigation tools—the toolbar with navigation buttons, online help, and the document button bar.

A search facility allows you to jump directly to the information that interests you. The CD-ROM also provides several ways to return to documents that you have previously looked at. A history facility allows you to keep track of the documents that you have looked at in the past 60 days. You can also save the location of documents that you reference regularly by adding them to a bookmarks list. The CD-ROM package contains the following documentation in HTML format:

- Cisco IOS release notes, configuration guides, command references, and command summaries
- A debug command reference and system error messages
- Cisco's *Management Information Base (MIB) User Quick Reference* and *Access Services Quick Configuration Guide*
- The Cisco product catalog
- Router and hub installation and configuration guides
- Switch installation and configuration guides, switch command reference guides, and switch MIB reference guides
- Client/server software installation guides
- Configuration notes for memory upgrades, network interface cards, rack-mount kits, and other field upgrade products

The online documentation includes the product manuals, white papers, product spec sheets, Quick Starts, technical tips, field notices, sample configurations, and more.

Cisco's Quick Starts provide quick hardware installation and software configuration information for experienced users. Streamlined navigation, task-oriented procedures, and enhanced graphics provide specific information quickly and efficiently, reducing the time it takes to get up and running. At the time this book was written, the following Quick Starts were online:

- Catalyst 5002 Quick Hardware Installation Guide
- Catalyst 5000 and 5505 Quick Hardware Installation Guide
- Catalyst 5509 Quick Hardware Installation Guide
- Catalyst 5500 Quick Hardware Installation Guide
- Catalyst 2926 Quick Start
- Catalyst 8510 Animated Quick Start
- Catalyst 8540 Animated Quick Start

You can also search or browse through a large collection of technical tips gathered from Cisco's Technical Assistance Center (TAC) experts.

Cisco Press

You can find information on Cisco Press at www.ciscopress.com. This site uses Web browser technology to provide navigation, document viewing, and document searching. Search and Seeker Agent technology is provided by Verity, Inc.

This site presents published selections from Cisco Press books. For a listing of available publications, you can visit Cisco Press Online, hosted by Macmillan Computer Publishing. Additional Cisco Press title information can be found at www.ciscopress.com.

CCO MarketPlace

CCO MarketPlace, through the IPC, allows you to purchase software products over the Internet. The IPC offers numerous benefits, including access to extensive product configuration and pricing information, order verification, and online order submission capabilities. The IPC uses Cisco Commerce Agents, which are applications that have been designed specifically for Cisco customers and partners:

- Status Agent provides access to current information on Cisco orders. This application simplifies and enhances the ability to track the progress and status of Cisco orders 24 hours per day, 365 days per year.

- Pricing Agent gives you direct access to Cisco's online price list. Price searches can be based on product family, product description, or product number. An additional feature enables you to download the entire price list to a computer.

- Configuration Agent offers searches of configurable Cisco products and the creation of product configurations online.

- Service Order Agent helps you get real-time access to the status of your service orders based on your service order number, PO/reference number, or TAC case number. The Service Order Agent has three parts:
  - Service Order Submit
  - Service Order Status
  - Service Parts Agent (also called FRUFinder, for Field Replaceable Units, which are parts that can be replaced in the field)

To access the IPC, you need to register for Commerce Agents via CCO Users. To do this, go to www.cisco.com, click on Register, select Commerce Agents, and complete the user profiles. For security purposes, you will be prompted for a valid purchase order number and billing address.

CCO Software Center

The CCO Software Center is the new version of the Software Library service that lets you obtain upgrades and learn more about Cisco's broad and growing range of software products.

Over the years, the Software Library, now the Software Center, has grown from a simple FTP service for delivering software fixes to customers, to a location for all phases of Cisco software product life cycles. Depending on your Cisco or Cisco Partner software service agreements, you can use support resources such as the following:

- Get major upgrades and maintenance releases of Cisco software products.

- Get selected demonstration and beta distributions for Cisco's latest products, so you can try before you buy or test before you invest.

- Consult software upgrade planners that collect and present product literature, release information, documentation, and release notes.

- Use checksum and MD5 (Message Digest 5—see RFC 1321, "MD5 Message-Digest Algorithm") values for software files to ensure software file integrity.

- Use software checklists to ensure the current availability and compatibility of Cisco software products for your internetworking platforms.

- Browse CCO's Software Image Library via the Web to locate the topic that contains the file(s) you need and then execute a software download.

- Try out custom-file-access postings of software not generally or publicly available (such as critical, customized defect fixes).

Using CCO to Correct Problems

CCO offers a number of resources to help you correct problems:

- Bug Toolkit II is CCO's popular bug searching tools. It is a set of integrated applications that can be used to identify, evaluate, and obtain a status report on defects that have real or potential impact on your network.

- The CCO Troubleshooting Engine can resolve a variety of common networking problems using an intuitive Web interface. This tool supports a wide variety of network protocols, Cisco platforms, and WAN protocols, and specializes in the areas of hardware, configuration, and performance.

- If you need to find out what happened on a Cisco product before it failed, use the CCO Stack Decoder. Analyze a stack trace (by using the **show stacks** command) on Cisco router platforms and receive a comprehensive set of diagnostic results, including hardware failures and candidate software defects.

- CCO's Open Forum provides an online question-and-answer mechanism for Cisco customers to receive answers to common technical questions.
- If you need to open a service case with Cisco TAC, you can use the CCO Case Management Toolkit. It provides direct access to TAC for case open, query, and update purposes. TAC can also be reached via phone at 408-553-6387.

Cisco's Bug Toolkit II

Cisco's Bug Toolkit II includes three tools:

- Bug Navigator
- Bug Alert
- Bug Watcher

Together these three tools allow you to locate (by using Bug Navigator) and subscribe to either specific defects (by using Bug Watcher) or defects matching a network profile that you create (by using Bug Alert).

You can use Bug Navigator II to search for known bugs based on software version, feature set, and keywords. If you know the specific ID number of a bug and need more information, you can quickly access it by using this tool.

Bug Navigator II allows you to save the results of a search in watcher bins and to create persistent Alert Agents that can feed the watcher bins with new defect alerts.

You can define any number of named profiles of your network environments, and Bug Toolkit's powerful search agents constantly monitor defects of interest, as well as any new defects that match your named agent profiles.

With Bug Watcher, you can create multiple named "bins" in which you can "watch" or monitor the status of any number of defects.

CCO Troubleshooting Engine

The Troubleshooting Engine is designed to be a simple and productive method for resolving the most common configuration and performance issues involving Cisco products. Although the tool is designed to provide a complete resolution to a submitted problem, it is also useful as an aid in further refining and defining the nature of the problem via hyperlinks to related documents and issues. In this way, the utility of the tool does not hinge on always having an answer, but rather on acting as a productivity enhancement in general troubleshooting methodology.

You should be able to solve common, simple problems by using the Troubleshooting Engine; however, you can't use it to solve complicated problems that require extensive debugging or troubleshooting.

To use the Troubleshooting Engine, select a high-level problem domain area and enter a concise description of your problem. The application prompts you for questions to help narrow down the problem. Possible suggestions are retrieved after you submit your description and every answer. As you continue answering questions, more likely suggestions are retrieved and are scored according to their likelihood of solving the problem. The maximum score possible for a suggestion is 100, so a score of 90 or higher indicates a very likely solution to the problem.

CCO Stack Decoder

Stack Decoder helps in those rare circumstances when a Cisco router encounters a set of conditions it has not been programmed to handle (for example, during a hardware failure) and the router generates a stack trace. The stack trace is an important feature of the Cisco IOS software that allows the subsequent diagnosis and repair of the underlying cause. You can display stack traces by executing the **show stacks** privileged command from the EXEC prompt of the router.

Cisco considers any situation that results in a stack trace and restart (often called a crash) that is not due to a hardware failure to be a software defect, even if the root cause is in fact another malfunctioning device on the network.

Stack Decoder decodes the stack trace that the device generates and creates a symbol file. The symbol file, plus the other information in the trace, usually provides enough information to isolate the cause of the stack trace.

Before Stack Decoder became a reality, you had to send the trace to the TAC to decode the trace; analyze the related data; and compare the results to Cisco's bug-tracking database, diagnostic rules, and hardware address information. Thanks to CCO's Stack Decoder, you can use the same techniques that the TAC uses and automate the process. After the trace has been analyzed, Stack Decoder presents an ordered results list of candidate diagnoses. The results list usually includes a list of bug IDs or a hardware diagnostic.

The first few defects listed in the results list usually contain the root cause of the problem. Occasionally, however, the diagnostic shows no clear winners. It is important that you pay careful attention to the software release levels, protocols, and conditions described in the bug citation. After you compare all the data, it is usually easy to identify the root cause.

CCO Open Forum

CCO's Open Forum provides an online Q&A mechanism for Cisco customers to receive answers to common technical questions. These answers can come in three ways:

- Browsing the CCO's Q&A database (much as you would do in an Internet service such as Yahoo!)

- Entering a single natural-language text question that the forum software parses and submits to a CCO search engine

- Sending questions to the Open Forum. This is a system for communicating in real time with other people on the Web. You can send messages with text, pictures, and live Web links.

NOTE   The Forum's responses come from Cisco Network engineers who may or may not work for Cisco. Open Forum is provided to Cisco customers as a service, and the answers provided do not necessarily represent the views of Cisco.

When the search is complete, you are given a list of potential answers to your question. These Q&A pairs are weighted based on the keywords you provided, and the "score" is provided in the left column: The higher the score, the greater the likelihood that the answer will help you.

If the system cannot find Q&A pairs that include keywords contained within your search question, you are notified that there were no valid Q&As for your query. At this time, you can either send the question to the Open Forum or return to the Open Forum home page to rephrase the question.

NOTE   Part of the Open Forum is the CCIE Chat Forum, which was designed to allow CCIEs the opportunity to open a real-time dialog with another CCIE, aiding in dissemination of information and problem resolution. This option is restricted to CCIEs only.

TAC

For Cisco service and support, the TAC provides warranty, contracted, or billable technical assistance with Cisco products, and monitors the service problem from initial call to closure.

The best way to work with TAC is to first perform all the troubleshooting that you can. Use the support resources for troubleshooting (including those in CCO) and the knowledge (including from this course) to troubleshoot the problem yourself.

If you solve your own networking problem, chances are the return to full operation on the network will occur faster than if you take the time to open a case and communicate the details of the problem to TAC. However, there may still be times when you need to escalate the problem to TAC. You can request service from the Cisco TAC via phone, fax, the Web, or e-mail.

Be sure to have all the necessary information ready before you open a case. The information can vary based on the type of network, products, and service arrangements you have. In general, you should do the following:

1   Gather all the associated facts to define the problem. Get the output from all affected devices by using the **show tech-support** command (Cisco IOS software Release 11.0 or later). This command combines the output from several troubleshooting commands. These troubleshooting commands are covered in Chapter 5, "Cisco Management and Diagnostic Tools." Add other facts such as the following:

— Recent configuration changes

— Debugs

— Protocol analyzer traces

2   Have information about your warranty equipment:

— Company name

— Contact name, address, and telephone number

— The serial number, model number of the unit that is experiencing the problem

— The problem priority level of the call. The following are the priority levels:

— Priority 1—Production network down

— Priority 2—Production network severely degraded

— Priority 3—Network performance degraded

— Priority 4—Information needed on Cisco product capabilities, installation, or configuration

3   Contact the TAC serving your area. Open a case to implement an action plan.

4   When you contact the TAC, the TAC customer support engineer (CSE) assigns a case number to your problem. You should record this number for any future references to this case. Your problem will be routed to the appropriate Customer Engineering Response Team for resolution, depending on the type of problem and the priority level.

5   You can use the Case Management Toolkit in CCO to interact directly with Cisco's TAC. The Case Management Toolkit has three distinct tools:

— Case Open lets you request technical assistance by opening a case with TAC.

— Case Query allows you to check the status of cases you have opened with TAC.

— Case Update lets you send your own notes to a case you have opened with TAC.

The Case Management Toolkit can also link to the Cisco MarketPlace and the Service Order Agent of the IPC. Cisco MarketPlace provides status of any field replacement parts ordered to bring up hardware that has malfunctioned.

6   TAC works to deliver service. After implementing the service action plan, the CSE works with you to observe the results. The CSE confirms with you that the problem is resolved and closes the case.

CCO Training Information

CCO lists training courses and certification programs for customers and resellers. The customer training section offers tools to locate the Cisco course you are looking for:

- Instructor-Led Courses—See the full list of instructor-led training courses, which includes a brief description of the course and the prerequisites, who should attend, and the course outline.

- Self-Study Materials—See the full list of self-study materials, which includes self-study guides, CD-ROMs, books, and computer-based training.

- Class Locator—If you already know what course you want to take, use the Class Locator to find a class at a convenient time and location. The Class Locator is a powerful search engine that allows you to search on the following criteria: course, training partner, city, state/province, country, region, language, start date, and end date.

- Cisco Career Certifications—Complete information on Cisco Career Certifications, including career track descriptions, recommended preparatory classes, and testing requirements.

Summary

You will find that CCO is one of the most comprehensive support sites on the Internet. The best way to get to know what's available is to browse through CCO and see what information is available.

References and Recommended Reading

This appendix lists relevant books, periodicals, technical publications, and standards. The "editors' picks" have been marked with an asterisk (*).

Books and Periodicals

Apple Computer, Inc. *AppleTalk Network System Overview.* Reading, Massachusetts: Addison-Wesley, 1989.

Apple Computer, Inc. *Planning and Managing AppleTalk Networks.* Reading, Massachusetts: Addison-Wesley, 1991.

Black, U. *Data Networks: Concepts, Theory and Practice.* Upper Saddle, New Jersey: Prentice Hall, 1989.

Black, U. *Physical Level Interfaces and Protocols.* Los Alamitos, California: IEEE Computer Society Press, 1988.

Case, J.D., J.R. Davins, M.S. Fedor, and M.L. Schoffstall. "Network Management and the Design of SNMP." *ConneXions: The Interoperability Report,* Vol. 3, March 1989.

Chappell, L. *Novell's Guide to NetWare LAN Analysis.* San Jose, California: Novell Press, 1998.*

Coltun, R. "OSPF: An Internet Routing Protocol." *ConneXions: The Interoperability Report,* Vol. 3, No. 8, August 1989.

Comer, D.E. *Internetworking with TCP/IP: Principles, Protocols, and Architecture,* Vol. 1, 2nd ed. Upper Saddle, New Jersey: Prentice Hall, 1991.*

Davidson, J. *An Introduction to TCP/IP.* New York: Springer-Verlag, 1992.

Ferrari, D. *Computer Systems Performance Evaluation.* Upper Saddle, New Jersey: Prentice Hall, 1978.

Garcia-Luna-Aceves, J.J. "Loop-Free Routing Using Diffusing Computations." Publication pending in *IEEE/ACM Transactions on Networking,* Vol. 1, No. 1, 1993.

Green, J.K. *Telecommunications,* 2nd ed. Homewood, Illinois: Business One Irwin, 1992.

Jones, N.E.H., and D. Kosiur. *Macworld Networking Handbook.* Foster City, California: IDG, 1992.

LaQuey, T. *The Internet Companion: A Beginner's Guide to Global Networking.* Reading, Massachusetts: Addison-Wesley, 1994.

Leinwand, A., and K. Fang. *Network Management: A Practical Perspective.* Reading, Massachusetts: Addison-Wesley, 1993.

McNamara, J.E. *Local Area Networks: An Introduction to the Technology.* Bedford, Massachusetts: Digital Press, 1997.

Malamud, C. *Analyzing DECnet/OSI Phase V.* New York: Van Nostrand Reinhold, 1991.*

Malamud, C. *Analyzing Novell Networks.* New York: Van Nostrand Reinhold, 1991.

Malamud, C. *Analyzing Sun Networks.* New York: Van Nostrand Reinhold, 1991.

Martin, J. *SNA: IBM's Networking Solution.* Upper Saddle, New Jersey: Prentice Hall, 1987.

Martin, J., with K.K. Chapman and the ARBEN Group, Inc. *Local Area Networks. Architectures and Implementations.* Upper Saddle, New Jersey: Prentice Hall, 1989.

Meijer, A. *Systems Network Architecture: A Tutorial.* New York: John Wiley & Sons, 1987.

Miller, M.A. *Internetworking: A Guide to Network Communications LAN to LAN; LAN to WAN,* 2nd ed. San Mateo, California: M&T Books, 1995.

Moy, John T. *OSPF: Anatomy of an Internet Routing Protocol.* Reading, Massachusetts: Addison-Wesley, 1998.

O'Reilly, T. and G. Todino. *Managing UUCP and Usenet,* 10th ed. Sebastopol, California: O'Reilly & Associates, 1992.

Perlman, R. *Interconnections: Bridges and Routers.* Reading, Massachusetts: Addison-Wesley, 1992.*

Rose, M.T. *The Simple Book: An Introduction to Management of TCP/IP-Based Internets.* Upper Saddle, New Jersey: Prentice Hall, 1991.*

Ross, F.E. "FDDI—A Tutorial." *IEEE Communications Magazine,* Vol. 24, No. 5, May 1986.

Schlar, S.K. *Inside X.25: A Manager's Guide.* New York: McGraw-Hill, 1990.

Schwartz, M. *Telecommunications Networks: Protocols, Modeling, and Analysis.* Reading, Massachusetts: Addison-Wesley, 1987.

Sherman, K. *Data Communications: A User's Guide.* Upper Saddle, New Jersey: Prentice Hall, 1990.*

Sidhu, G.S., R.F. Andrews, and A.B. Oppenheimer. *Inside AppleTalk,* 2nd ed. Reading, Massachusetts: Addison-Wesley, 1990.

Spragins, J.D., et al. *Telecommunications Protocols and Design.* Reading, Massachusetts: Addison-Wesley, 1991.

Stallings, W. *Data and Computer Communications.* New York: Macmillan, 1991.

Stallings, W. *Handbook of Computer-Communications Standards,* Vols. 1–3. Carmel, Indiana: Howard W. Sams, 1990.

Stallings, W. *Local Networks,* 3rd ed. New York: Macmillan. 1990.*

Stevens, W.R. *TCP/IP Illustrated,* Vol. 1. Reading, Massachusetts: Addison-Wesley, 1994.*

Sunshine, C.A. (ed.). *Computer Network Architectures and Protocols,* 2nd ed. New York: Plenum Press, 1989.

Tannenbaum, A.S. *Computer Networks,* 2nd ed. Upper Saddle, New Jersey: Prentice Hall, 1988.*

Terplan, K. *Communication Networks Management.* Upper Saddle, New Jersey: Prentice Hall, 1992.

Zimmerman, H. "OSI Reference Model—The ISO Model of Architecture for Open Systems Interconnection." *IEEE Transactions on Communications* COM-28, No. 4, April 1980.

Technical Publications and Standards

Advanced Micro Devices. *The Supernet Family for FDDI.* Technical Manual Number 09779A. Sunnyvale, California, 1989.

Advanced Micro Devices. *The Supernet Family for FDDI.* 1989 Data Book Number 09734C. Sunnyvale, California, 1989.

American National Standards Institute X3T9.5 Committee. FDDI Station Management (SMT). Rev.6.1; March 15, 1990.

American National Standards Institute X3T9.5 Committee. Revised Text of ISO/DIS 8802/2 for the Second DIS Ballot, "Information Processing Systems—Local Area Networks." Part 2: Logical Link Control. 1987-01-14.

American National Standards Institute T1.606 Committee. Integrated Services Digital Network (ISDN)—Architectural Framework and Service Description for Frame-Relaying Bearer Service, 1990.

American National Standards Institute T1.617 Committee. Integrated Services Digital Network (ISDN)—Signaling Specification for Frame Relay Bearer Service for Digital Subscriber Signaling System Number 1 (DSS1), 1991.

American National Standards Institute T1.618 Committee. Integrated Services Digital Network (ISDN)—Core Aspects of Frame Protocol for Use with Frame Relay Bearer Service, 1991.

ATM Data Exchange Interface (DXI) Specification, Version 1.0. Document ATM_FORUM/93-590R1, August 4, 1993.

Banyan Systems, Inc. *VINES Protocol Definition.* DA254-00, Rev. 1.0. Westboro, Massachusetts, February 1990.

Bellcore. *Generic System Requirements in Support of a Switched Multi-Megabit Data Service.* Technical Advisory, TA-TSY-000772, October 1989.

Bellcore. *Local Access System Generic Requirements, Objectives, and Interface Support of Switched Multi-Megabit Data Service.* Technical Advisory TA-TSY-000773, Issue 1, December 1985.

Bellcore. *Switched Multi-Megabit Data Service (SMDS) Operations Technology Network Element Generic Requirements.* Technical Advisory TA-TSY-000774.

Chapman, J.T., and M. Halabi. *HSSI: High-Speed Serial Interface Design Specification.* Menlo Park, California and Santa Clara, California: Cisco Systems and T3Plus Networking, Inc., 1990.

Consultative Committee for International Telegraph and Telephone. *CCITT Data Communications Networks—Services and Facilities, Terminal Equipment and Interfaces, Recommendations X.1–X.29.* Yellow Book, Vol. VIII, Fascicle VIII.2, 1980.

Consultative Committee for International Telegraph and Telephone. *CCITT Data Communications Networks—Interfaces, Recommendations X.20–X.32.* Red Book, Vol. VIII, Fascicle VIII.3, 1984.

DDN Protocol Handbook. Four volumes, 1989.

Defense Communications Agency. *Defense Data Network X.25 Host Interface Specification.* Order number AD A137 427, December 1983.

Digital Equipment Corporation. *DECnet/OSI Phase V: Making the Transition from Phase IV.* EK-PVTRN-BR, 1989.

Digital Equipment Corporation. *DECserver 200 Local Area Transport (LAT) Network Concepts.* AA-LD84A-TK, June 1988.

Digital Equipment Corporation. *DIGITAL Network Architecture (Phase V).* EK-DNAPV-GD-001, September 1987.

Digital Equipment Corporation, Intel Corporation, and Xerox Corporation. *The Ethernet, A Local-Area Network, Data Link Layer and Physical Layer Specifications.* Version 2.0, November 1982.

Garcia-Luna-Aceves, J.J. "A Unified Approach to Loop-Free Routing Using Distance Vectors or Link States." ACM 089791-332-9/89/0009/0212, pp. 212–223, September 1989.

Hemrick, C., and L. Lang. "Introduction to Switched Multi-Megabit Data Service (SMDS), an Early Broadband Service." *Proceedings of the XIII International Switching Symposium* (ISS 90), May 27–June 1, 1990.

Hewlett-Packard Company. *X.25: The PSN Connection: An Explanation of Recommendation X.25.* 5958-3402, October 1985.

IEEE 802.2. *Local Area Networks Standard, 802.2 Logical Link Control.* ANSI/IEEE Standard, October 1985.*

IEEE 802.3. *Local Area Networks Standard, 802.3 Carrier Sense Multiple Access with Collision Detection.* ANSI/IEEE Standard, October 1985.*

IEEE 802.5. *Local Area Networks Standard, 802.5 Token Ring Access Method.* ANSI/IEEE Standard, October 1985.*

IEEE 802.6. *Local & Metropolitan Area Networks Standard, 802.6 Distributed Queue Dual Bus (DQDB) Subnetwork of a Metropolitan Area Network (MAN).* ANSI/IEEE Standard, December 1990.

International Business Machines Corporation. *ACF/NCP/VS Network Control Program, System Support Programs: General Information.* GC30-3058.

International Business Machines Corporation. *Advanced Communications Function for VTAM (ACF/VTAM), General Information: Introduction.* GS27-0462.

International Business Machines Corporation. *Advanced Communications Function for VTAM, General Information: Concepts.* GS27-0463.

International Business Machines Corporation. *Dictionary of Computing.* SC20-1699-7, 1987.

International Business Machines Corporation. *Local Area Network Technical Reference.* SC30-3883.

International Business Machines Corporation. *Network Problem Determination Application: General Information.* GC34-2010.

International Business Machines Corporation. *Synchronous Data Link Control: General Information.* GA27-3093.

International Business Machines Corporation. *Systems Network Architecture: Concepts and Products.* GC30-3072.

International Business Machines Corporation. *Systems Network Architecture: Technical Overview.* GC30-3073-1, 1985.*

International Business Machines Corporation. *Token-Ring Network Architecture Reference.* SC30-3374.*

International Business Machines Corporation. *Token-Ring Problem Determination Guide.* SX27-3710-04, 1990.*

International Organization for Standardization. *Information Processing System—Open System Interconnection; Specification of Abstract Syntax Notation One (ASN.1).* International Standard 8824, December 1987.

Novell, Inc. IPX Router Specification, Version 1.10. Part Number 107-000029-001, October 16, 1992.*

Novell, Inc. NetWare Link Services Protocol (NLSP) Specification, Revision 0.9. Part Number 100-001708-001, March 1993.*

StrataCom. *Frame Relay Specification with Extensions.* 001-208966, Rev.1.0, September 18, 1990.

Xerox Corporation. *Internet Transport Protocols.* XNSS 029101, January 1991.

Problem-Solving Checklist and Worksheet

To isolate problems in your internetwork, you must first compile all the relevant facts and then methodically address each suspected problem. This appendix provides a troubleshooting checklist and general worksheet to help you in this process. Use the checklist and worksheet as a guide for creating your own checklists and worksheets, which are tailored to your own internetworking environment.

Troubleshooting Checklist

Before you make any changes to your internetwork, be sure you can answer the following questions positively:

☐ Have you identified and compiled a list of all the reported symptoms on your internetwork?

☐ Do you know your internetwork? Do you have an accurate physical and logical map of your internetwork?

☐ Do you have a list of all the network protocols implemented in your network?

☐ Do you know which protocols are being routed?

☐ Do you know which protocols are being bridged?

☐ Do you know all the points of contact to external networks?

☐ For every symptom, have you developed a list of potential problems and causes?

☐ For each problem, do you have a plan of action?

☐ Do you have a disaster recovery plan if your network fails?

If you can answer yes to these questions, you can begin to isolate problems. Be sure to eliminate one problem at a time.

Troubleshooting Worksheet

1 Symptoms reported:

_____

_____

_____

_____

2 Network topology map—attach separate sheet(s):

3 Protocols routed:

_____

_____

_____

_____

4 Protocols bridged:

_____

_____

_____

_____

5 Media used in your environment:

_____

_____

_____

_____

6 Internetwork equipment (including network address, vendor, model, and function):

_____

_____

_____

_____

7 Suspect end-system and internetwork nodes (including network address, vendor, model, and function):

_____

_____

_____

_____

8   Applications used on the network (FTP, sendmail, NFS, NetWare, and so on):

_____

_____

_____

_____

9   Symptoms and possible problems:

Symptom	Possible Problems

Symptom	Possible Problems

10 Action plan for each problem:

Problem	Action Plan

Problem	**Action Plan**

11 Action outcomes:

Problem/Action	**Result/Outcome**

Problem/Action	Result/Outcome

INDEX

Numerics

A

I

Q

R

T

U

V

W

X

Z

CCIE Professional Development

Routing TCP/IP, Volume I

Jeff Doyle, CCIE

1-57870-041-8 • AVAILABLE NOW

This book takes the reader from a basic understanding of routers and routing protocols through a detailed examination of each of the IP interior routing protocols. Learn techniques for designing networks that maximize the efficiency of the protocol being used. Exercises and review questions provide core study for the CCIE Routing and Switching exam.

Advanced IP Network Design

Alvaro Retana, CCIE; Don Slice, CCIE; and Russ White, CCIE

1-57870-097-3 • AVAILABLE NOW

Network engineers and managers can use these case studies, which highlight various network design goals, to explore issues including protocol choice, network stability, and growth. This book also includes theoretical discussion on advanced design topics.

Large-Scale IP Network Solutions

Khalid Raza, CCIE; Salman Asad, CCIE; and Mark Turner

1-57870-084-1 • AVAILABLE NOW

Network engineers can find solutions as their IP networks grow in size and complexity. Examine all the major IP protocols in-depth and learn about scalability, migration planning, network management, and security for large-scale networks.

Cisco LAN Switching

Kennedy Clark, CCIE; Kevin Hamilton, CCIE

1-57870-094-9 • AVAILABLE AUGUST 1999

This volume provides an in-depth analysis of Cisco LAN switching technologies, architectures, and deployments, including unique coverage of Catalyst network design essentials. Network designs and configuration examples are incorporated throughout to demonstrate the principles and enable easy translation of the material into practice in production networks.

Cisco Career Certifications

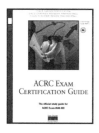

ACRC Exam Certification Guide
Clare Gough, CCIE

0-7357-0075-3 • AVAILABLE NOW

This book is a comprehensive study tool for the ACRC Exam #640-403 and part of the recommended study program from Cisco Systems. *ACRC Exam Certification Guide* helps you understand and master the exam objectives. Instructor-developed elements and techniques maximize your retention and recall of exam topics, and scenario-based exercises help validate your mastery of the exam objectives.

Advanced Cisco Router Configuration
Cisco Systems, Inc., edited by Laura Chappell

1-57870-074-4 • AVAILABLE NOW

Based on the actual Cisco ACRC course, this book provides a thorough treatment of advanced network deployment issues. Learn to apply effective configuration techniques for solid network implementation and management as you prepare for CCNP and CCDP certifications. This book also includes chapter-ending tests for self-assessment.

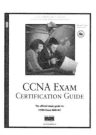

CCNA Exam Certification Guide
Wendell Odom, CCIE

0-7357-0073-7 • AVAILABLE NOW

This book is a comprehensive study tool for CCNA Exam #640-407 and part of a recommended study program from Cisco Systems. *CCNA Exam Certification Guide* helps you understand and master the exam objectives. Instructor-developed elements and techniques maximize your retention and recall of exam topics, and scenario-based exercises help validate your mastery of the exam objectives.

Introduction to Cisco Router Configuration
Cisco Systems, Inc., edited by Laura Chappell

1-57870-076-0 • AVAILABLE NOW

Based on the actual Cisco ICRC course, this book presents the foundation knowledge necessary to define Cisco router configurations in multiprotocol environments. Examples and chapter-ending tests build a solid framework for understanding internetworking concepts. Prepare for the ICRC course and CCNA certification while mastering the protocols and technologies for router configuration.

CISCO SYSTEMS

CISCO PRESS®

www.ciscopress.com

Cisco Press Solutions

Internetworking SNA with Cisco Solutions
George Sackett and Nancy Sackett
1-57870-083-3 • AVAILABLE NOW

This comprehensive guide presents a practical approach to integrating SNA and TCP/IP networks. It provides readers with an understanding of internetworking terms, networking architectures, protocols, and implementations for internetworking SNA with Cisco routers.

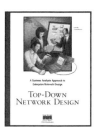

Top-Down Network Design
Priscilla Oppenheimer
1-57870-069-8 • AVAILABLE NOW

Building reliable, secure, and manageable networks is every network professional's goal. This practical guide teaches you a systematic method for network design that can be applied to campus LANs, remote-access networks, WAN links, and large-scale internetworks. Learn how to analyze business and technical requirements, examine traffic flow and Quality of Service requirements, and select protocols and technologies based on performance goals.

Internetworking Technologies Handbook, Second Edition
Kevin Downes, CCIE, Merilee Ford, H. Kim Lew, Steve Spanier, Tim Stevenson
1-57870-102-3 • AVAILABLE NOW

This comprehensive reference provides a foundation for understanding and implementing contemporary internetworking technologies, providing you with the necessary information needed to make rational networking decisions. Master terms, concepts, technologies, and devices that are used in the internetworking industry today. You also learn how to incorporate networking technologies into a LAN/WAN environment, as well as how to apply the OSI reference model to categorize protocols, technologies, and devices.

OSPF Network Design Solutions
Thomas M. Thomas II
1-57870-046-9 • AVAILABLE NOW

This comprehensive guide presents a detailed, applied look into the workings of the popular Open Shortest Path First protocol, demonstrating how to dramatically increase network performance and security, and how to most easily maintain large-scale networks. OSPF is thoroughly explained through exhaustive coverage of network design, deployment, management, and troubleshooting.

CISCO SYSTEMS

CISCO PRESS

www.ciscopress.com

Cisco Press Solutions

Internetworking Troubleshooting Handbook

Kevin Downes, CCIE, H. Kim Lew, Spank McCoy,
Tim Stevenson, Kathleen Wallace

1-57870-024-8 • **AVAILABLE NOW**

Diagnose and resolve specific and potentially problematic issues common to
every network type with this valuable reference. Each section of the book is
devoted to problems common to a specific protocol. Sections are subdivided
into symptoms, descriptions of environments, diagnosing and isolating problem
causes, and problem-solution summaries. This book aims to help you reduce
downtime, improve network performance, and enhance network reliability
using proven troubleshooting solutions.

IP Routing Primer

Robert Wright, CCIE

1-57870-108-2 • **AVAILABLE NOW**

Learn how IP routing behaves in a Cisco router environment. In addition to
teaching the core fundamentals, this book enhances your ability to troubleshoot
IP routing problems yourself, often eliminating the need to call for additional
technical support. The information is presented in an approachable,
workbook-type format with dozens of detailed illustrations and real-life
scenarios integrated throughout.

Designing Network Security

Merike Kaeo

1-57870-043-4 • **AVAILABLE NOW**

Designing Network Security is a practical guide designed to help you
understand the fundamentals of securing you corporate infrastructure. This
book takes a comprehensive look at underlying security technologies, the
process of creating a security policy, and the practical requirements necessary
to implement a corporate security policy.

For the latest on Cisco Press resources and Certification and

Training guides, or for information on publishing opportunities, visit

www.ciscopress.com.

**Cisco Press books are available at your local bookstore,
computer store, and online booksellers.**